The Original
DOG BIBLE ™

2nd Edition

The Definitive Source for All Things Dog

Edited by Kristin Mehus-Roe

BOWTIE
P R E S S ®

Irvine, California

This book is intended as a reference source only. It is not intended to substitute for veterinary advice, training expertise, breeder recommendations, or your own judgment. It should be used as one of the many sources of information you will consult as you guide your dog safely through his life. Always seek the help of a veterinarian or professional trainer if your dog displays symptoms of a medical or behavioral disorder.

Cover photographs © Gina Cioli and Pamela Hunnicutt/BowTie Inc., left; Isabelle Francais/BowTie Inc., top, middle, and bottom right.
Text copyright © 2009 by BowTie Press®

Library of Congress Cataloging-in-Publication Data

The original dog bible : the definitive source for all things dog / [edited] by Kristin Mehus-Roe. — 2nd ed.
        p. cm.
 Includes bibliographical references and index.
 ISBN 978-1-933958-82-8 (alk. paper)
 1. Dogs. I. Mehus-Roe, Kristin.

 SF426.O75 2008
 636.7—dc22
                                        2008044402

BowTie Press®
A Division of BowTie, Inc.
3 Burroughs
Irvine, California 92618

Printed and bound in Singapore
15 14 13 12 11 10 09   1 2 3 4 5 6 7 8 9 10

Contents

Section I: The Dogs in Our World

Section II: A New Dog

Section III: Life with a Dog

Section V: Health

Section VI: Daily Care

Section VII: Training and Behavior

Section VIII: Dogs and Work

Preface

Why another book about dogs? Because although there are thousands of books about dog care, dog breeds, and dog health, no one book combines this information—along with the latest information on behavior, training, grooming, nutrition, and canine work and activities—into one comprehensive and usable package. Tying together the experience of top dog writers with the knowledge of dog experts and breed clubs, in this new edition we present the most accurate and up-to-date information on dogs available.

Having a dog is equal parts play and work—and your family, friends, veterinarian, trainer, groomer, and pet sitter are all part of the team that will make your friendship with your dog a valuable and long-lived experience. We hope this book will help you bring it all together.

Acknowledgments

Good books about dogs are never just technical. Without fail, authors, editors, photographers, and illustrators bring their personal experiences and knowledge into play. *The Dog Bible* is no different. Everyone who worked on this book is a true lover of animals, and their years of personal and professional experience with dogs contributed greatly to its final success.

Thanks to the great work of the authors—Kim Campbell Thornton, Audrey Pavia, Kathy Salzberg, Siri Mehus, and September Morn—and editors Amy Fox and Rebekah Bryant. Author Kim Campbell Thornton multitasked as editor, bringing her broad knowledge of breeds to the breed descriptions. Special acknowledgment goes to Ruth Strother, who not only almost single-handedly copy edited the entire book but also served as my mentor, helping to guide this book from its earliest beginning to its final completion. Thanks, as always, to the current and former staff of BowTie Press: Nick Clemente, Karla Austin, Michelle Martinez, Rebekah Bryant, Erin Kuechenmeister, Jim Fisher, Jennifer Dodd, and to layout designer Monika Stout. Vicky Vaughn's exceptional design is especially worthy of mention. The tenacious research abilities of Vicki Hogue brought the text to an even greater level. And Deborah Eldredge, DVM, deserves kudos for the guidance and technical knowledge she brought to the health section.

Thanks especially to Norman Ridker; without his vision and commitment, *The Dog Bible* would not have happened.

All of the photographers were patient and generous with their supplies of slides—never complaining even as weeks stretched to months and beyond. Art supply company Art Resources supplied excellent historical images on short notice. A very special nod goes to the amazing work of anatomical illustrator Laurie O'Keefe. She was exceedingly generous with her time and talent.

Without the liberal help of breed clubs across the United States and abroad, the breed section would not be what it is. Their contributions helped bring this book to a level unprecedented and provided a nuanced and accurate view of the many rare and wonderful breeds in existence. I can't thank them enough for their contributions.

Finally, I'm thankful to the wonderful dogs I've known and loved and the two great dogs in my life now, Desi and Muddy. The unswerving support of my family, and especially my best friend and husband, Andrew, is as always my lifeline. This book is especially poignant to me as its summation coincided with the death of my office buddy and true and loyal companion, Tramp. Even as I write this, I miss her soft presence under my desk, so this book is truly in her memory.

Introduction

Adopting a dog is one of the most profound experiences you will have in your life. It rates right up there with getting married, buying your first house, and having a child. If that surprises you, you are just the person to be reading this book. Over the course of your dog's lifetime, he will bring you infinite joys but also moments of despair. He will provide you with constant companionship, a warm head to rest your hand on, and unquestioning devotion.

A dog also brings responsibilities. No more stops at the gym on your way home from work; you have a dog who needs to eat and be taken outside. How about those weeklong ski trips you once relished? Now you need to find a dog-friendly lodge, a good boarding kennel, or a reliable pet sitter. Then there are the moments of panic and frustration: Is he loose? Has he eaten the pound of dark chocolate you left on the table? Why won't the dogs get along?

No one said having a dog is easy, but knowing how and where to find the type of dog who will fit into your life and how to prepare yourself and your home for him will lighten your load. Proper training, grooming, and health care will keep your dog physically and mentally healthy. Having the tools to properly care for a dog will make your experience infinitely better.

Whether you choose an adult dog or a puppy, buy a purebred from a reputable breeder or adopt a mixed breed, and feed a raw food diet or the best commercial food you can find, there are decisions to make and precautions to take. Making your home and garden safe for your pet and your pet safe for the rest of the world is all part of this responsibility. With help and perseverance, your dog will be your best friend and live a long and happy life.

The Dogs in Our World

Humans and dogs first crossed paths more than 10,000 years ago. Since then, dogs have lived at the edges of our villages and within them, worked with us and guarded us, shared our leisure time and our family lives. Dogs share our lives more completely than do any other animals.

The role of dogs in human society has changed dramatically since we first encountered one another, but throughout recorded existence dogs have been significant: in our myths and folklore, religions, and cultural memories. In modern times, dogs are celebrated in movies and art, from comic strips to great literature. Yet, their presence in our lives is not always simple. Our sometimes disparate needs have necessitated that we protect dogs from humans and humans from dogs through animal rescue efforts and through laws.

CHAPTER 1

Dog Genetics and Development

Where do dogs really come from? Are they descended from wolves or foxes, coyotes or jackals? The mystery of canine origins fascinates scientists and dog fanciers alike. We do know that domestic dogs are of the family Canidae, as are wild dogs, wolves, foxes, jackals, coyotes, and dingoes. There are 39 canids in all, and most of them are subspecies of the genus *Canis*. While the wolf is known as *Canis lupus*, the domesticated dog is called *Canis familiaris*.

Canids are all mammalian carnivores of the order Carnivora. It is believed that all of the canids and felids (members of the Felidae family, or cats) were descended from a prehistoric mammal called the Miacis. The canids separated from the cats when canids evolved into a new species, the Cynodictis. From here, scientists say, there came a new division, that of the Cynodesmus, from which hyenas are descended, and the Tomarctus, from which all of the canids are descended.

Many of us like to believe that our dogs are the direct descendants of noble wolves, and much has been made of this connection in the training and care of the dog. Based on DNA evidence, most scientists now agree that the dog is probably directly descended from the wolf. However, some scientists believe that dogs and wolves, as well as the other canine species, all descended from one canid but developed distinctly from one another. Of the canids, the wolf, coyote, jackal, dingo, wild dog, and domestic dog can interbreed. Rarely, the fox breeds with other canids. The DNA makeup of all the canids is almost identical. In addition to almost identical DNA sequences, the canids all share several other features, including a 63-day gestation period and 42 teeth.

Some scientists are so convinced that the dog and wolf are essentially indistinct that they term the dog *Canis lupus familiaris*, essentially saying that dogs are really a subspecies of wolves rather than a distinct species in the genus *Canis*. Other scientists dispute this theory, saying that wolves and dogs are as similar to coyotes and jackals as they are to one another. Because of this, they say, it is more likely that all of the canids evolved from the same ancestor, rather than that one evolved from one or several canids. Some scientists dispute the idea that the interbreeding canids are separate species, arguing that the ability to interbreed negates speciation.

If wolves, coyotes, and dogs can interbreed, why aren't there more hybrids? Scientists say that this is because all of the canids live within different social niches.

Dog Taxonomy	
Kingdom: Animalia	Family: Canidae
Phylum: Chordata	Genus: *Canis*
Class: Mammalia	Species: *Canis familiaris*
Order: Carnivora	(Subspecies: *Canis lupus familiaris*)

None of the species (or as some scientists would prefer, subspecies) inhabits any one niche at any one time. The rare times species do interbreed are when one or both parties cross niches. Often, this is the result of outside forces; for example, a captive wolf being bred with a domestic dog.

The question of whether dogs are descended directly from wolves brings some of our assumptions about dogs into question. If, in fact, they are not descended from wolves, how does that alter our understanding of dogs as pack animals? Does this change the way we should interact with them? Not really. Both trainers and behaviorists work with dogs with an eye toward the framework of our human-dog relationship. They may use the idea of wolf social interaction as a way to illustrate canine behavior, but most training techniques aren't based on how a wolf would be trained but, rather, on the techniques that have worked to train dogs in the past. Whether they are descended from wolves or share another common ancestor, dogs differ greatly from wild animals. Dogs are domesticated, trainable creatures who depend on us for their survival. Wolves don't live in our homes, and experts say that even bottle-fed wolves are never completely tamed. Yes, dogs descend from some wild animal, but which one doesn't make a great deal of difference in our relationship with them.

Domestication of the Dog

Since dogs descended from a common canid species, how then did they go from wild animals to domesticated ones? Scientists differ about the age of dogs. Did they diverge from wolves or a wolflike ancestor 135,000 years ago as one scientist argues, or did they come into being 12,000 to 15,000 years ago, when the first evidence of their existence is dated?

Domestic Dogs Versus Wild Dogs

Dingoes, African wild dogs, raccoon dogs, Carolina Dogs, Canaan Dogs, New Guinea Singing Dogs, wolves, wolf hybrids—how are they different, and how are they the same?

The dingo is believed to have been a domestic dog who became wild. DNA studies have shown that dingoes are closely related to domestic dogs in East Asia. Scientists think that Chinese explorers were sometimes accompanied by dogs; dogs may have been kept for companionship but most likely were brought aboard Chinese ships as guards, workers, and food. About 3,500 years ago, some of these dogs ended up in Australia. The dogs bred together and eventually became the dingo we know today. Dingoes are carnivorous predators; they eat a range of animals, from small lizards and rodents to kangaroos! Although dingoes are wild animals, some dingoes have been kept as pets by the Aboriginal people of Australia and occasionally by others. It is believed that dingoes were also introduced into some lines of domestic dogs, including the Australian Cattle Dog.

Wolves have also been introduced to lines of domestic dogs. Some people have what are called wolf hybrids as pets. These are animals who are part wolf and part dog. Keeping wolf hybrids, or wolf dogs, as pets is controversial. Many wolf experts say that wolf dogs are unpredictable. Wolves might be part of the lineage of some domestic dogs, such as Siberian Huskies and Alaskan Malamutes, however, this is not known for sure. (These dogs are considered ancient dogs, among the breeds closest to wolves in DNA.)

> "Dogs are the only animals who will answer to their names and recognize the voices of the family. . . . Next to man, there is no living creature whose memory is so retentive."
>
> —Pliny the Elder (A.D. 23–79)

Did the domestic dog as we know him today evolve into his current existence only after humans began making permanent settlements, approximately 15,000 years ago? Whether they became a separate species around 100,000 years ago or 10,000 years ago, we do know that dogs weren't the domesticated creatures as we know them today until their lives intersected with those of humans.

It is generally accepted that the dog's ancestors were first attracted to human settlements for the scavenging opportunities. They came to eat the scraps of food and garbage, as well as the human waste, that were thrown into refuse piles. Over time, the villagers became accustomed to these scavengers; perhaps they even valued the elimination of food and waste that would attract undesirable scavengers, such as vermin. As the scavenging dogs became territorial over their refuse heaps, they probably began to bark at approaching animals and strangers. Likely, the villagers grew to appreciate these early warnings and that the barks and territorial behavior served as a deterrent to other, more dangerous or irksome animals.

Over time, the villagers may have come to recognize certain village dogs—perhaps naming

Archaeologists have translated some of the names of ancient Egyptian dogs. They include Good Herdsman, Blackie, One Who Is Fashioned as an Arrow, She of the Town, and Useless. *Abu* or *jwjw*, meaning "bow-wow" and "howler," respectively, preceded or followed the dogs names.

them or capturing a cute puppy for a child's amusement. Somehow, over the course of many years, the dogs became part of the village—living within its borders rather than simply on the periphery. Eventually, hunters discovered that the dogs could track scent, or maybe help take down large game. They began to bring these dogs with them when they hunted, utilizing the dogs' superior olfactory power and speed to find and capture prey. At some point, when villagers began raising their own livestock, dogs' prey drive was redirected into herding and livestock guarding. For the next 10,000 years, dogs became helpers across the continents and in many different capacities. They were trained to guard people and livestock, to hunt, to herd, and to pull sleds and other cargo.

The domestication of dogs emerged at similar times throughout the world—seemingly with no connection to one another. It appears that villagers on the Asian, African, and European continents all began their relationships with dogs in a similar, coincidental manner. Interesting, however, is that some dogs did not evolve in the same manner as others. There are two types of *Canis familiaris*, although they're not technically subspecies: pariah dogs and truly domestic dogs. The pariah dogs continue to exist on the peripheries of civilization, surviving through scavenging behavior in much the same way as their ancestors did. At the same time, their close relatives, the domestic dogs, live within our homes and share their lives with us. Pariah dogs live in urban areas, in dumps, and in vacant lots. They may also live in rural areas. They are commonly seen in underdeveloped countries but also exist in developed countries, especially in areas of poverty. Domestic and pariah dogs cross paths often, and it's not uncommon for one to become another within a generation or two.

Domestication Timeline

Recent research shows that dogs have been domesticated for 10,000 to 15,000 years. This same research indicates that dogs even accompanied people over the Bering Land Bridge some 13,000 years ago, when the first humans made their way from Asia to continental America. Between 10,000 B.C.E. and

Dogs have served as workers and companions for thousands of years.

4000 B.C.E., dogs were found throughout Mesopotamia, the region that now comprises Iraq, Syria, and Turkey. A grave in northern Israel that held a human skeleton and a puppy skeleton was dated at about 12,000 B.C.E. The first evidence of dogs and humans living together dates from about 7000 B.C.E.

Since their domestication, dogs have accompanied and served us in many ways. They have been our companions and our working partners. They have sometimes been our slaves. In some cultures we have eaten dogs; in others we have pampered

them. Dogs are found throughout ancient literature and art, and a few ancient cultures even prayed to them.

Dogs looking much like modern sighthounds are depicted in Egyptian art from about 4500 B.C.E. Ancient Egyptian dogs were well respected and sometimes considered to be messengers of the gods. Some gods were even depicted as part dog, such as the jackal-faced god, Anubis, and the god Seth, who had the body of a dog. It was not uncommon for dogs to be mummified. The Egyptians kept dogs as companions and hunting partners, but they also used mastiffs in battle. Not all dogs found in ancient Egypt were domesticated, however. As in most areas of the world, there were also feral, or pariah, dogs, who received treatment far different from the Egyptian's domestic dogs.

Depictions of dogs in Greek and Roman art are found as far back as 300 B.C.E., although not as commonly as in Egyptian art. They were mentioned by both Aristotle and Homer in their writings and were portrayed on Greek and Roman coins. Dogs were an accepted part of society in ancient Greece and Rome. They were used for both hunting and guarding. Greeks and Romans used war dogs widely, outfitting large mastiffs with spiked collars and sending them into battle. Romans also cherished their lap dogs, even breeding them for specific looks in much the same way modern dog fanciers do. Companion dogs were considered status symbols, and many noble people kept both hunting dogs and small companion dogs.

The board game known today as Hounds and Jackals was a favorite game of the ancient Egyptians. It first appears in records around 1300 B.C.E. An original board was found in a tomb along with 10 game pieces—5 with the head of a hound and 5 with the head of a jackal.

Explorer Dog

When explorers Meriwether Lewis and William Clark set out on their 8,000-mile trek into the uncharted wilderness of the American West in 1804, they brought along a shaggy black Newfoundland named Seaman. The dog helped the explorers by alerting them to grizzlies, accompanying Lewis in the hunt for food, and once redirecting the course of a buffalo that charged into camp, saving several men from being crushed. Seaman also experienced some travails along the way, including suffering near starvation one winter and being bitten by a beaver.

One reference to Seaman in Lewis's journal describes an encounter with a young buffalo. "Walking on shore this evening, I met with a buffalo calf which attached itself to me, and continued to follow close at my heels, until I embarked and left it. It appeared alarmed at my dog, which was probably the cause of its so readily attaching itself to me."

Seaman is mentioned several other times in both Lewis's and Clark's journals, but no reference to Seaman is made after July 1806. No one knows what became of him.

Dogs were also valued pets and fierce fighters in ancient Asia—as early as 1000 B.C.E. In China, they were cherished by royalty, who bred small dogs called sleeve dogs as companions. The dogs were said to be so small they could fit into the flowing sleeves of a nobleperson. It was also in Asia that Buddhists began to breed small dogs to emulate the lions that were said to be loyal to Buddha. In India, Buddha's Lion Dogs, or Fo Dogs, were believed to be actual lions with doglike submissiveness. There were no lions in Asia, though, and the image of a doglike lion gradually became a lionlike dog. In China, Japan, Korea, and Tibet, the Fo Dog was embraced, and believers began to breed small dogs to look like tiny lions. Among these dogs were the Pekingese, the Lhasa Apso, the Tibetan Terrier, and the Shih Tzu. Later, East Asians prized hunting dogs, guard dogs, and war dogs, as well.

In medieval Europe, dogs served as hunters and were cherished by noble people, some of whom owned hundreds of dogs. So much value was placed on hunting dogs that commoners were not allowed to own dogs who could course, or pursue, game—commoners' dogs had to be under a certain size or hobbled so that they and their handlers could not poach game from landowning gentry. According to some sources, this is the root behind the terrier group—dogs bred adequately small to be kept by commoners legally but still keen enough to hunt small prey.

Later, particularly during the Renaissance, dogs became status symbols among European royalty. Europeans still used hunting dogs, but they also bred small dogs as companions and fierce dogs to fight bulls, bears, and one another as blood sport. Small companion dogs were pampered by the aristocracy and lived in the lap of luxury.

Native Americans are believed to have kept dogs since humans first crossed the Bering Land Bridge. Different tribes kept dogs either as companions, as hunters, or for meat. There were also pariah dogs who lived on the outskirts of villages.

Dogs also lived among African tribespeople, both as scavengers at the village edge and as hunting dogs. Rhodesian Ridgebacks were developed from the dogs kept by the Khoisan people of South Africa. Semiwild dogs, dogs who were feral in some areas but used for hunting or livestock guarding in other areas, were also common in North Africa and the Middle East.

Throughout the second millennium, dogs were embraced as workers in Europe and on the American continent. They were bred and trained to serve in a variety of capacities: from war dogs to drafting dogs to hunters to rescue dogs. Their work ranged from herding and livestock guarding to drafting—pulling carts laden with wares or people and pacing endlessly to operate grain wheels or cooking spits.

As Western lives shifted from agrarian to urban during the Industrial Revolution, dogs fell out of favor as workers and took on deeper significance as companions. As dogs became less depended upon for work, more emphasis was placed on their looks, which gave rise to the so-called dog fancy and the sport of dog conformation. By the mid-1800s, breed clubs and breed shows were established in Europe and quickly crossed to the United States.

By the mid-twentieth century, most U.S. dogs lived in urban and suburban settings—leashed and kept behind tall fences. As dogs became accepted as family members rather than beasts of burden, animal welfare groups also arose. Animal cruelty laws prevented the use of dogs as drafting animals within urban settings, further reducing their use as working dogs. In the latter half of the twentieth century, however, European and U.S. dogs reemerged as working animals, used as assistance dogs, detection dogs, and police and military dogs.

While the development of domestic dogs has been mapped throughout history, their status has remained virtually unchanged in some areas of the world. Throughout both industrial and agrarian societies, there are dogs who continue to live in much the same manner as did the village dogs of 10,000 to 15,000 years ago.

Genetics

Domesticated dogs are members of the species *Canis familiaris*. Even breeds that look very different from each other, such as the Great Dane and the Chihuahua, are essentially the same type of animal. In fact, if dogs of 10 different breeds were left to breed

Village dogs were found, and continue to be found, in cultures throughout the world.

unchecked for several generations, the resulting dogs would look basically the same: medium-sized with prick or semi-erect ears, neutral coloring, catlike (compact) paws, and a sickle-shaped tail. In other words, they would have the characteristics of the native dogs that are found around the world.

That dog breeds are not separate species is sometimes a surprise to dog fanciers, and it creates a dilemma for those committed to preserving breeds. Because breeds are not separate species, they do not come under any sort of endangerment laws or provisions. In fact, some scientists argue that the effort to strictly preserve breeds can lead to their decimation. They argue that the limited genetic diversity in a given breed makes purebred dogs susceptible to a host of genetic diseases. When breeders develop a breed and enter the breed into a registry, the stud book is usually closed. That means only dogs who are deemed to be of this breed—descended from a certain number of dogs of this breed—can breed together to create a descendant of the breed. There may have been thousands of dogs when the stud book was closed, or fewer. The number of dogs entered into a stud book limits the genetic lineages available to a purebred fancier.

The limited genetic diversity that can lead to many genetic problems is further exacerbated when a particular dog or kennel becomes popular, a war or natural disaster decimates a particular breed population, or breeders focus more on looks than utility or health. One dramatic example is the Lundehund, or puffin dog, a Norwegian breed that was virtually wiped out during World War II after distemper struck the small island where the breed had been developed. At the end of the war, fewer than a dozen dogs were still alive. Although the breed has substantially recovered since then, the extremely small gene pool has led to a rampant genetic intestinal disorder, so common that it is coined Lundehund syndrome. It is believed to affect more than 70 percent of these dogs.

To battle the problem of genetic disease in both humans and dogs, scientists at a number of research institutes are mapping canine DNA. In addition to the benefits for human medicine, they hope that by mapping canine DNA, they can exclude dogs with mutated genes from future breedings. Because dogs exhibit such a large range of physical and behavioral variances, scientists also hope that they will learn some universal truths about mammalian DNA by mapping canine chromosomes. Many scientists and dog experts believe that the only way to cut down on the number of genetic problems so prevalent in purebred dogs is by introducing new blood, or by crossbreeding.

In 2003, a rough sketch of the first dog genome sequence was unveiled by scientists at The Institute for Genomic Research and

The merle coat shown here is carried by a gene that lightens the pigmentation of both the coat and the iris.

the Center for Advancement of Genomics. The genome belonged to a family pet, a male Standard Poodle named Shadow. By 2004, scientists at the Broad Center/MIT Center for Genome Research released a more detailed dog genome map, this time the genome belonged to a female Boxer, Tasha. Tasha's genome sequence has been posted on the Internet to allow other researchers to use the results to further research in canine and human genetics.

In the spring of 2004, researchers at the Fred Hutchinson Cancer Research Center furthered canine DNA research when they released findings from a study comparing 414 individual dogs from 85 breeds. The study revealed that through their DNA, individual purebred dogs can be traced to their breed with 99 percent accuracy. The scientists were also able to group the 85 breeds into four groups based on geography and morphology. Although many of the individual breeds in the four groups were expected, there were surprises among the relatives, such as the placement of the Greyhound and Saint Bernard among the herders.

Purpose, Personality, and Pinups

To develop a breed, dogs from several different breeds or breed mixes are brought together for that specific purpose. For example, the Australian Cattle Dog was bred in the nineteenth century to serve as a cattle herding dog in the Australian outback. There were a number of requirements for a dog of this breed to be good at his job. He needed to be small enough not to tire quickly, agile enough to make sharp turns to avoid kicks, and tenacious and enduring enough to herd cattle in the hot sun all day and across many miles. For this job, ranchers bred together several types of dogs: Australian Kelpies for their herding ability in Australia's particular climate, Rough Collies for their tenacity, Dalmatians for their loyalty,

Relatives of the Dog

Coyote: The highly adaptable coyote is the only large predator that has increased its range since the first European settlers arrived in North America. Sharing the same genus as the gray wolf and the domestic dog, the coyote is found from Alaska to Costa Rica and lives in every U.S. state except Hawaii. In addition to the high-pitched howl that most people associate with the coyote, the animal uses at least 10 other distinct sounds to communicate. Jackrabbits, ground squirrels, and other small rodents account for the majority of the coyote's diet. Coyotes hunt in packs to capture larger animals such as elk and deer.

Dingo: The dingo is a member of the domestic dog family, although it has lived in the wild in Australia for thousands of years. How the dingo first arrived in Australia is not known, but there are several theories. Some people believe that dingoes came with aboriginal people; others theorize that they arrived with Asian seafarers or Indian traders. Dingoes are still sometimes kept as pets by native peoples. Features of the dingo that distinguish it from domestic dogs include a longer muzzle, larger molars, and longer canine teeth. It has a lithe, deep-chested body made for long-distance running.

Fox: A more distant relative of the dog than the wolf, jackal, and coyote, is the fox. There are 21 species of fox throughout the world, including the red fox, gray fox, Arctic fox, and bat-eared fox. Foxes hunt alone rather than in packs, although they often live in small groups. Foxes vocalize by yapping, howling, barking, and whimpering. Their food sources include small rodents, rabbits, wild fruits and berries, and insects.

Jackal: There are four species of jackal: the side-striped jackal, the black- or silver-backed jackal, the golden jackal, and the rare Simien jackal. The side-striped, black-backed, and Simien jackals are found in Africa; the golden, or common, jackal lives from the Balkans to Burma. Jackals have a large vocabulary and use yips, growls, and hisses to communicate. Much of their social behavior is similar to that of domestic dogs, using submissive to aggressive postures to communicate their hierarchy in the pack. They are both predator and scavenger, with some species following lions to scavenge from their kills.

Wild dog: The term *wild dog* is usually used to describe the African wild dog and the dhole of Asia, both endangered species. The African wild dog is so endangered it is now listed as being threatened with extinction. Both of these wild dogs are pack animals, living in groups averaging between 8 and 15 dogs. They are communal hunters. The African wild dog is one of the few mammals to care for its old, sick, and disabled. Wild dogs weigh between 35 and 70 pounds.

Wolf: The gray wolf, *Canis lupus*, is the best known of the wolves. It is also the largest, with an average weight of 120 pounds, increasing to as much as 175 pounds. The largest of the gray wolves are usually found in North America. Subspecies of the gray wolf include the Mexican wolf, timber wolf, Arctic wolf, Rocky Mountain wolf, and Asiatic/Arabian wolf.

 The red wolf, *Canis rufus*, is smaller than the gray wolf, weighing about 40 to 80 pounds. The endangered red wolf is the subject of reintroduction programs in Tennessee and North Carolina. It is often debated whether the red wolf is a true wolf or a coyote-wolf hybrid.

New research indicates that purebred dogs not only look different from one another but also have distinct genetic makeups.

Most Popular Dogs of the Twentieth Century

1. Fala, the Scottish Terrier owned by President Franklin D. Roosevelt

2. Togo, a Siberian Husky who was a lead dog in the Nome Serum Run in 1925

3. Snoopy

4. Rin Tin Tin

5. Lassie

6. Scooby Doo

7. Balto, a husky mix who was a lead dog in the Nome Serum Run in 1925

8. Eddie from TV's *Frasier*

9. Old Yeller

10. Gidget, the Taco Bell Chihuahua

Source: From a 1999 survey

The well-known presidential pet Fala was Franklin D. Roosevelt's constant companion.

Bulldogs for their bite, even, some say, dingoes for their silent working ability. The original Australian Cattle Dogs were what we would now call mixed breeds. The stud book was closed in the early 1900s, and a breed description was drawn up. From that point on, there was an official Australian Cattle Dog and no further crossbreeding was acceptable.

In this way, there have been scores of new purebred dogs created, each embodying different attributes pulled from different breeds to enhance their working ability. It's rare for a new breed to be developed for its looks alone; generally, the looks we associate with purebreds are a byproduct of the working skills breeders selected for. That is, the Australian Cattle Dog gained its tenacity from Collies, but the breed also lent its merle coat. Darwin termed this artificial selection—essentially altering a species' evolution through the specific selection of genes (or traits that correspond to specific genes).

Interestingly, one scientist who has worked to breed tame foxes, selecting for docility and amenability, has encountered a side effect: after generations, the selectively bred foxes have developed piebald coats, floppier ears, curlier tails, and almost dog-like faces.

CHAPTER 2

Dogs in Religion and Folklore

Dogs haven't always fared well in the major religions. They've often been viewed as unclean or impure, probably because at the time that the tenets of the modern religions were written, most dogs were scavengers who fed on garbage or even corpses. Some of these ancient religions and cultures tolerated dogs' existence at the periphery of society because they served a function: to keep the streets clean of refuse and carrion.

Religion

Many religions have had a love/hate relationship with the dog. Although some considered dogs to be impure, others valued

In Greek and Roman mythology, a three-headed dog, Cerberus, guards the gates to the underworld.

dogs as noble comrades, workers, or simply as innocents. In religious writings, dogs are often associated with death or with the afterlife. Some worshipers believed that dogs had a heightened sensitivity to death and that their barking could either ward off, or be a harbinger of, death. Other cultures related tales in which dogs helped create civilization, affected the way humans experienced death, or were even the forbears of humankind.

The question of whether dogs have souls has been something that modern religions have sporadically tackled, generally concluding that they do not. However, many ancient peoples, such as the Egyptians, did believe that dogs had souls. They manifested this belief by burying dogs with their owners for protection and companionship in the afterlife and even by worshipping canine demigods.

Dogs have often taken on the cloak of good or evil—their presence being either good or evil omens. In some religions they've been considered minions of the devil and other evil deities, while in other religions they are considered messengers of gods or even gods themselves.

Judaism

In Judaism, dogs are considered unclean; at the time the Torah was written, dogs often traveled in packs, scavenging human garbage and, sometimes, human corpses. These packs of feral dogs often carried disease and could be dangerous, so the Talmudic disdain for dogs was partially the result of social mores that were established to keep humans free from canine-born disease.

However, dogs aren't all bad in Jewish tradition. Because the dogs stayed silent when the Israelites began their exodus from Egypt, the Talmud instructs Jews to "tolerate" dogs. In addition, the Talmud extols dogs as faithful to their masters and as protectors: God gave Cain a dog as a symbol of protection.

Christianity

Although there are some negative depictions of dogs in Christianity, among the major religions it is the most tolerant of dogs. Some

Dogs are often depicted in Nativity scenes along with other barnyard animals. Some Christians believe dogs accompanied the three wise men.

Christians believe that the shepherds who visited Jesus brought dogs with them. Often, dogs are depicted in nativity scenes because of this belief. In Grenada, Christians believe that the shepherds had three dogs with them: Cibila, Lubina, and Malampo.

Many saints are depicted as having canine companions. Saint Patrick was believed to have been guided several times during his life by a large gray dog, whose chest bore a mark in the shape of a white cross. Saint Margaret of Cortona is often depicted with a dog pulling at her skirt because, lore says, she was first pulled to the church by a dog. Grigio, a gray mongrel, was the protector of Saint Giovanni Melchior, or Don Bosco. Bosco was a priest who served the children in the slums of Turin, Italy. Grigio was said to have saved the life of Don Bosco several times. Throughout the stories of the saints and their dogs, there is a running theme that the dogs served as messengers of God, leading saints to safety or testing their loyalty.

Islam

Dogs are considered so impure in the religion of Islam that fundamentalists believe that touching a dog requires ritualistic purification. A bowl that a dog has eaten from cannot be used until it has been washed seven times and then scrubbed with earth.

Although dogs are considered unclean, the prophet Mohammed opted not to exterminate all dogs for two reasons: one, because Allah created them and only Allah can destroy them; two, because of their proven skill in assisting hunters and shepherds in their work. Mohammed, it is said, even had his own hunting dog. He did, however, condone the killing of all black dogs with light markings above the eyes because these markings were considered signs of the devil.

In one Islamic scripture, a Muslim man provides water to a thirsty dog. A member of his

An interesting fact for dog spotters: Did you know that dogs are mentioned in the Bible (Old and New Testament) 24 times? Cats aren't mentioned at all.

group complains to Mohammed that the man is impure because he has touched a dog. Mohammed chastises the man who complained, saying the first man is a better Muslim than the second because of his compassion and kindness to animals.

Buddhism

Dogs occasionally appear in Buddhist writings to illustrate the need to be kind and generous at all times. The monk Asanga, for example, longed to encounter the Buddha Maitreya so that he could learn from him. After meditating for 12 years, Asanga emerged from a cave with a heightened sense of consciousness. Encountering a dying dog covered with maggots, Asanga tried to help the dog by skimming the maggots off of the animal with his tongue to relieve the dog's pain but not injure the maggots. At that moment, Bodhisattva Maitreya, the Buddha of the future, appeared in the dog's place and praised Asanga for his compassion and his purity of mind. He agreed to become Asanga's teacher because by licking the maggots off the dog, Asanga had proved he was ready.

Dogs took on an even bigger role as Buddhism spread throughout Asia. The Buddhist symbol, the Fo (meaning Buddha) Dog, represents a lion that Buddha is said to have trained to mind him like a dog. The Fo Dogs are often seen at the entrances of temples: on one side is the male Fo Dog with his right paw resting on a sphere; on the other side is the female Fo Dog with her left paw resting on the mouth of a cub. In Buddha's birthplace of India, lions are well-known and respected animals. When Buddhism traveled to East Asia, however, the Chinese had a different take on the ubiquitous figure. Because there are no lions in China and few Chinese had seen or heard of the creatures, they adapted the concept of the Fo Dog to an animal they were familiar with: the dog.

The Han emperor Ming Ti was the first Chinese emperor to embrace Buddhism. However, he wanted a tame lion of his own, so he announced that the Pekingese looked like a lion and called it Lion Dog, or Fo Dog. These small dogs eventually came to represent Buddhism and Ming Ti. Later, in Tibet and Japan, Lhasa Apsos, Tibetan Spaniels, and Shih Tzu also came to represent the Fo Dog. Over time, these breeds took on such significance in China that they came to be considered royalty and could live only within the walls of the Forbidden City. One emperor, Ming of the Tang Dynasty, even legally married a Pekingese.

Hinduism

Dogs are associated with the Hindu god Shiva, who is frequently depicted with four dogs. The animals represent the Vedas, which are the most ancient of Hindu scriptures.

The *Mahabharata*, an ancient religious epic, prominently features a dog. In it, the Pandava brothers are ascending to heaven, or Swarga. They are followed by a dog on their journey. The journey is treacherous, however, and one by one the brothers die until only one is left, Yudhishthira. Indra, the ruler of heaven, appears in a golden

Canine Constellations

Dogs can be found in the heavens as well as on earth. The constellations Canis Major (Greater Dog) and Canis Minor (Lesser Dog) are the constellation Orion's hunting dogs. Canis Major contains Sirius, the Dog Star. In another part of the sky, the constellation Canes Venatici (Hunting Dogs) is said to be held on a leash by the constellation Boötes (Bear Driver) as he hunts the bear constellations Ursa Major and Ursa Minor.

In Asia, small companion dogs were pampered and adored. Some were even bred to resemble the revered Buddhist Fo Dog.

chariot and offers Yudhishthira a ride into Swarga. Yudhishthira, however, will not leave the dog, who is his only surviving companion. Indra argues that dogs are unclean and cannot enter Swarga, but Yudhishthira insists that he won't abandon his faithful companion. Suddenly, the god Dharma (or

The Year of the Dog

In Chinese astrology, the Year of the Dog occurs every 12 years (in the 20th and 21st centuries, the Year of the Dog occurred in 1922, 1934, 1946, 1958, 1970, 1982, 1994, and 2006). Those born in the Year of the Dog tend to be loyal, honest, leaders, affluent, critical, and aloof.

in some tellings, Yama, the god of death) appears from the dog's form and blesses Yudhishthira for his loyalty and compassion for the dog.

Indra also had a dog, Sarama, who served as the deity's messenger. Sarama was sometimes associated with the dawn, announcing Indra's arising. Sarama also found cows that had been stolen from Indra and brought them home. Sarama was said to have mothered the dogs owned by Yama, god of the dead. These dogs serve as messengers between the land of living and dead, summoning humans to their death. Prayers for long life include lines about not following the dogs of Yama. Varuna, Hinduism's sky deity who upholds heaven and earth, also has a dog.

Ancient Religions and Cultural Folklore

Dogs (and other animals) often played greater roles in ancient religions than they do in the modern religions. In polytheistic religions, many gods and demigods were even represented by dogs, and images of dogs were often found in religious depictions. The ancient Egyptians, for example, worshipped the dog god, Anubis. Anubis was the judge and lord of the afterlife. King Tutankhamen was buried with his faithful

In ancient Egypt, sighthoundlike dogs were held in high esteem and often depicted in artwork.

The faithful Argos was the only member of Odysseus's household to recognize him after his 19-year absence.

dogs, and the wild dogs in the hills of Punjab are called hounds of God and are not supposed to be killed.

Dogs also feature prominently in some Native American cultures. The Kato tribe of California depicted the creator, Nagaicho, as having a dog before even the earth existed. Because of this, the Katos gave greater respect to dogs than most other Native American tribes did, giving dogs names and allowing them to sleep indoors. The Shawnee believed that their creator was a female god named Our Grandmother, Kohkumthena. Kohkumthena was followed by her grandson and her dog while she put the finishing touches on the earth. In Shawnee folklore, Kohkumthena sits on a roadside near the land of the dead weaving a basket, but each night her little dog unravels it. In this way, her dog prevents the world from ever being finished.

The Ifugao people of the Philippine Islands also depict creation as featuring a

canine companion, Abuwitiyuw, so that the dog could accompany him into the afterlife. Other ancient cultures and religions also buried dogs with loved ones, apparently to serve as their protectors in the afterlife. Some dogs were even buried with money of their own.

The ancient Greeks often depicted dogs as messengers of gods or demigods. For example, the location of the most famous altar to Heracles, Cynosarges, was chosen because a white dog grabbed a priest's offering from the original altar and moved it to that spot. The name Cynosarges means "white dog."

Dogs feature prominently in the folklore of many cultures. Dogs have been seen as both positive and negative. Black dogs, in particular, are often considered evil or harbingers of death in cultural and religious stories. In India, however, the Bengals give deference to black

An ancient sculpture of the dog god, Anubis, adorns this golden crypt from the ancient city of Tebe, Egypt, containing an Egyptian noble and his faithful dog.

Archaelogical discoveries from Egypt support the belief that the ancient Egyptians revered the dog god, Anubis. Two images of Anubis guard the burial chamber of Pashedu, dated circa 1200 B.C.E.

dog. The god of the skyworld, Kabigat, came to earth with his dogs to hunt. But because the earth was so flat and featureless, he could not hear them barking at the prey. To hear his dogs bark, he created mountains, hills, and valleys.

There are many African myths about dogs, both positive and negative. The Nandi people of East Africa believe that death to humankind was brought on when a dog asked villagers for a drink of milk through their straw. They poured the dog's milk into a hollowed stool instead. The dog was offended and created death for people. People of the Dahomey African tribe tell a myth about a dog mediating an argument among three gods. In return, the gods granted the dog three blessings, making dogs the guardian of women, leader of all spirits, and guide to men.

In Germanic and Nordic cultures, the god Odin was said to have dogs or wolves who protected him. The Sami of the northern regions of Finland, Sweden, and Norway, believed that they were descendants of either dogs or reindeer. The Mongols also believed they were either descendants of a dog or created from a tree and then nursed by a dog.

The Koryaks of Siberia, however, believe dogs were created directly by the creator, Eme'mqut, and his wife, Miti. He created one dog from his penis, and she created another from her vulva. When the two gods were separated, they gave their dogs the power of speech and sent them back and forth as messengers.

CHAPTER 3

Dogs in Popular Culture

No other animal has been so prominently featured in popular culture as the dog. Dogs show up in literature, art, the media, television, film, and on the Web. Their depictions were found on cave walls, and they're still the best-selling cinema animal in Hollywood. The prevalence of dogs in popular culture isn't surprising considering how much a part of our lives they are. There are more than 70 million pet dogs in the United States, so this is one character we can almost all relate to. And even today, dogs hold great symbolism for us; in movies and books they are used to convey moral lessons and tales of courage, and we rely on them to personalize events of great cultural significance, such as the tragedies of 9/11 and Hurricane Katrina.

Dogs in Literature

From great authors to kitschy puppy stories, dogs are often featured in the written form. Children's books may be the most common genre for dogs, from the classic books *Where the Red Fern Grows* and *Old Yeller*, to such modern-day tales as *Good Dog, Carl,* and *Clifford the Big Red Dog.*

One of the most famous dogs in literature is Charley, from John Steinbeck's nonfiction travelogue *Travels with Charley: In Search of America.* The acclaimed author traveled across the United States in a trailer with his Standard Poodle, recording his trip along the way. Some other classic dog books are *The Call of the Wild* and *White Fang.* These two novels by Jack London depict the dog as a noble and faithful friend, as did books by London's contemporary Zane Gray, such as *Riders of the Purple Sage* and *The Man of the Forest.*

Dogs in literature date back several thousands of years. In *The Odyssey* by Homer, Odysseus' dog, Argos, is the only member of the household to recognize him after his 19-year absence. Ancient Indian and Persian literature mentions dogs, and several of the Greek philosophers, including Plato, discuss the role of dogs in society. Dogs are also found in the literature of the Vikings and the Celts. Aesop, the great Greek fabler, features dogs in many of his fables, including *The Dog and the Cook* and *The Fox, the Cock, and the Dog.*

COME ON-JOIN NOW
15,000,000 MEMBERS BY CHRISTMAS

Dogs have been used in advertising and other popular media for centuries.

Edwin Landseer, English, 1802–1873; "Terrier in a Kennel," *Oil on panel, 8 x 6 inches, private collection; Courtesy William Secord Gallery, Inc., NY.*

Later, Chaucer writes about dogs, and Shakespeare mentions dogs in several of his plays. One play, *The Two Gentleman of Verona*, even boasts a canine character, Crab.

Dogs are also featured in the poetry of Walt Whitman and Rudyard Kipling and in the epitaph for Lord Byron's Newfoundland, Boatswain. The famous lines, including, "The

---

Doggy Memoirs

Travels with Charlie, John Steinbeck
Marley and Me, John Grogan
A Dog Year: Twelve Months, Four Dogs, and Me, Jon Katz
Pack of Two: The Intricate Bond Between People and Dogs, Caroline Knapp
Amazing Gracie: A Dog's Tale, Dan Dye and Mark Beckloff

---

poor dog, in life the firmest friend, The first to welcome, foremost to defend," are commonly attributed to Byron but were actually written by his friend and fellow poet, John Cab Hobhouse. In *Peter Pan*, the Darling children are tended to by a Newfoundland named Nana because the family is too poor to afford a nanny.

Dogs in Art

From the cave drawings of North Africa to this week's Sunday comics, dogs have been depicted in art as long as humans have been creating art. Some of the first drawings of dogs depict hunters and their dogs. The oldest known drawing of a dog was found in Persia, the region that is now Iran, and is dated to about 7000 B.C.E. It depicts a dog assisting a human on the hunt.

The dog-loving English have been leaders in the area of dog art, favoring hunting

Maud Earl, English, 1863–1943; "Foxhounds Giving Tongue," *ca. 1905; Oil on canvas, 28 x 18 inches, private collection; Courtesy William Secord Gallery, Inc., NY.*

Christine Merrill, "The Three Graces," *Oil on canvas, 22 x 20 inches, private collection; Courtesy William Secord Gallery, Inc., NY.*

ing protected by dogs; and Chinese Buddhists have two Fo Dog statues guarding the entrance of most temples. Although the original Fo Dog was actually a tame lion, several of the small Asian dogs, including the Pekingese, became known as Fo Dogs.

Photography has taken over much of dog art in recent years. Dog photography books range from the well-received *Dogs* by Elliot Erwitt, featuring more than 500 photos of dogs throughout the world, to the comically posed Weimaraners of William Wegman.

scenes and other depictions of gun dogs. Especially popular during the Middle Ages were tapestries that showed royal dogs coursing game. Sir Edmund Landseer was one well-known English artist who often painted dogs. He depicted his black-and-white Newfoundlands so often that his name became synonymous with the dogs. Black-and-white Newfoundlands are now known as Landseer Newfoundlands.

Dogs are also featured in religious art in almost every known religion. The Christians depict dogs as companions to saints; the Hindus depict some of their deities in the form of dogs, being carried by dogs, or be-

Early twentieth-century sports cartoonist T. A. Dorgan drew a Dachshund on a bread roll to depict a frankfurter, thus the nickname "hot dog." This characterization may have been an allusion to the popular notion that franks, which were brought to the United States via Germany, were made of dog meat.

During his presidency, Calvin Coolidge was often depicted with a family dog.

Stubby, America's First War Dog

Stubby, a Bull Terrier mix, served in World War I and is the most decorated war dog in U.S. history. A stray dog, Stubby was smuggled aboard a troop ship to France. He served 18 months in Europe and participated in seventeen battles on the Western Front. Memorably, he roused sleeping soldiers to warn of a mustard gas attack, giving the men time to don gas masks. On another occasion, he caught a German spy, quite literally by the seat of the man's pants. With his excellent hearing, he was able to routinely warn soldiers of incoming shells, and his presence served to comfort many of the wounded. Stubby's valor did not go unnoticed. His heroic deeds were known throughout all branches of the military, and he made the front pages of every major U.S. newspaper.

At the war's end, Stubby shook hands with President Woodrow Wilson and also met Presidents Calvin Coolidge and Warren G. Harding. General John "Black Jack" Pershing, who commanded the American Expeditionary Forces during the war, presented Stubby with a gold medal made by the Humane Society, declaring him to be a "hero of the highest caliber."

Stubby was made an honorary Sergeant, and the Red Cross, American Legion, and YMCA all gave him lifetime memberships. His YMCA membership card stated it was good for "three bones a day and a place to sleep." Stubby toured the country and probably led more parades than any other dog in American history. He later became the mascot for Georgetown University. This well-heralded dog died of old age in 1926, and his remains are displayed in the Smithsonian in Washington, D.C.

Dogs in the Media

Because dogs humanize people so well, they are often embraced by public figures. Politicians, for example, are known for their well-timed use of a family dog to ingratiate themselves to the public. During the Monica Lewinsky scandal, President Bill Clinton bought a chocolate Labrador Retriever named Buddy, who was specially chosen for his breed and coloring to enhance Clinton's image as a family man. President Richard Nixon epitomized the use of a dog in enhancing a public image in the so-called Checkers speech. After being accused of taking illegal political gifts, Nixon went on television with Checkers, his family's Cocker Spaniel, appealing to the American audience that the only gift he'd ever received from a lobbyist was Checkers. His daughters loved the dog, he said, and he wasn't going to return him, even if it was a crime. He won the hearts of TV viewers and probably both the vice presidency and the presidency with that one speech.

Another president, however, was stigmatized when he tried to lift his Beagle, Him, off the ground by his ears. The ignominious photograph of President Lyndon Johnson pulling Him's ears while the animal seemingly yelped in pain permanently sullied Johnson's public image.

Dogs have also entered the media in other ways. The plight of a single dog or litter of puppies has always managed to appeal to wide audiences. For example, the rescue of a dog abandoned on a sinking Japanese fishing boat in 2002 made the news for weeks, while the 2000 killing of a Bichon Frisé in a road rage incident galvanized animal rights activists and animal lovers.

In times of crisis, dogs are also frequently depicted in the media. For example, rescue efforts for dogs trapped in floods or other natural disasters are frequently aired. And in the aftermath of the Oklahoma City bombing in 1996 and the September 11, 2001, terrorist attacks, disaster search and rescue dogs were

War heroes, presidents, and other national figures have long been associated with the faithful dog. Here, General Custer is shown with a battlefield canine companion.

featured prominently in media coverage. During the tragedy of Hurricane Katrina in August 2005, photos of dogs on rooftops and up in trees, flood waters rising beneath them, touched the hearts of millions of dog owners. Throughout the nation, people opened their homes and wallets to help ensure that pets who were rescued from the flood were either reunited with their people or placed in new homes. And the story of Snowball, whose young owner was forced to leave the little white dog behind by evacuation personnel, brought about federal and state legislation to ensure that pets would not be left behind or separated from their owners in the event of a disaster.

Dogs are also prominently featured in advertising. Whether to show a company or organization in a more sensitive light or to humorously spotlight a product or message, plaintive hounds have begged for donations,

hawked everything from trucks to toilet tissue, and even been used to generate patriotism during times of war or strife. Whether the message is commercial or patriotic, the perception of dogs as uniquely American has made them popular spokesmodels.

Dogs in the Movies and Television

From Lassie to Benji to Rin Tin Tin, dogs have appeared in motion pictures since the beginning. Dogs are still the most common animal seen on either the big or small screen. Their

The original Pete the Pup of the *Our Gang* movies also starred in the *Buster Brown* series, where he got the ring around his eye. It was painted on with permanent dye and would not come off. Several dogs played Pete over the years, and each had his own distinctive look with his own carefully painted ring.

Popular Dog Songs

"Hound Dog," Jerry Leiber and Mike Stoller (made famous by Elvis Presley)
"Sick as a Dog," Aerosmith
"How Much Is That Doggie in the Window?" Bob Merrill (made famous by Patti Page)
"Who Let the Dogs Out?" Baha Men
"Bird Dog," The Everly Brothers

acting chops go back to the silent film era. America's biggest canine star was Rin Tin Tin. According to lore, Rin Tin Tin was a German Shepherd Dog found by a U.S. serviceman in France in the aftermath of World War I. Rin Tin Tin first found fame in the silent movie *The Man from Hell's River* but was able to make the jump to talkies, unlike many human stars. In fact, his string of successful movies is said to have saved Warner Brothers Pictures from bankruptcy. Rin Tin Tin's career didn't even end with his death in 1932. Since then, his descendants (as well as some other German Shepherd Dogs) have served as Rin Tin Tins in films, TV, and promotional appearances. The current Rin Tin Tin is, in fact, Rin Tin Tin IX.

That Rin Tin Tin has been played by many canine actors isn't unique; it's common for a movie or television show to use several look-alike dogs to depict a canine character. One dog may be excellent at tricks but not as good at facial expressions. Or several dogs may be used because of the long hours of filming. Trainers may breed successful dog actors in the hopes of having look-alike descendants, as was done with Rin Tin Tin, Lassie, and the canine actor, Buddy, from *Air Bud*, who had to be replaced when he was diagnosed with bone cancer. (Buddy eventually succumbed to the disease.) Even Eddie from *Frasier* has a doppelgänger, his son Enzo. In other instances, trainers simply scout for a similar-looking dog, as in the case of Benji and Sandy from *Annie*. However it's done, chances are your favorite screen dog isn't just one animal, but two or three.

Dogs on the Web

Dogs have a high presence on the Internet, with Web sites, Web logs (blogs), message boards, and list serves. Dog caretakers use the Internet to ask questions about their dog's health, training, behavior, and general care

Laura Bell Bundy as Elle Woods and her canine co-star Chico as Bruiser, in Broadway's Legally Blonde: The Musical.

and sometimes just to relate anecdotes and show off their pups' photos. Enter almost any dog-related subject into an Internet search engine and you're bound to pull up a page or 10. Experts, however, caution that much of the information on the Internet is untried or untested or from questionable sources. For veterinary or behavior questions, it's safer to visit a qualified veterinarian or trainer. At the same time, researching a breed or a new activity is a snap with the Internet and undoubtedly has led to a greater knowledge of our canine companions.

CHAPTER 4

The History of Dog Rescue and Welfare

Organized animal welfare didn't begin until 1824 in Britain, when 22 philanthropists founded the Society for the Prevention of Cruelty to Animals. At the time, animal welfare was considered a waste of time and money—animals were not accepted as sentient beings by most people. However, with education and hard work, the first SPCA gained such momentum that by 1840 Queen Victoria granted permission to rename the organization the Royal Society for the Prevention of Cruelty to Animals, which it continues to be called today.

Animal rescue found its way to the United States by 1866, when Henry Bergh founded the American Society for the Prevention of Cruelty to Animals (ASPCA) in New York City, in part because of the hard life of the carriage horses he observed there. Other rescue organizations followed, and within three years there were anticruelty laws and humane societies in at least six U.S. states. Then national organizations formed, including the American Humane Association (AHA) in 1877 and the Humane Society of the United States (HSUS) in 1954. While some of the national organizations ran animal shelters as well as conducted animal welfare campaigns and education programs, most did not.

The first animal shelters appeared in the United States in the 1700s, but they were largely used to warehouse animals before they were euthanized. Until the early 1900s, stray animals, especially dogs and cats, were considered a public health threat rather than an animal welfare problem. Packs of stray dogs often carried diseases, including rabies. Following the establishment of the ASPCA, however, the public began to support animal rescue and welfare efforts. In 1869, one of the first true U.S. animal shelters was established, the Women's SPCA of Pennsylvania. In 1894, the ASPCA took on the role of sheltering the stray cats and dogs of New York City; and in 1903, the Bide-A-Wee Home Association (now just Bide-A-Wee), an animal shelter, was established in Manhattan.

Humane Societies and Nonprofit Shelters

Unfortunately, most municipal shelters continued to warehouse and euthanize animals with little effort made to rehome them. The 1960s and 1970s found animal advocates starting shelters of their own. These nonprofit shelters worked not only to get strays off the street but to rehome them, as well. They were less concerned with the public

Until the mid- to late twentieth century, municipal animal shelters were mostly used to warehouse stray animals until they were euthanized.

health threat of stray dogs than with the welfare of the stray dogs themselves.

Being nonprofit didn't mean a shelter was ideal. Many were, and still are, no more than rows of cages on concrete floors. Despite

There are many private groups working toward the protection of domestic animals.

workers' best intentions, the animals were given days or weeks to be adopted and then were euthanized. There was still little effort made to market the adoptable animals to the public, and the kennel workers rarely knew anything about the animals under their care.

Increasingly, however, well-managed progressive animal shelters began to appear. The Progressive Animal Welfare Society (PAWS) in Lynwood, Washington, took on the principle of not just warehousing animals but also actively working to rehome them. Although the shelter still euthanized animals, they were given more time, and PAWS made an effort to both market the animals to the public and to get to know the traits of the animals in its care. It and other humane societies were also taking time to screen prospective adopters, rather than automatically adopting out an animal to the first family to come along. In fact, most progressive shelters placed great emphasis on the appropriateness of adopters.

Today, at private or nonprofit shelters, prospective adopters are expected to fill out lengthy applications and may even be subject to a home inspection. Although many advocates argued that the strict application process prevented dogs from being mistreated or abandoned again, others suggested that the rigorous application process gave the shelters an adversarial image in the community and inhibited both donations and potential adopters. This is currently an area of debate among shelters, both municipal and nonprofit. Many shelters now are recasting their application policies to be educational rather than adversarial.

Breed Rescues

At the same time that humane societies and progressive shelters were taking a more proactive role in sheltering, another version of dog rescue was slowly gaining momentum. As the AKC opened its registry to more breeds, many began to experience overwhelming popularity. A movie featuring Border Collies, for example, could increase the number of Border Collie puppies being bred and, subsequently, being abandoned by the thousands. Unethical breeders exacerbated the problem by providing inadequate information to puppy adopters, increasing the likelihood that the dog would later be abandoned. Shelters were filling not only with random-bred dogs but also with purebred dogs bred specially for quick sales. Today, 25 percent of the dogs in animal shelters are purebreds.

According to the Humane Society of the United States, 20 percent of family dogs have been adopted from animal shelters.

In response to the high number of pure-breds being abandoned, many of the AKC breed organizations began establishing their own breed rescues. Most of these were and continue to be organized groups of foster homes. Some are very large, with hundreds of foster homes taking in thousands of dogs a year. Others are quite small, with fewer than 20 foster homes and fewer than 100 dogs sheltered each year. Some of them have even invested in their own kennels. The Delaware Valley Golden Retriever Rescue, Inc., for example, is housed in a state-of-the-art facility on 4 acres of land.

Breed rescues generally charge more than double what a municipal shelter or nonprofit shelter charges; advocates, however, say it's worth it. Not only is every dog spayed or neutered, temperament tested, and treated medically, most dogs receive training and socialization by being fostered in a home environment. Those interested in purebreds get the benefit of saving a life while still adopting the breed of their choice. You may, however, have to wait for an appropriate dog to become ready for adoption.

Rescue organizations are also known for their strict adoption policies, often requiring home visits, references, and a lengthy adoption application. Many breed rescues assert that particular breeds fare best in certain types of households.

Multibreed Rescues

There are also private rescue organizations that rescue more than one breed. They may serve mixed breeds of one or several breeds, or they may serve a geographical area or a type of dog such as small dogs or herding

---

October is Adopt-A-Dog Month. This yearly nationwide effort encourages dog lovers to provide homes for homeless dogs and puppies.

---

dogs. The ForPaws Corgi Rescue is a breed rescue that specializes in Corgi mixes rather than purebreds. Many of these rescue groups strive to serve a dog population that they believe is underserved by the breed rescue or shelter community. Other nonbreed rescue groups cater to dogs with medical problems or behavior issues.

No-Kill Shelters

Because of effective spay and neuter programs, fewer dogs are showing up in shelters. Many shelter workers oppose euthanizing perfectly healthy dogs. This combination of factors has given rise to a new type of shelter: the no-kill shelter. No-kill shelters do not euthanize any adoptable animal. That means they euthanize only animals that are very old, seriously injured or ill, or aggressive toward people or other animals. These shelters also will not kill an animal for space. That means, however, that they are unable to accept every animal that comes to their door.

It's important to keep in mind that it's not that fewer dogs are being euthanized, only that fewer dogs are being euthanized by no-kill shelters. Many animal welfare advocates feel that calling shelters no-kill gives the public the false sense that healthy, adoptable dogs and cats are no longer being euthanized anywhere, which is untrue. Opponents of no-kill shelters point out that when a shelter becomes no-kill, it merely transfers the responsibility of euthanizing adoptable animals to another agency. No-kill shelter proponents argue that these shelters help galvanize communities to protect their animals and that their goals are achievable.

Spay/Neuter

Spaying and neutering is arguably the biggest single issue in domestic animal welfare. Most animal welfare organizations have placed an emphasis on education about the pet overpopulation problem. The effect of the spay and neuter education campaigns has been astounding, especially in urban areas and on the coasts. The number of homeless dogs in the United States has dropped considerably in the last 10 years. Although there are approximately three to four million dogs and cats euthanized each year today, in 1990 the number was more than twice that.

New information on the relative safety of early spaying and neutering has been a boon to shelters, which can now alter even eight-week-old pups before they go to their new homes. Most shelters and rescue organizations in urban areas now require that dogs be spayed or neutered before being placed in an adoptive home. Previously, shelter workers often saw the puppies of dogs they had adopted out coming through a year or two later.

Although southern and rural regions have benefited less from spay and neuter education, overall the effects have been phenomenal. In fact, shelters say that the number of puppies and kittens in urban shelters is so low that some only rarely have them available for adoption. The shelters began bringing in young animals from less-fortunate outlying regions to supply the demand. Most of the dogs in shelters these days are adolescents or adults. Many of

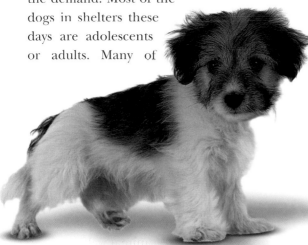
To fight the problem of pet overpopulation, young shelter puppies are often spayed or neutered before being placed in adoptive homes.

Pet Overpopulation in the United States
Number of dogs and cats entering shelters each year: 6–8 million
Number of dogs and cats euthanized by shelters each year: 3–4 million
Number of dogs and cats adopted from shelters each year: 3–4 million
Number of animal shelters in the United States: Between 4,000 and 6,000
Average number of litters a fertile dog can produce in one year: 2
Average number of puppies in a canine litter: 6–10
Number of dogs and cats reclaimed by owners from shelters each year: Between 600,000 and 750,000, which is about 30 percent of dogs and 2–5 percent of cats entering shelters
Source: Humane Society of the United States

them are from the working breed lineages, both purebred dogs and mixes. Depending on the geographic region, the dogs who are seen most at shelters might be pit bull types, herding dogs, or gun dogs. The similarity is that they lean heavily toward highly active dogs who are between nine months and two years old. For dog-experienced people who are willing and able to put in the time these young, enthusiastic dogs need for training and exercise, they make wonderful companions.

Shelters Today: A Middle Ground

The role of rescue organizations has changed substantially over the past 30 years. It's gone from municipal pounds serving as unwanted animal depositories, where the vast majority of animals were euthanized after a few days in holding kennels; to progressive shelters, where potential adopters ran the gantlet when trying to adopt; to where it is now. Although there are many shelters in the various stages of rescue evolution, most progres-

Despite education and awareness campaigns, there are still three to four million homeless dogs and cats euthanized each year in the United States.

sive animal shelters and rescues today are rethinking their role and trying to balance between finding the right home and just finding a home.

Dog rescue still ranges greatly in its efficacy. In some countries, stray dogs are simply rounded up and euthanized by both humane and inhumane methods, from gassing to shooting. Even in the Unites States, many shelters still exist that are simply holding areas for dogs (and other domestic animals) before they are euthanized. In some rural areas and crowded urban areas, strays are jammed into overcrowded kennels, subject to disease, attack, and undue stress.

Although the influx of private nonprofit rescue organizations has been a boon for many abandoned animals, it's also created a new breed of animal abusers—so-called col-

lectors who may start out with good intentions but eventually become so overwhelmed by the needs of the animals that they are incapable of refusing. Eventually, the animals are living in worse conditions than they were—in filthy cages, lacking food and water, and not being exercised or socialized. When these "rescue" organizations are exposed, officials frequently find carcasses in varying states of decomposition—and scores, sometimes hundreds, of starving and neglected animals.

Municipal shelters that once only warehoused animals now work to screen dogs, market them to the public, and even train them when they can. These shelters are subject to municipal codes that private shelters are not. Often, municipal shelters function as both adoption shelters and holding areas for strays and dogs under quarantine. They also are restricted as to the questions they can ask potential adopters. Unless a potential adopter admits to actions that are illegal, such as abandoning an animal or, in some cities, chaining an animal, the shelter cannot prevent the person from adopting a dog. However, many of these shelters are putting more emphasis on working with adopters to match them with the right dog for their lifestyles.

At the same time, many nonprofit shelters are revamping the ways they work with the public. Instead of presenting an adversarial front, they are putting their efforts into public relations—working with adopters rather than fighting them. Many of these shelters say they have found that intensive screening of adopters didn't guarantee an appropriate home but did set up an antagonistic relationship between the shelter and adopter. Adopters were less likely to come to the shelters with questions, work with shelters to keep a pet, or approach a shelter when looking to adopt. They were also less likely to donate

High-energy purebred dogs such as this Australian Cattle Dog may end up in private rescues or animal shelters when busy families realize they are unable to meet the dog's needs.

money to a shelter they felt had treated them unfairly. Whereas many shelters once looked for reasons not to adopt to a person, they now look to make the best match. For example, instead of refusing an adoption to a homeowner with no fence, they advise the adopter about building a fence or recommend a senior dog who can be exercised adequately on leash.

Ultimately, both municipal and nonprofit shelters say that the best way to find the right home and keep the animal in the home is threefold: a good workup of the animal, a good match between dog and adopter, and good follow-up. That means they are spending more time screening animals before placing them for adoption, and they're working with dogs who have particular behavior issues. Many shelters now have special training programs for adolescent dogs or dogs with high activity levels. Other shelters train every dog who comes through their doors—asking the dog to sit for a treat or shake hands. This type of ongoing training is believed to make a dog more attractive to potential adopters and better able to adjust to his new home.

To match the right dog with the right person, shelter workers try to find out as much about each animal as they can. They work with the relinquishing family to get insight into what the dog is like and why they are giving him up, and they spend time observing the dog themselves. They may place this information on cards on the front of kennels or even post the information on the Internet through their own Web site or through Petfinder's site, www.petfinder.org. When potential adopters arrive at the shelter, trained counselors talk to them about what they are looking for in an animal. Do they want a jogging buddy, or will they be leaving the dog alone for long periods of time? Are they agility hobbyists, or do they lead a particularly sedentary lifestyle? The counselors then try to match the adopters' lifestyle with the type of dog that would fit into this lifestyle best.

It's in the weeks after an adoption that problems often begin; house-training lapses, digging, nipping, and chewing can all end a beautiful friendship. Many shelters now make themselves available to adopters for questions about training and behavior. Some even offer free or discounted training classes. There are even shelters that require training for particularly high-energy dogs. Follow-up may also include a postadoption home visit or access to a 24-hour hotline for worries or concerns.

Shelters also are making it easier for a family to return a dog in the days or weeks following adoption. Although shelter workers don't want to see a dog come back into the shelter, they'd rather see it happen early and before the dog learns any bad habits or is relegated to the backyard. They'd also like to see that the adopters ultimately go home with the right dog for them.

According to a 2007 survey by the American Pet Products Association, three-quarters of all dogs have been spayed or neutered.

CHAPTER 5

Dogs and the Law

There are many laws associated with our canine companions. Some of them benefit dogs, some of them harm dogs. Some are for the protection of humans or other animals; others are for the protection of dogs. Canine laws have been among the most controversial aspect of our relationship with dogs because they affect where and how we interact with dogs.

Breed Bans

Breed bans are laws that have arisen in recent years in response to actual or perceived threats by certain breeds of dogs. These laws have especially targeted pit bull–type dogs, but other guardian breeds have been targeted as well. Rottweilers, Doberman Pinschers, Mastiffs, and German Shepherd Dogs have all been banned by breed laws, whether by countries, states, cities, counties, or even neighbor-hoods. Germany has been at the forefront of the movement, banning all bully breeds from Miniature Bull Terriers to American Staffordshire Terriers.

The majority of the breed bans have been in response to specific incidents involving severe attacks. Although fatal dog attacks are rare, they receive a great deal of media attention and often incite public support for severe consequences. Proponents of breed bans say that certain breeds have a propensity for violence toward people, so banning these breeds will reduce the incidence of fatal or severe dog attacks. Opponents of breed bans argue that dog bites are unrelated to breed—all breeds of dogs are capable of biting. And although larger, stronger dogs are capable of inflicting more severe bites than small dogs are, it's not the type of dog that leads to severe attacks but rather the training and treat-

The Rottweiler is just one of the many breeds that have been banned by counties, states, municipalities, and gated communities.

A properly raised Presa Canario will form a loyal bond with his human family but will always possess an innate distrust of strangers.

ment that the dog receives. For example, many of the powerful guardian breeds have become popular among those seeking a dog for protection, fighting, or projecting a macho image. Dogs owned by these types of people generally receive substandard training and may even be trained to harm people or other animals. Often, aggressive dogs are bred to aggressive dogs in order to increase the likelihood of aggressive offspring. In addition, dogs who are mistreated, neglected, or abused are far more likely to bite than are dogs who are not. Opponents of breed bans say that a well-bred, well-trained, and well-socialized American Pit Bull Terrier is just as friendly as an equally well bred and well-trained Labrador Retriever.

In addition to outright breed bans passed by municipalities, many breeds are banned from certain apartment buildings or housing complexes. A more subtle form of breed ban has arisen with insurance companies that will not insure homeowners with certain breeds of dogs. These companies claim that the new bans stem from a rise in lawsuits over bites. The opponents of breed bans argue that the rise in dog-bite lawsuits is not exclusive to specific breeds.

The Myth of the Pit Bull

There is no such breed as the pit bull. Instead, the term *pit bull* refers to a group of similar dogs that descend from the bull and terrier dogs. These are dogs whose ancestors were Bulldogs and terriers crossed together. Some of the so-called pit bull–type dogs are the Staffordshire Bull Terrier, the American Staffordshire Terrier, the Bull Terrier, and the American Pit Bull Terrier. Other similar dogs are the American Bulldog, the Dogo Argentino, and the Boxer. In addition, there are many mixes, which may or may not have one or more of these breeds in their background, who may have similar looks. All of these dogs are frequently lumped into the pit bull category.

Noise Ordinances

Most cities have noise ordinances, and dog barking falls under those ordinances. Dogs left outside all day and night or while their owners are at work often bark excessively. This can be extremely irritating to neighbors and may prompt them to complain to the local police department or animal control agency. Owners of barking dogs are usually given a written or verbal warning, followed by cash fines if the barking continues. Sometimes dogs are even impounded for excessive barking.

Leash Laws

Leash laws work to protect citizens from dog bites and the threat of communicable diseases such as rabies, and to protect livestock from attacks. They also work to protect dogs

Many cities have created specially designated dog zones where dogs can be off leash. However, owners must adhere to all other municipal laws.

from traffic, becoming lost, and theft. In most cities in the United States, laws require that dogs be on a leash less than 6 feet long and under their owner's control when in public places. People who don't keep their dog on a leash or who allow their dog to roam are subject to warnings, fines, and even confiscation of the dog.

In the majority of urban areas, dogs are allowed off leash in public places only in specially designated off-leash areas. These off-leash areas have become increasingly popular in recent years. Most of them have certain requirements: dogs must be current on all vaccinations, licensed, and friendly with other dogs and people. Poop scoop laws apply within off-leash areas, and dogs must be kept on leash until they are within the fenced or designated off-leash area.

Livestock and Dogs

In agricultural and rural areas, dogs at large are considered a predation threat to livestock. For this reason, dogs can be legally shot for harassing or injuring livestock, including poultry. Often the laws are written so that peace officers have no alternative but to euthanize a dog if he is seen killing livestock. In the case of licensed dogs, some rural communities have laws that require livestock owners or peace officers to notify the dog's owners before euthanizing the dog. Dog owners may also be asked to compensate a rancher or farmer for their losses.

Animal Cruelty Laws

Although the majority of dog laws are enacted to protect property and people from dogs, animal cruelty and neglect laws protect dogs from the harm humans can and do bring upon them.

The first animal cruelty laws in the United States were enacted in the mid-1800s to prevent the abuse and mistreatment of working animals, including dogs, who were commonly used for drafting labor at that time. Animal cruelty laws vary widely. In some cities, animal cruelty or neglect can lead to felony convictions with stiff penalties and jail time. In other areas, animal cruelty is a misdemeanor with

Although serious dog bites are rare, experts believe the overall rate of dog bites is at an epidemic level in the United States.

minimal penalties. The definition of *animal cruelty* may range from intentionally injuring or killing an animal to not providing adequate food, water, or shelter or, in some instances, chaining an animal.

Dogs are protected from abandonment in most counties and cities. Perpetrators are subject to fines and imprisonment.

Recent studies that have connected the torturing and killing of animals with the torturing and murdering of children have helped to establish and strengthen animal cruelty laws.

Chaining and Tethering

Chaining or tethering a dog makes the animal vulnerable to attack by predators and other dogs; encourages him to behave aggressively toward other animals and people, especially children; and subjects the dog to a poor standard of life with limited exercise and social interaction. In recent years, many municipalities have created laws restricting or barring the use of chains or tethers as a means to confine a dog. They may bar tethering or chaining a dog to a stationary object altogether or provide a time limit—anywhere from one to five hours. These laws do not apply to leashes held by a person or to overhead trolleys that are at least 10 feet long. Some laws also provide a minimum enclosure for confining a dog—usually about 150 square feet.

Bite Laws

Dog bites are a national epidemic. Estimates by the Centers for Disease Control and Prevention (CDC) put the number of dog-bite-related emergency room visits at 386,000 annually, with an additional 414,000 people seeking nonemergency medical treatment. There are approximately 12 dog-bite-related deaths each year, about .0002 percent of those bitten. Legislators have resorted to many methods to

Insurance Resources

Some insurance companies will not provide homeowner's coverage to people with certain dog breeds or breed mixes they deem dangerous. Bull Terriers, American Pit Bull Terriers, American Staffordshire Terriers, Presas Canarios, Rottweilers, Doberman Pinschers, Akitas, and Chow Chows are a few of the breeds commonly discriminated against by insurance companies. Finding coverage for owners of these dogs can be a challenge. Here are a few resources for finding dog-friendly coverage:

- Contact the insurance commissioner in your state for a list of all insurance companies doing business in the state and for any other information that may be helpful to dog owners looking for insurance. Let the insurance commissioner know if you have been discriminated against by an insurance company because of your dog and ask what can be done about this practice.

- The Insurance Information Institute has information on homeowner's insurance and dogs. Go to www.iii.org.

- The Humane Society of the United States (www.hsus.org) and American Society for the Prevention of Cruelty to Animals (www.aspca.org) can provide information about insurance discrimination practices.

- The American Dog Owner's Association, Inc., provides information on pending dog legislation throughout the country, including insurance legislation. Go to www.adoa.org.

- Contact the American Kennel Club for information on insurers and their policies regarding dog breeds.

- Contact breed clubs and breed rescue groups that work with your breed of dog. Ask them to suggest ways to find breed-friendly insurance coverage.

- Investigate company policies, as well as general industry information, on insurance comparison Web sites such as www.insurance.com, www.insure.com, or www.insweb.com.

- Talk to friends, neighbors, and others with dogs, especially with your breed of dog, about the type of insurance they have and ask if they had any difficulties obtaining it.

Poop scoop laws are now common in most U.S. cities.

address the problem. Suggested solutions have ranged from breed bans to imprisonment for owners of dogs who bite.

Dogs who bite are subject to confiscation, quarantine, and euthanasia. Their owners may also be subject to lawsuits or criminal prosecution and may be held responsible for medical bills as well as compensation for pain and suffering. Many communities have a one-bite rule, which states that owners of previously gentle dogs cannot be held criminally liable for the dog's first bite. The dog is also exempt from consequences for the first bite. There may be exceptions, however, if the bite is severe.

In first-time cases involving bites that draw blood but are not severe, dog owners may receive a warning or be fined. The dogs are sometimes quarantined, particularly if the bite

The passage of the ADA ensured public access to people with disabilities, including those who utilize assistance dogs.

is serious. Second bites may lead to additional fines as well as confiscation and quarantine of the offending dog. Depending on the severity of the bite, the dog may be euthanized or the owner may be required to provide additional security to ensure that the dog does not come into contact with people. Severe or multiple instances of bites generally lead to euthanizing the dog and criminal prosecution of the owner if negligence or intention is shown.

Dog bite laws are not restricted to attacks on humans only. Dogs who attack other dogs or other domestic animals causing injury or death are also subject to confiscation, quarantine, and euthanasia. Owners may be held criminally or civilly responsible or both.

Poop Scoop Laws

The poop scoop law, which is in effect in most urban areas within the United States, is a fairly recent phenomenon. Until 20 years ago or so, it was not a requirement to clean up dog feces in most places, and this continues to be unusual in most other countries and in many rural areas in the United States. But now it's recognized that aside from their unpleasant sight and odor, ani-

mal feces create both public health and environmental hazards. Most urban areas impose cash fines on owners who do not pick up feces in public areas. These fines can range anywhere from $25 to $1,000, depending on how serious a municipality deems the infraction.

Some cities have also passed laws that require dog owners to remove dog feces from their own properties within 24 hours. The reasoning behind such laws is that feces pollute groundwater and attract disease-carrying pests.

Americans with Disabilities Act

The passage of the Americans with Disabilities Act (ADA) in 1990 brought a new level of acceptance for the use of service dogs in public. The ADA requires that all public places be accessible to disabled people, including those people who use a service dog. This means that people with service dogs are granted access to public places just as are people confined to wheelchairs.

Although many restaurants and hotels post signs allowing only guide dogs into the establishment, in fact all service dogs are covered under the ADA. This includes dogs who assist people in areas of mobility, hearing, seizure detection, and mental illness support. Under the ADA, dogs are not required to wear vests nor are service dog users required to carry papers registering their dogs as service dogs. However, most service dog users do carry both papers and outfit their dogs in vests or collars indicating their work.

Other than accessibility, service dogs are subject to the same laws as other dogs are: they must be leashed, cleaned up after, and they cannot be aggressive.

Laws for Working Dogs

Working dogs are subject to the same laws that apply to companion dogs, including bite and leash laws and neglect and abuse laws, but they have additional laws that protect

Many breeds possess the ability to be trained for service and assistance work.

etary fines. To be licensed, dogs must be up-to-date on their rabies vaccination. The cost of licensing often depends on whether an animal is spayed or neutered. The owners of unaltered dogs pay more to license their dogs.

Licenses protect dogs. Lost unlicensed dogs are at greater risk of being euthanized. In many rural areas, peace officers must contact the owner of a licensed at-large dog before euthanizing him. In urban areas, shelters are required to attempt to find the owners of licensed dogs before euthanizing them or placing them up for adoption.

The spay and neuter laws arose in response to the crisis of pet overpopulation. They appear to be having a dramatic effect in reducing the number of adoptable dogs and cats euthanized by animal shelters each year.

In addition to laws that require owners of unaltered dogs to pay a higher license fee, some governments require all shelter dogs to be altered before they are placed into adoptive homes. Additionally, some cities now prohibit breeding within their boundaries.

The Animal Welfare Act

The Animal Welfare Act (AWA) was first passed in 1966 and then revised in 1970, 1976, 1985, and 1990. Administered by the USDA and the Animal and Plant Health Inspection Service (APHIS), the AWA was enacted to protect commercially used animals from mistreatment. These include animals sold in commerce, used for exhibition purposes, and used by laboratories for scientific testing.

The AWA also regulates the dealers who sell animals for scientific research. Laboratories that use animals and the dealers who supply them are required to record the names and addresses of all their animal sources to discourage these dealers from stealing companion animals and selling them to laboratories. They must hold animals for at least five days to

them. Working dogs are protected from being overworked or abused in the course of their training or work. Dogs cannot be used for drafting work within urban areas. Some states have banned Greyhound racing as well as some forms of hunting.

Law enforcement dogs are also protected in their work: they cannot be willfully distracted or prevented from doing their jobs. They and their handlers are also protected from prosecution if a dog bites in the course of his work.

Licensing and Spay/Neuter Laws

Almost every U.S. government, county, or municipal requires the licensing of dogs. The owners of unlicensed dogs are subject to mon-

give owners the opportunity to claim lost or stolen animals.

Pet Theft

The theft of a dog is prohibited and punishable by monetary fines, imprisonment, or both in most areas. The laws covering pet theft are enacted at the city or county level. In most instances, dog theft is considered the same as theft of personal property, although there are many who argue that the theft of a pet should be punishable under more stringent laws.

The thefts of animals by dealers or bunchers—who supply animals to animal testing laboratories—are covered by the Animal Welfare Act.

Antifreeze Laws

Antifreeze is an extremely toxic and usually fatal substance that causes the kidneys to fail. Unfortunately, thousands of dogs die from antifreeze poisoning each year because the substance has a sweet taste that they're attracted to. In some states, including California, there is a law requiring antifreeze manufacturers that include more than 10 percent ethylene glycol in antifreeze to add a bitter agent that makes the toxic substance less palatable to dogs. Wholesale antifreeze, however, is exempted from the law, meaning that most mechanics do not use the new antifreeze.

Laws for Airlines

The USDA imposes several restrictions for transporting dogs by airplane cargo. They must be in adequately sized and ventilated kennels with clear markings and handles. They must be provided food and water, regardless of the length of flight, and the airline must feed and water adult dogs at least once every 24 hours. Young puppies must be fed and watered once every 12 hours. Puppies under eight weeks old are prohibited from airlines.

In response to publicity surrounding the dangers of animals flying as cargo on commercial airlines, the U.S. Congress passed legislation requiring airlines to report any and all injuries, deaths, or incidents that occur to pets when they are being transported by passenger airline.

Estate Planning

If you are concerned about what would happen to your dog if you died or were incapacitated, take steps now to ensure that he would be cared for. You can name a guardian in your will or set up a pet trust that will be funded by some of the proceeds from your estate. Speak first to the person you choose as guardian to make sure that he or she is willing and able to take on the responsibility of your dog. Name an alternate guardian as well, in case your first choice is no longer in a position to care for your dog. Your lawyer can advise you on the best way to word your wishes to ensure your dog's comfort and happiness. The Humane Society of the United States also offers information on writing a will to protect your dog.

You may wish to look into the possibility of placing your pet in a retirement home for animals whose people have died. These include the Pet Survivors Life Care Program, managed by the SPCA of Texas and the Perpetual Pet Care Program, administered by Kansas State University College of Veterinary Medicine. Other programs exist as well. Costs usually range from $10,000 to $25,000.

The laws governing companion animals change often and range widely depending on whether you live in the South or the North, the East or the West, or the city or country. To learn what your specific rights and responsibilities are as an animal caretaker, contact your local animal control facility.

CHAPTER 6

The Problems Surrounding Dogs

Dogs have been our trusted companions for thousands of years, helping us by herding our livestock, guarding our possessions and providing us with unconditional love. Humankind has not always been so generous in return, however.

Dogs have been used and abused for centuries. Even today, dogs are treated unfairly. Problems continue to plague the canine race, from overbreeding to dog fighting to breed bans. But dog lovers are working hard to help overcome the injustices that dogs continue to suffer in our society.

who have nowhere to go. Abandoned and unwanted, thousands of these "excess" dogs are euthanized every year in the United States. Five out of every ten dogs who end up in animal shelters are destroyed simply because no one wants them.

Animal welfare groups around the country educate the public as to the importance of spaying and neutering pet dogs. Some progress has been made, as the number of animals in shelters has declined in recent years, but much more work needs to be done in this regard.

Overpopulation

One of the greatest tragedies concerning dogs in modern times is overpopulation. More dogs need homes today than exist for them. Animal shelters are filled with dogs

Spaying and Neutering

As a dog owner, you can do a lot to help with the problem if dog overpopulation. By spaying or neutering your pet, you will help reduce the numbers of dogs competing for homes.

Fact and Fiction About Spaying and Neutering

Many myths exist on the subject of spaying and neutering dogs. Some of the notions people have about spaying and neutering are simply not true.

- Myth: *Dogs who are spayed or neutered get fat*. This is a common misconception based on the fact that most dogs are neutered when they are fairly young and tend to put on weight as they get older. People associate the weight gain with the spay or neuter, when in reality the dog's metabolism has slowed down because it is no longer a puppy. Dogs who are spayed or neutered can maintain a healthy weight if they are not overfed and are given plenty of exercise.

- Myth: *Female dogs need to have a litter first before they are spayed*. Some people believe that in order for a female dog to be well adjusted, she must experience motherhood at least once before being spayed. The truth is that dogs do not need to be mothers in order to be happy dogs. Plus, waiting until a dog gives birth to a litter adds to the pet overpopulation problem and puts the dog at risk for certain types of cancer.

- Myth: *My dog is a purebred, so he or she should reproduce*. Animal shelters are filled with purebred dogs who came into the world under this false assumption. Only responsible breeders with well-planned breeding programs should be breeding their dogs.

- Myth: *It's cruel to spay or neuter a dog*. Dogs do not have sexual identities like those of humans, and they don't know the difference after they have been spayed or neutered.

Greyhounds have some of the most active rescue programs in the United States, as many racing dogs are in need of loving homes after their short careers are over.

In addition to cutting down on the number of dogs needing homes, spaying or neutering your dog will also improve your pet's life and behavior. Dogs who have been spayed or neutered are less likely to roam in search of a mate. Dogs who have been altered are also healthier because they are at less risk of developing cancer of the reproductive organs.

Animal Abuse and Neglect

Another tragedy taking place in the world of dogs is abuse and neglect. All you need to do is read the paper or listen to the news on the radio to hear about these kinds of cases. Often, disturbed individuals take out their rage on helpless dogs, inflicting abuse that maims or kills the animal. More often, people simply neglect their dogs by tying them up and leaving them without food or water, failing to take them to the veterinarian when they are sick, and generally disregarding their needs.

The abuse and neglect of dogs is against the law in most states and counties, and people who commit these heinous acts are subject to prosecution, fines and sometimes jail time. People who care about dogs have a responsibility to report suspected cases of animal abuse to the authorities. The authority to enforce animal cruelty laws falls on Animal Control agencies in most cities and municipalities. In areas where Animal Control agencies do not exist, the local police department is responsible for handling these situations

Unethical Uses

Throughout human history, dogs have been used in ways we consider unethical today. In the past, dogs were used to subdue and control entire civilizations. The Spanish conquistadors used attack dogs to keep the conquered Incas in line. Plantation owners used dogs to keep slaves from running away. Dogs also played a role in keeping East Germans from scaling the Berlin Wall to freedom. Stationed as sentries along the wall, these dogs of German breeding helped the oppressive East German government maintain control over its citizens. In the more recent past, dogs were used to intimidate civil-rights workers.

These days, the unethical use of dogs still persists. Dogs are bred like livestock in puppy mills, where they are kept in cages stacked on top of each other, often in filthy conditions. In certain parts of the world, dogs are killed for their fur. In other places, dogs are slaughtered for their meat.

Dogs are used in certain sports today that are controversial. Greyhound racing, which may seem innocuous enough, is responsible for the death of thousands of Greyhounds every year. At disreputable establishments, dogs who don't win consistently are euthanized. A small but lucky percentage are placed in adoptive homes when their racing days are done.

Another controversial sport in the world of dogs is dog-sled racing. Each year in Alaska, the Iditarod dog-sled race, which calls for teams of dogs to travel over 1,150 miles of frozen ground, draws the ire of animal welfare groups who believe the event is abusive to dogs. Dog-sled racing aficionados counter that their dogs love to run and that they take good care of them.

People who care about the welfare of dogs are working hard to pass laws to stop the abuse of dogs in sports, as well as to make puppy mills illegal. They are also putting pressure on foreign governments to stop the killing of dogs for fur and meat.

Breed-Specific Legislation

Over the past few decades, certain breeds of dogs have attained international attention for their misdeeds. American Pit Bull

Many pit bulls are loyal and affectionate companions; however, due to the actions of some irresponsible owners, the public's perception of the breed has suffered greatly.

What Is a Dangerous Dog?

How do you know if a dog is dangerous? Local laws define dangerous dogs according to a description stated in local statutes. The exact definition of a dangerous dog varies from place to place, depending on the legislation that has been enacted. Typically, a dangerous dog is one who has attacked and bitten a person or animal without provocation or has chased a person or animal with the intent to do harm.

In most places, a dog who is deemed to be dangerous must be securely confined. The owner may be required to purchase a bond and liability insurance. If these safeguards do not prevent the dog from attacking an animal or person, the dog may be euthanized. The owner may also be charged with a misdemeanor or felony.

Terriers and Rottweilers are just two of the breeds that have made headlines in vicious dog attacks that result in the death or severe maiming of human beings.

The result of the news media's fascination with dog attack stories particularly offenses committed by so-called pit bulls—has been a knee-jerk reaction from legislators to ban these breeds from cities and municipalities. Laws have been enacted around the country making it illegal to own certain breeds of dogs.

The injustice of this legislation is obvious to those who know and love the breeds being banned. Certain breeds of dogs are not inherently bad. Rather, these breeds fall victim to the whims of people who breed and train the dogs to be vicious.

Dog attacks most often happen in high-crime areas where drug dealers and others on the wrong side of the law use the dogs as part of their illegal activities. The dogs are often mistreated and deliberately trained to be aggressive toward humans. The media, legislators, and the public blame the dog's

Breed-specific legislation is harmful to all purebred dogs, not only the so-labeled dangerous breeds. When common sense falters, companion breeds like Bulldogs and Pugs could be the next banned breeds on your block.

breed for the attacks—not the criminals who are truly responsible.

People who know and love dogs are fighting to eliminate breed bans, instead insisting that each individual dog be judged on his or her behavior.

Puppy Mills

One of the most inhumane situations facing dogs today in America is the puppy mills. Large breeding facilities where dogs are treated like livestock and kept in cages their entire lives, puppy mills provide dogs to pet shops around the country. Females are forced to have litter after litter until the constant reproduction destroys their health. Both male and female breeders are confined to cages, often in filthy conditions.

The puppies that result from these breedings are not properly socialized and are kept in cages until they are shipped to pet stores around the United States. Many of these puppies suffer from genetic disease (the result of indiscriminate breeding) or

from ailments such as parvovirus or distemper. Because they spend their early weeks in cages, they are difficult to house-train because they are used to eliminating in their living area.

Although animal welfare advocates have fought long and hard to shut down puppy mills—most of which are located in the Midwest—these breeding facilities are still in operation. As long as the public continues to buy puppies from disreputable pet shops, puppy mills will continue to thrive.

To help fight puppy mills, do not buy puppies from questionable pet shops. Talk to your friends and educate them. If you want a purebred puppy, look into obtaining one from a responsible breeder, preferably one who is local.

Dog Fighting

The cruel act of dog fighting is an old one. The so-called sport reached its popularity in England in the 1800s, when a number of fighting breeds were developed. The descendants of these fighting dogs still exist today. In the right hands, these dogs are gentle and obedient companions who love people. In the wrong hands, they are vicious fighters who will tear each other to shreds for the amusement of spectators.

Organized dogfights take place in pits, which are small arenas surrounded by plywood walls. Spectators watch while dogs are put together in the pit to fight. Bets are placed, and fights last anywhere from one to two hours. The fight ends when one of the dogs refuses to fight anymore or is so severely injured he can no longer do battle.

Unorganized dogfights are also catching on in popularity in urban areas, and usually involve a handful of individuals watching as two dogs fight. Dogs used in dogfights receive injuries so severe that the wounds are sometimes fatal. Bruises, broken bones and deep puncture wounds are common.

An unsettling reminder that dog fighting is alive and well in the United States was the arrest of professional football player Michael Vick in 2007. Vick pleaded guilty to federal dog-fighting charges and was sentenced in 2008 to 23 months in prison. Vick's dogs were seized by the court. Some were euthanized; others were turned over to rescue groups for rehabilitation.

Pit bull–type dogs suffer the most from dog fighting, which not only is inherently cruel but also results in tremendous suffering for dogs in training. Dogs who won't fight or who fight poorly are often beaten and killed, while other dogs are used as virtual punching bags by dogs being trained to be more aggressive. Other animals are used to train fighting dogs as well, including cats, rabbits, and small dogs.

Dog fighting is illegal in all 50 states. In 2008, Wyoming became the last state to make it a felony instead of a misdemeanor.

Dog Bites

The simple fact is that dogs bite more than 4.7 million people in the United States each year. Children and other vulnerable people incur many of those bites. And against popu-

Socialize your new puppy to children within his first few months of life. Well-socialized dogs are far less likely to bite.

Steps to Prevent Your Dog from Biting

- If you are buying your dog from a breeder, ask to meet the dam. Do not buy a dog if the mother is aggressive or overly fearful.
- Spay or neuter your dog.
- Do not allow your dog to nip or bite when playing.
- When playing tug-of-war or other aggressive games, you should always be in control of the game. Teach your dog to drop the tug object when asked.
- Start socializing your dog early in puppyhood to a lot of different types of people.
- Train your dog to follow basic commands and to respond to you when you call his name.
- Do not allow your dog to be possessive of food or toys. To reinforce the idea that people provide food, drop occasional treats in his bowl as he eats.
- Be cautious when introducing your dog to new situations

lar belief, most dogs bite people they know, often members of their own families. Even otherwise reliable dogs can bite under extreme circumstances.

Although there are ways to curb aggressive behavior in dogs, we can't prevent all bites. Sometimes dogs bite because they have a dominant temperament or they become aggressive because they are fearful, which is called fear aggression. Other times dogs bite because they're in pain or are panicked.

There are also times when we encounter unknown dogs who may potentially bite, so it's important to know what to do when you are meeting a dog and how to avoid being bitten by one.

Why Dogs Bite

There are certain situations in which dogs feel trapped or fearful, causing them to growl or bite. Use caution when waking a sleeping dog or taking away an especially tasty bone. Do not allow situations to develop in which your dog feels cornered. Although you can condition a dog to accept such acts as touching his food bowl or taking away a toy, you should always exercise caution when doing so.

Dogs may also exhibit aggressive behaviors when ill or injured. If you or a family member is bitten when petting or touching an otherwise trustworthy dog, visit your veterinarian to ascertain whether the dog acted out of pain or discomfort. Once you've ruled out a medical explanation for your dog's aggressiveness, see a trainer. The sooner you deal with this, the better. There are many types of aggressiveness that can be alleviated with careful training and socialization. A professional trainer can guide you through this process.

Don't allow your puppy to nip. Encourage him to chew on safe, appropriate toys instead.

To prevent food possessiveness, periodically feed your dog from the bowl and add tasty bits as he is eating.

If your dog is suffering from an illness or injury that you know about, take precautions when petting or moving him. If he seems uncomfortable or in pain, minimize your contact with him unless he seeks it out. Heed his warnings. If he growls, he does not want you to touch him. If you need to move him, use a soft muzzle or tie a length of gauze around his snout. Better safe than sorry when it comes to the sharp end of a dog's discomfort.

Unknown Dogs: Precautions

Although more than half of all bites are from a dog the victim knows, there are still legitimate concerns about unknown dogs. You do not know a stray dog's temperament or background, and a dog on the loose is often lost and scared or may be injured.

When you encounter a stray dog, never approach him. If he appears to be injured, call your local animal control office. If you

---

One-third of all liability claims against homeowners stem from dog bites. The insurance industry claims that bites involve a total payout of $310 million annually. As a result, many insurance companies will not insure large, powerful breeds such as Rottweilers, German Shepherd Dogs, Dobermans, and pit-bull types.

---

are worried about his safety, speak to him calmly and call him to you. If he refuses to come to you, keep an eye on where he is and call animal control. If he approaches you in a friendly manner, allow him to sniff you. Do not make any sudden moves. Once the dog seems comfortable, you may coax him to follow you or check his collar for identification.

If an unknown dog acts threateningly toward you, stop and stay very still. Do not make eye contact with the dog but do not turn away from him either. Talk gently to the dog—do not raise your voice. Back away from the dog slowly. Never run. A running person looks like prey to an aggressive dog. If the dog attacks you despite these efforts, drop to the ground and curl into a ball, protecting your head and neck with your hands.

If a dog chases you while you are riding a bicycle, stop and dismount, keeping your bike between you and the dog at all times. Slowly wheel your bicycle away.

What to Do If You're Bitten

A dog bite isn't the same as other cut injuries, even if it looks fairly innocuous. If your own dog bites you, double-check his vaccination records, and make sure he is up to date on rabies shots. If the bite is from a dog you know, ask the owner for proof of up-to-date vaccines. If a free-roaming dog bites you, contact your local animal

Resist the urge to let your dog give you a kiss on the lips; a dog's mouth harbors germs, so stick to cheek kisses.

Is it true that dogs' mouths are cleaner than those of humans? No. In fact, dogs' mouths can host many disease-causing bacteria, including *Pasteurella*, *Streptococcus*, *Staphylococcus*, and *Capnocytophaga*. And dogs are much more likely to eat things like garbage, rotten food, and feces than are humans. However, human bites are still more dangerous to other humans than dog bites are. That's because, although our mouths are comparatively cleaner than dogs' mouths, we host more bacteria that cause disease in humans.

control office. If the dog is not found and tested for rabies, you may need to be prophylactically treated for the rabies virus. Rabies is almost 100 percent avoidable if treatment begins before symptoms appear. Once symptoms begin, however, rabies is almost always fatal.

A dog's mouth harbors germs, so visit your doctor even if you do not need stitches. If the bleeding does not stop with gentle pressure on the wound, go to the emergency room. If you were bitten on the face, on the hand, or on a joint, go to the emergency room; you may require plastic surgery or X-rays. Bites on the hand are more likely to become infected.

If you do not need immediate care, visit your doctor by the next day. Most clinics have an urgent care center where you can be seen by a doctor, physician's assistant, nurse practitioner, or medic. If you are not up-to-date on tetanus boosters, you will need a tetanus shot. The doctor will also clean the wound and might dress it. Because of the potential for infection from any animal bite, you'll also receive a prescription of antibiotics. It's important to keep an eye on a bite wound for the first few days to ensure that it does not become infected. If you see a red line forming from the wound, go to the emergency room.

Once you've been treated medically for the bite wound, it's up to you to take any legal or behavioral actions. If the dog who bit you was your own, you need to address the reasons behind his aggressiveness, whether medical or behavioral. If your dog bit someone else, fully cooperate with the victim and authorities, providing your dog's veterinary history and quarantining your dog, if necessary. If you were bitten by a dog who is not your own, you may wish to file a report with your local animal control agency. The dog may be quarantined or even euthanized, depending on his history and the owner's wishes.

A New Dog

Bringing a new dog into your home is a life-changing decision. Whether you have a household of animals or are adopting your first pet, a new dog brings a variety of adjustments.

Before proceeding, examine your lifestyle and personality, and carefully research the type of dog that will fit into your life best. Being a parent, having a full-time job, and having experience with dogs are all factors when adopting. Obtaining your dog through a reputable source, such as a respected breeder or recognized animal shelter, helps establish a healthy and lifelong friendship.

Knowing how and when your dog is going to enter your life, realizing both the benefits and responsibilities of a new pet, and preparing your home and family for your new addition will smooth the transition immeasurably.

CHAPTER 7

Is a Dog Right for You?

Before you begin the search for a dog, you need to ask yourself the most important question of all: is this the right time to bring a dog into my life? Sharing your home with a dog is a life-changing experience. A dog contributes a special kind of companionship, but it also requires a daily, long-term commitment in the form of regular mealtimes, playtime, exercise, veterinary care, grooming and training.

This is when you need to take a hard look at yourself and your life. Welcoming a dog into your home is a huge step. Adopting a dog is accepting a 10- to 15-year commitment—or longer—to substantially change your way of life. Just as graduating from high school, getting married, buying your first house, and having a child will lead you to change many parts of your life, so will having a dog.

Pros and Cons of Dog Ownership

We all know the great things about dogs. They give us unconditional love and friendship. They contribute to our health by always being ready for a walk or a game of fetch. They provide instant stress relief and lower our heart rate. They're always thrilled to see us, even if we've only stepped out for five minutes. They're trustworthy confidantes who never tell our secrets. And they make us laugh.

While living with a dog has its benefits, it can also restrict the amount of time you spend away from home and the amount of money you have for discretionary spending. Dogs need to be fed and walked at approximately the same time each day, so those spontaneous after-work get-togethers are more difficult to attend. Planning a trip requires the additional step of deciding whether to board the dog, hire a pet sitter, or take the dog with you—and then finding a boarding kennel, pet sitter or vacation spot that meets your needs as well as those of your dog. Veterinary expenses are generally manageable unless an emergency comes along. Do you have the financial resources to purchase pet health insurance or set aside money for a pet health savings account? Think about what you're willing to sacrifice and what you're not willing to sacri-

Every dog has a perfect owner. Take the time to find the right dog for you.

fice to maintain your dog's health and give him the best food and day-to-day care.

Are You and Your Family Ready for a Dog?

Consider the other people in your life. Your spouse or significant other as well as your children may have their own thoughts on whether a dog is a good addition to the family. If everyone isn't on board with the idea of acquiring a dog, it can cause tension and disagreements. In a worst-case scenario, the dog becomes the victim when the family decides it's too much trouble and gets rid of him.

If you have children, it's vital to choose a dog who is kid friendly. This may mean finding a puppy you can raise yourself, or it might mean visiting a shelter or rescue facility for an adult dog who's been temperament tested with children.

Do you have other dogs or cats? If so, are you sure they will accept another dog in the home? Is the new dog you've found friendly toward other animals? If you have cats, you need to realize that not all dogs are appropriate for households with cats. Some breeds have predatory instincts that make them unsuitable to live with a cat if they have not been properly socialized. Siberian Huskies, Greyhounds, and Jack Russell Terriers, for example, are known for their interest in small, fast, furry things— not the situation you want for Misty.

The Right Time to Get a Dog

Your stage of life can also factor into the decision. Are you a college student? A busy parent with two young toddlers? A jet-setting business traveler? It's essential to consider how a dog will fit into your lifestyle. Any friendship, including one with a dog, requires nurturing and quality time. Will your busy schedule allow you to give a dog the care and companionship he needs?

Housing a Dog

Where you live can also determine whether it's a good time for you to acquire a dog. Homes, condos and apartments can all accommodate dogs, but some dogs are more suited to each type of housing than others are.

For many breeds, a single-family home with a yard is most appropriate for their size and energy level. For instance, sporting or gun dog breeds such as Golden Retrievers and Labrador Retrievers do best when they have a yard where they can chase tennis balls or even a pool where they can swim. They can do well in condos or apartments, however, if you're committed to giving them daily exercise.

In terms of size, small dogs fit well into any type of housing, but sometimes other traits can make them unsuited to life in apartments or condos. Shetland Sheepdogs might seem just right for apartment life because of their small size, but they love to bark and they're highly active. Those characteristics can make them unwelcome neighbors in multifamily living environments.

Many giant breeds have low energy levels that make them suited to condo or apartment life, as long as the unit isn't so small that you're always tripping over the dog. Take into account whether there are many flights of stairs. Often, giant breeds such as Mastiffs or Scottish Deerhounds have difficulty navigating steps. Unless you're a giant yourself, carrying them isn't really an option.

Rental housing that permits pets is sometimes difficult to find. When it is available, a large pet deposit or monthly pet rental fees may be required. Don't overlook valuable resources in your search for an apartment that permits pets. Some humane societies, such as the San Francisco SPCA and the Riverside County Department of Animal Services in Riverside, California, provide lists of pet-friendly apartments on their Web sites. And before you sign a lease, be sure that it includes written permission to have a dog.

College students often long for a dog but are limited by dormitory life or the constraints of having a roommate. Some colleges have dormitories that accommodate students with pets, but those are few and far between. At this ever-changing time of life, it may be best to set aside the idea of dog ownership for a time when your living situation is more stable.

Should Allergies Keep You from Having a Dog?

When you pet a dog or even enter a room where there's a dog, do your nose and throat itch or do your eyes water and get puffy? People with allergies make up about 20 percent of the population, and of those, about 30 percent are allergic to dogs or other pets. Whether they're furry or hairless, wire-coated or single-coated, all dogs produce saliva, urine, and dander (dead skin flakes) that carry allergens.

A number of breeds lay claim to being hypoallergenic, most commonly Bichons Frises, Portuguese Water Dogs and various terrier breeds. Their coats have a slower shed cycle than do those of other dogs. For this reason, they shed less and their coats do not stop growing at the 2 to 3 inches typical with most dogs. Dogs with low-shedding coats require regular, often expensive grooming, but they may trigger fewer allergy problems. That said, the important thing to remember is that dogs and people are individuals. All dogs produce allergens, but some make more allergens than

---

Finding Dog-Friendly Rental Housing

To find rental housing that accepts dogs, you need to pull out all the stops. Here are some tips that will help:

- Tell family and friends that you are looking for dog-friendly housing. Ask them to keep their eyes open and to let you know if they hear of anything.

- Mention your quest for housing to your veterinarian, groomer, and the staff at your pet supply store. Dog lovers are often friends with other dog lovers who may live in a dog-friendly building or own a dog-friendly unit.

- When looking at newspaper and online rental housing advertisements, check out the ads that say dogs are welcome and also those that do not mention dogs, which often indicates that the landlord can be convinced to accept dogs.

- Visit local real estate offices and ask about dog-friendly rentals and lease arrangements. Taking the extra step to introduce yourself may prompt a realtor to do a little extra digging for you.

- Get in your car or on your bike and look for rental signs. Home owners who rent out back units or have other small properties do not always pay for advertising. These more casual landlords are often more willing to accept dogs.

- Develop a résumé for your dog to let prospective landlords know about his good behavior. Include letters of reference from previous landlords and your dog's veterinarian and trainer.

- Provide your potential landlord a copy of your dog's Canine Good Citizen certification from the American Kennel Club. Get information on training and testing for the CGC from www.akc.org.

- When visiting an open house, bring your dog along. Ask a friend to wait with him outside while you speak with the landlord. If your dog is well behaved, meeting a prospective landlord may just be the clincher.

Human Allergies

Many people have allergies to dogs. Symptoms of allergies include sneezing; coughing; red, itchy, watery eyes and nose; scratchy or sore throat, and wheezing or breathing difficulty.

If an allergy specialist has diagnosed you or a family member with a dog allergy, it doesn't mean you have to give up your pet. You can discuss the possibility of allergy shots or medication with your doctor, but there also are ways to reduce the allergens in your home so that you can continue to live happily with your beloved dog:

- Keep the bedroom dog free to ensure a good night's sleep void of allergens. Use dust mite covers on your mattresses and pillows.

- If you have forced air heating and air conditioning in your home, the air currents may spread allergens throughout the house. Fit your home with a central air purifier that uses a HEPA (high-efficiency particulate arresting) filter, and use it at least four hours a day to remove a significant amount of pet allergens.

- Vacuum floors and furniture daily using a machine with a HEPA filter. Regularly clean walls with water to further reduce exposure to allergens and dust.

- Stick to washable blinds or shades and cotton-covered furniture, and limit the number of rugs, upholstered furniture, and drapes in the home. Opt for hardwood floors or tile rather than wall-to-wall carpeting.

- Clean dog bedding and crates at least weekly. Wash clothes that you wear while interacting with dogs before putting them back in the closet or drawer.

- Bathe your dog weekly, and brush or comb daily. Weekly baths can greatly reduce the level of allergens on fur.

- Wipe your dog's coat with large baby wipes several times a week. Ideally, this should be done outdoors by someone who's not allergic to the animal.

- Look for symptoms of dermatitis in your dog, which often leads to accelerated skin sloughing and fur shedding. Always wash your hands after touching your dog, and do not touch your eyes or other areas of your face before your hands are washed.

- Wear a dust mask to reduce exposure to allergens while you groom your dog and do housework. If possible, have a professional or family member without allergies take over these tasks.

- Keep over-the-counter antihistamines on hand. Liquid Benadryl works the fastest, followed by the chewable type.

---

others do, and some people are more susceptible to allergens than others are. You may find that you can tolerate certain dogs but not others, even within the same breed.

Before you decide to try your luck with a so-called hypoallergenic cat or dog, remember that allergies can build over time. You may not react to a particular animal on first meeting but develop an allergy after living with it for days, weeks, or even months.

If you have allergies and still want a dog, have a contingency plan ready if the situation doesn't work out. You must find some way to either coexist with the dog by taking medication or adjusting your cleaning routine or you must have a solid alternative home lined up. It's not fair to a dog to get rid of it because you made a poor decision.

Finally, accustom yourself to a stuffy nose and puffy eyes. For most people, the companionship is worth it.

None of these issues need stop you from acquiring a dog if that's your heart's desire, but thinking about them can help you make a good choice when it comes to selecting a dog.

CHAPTER 8

Choosing a Dog

The wonderful thing about dogs is that they come in so many varieties. There's a size, shape, color, coat type, activity level, and temperament to suit just about anyone and any environment. And it's essential to take all of those elements into account when selecting a dog. Making the wrong decision can turn dog ownership from a delight to a disaster. Factors to consider include breed, age, background, and temperament.

All Agreed

Before you go out looking for a dog, be sure your entire household is on the same page. Does everyone agree that a Great Dane is the right dog for you, or does someone desire a Chihuahua? Sit down and talk as a family about each member's expectations, desires, and concerns. Does everyone want a dog? Is there a particular type of dog that family individuals want? Who is going to care for him? Ask each family member to write a list of hopes and concerns and share it with the rest of the family. Ironing out concerns and ensuring that everyone is in agreement will save everyone a great deal of frustration once the new dog is home.

Age

Choosing between a puppy and an adult dog is difficult. Many of us relish the idea of watching a puppy grow but realistically don't have the time for an active puppy. Others are drawn to an adult dog but have a partner who is yearning for a pup. If you want to adopt a dog from a shelter or rescue facility, in some areas you may need to search to find a puppy, although there are always plenty of adult dogs available.

Before making this difficult choice, take stock of your life. Puppies require an extraordinary amount of time and patience. Do you have both in sufficient amounts to raise a new puppy? If you have a high-stress job with long hours and a lot of travel time, a puppy probably isn't for you right now. Take comfort, though, because there are loads of eligible adult dogs out there—in foster homes and shelters—looking for a home to call their own.

The good thing about an adult dog is that what you see is what you get. You'll know his size, temperament, and exercise level right from the start. An adult dog—especially one who is past two or three years old—also requires far less work than a puppy. Most adult dogs come into the home house-trained. Even if they aren't, it's usually a fairly painless process with adults. They may even know some basic commands such as *sit* and *down*.

Consider adopting an adult dog from an animal shelter. You'll save a life and have an instant companion.

Choosing an Adult Dog with the Right Temperament

Understanding a dog's temperament helps determine how much training he may need. If you don't have the time, interest, patience, or knowledge to work with a dog who is poorly socialized, suffers from separation anxiety, does not get along with children, or is nervous or excitable, it is not fair to the dog—or to you—to take him home. It is better for that dog to be adopted by someone who can put in the extra training effort and for you to select a dog who is a better fit for your lifestyle. To help determine a dog's temperament, try these tips:

- Check the dog's sociability. If you want your dog to be your best pal and an integral part of your family, look for one who loves people. Ask to visit with the dog privately in a quiet area. If he is a people dog, he will solicit your attention by approaching you with tail wagging and licking or nudging you. He should also approach your child in a friendly manner. This is a good sign that he is at least tolerant of children.

- Check the dog's tolerance of physical affection. To determine how much contact a dog will tolerate, pet him a dozen times. Does he lean in for more or does he pull away? A friendly dog will lean in for more affection.

- Test the dog's excitability level. Jump around and make noise for several seconds. How excited does the dog get? How long does it take him to calm down? If he gets excited, jumps on you, and takes a long time to settle down, he probably requires an owner with some patience who can give him extra attention. If he becomes aggressive or predatory, he requires a home where he can receive special training. If he gets excited and playful but calms down quickly, he could be an excellent choice for a family with young children.

- Determine if the dog suffers from separation anxiety. Leave the dog alone for a few minutes. When you return, observe his behavior. If the dog seems stressed or out of breath, he may suffer from separation anxiety, which requires additional training.

- Check the dog's response to new situations. Take the dog for a short walk and observe how he reacts to noise and traffic. Is he frightened or curious? Does he try to chase moving objects? Dogs who are fearful in new situations often need socialization and training or even medication to remain calm. Car, bicycle, or cat chasers are a danger to themselves and sometimes to others—they can be killed by traffic or they can injure small animals. These dogs need special training, secure fencing, and a good leash and collar.

The downside to an adult dog is that you often won't know much about his past. If he was abused or neglected, he may bring baggage, and many adults have developed some bad habits that need to be addressed. Adult dogs who haven't been allowed in the house in the past can have some difficulty adapting to home life, and it may take some time before they're comfortable on a leash. Fortunately, old dogs can learn new tricks, and older dogs usually adjust to their new life quickly.

Not everything is going to be perfect: your new friend may be aggressive toward dogs or cats or have separation anxiety; a good shelter or rescue group should have a sense of this before adopting the dog to you, but surprises always come up. Sometimes adult dogs go through a honeymoon period in their new home; behavior problems may not always be apparent for several weeks or even months after Fido moves in. Enroll your new adult dog in training classes as soon as he comes into your life. These classes will help prepare you for any transition issues, and you'll be surprised how much a dog can learn and unlearn.

Puppies need you to be with them a great deal. To become a healthy, well-adjusted adult, a puppy needs your guidance and support—and that doesn't mean just half an hour when you get home from work. Puppy kindergarten, crate-training, and socialization go a long way toward developing a well-adjusted adult. If you work full-time and there's no one else in the home who can help out, an adult dog may be your best bet.

Purebred or Random-Bred

There are diehards who want a purebred only and others who refuse to accept anything but a mixed breed. You can get a happy, well-adjusted, friendly pet whichever route you choose, but there are some pluses and minuses with both.

When you buy a purebred puppy, you know what your dog will look like as an adult and may have a general sense of his personality. Although dogs are individuals, they were bred for specific tasks, and dogs of a particular breed have some similar personality traits. On the downside, purebred dogs are believed to suffer from more genetic problems such as hip dysplasia, skin allergies, and eye and heart problems than are random-bred dogs.

If you adopt a random-bred puppy, though, chances are you won't know what he will look like as an adult. Mixed-breed aficionados think this is half the fun, but others want to be prepared for the size and personality of their grown-up dog. Even if you know the breeds that went into the mix, it's difficult to say what physical or temperamental traits will predominate.

Breeds and Breed Groups

Whether you choose a purebred or a random-bred, your dog's ancestry will come into play in your life together. Although every dog exhibits a variety of qualities, there are certain traits representative of your dog's breed(s) that will likely show up in your pet. A dog with several breeds in his mix may exhibit traits from one or all of them, although one breed

Which breed will fit into your lifestyle best? Learn as much as you can about different breeds so you can make an informed decision.

tends to dominate. Before choosing a breed, spend some time looking at breed descriptions. Determine the exercise needs, kid appropriateness, size, and best family situation for each breed you consider before making a decision. Don't base your choice of breed on looks alone. Be sure you understand the temperament and characteristics that come inside the pretty package.

If you're adopting your dog from a shelter, where many dogs are so randomly bred that it's difficult to determine what breeds are dominant in an individual, ask for help from shelter workers or volunteers. Describe what you want in a dog, and ask the workers to steer you toward the right dog for your lifestyle. Even if the workers don't know an individual dog's breed, they can probably tell you quite a bit about a dog's personality and needs. A good shelter tries to determine the dominant breeds in each mix, but there are no guarantees, and puppy looks can be deceptive.

In general, smaller dogs are bred to be companions, but this isn't always the case. While a Chihuahua makes a great apartment dog with few exercise requirements, a terrier is super active and intelligent. If you don't give him a job, he will find one on his own, usually something that you won't appreciate, such as chewing your shoes, digging holes in your car pet, or making mad dashes out the front door. And what about a Chihuahua/Norwich Terrier mix? There's no telling what personality traits will dominate in an adult, so you must be prepared for those of either breed.

Fortunately, there are some general rules you can follow with most dog breeds. Determining the group that a breed is part of is also helpful. Each breed registry categorizes breeds by a number of groups. Although the group names of the American Kennel Club (AKC), United Kennel Club (UKC), and Fédération Cynologique Internationale (FCI) differ, they follow fairly standard lines and can tell you a great deal about the dogs included within them.

It's human nature to look for patterns and to group objects or animals by their common characteristics. Dogs are no exception to this tendency. Over the centuries, people have divided dogs into a number of different categories. Some of these are based on the dogs' purpose in life, such as the hounds, developed to scent or sight game, or the herding breeds, whose job it is to keep flocks together and direct them according to the shepherd's instructions. Understanding which group a dog belongs to as well as its original purpose can help you choose the breed or mix that's right for your family and lifestyle. Following are descriptions of the various breed types, which can help you narrow your choice.

For this book, we are using the following group guidelines: companion dogs, guardian dogs, gun dogs, herding dogs, hounds (scenthounds and sighthounds and pariahs), northern dogs, and terriers. There are some general descriptions of dogs from each group, although, of course, there are exceptions within individual breeds and dogs. No one dog exhibits every trait associated with a particular breed. There are aggressive Labrador Retrievers and mellow Norwich Terriers; Siberian Huskies, who stick close to their people, and independent Golden Retrievers.

When looking at the different groups and breed descriptions, match your interests with the dogs' needs. Make a list of what you are looking for in a dog. Although you may think you want an Australian Shepherd, after comparing your list and the dog's traits, you may find that an Alaskan Malamute is more to your liking. For detailed descriptions of each breed, see chapter 18 on page 208.

Companion Dogs

Companion dogs are generally small, although there are some exceptions, and they

The bully breeds often make excellent companions for children, but they may not get along with other dogs.

More than 10 million dogs in America sleep on their owners' beds, according to a 2003 online survey by the American Pet Association.

Most companion dogs make great pets. After all, that is what they were bred for.

or field dogs. Among the breeds that have served as companions are Marie Antoinette's Papillon and the Shih Tzu—a favorite of Chinese royalty during the Manchu dynasty.

After generations of life as companions, many of these dogs are excellent house pets who get along with almost anyone. Some, however, tend toward nippiness and anxiety if not properly socialized to accept people and trained to have the basic manners necessary for every dog. They are often overly coddled instead of being allowed to be the real dogs that they are. This is a mistake, leading to dogs that become possessive, needy, and even aggressive.

If you're elderly, lead a sedentary lifestyle, live in an apartment, or travel, a small companion dog could be an excellent friend for you. Because of their size, their exercise needs are minimal—a walk or two a day is fine. They are also easier to handle in a small apartment because they eat and eliminate smaller amounts and require less space than the larger breeds do. They're lightweight, and their mobility makes them easy to bring along when traveling by car or airplane and easy for a person who is disabled or elderly to lift and carry.

bond easily with their owners. All breeds were developed for a job, and the companion dogs are no exception. Some of them originally held a job or are miniature versions of larger working dogs, like the Boston Terrier and French Bulldog, which are scaled-down versions of the bull baiters. The little Schipperke was bred to work on canal barges, catching vermin and keeping guard. Even some of the very small companions were bred for work and can require more training and exercise than the other companion breeds do. Yorkshire Terriers, for example, were bred as ratters and so tend to be bold and assertive. Despite their tiny size, they believe they can take on even the biggest threat. The companion dog group also includes several breeds that are larger or were originally bred for other uses. The Dalmatian, for example, was bred to accompany carriages on what could be 60- to 70-mile trips. It has sometimes had difficulty transitioning into its role as a companion because its protective instincts and high energy level remain intact. It requires an experienced owner who can provide it with structure and exercise.

But many companion dogs were bred simply to keep people company. In many cultures of the past, royalty and noble people bred dogs to serve as companions rather than as workers

Guardian Dogs

Sometimes known as working dogs, guardian dogs were bred to guard homes, people, and valuables as well as livestock. While they might sound like a useful sort of dog to have around, they are not for everyone. Large and reserved in nature, the guardian breeds are gentle with family and friends but fierce when provoked.

Some, such as the Rottweiler and the Doberman, were bred to live closely with people as personal guards. Although their guarding instincts can work for you, they can also work against you if your dog is poorly bred, poorly socialized, or untrained. These guardian dogs bond tightly with their families but can be wary of strangers, even when socialized. If you love to entertain and thrive on having guests in and out of your home, your guardian dog must be very well socialized and always supervised with guests. This is especially true if you have children who frequently have friends over. It's not unusual for guardian breeds to mistake friendly wrestling for an attack on "their" child and to leap to his defense. Consider whether this type of dog is really appropriate for your lifestyle.

The livestock guardians were bred to live largely independent of people. They bond with livestock rather than with people or other dogs, defending them with their lives. Guardian dogs bred to protect livestock rather than humans include the Anatolian Shepherd of Turkey and Kuvasz of Hungary.

Guardian breeds can be excellent family dogs. However, they may be wary of strangers and need supervision and socialization.

Many are still used in these roles today, in both their countries of origin and on farms and ranches across the United States. The protective instinct of these guardian dogs sometimes puts them at odds with a human household. They make excellent watchdogs because they see their owners as their herd, and their job is to protect their herd. They can overwhelm a family not experienced with dominant dogs, however, and they may be wary of strangers and strange animals. Many experts suggest that livestock guardians be chosen only by individuals who are experienced with guardian-type dogs and have an understanding of their special needs.

Other guardians include the relatively gentle Newfoundlands and Saint Bernards. Instead of guarding against human or animal predators, these traditional search and rescue dogs held the job of aiding the lost and injured. Despite their large size and propensity to drool, both make excellent and dependable pets, being friendly and outgoing. But even very friendly working dogs should receive obedience training; their sheer size can be dangerous to both young children and senior citizens if they do not learn how to behave in a restrained manner.

Size should also be considered when deciding whether to bring a guardian or working dog into your family. Although most are sedentary, a 150-pound dog takes up a lot of room in a small apartment. And several, such as Black Russian Terriers, are highly active and need a family who can provide them with an outlet for their active bodies and minds.

These giant dogs also have giant-size needs: they require more food and more frequent cleanup, and boarding, grooming, and veterinary costs are considerably higher than are those for their smaller relatives. And giant breeds tend to have shorter life spans than other dogs do. They are often old at 5 or 6 years of age and may die by 8 or 10 years.

Guardians demand a dog-experienced owner who can provide them with consistency and structure. With most of these dogs, physical correction is not necessary or recommended—you are not going to win physically. However, firm, consistent training will garner their respect and loyalty. Guardian breeds can and do make excellent family companions, but be sure to consider their special needs before you acquire one.

Gun Dogs

These are the quintessential family companions. As a rule, they are loyal, friendly, active, and affectionate. Also referred to as sporting dogs, gun dogs were bred to accompany hunters in the field and to work closely with people and other dogs. For this reason, they tend to get along well with everyone, including children. Gun dogs love the outdoors and being with their families, making them the ultimate hiking and boating companions, with energy and stamina to spare. If you have an interest and love for physical activity, then these superactive dogs are the companions for you.

Generally speaking, the gun dogs tend to be gentle, with soft mouths and an easygoing disposition, but a few are sharper and more intense, such as the pointers and the Chesapeake Bay Retriever. The downside is that many do not calm substantially with age—there are 11-year-old Irish Setters who have the same boundless energy as rambunctious pups. Labs retain puppylike energy well after most dogs have settled into adulthood, and some never calm down. This energy can make them anxious in the home if they don't get enough exercise. None of the gun dog breeds are sedentary, and few will fit into apartment life. Even the Cocker Spaniel has a strong need for exercise and play.

Be aware as well that some gun dog breeds, such as English Springer Spaniels and Labrador Retrievers, are bred along show lines, while others are bred along field lines. Dogs from field lines tend to be more agile with a stronger drive to hunt and may be smaller or otherwise differ in appearance from show-bred dogs. This is something to discuss with a breeder or to ask the breed club about.

Within the gun dog group are breeds so disparate as Golden and Labrador Retrievers

The retrievers are known for their affability and family-friendly nature. However, every retriever has a unique personality.

and German Shorthaired Pointers. While the retrievers often make affable family pets, are usually gentle, and tend to mellow with age (despite a continued love of long walks and playtime), the various pointers have more energy and tend to be more difficult to train. Many gun dogs are notorious runners; without consistent training, don't expect them to come happily back to you after fun in the park. Despite their gentleness with people, their strong chase instincts mean the gun dogs can be dangerous with small animals such as cats.

For people who can provide the exercise and training they need, gun dogs can't be beat as trustworthy companions for active families. Like all dogs, they need early socialization to ensure that they are friendly with everyone.

Unfortunately, because of their popularity, there are a number of puppy mills, pet stores, and backyard breeders that are eager to make a dollar off these dogs. Be picky when choosing a breeder, or work with an accredited rescue or animal shelter. And do your research; you'll be thankful in the long run.

Herding Dogs

Highly intelligent and highly active, herding dogs require jobs probably more than any other group does. With their quick minds and endless endurance, they require people who have the time, energy, and smarts to keep up with them, and they chomp at the bit in a home where TV rules. If you enjoy running and hiking, Border Collies,

Herding dogs are high-energy animals with quick minds and a zest for life. They require families that have both time and energy to expend on them.

Australian Cattle Dogs, and Australian Shepherds will all make eager companions—there is nothing they love more than hours of fun and exercise with their favorite person. If you want to get involved in a sport such as herding, agility, or flyball, a herding dog may be the perfect dog for you. On the downside, all this energy and intelligence can lead to a truly out-of-control dog in the wrong hands. Even a short-statured Corgi is a handful when there is a breakdown in training or socialization. A herding dog without a job to do will make one up for himself, and it will probably be something you do not want him to do, such as digging up your plant beds and chewing holes in your favorite shoes.

Because herding dogs regularly herd animals much larger and stronger than themselves, they must be brave and even a little foolhardy. Although they are rarely aggressive, the herding breeds are hard dogs who may have a tendency to nip in the same way they might nip at cattle or sheep to move them along. You must teach them that this is not acceptable behavior. They are also adventure seekers and will find their own entertainment if you don't provide it. Some of these dogs will accept nothing less than a 3-mile run and an hour of aerobic play each day. Keep this in mind when you find yourself lulled by that incredibly sweet ball of fluff. If you cannot provide your herding dog with sheep to herd or cattle to drive, consider training him in agility or flyball. Regular organized activities can take the place of a traditional job and keep your dog physically and mentally satisfied.

Physical correction will only cause these dogs to dig in their heels. Give them firm, positive, and consistent training rather than harsh reprimands. Because of their special needs, they do best in homes with a dog-experienced owners.

Herding dogs tend to pick one person as their own. If you are adopting only one dog for a family of four, be prepared that a herding dog will most likely choose one person to bond with—and that won't always be the person intended.

Hounds

Hounds are sometimes erroneously thought to be perfect companions for mellow dog lovers. It's easy to picture the lethargic hound slumbering in front of the general store depicted in so many Hollywood movies. The truth is, there are actually two types of hounds—scenthounds and sighthounds (and pariahs)—and among the two are many different personalities.

Scenthounds aren't always the easygoing dogs Hollywood depicts. They need structure and exercise.

Scenthounds

Scenthounds are what we're usually thinking of when the word hound comes to mind. Scenthounds tend to be rangy dogs with pendulous ears who keep their nose to the ground. Despite the image of the lazy hound lolling on a porch, not all scenthounds are canine narcoleptics. Far from it. Most of them are intense and fearless hunters who can be active and single-minded when it comes to tracking. For these dogs, nothing makes them happier than sniffing out a varmint, be it human or animal. The entire makeup of a hound is bound to hunting: even the long ears and facial wrinkles are said to help catch and direct scent. These dogs were bred to help hunters in their search for anything from foxes and rabbits to bears and mountain lions. Once they catch a scent, they will pursue it relentlessly, even if that means crossing busy roads or traveling tens of miles. For their safety, it is crucial that scenthounds be kept on leash or within a securely fenced area. Among the scenthounds are dogs large and small, including the Black and Tan Coonhound, Beagle, Basset Hound, and Bloodhound.

Scenthounds were developed in Europe and North America to track and pinpoint prey. Some were specifically developed to trail injured prey, whereas others were developed to tree prey, driving raccoons or opossums into trees and keeping them there while alerting the hunters by baying. Because of this background, they tend to be very vocal and can make unpopular neighbors in apartments. On the plus side, hounds were traditionally hunted in packs, so they get along well with other dogs and are almost universally friendly toward people. They are largely dependable with rambunctious children and playful puppies alike. That said, the exuberance of large hounds can be a bit much for small children.

Besides their love of sniffing, hounds tend to have another common characteristic: single-mindedness. This is sometimes translated as stubbornness, but it is indicative of their ancestry: they were bred to sniff out one thing despite cut backs, distractions, and diminished trails. Once a hound has something on his mind, or in his nose, you can bet that little will distract him. This can be difficult with a large, powerful dog such as the Bloodhound. Fanciers are adamant about Bloodhounds being kept on a leash; otherwise they may be gone two days on a scent before their owners see them again—if they see them again.

Although many of the hounds are large and leggy, there are several dwarf varieties, including the Basset Hound and Dachshund. Despite their short stature or small size, dwarf hounds retain the hunting traits of their larger cousins. They can be equally vocal and single-minded.

Bloodhounds and other large hounds tend to be exuberant youngsters, and with their ungainly trot, whipping tail, and drooping flews, they can cause a bit of a ruckus in a small or cluttered house. That's not to say large hounds don't make good housedogs; often they do, but for the right person.

Scenthounds, such as the Basset Hound, Beagle, or Foxhound, can have widely disparate personalities. Basset Hounds do not make good apartment dogs even though they're slow-moving and require less exercise than most hounds. They have a propensity for vocalization—as do most hounds—and can injure their backs by climbing stairs, which most apartments have. Beagles, while small, require a good deal of exercise and can be stubborn. Fortunately, most scenthounds are food mad, which can help with training.

Hounds also have special health issues. Their long, droopy ears are prone to infection, and they can develop skin infections related to their heavy wrinkles and loose skin. The long-backed, short-legged dwarf breeds may suffer disc and spinal problems. Clean the ears and skin folds regularly, and teach your hound not to jump on and off the furniture, which can injure his back.

Many hunting hounds are kept as kennel dogs, but they are happiest when part of the family. Although they love to hunt, they also enjoy using their innate talents in other areas, such as search and rescue and therapy work. If you have a good-size yard, patience, and a sense of humor, you may want to consider a hound as your next dog.

Sighthounds and Pariah Dogs

The sighthounds are possibly the world's oldest type of dog. Evidence of sighthounds has been found as far back as the eighth century B.C.E. Originating in the Middle East and Asia, they were bred to hunt by sight and to course prey. They retain these abilities, making them the runners of the dog kingdom.

Sighthounds love nothing as much as to run; they make good pets as long as they are kept securely fenced.

All of the sighthounds look quite similar, elegant with long, narrow bodies and deep chests. Most of them are quite large: think Greyhounds, Afghan Hounds, and Irish Wolfhounds. They are active and keen in the field but restful in the home. Sighthounds will run after anything that moves, whether it's a rabbit or a radio-controlled car, so they should always be leashed or confined to a securely fenced yard. Many are not trustworthy with small animals such as cats.

Like scenthounds, sighthounds are incredibly single-minded. That combined with their amazing speed can spell danger. Owners caution that sighthounds must always be on leash when in unfenced areas. Despite this, sighthounds make excellent companions. They are lovable dogs who can easily switch between work and relaxation mode. In health matters, the sighthounds are often sensitive to anesthesia as well as being susceptible to bloat—also known as gastric torsion—because of their deep chests. The very large members of the group, such as the Irish Wolfhounds and Scottish Deerhounds, tend to be short lived.

Pariah dogs are often grouped with sighthounds. These are primitive dogs who tend to live at the periphery of civilization. They are the closest to being wild among the species *Canis familiaris*. Some of the pariah dogs, such as the Carolina Dog, exist as feral dogs with some domesticated individuals. Others are largely domesticated, such as the Basenji, a quick, clever, and highly mischievous dog that has become an increasingly common choice for a family pet. The Canaan Dog of Israel was documented as a domestic breed more than two thousand years ago. After the exodus of the Jews, it became feral except for individual dogs kept by the nomadic Bedouins. In the twentieth century, it gained popularity among Israelis and is again kept as a domestic dog.

Pariah dogs tend to have similar looks, being of medium size with prick or rose ears, curled tails, and compact feet. Many of them are described as catlike, fastidious, and primitive in their behaviors. For instance, female pariah dogs tend to come into estrus only once a year rather than twice a year like the typical domestic dog.

Pariah dogs are not for every family. They require an experienced dog owner. Although some pariah dogs have a long history of domestication, others are closer to their wild roots and may have problems adjusting to a home life without concentrated socialization and training.

Northern Dogs

Northern breeds, also known as spitz dogs, are defined by their geographical background. They were all born of the north, suited to the harsh, cold climate of the Arctic or near-Arctic. Most of these dogs from northern climes have a decidedly similar appearance, with prick ears, a thick double coat, a sharp, foxlike face, and a tail that curls over the back. Many of these dogs are multipurpose, serving as hunters, herders, and sled dogs as well as companions. The smaller spitz dogs of Scandinavia were generally used to herd and guard reindeer, while the larger dogs, such as the Siberian Husky and Alaskan Malamute, were primarily sled dogs. Many of the Asian spitz breeds, such as the Chow Chow, Chinese Shar-Pei, and Akita, were originally guarding or fighting dogs. Whatever their use, all the northern breeds have a tendency toward independence.

Many northern breeds are aloof with people, rarely forming strong one-person relationships. Most have an innate desire to roam. Siberian Huskies, for example, are the quintessential escape artists. Owners have been known to resort to concrete and steel dog runs to keep

If you live in a cool climate, consider a northern breed. These dogs love the cold and will thrive when allowed to participate in winter sports such as skijoring.

them from escaping. Some northern breeds have predatory instincts, so they should be supervised with small animals and even babies, whose cries can sound like injured prey.

These dogs have energy to burn, so getting them involved in some sort of activity is suggested. Huskies and Malamutes do well with skijoring or sledding. Because some are wary with strangers, it's advised that these dogs be socialized early and thoroughly. Northern breeds are independent, yet they affiliate strongly with other dogs—they are true pack animals and will be ready members of your pack as long as you establish the hierarchy early.

The northern breeds do very well with active families who are experienced with dogs. A northern breed would probably work well in your life if you hike, skijor, or bike; live in a cool climate; and have the time for training and exercise.

Terriers

The name *terrier* comes from the Latin word *terra*, meaning "earth," and it stems from their traditional work of entering tunnels or dens to chase small prey and vermin. Some were bred to bolt the prey from the tunnel so it could be caught by the hounds, while others were bred to catch and kill the animals themselves. Tunneling, known as going to ground, was the motivation for developing the terriers' distinctive looks and traits, from their protective wiry hair and docked tails to the keen expression and lively and tenacious nature. The larger terriers were also used as guard dogs.

Terriers were developed primarily in Great Britain, especially beloved by the people of the working class. They were first imported to the United States by English immigrants in the late 1800s. Depending on their use, they were small and short-legged or large and long-legged. The Airedale is the largest of the terriers, while the Australian and Silky Terriers, along with the Miniature Schnauzer, Toy Fox Terrier, and Norfolk and Norwich Terriers, vie for the title of smallest. There are two distinct types of terriers: the traditional terriers and the bull and terrier types, nicknamed the bully breeds.

The traditional terriers include the Norwich Terrier, the Border Terrier, and the Cairn Terrier, as well as the larger Airedale Terrier. The bully breeds include Bull Terriers, Staffordshire Bull Terriers, and American Pit Bull Terriers. All of these breeds were originally ratters—dogs bred to kill vermin for practicality or sport—but the bully breeds were also used in other blood sports, including bull baiting and dog fighting. Because of this background, as well as their continued use in illicit dog fighting, there are concerns about their temperament. Bully-breed fanciers, however, argue that most of the breeds are extremely people-

Many terriers are high-energy little dogs that require attention and exercise.

oriented and especially good with children. What they are not reliably good with are other dogs. Although there are bullies who love their fellow canines without any special training or socialization, owners are encouraged to expose their young bully puppies to as many good dog experiences as possible.

Not surprisingly, the terriers can be dangerous with small, furry creatures, from cats to rats. With ample socialization and training, however, some can learn to live peaceably, at least with cats. Others are entirely untrustworthy.

Most terriers are passionate diggers and will journey down rabbit holes in pursuit of quarry. Many terriers have met their demise by being caught in a tunnel collapse—terrier fanciers are quick to advise fellow owners to keep a leash on their pets in unfamiliar terrain.

If you want a bold and lively dog, consider a terrier. Although terriers are generally small, they are high-energy dogs with a love of exercise and play. They're also intelligent and will find something to keep them busy if you don't. The downside is that some can be snappy and reactive.

Energy Level

After looking at the groups and individual breed descriptions, you should have a fairly good sense of each breed's energy level and exercise requirements. If you will be adopting a puppy or adult from a shelter or rescue organization, the volunteers or staff members should be able to help you determine an individual dog's activity needs and at least guess at what a puppy will be like as adult.

Think about what you want: a dog who needs a couple of 10-minute walks a day, a dog who thrives on longer walks or runs with a half-hour of ball playing thrown in for good measure, or a dog who is not happy without a good long run every day as well as an hour of agility or other mind/body task. Ask about the dog's personality: active, mellow, or somewhere in between? Then ask yourself about your personality. What's your dream day: lounging on the couch with the remote control and a beer, or taking a 10-mile walk in the mountains? Are you a runner or long distance walker, or is your

exercise limited to a monthly trip to the gym? How about time: are you home from work in time to take a long walk every day, or is it more likely that you'll have to cram in the time to take a jaunt around the block?

Different dogs have very different exercise needs and desires. If you long for a dog with whom to do agility, you may be disappointed with a Pug or a Mastiff, who probably wouldn't be competitive and may not even enjoy the activity. On the other hand, if you want a couch buddy, a young Australian Cattle Dog will be chomping at the bit to get out into the action and can make your life miserable. Active dogs who do not have an outlet for their energy often become destructive and may exhibit neurotic behaviors such as digging, barking, and chewing. They're unhappy and make you unhappy at the same time. Even if you do summon the energy to provide the exercise an active breed requires, is it what you want to do? The last thing you want is to feel that fulfilling your dog's needs is a burden. It's no way to spend the next 10 to 15 years of your life. And it's disappointing when you long for a dog with whom to participate in sports and outdoor activities, and instead you have a dog who needs a break every 15 feet. Good owners adjust, but why stack the cards against a wonderful lifelong relationship? Think about your activity level and your potential dog's before you choose.

All puppies have energy to burn; however, many breeds mellow as they age.

Rural, Suburban, Urban

Some breeds and individual dogs are more amenable to city, country, or suburban living. Many of the livestock guardian dogs, for instance, are difficult to keep in the city. They are large and powerful, so a small house or apartment can be confining and lead to a lot of broken glass. Guardian dogs are often wary of strangers and highly territorial, so they can be problematic at the dog park or in an apartment, where they are in close proximity to strangers. They're only doing their job, but most neighbors won't appreciate the barking and will be disarmed by a 150-pound dog growling at them in the elevator. Small companion dogs, however, may not be the best choice for rural life. There are dangers from wild animals, extreme weather, and rough terrain. In addition, smaller dogs may simply be disinterested in your rural lifestyle. So keep in mind that a Pomeranian isn't going to make a great ranching companion and a Maremma Sheepdog isn't going to be the best dog for a studio on the seventeenth floor of a Manhattan apartment building.

There are also other considerations. Large, rural properties often don't have secure fencing. This may work with a 12-year-old Lab, but a younger, more active dog is going to wander and may be hurt or killed by wildlife, traffic, uncovered wells, poison, animal traps, or any number of other dangers. Many dogs who do well living the rural life are born herders and hunters. However, their instincts are to chase livestock, and most farming communities allow property owners to shoot dogs who harass their livestock. If you live in a rural area, even if there is no leash law, do yourself and your dog a favor and install secure fencing or a dog run to keep your dog safe when he is outside on his own.

Most dogs do well in suburban settings or residential city neighborhoods, where there are large yards, some distance between neighbors, and a number of parks. This type of neighborhood can play host to dogs from tiny Yorkies,

Gun dogs, herding dogs, and guardian dogs can all make good ranch companions.

Some breeds make better city dogs than others. Keeping a dog in an apartment demands special considerations.

For some dogs, a country life is a dream come true; for others, there are too many dangers.

who spend most of their time in a loved one's arms, to large Rottweilers and German Shepherd Dogs, who may alternate between playing in the yard and sleeping next to the sofa.

Companion dogs are the best of all urban dogs because their generally small size, affability, and somewhat lower exercise needs are ideal for a smaller environment, where they're in close proximity to many people and other dogs. Also, small dogs need less space in the home (their crates, beds, bowls, and play spaces are smaller) and produce less waste. This may seem petty, but it can become an issue for indoor dogs without access to an outdoor potty area.

Guardian dogs, herding dogs, and gun dogs are good country dogs. These breeds enjoy romping in the woods and helping out on the farm, and they have the energy, protective coat, and gumption to enjoy a long day in the outdoors. They would probably be exponentially happier in the country than their urban counterparts because their often high exercise needs and desire for room are met.

Dogs who require a high level of grooming are not the best dogs for a rural environment. In the country, dogs can get into a host of messes: rolling in dead animals, getting burrs caught in their coats, and having various twigs, grasses, and pine needles find their way into ears and between pads. Dogs bred to be outdoors have more protection from burrs, and it's easier to groom a wash-and-go Lab after a skunk's made its mark than to groom, say, a Samoyed.

Size

People often have distinct ideas about the type of dog they want before they start looking for one. You might want a dog who is large, small, or somewhere in between. Although every dog requires much the same care, there are distinctions among sizes that will affect your life together.

Large dogs sometimes get a bad rap. Although we think of them as having high energy and even being destructive, this is only sometimes correct. In reality, many large dogs, especially the giant breeds, are among the mellowest dogs. Like any dog, they can be a handful during puppydom, but very large dogs such as Newfoundlands, Mastiffs, and Saint Bernards tend to mellow once they hit adulthood. As far as energy level, some of the giant dogs are more appropriate for apartment life than are small, spunky terriers. These large dogs are generally happy with a daily walk and maybe a couple games of fetch. Most are content to hang out by your feet while you watch TV and are always quick to accept a cuddle session. In fact, despite their size, they are the want-to-be lap dogs—content to while away their days with a head on your lap, snoring contentedly.

That said, giant breeds aren't always easy. They tend to slobber (think Saint Bernards, Great Danes, and Bloodhounds) and they're big, so they have big needs. Food must be plentiful and the expense can add up quickly. And as size increases, so do the prices of accessories, crates, beds, treats, toys, grooming, and kenneling. These dogs are also likely to have more health problems than most other breeds do. Hip dysplasia and other joint and arthritic disorders are common. Giant breeds carry a great deal of weight, which can be a liability if they are not bred carefully. They are also the shortest-lived dogs—many enter old age at six or seven years. Advances in veterinary science, however, are increasing their life span, and many fanciers say that with a good diet, regular exercise, and veterinary care, large dogs can live much longer than they have in the past. Many are now breaking the 10-year mark, even living for a few years beyond it.

Even country dogs should have the benefit of secure fences. Roaming dogs can get themselves into trouble.

Giant breeds also have space needs that you should consider. Although most giant breeds are somewhat sedentary, you need to determine whether your home is conducive to having a large dog. If you live in a studio apartment, chances are that a large dog is going to take up a big portion of that space, and you'll be tripping over him more than you'd like. And even a mellow giant breed dog can cause havoc with just a few swishes of his tail.

With giant dogs and giant amounts of food come giant waste. These dogs produce a lot of waste, so daily scooping is a must. You might also find it's difficult to maintain a giant dog in an apartment because of this.

Medium to large dogs have some of the disadvantages and advantages of giant dogs but also some characteristics of their own. Medium to large dogs, such as German Shepherd Dogs, Labrador Retrievers, Australian Cattle Dogs, Standard Poodles, Border Collies, and Golden Retrievers, share similar qualities. Most are active dogs: they enjoy running, jumping, swimming, fetching, and a lot of other canine games. For someone with an interest in canine sports and a vigorous recreational life, these are the dogs to choose. While they vary in individual temperament and energy level, most dogs this size make great hiking and sporting companions. After a couple years, most mellow out and become good house buddies; they are up for a cuddle as well as a walk.

There's a wide range of grooming and exercise needs, as well as common veterinary ailments and longevity among dogs of this size. In general, medium and large dogs have fewer hip and joint problems than do giant breeds, but they have more than the small breeds do. Most, if not all, need more exercise than do both giant and small breeds. Depending on the individual dog, these breeds can fit into urban, suburban, and rural lifestyles. As long as their exercise needs are met, they don't share the space issues of the giant breeds, although they may prefer a house with a yard. Medium to large dogs are routinely kept in apartments in large cities such as New York and Chicago without much difficulty. They usually live longer than giant breeds but not as long as small breeds do. They're also easier to transport than are giant breeds. Medium and large dogs fit easily into a car and can fit into the lifestyle of a family that goes boating or travels by RV—something that's difficult for a 150-pound Mastiff. Their food, crate, bedding, kenneling, and grooming needs fall into the medium range of cost. This is the size that fits best into most people's lifestyles and expectations.

It's said that small breeds are the ultimate travel companions. They're small enough to fit into any car and boat and have the added bonus of being able to ride with their owners in the passenger cabin of most airlines—at least if they're small enough for their travel crate to fit under the seat. For this reason, many frequent fliers favor small dogs. In general, small dogs are the most convenient of dogs: they can be picked up and moved, tucked into a portable dog carrier, or simply held in a person's arms when out and about. At the same time, their small size leaves them vulnerable to people and other animals. While an errant step would barely cause a Newfoundland to budge, it could kill a 4-pound Chihuahua.

Small dogs are often purported to be excellent apartment dogs and ideal companions for the elderly. This is often true but must be tempered with reality: many of the small

Small companion dogs often make excellent pets for the elderly or for those with sedentary lifestyles.

breeds are big dogs in small bodies. For example, a dog like the Norwich Terrier requires an owner as active and involved as that of the most energetic Border Collie. The same goes for the intelligent Corgi. Terriers are usually small, but they are intelligent, active, and headstrong dogs with strong predatory drives. These aren't the right dogs for people who want an easy-to-raise, instant couch potato.

On the plus side, many small breeds do fit well into apartments and into senior-paced lives. The exercise needs for many are minimal—a walk or two a day is ample. The small companion dogs are especially well suited for a sedentary lifestyle. They've been bred for centuries to fit into just such an environment. Their small size means they need less room; their beds, crates, and food bowls take up but a fraction of your space; and the limited amount of waste they produce means low-hassle cleanup. Accordingly, their supplies are less expensive than are larger dogs': less food, cheaper accessories, and less expensive grooming and kennel-

> "For some people a home isn't a home unless it has a piano, or a fireplace, or some other natural adjunct. For me a house or an apartment becomes a home when you add one set of four legs, a happy tail, and that indescribable measure of love we call a dog."
>
> —*Roger Caras*

ing costs. On the other hand, small dogs have veterinary problems their larger brethren don't: dental, anal sac, and eye problems among them. They're also more sensitive to anesthesia, so treatment can be a bigger risk.

If you start out looking for a Miniature Poodle, don't be surprised if you find yourself drawn to a Standard. Most dogs of any size can be accommodated. Think about the differences the size will entail, but don't let it scare you.

Coat Care

A dog's coat isn't something we usually give a lot of thought to when choosing dogs, but we should. If you're a neat freak, a heavily shedding dog is going to make you miserable. Dogs with heavy coats can exacerbate human allergies, and some coats require extra care to keep the dog happy and healthy.

Double-coated, longhaired dogs are among the hardest to groom. Dogs such as Australian Shepherds lose huge amounts of hair, especially when they blow coat (shed), which happens twice a year. If you don't keep up with the brushing, your house will be adrift with Aussie fur. Some double-coated dogs have fairly short and coarse hair. However, they shed their fuzzy undercoat almost year-round, leaving giant dust bunnies in their wake.

Another notorious shedder is the Labrador Retriever. Despite having a low-maintenance reputation, Labs shed throughout the year. Wear a pair of black pants when you pet your next yellow Lab, and you'll experience the bane of Lab owners everywhere: short, spiky hairs stuck to you in copious amounts. Even the most conscientious brushing won't prevent their hair from appearing just about everywhere.

Some of the dogs who shed the least are the setters. They have a single coat, and although their fur is long, it is fairly thin, almost like human hair. Setters shed minimally, but they do need to be brushed regularly to avoid getting tangles in their feathering.

Some dogs are known for having low-shedding coats. These coats have a slower shed cycle than do other coats. For this reason, the dogs shed less and their coats do not stop growing at the 2 to 3 inches typical with most dogs. Low-shedding coats require regular grooming and haircuts, but they may trigger few problems in people with dog allergies. Some dogs with low-shedding coats are Poodles and Bichons Frisés. And a dog can have a coat that is perfect for one person but a nightmare for another. For example, Poodles don't shed much, so allergy sufferers find that they have fewer symptoms when they keep Poodles. On the other hand, Poodles require regular brushing and clipping. Their tightly curled coats can quickly become matted if grooming lapses. For those without the time or money to maintain a high-maintenance coat, a Poodle is the wrong dog to choose.

Grooming needs are important considerations when choosing a dog. All breeds, no matter the coat, should be brushed at least weekly.

Many terrier breeds have wiry coats that are somewhat rough-textured.

infections, so be sure to clean their ears regularly with a cotton ball and an ear-cleaning solution—never use cotton swabs or any cleaning utensil small enough to fit into the ear canal. Dogs who aren't walked on concrete need to have their nails clipped because they aren't worn down naturally from a tough surface. And ideally, you should brush your dog's teeth daily or at least weekly.

Other Pets in Your Household

Too many of us forget about our current pets when we go in search of a new companion. Some dogs just will not get along with other dogs, cats, or other household pets. However, there are ways to introduce new pets to pro-

All dogs should be brushed at least weekly. Breeds such as the Australian Shepherd or the Belgian Malinois do best with daily brushing as a way to keep shed hair to a minimum. Unless they spend a lot of time rolling in the mud—or in other less appetizing substances—dogs don't need a bath more than once a month. Dogs have natural oils that keep their bodies warm and their skin healthy. Too much bathing can wash away these oils and lead to dandruff and other skin conditions. However, dogs with severe skin allergies may benefit from weekly shampooing. Weekly shampooing can also help decrease allergies in owners.

Other regular grooming needs to consider include ear cleaning, nail clipping, and teeth brushing. Dogs with drop ears, such as Labs or Golden Retrievers, are prone to ear

Not all dogs get along with cats. Find out whether a new dog is cat-friendly before bringing him into your home.

Introducing an adult dog to a home where there are already pets can pose challenges, but they are usually resolved with patience.

vide the best chance for a smooth transition for everyone in your household.

If you already have a dog in the home, think long and hard about whether a new companion will make him happy. Does he love other dogs or is he afraid of them? Is he good at sharing or is he food or toy possessive? Is he a dominant or submissive dog, and how do you think he will handle sharing your affection? If you have a partner, consider allocating one dog for you and one dog for him or her—dogs like to have a person they can call their own.

Make sure your dog is going to be welcoming to a new pet by bringing other dogs into your home and seeing how he reacts. Is he friendly or hostile? Keep things slow, gentle, and jovial—this is just a test. If your dog does get along with other dogs, doesn't have possessiveness issues, and isn't overly dominant or submissive, start thinking about the type of dog he'll get along with best. If you have a female, experts say a male would make the best companion: they tend to get along better than same-sex companions, who may be more prone to fighting. Altering both dogs will help you keep relations friendly and will also prevent an accidental mating.

Now that you know that you do want another dog and have decided on the sex of the dog you want, it's time to think about age. If you're buying a puppy, talk to the breeder about the litter. You don't want the most dominant or most submissive one in the bunch. You'll want an even-tempered, friendly pup who seems to get along with other dogs well. The new puppy is, of course, usually only eight weeks old, so it'll be up to you to mold him to be a good companion for your older dog. Remember, the older dog in the home is your priority and it's important that you not ignore him in favor of the new pup—this will only cause problems for both dogs. If you don't think you can do this, please don't bring a puppy into your existing dog's life. There is nothing more tragic or senseless than a family abandoning an older dog because he "doesn't get along with the new puppy." A good breeder, shelter, or rescue organization will encourage you to bring your dog to visit with the new pup before making a final decision.

If you are adopting an older dog, there are even more things to think about. The shelter or rescue organization that you are adopting your adult dog from should know enough about the temperament of the dogs in their care to guide you toward an appropriate animal. Some dogs are not always trustworthy with other dogs, and some individuals are either afraid of or inappropriately dominant toward other dogs. The shelter or rescue

During their first year of life, children in homes with two or more dogs or cats may be less likely to develop allergies than are children in homes without pets, according to a study in the August 2002 *Journal of the American Medical Association*. Researchers found that children exposed to multiple pets were on average 66–77 percent less likely to be allergic to common allergens.

staff should be able to provide you with that information. Nowadays, most good shelters do test their dogs' attitude toward other dogs.

It's very important to bring your existing dog to meet his new companion before making a final decision. If they don't get along on neutral territory, they probably won't get along in your home. Most shelters now provide a special area for family dogs and potential adoptees to get acquainted. Make use of it.

If you have a cat in your home, you should first ascertain whether she will get along with a dog. If she's never been around dogs, is highly fearful of them, and is active and reactive, you will want to adopt a dog who is comfortable with cats and not prone to chasing or teasing. A puppy can be a good fit in a cat friendly home because both puppy and cat will learn to get along as the puppy grows. Most adult cats will also lay down the law when a new puppy arrives on the scene. However, a high-energy puppy with a strong chase instinct can make your adult cat's life miserable.

Most cats will eventually get along with most any adult dog—or at least learn to stay out of his way. The larger question is finding a dog who will get along with the cat. Again, you need to work with the shelter or rescue group to determine that the dog you've chosen is cat friendly. Many shelters temperament test their dogs with cats, and rescue groups often foster their dogs in homes that have cats.

Some breeds tend to be worse with cats than others are: terriers are potentially dangerous in a cat home. An adult terrier who has not lived with or been temperament tested with cats is a bad risk. This is also the case with Greyhounds—retired racing Greyhounds have been trained to chase after small fuzzy things, and a running kitty

This guinea pig and Bull Terrier make a sweet picture, but small furry pets incite most dogs' prey drive and thus don't make good playmates.

fits the bill. Talk to the Greyhound rescue group you are working with to find the right pet for you, as some Greyhounds get along famously with cats. Some gun dogs can sometimes be dangerous with cats as well—again, it's all a matter of the individual.

These considerations extend to other small animals such as hamsters, gerbils, and birds. Don't put your pocket-size pets in harm's way—make sure the dog you bring home is friendly with animals of all shapes and sizes, and keep your pocket pets safely enclosed in cages and hutches.

Spaying or neutering your new companion by six months to a year of age can help reduce territoriality and aggression. Dogs who are altered are less likely to bite, to roam, or to inappropriately mount. They also tend to bond more closely with their people. Altering your new companion is just one of the many ways you can stack the odds in your favor.

CHAPTER 9

Kids and Dogs

What do *Big Red*, *Old Yeller*, *Where the Red Fern Grows*, *Lassie Come-Home*, and *Because of Winn-Dixie* have in common? All are stories about children and dogs. If this small sampling of kid-dog literature is reflective of our culture (there are many more books with a similar theme), it is obvious that friendships between children and dogs are as natural as chilled lemonade on a sweaty-hot day. In fact, according to a recent survey by the American Pet Products Association, Inc., an estimated 71.1 million U.S. households own pets; 44.8 million of those families own nearly 75 million dogs.

Given the inevitable pairing of children and dogs in the United States, parents, future parents, and guardians are wise to consider the relationship between the two to ensure an ending as happy as *Lassie Come-Home* —and avoid a sad *Old Yeller* finish. After all, children are, well, children: they are immature and impulsive. And dogs are dogs, not little people with fur coats. The combination of the two is sometimes oil and water. Usually, a child-dog mix is playful, endearing and happy, just like Winn-Dixie and Opal, but not always, and never without thought, teaching, and training.

If you have children in your family—or plan to have them anytime in the next 10 to 15 years—take them into consideration when choosing your new four-legged companion. Kids and dogs can be great friends, but this combination can also lead to problems. Following is a bit of information that will help you—whether you are a parent or a parent-to-be—make sure that the children and dogs in your life are best pals.

Choosing a Family Dog

"What breeds are good with children?" This is probably the most frequently asked question by parents considering a family dog. It's a great question—but there's no definitive answer. Got that? *No definitive answer.* There is no "list" of kid-friendly breeds from which to choose. Parents and parents-to-be must know that achieving a successful dog-child friendship in a family is more complex than asking whether a Border Collie or Beagle, for example, is good with kids. Rather, a successful

You cannot expect a child to be the primary caretaker for a dog. Be prepared to take over pet-related chores if your child cannot perform certain tasks or if your child becomes disinterested.

Most children adore the company of dogs, especially furry, fun ones who make everyday activities exciting and memorable. This pair of Samoyeds has enchanted their young charge.

family pet friendship involves many factors, including the dog's background and genetic makeup; if he is well socialized and well trained; his age and health; the age and maturity of the child; if the child is educated in humane handling of pets; and parental supervision.

Now it is true that certain breeds are *sometimes* better suited to children than others are, but there are many exceptions. No breed or mixed breed is always the perfect child companion. Although the Labrador Retriever and the Golden Retriever are usually wonderful children's companions—patient, playful, and gentle—there are Labs and Goldens that are better suited to an adult home because of their lack of socialization and training in their early years. American Pit Bull Terriers are often purported to be dangerous with children, but bully breeds often make excellent child companions. (The bully breeds are sometimes called "nanny" or "nursemaid" dogs because of their fondness for children.) All breeds need proper socialization and training to grow up to be friendly toward children.

Years ago, doctors recommended that families, especially those with a history of allergies and asthma, not own pets while children are very young because they believed kids were likely to develop allergies and asthma later on. However, a recent study in the *Journal of the American Medical Association* suggests that such recommendations may not be necessary. In fact, the study concludes that having two or more dogs or cats around during the first year of life actually decreases a child's chances of developing allergies. Research shows that 33 percent of children with no exposure to animals and 34 percent of children with only one dog or cat in the household tested positive on allergy skin tests, but only 15 percent of the children with two or more dogs or cats had allergies. Children with several pets are less likely to develop allergies.

Another recent study concludes that childhood exposure to cats was associated with a significant decrease in sensitization to cats in adulthood, particularly among those with a positive family history of allergies. Other studies have shown a decrease in allergies and asthma among children who grew up on a farm and were around a lot of animals.

While these studies are not conclusive, and more studies are necessary, the data certainly suggests what animal lovers have know all along: pets are good for you!

Although almost any dog can make a great companion (and every dog can be a potential sourpuss), a few breeds have tendencies of which you should be aware. Some dogs have strong predatory instincts, such as terriers and northern breeds. Although it's rare, such a dog can misinterpret the sound of a crying baby as wounded prey and attack. Herding dogs (such as the Border Collie) are bred to herd, and family dogs will herd chil-

A good relationship with a dog can establish a lifetime of wonderful memories. Help facilitate this friendship for your child.

Publisher's Weekly All-Time Best-Selling Children's Dog Books

1. *The Pokey Little Puppy*, Janette Sebring Lowrey. 1942.

2. *Where the Red Fern Grows*, Wilson Rawls. 1973.

3. *The Incredible Journey*, Sheila Burnford. 1984.

4. *Fox in Socks*, Dr. Seuss. 1965.

5. *Go, Dog. Go!* P. D. Eastman. 1961.

6. *Stone Fox*, John Reynolds Gardner. 1983.

7. *Sounder*, William H. Armstrong. 1972.

8. *Just Me and My Puppy*, Mercer Mayer. 1985.

9. *101 Dalmatians*, Dodie Smith. 1976.

10. *Clifford the Big Red Dog*, Norman Bridwell. 1985.

11. *Clifford the Small Red Puppy*, Norman Bridwell. 1990.

12. *Shiloh*, Phyllis Reynolds Naylor. 1992.

13. *Puppies Are Like That*, Jan Pfloog. 1975.

14. *The Werewolf of Fever Swamp*, R.L. Stine. 1993.

15. *The Barking Ghost*, R.L. Stine. 1995.

dren as well as livestock. This can be annoying or frightening to children because herding dogs often nip when gathering livestock. Such nips can result in bruising and a scared child. Large, powerful breeds such as the Akita, Doberman Pinscher, or Mastiff can be wonderful protectors of children. However, their great strength can be intimidating, even dangerous if a large strong dog knocks over a young child in his exuberance.

Before choosing a dog, consider your children's ages, the number of children in your household, and their personalities. Take time to think about this, since you, your child, and the dog all lose if you make a poor match. Consider the child's maturity level. Some 7-year-olds are ready to assist in the responsibility that comes with dog ownership, while some 13-year-olds are not so reliable. Be honest in your evaluation: Is your child ready for a dog? Is he or she prepared to help with feeding, training and clean up? Are you ready for a dog? Are you prepared for the feeding, training and clean up, as well as around-the-clock supervision of the dog and your child?

Timing is everything. If you have three children under the age of 5, now is probably not a good time to acquire a dog. Wait until the children are older. In fact, many reputable breeders refuse to place dogs in homes with infants or toddlers because they are rightly concerned that the dog will not receive adequate attention. Infants and toddlers are extremely time-consuming and exhausting to parents. They require constant attention. Add a puppy or dog to a family with very young children and you are likely to see a canine who doesn't receive a fair shake. In addition, toddlers are normally clumsy and uncoordinated; unintentionally, they are often too rough with puppies or small dogs.

If you think you have adequate time and energy to supervise child-dog interactions and make sure every family member receives adequate care, exercise, and affection, consider what type of dog will suit your family. If your child is rambunctious and full of fun, a small, delicate dog—a five-pound Yorkie, for example—is probably not the best choice. A few good choices for an active child might include an adolescent or adult Labrador Retriever, Golden Retriever, or Boxer. These dogs relish days of endless play with young human friends.

An upbeat youngster may have a lot of friends visiting. For this reason, be sure the dog you adopt is neither an escape artist nor wary of strangers. As anyone who has owned a Siberian Husky or Irish Setter knows, some dogs just want to run. Despite your best efforts, certain children (who might forget to latch at gate) and dogs (who are seasoned escape artists) aren't the best combo. Some guardian breeds may be inappropriate as well, because while they make excellent companions for

What to Do . . .

If you or your child is approached by an unknown dog, do not run away. The dog's prey drive will cause him to give chase. Do not make eye contact with the dog; he could interpret staring as a canine sign of aggression. Instead, stand still with your arms at your side, or back away slowly and quietly. In a loud, commanding voice, tell the dog to "Go away!" If you are attacked, give the dog an object such as a jacket or backpack to bite. If you fall or are knocked to the ground, curl into a ball. Protect your face by covering your head and neck, and put your hands over your ears.

your own children, they can be overly protective. Might the dog misinterpret a friendly wrestling match between your child and a friend? What might the dog do if a neighborhood friend with less-than-perfect manners lets herself into your home without knocking?

What about the bookish, quiet child? Such a child may adore a small companion dog. If your child prefers spending free time indoors, a Pomeranian, Cavalier King Charles Spaniel, or Miniature Poodle are possible choices, these dogs love nothing more than snuggling with a youngster while she reads or draws.

No matter what the child's personality is, he or she should be excited about and willing to assist in the responsibilities caring for the dog. Of course, responsibilities must be age appropriate. But what if your child won't do dog chores, despite his or her promises, or doesn't do them very well? Then you are the feeder, walker, trainer, pooper-scooper. That is why it is important to think about whether or not *you* want to add a dog to your family. Ultimately, the parent or adult is responsible for the care of the dog and is responsible for teaching the child to care for the dog. Because kids are kids, they sometimes don't complete tasks very well, or they lose interest

What do kids and dogs have in common? They both love to play. You can ensure safe play between your children and the family dog by sticking to games that do not include wrestling, chasing, or mouthing. You can make up your own games or follow these suggestions to get started. Have fun!

Soccer. Dogs are amazing soccer players (think *Air Bud: World Pup*). An athletic child and an athletic dog can have a great time passing a soccer ball back and forth. The child kicks or tosses the ball, the dog traps it with his front feet and rolls it with his nose. To start, get a soccer ball or any other sort of soft ball, making sure it is too large for the dog to pick up in his mouth. Have your child gently kick the ball so it rolls on the ground toward the dog. If necessary, have your child encourage the dog to get the ball. At first, the dog may try to pick up the ball but will quickly realize that he must push it with his nose for it to move. When he does this, the child should give him a lot of praise. (Caution: some dogs are ball hogs!)

Find It. This fun game is a variation of old-fashioned hide-and-seek. A parent holds the dog while the child hides with treats. The dog is sent to "Find Timmy." At first, encourage your child to help the dog find her by calling him. When the dog finds the child, she should make a big deal over him, offering lots of pats, hugs, and praise as well as his treat. Eventually, your dog will be able to play the game without having his name called. A bit of training is necessary at first, but this game is intellectually and physically challenging for all dogs. Another way to play is to teach the dog to find an object such as a treat, toy, or ball. To teach this game to your dog, put him in a sit and stay position, or hold him if he doesn't know these commands. Have your child hide the object, letting the dog see where it is placed, and then tell him to find it. A lot of praise should be lavished on the dog when he is successful. Allow him to eat the treat or play with the ball or toy when he finds it. After doing this several times, your child can hide the object in a less visible location.

Fetch. A ball plus dog plus child equals an afternoon of fun. Dogs love to chase and fetch all sorts of different items, including balls, toys, and Frisbees. If playing with a ball, be sure that it is small enough to fit comfortably in the dog's mouth but not so small that he could choke or swallow it. Have your child throw the item while telling the dog to fetch. When the dog returns with the item, tell your child to give him the *drop it* command. She should give him a lot of praise when he drops the item. Make sure your child knows never to try to take the toy out of the dog's mouth because she could be bitten. If the dog won't drop the item, have your child throw something else for him to chase, which will probably cause him to drop what he has in his mouth.

Walk. A simple walk around the neighborhood is always a fun activity for dogs and children.

Tricks. Who doesn't love a dog who shakes? Teaching tricks is a great way for a child to bond with his dog. See Chapter 31 for tips on trick training.

or they forget. This is normal. Just be sure you are willing to assume all care for the dog if necessary.

And if you don't want to assume that responsibility, for heaven's sake, don't get a dog. Forcing a reluctant child to care for a dog will only lead her to resent the dog. Dogs are frequently abandoned at animal shelters or to the backyard because a child loses interest and the parent either doesn't want the burden of caring for the animal or wants to "teach the child a lesson." Unfortunately, the real lesson the child learns in this case is that abandoning an animal is OK. Please keep this in mind before acquiring a dog or any living creature.

Sometimes an old-fashioned tea party is the best game of all for a child and her faithful companion.

Supervision Matters

Regardless of the breed you choose, the essential element in a happy dog-child friendship is your supervision. Be prepared to supervise all dog-child interactions. This sounds like a lot—it is. But it is key to the success of your child's relationship with the family dog. You must supervise to ensure the safety of both child and dog.

How much supervision is necessary depends on the age and maturity of the child and the age and personality of the dog. Babies and toddlers need constant supervision with pets. Toddlers are especially problematic because they are highly curious, wanting to touch and explore everything. However, they lack coordination. A toddler can fall onto a dog, startle him, or frighten him. Children and dogs should be separated when you're not in the room: baby gates, crates, X-pens (portable stand-alone dog fencing), and playpens work well for this.

As the child grows and matures, direct supervision can be decreased. Children over the age of eight or nine can probably play safely in the yard, as long as you are within earshot. You need not be in the center of the game, but close by.

Instruction goes hand in hand with supervision, so be prepared to teach your child how to treat pets with kindness. Children are not born knowing how to handle, pet, or play nicely with animals (or each other). They have to be taught. Modeling correct behavior is the best way to teach this behavior. If your child sees you handling your dog carefully, touching gently, and speaking softly, he or she is more likely to adopt the same behaviors. But don't expect your gentle handling of pets to miraculously rub off on your child. Show the child how to pet with an open hand (not grab), sit on the floor to hold a puppy, and speak normally (not yell). Demonstrate and ask the child to give it a try.

Introductions

Good first impressions are essential. When you are bringing a puppy or dog into your family, it is important to ensure a proper introduction and homecoming. You want your new puppy or dog to feel welcome in your home and friendly toward your children. And you want your children to feel friendly and loving toward their new pet.

Ideally, your child has participated in selecting the dog. The next step is to make sure the pet's first few days in your home are happy and secure. Adopting a pet can be stressful for everyone, including the dog. You can minimize stress by being prepared. Buy supplies, and arrange bedding, eating, and "bathroom" areas before you bring home the dog. Learn as much as you can about the dog's likes and dislikes, and try to follow his established routine.

A new pet is terribly exciting for children. Be careful to not allow a child's excitement to overwhelm the dog. Don't let the child "rush" the dog when he comes home, and don't allow a gathering of neighborhood friends just yet. Give the dog time to adjust and bond to his new family. Supervise carefully.

A Baby on the Way

What if you already have a dog and are expecting a baby? Again, proper introductions are in order. It's wise to prepare your dog to accept the new baby well before the baby is born or adopted. First, take your dog to the veterinarian for a routine health exam, and make sure your dog's vaccinations are up to date. Talk to your veterinarian about introducing your dog to the upcoming bundle of joy. If your dog is prone to fear, anxiety, or other behavioral problems that might lead to aggression, consult a trainer or animal behaviorist for assistance prior to the baby's arrival. Train your dog not to jump up on you or others and to remain calmly on the floor beside you.

Expose your dog to babies and the smells and sounds that accompany them. Ask friends with babies and young children to visit, and let your dog spend supervised time with them. Rub baby lotion or other baby products onto your skin so your dog becomes used to these baby-ish smells. Sing lullabies that you'll soon share with your infant. Say the baby's name when you talk to your dog so he becomes familiar with it. Buy a baby doll that cries so the dog will become accustomed to the sound of crying.

Once the baby is home, much time will be devoted to caring for her. A sudden, drastic reduction in the amount of time you spend with your dog can cause him stress. Begin to gradually reduce the amount of time you spend with your dog *before* your baby is born, but, of course, do not neglect your dog. If the expectant mom is the primary caregiver of the dog, another family member should take over that role before the baby is born. If your dog currently sleeps in your bedroom or in a room that the baby will sleep in and you don't wish to continue this once the baby is born, move the dog into new accommodations now. This will prevent him from associating the eviction with the baby.

After the baby is born, introduce her to the dog slowly. Bring a baby blanket or an item of clothing home from the hospital for your dog to smell before the baby arrives. Upon arriving home, the new mother should greet the dog without the baby, being quiet and calm. Following the greetings, let the dog sit next to you and the baby, and reward the dog with yummy treats for good behavior. Never force your dog to be near the baby, and always supervise interactions closely. Do not exclude your dog from your family now that the baby is home. Keep your routine as

Commonsense Rules for Kids and Dogs

- An adult or parent must supervise all child and dog interactions.

- Do not allow children to be in charge of training or correction. Training is an adult responsibility, although children can assist in training their pets.

- Never leave a baby or young child alone with any breed of dog.

- Teach children to be gentle with pets. Yelling, foot stomping, and arm waving are inappropriate, as is teasing, poking, and pulling a tail, ears, or nose.

- Children should not bother a dog while he is sleeping or eating.

- Do not allow a dog to steal snacks from children. Separate child and dog during snack time.

- Teach children to never approach an unknown dog, especially if the dog is on the other side of a fence, tied with a rope or chain, or in a parked car.

- Always ask the owner's permission before petting a dog.

normal as possible, and be sure a family member plays with and exercises the dog each day. Teach your dog that the baby is a positive addition to the household and with the baby come treats, walks, and playtime in the park.

Keep both dog and baby safe by setting clear boundaries. Gate the baby's bedroom door so that your dog cannot enter that room without you. Keep the baby's toys and other possessions away from your dog, and don't let the baby play with the dog's toys. Once your baby starts crawling, keep canine food bowls in an area inaccessible to the baby. No dog of any breed should ever be left alone with a child.

Bites Happen

Most owners don't like to think that their dog might bite, but bites do occur, especially with children. According to the American Humane Association, children under 15 years of age are most commonly bitten by dogs; 70 percent of all dog bite vic-

Dogs and children can make excellent playmates if they are both taught good, gentle behavior.

To find a child-friendly dog, consider the breed, individual personality, and early training and socialization.

tims are children. Dog bites are a greater health problem for children than is measles, mumps, and whooping cough combined. There is no need for alarm, though. Bites can be prevented. Here's how.

First, acquire a dog with a trustworthy temperament. Buy or adopt from a reputable breeder or organization. Research the temperaments of the dog's parents and relatives.

Socialize and train the dog. Attend training classes that teach you how to teach your dog to be a respectable canine citizen. Do not allow or encourage mouthing or biting; in fact, it is a good idea to teach "bite inhibition," a concept that says the dog is not allowed to put his mouth on the human body and, in the rare cases it might occur accidentally, the dog knows not to bite. Do not allow children to play rough games that include mouthing. Although they are traditional favorites, games like tug-of-war and wrestling are not recommended because they can encourage aggression in some dogs.

Children should never bother a dog when he is eating or sleeping, although it is a good idea to teach a dog to accept being handled when he is eating (this tolerance is best taught during puppyhood). Do not allow a child to interact with an unknown dog. Teach your child to always get permission from the dog's owner before petting any dog, even dogs at dog parks. Teach youngsters to pet gently and to always stroke the dog's body rather than pat the dog's head and face.

Consider both dog and child behavior before selecting a family pet. Most dogs do not bite unprovoked. There is usually a trigger, such as the child poked, prodded, or hit the dog; or the child is too close to the dog's food bowl or toys. Until your child is old enough to interact with your dog reliably, all child-dog play must be supervised. Be on the lookout for trouble, such as occasional growls and snaps. Don't ignore such behaviors. Instead, consult a trainer and work toward changing the behaviors.

CHAPTER 10

Finding Your Dog

You've done your research and know what kind of dog is right for you. But where do you find him? Choosing where to obtain a dog may be even more important than choosing the right breed for you. There are a number of poor sources for dogs that can lead to heartbreak. Buying from these sources also contributes to the continuing overpopulation of companion animals and even to animal neglect and cruelty. If you stick to some simple rules, however, you can bypass these unreliable and unethical sources completely.

1. Buy or adopt a dog only from an ethical breeder, established rescue group, or accredited shelter. Research your options.
2. Do not buy a dog from a backyard breeder, or puppy mill.
3. Never buy a dog who appears ill. If you are concerned about a dog's welfare, contact your local animal control office.
4. Research your adoption options before you begin looking. It's hard to say no when your heartstrings are being pulled.
5. Bring a checklist with you—a list of things to look for at the facility or breeder's home, and a list of questions to ask the shelter staff or breeder.

Consider what is important to you about buying or adopting a dog before deciding which avenue is right. At a municipal shelter you will definitely save a life, but you probably won't have the comfort of knowing your pup's background. With a purebred rescue organization, you may be able to get more information about a dog than at a shelter, and although most rescue groups do not euthanize dogs for space, adopting a rescue dog will free up space for another abandoned dog. You will get the most information about a dog from a breeder, but buying from a reputable breeder can be expensive.

Deciding what you're most comfortable with is important. While some people want a purebred, others are as happy, or happier, with a random-bred dog. About a quarter of the adult dogs at shelters are purebred. There are many breed-specific rescue groups as well.

Ultimately, a good breeder, rescue group, or shelter will provide you with a

To find an excellent breeder, ask for advice from breed parent clubs, trusted animal professionals, and friends.

friend for life, regardless of his pedigree. None are perfect, but all provide support and honest information. Regardless of which choice you make, being prepared and knowing what to look for will make for a far more satisfying adoption or buying experience for both you and the dog you bring home.

Breeders

Before buying a purebred puppy from a breeder, do your research. First, decide what

When buying a purebred dog from a breeder, it's vital that the breeder supply you with the puppy's health records; a written guarantee; an AKC registration; a copy of your puppy's pedigree; and certification of deworming, first immunizations, and altering (if done before going home). The written guarantee should allow you to bring the puppy back for a full refund or for another puppy if the vet detects any health problems, genetic or otherwise, at the puppy's first visit, which should happen within 48 hours of bringing the pup home.

In addition, all good breeders will give you health test results for the parents, such as Canine Eye Registration Foundation certification, BAER certification (hearing test), and Orthopedic Foundation for Animals certification. Depending on the breed, the breeder may also provide certification of healthy patellas (knees), especially in smaller dogs, and liver shunt and cardiac tests.

breed of dog you are looking for. Once you've determined your breed of choice, it's time to find a breeder. To find a reputable breeder, look to your veterinarian or a breed club in your region. Do you know someone with a friendly and beautiful Irish Setter? Ask her where she bought her dog. Visit dog shows or other dog events, and talk to owners of the breed you're interested in. Ask them if they can recommend several breeders so that you have a few to pick from.

Just because a breeder is advertised in a national magazine or has a Web site does not make him or her reputable. Anyone can buy an ad or design a Web site. Although most magazines will bar an advertiser with substantiated complaints against it, this is a long process. The AKC and UKC may provide lists of breeders, but again, these breeders aren't screened, so this is just an informational service, not an endorsement.

Not all breeders are equal; some are wonderful, others are not. Talk to several breed-

ers before making your choice. Over the phone, ask them how many types of dogs they breed, how many litters they have a year, and whether their dogs have titled in conformation, obedience, or other activities—championships indicate a commitment to the breed. Danger signs include breeders who raise several different breeds; breeders who always have multiple litters available; and breeders whose dogs have never participated or titled in any activities. Ask them for several references as well—people who have purchased dogs from them. A good breeder will be happy to provide them to you.

Try to glean as much information from references as possible. When was the dog bought, how old is he, what is his name? Did they meet the dog's siblings and parents; did

When you visit a breeder, be prepared to answer questions about your home and lifestyle. A good breeder wants to know where her pups are going.

A happy, healthy, friendly dam is a good sign. Personality characteristics are often passed from one generation to the next.

they visit the kennel and what did they think of it? Has their pet had any health or temperament problems; if so, has the breeder been helpful? Would they buy from this breeder again? Be concerned if you detect any hesitancy or if the answers sound false.

If possible, buy your puppy locally. Shipping a puppy can be complicated, but what's worse is that you don't get a chance to meet the pup, his siblings, or his parents before you make a decision. If you are buying a pup long distance, do yourself a favor and pick him up. If he's small enough, he can even ride in the airplane cabin on the way home with you.

Visit several breeders before making a decision. A good breeder will limit the number of litters each year. That means a particular breeder may not have puppies when you're looking. Be prepared to wait. Most good breeders also have waiting lists, so your wait may be extensive. There are big breeders and small breeders—some have large kennels, some breed their dogs out of their homes. Most dog experts believe that puppies raised in the home are better socialized than are those raised in a kennel.

Look around the breeder's home or kennel: is it clean, does it smell good, are the dogs groomed and healthy looking? Is waste picked up, and does every dog have a comfortable safe place of his own? Does the breeder feed a premium food; is there fresh water available? How about exercise—do the dogs live their life in small kennels, or do they get exercise and interaction?

Meet the pup's siblings and parents, if possible. There's no excuse for not meeting the puppy's littermates and dam (mother). The sire, or father of the litter, may have been a stud dog owned by another breeder, so he may not be available to meet. However, you should be able to get information about the stud, his owners, and any championships he has of his own or in his lineage.

Pet Stores and Internet Sales

A puppy's health and temperament are dependent on the knowledge and values of the breeder. The benefit of buying directly from a breeder is that you can meet her and her dogs, evaluate the temperament of the mother, and see how the puppies are raised

Pet stores and Web sites with puppies for sale may charge as much as or more than what breeders charge for puppies, but you don't get to meet the parents and see the conditions in which the puppies are raised. Without that context, it's difficult to judge a puppy's temperament and potential health.

Some pet stores and Web sites promote their breeders as being USDA licensed, but USDA regulations don't address socialization—the handling and exposure a puppy needs during the first weeks of life to develop properly—or the health, temperament, and quality of the parents.

Registration papers are no guarantee either. All they certify is that both parents were of the same breed. No dog registry or government agency requires breeders to socialize puppies or health-test their parents for orthopedic, eye, or heart problems or even to be knowledgeable about the breed or about dogs in general.

When meeting a new puppy, bring the entire family. Make sure everyone gets along with your future charge.

Do all the puppies look clean and healthy? Are they too skinny or too fat? Are their eyes bright, and do they express curiosity and friendliness? A good breeder will help you pick the right dog in the litter or will have already selected one or two puppies who are most suitable to your living situation. Some puppies may be boisterous and others more shy. An energetic, dominant male pup may not be the right dog for you if he's your first. If you want a

Puppies should have bright eyes; curious expressions; and clean, soft skin.

great guard dog, however, the meek runt may be a little too timid. Look for a breeder who will help you make these decisions.

What about the mom? Is she friendly or shy? Does she greet you with a tail wag or a growl? Parents can pass on important personality traits to their pups. An aggressive, shy, or skittish dam is a good reason to pass on a litter.

When you arrive at the breeder's home, you should have plenty of questions for her. If she's a good breeder, she will have plenty for you. She'll want to know something about your family and your lifestyle. She'll also ask questions about the size of your yard, whether it's fenced, and where the pup will be during the day and at night. Good breeders will require you to keep your dog in the house, and some will even insist that one person be home during the day. Many breeders will ask to talk to all adults in the household and meet the children in the family, as well as other dogs. They may also visit your home to ensure that it's the best place for their pup.

A good breeder will be open about any genetic problems in the breed. Every breed has some genetic health problems, so an unwillingness to discuss these or insistence that the breed has no health concerns is a serious red flag. The breeder should supply you with proof that she's performed the tests for hip or eye or ear problems. She'll supply records with the pup's first vaccines and worming. Depending on whether you are looking for a dog as a pet or for conformation, the breeder may ask that you alter the dog or insist that you do not (AKC conformation does not allow altered dogs). Some breeders may even require that you allow them to show the dog if he proves to be a contender. Depending on whether the dog is pet or show quality, the price will be affected. Pet-quality dogs tend to be less expensive, but some breeders charge the same amount for pet-quality and show-quality puppies, noting that they all come from the same health-tested parents and are raised with the same good nutrition and veterinary care. The primary difference is cosmetic, not quality of health or temperament.

The downside of buying from a breeder is that well-bred dogs cost a fair amount of money, although rarely as much as poorly bred dogs found at unreputable pet shops. It's also difficult to determine whether a breeder is good or not without a lot of research on your part.

Questions to Ask a Breeder

- When were the puppies whelped? How old will they be before you will adopt them out? Puppies should be at least eight weeks before going to their new homes.
- Is there a waiting list? Most good breeders will have some waiting list.
- Have the pups, their dam, and their sire been health cleared—hips/eyes/ears? Insist on documentation. Have the pups received their first shots and been wormed? Pups should receive this basic veterinary care in their whelping home.
- Does the breeder require the pups to be altered? A good breeder will require pet-quality puppies to be altered.
- Has there been any sign of genetic disease in previous litters? What types of genetic diseases occur in the breed? There is genetic disease in nearly every breed; a good breeder will be up front with this information, and provide documentation that the sire and dam have been cleared of genetic disease and that previous litters have not been abnormally affected by genetic disease.
- What is the return policy? If something happens requiring you to give up the puppy, can you return him to the breeder? All good breeders insist that puppies or even adult dogs be returned to their care if the new owners can no longer keep them.
- Will the breeder replace a puppy with severe health problems? This should be included in the sales contract.
- How long has the breeder been breeding? Look for a breeder with at least a few years of experience under her belt.
- How many breeds does she breed? Legitimate breeders generally do not breed more than two breeds of dog.
- How many litters per year does she have?
- A breeder with multiple litters at once would have a hard time doing justice to them all and socializing them all, so look for a breeder with time to devote to each puppy.
- Do her animals have any championships of their own or in their pedigree? Championships indicate a commitment to the breed, whether they be in conformation, agility, field trials, or obedience.

What to Look for at a Breeder's

- Is the home or kennel clean?
- Does the kennel area and home smell pleasant?
- Is water readily available?
- Do the animals have adequate bedding and toys to keep them occupied?
- What is the exercise area like? Is it large and secure?
- Are the kennels and exercise areas kept clean of feces?
- Do the puppies and adult dogs look healthy?
- Are the puppies' eyes clear and skin elastic?
- Do the skin and ears smell clean?
- Are the pups' bellies slightly plump but not turgid?
- Is the anus clean of feces?
- Are the puppies active and curious?

Sadly, older dogs do land in breed rescues and animal shelters. If you're looking for a mellow, well-behaved buddy, an older dog may be perfect for you.

• Are the adult dogs, especially the dam, friendly?

If you answer no to any of these questions, this may not be the puppy for you. Breeders' homes and kennels should be clean, smell pleasant, and be clear of feces. Puppies and adult dogs on the premise should appear healthy and be friendly.

Breed Rescues

With a large pet overpopulation problem in the United States, many breed clubs and individual fanciers have become involved in breed rescue. Breed rescues may be housed in individual homes or in private kennels. A breed rescue charges more than a shelter but less than a breeder does—usually a few hundred dollars. Dogs are always altered before they leave the rescue, and they may also receive other medical treatment. Because most live in foster homes while they await

adoption, they generally receive more socialization and training than shelter dogs do. Rescue organizations also provide more information about the pets they are adopting out than do most shelters. After a dog has lived with a foster family for weeks, months, or even years, his personality traits are well known to the family members. In addition, many of the dogs are owner turn-ins, so the rescue group is able to glean a great deal of information about a dog's former life.

Although most rescue organizations are breed specific, there are also many that cater to certain types of dogs, small, large, pit bull–types, herding types; or cater to geographical regions. Many rescue groups search shelters for dogs to adopt before their time is up as well as accept owner turn-ins.

To find a rescue, talk to your veterinarian, local animal shelter, or breed club. Most rescue groups screen their dogs rigorously, placing only those who are well socialized and healthy.

Most pet Greyhounds in the United States were adopted from rescue groups after their racing careers ended. Although they may need to be taught some basic manners, they adjust quickly.

Some private rescue groups focus on certain breeds, while others may specialize in small or older dogs.

The rescue staff members will probably have a lot of questions for you, as you should for them. Many rescue groups work hard to match the right dog with the right family. They want to know what your activity level is, how often you're at home, who lives in your home (including other animals), how secure your fence is, and what type of dog activities you plan to include your new pet in. Depending on their philosophy, they might insist that you feed a certain type of food, be involved in a particular activity, or even that one family member not work outside the home.

Because the dogs in rescue groups have been abandoned at least once, volunteers are committed to keeping the dogs from being abandoned again. Most groups will ask you to fill out an extensive application and agree to be interviewed. They do their best to match dogs with families in order to avoid the problems that landed the dogs in the rescue in the first place. Adopting from a breed rescue is an excellent way for an individual or family to find the exact breed of dog they desire, while still saving a life.

Other Rescue Options

There are other rescue options for people looking for a well-trained dog. Organizations that train service dogs, detection dogs, search and rescue dogs, and even movie dogs all offer dogs for adoption when they are retired or if they are unable to complete their training. Retired dogs have lived and worked with a handler for anywhere from one to ten years and are retired for medical reasons or age, although there are some dogs who simply decide they are no longer interested in working. Dogs who do not make it through training are not bad dogs; rather, they are dogs who were determined to be inappropriate for a work environment. They may have reacted poorly to the kennel environment, been too skittish to work in public settings, or simply have been more interested in playing ball than in guiding a blind person. The standards for working dogs are extremely high, and of

A sign outside a shelter invites people in to meet the animals in need of new homes.

the many dogs bred or recruited for work, fewer than 25 percent of them make it through any program.

The upside for adopters is that these dogs are highly trained when they arrive at their new home—not only do they have excellent manners but they can hold a sit- or down-stay for long periods; are house-trained and crate-trained; have received high levels of socialization so they are comfortable with kids, other animals, and in crowds; and are highly intelligent. Most organizations have long waiting lists of people interested in adopting their retirees and career-change dogs.

Shelters

Adopting a dog from a shelter is one of the most satisfying things you can do. It's win-win because you gain a companion at the same time you save a life. Many shelter dogs are wonderful, happy, healthy dogs. Most people give up dogs because of inconsistencies in their own life, rather than any fault of the dog. That said, many of the dogs in shelters are high-energy adolescents, so be prepared to bring home a dog who needs immediate training and attention.

The downside of adopting a dog from a shelter is that you know less about the dog than when you adopt from a private rescue or buy from a good breeder. You also will not be sure of the breed or mix of breeds. If the dog is a puppy, you will have no guarantee of his size or appearance as an adult.

There are several types of shelters: private/ nonprofit, progressive, and municipal. Private/ nonprofit and progressive shelters are usually small, housing fewer animals than municipal shelters. They may have better kennel facilities and employ a number of volunteers and staff members who work not only to feed and shelter the animals but also to do some training, socialization, and adoption counseling. Municipal shelters usually serve as both animal control facilities and animal shelters, taking in strays and owner turn-ins as well as adopting dogs out. Municipal shelters usually must euthanize a greater number of the dogs in their care than do private/nonprofit shelters and may be understaffed and overcrowded.

Many animal lovers, therefore, prefer to adopt from municipal shelters, feeling that they are able to make the greatest impact there. Other people like the support and counseling that they receive through a private or progressive shelter. It's best to make a decision based on your comfort level.

Many cities now require that shelters alter animals before they are placed for adoption.

Mixed-breed puppies are often found in animal shelters. Ask shelter workers for advice about breed mixes.

Puppies in shelters often have minor health problems, such as worms or malnutrition. Take a new puppy to see a vet shortly after adoption.

Research has shown that early spaying and neutering is safe for most animals, so even an eight-week-old pup goes home altered. This policy has had a dramatic effect on the number of unwanted animals born in the United States each year. Because many shelters alter animals once they've been adopted, you may have to wait a day or two to pick up your new buddy.

While municipal shelters may only ask for basic information from you, such as your name and address, progressive shelters are much like rescue groups in their adoption process. They may ask you to fill out a lengthy application and also provide you with adoption counseling, helping match the right dog with your family. Many shelters now provide get-acquainted rooms where you can spend time with a potential pet before bringing him home. They may also encourage you to introduce your existing pets to the new dog before making a final decision. Some shelters have begun allowing a grace period, a short period of time to keep the dog in your home before

you officially adopt him to help ensure that this is a good match for everyone.

Questions to Ask When Adopting

- Was the dog an owner turn-in, a stray, or a shelter save? The shelter or rescue will likely have more information about a dog that was an owner turn-in.
- If he was an owner turn-in, why was he given up? Did the family provide any information about the dog? Find out what you can about your new dog's past; it will be helpful in training him.
- How old is the dog (may be approximate)? Rescue dogs range in age from 8 weeks to more than 15 years.
- How long has the dog been in foster care or in the shelter? A dog who has been in a shelter for a long time may experience some kennel-related behavior issues, such as a need for remedial house-training. If a dog has spent substantial time in a foster home, the foster family can likely give you good information about him.

If a particular dog catches your eye, ask a shelter worker to take him out of his kennel so you can get to know him a little better.

- Did he have any medical or behavioral problems on arrival? These may or may not be serious.
- What medical treatment has he received? Find out whether the treatments must be continued or whether there are any long-term effects.
- Has he received training and socialization while in his foster home or the shelter?
- Does the dog have any training or behavior issues that will need to be addressed, such as house-training or dog aggression? Determine whether these are issues you can handle.
- What is the dog's activity level? What are his exercise needs? Choose a dog whose activity level complements your own.
- Is this dog compatible with your lifestyle (you're quiet, outgoing, athletic, etc.)? A rescue or shelter should be able to help you match your lifestyle with a certain dog.
- Has the dog shown any sign of aggression toward people or animals? A dog

Top Reasons Given for Surrendering Dogs to Shelters

1. Moving
2. Landlord issues
3. Cost of maintenance
4. No time for the dog
5. Inadequate facilities
6. Too many dogs in home
7. Dog is ill
8. Personal problems
9. Biting
10. No homes for litter

with aggressive behavior requires special training. If you are not experienced in training dogs with aggression or if you have children, do not choose this particular dog.

If you have your heart set on a purebred but still want to save the life of an animal, consider adopting through a private breed rescue group.

- Does the dog show a preference for certain types of people—men, women, children, the elderly? Dogs are adaptable, but try for a good match.
- Has the dog been socialized with children? Has the shelter or rescue group temperament tested the dog with children? If you have children and are adopting an adult dog, make sure he does not have any fear or aggression toward children.
- Does the dog require a dog friend in the home (or a home with no other animals)? Don't forget about your existing pets when adopting.
- What is the rescue group or shelter's return policy? If the new home doesn't work out or the dog is found to have a major medical problem, will the rescue or shelter take the dog back? A good shelter or rescue will accommodate a return if the pet is found to have serious medical or behavior problems.
- Has he been altered, and has he received his shots and first worming? Ideally, this will be done. However, many municipal shelters provide only the bare minimum.
- What kind of pre- or postadoption help does the shelter or rescue provide? This may include training classes, 24-hour behavior hotlines, adoption counseling, or home visitations.

What to Look For

With a rescue group, you may or may not have the opportunity to visit the foster home or kennel. Often, rescue dogs are made available through pet adoption days at local pet supply stores or parks. Look for signs that the dog is healthy and happy. Although many dogs come into rescue groups or shelters injured or undernourished, the organization should be forthright with this information and willing to tell you any medical or behavioral needs the dog might have. If a shelter is dirty, water is unavailable, or you observe any signs of neglect or abuse, contact your local animal control or animal advocacy organization. Here are some other things to look for:

- Does the dog appear healthy? Is he too thin or too fat; is his coat shiny or dull?
- Are his eyes clear and bright, and are his nose and ears clean?
- Does the dog show any signs of lameness or discomfort?
- Is the dog energetic or listless?
- Does the dog seem friendly? Does he approach you readily, or does he shrink away from you?
- When you pet the dog, does he lean into you or does he stiffen?
- Does the dog indicate discomfort or aggression when you interact with him?
- How does the dog interact with other animals?

When adopting from an animal shelter or rescue, you may well fall in love with a dog

You won't know which breeds will be predominant in a mixed-breed puppy, but that can be part of the fun.

who is not completely healthy. That's OK. But before leaping into a long-term commitment, know what you're getting into. If a dog appears to be seriously ill or injured, he should see a veterinarian before you make a final decision. He may have an illness that will cost a great deal of money to treat or cannot be treated.

Many shelter dogs have internal or external parasites, dehydration or malnutrition, or skin allergies. There's no reason to reject a shelter dog for minor illnesses, but see a veterinarian before making a final decision.

Many rescues and shelters now try to place dogs who in the past may have been euthanized for medical or behavioral problems. Some of these conditions include chronic diseases such as diabetes or epilepsy, mild food or dog aggression, and separation anxiety. One of these "special needs" dogs may or may not be right for you and your family. A dog who is aloof or frightened may not suit your lifestyle.

Adult dogs who are adopted from rescues or shelters sometimes go through what is called a honeymoon phase. This means that the behavior they exhibit in the kennel or foster home or during their first few weeks in your home may not necessarily be their typical behavior. Some dogs may seem passive and submissive in the kennel and when they first arrive in your home, but as they become more comfortable they begin to display more dominant tendencies. Other dogs who seem shy in a kennel environment become confident, boisterous dogs. Although the honeymoon transition generally works itself out with patient training and socialization, this is something to discuss with the shelter or rescue group. A good trainer can also help guide you.

If you have children, are not dog experienced, or do not feel you are able to spend the extensive time entailed in training a dog with behavior issues, look for a dog who can come

Many rescue dogs spend time in foster homes, where the foster families can learn about the dogs and provide valuable information to prospective owners.

into your life with a minimal adjustment period. The ideal dog will be friendly and interested in you. He will respond appropriately to your children and interact nicely with your other pets. He will not stiffen, show his teeth, growl, or shrink away from you when you attempt to interact with him.

Adopting from a rescue group or shelter rather than buying from a breeder helps alleviate the chronic overpopulation problem among pets in the United States. Some breed fanciers have a policy of adopting a shelter pet for every purebred dog they purchase. The late, great animal writer and voice of the Westminster Kennel Club Dog Show, Roger Caras, famously urged his audience to adopt an animal from a shelter after they have "their champion."

CHAPTER 11

Bringing Your Dog Home

Bringing your dog home is an important first step in your life together. You do not want his first impression to be traumatic or for him to be exposed to any dangers. For a puppy, this may be the first time he's been away from his mother and siblings. For an older dog, entering a new home, especially after spending time in a kennel, can be intimidating. Before you bring your pup home, prepare your home, your family, and yourself for a safe and joyous homecoming.

Pet Proof

Before welcoming your new pet, you must pet proof your home. If you already have an older, mature dog, you may have forgotten those stressful first days of puppy ownership. Remember them now. There was a time when you couldn't leave shoes, books, or toys on the floor without puppy teeth shredding them. There was also a time when your fuzzy bundle of joy needed constant vigilance to avoid indoor messes. Remember the puppy pads and the pee cleaner? It's time to stock up again.

Outside

There are many areas outside of your home to which your puppy will have access. Perhaps you have a fenced backyard and an open front yard; if so, take a look around your property, and inspect the plants that are growing. Are any of your plants toxic to animals? If you don't know what type a plant is, take a sample to your local nursery and have it identified. Then compare it to our list to determine its risk to your pet. If it is toxic, remove it or transplant it to an area of the yard where your dog does not have access, like that unfenced front yard. You can also fence in a designated plants-only garden area where dogs do not have access. And if

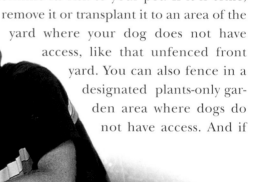

The entire family should be in full agreement before adopting a new dog.

Shopping Checklist for a New Dog

Prepare for your new dog by purchasing supplies ahead of time. Here is a checklist of recommended items:

__Dog food: Choose a high-quality food that is appropriate for your new dog's age and size. Ask your veterinarian for recommendations.

__Food and water bowls: Food and water bowls should be heavy so that they can't be easily tipped over. Stainless steel and ceramic bowls are best, although stainless steel bowls become hot if left in the sun. Plastic bowls can harbor bacteria. Raised bowls are ideal for larger dogs and older dogs who have trouble stooping.

__Toys: Buy a selection of toys. High-quality rubber and nylon bones provide dogs relief from teething. Unstuffed lambswool and interactive toys like balls or Kongs keep dogs busy.

__Grooming tools: A brush, flea comb, shampoo, and nail clippers are grooming regimen basics.

__Toothbrush and toothpaste: It is important to keep your dog's teeth clean and healthy. Brushes and paste especially for dogs can be purchased at the pet supply store or from your veterinarian.

__Crate: Choose a crate large enough so your dog can stand up and turn around in it comfortably but not so large that he can get away from any mess he makes. Some crates can be purchased with dividers that make the crate temporarily smaller, which may be a good choice for puppies. The crate will grow with them as they grow. A crate provides a comfortable spot in which to sleep and relax but is also an excellent tool for house-training and keeping your dog safe when traveling. Cushion the floor with a blanket or fleece mat.

__Bed: If your dog isn't sleeping in a crate, he'll need a comfortable dog bed.

__Collar and leash: Purchase an adjustable nylon or flat leather collar and check its fit often, especially if you are adopting a quick-growing puppy. You should be able to fit two fingers under the collar, but it should be tight enough that it won't slip over your dog's ears. Use a 4- to 6-foot leash for walks.

__Identification tag: The ID tag should include only your name, your dog's name, your address, and your phone number. If the tag allows for only two lines, they should be your name and your phone number.

__Canine first aid kit: A basic first aid kit helps you deal with minor emergencies.

__Treats for training: Healthy soft treats positively influence a dog's learning experiences.

__Baby gates: Use gates to block stairs or any area that is off-limits to your dog.

__Urine cleaner: Specially made urine cleaner uses natural enzymes to neutralize staining and odor from puppy pee. It's vital that puppy accidents are cleaned up immediately and thoroughly to prevent the culprit from returning again and again to the same spot.

__Puppy pee pads: These pads soak up urine and make clean up quick and easy. If you must return to work and leave your pup alone for more than two hours at a time, place these pads inside a gated area outside the pup's crate. (Pups cannot hold their bladders for more than two hours at a time and should not be left inside a latched crate for more than that amount of time.)

you place special value on any of your plants, you should transplant them to a safe place away from adventurous pups or fence them in, at least until your new dog has learned all of the outdoor rules.

Move on to your vegetable garden. A lot of dog owners assume that because vegetables are edible, so are the plants. That's not always true. Tomato plants, for example, are members of the nightshade family, and their stems

The plants and vegetables growing in your garden can be tempting for a curious pup.

ing is assembled in much the same way as chicken wire is.

If you need a fence right away, go for the wire fencing. With a friend, you can have your entire garden protected in an hour's time. Wire fencing can also be used to protect plantings in immature garden beds. Form the fencing into a hoop and attach it at either side of the bed. The plants can grow through the wire, but the pup can't reach the plant's roots. Putting up any of the wire fencing methods is an easy afternoon job, and the materials are readily available at any hardware or garden supply store.

Chicken wire and wire fencing, however, are not attractive, so some gardener/pet owners opt to go for nicer permanent fencing—either all wood or a wood/cyclone fencing combo. Some even splurge for sculptural iron or Grapewood fences. All work but there's a big difference in price and time commitment.

Other Outdoor Dangers

Additional dangers can be found in gardens. Get rid of slug or pest poisons. Throw them out and as long as you have a pet, don't buy more. Many dogs and cats are poisoned and die because of these products each year. Don't risk it. Talk to

and leaves are toxic. Of course, we'd never gnaw on a tomato vine, but our puppies might. There are other reasons to keep your pup out of the vegetable garden. Puppy feet can quickly trample and destroy plants. Dogs love to dig up soft earth and find joy in rolling around patches of sweet basil. In addition, dogs in the veggies aren't good for us. Dogs don't know vegetables are food and treat them no differently than they do any other area of the yard. That means they'll urinate or defecate just as likely there as anywhere else. Urine can burn and kill tender plants— notice those burned spots of grass in your lawn—and feces can contaminate our food with *E. coli* and other dangerous bacteria.

Fencing Options for Gardens

It's easy enough to keep dogs out of the garden; it just takes a little forethought. The options range from simple but not particularly aesthetic to complicated and attractive. Chicken wire works to keep young pups out of the garden and is easy to set up. Just unfurl the roll and attach to stakes placed about a foot apart. Or you can go a step further and use wire, or hurricane, fencing—it comes in a variety of heights. Wire fenc-

Before bringing your new dog home, be sure your yard is securely fenced.

Toxins

Many products commonly found around the house and yard are dangerous to dogs. Ingestion of toxic substances can lead to upset stomach, vomiting, diarrhea, seizures, and even organ failure and eventual death. Some substances such as pesticides and acetone, the active ingredient in nail polish remover, can be dangerous even if a dog does not ingest them. They can cause harm by being inhaled or absorbed through the skin.

Human medications are the number one cause of animal poisonings, surpassing pesticides. They can be lethal to dogs and should be kept out of reach. Advise overnight guests to keep any medications locked away. Even common pain relievers can be dangerous to dogs. One regular strength 200-milligram ibuprofen tablet (Advil, Motrin) can cause stomach ulcers in a 10-pound dog; ingestion of two or more tablets of ibuprofen can cause seizures and coma. The most commonly reported medications involved in animal poisonings are non-steroidal anti-inflammatory painkillers such as ibuprofen; antidepressants; cold and flu medicines; and diet pills.

Commercial pesticides are another common cause of dog poisonings. Fly baits containing methomyl, such as Stimukil, and slug and snail baits containing metaldehyde, such as Snarol, Buggetta, and Slugit Pellets, are particularly dangerous. Methomyl is rapidly absorbed into the skin, lungs, and gastrointestinal tract and is broken down in the liver. Vomiting, seizures, and death are the most common signs of ingestion. Metaldehyde is a neurotoxin, a poison that affects the nervous system. Ingestion of less than a teaspoon of a 2 percent metaldehyde product by a 10-pound dog can cause harm. Mole and gopher baits and rat poisons are also dangerous to dogs. Do not use these if you have pets.

Seasonal products that contain toxins include antifreeze, Christmas tree water, and liquid potpourris. Ingestion of just a small amount of antifreeze can be fatal to a dog. Keep driveways and garages clean of car drippings. Christmas tree water contains fertilizers that can upset the stomach. Stagnant tree water also can breed bacteria, leading to vomiting, nausea, and diarrhea if ingested. Liquid potpourris are caustic. Licking or ingesting potpourris can result in chemical burns, vomiting, retching, hypersalivation, or depression.

Hazards to beware of during warm weather months include lethal strains of blue-green algae usually found in stagnant bodies of water. Ingesting even a small amount can kill a dog within an hour. Cocoa bean mulch, often used in gardens, contains the substance theobromine, which is also found in chocolate. A 50-pound dog who eats 2 ounces of cocoa bean mulch may suffer stomach upset; eating 9 ounces or more would probably be fatal. Another garden hazard is compost, which is filled with decaying matter harboring dangerous bacteria that can make a dog sick. Fertilizers, too, are hazardous. They contain heavy metals such as iron. Ingesting a large amount of fertilizer can cause gastrointestinal upset and possibly obstruction, and may even affect the heart and liver. Swimming pool cleaning supplies may contain harmful chemicals, and citronella candles can cause gastrointestinal inflammation if a dog eats them.

Other toxic products include household cleaners, rubbing alcohol, ice-melting products, batteries, paint, boric acid, hair coloring, and other human grooming products such as shampoo and petroleum products. The best prevention is to keep these items out of your dog's reach.

your nursery about less toxic ways to combat pests. And don't fertilize or use weed killer in your yard or garden in the weeks prior to bringing your new pet home. Puppies are especially susceptible to the nutrients and chemicals found in these substances, but you should continue to be vigilant throughout the life of your pet. If you use fertilizer or weed killers on your lawn, keep your pet away for at least a few days.

Assuming you have a fenced yard, take a walk along its periphery and look for any possible escape routes. Puppies can squeeze through very small spaces. Any hole that is more than 3 inches in diameter should be blocked. Look for loose wood slats in your fencing and repair them. How tall is your fence? If you're bringing home a medium to large adult dog, you need a 5-foot-tall fence

Animal Poison Control Centers

When calling a poison control center, be prepared to provide as much information as possible, including the substance ingested; the time the substance was ingested; the appearance and smell of the vomit, if applicable; the dog's other medical conditions, if applicable; and the dog's current behavior. Keep a list of emergency hotlines close to your phone:

Animal Poison Control Center
American Society for the Prevention of Cruelty to Animals
888-426-4435 (888-4ANI-HELP)

The Animal Poison Control Center of the ASPCA provides 24-hour veterinary diagnostic and treatment recommendations. The Center's staff consists of 25 veterinarians, including 4 board-certified veterinary toxicologists and 10 certified veterinary technicians. The center handled more than 130,000 cases in 2007. The fee for each consultation is $60.

Animal Poison Hotline
PROSAR International Animal Poison Center and North Shore Animal League America
888-232-8870

The Animal Poison Hotline is staffed 24 hours a day by licensed veterinary professionals and experts on toxicology and pharmacology. The center provides care to more than 35,000 animals each year. The fee for each consultation is $35.

Comparative Toxicology Laboratories
Kansas State University College of Veterinary Medicine
785-532-5679 (day); 785-532-4100 (after-hours emergency desk)

Kansas State University's College of Veterinary Medicine has operated a poison control center since 1969. The primary focus of this center is to help animals who have been exposed to poisonous substances. Veterinarians staff the poison control hotline 24 hours a day. The hotline receives an estimated 50 calls a week. There is no fee for this service.

National Capital Poison Center
The George Washington University Medical Center
800-222-1222

In addition to the poison control centers that specialize in animals, human poison control centers such as the National Capital Poison Center can often help with animal poisoning cases. If they are unable to help, they will refer callers to one of the animal poison control centers. The National Capital Poison Center does not charge callers. Other human poison control centers are listed in the front of local telephone books.

at a minimum. Even if your new pet is a puppy, consider the height he will eventually reach and go ahead and install a new fence now. You'll have to build a fence eventually, and it will be a bigger hassle to be under construction when your dog is grown. How about under the fence? Does your fencing reach all the way to the ground? If not, add chicken wire to cover

the gap between the fence and the ground. Once you get your pet home, you may find that even these precautions aren't enough. If a dog can't get over or through, sometimes he'll just tunnel under. In a matter of moments what seemed like secure fencing can become an access to the wider world. If you find you have a tunneler, you might need to pour con-

Cleaning Up After Puppy

When a puppy has a house-training lapse, it is important to thoroughly remove the odor from spots where the accidents have occurred. A thorough cleaning helps prevent the puppy from returning to the same location and resoiling.

To clean carpet or upholstery, first soak up as much of the urine as possible using a thick layer of paper towels or newspapers. Refresh this layer until the area is almost dry. The more urine you can remove before it soaks into your carpet, the better you will control the odor. Once the fresh urine has been soaked up, rinse the spot with cool water. Blot the water up with paper towels or remove with a wet vacuum.

To clean the spot, use an odor neutralizing commercial enzyme carpet cleaner and deodorizer, which are available at carpet and pet supply stores. These cleaners can be used for urine as well as feces. If the carpet has been previously cleaned with a chemical, the efficacy of enzyme cleaners is inhibited. Remove all traces of the old cleaning product with a wet vacuum using plain water. In some cases, the carpet padding may have to be replaced to thoroughly remove urine odors.

While carpet is the most difficult flooring from which to remove odors, unsealed concrete floors such as those found in garages and basements allow urine to seep in. Clean concrete floors with a disinfectant, and allow it to sit and seep into the floor. Rinse with water. When the floor is completely dry, seal it to prevent future absorption. Sealed floors can be cleaned with commercial cleaners or a mixture of ¼ cup white vinegar, a quart of warm water, and a squirt of liquid dish detergent. Scrub the area with this solution and finish with an enzyme cleaner.

If your puppy makes a habit of eliminating in specific areas of the house, close the door to that room or block the entrances with baby gates. Move furniture over frequented spots. Placing water bowls and toys in previously soiled spots can also discourage a puppy from eliminating there in the future.

---

crete under the fence or bury bricks along the periphery. Some dogs are such notorious escape artists—they climb, dig, chew, or do just about anything else for their freedom—that they must be kept in covered, reinforced dog runs when outdoors and unsupervised.

Next, take stock of your yard and look for anything that might be dangerous or that you don't want to be destroyed. Hoses? Use a shelf to store them out of pup's reach. Sprinklers? Keep them in the garage or toolshed when they are not in use. The same goes for gardening tools. Are there any shards of glass or plastic, nails, or jagged edges of metal? Clean them up. Do you have a barbecue area? Keep charcoal and lighter fluid out of pup's reach. How about old paint cans and chemicals that you've kept because you don't know what to do with them? Call your city trash department to find out where these should be taken. (Never pour old chemicals down the sink or onto your soil—they'll find their way into storm drains and even-

tually into our streams and oceans.) Once you feel confident that your yard is completely safe for a new puppy, take another walk through it—you might be surprised by what you find. And if you don't have a fence, build one now.

Garage

Just as you did in your yard, look around your garage, and make sure all chemicals are stored up and out of a dog's reach. Keep the floor of your garage clean of tools and other equipment. Clean any spills or car drippings. Antifreeze is one of the most common causes of poisoning in cats and dogs. It has an attractive sweet taste and is highly toxic. Don't take this risk lightly. Even a very small amount, less than a teaspoon, can kill a dog. Use a less toxic brand of antifreeze, one made with propylene glycol rather than ethylene glycol. One option is Sierra Antifreeze.

Remove any set rattraps or mousetraps that are at ground level, and never use poison anywhere on your property. You'd be surprised at what a dog can get into. Dogs have even died from rat poison dripping from out-of-reach spots during a rain.

And even when you think it's completely safe, don't let your dog in. A garage is no place for a dog—there are just too many hidden dangers.

Inside Your Home

Inside your home are a host of potential dangers and attractions for a new dog. Go through your house room by room and remove everything from the floor. There should be nothing but furniture on the floor. Place pillows, shoes, toys, and video games out of reach. Remember, anything that your puppy or untrained adult dog chews is your fault. If you leave it out, he thinks it's fair game. If he is allowed to chew your things as a puppy, chances are he will continue to do it as an adult. Don't establish bad habits, and don't risk the well-being of your dog or of your property. Until you start training him, a dog should not have access to any of your belongings and should never be allowed to have free run of the house.

Bedroom

Keep clothes, books, and shoes off the floor. Store all loose items in closets and on shelves, and keep closet doors closed securely. If necessary, get child safety latches to keep closet and cabinet doors shut. Always keep the door to the room shut when you're not in it so the pup doesn't have a chance to wander in unsupervised. Clean under the bed—pups like to get under there and will wreak havoc with anything you've allowed to pile up.

In 2007, pet owners spent $9.8 billion on pet supplies and over-the-counter medications, according to the American Pet Products Association. That number was projected to increase to $10.3 billion in 2008.

Puppy teeth are made for chewing. Keep your valuables off the floor and out of the dog's mouth.

Be sure bedding doesn't hang on the floor or have any tassels a puppy might find tempting; tuck in corners to keep hanging fabric to a minimum. How about pills next to the bed: aspirin, vitamins, and cough medicines are common nightstand items. Keep them in a drawer safely out of reach.

If you have kids, clean their toys off the floor. The toy battle is trying for kids and dogs: they're both loathe to give them up. This conflict can cause a dog to be possessive of his toys, which can be dangerous for your child. Your puppy must be taught that kid toys are only for kids; puppies have their own toys. If he is allowed to play with your child's toys, he will not learn this important lesson. There are also dangers lurking in children's toys. Small plastic parts and toy stuffing are not made puppy safe. These are choking and ingestion hazards. Avoid favorite toys being chewed up, pups getting ill, and battles between child and pup over toys by keeping floors picked up and bedroom doors closed to the puppy. Dirty diapers can be a particulary dangerous attractive nuisance, so keep diaper pails securely shut and latched.

Bathroom

Bathrooms can pose many dangers for dogs. Keep medicines in high medicine cabinets

The poinsettia gets a bad rap. More than 80 years ago, a child was poisoned by a plant that was rumored to be a poinsettia (there was no proof), and the reputation stuck. This common holiday plant is not the killer that many believe it to be. A review of 22,793 cases (mostly involving children) of unspecified poinsettia exposure reported to the American Association of Poison Control Centers revealed that 92 percent of the patients did not become ill. The most common symptoms of exposure to poinsettias reported to the ASPCA's Animal Poison Control Center are vomiting, anorexia, and depression, which can be resolved by limiting food and water for a couple of hours to reduce stomach irritation.

far out of your dog's reach. Don't keep them in your lower cabinet drawers—you'll be surprised by what an enterprising dog can open. Use childproof latches on bathroom cabinets and drawers. You can't be too cautious about medicine. Even common, over-the-counter medications can be toxic for dogs. Ibuprofen (Advil) and acetaminophen (Tylenol) are both potentially fatal for dogs.

Keep shampoos, soaps, bath beads, and other such goodies out of pup's way. They probably won't kill him if he gets hold of them, but they will cause tummy upset, and you won't appreciate the mess or the loss of expensive toiletry. In addition, plastic or glass containers can be dangerous if chewed, ingested, or stepped on.

The wastepaper basket is also a temptation for dogs. They can have hidden dangers such as discarded medications. A dog who gets into the wastepaper basket can cause a big mess, strewing garbage around your house. Keep wastepaper baskets out of reach.

Kitchen

The kitchen is another danger area. Many of us keep our household chemicals under the sink. If you have a dog, you can't do that. Move all cleaners into an upper-level cabinet. Buy childproof locks for your lower-level cabinets and pantry doors.

Young adult dogs still have plenty of puppy energy and curiosity.

Toxic Plants

Common Name	Scientific Name	Toxic Parts
aloe, medicinal aloe	*Aloe vera*	latex under the skin
amaryllis	*Hippeastrum* spp	bulb
American bittersweet, climbing bittersweet, staff tree, staff vine	*Celastrus scandens*	entire plant
American holly	*Ilex opaca*	fruit
angel wings, elephant's ear, heart of Jesus, mother-in-law plant	*Caladium bicolor* (synonym: *Caladium hortulanum*)	leaves and stems
arrowhead vine, goosefoot	*Syngonium podopyllum (Nephthytis triphylla)*	entire plant
Australian nut, macadamia nut, Queensland nut	*Macadamia* spp	nuts
Australian ivy palm, octopus tree, Queensland umbrella tree	*Schefflera actinophylla* (synonym: *Brassaia actinophylla*)	leaves
autumn crocus, meadow saffron	*Colchicum* spp	entire plant, including the bulb
be-still tree, yellow oleander	*Thevetia peruviana* (synonym: *Thevetia neriifolia*)	entire plant, especially the seeds
bird-of-paradise shrub	*Caesalpinia gilliesii* (synonym: *Poinciana gilliesii*)	seeds
buckeye, horse chestnut	*Aesculus* spp	nuts and twigs
Buddhist pine, kusamaki, southern yew	*Podocarpus macrophyllus*	seeds and leaves
castor bean	*Ricinus communis*	seeds are the most dangerous, all parts of the plant are toxic
ceriman, Mexican breadfruit, Swiss cheese plant, windowleaf	*Monstera deliciosa*	leaves, stems, stalk
chinaberry, bead-tree, Persian lilac, pride of India	*Melia azedarach*	fruit and bark
Christmas rose	*Helleborus niger*	entire plant
daffodil	*Narcissus* spp	bulb
deadly nightshade, belladonna	*Atropa belladonna*	entire plant
devil's ivy, golden pothos	*Epipremnum aureum* (synonym: *Scindapsus aureus*)	entire plant
dumb cane, mother-in-law's tongue	*Dieffenbachia* spp	leaves
flamingo flower, tail flower	*Anthurium* spp	leaves and stems
florist's cyclamen	*Cyclamen persicum*	entire plant
foxglove	*Digitalis* spp	entire plant
gladiolus	*Gladiolus* spp (synonym: *Acidanthera, Homoglossum*)	bulb
hyacinth	*Hyacinthus* spp	bulb
hydrangea	*Hydrangea* spp	flower bud
iris	*Iris* spp	rootstock
ivy	*Hedera* spp	leaves and berries
lily-of-the-valley bush	*Pieris japonica*	leaves and nectar
mistletoe	*Phoradendron* spp	berries
morning glory	*Ipomoea* spp (synonym: *Mina, Pharbitis*)	seeds
mountain laurel, calico bush	*Kalmia latifolia*	entire plant
nightshade (A highly cultivated genus in the nightshade family that includes tomato, eggplant, potato plant, Jerusalem cherry, winter cherry, and potato vine.)	*Solanum* spp	toxic parts vary between plants; plant and flower parts, fruits or berries, or immature fruits or berries may be toxic depending upon the plant
old man's beard, traveler's joy, virgin's bower	*Clematis* spp (synonym: *Atragene*)	entire plant
oleander, rose bay	*Nerium oleander*	entire plant
peace lily	*Spathiphyllum* spp	entire plant
philodendron (all species, including fiddleleaf, panda plant, tree philodendron, heart leaf, sweetheart plant)	*Philodendron* spp	leaves
rhododendron, azalea	*Rhododendron* spp (synonym: *Azalea*)	entire plant
rosary pea	*Abrus precatorius*	seeds
shrub verbena, lantana	*Lantana* spp	immature green berries
tulip	*Tulipa* spp	bulb
yesterday, today and tomorrow	*Brunfelsia pauciflora* (synonym: *Brunfelsia calycina, Brunfelsia eximia*)	entire plant
yew, Japanese yew	*Taxus* spp	seeds and foliage

Some plants are toxic to dogs, causing symptoms that range from irritation of the mouth to vomiting, organ failure, or death. Whether an entire plant or just a certain part of a plant is toxic varies among plant species. If your dog ingests a toxic plant, contact a veterinarian or poison control center immediately. The following is a partial list of plants that can be dangerous to dogs. Just because a plant is not included on this list does not mean it is safe. Please consult your nurseryperson or a poison specialist for complete information.

Level of Toxicity	Symptoms
mild	vomiting
mild to severe	nausea, vomiting, diarrhea, excessive salivation, tremors
mild	vomiting, diarrhea
mild	nausea and vomiting
mild to severe, depending upon the quantity ingested	intense pain and irritation of the mouth, swelling, dermatitis
mild	swelling and burning of the mouth and throat, possible gastroenteritis
severe	vomiting, muscle tremors, depression, staggering, weakness, elevated body temperature and heart rate
mild	burning of the mouth and tongue, drooling, vomiting
severe	pain in the mouth and throat, vomiting, nausea, abdominal pain, severe diarrhea, possible shock, occasional renal damage
fatal	nausea, vomiting, abdominal pain, diarrhea, cardiac problems, possible death
mild	nausea, vomiting, diarrhea
fatal	severe gastroenteritis, death possible with frequent exposures
mild	vomiting, diarrhea
fatal	bloody diarrhea, stomach pain, muscle twitches, convulsions, coma, death
mild	burning and irritation of mucous membranes, drooling, vomiting
fatal	lethargy, stupor, vomiting, diarrhea, shock, labored breathing, convulsions, paralysis
severe	mouth irritation, abdominal pain and nausea, cramping, diarrhea, vomiting, convulsions
mild	nausea, vomiting, diarrhea
fatal	dry mucous membranes, fever, urine retention, respiratory paralysis, coma, possible death in high doses
mild	burning of the lips, mouth, tongue, and throat; drooling; difficulty swallowing
mild	dermatitis, oral irritation, diarrhea, vomiting
mild	burning of the mouth, tongue, and throat
mild	nausea, vomiting, diarrhea, contact dermatitis
severe	dizziness, nausea, abdominal pain, vomiting, diarrhea, irregular heartbeat
severe	vomiting, diarrhea, depression, hypersalivation, abdominal pain
fatal	nausea, diarrhea, vomiting
fatal	abdominal pain, lethargy, vomiting, convulsions, bowel incontinence, coma, and possible death in high doses
mild	abdominal pain, nausea, vomiting, diarrhea
severe	burning in the throat, vomiting, diarrhea, muscular weakness, incoordination, difficulty breathing
fatal	burning in the mouth, hypersalivation, vomiting, diarrhea, coma, convulsions, possible death
fatal	vomiting, cramping, diarrhea, labored breathing, heart failure, death
severe	diarrhea, nausea, increased urination, hallucinations
fatal	vomiting, diarrhea, hypersalivation, muscular weakness, difficulty breathing, convulsions, possible death
fatal	abdominal pain, vomiting, lack of appetite, diarrhea, difficulty breathing, weakness, incoordination, collapse, convulsions, possible death
severe	pain and inflammation of the mouth, hypersalivation, bloody vomit and diarrhea, convulsions, mental confusion, paralysis in severe case
fatal	vomiting, diarrhea, cardiac problems, collapse, possible death
mild	swelling and burning of the mouth and throat, nausea, vomiting
mild	pain and burning of the mouth, tongue, and throat; contact dermatitis
fatal	vomiting, diarrhea, hypersalivation, weakness, convulsions, coma, possible death
fatal	vomiting, nausea, diarrhea, ulcers in the mouth and throat, hemorrhaging in the stomach, loss of intestinal function, possible death
severe	weakness, lethargy, vomiting, diarrhea
mild	vomiting, diarrhea, depression, hypersalivation, lack of appetite
severe	vomiting, depression, diarrhea, increased urination, incoordination, convulsions
fatal	vomiting, diarrhea, abdominal pain, irregular heartbeat, weakness, coma, cardiac or respiratory failure, death

Safe and Hazardous Toys

Toys provide dogs with mental stimulation and exercise, and they can keep dogs occupied while their people are away. But it's up to you to buy toys that won't harm your dog. The following list discusses which toys can be dangerous and which are safe.

- Give your dog toys made especially for dogs. Toys made for children or other animals and items found around the yard or house can be dangerous.

- Give your dog toys that are the appropriate size for your dog. A dog can choke on balls or toys that are too small.

- Avoid giving your dog sticks, wooden toys, and cooked bones. They can splinter, causing damage to a dog's teeth and mouth, choking, vomiting, ulcers, and intestinal perforation. Hard bones can damage teeth. Some people feed their dogs uncooked bones as part of a raw food diet. While they usually don't splinter as easily as cooked bones do, uncooked bones may harbor bacteria such as salmonella, which can lead to illness.

- Give your dog bones and toys made of hard rubber and nylon. They are safe and especially good for teething puppies.

- Do not allow your dog to chew towels, socks, shoes, and other pieces of discarded clothing. They can be swallowed, in part or whole, and cause intestinal obstructions. Allowing your dog to chew old clothing also sends a message that it is OK for him to chew all clothing that bears your scent.

- Avoid giving your dog toys with small parts, with squeaking mechanisms, or made of soft latex. Small parts and squeaking mechanisms can cause choking and intestinal obstructions. Soft latex toys can shred.

- Do not allow your dog to chew rocks. In addition to damaging the mouth and teeth, rocks can also block the intestines if swallowed.

- Purchase only high-quality, 100 percent rawhide chews from reputable pet supply stores. Inexpensive rawhide bought at swap meets and other discount venues may be preserved with arsenic, which is toxic. Give your dog rawhide only when you can supervise him. Throw away small pieces of chews so your dog doesn't swallow them, potentially causing choking or intestinal obstruction.

Garbage is another big kitchen attraction. A dog can create quite a mess with it, and it can be a real danger to your dog. Cooked chicken bones, plastic bags, and broken glass are all items commonly found in trash cans, and they all can be seriously injurious to a dog. Keep the trash can inside a cabinet with a childproof latch.

There are also many human foods that are dangerous for dogs. Chocolate, alcohol, grapes, raisins, onions, and garlic are just a few of the people foods dogs shouldn't eat. Keep them out of reach of your dog.

Once properly puppy proofed, the kitchen can be a great place for the dog to hang out. Tile floors and quick accessibility to the outdoors are puppy pluses. Most families spend a lot of time in the kitchen, too, so the new addition will enjoy a lot of traffic. Keep his crate in the kitchen, and buy a toddler gate to keep him out of other rooms when he's not in his crate or

Crate your new puppy whenever you can't supervise him.

accompanied by you. During the first month or two of your dog's life with you, especially if he is a puppy, the kitchen should be the only room in which he's allowed to roam freely.

Living Room, Den, and Family Room

These are the rooms where most people keep their valuables—the type of stuff a pup loves to chew. If you have precious Oriental rugs, do yourself a favor and roll them up and put them in storage for at least the first few months of your puppy's life—house-training accidents and puppy teeth can cause a lot of damage. Keep decorative pillows, candles, and other display items off of low tables. Even if you're with your pup, you may not be giving him your full attention; you'd be amazed by the havoc a puppy can wreak when you're engrossed in a TV show.

There are also plenty of tantalizing wires around the TV, stereo, and computer. Keep these wrapped up and out of the way. They

Wires are dangerous play toys. If your pup develops a taste for chewing wires, use a bittering agent to dissuade him—before electricity does.

are far too attractive to the average dog and can be dangerous and expensive to replace.

Household Cautions

Wires, wires, wires: these can be a dog's worst enemy. They're dangerously appealing; they feel good to chew and look so inviting. Unfortunately, they pack a wallop and can seriously injure or even kill a small dog or puppy. Some dogs never develop a taste for wires—others cannot keep their teeth off of them. If you notice that your pup is taking an interest in wires, coat them with Bitter Apple or another foul-tasting agent to deter him from chewing them. And unplug wires whenever you're going out. It's a safety precaution that could save your puppy's life or save your house from fire.

Houseplants are another indoor liability. Go through your home and mark down all the indoor plants you own. Cross-reference them against our list of dangerous houseplants. Dogs like to chew plants. Any accessible household plants will be chewed at some point or another. Even nontoxic plants should be kept out of reach because there's nothing more irritating than coming home to an overturned pot with soil spilled out all over the carpet.

Before Fido Comes Home

In addition to dog proofing your home, there are several things you should do before your new dog arrives. Schedule time to introduce your pooch to his new home, buy the necessities before he arrives, and talk to your family about expectations and responsibilities.

There are plenty of things to shop for when bringing a new pup home. Take a checklist with you to the store so you won't forget anything.

If you are buying a puppy from a breeder, it's easy to have everything ready before he comes home. Puppy proof your house and do all your shopping the week before your puppy arrives—this way you won't have to dash out for more supplies and can spend your pup's first day home completely relaxed and getting to know him.

If you're adopting from a shelter, it's not as easy to plan. You may not expect to bring home a dog that day, but you end up finding your dream companion. Or you may find it takes several weeks of searching before you find the right dog. Still, once you decide to start looking for a dog, pet proof the house. It's far easier to do it before bringing a dog home, and once it's done, it's done. If you're adopting from a shelter, however, you will not know the dog's size, age, breed or mix of breeds until you find the one for you. Wait on buying collars, beds, crates, food bowls, and other size- or age-specific products until you've made a final decision.

If you're buying your pup from a breeder, schedule a vet appointment for a couple days

Dog and Puppy Proofing Checklist

Use this checklist when dog or puppy proofing your home:

__ Remove poisonous plants in the house and yard or move them safely out of reach.

__ Install childproof locks on doors where cleaning supplies, pesticides, and other chemicals are kept. Store all household toxins up high, where your dog can't reach them.

__ Invest in indoor and outdoor trash cans with secure lids, or keep trash where your dog can't get to it.

__ Pick up small objects that could be choking hazards or cause intestinal blockages, including loose change, paperclips, rubber bands, and dental floss.

__ Cover electrical cords with rugs or plastic cord guards or tape them to baseboards to keep dogs from chewing them.

__ Secure or move lamps, statues, and other breakable objects placed on unstable tables or bases. A frisky dog could easily knock these items over.

__ Make sure screens are secure on low windows. Install springs on screen doors and gates so that they can't be left open.

__ Use tall baby gates to block stairs and access to other areas you don't want your dog to venture.

__ In the yard, fix fence holes and gaps; remove choking hazards, dangerous plants, and other toxic substances. Keep garbage cans out of dog's reach.

__ Fence or cover hot tubs, swimming pools, deep fountains, and ponds.

__ Clean driveway and garage floors to remove any antifreeze or other car drippings.

---

after homecoming. That'll give the pup a few days to settle in before being exposed to new and possibly frightening sights and sounds. If you're adopting from a shelter, it may require that the dog be spayed or neutered before leaving the shelter or it will ask you to spay or neuter your pet within a certain time period. Call your vet to make an appointment once you have your new dog home.

Arrange to take the first week off work, or at least take a four-day weekend, when you first bring your new dog home. Spending the first week at home with your dog will go a long way toward establishing proper behaviors, easing him into your family's lifestyle, and house-training him. If you adopt your dog from a shelter, arranging for time off work may be difficult. Breeders and rescue groups are usually happy to accommodate your schedule, but shelters don't always have that liberty. Before looking for a dog, let your supervisor know that you may have to take off an unexpected day or two when you make your match.

Once you go back to work, try to come home during your lunch hour—this will ease separation anxiety and also help with house-training. If you can't come home, arrange to have a friend, neighbor, or professional dog walker visit at lunchtime for at least the first couple of weeks.

A short name with two syllables is the best choice for a new puppy. It is easy to say, and two syllable names won't be confused with one syllable commands such as *sit*, *stay*, or *no*.

If you can't take time off work at the spur of the moment, try to visit the shelter on a Friday so you'll have the entire weekend ahead of you to get acquainted with your dog, should you pick one up that day. Or if you visit the shelter on a weekday and find the pet of your dreams, find out if you can arrange a later pickup time. This may work out well if the dog requires altering before leaving the shelter. Most shelters will hold an adopted animal until the weekend, when you'll have at least two days to get acquainted before getting back to your normal schedule.

Bringing a new dog into your home requires careful planning and a lot of patience. Dogs are not instant companions, even when they're adults.

New Dog Necessities

Your new dog requires a number of items to help him fit into your household. He needs food, a place to sleep, a collar, and an ID tag or some other form of identification. If possible, do your shopping before picking him up, or ask a family member to run to the store while you're visiting with your new adoptee.

Family Meeting

Before you bring home your new pet, have another talk with your entire family. Just as you discussed the type of dog everyone wanted, now is the time to sit down and work out what it means to each family member to have a new dog in the home. Are there expectations or concerns that you need to address? Are chores and responsibilities allocated, and does everyone agree to the terms? Parents must be aware that even if a child desperately wants a puppy, he or she won't necessarily take on the responsibility. Don't turn dog care into a punishment. The dog will suffer for it.

This is also a good time to set up house rules. Decide whether to allow the dog on furniture, in certain rooms, or on beds. Where will he sleep? Where will you keep his food and water bowls? How will all of you work together to train the puppy not to jump up, nip, or beg? Consistency in training is vital.

Your new canine addition should have a safe place to call his own when things get overwhelming. A crate or doggy bed works well.

Make sure everyone in the family is comfortable with the decisions made.

Homecoming for Pups

The day you bring your new pup home is an exciting one for you, your family, and your puppy. This may the first time that he's been away from his mom and siblings. At first, your puppy will be overwhelmed by everything he is exposed to, so it behooves you to make the transition as easy as possible.

An eight-week-old pup has huge bursts of energy that alternate with periods of sound sleep. By pet proofing your home, you've made it safe for your pup to career around wildly during energy bursts. To keep him snug and safe during sleep time, you've bought a cozy crate in which he can bed down. After potty breaks, eating, play sessions, and general puppy freak-out time, put your pup in his crate with a warm blanket and a soft toy.

During the first night or two, puppies may cry and whimper, missing the warmth and comfort of their mom and siblings. Some people provide a hot water bottle or ticking clock for the first couple of nights as a surrogate for his mom and siblings' warm bodies and comforting heartbeats. A soft, fuzzy toy will also help him feel cozy. If you do not want your adult dog sleeping with you, resist your puppy's heartrending cries, and do not let him on your bed.

When introducing a new dog to an existing household dog, keep things calm but upbeat.

Sleeping on furniture is a difficult habit for your dog to break. If you do want him to sleep with you, wait until he's comfortable sleeping alone so that he doesn't develop sleep phobias.

For the first couple weeks, puppies should stay in your bedroom because they are fearful and because they need to relieve themselves fairly often. Expect to be awakened every few hours by puppy whines. When this happens, bring your puppy outside and wait while he relieves himself, giving him enthusiastic praise when he does. Then back to bed to start all over again. Having a new puppy is a little bit like having a baby—sleepless nights and all.

Homecoming for Adults

Bringing a new adult dog into the home has its own share of issues. Some adult dogs may not have any house manners or may not have been inside a house at all. Some retired racing Greyhounds must be taught to climb stairs because their previous lives were limited to their kennels and the racetrack. Other dogs are mannerly and house-trained. You won't know how your new dog will do until you get him home. Dog behaviorists call the first couple of weeks an adult dog is in a home the honeymoon period. It generally takes a period of time before the dog relaxes enough to expose his personality quirks to you—so dog aggression, food possessiveness, and other negative as well as positive characteristics may take some time to surface.

It's important for a new dog to have a place to retreat to; that's where a crate can come in handy, although he won't need to spend as much time in it as a puppy would. Show your new dog that he has his own spot in an out-of-the-way place, where he can retreat when things get a bit much. Baby gates come in handy to keep your new dog out of certain areas—he may still be in a chewing stage if he's young, and anxiety can lead to destruction.

And too much freedom can overwhelm a recently adopted dog.

It's also important that you keep a new adult dog on a leash whenever you are outside your securely fenced yard. A new dog is prone to running away, so don't set yourself up for heartbreak.

Introducing a New Dog to Your Pack

It's natural for a dog to chase other dogs away from his home territory, but most dogs can learn to accept and enjoy canine housemates. Two dogs of opposite sexes often get along better than same-sex pairs, but not always. Some get along with both sexes, while other dogs will reject a newcomer of either gender.

Adult dogs are usually more tolerant of a puppy than of another adult. Pups under six months don't normally challenge an adult dog's authority, which allows the resident pooch to set the rules of the relationship. On the other hand, a pup's natural exuberance can be annoying to some older dogs, who may growl or snap if a rowdy pup comes too close. Most pups respect that message, but some act as though it's a game and dodge away only to come back and bother the old dog again, hoping for another thrill. Until they work out a peaceful relationship, keep the pup and the senior dog separated except when they're being supervised.

If your resident dog isn't used to other dogs or chases away those who trespass on his turf, introducing him to the new dog in a neutral place, like a park or friend's yard, will help.

Your new dog's first night in your home can be traumatic. Take him into your bedroom at night so you can keep a close eye on him.

Have someone else handle the new dog while you manage the current resident. Bring the dogs into the area leashed. Let them observe each other from a distance for a few minutes. Bring them closer together to the point where they're interested and curious about each other, but leave sufficient distance between them so that neither feels crowded or cornered. You and your helper should then walk the dogs along parallel paths, keeping a safe distance until both dogs relax. Gradually bring your paths closer together, keeping the mood light and positive. When the dogs accept being walked several feet from each other, then you can allow them to meet. When the two are comfortable together in this neutral place, take them home and reintroduce them there, going through the same steps. As long as you begin the process with the dogs far enough apart, they should not exhibit any leash aggression. If either dog has leash aggression, you may need to introduce the two dogs off-leash in a securely fenced area. Remember to always present a calm, positive demeanor when introducing dogs to one another. If either senses anxiety from you, he may react aggressively toward the other dog.

If you must introduce dogs without an assistant's help, confine the new dog behind a fence or gate and calmly walk your resident dog nearby on leash until the two become used to the sight and smell of each other. If neither behaves aggressively or defensively, pet each one, then let them sniff each other's scent on your hands. If that doesn't seem to bother either dog, allow them to sniff noses through the barrier. If they act friendly, with happy wagging, relaxed and slightly open mouths, and attempt to lick each other through the fence, allow them to meet.

If you have more than one resident dog, introduce them to the newcomer one at a time so they won't overwhelm him. Introduce the friendliest resident dog first. Once he's said hello and played, take him inside and bring out the next resident to be introduced. After the new dog meets each member of your group individually, start again with the friendliest, and add the other dogs one by one until all are interacting peacefully.

Never leave a puppy and older dog alone together until you are confident that the older dog will not injure the pup. Often, the senior dog takes on a dominant role with a new pup and can come across strong. That said, don't overcorrect your older dog for correcting the puppy. Blatant aggression is not OK, but correction when a puppy is out of line is fine, even good. Now that there is no mom or siblings to let the puppy know when he's exhibiting rude behavior, it's up to the senior dog of the family.

It's important that you do not overcoddle the new dog. The family dog is the king of the house, at least for now, so make sure he feels special. The two will work out their issues of dominance in the weeks and months to come.

Putting It All Together

Bringing a new puppy or adult dog into your life is a time of great joy and change. From researching breeds to picking out a properly sized crate, your journey will include both pitfalls to avoid and precautionary measures to take. Take your time to find your dog. There's no question that your heartstrings will dictate part of your decision, but try to use your brain as well. Know what you are looking for before you begin talking to breeders and visiting animal shelters. Even if you are looking for a Labrador puppy and end up coming home with a geriatric Poodle, your research will help you keep your expectations in line with reality.

Don't forget to plan ahead—dog proof your house and buy a crate and food before the big day. Bringing your new dog into a home that is prepared for him will keep him safe, keep you sane, and allow you to spend your first few days together the way you should: having fun.

Small pets such as mice and rabbits may evoke a predatory response in some dogs. Keep all your pets safe from one another.

Life with a Dog

You and your dog will spend many years together, probably 10 or more. During this time there will be a number of opportunities for fun and exploration, and inevitable moments of panic and despair. Together, you may travel, play at the beach, maybe even participate in dog sports such as agility or flyball. You may also face personal and widespread calamities and will need to know what to do if your dog becomes lost or injured, or if a fire or flood threatens your home.

Finally, the inevitable reality of the human-dog bond is that dogs just don't live as long as we do. You will need to say good-bye to your devoted friend. Caring for your dog and knowing when to say good-bye will be your greatest gifts to him.

CHAPTER 12

Pet Care Partners

You will need to turn to someone else to care for your dog many times throughout his life. You have options to consider, whether your dog needs regular day care because you work long hours and can't be home to walk or feed him or you need long-term care because you receive a work assignment in another city for a month or more—or you simply need someone to watch your dog while you vacation for a week. Although some dogs do best in their own home with a pet sitter, others do better in a boarding kennel. Consider your dog's personality and temperament before making a decision. If you aren't comfortable having a stranger take care of your dog, perhaps you can find a friend who is willing to care for him in your home for a fee.

Above all, ensure that the facility or caretaker you are hiring will keep your animal safe. Price, comfort, and health and safety are all valid concerns when choosing a caretaker for your dog. After all, you're entrusting someone with one of the most emotionally valuable things of your life, so it's only normal that you feel wary.

Although some dogs do well in a boarding kennel, others do best at home with a pet sitter.

energy dogs alone for too long every day. As a result, many people, especially in urban areas, are turning to doggy day care centers. These are organizations that provide daytime kenneling and activities for "latchkey pups." In addition to day boarding, some doggy day cares provide play groups, trips to dog parks, organized games, and training. Day care providers often also serve as overnight boarding kennels.

Doggy Day Care

When an overworked lawyer adopts a one-year-old Border Collie, they're in for trouble. This combination of long work hours and, in some cases, poor lifestyle matches leaves many high-

The state of Rhode Island and communities in California, Colorado, Louisiana, and Wisconsin designate owners of dogs and other domesticated pets as *guardians*. This term recognizes pets as companions rather than as property.

Dog Walkers

Not all dogs require full-time day care, but owners are turning to dog walkers to give their dogs a break from the monotony of spending the day alone. Dog walkers are also helpful if you have a dog with special needs: an incontinent senior, a dog who needs medicine, or a puppy with energy to burn. Although dog walking got its start in New York, where many dogs live in high-rise apartments, it's caught on in most urban areas; urban dog parks are often filled with dog-walking clientele.

The two top dog-owning countries in the world are the United States and Brazil. According to a 2007 survey by the American Pet Products Association, there are approximately 74.8 million pet dogs in the United States in 71.1 million households. Although the number of pet cats is greater than that of dogs, a higher percentage of households own dogs than cats. The same survey says that people consider pets a part of the family and treat them accordingly, buying specially formulated or organic pet food, giving gifts to pets, and rewarding them with treats and toys.

Questions to Ask Pet Sitters and Dog Walkers

- Are you accredited?
- Are you licensed and bonded?
- What is your experience/training?
- Will you provide references?
- Have you worked with (aggressive, medically fragile, senior) dogs before? How do you adjust your services?
- What is your pay scale?
- What does pet sitting/dog walking involve—playing, walking, and feeding?
- Will you visit the dog at a regular time each day—how much leeway is there?
- Will you administer medicines; if so, is there a charge?
- Do you have transportation to take the dog for veterinary care if necessary?
- What other services will you provide: taking in mail and watering?
- How much do you charge for additional services?
- Are you willing to spend the night in the home?

Pet ownership is currently at its highest level, with 63 percent of total households owning at least one pet, according to a 2007 survey by the American Pet Products Association. In a 2006 pet ownership survey by the American Veterinary Medical Association, about 49.7 percent of survey respondents consider pets to be family, and 48.2 percent consider pets to be companions.

Boarding Kennels

Boarding kennels are used for overnight stays, which can last one night to one month or longer. It's important that you visit any boarding facility you're considering before boarding your dog. A good boarding kennel will welcome you and be happy to show off its facility and other amenities, even without notice.

Most veterinarians have kennels where they board clients' dogs. Although the facilities tend to be limited, with small kennels and minimal opportunity for exercise, many owners, especially those who have dogs with medical problems, feel most secure leaving their dogs there.

Wherever your dog stays while you are out of town, be sure that he is kept safe and secure.

Other owners turn to private boarding facilities, which range from sparse to elaborate. Bare-bones facilities aren't much different from a veterinarian's—dogs stay in small kennels with concrete floors. They usually receive two walks a day. Upscale facilities may offer longer walks or provide grooming and interactive playtime. A popular trend is doggy hotels, where dogs receive as much pampering as their owners do on their own vacations. These dog hotels, sometimes called doggy spas, boast luxury kennels with everything from raised beds to color television and soundproofing, playtime with wilderness walks or group activities, and even swimming pools. Most include grooming and a lot of interactive time with both staff and other doggy clients. Some even offer bedtime partners—dogs with separation anxiety can have a staff member sleep with them (in a human-size bed, of course).

Regardless of the boarding facility, the most important consideration is the health and safety of your dog. After ensuring these most important elements of dog care, details such as price and extra pampering can be examined.

You will also want to ask a prospective boarding kennel details about the service they provide, including what types of add-on services they offer, how much exercise your dog will receive, what you can bring with your dog (food, bedding, toys), and whether there is a charge for administering medications or supplements. Before leaving your dog in the care of any facility, insist on a tour of the kennel, and ask the following important questions.

What to Ask Day Care or Boarding Kennels

- How often are dogs exercised and allowed to relieve themselves?
- How often are they fed? Is there an extra charge for additional feedings?
- Will the facility administer medications, and is there an extra charge for this?
- Is grooming provided or available?
- What veterinarian does the facility contract with?
- What happens if my dog becomes ill or is injured?
- Can my dog's special needs (medical problems, aggression, etc.) be accommodated?
- What activities are available, and who conducts them?
- Are all staff members experienced, and can they provide references?
- Is the boarding facility accredited with the American Boarding Kennels Association?
- What vaccinations are required?
- Can I bring my own bedding, food, and toys for the dog?
- Is the facility licensed and bonded?

The amount of time dogs spend sleeping varies among individuals and breeds. On average, dogs sleep 14 hours a day, but big dogs like Saint Bernards and Newfoundlands sleep even more—up to 18 hours a day.

What to Look for at a Day Care Center or Boarding Kennel

- Clean facilities
- Adequate ventilation and lighting
- Comfortable temperature
- Resting areas for dogs off of the concrete
- No feces or urine in kennels or play areas
- No strongly unpleasant smells
- Individual kennels are large enough for the dog to move around freely
- Location of kennels is appropriate for the climate. In warm climates, the kennels should be in an air-conditioned building. In cool climates, the kennels should be in a heated building. In mild climates, the kennels may be indoors with access to the outdoors.
- Clean, comfortable bedding
- Easy access to clean water
- The staff member's behavior with the animals—do they speak harshly, hit, smack, or manipulate the dogs roughly? Do they indicate a dislike for a certain dog or speak derogatorily of any animals? These are all warning signals.
- Noise level. Although it's impossible to prevent dogs from barking (especially while someone is walking through the facility), the kennel should not be overcrowded to the point where dogs are continually barking. Think about your dog's own personality as well—will a kennel full of barking dogs frighten or stress him? Is a soundproof kennel available, which may be more comfortable for your dog? (These generally cost more.)
- Type of exercise area. Is it roomy and secure? Are there any areas where a dog could escape? Is it grass, concrete, or dirt? Are feces picked up promptly?
- Observe any activities that are offered. How does the staff interact with the dogs? How many dogs do they turn out

Introduce your dog to the pet sitter before leaving on vacation. Observe their interactions and clarify services and prices.

together? Are there any aggressive dogs or situations in which dogs may fight? Are the dogs observed closely, and are all the activities safe? If there is a pool, is it easy for a dog to get out of? Does a staff member keep close watch on it?
- Listen to your gut instinct. Does it feel good or bad to you?

In-Home Pet Sitters

Some dogs just don't do well in boarding kennels—whether they're nervous or scared, the kennel environment causes them undue stress and makes your time away a nightmare for them. One alternative to boarding your dog at a kennel is to hire a pet sitter. Pet sitters' experience can range from professionals with accreditation to friends or neighbors who are willing to house-sit. No matter how

Using a Doggy Door

A doggy door can be a great convenience. It allows your dog to go in and out of the house as he pleases. Of course, dog doors should open only into a securely fenced area.

There are a variety of doors in a variety of price ranges available at pet supply stores. The doors come in different sizes to accommodate dogs from small to extra large, and the frames come in different colors such as white, silver, gray, or brown. Some doors need to be installed in existing walls or doors; others come on a separate panel that is used as an extension to a sliding glass door. There are doors made of see-through Plexiglas panels that slide open with a gentle push from a dog, doors with acrylic flaps that open as a dog walks through, and even motorized electronic doors that are activated by a sensor in a dog's collar. Most dog doors can be locked to keep your dog inside or outside if necessary and to keep your home secure. Your doggy door should be taller and wider than your dog so he has plenty of room to get through.

Teaching your dog to use a dog door is fairly simple. Just use his favorite treat to lure him through the door several times. In a short while, he will be going in and out on his own.

---

close your relationship may be with someone, don't expect that person to take care of your dog for free. It is more likely that your dog will be cared for properly if you pay for pet-sitting services.

Some people opt to have a pet sitter simply stop by twice a day for morning and evening feedings and walks; others want someone to stay in the house with the dog overnight. Whichever you prefer, be sure to stipulate what you are paying for: feeding, walking, socializing with the dog, and providing medications. Talk about any additional expectations you may have, such as watering plants, picking up mail, or turning on and off lights. Be prepared to pay accordingly for additional services.

Professional pet sitters should be accredited by a professional organization, such as the National Association of Professional Pet Sitters or Pet Sitters International. They should also be able to provide you with references and information on their training background and experience.

Introduce your dog to the pet sitter before you leave. Observe them together. Does your dog seem comfortable; is the pet sitter friendly and relaxed? A good pet sitter will interact with your dog and work to establish a relationship before returning when you are gone. Ask the pet sitter to feed your dog a few treats to establish a rapport so that he remembers her when she comes to the house.

CHAPTER 13

Emergencies

Life is full of the unexpected, and that's true of your dog's life, too. Personal and community emergencies can and do happen. Because the only predictable thing in life is that life is unpredictable, we should all be prepared for emergencies. To keep your puppy safe, take a three-prong approach to emergencies: prevent, prepare, and respond. Try to prevent emergencies as much as possible, but prepare for their possibility. When there is an emergency, stay calm and respond quickly and efficiently.

Personal Emergencies

Unfortunately, there is no dog 911. If your dog is hit by a car or chokes on a ball, it's up to you to save him. So the first step to take when it comes to emergencies is to do everything you can to prevent them.

Prevention

There are ways to prevent many tragedies, including choking, poisoning, injuries, and even some illnesses. Choking is common. One way to prevent choking is to buy toys that are made specifically for dogs. Keep in mind that toys with moveable parts or sewn-on features are a hazard. Take a close look at balls and other chew toys. Make sure they are too large to be swallowed before allowing your dog to play with them. Of course, small dogs need smaller balls and toys than do larger dogs. If you have dogs of diverse sizes, don't allow your larger dog access to the smaller dog's toys. Bones are also a choking danger. Never give your dog cooked bones, as they can easily splinter and cause choking. Keep the kitchen garbage well out of reach.

Getting into poisons is another household danger. We encounter many poisons and toxins every day without even thinking about them. Many of these can be dangerous or even fatal for our dogs. There are also household items that are safe for us but not for our dogs. Indoor and outdoor plants, fluids dripping from cars, cleaning supplies, pesticides, rat and mouse poisons, even certain human foods such as chocolate and onions can be toxic to dogs. Keep these and other questionable items well out of a dog's reach.

Injuries, such as sports injuries, falls, or traffic-related injuries, are often preventable.

Do your best to prevent emergencies by taking precautions.

Canine CPR

Should your dog's heart or breathing stop as the result of injury or illness, would you know what to do? Cardio-pulmonary Resuscitation (CPR) and the Heimlich maneuver can be used on dogs as well as on humans. If possible, sign up for a canine CPR course in your area. If there is none available, ask your veterinarian for a tutorial. Follow this step-by-step procedure in case of an emergency:

1. Ascertain whether your dog is breathing. To do so, look to see if his chest is moving up and down. You can also place your hand in front of his nose to check his breath.

2. Ascertain whether your dog has a heartbeat. Do so by placing your ear against the dog's chest to listen for a heartbeat. His heart is located where the left elbow touches the chest.

3. If your dog is not breathing but has a heartbeat, you will need to give him artificial respiration. To do so, first clear his airway by pulling his tongue forward out of his mouth. Run your finger through his mouth to make sure there are no foreign bodies or mucus blocking his airway. Be careful not to push a foreign object farther into his airway. (Protect yourself from being bitten as well; even unconscious dogs can bite.) Gently bring his head in line with his neck to open the airway.

4. With one hand, hold the dog's muzzle closed. Put your mouth over the dog's mouth and nose, creating a seal, and blow into his nose. Watch to see if the chest expands. If it does, continue to breathe into his nose, giving one breath every three seconds. Continue artificial respiration until the dog breathes on his own or until you reach emergency help.

5. If the chest does not rise when you blow into your dog's nose, something is blocking his airway. Sweep your fingers through his mouth again to check for foreign objects. Open his mouth and try to find the blockage visually. If you cannot see or touch the blockage, you must do the Heimlich maneuver. Lift your dog upside down with your arms around his abdomen under his rib cage and his tail toward your face. Give five sharp hugs. The strength of the hugs should depend on the size of the dog. If this does not work, lay your dog on his side with his hindquarters under a pillow. Give five strong thrusts under his rib cage, using one hand for a small dog and two hands for a larger dog. Once the object is dislodged, check your dog's heartbeat and breathing. Begin CPR, if necessary.

6. If your dog does not have a pulse, you must begin chest compressions. Place your dog on his right side. Place the heel of your hand over his heart— on his rib cage just below the elbow. Place your other hand palm down on top. Compress the chest 30 times, about 3 compressions every 2 seconds. Adjust the strength of your compressions based on the size of the animal. Give 2 breaths every 30 compressions. Repeat until you feel a heartbeat and the dog begins breathing on his own or until you reach emergency help.

7. Get your dog to a veterinarian immediately.

Always keeping your dog under your control, whether within a secure fenced-in area or on a leash, is the best injury preventive. To avoid pulled muscles, heatstroke, and other exercise-related injuries, pay attention to your dog's needs, and keep him in good condition. Don't be a weekend warrior, hanging out on the couch 95 percent of the time and then running your dog into the ground one day a week. Don't exercise your dog during the hottest times of the day, and always keep fresh water available.

Some serious illnesses seem to come from nowhere. Many illnesses, however, can be treated before they turn into an emergency. If your dog shows signs of illness—coughing, vomiting, or having diarrhea—don't just hope it will go away. Call your vet and describe the signs. The sooner you treat an ill-

Moving an Injured Dog

Follow this procedure for safely moving and transporting an injured dog who cannot walk:

- Assess the situation. If your dog seems to be very agitated and reacts aggressively to your attempts to touch him, restrain him with a muzzle. Even the most trustworthy dogs will bite if they are in great pain and very afraid.

- Find a door, board, blanket, or floor mat to use as a stretcher for the dog. Small dogs may be moved inside a sturdy box or wrapped in a blanket or towel and carried.

- Lift the dog gently and with help. One person should support the chest and the other the rear end when lifting the dog. Transport the dog carefully.

- Be mindful of fractures. If a limb is broken, keep the limb still and supported. Move the dog as little as possible. If you are experienced in first aid, a properly applied splint helps reduce further injury. Getting your dog to a veterinarian should be the first priority.

ness, the better your dog's chances of a quick recovery, and the less likely the illness will become serious.

Preparation

Don't wait for a medical emergency to find out where the closest emergency clinic is. Instead, have the name, number, and address of a reputable 24-hour emergency clinic close at hand at all times. Drive the route at least once before an emergency strikes. When in a panic, it's easy to forget how to get to a location or become so flustered that you can't figure out an address. Don't leave anything to chance. Keep a well-stocked canine first aid kit available at all times as well.

Traffic injuries are common. Know what to do if something happens to your dog.

Response

Sometimes emergencies just happen despite your best attempts to prevent them. Experts say the most important thing you can do when your dog is injured or ill is to remain calm. Losing control puts both you and your dog in further danger. Instead of losing your head, stop for a moment, take a deep breath, and observe the situation. Collect yourself before rushing to your dog. Many dog owners have been injured or even killed because they panicked and rushed into the street after an injured animal. Proceed cautiously.

Determine if your dog is seriously injured or ill. If he is, the first thing you must do is stabilize him. If he's been hit by a car and is in the street, you must stop traffic to move him out of harm's way. You might need help to do this. Flag down drivers traveling in the opposite direction and ask them to block the street while you move your dog. Keep in mind that your dog may act aggressively toward you due to pain and fear, so find a length of gauze or a strip of cloth to tie around his muzzle. Your dog may have a neck injury, so you need to take special care when you move him. Find a large, sturdy piece of wood or a sheet that will support the

If you don't have a commercial muzzle available and need to immobilize your dog's mouth to treat an injury, you can fashion one out of a strip of soft cloth, rope, gauze, a necktie, or a nylon stocking—anything strong and approximately 2 feet long. Firmly, but not too tightly, wrap the cloth over the top of the nose. Cross the two ends under the chin and tie behind the ears. Take care not to impede breathing by covering the nostrils. Allow the dog to pant periodically by loosening the muzzle.

Use the muzzle only while you are moving or treating your dog. A muzzle can increase an injured dog's distress. Remove the muzzle immediately if the dog begins to vomit or has difficulty breathing. Keep scissors handy in case you need to remove the muzzle quickly.

dog's weight. With help, gently maneuver him onto the sturdy board or taut sheet. Be careful not to jostle him.

Once out of direct danger, assess your dog's condition. Is he conscious, in pain, bleeding? If he is bleeding, apply direct pressure to the wound to stem the blood flow. If he is breathing with difficulty, sweep his mouth to remove any foreign bodies, and then perform mouth-to-mouth resuscitation. If you cannot obtain a pulse, perform CPR. Talk to your veterinarian about the proper method to administer mouth-to-mouth resuscitation and CPR. She may also be able to refer you to a canine first aid training course.

Once the dog is stabilized, gently load him into your car. Call your vet or the closest emergency clinic to let the staff members know you're on the way. Give them as much information on the dog's condition as possible and your probable time of arrival. Be sure to bring a checkbook or major credit card with you so there is no issue with payment. If possible, bring a friend or neighbor to monitor your dog's condition as you drive.

Disasters

Natural or intentional disasters are another unfortunate part of life. For every human life affected by a disaster such as a fire, tornado, or explosion, many animal lives are affected as well. There is nothing you can do to prevent a widespread disaster, but you can be prepared to act in your dog's best interests. Many cities are now taking that into consideration and include family pets into emergency response plans. However, saving human lives and structures are firefighters' top priorities, so you are largely responsible for your own dogs. Most cities have an animal control division or humane societies that will assist in animal rescue in the case of a disaster, but help may arrive late or not at all. Be prepared to assist all of the animals in your care in the case of a disaster.

Disaster Preparation

As with personal emergencies, being prepared for a disaster is key to the survival of your dog. In the case of an earthquake or tornado, you may

In the case of a personal or community emergency, your dog is dependent on you for salvation. There is no canine 911.

not have water or power for several days, even weeks. It's vital you have at least a three-day supply of food and water for both you and your dog. Store an extra 10-pound bag of dog food in a watertight container along with three sealed gallons of water earmarked for your dog. Rotate the food and water every so often to make sure you always have an in-date supply.

Although the situation has changed since Hurricane Katrina, when many people endangered their lives by refusing to evacuate without their pets, not every emergency shelter allows pets, so you cannot automatically rely on them to house you and your animals. It's a good idea, then, to have a safe house lined up where you can go with your pets in case of an emergency. This may be the home of a friend or family member, or it may be a boarding kennel or a veterinary clinic. Because a disaster may strike several hundred miles of territory, have alternatives lined up in the event that your original safe house is also affected by the disaster. Remember, too, that many hotels and motels relax their rules about pets in times of crisis. You will be able to find some way of housing your pets if you bring them with you. If you leave them behind, however, there's no guarantee that they will survive or that you will be able to have them rescued in a timely manner. For more information, go to www.fema.gov/plan/prepare/animals.shtm.

Even if you don't normally use a crate for your dog, keep one on hand. Some shelters require that your dog be crated, and a crated dog is more secure than one on a leash. Make

Veterinary Medical Assistance Teams (VMAT) help dogs and other animals endangered by catastrophic events such as floods, hurricanes, fires, and earthquakes. Established by the American Veterinary Medical Association and sponsored by the American Veterinary Medical Foundation, the VMATs respond within 24 hours to federally declared disasters.

Acclimate your pet to a crate before a disaster strikes. Many emergency shelters will accept only crated dogs.

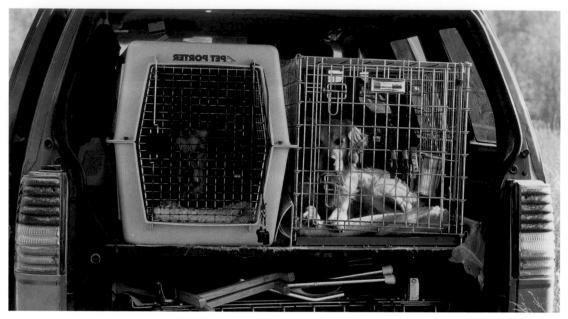

If you have animals, evacuate your home before it becomes mandatory.

sure your dog is comfortable in his crate by regularly feeding or giving him treats in it.

In the event that your dog cannot accompany you to a local shelter and your safe houses cannot be reached, have a list of second tier alternative resources. These should include your local animal shelter or animal welfare society, which may have resources during a disaster; names and phone numbers of local hotels/motels that accept pets; and names and numbers of friends and relatives who are willing to board your dog should that prove to be necessary.

Always keep a disaster kit fully stocked. In it you should have your dog's medications: a doggy first aid kit; emergency phone numbers (including your regular vet, emergency vet, alternate dog caretaker); an extra leash and collar; an ID tag with open space to fill out; grooming equipment: comb, brush, dog shampoo, nail clippers, ear cleanser, cotton balls; a towel; a toy or two (such as a tennis ball and chew toy); a bottle of water; a one-day supply of food; and bowls for food and

water. Your disaster kit should also include an up-to-date photo of your dog, which will be useful if you are separated from him. Finally, keep an up-to-date medical history of your dog with proof of recent vaccines, especially rabies, in your kit. This may be required if you need to find alternate housing.

Tornadoes have been known to rip collars right off of dogs, leaving them disoriented and without identification. So in addition to wearing a collar with ID tags, your dog should be either tattooed or microchipped. These permanent forms of identification will be a lifesaver if your dog loses his collar or tags in the havoc of an emergency.

Certain disasters are more likely to occur in certain regions, so be aware of which disasters are likely in your region and practice for them. People living in California should have a place in the house where everyone in the family knows to go during an earthquake. They should also have a three-week supply of food and water for every family member, and alternate plans for meeting outside the home

The Legislative Aftermath of Hurricane Katrina

When Hurricane Katrina struck the Gulf Coast in 2005, many people endangered their lives by refusing to evacuate without their pets. Pets that were left behind, an estimated 250,000, drowned or faced starvation, forced to fend for themselves in an abandoned city. The lucky ones, approximately 15,000, were rescued by humane organizations, dog and cat breed or rescue groups, and individual volunteers.

The hurricane laid bare the dichotomy between people's attachment to their animals and the unwillingness or inability of shelters, police, and other rescue officials to accommodate pet owners. Because of this situation, Congress passed the Pets Evacuation and Transportation Standards (PETS) Act, which requires local and state disaster plans to include provisions for household pets and service animals in the event of a major disaster or emergency. To date, 24 states have enacted animal disaster plans, and 10 are in the process of writing plans. To find out if your state has a plan and what it is, visit www.friendsofanimals.org/programs/animal-disaster-plans/.

in an electrical wire–free zone in the event that the house structure is undermined.

In Florida, hurricanes are common, and families there know to hide in an interior room with no windows—if that's a bathroom, make sure everyone can fit, dogs included. Keep emergency and first aid supplies in this safe place.

In dry wooded or brush areas where wildfires are a risk, have plans for evacuation from the immediate vicinity—how long does it take to load your human and canine family into the car to make a quick getaway? How long does it take for you to get out of the danger zone on foot? Discuss an evacuation route and procedures with every member of your family.

© Dogphoto.com

Animal-control officers and pet rescuers are specially trained to help evacuate pets when necessary.

In every family, one person should be responsible for the dogs so no other family member is put at risk looking for them. Include the family dogs in fire drills and natural disaster drills. Check fire alarms monthly, and keep a towel close to your bed to cover your nose and the noses of your canine or human charges when leaving the house. Be sure that all windows open easily and that every room has at least two exits. Never lock your dog's crate in case he must be rescued; do not keep dogs in areas that you cannot easily access from outside the home.

When Disaster Strikes

When a disaster strikes, the normal reaction is to panic. To protect your family, human and canine, maintain your calm until everyone is safe.

If an earthquake hits, the safest place to be is under a desk or table away from outside walls. If there is no desk or table, crouch against an inner wall that is far from unsupported bookshelves, glass doors, and windows. This applies to your dog, too. Call him to you. If he won't come, don't leave your safe niche to chase after him—you'll only risk injury to both of you. If you need to leave the house, try to grab a leash and secure your dog on the way out. Keep leashes at every exit of your home so if you can't reach your disaster pack, crate, or your dog's normal leash, you won't have to look for it or leave the house without your dog secured.

Never leave your dog in the house if you are evacuated. According to the Federal Emergency Management Agency, if you do not take your dog with you when you are evacuated, chances are he will not survive. However, if you absolutely can't bring your dog, there are a few things that may increase his odds of survival. Keep all of your animals in a room with access to fresh water and away

Keeping your dog safe is part of the responsibility you accept when you first bring him home. Think of it as payment for all the joy he will give you throughout his life.

from hazards such as glass and windows that can break, unattached bookshelves that can tip over, and large picture frames that can fall. If there is a risk of flooding, keep your dog in a room that has high counters or furniture he can retreat onto. Post a large sign outside

The American Veterinary Medical Foundation provides grants for training to help ensure that every state is disaster-ready and helps provide animal care and treatment through disaster preparedness programs. In the past decade, AVMF has awarded grants totaling more than $7 million in support of that mission.

Do all you can for the pet you love; always be prepared to keep him safe.

who are left behind may be alone for weeks or even months. In New Orleans, thousands of animals perished unnecessarily. New national and state legislation should help ameliorate this problem in future disasters, but it is still largely up to individual owners to protect their pets. Have a plan for your pet in the event of a disaster. It is vital. Leaving your dog in your home in the event of an evacuation is never a good option.

Evacuations

Many people lose their dogs because they are forced to leave a burning or flooding home without their beloved animals. So as soon as the possibility of evacuation is indicated, begin preparing for it. In the case of wildfires, floods, and hurricanes, a voluntary evacuation can become mandatory rapidly. Both dogs and cats can be difficult to capture when an evacuation is immediate. If you are given only five minutes to leave your home, getting your dog out may be a difficult task. So as soon as there is the slightest indication of an impending evacuation, start moving. Place all of your animals together in one room, along with their disaster kits, leashes, and crates.

Prepare yourself to leave as well; pack your car and be ready to go at a moment's notice. As soon as a voluntary evacuation is in effect, leave. While those without dogs may opt to stay at their homes as long as possible, dog owners do not have this liberty. Evacuating with dogs is much more difficult than without them.

The Federal Emergency Management Agency cautions that even if you do not have to evacuate your home during a disaster, there are precautions you should take in the days following a catastrophic event. Because dogs may be shaken or stressed, be sure they are properly secured at all times. The presence of new odors, changes in once-familiar land-

your house in a prominent place indicating that your dog is indoors. Inside, leave information about your dog: his name, medications, temperament, your evacuation location, and feeding instructions. Contact your local animal shelter to help you get your dog evacuated. If you do have to leave your dog, try to keep him as calm as possible by leaving him with his own bedding and a favorite toy or two. Again, leave your dog only if you have absolutely no other option. As we now know from the events in New Orleans following Hurricane Katrina, not all disasters can be wrapped up in a few days or even weeks. Dogs

Your dog may get himself into a precarious situation if he panics and tries to escape from danger.

marks, and their own panic may cause them to get lost if they run away. Even well-behaved dogs can act uncharacteristically erratic when frightened.

If You're Not Home

Sometimes a disaster strikes when you are not at home, leaving you unable to reach your dog; plan for this possibility every time you leave your house. Always fill your dog's water bowl before you leave home. In addition, leave at least one toilet bowl open so if your dog is left alone for several days, he will have access to water. Never use any additives such as bleach or antifreeze in your toilet tank. Although dogs can survive without food for up to a week, some people who live in earthquake zones or other areas with a high incidence of natural disasters

feed their dogs with timed feeders so that if an emergency should occur, the animals will not be deprived of food.

Provide a trusted neighbor with a key to your house. Make sure he or she knows your dogs and your dogs trust him. Even if your neighbor can't evacuate your animals, he may at least be able to stop and feed them and make sure they are safe. If you live in an area where there is a high risk of wildfire, arrange with a friend or neighbor to evacuate your dogs if you aren't able to. Do not release them to fend for themselves—fire is disorienting and often dogs will run straight into the flames they are trying to flee. Even if they escape the flames, it is likely they will become lost, and they could be killed in traffic.

CHAPTER 14

Lost Dog

Your dog is lost; what do you do? Most dog owners find themselves in this scenario at one point or another. Usually the errant dog is just trapped in the garage or down the street playing with a canine friend, but not always. There is nothing like the sense of panic and hopelessness that accompanies the discovery of a lost or runaway dog—but there is plenty you can do.

You can take steps to prevent your dog from running away, but you should also prepare for the worst. If the worst does happen and your dog is gone, quick, decisive action is paramount: your best chances for bringing him home come in the hours immediately following his disappearance. Be thorough and don't give up. Don't skip searching a neighborhood because you think your dog wouldn't go there—animals surprise us all the time. And don't stop looking just because your dog has been gone for several days or weeks; there is still a chance of bringing him home.

Security

To prevent a tragedy, ensure your dog is well secured at all times. Even the best trained, most sedentary dogs will make a break for it under the right circumstances, such as seeing a cat running by, being disoriented due to age or illness, or being left in an unfamiliar place.

Teach your dog an excellent recall. Not just a saunter-over-at-my-own-convenience recall, but a drop-everything-and-coming-running-instantly recall. Always keep your dog on leash when outside of your yard. Even at the park, take your dog off leash only when you have him in a securely fenced area.

Fence your yard. The fence should be at least 5 feet high and reach to the ground with no gaps. If your dog's a jumper, you may want to go higher. Walk the perimeter regularly to make sure there are no nooks or crannies where an intrepid dog could escape. To prevent an under-the-fence escape, pour concrete around the base of the fence or use bricks as a stopgap. Some people use buried electric wire, but some municipalities prohibit this.

If you leave your dog at a friend's or relative's home, be sure that he is completely secure. Dogs can panic when left at a home or a location they are unfamiliar with. Check that the fencing is secure, and ask the homeowner to keep your dog on a leash whenever he is not fenced.

Even with the best security, dogs can escape. Maybe a visitor leaves a door open or your dog jumps out of the car when you stop for gas. Chances are this will happen at least once in your dog's lifetime. Dogs have even been stolen from their own yards. In the event

Prevent a dog escape by building a secure fence around your entire property.

your dog gets lost, you want to act quickly. Keep a current, well-lit photo of your dog on hand to use for posters. Also, keep a list of vets, animal shelters, and humane agencies in your area so you can begin your search immediately. To increase the chances of your dog's return, there are several things you can do.

Identification

However your dog gets loose, his best chance for return is proper identification. There are three main forms of identification: tags, tattoos, and microchips. Because tags can be removed or lost, dogs should have at least one other form of identification—either a tattoo or a microchip.

There are two tags your dog should wear at all times: an ID tag stating your dog's name and your phone number, and a license from the city or county within which you live. An ID tag can keep your dog's time away from home short and sweet. If a neighbor finds him and calls your number, you can be reunited pronto. When vacationing with your dog, affix a temporary ID to his collar. You can securely tape a piece of paper with your local or cell phone number on it; or if you are in one location for an extended period, you can get a regular ID tag with your temporary or cell phone number on it.

Besides being required by law in most counties, a license can quickly reunite owner and dog

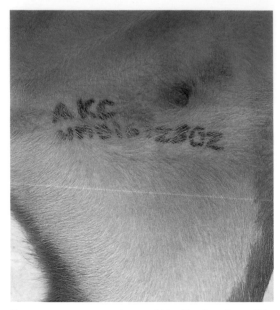

Tattoos are permanent forms of identification; they will be invaluable if your wandering dog loses his collar.

if the dog is picked up by animal control. Licensing your dog will save you sleepless nights and reduce the chances of your dog being euthanized or adopted before you find him. In agricultural communities, licensing has another benefit. Many counties require ranchers and farmers to notify animal control before shooting free-roaming dogs, even if they are harassing livestock. You can buy licenses through your city animal control office; ID tags are available through most major pet supply stores.

Stolen Dog

Unfortunately, not all dogs are lost by accident; sometimes they are stolen. One of the most important things you can do to prevent your dog from being stolen is to have him tattooed or microchipped or both. The Animal Welfare Act makes it a federal offense to buy, sell, exhibit, use for research, transport, or offer for transportation any stolen animal, and all research laboratories are required to check to see whether a dog is tattooed or microchipped. If the dog is resold to a private party, there is a good chance that a vet will check for a microchip at one point or another—another opportunity to reunite you and your best friend.

If you know your dog has been stolen and hasn't just wandered away, the first call you should make is the police. In many states, dog theft is a felony and is treated very seriously. Call your local TV and radio news and the local newspapers. Many stations and newspapers will feature stolen pets on their broadcasts or local news section. Even if this doesn't eventually reunite you with your pup, it will help educate the public to the dangers of dognapping and warn other dog families.

Microchips are the newest thing in pet identification. The chips, placed under the skin, work for 25 years.

A tattoo is one form of permanent identification that can be used with an ID tag. It consists of a series of numbers that are registered with a national database. These numbers are tattooed on the inside flank of the dog or sometimes on the ear. Getting a tattoo is relatively painless for dogs and can be done at pet fairs, humane agencies, or through your veterinarian.

Animal control is required to attempt to contact the owners of dogs with tattoos before euthanizing them or placing them for adoption. Animal research facilities routinely check for tattoos as well. The downside to tattoos is that whoever finds your dog needs to know to look for one. Tattoos can also fade and become difficult to read.

Microchips have largely replaced the use of tattoos—they're quick and easy to place. Like a tattoo, a microchip carries numeric information that is registered with a national database. About the size of a grain of rice, the microchip is inserted between the shoulder

blades by a veterinarian. This should cause no more pain than receiving an inoculation, although many vets try to place microchips when dogs are already under anesthetic for altering or dental cleaning. The microchip is so small that the dog never even knows it's there. The chips have a life span of 25 years.

Most veterinarians, animal control offices, and animal shelters have handheld scanners that they use for checking incoming stray dogs. If a microchip is found, the registry is informed and the owner is contacted. As with tattoos, animal control and animal research facilities routinely check for microchips before a dog is euthanized, placed for adoption, or used for research. The negative of microchips is that the person who finds your dog must take the dog to a local shelter or veterinarian to have him scanned. In addition, microchips are not universal; not all

A lost dog can become confused and disoriented. Don't be surprised if your dog wanders very far from home.

scanners can detect all microchips. Talk to your veterinarian and local animal shelter about the appropriate microchip before having one placed in your dog.

Your Dog Is Gone

Despite all of your preventive measures, your beloved dog is gone. The first thing you must do is begin the search. Recruit friends, relatives, and neighbors to help. Leave one person at home in case the dog comes back or a Good Samaritan finds him and calls. The rest of you, fan out.

In the first hour or two after you notice your dog is missing, one or two people should search the neighborhood while another person gets in a car and looks farther out. You may be surprised by how far away your dog can get in a short time. Use a car familiar to your dog—most dogs recognize the sound of their owners' cars and may approach them on their own. Call your dog's name frequently and stop to listen: he may be stuck somewhere and will bark or whine when he hears the sound of your voice.

Besides the legwork, there are other plans of attack you can take to find your dog. Place lost dog ads in your local papers and on petfinder.com as soon as you know

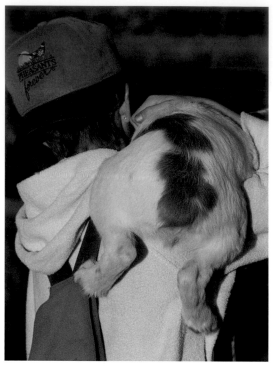

Moving can be traumatic for people and pets alike. Take precautions to keep your dog safe throughout the move.

your dog is missing. Don't wait several hours in case he comes home, take action immediately.

Create a flyer. Scan a photo of your dog and print it on small poster paper. The top should read LOST DOG in large, bold letters. On the

---

Pet Detective

If your dog is lost, consider hiring a pet detective. For any number of reasons, you or your family may not be able to conduct a thorough search. A pet detective can post flyers, check shelters and rescue groups, perform Internet searches and post information on lost-pet Web sites, interview neighbors and follow up on potential sightings, set humane traps to capture a panicked dog, or even follow a trail using trained search dogs.

After compiling information about your pet, pet detectives use techniques that include posters, direct mail, and networks of paid and volunteer searchers. Posters go to veterinarians, kennels, groomers, medical research labs, police agencies, humane societies, animal control agencies, and pet supply stores not only in your city or county but also in the surrounding area. Many dogs are found more than 30 miles from home.

Postcards with the pet's photo may be sent to residents in the immediate neighborhood as well as to veterinary hospitals within 10 miles and animal shelters within 30 miles. The idea is to create a network of individuals—the mail carrier, neighbor kids, garbage collector, utility workers—who will keep an eye out for the dog. Ideally, all of this is done within the first 24 hours of the dog's disappearance.

bottom, include pertinent information about your dog, including a description of him and his name. Be sure to include your phone number at the bottom of the poster and offer a nonspecific reward. If you have a good computer setup at home, you can do this on your own. Otherwise, ask a local copy center to do a rush job.

Make giant fluorescent posters to place on major roadways in the immediate area of the escape. Use five words that people driving by at 55 miles per hour can read and visualize: REWARD LOST DOG RED/WHITE SPANIEL. Those are five words that a driver can read, interpret, remember, and convey to others if they see such a dog or know someone who did. More information on making an effective poster and flyer is available on the Web site lostapet.org.

Plaster your neighborhood with the posters—affixing them to light poles and bulletin boards within a several-mile radius. Take additional posters and distribute them door-to-door, to businesses, and at parks. Talk to everyone you meet on the street –the more people who know your dog is missing, the better your chances are of finding him.

You should also call and visit every veterinary hospital in your city and surrounding cities, as well as visit every animal shelter, private and municipal, in your area. Distribute posters to all of these places. Sometimes people bring strays to shelters outside of the city limits, so be thorough. Visit every shelter every day. Look at the animals yourself; do not take the shelter staff's word for it; someone else's description of your dog can sound very different from your own.

High tech is going to the dogs. Global Positioning System satellites are now being used to track pets. Electronic pager collars send and receive data via satellite, allowing users to monitor their pets' location via the Internet.

Photo courtesy of Zoombak.

A recent development in pet-product technology is a GPS device that attaches to the collar and alerts you to your dog's location.

The point is that you never know where your dog may go, so look anywhere and everywhere. Sometimes dogs return to their previous home, so drop off posters in your old neighborhood. Don't assume your dog won't be in an area where you've already searched. Revisit these areas constantly.

Don't lose hope. Dogs are unpredictable and can wander far. In addition, someone may find your dog but not report it to animal control for many days. Keep searching for several weeks after your dog has disappeared. Dogs have been found even months after their disappearance.

Moving

Moving can be hard on a dog and is one of the most common times for a dog to become lost. To ensure his safety, whether you're moving via plane or car, keep your dog well secured and his ID updated. Avoid stops along the way, but if you must stop overnight before moving into the new house, keep your dog securely on leash or in his crate at all times. The actual process of moving from point A to point B isn't the only concern. The hustle and bustle of packing and rearranging can also be stressful for a dog. Familiarity breeds comfort and disruption can be frightening.

When preparing to move, packing boxes and rearranging furniture, keep one room relatively unscathed. This is where your dog can sleep and relax while turmoil is going on in the rest of the house. The room should have a door that can be shut securely when movers or packers are in the house. The day before the move, take everything out of his room but his bed, bowls, and toys.

On the day of the big move, keep your dog in his special room throughout the day. If he's crate-trained, keep his crate in the room—it can serve as an extra security blanket for him. Shut the door to the room securely and post a large sign: DOG IN ROOM, DO NOT ENTER. Once the rest of the house is emptied and the movers have departed, you can let your dog out, but only if the rest of the house is securely closed with windows and doors shut. Even if your dog has never run away, being faced with a big, empty house can confuse and panic him.

It is best to wait until the movers leave your new home before moving your dog there. If you have to bring your dog to the new house while the movers are still there, again, find a secure room for your dog's bed, crate, toys, and food and water bowls. Settle him in his room and post your caution sign on the door. Reiterate to everyone entering the house that your dog cannot be let out of the room.

Because moving is stressful for both you and your dog, you may want to find an alternative place for him to stay during the days before and after your move. If you have family or close friends in the same city and your dog is familiar with their home, ask if he can stay

Allocate an off-limits doggy room during a move. Keep your dog, along with his bed, crate, bowls, and toys, here until you are ready to load him into the car.

In the first weeks and months after a move, your dog may need extra attention and affection.

over for a few days around the time of the move. This will allow him to avoid much of the commotion, and it will give you a chance to dog proof your new home before he arrives. The other option is to board your dog at a kennel or your vet clinic for the days or week surrounding your move. This is the safest option and will relieve some of your stress and keep your dog out of danger.

Even after you've moved in, there are dangers in a new home. It often takes dogs weeks or even months to settle in. Occasionally, they may even try to escape and make their way back to their old home. If your dog runs away, your first stop should be your old neighborhood.

For the first weeks after moving in, give your dog extra attention. Again, allocate a special no-disruption room for your dog, and keep his bed, crate, toys, food and water bowls, and anything else that comforts him in this room. While you're unpacking boxes and rearranging furniture, your dog needs a respite so that he doesn't become stressed. It's common for dogs who have moved to have behavior changes such as increased aggression, anxiety, disobedience, house-training issues, or separation anxiety. For the first month after your move, limit your dog's access to the outdoors. Make sure your fencing is secure and that your dog won't bolt through an open door.

If, despite your best efforts, your dog becomes anxious after your move, consult your veterinarian. She may be able to provide medication or recommend a trainer who can help. Another option is one of the over-the-counter natural anxiety supplements, such as Rescue Remedy, available through most pet supply stores.

Dogs would rather vacation with their owners than stay home and await postcards from faraway destinations.

CHAPTER 15

Traveling with Your Dog

Traveling with your dog can be a great experience or a big headache. It all depends on your organizational abilities, flexibility, and sense of humor. Many people have romantic notions about bringing their dog on vacation, but reality is sometimes more complicated. Your mobility and spontaneity are limited when you travel with your dog, but at the same time you are open to experiences that you would never know if it were not for your dog.

Not all modes of transportation welcome dogs with open arms. There are a few cruise ships that allow you to travel with your dog. Small dogs are even allowed to travel in the kennel on some transatlantic cruises. Before booking a cruise, ask about the cruise line's pet policy as well as the policies of the countries you are visiting. Trains and private buses in the United States do not allow dogs except those covered by the Americans with Disabilities Act such as guide and service dogs. But travel by car or plane can be more dog friendly.

To keep your dog safe on trips, follow a few basic safety precautions. Keep a collar and up-to-date ID on your dog at all times. If you plan to be in one location for an extended period, affix a temporary ID to his collar. You never know when an escape may happen. Well-behaved dogs can act unpredictably when traveling; the stress and excitement can

Traveling by car can be a great way to see the country with your dog.

affect their behavior. Even if your dog comes reliably when called, keep him on leash or in his carrier at all times. The traffic, people, and noise at rest stops and airports can spook even the most serene dog.

Traveling by car will also allow you to seek out off-the-beaten-path attractions, which may be more welcoming to dogs. Public beaches and parks, quaint villages, and other rural destinations can add a new dimension to your travels.

Traveling by Car

Traveling by car is probably the easiest way to go when you decide to take your dog along. It's flexible and private—you get to choose where you want your pup to sleep and how

Now, Charley is a mind-reading dog. There have been many trips in his lifetime, and often he has to be left at home. He knows we are going long before the suitcases come out, and he paces and worries and whines and goes into a state of mild hysteria, old as he is. During the weeks of preparation he was underfoot the whole time and made a damned nuisance of himself. He took to hiding in the truck, creeping in and trying to make himself look small.

Source: Travels with Charley *by John Steinbeck*

Quarantine and Pet Travel Laws

Thinking of traveling to Hawaii or outside the United States with your dog? Be sure to do your homework about quarantine rules and other animal regulations. The following are dog-related laws for some popular destinations. For information on countries or locations not listed here, visit the Bureau of Consular Affairs Web site at travel.state.gov.

Hawaii: Hawaii has a quarantine period of up to 120 days. When specific pre- and post-arrival requirements are met, animals may qualify for a 30-day quarantine or the 5-Day-or-Less Program that went into effect on June 30, 2003. Some of the requirements include being microchipped, having had the OIE-FAVN rabies blood test, having fulfilled specific rabies vaccination requirements over the dog's lifetime, and having been treated for ticks. For complete checklists of requirements to qualify for the 30-day or 5-Day-or-Less Program go to http://hawaii.gov/hdoa/ai/aqs.

Canada: There is no quarantine for dogs traveling to Canada. All dogs older than three months require signed and dated veterinary certificates verifying that they have been vaccinated against rabies within the last three years. The certificate must clearly identify the animal. Dogs younger than three months do not need a certificate of rabies vaccination. All animals must be in good health when they arrive. For more information, go to www.inspection.gc.ca/english/anima/heasan/import/dogse.shtml.

Mexico: U.S. visitors to Mexico must present a pet health certificate signed by a veterinarian registered in the United States and stating that the animal has no communicable diseases, issued not more than 72 hours before the animal enters Mexico. Visitors must present proof that their dog was vaccinated against rabies, viral hepatitis, leptospirosis, and distemper not less than 15 days or more than one year before arrival, and vaccinated against parvovirus not less than 15 days or more than 150 days before arrival. For the most current information on traveling with pets to Mexico, contact the Mexican consulate in your area. To find the consulate office nearest you, go to www.mexonline.com/consulate.htm.

France: There is no quarantine for U.S. dogs traveling to France. U.S. travelers taking their dogs to France must show a valid rabies vaccination certificate given at least 30 days before entering France (21 days if it is the animal's first rabies vaccination) and within the previous 12 months, as well as an international health certificate executed no more than 10 days prior to travel. All dogs must be accompanied by original documentation. Dogs, cats, and ferrets must be at least 3 months old or, if younger, traveling with the mother. Some breeds are not permitted in France, so check beforehand. Dogs, as well as cats and ferrets, must be identified by an approved microchip such as HomeAgain from AKC Companion Animal Recovery or AVID-Eurochip. For more information, go to http://ambafrance-us.org/spip.php?article783.

Germany: There is no quarantine for U.S. dogs traveling to Germany. Dogs entering Germany must be identifiable with an approved microchip such as HomeAgain from AKC Companion Animal Recovery or AVID-Eurochip and must show proof of having been vaccinated for rabies within 12 months of entry and at least 30 days prior. For more information, go to http://www.germany.info/relaunch/info/consular_services/customs/animal_factsheet_10_2004.html. Germany has various dangerous breed regulations at both the national and state level. On the national level, dogs designated as dangerous are pit bull-types, Bull Terriers, American Staffordshire Terriers, and Staffordshire Bull Terriers. Importation into Germany of these dogs is forbidden. German states have varying dangerous breed regulations. Rhodesian Ridgebacks, Doberman Pinschers, and Rottweilers are just a few of the breeds affected by these regulations. Dogs accompanying travelers remaining in Germany for no more than four weeks and service dogs are exempt from these regulations. For the complete list of dog breeds affected by state regulations go to www.germanyinfo.org/relaunch/info/consular_services/customs/dogs.html.

Italy: Dogs may enter Italy with proof of current rabies vaccinations and an international health certificate issued by a U.S. veterinarian no more than 30 days before departure. Dogs younger than 3 months of age are not permitted as they are too young to have received a rabies vaccination. Dogs must also be identifiable by a microchip that provides the pet owner's name and address. There is no quarantine for U.S. dogs traveling to Italy. Dogs must be on a leash or muzzled when in public. Contact the Italian Tourist Board for more information at www.italiantourism.com.

United Kingdom: Through Britain's PETS (Pet Travel Scheme), travelers from the United States, Canada, and other qualifying countries are no longer required to quarantine their dogs for six months as long as they meet a lengthy list of specific requirements. If any of the requirements are not met, dogs will be placed in quarantine. Early release from quarantine may be permitted when PETS requirements are met. Pit bull–types, Japanese Tosas, Dogo Argentinos, and Fila Brasileiros are considered dangerous and are not allowed in the United Kingdom. These breeds may be seized and destroyed and the owner can be prosecuted. For regulations before you travel, visit the PETS Web site at www.defra.gov.uk/animalh/quarantine/pets/index.htm.

Japan: There is a 14- to 180-day quarantine period for U.S. dogs that are traveling to Japan, and a rabies inoculation certificate is required. Dogs should be given rabies shots at least 30 days before traveling to Japan. The vaccination period cannot expire before the pet's arrival, and the certificate must state its duration. Dogs must have a health certificate stating they are not suspected of having rabies or leptospirosis. For more on quarantine regulations, go to Japan's Animal Quarantine Service at http://www.maff.go.jp/aqs/english/animal/dog/index.html.

you want to accommodate him. Another benefit is that once you reach your destination, you won't need to worry about in-town transportation. Depending on the city, the laws for dogs on buses and in taxis differ; some restrict dogs to certain times of day or do not allow them at all.

Safety Precautions for Traveling by Car

Use a crate or a doggy seat belt whenever you are transporting your dog in a car. There are plenty of comfortable and convenient belts now on the market. Crates require your pup to be separated from you during the trip, which might change the experience, but it does allow your dog a cozy, safe space of his own. The crate can also be used when you reach your destination so your dog can be left alone in a hotel room. A crate can take up a fair amount of space, so if you're in tight quarters and won't need to keep your dog in a crate at your destination, then a seat belt is probably the best way to go. Never transport your dog in the back of a truck unless the vehicle is canopied and he is in a crate. Do not let your dog hang his head out the window while you are driving. As

Car Deaths

Dogs easily can become overheated if left in a car on a warm day. Even if it doesn't seem very hot outside or if the windows are left cracked open, the car can heat up quickly. Avoid taking your dog on errands during summer's heat unless he can leave the car with you.

- Be respectful to others. Not everyone is the dog lover you are. Do not impose.

- Bring only well-trained, well-socialized dogs when traveling. A vacation is no place for remedial dog training.

- Use a harness leash; it provides more security.

- Update your dog's ID tags, license, and vaccinations.

- Clean up after your dog; bring plenty of plastic bags for this purpose.

- Bring your dog's own food from home. You may not be able to find it in another city or country, and a quick change to new food can bring on digestive upset.

- Keep your dog's safety first. Do not take him off leash or push him into uncomfortable or frightening situations.

much joy as he derives from this activity, it's too easy for flying debris to injure an eye.

Rest stops are opportunities for danger when traveling with your dog by car. If your dog runs away at a rest stop, you're almost guaranteed tragedy. Not only is there an easily accessible ramp onto the freeway, but you're in the middle of unknown territory with no recognizable landmarks for your dog. So instead of playing fetch when you stop for a break, take your dog for a walk on a leash around the parking lot and allow him to relieve himself. Five minutes of leg stretching is probably fine. Because many dogs won't drink water or eat when in a moving vehicle, a break is a good time to offer a drink and a small snack.

Avoid pet potty areas where there is fresh excrement. Dog feces carry a lot of diseases, and these areas can be dangerous to your dog, especially if he is young, elderly, or immunocompromised in some way. Do be sure to clean up after your dog, and carry plastic bags with you for this purpose.

Cars themselves can excrete substances dangerous to your dog, particularly antifreeze and coolant. Both contain ethylene glycol. When letting your dog in and out of the car, keep him close and do not allow him to sniff or lick any car drippings—from your car or from any others. And never keep extra antifreeze inside the compartment of your car.

Remember, never leave your dog alone in a hot car. The temperature inside a car rises rapidly, and dogs can quickly overheat, leading to heatstroke or even death. Short-nosed dogs such as Pugs and Bulldogs are at special risk when left in cars, but all dogs can become victims. If traveling during a cool time of the year, dogs can be left for very short periods with the windows rolled down at least 3 or 4 inches and the car parked in a shady area.

Car Travel Hints

There are a number of things you can do to make car travel with your dog more pleasant. Before leaving on your trip, have him professionally washed and groomed. Both of you will be more comfortable with less shed hair covering the seats and dander in the air. This also keeps doggy smells to a minimum. Use slip-

According to the American Animal Hospital Association's 2004 pet owner survey, 63 percent of respondents traveled with their pets, and 45 percent stayed in hotels with them.

Car Sickness

Does your dog's stomach get upset when he rides in the car? The following tips will help prevent car sickness and give you both a smooth ride:

- Car sickness is often caused by anxiety, rather than motion. (Motion sickness is caused by fluid changes in the middle ear that affect the body's equilibrium.) Teach your dog that car rides are good. Have him sit in the car for a few minutes each day for about a week without going anywhere. Then each day for several days drive a short distance, such as around the block. Slowly increase the distance and time he rides in the car. Offer a lot of praise during this process. Don't put your dog in the car only for unpleasant trips such as going to the vet. Take him on rides to the park or to visit friends and your dog will soon associate the car with positive experiences.

- If your dog is fearful, try Rescue Remedy, Serene-Um, Pet Calm, or another natural remedy. These products use flower essences, herbs, vitamins, and minerals for natural calming and stress relief. Check with your pet supply store, local health food store, or veterinarian for more information.

- Don't feed your dog four to eight hours prior to a car trip. A dog with an empty stomach is less likely to vomit. Water is OK and may make your dog feel more comfortable. However, some dogs may feel better with a small amount of food in their stomachs; try giving a small amount of food if your dog has vomited on an empty stomach on previous trips.

- Keep fresh air flowing while your dog is in the car. Don't open the window far enough for him to get out or to stick his head through.

- Allow your dog to ride in the front seat where there is minimal movement (do not allow your dog to ride in the front seat if you have air bags). Some experts believe that allowing the dog to look outside, positioned so he can see out the front window in the direction the car is moving, may help prevent car sickness. Others believe looking outside actually increases car sickness and dogs should be confined to crates or made to lie down where they can't see out. If the first method you try with your dog doesn't work, try the other.

- Drive slowly and carefully, avoiding sharp turns and jerky movements. On longer trips, stop every hour or so and give your dog a quick walk and a little water.

- If all else fails, an antinausea medication called Cerenia is now available by prescription from your veterinarian. Clinical trials proved that it helped with motion sickness in dogs. Fresh air and a view of the horizon can also help minimize motion sickness.

covers over the seat your dog is sitting on. That way, you can wash the cover when you arrive at your destination, and you won't be embarrassed to have guests in the backseat. And it will be nice and fresh for the trip home.

Always carry water, a watertight bowl, food, and snacks for your pup. Avoid changing your dog's diet while on the road; a quick change can cause diarrhea and can exacerbate car sickness. Bring along a couple security toys—a ball or Frisbee will make visits to securely fenced parks and backyards more fun.

Bring your dog's bed or a comfy blanket that smells of home. You can use it if you stay overnight at a friend's house or in a hotel. It will help keep your dog feeling secure and cozy. Always cover guest or hotel beds with a sheet or blanket if you allow your dog to sleep with you. If your dog is predisposed to barking, accidents, or separation anxiety, do not leave him alone in a hotel room. If you do leave your dog in the room, provide him with a crate or ex-pen to keep him out of trouble. If a hotel has a good experience with your dog, its future acceptance of dogs will reflect this. Be a good ambassador and be conscientious of hotel owners and your fellow travelers.

Traveling by Airplane

Many people are flying with their dogs nowadays. If your dog is small enough for his crate to fit under the seat in front of you, he can even travel in the cabin. Larger dogs must travel in the baggage compartment, which, although pressurized, may not be temperature controlled or ventilated. Although the vast majority of dogs who travel in cargo

Plan ahead to make traveling with your dog as stress free as possible.

arrive unscathed, many dog owners feel that it is too much of a risk. Hundreds of animals transported as cargo are killed, injured, or lost each year when traveling by airplane. Dogs flying in the cargo area are put at risk because of the possibility of very hot or cold temperatures; suffocation; being dropped; or their crates being damaged, allowing them to escape. There are several airlines currently exploring the possibility of in-cabin pet kenneling areas, but none exist at this time.

Many commercial airlines no longer fly animals in very hot or cold weather. Some airlines place a moratorium on shipping animals during summer or winter; others have stopped shipping dogs as cargo altogether. Some airlines no longer fly the short-snouted brachycephalic dogs such as Bulldogs or Pugs, who are susceptible to a type of respiratory distress called brachycephalic respiratory syndrome. Many airlines no longer accept dogs as excess cargo and only ship them as cargo through a recognized air-shipping service. Before flying, talk to your airline about potential issues in transporting your pet. If you are uncomfortable with the airline's answers, you may wish to postpone a trip until another time of year or use another mode of transportation.

Airplane Safety Concerns

There are safety concerns for all dogs traveling by airplane, whether in the cabin or as cargo. Pay close attention to the cautions listed below, but also be careful when bringing your dog in and out of the airport.

If there's no other option for your travel plans than putting your dog in cargo, there are ways to minimize risk:

- Use a recognized air-shipping service.
- Use a USDA-approved crate that is large enough for your dog to stand up and turn around in.
- Freeze water in a bowl that is attached to the inside of the metal mesh at the front of the crate. It will prevent spillage when the crate is being loaded but be melted by the time your dog is thirsty.
- Tape a cloth bag with one meal's worth of dog kibble to the front of the crate in case there is an unexpected delay.
- Never lock the crate. Close it securely so airline staff can open it in case of an emergency. Affix Live Animal stickers to each side of the crate.

A USDA-approved crate is required when a dog travels by cargo. Small dogs can travel in the airplane cabin.

- Pen arrows on the sides indicating which side is up. This may seem unnecessary but when the airline is being loaded, everything looks like baggage to the workers.
- Never tranquilize your dog; it may cause breathing problems.
- Line the bottom of the crate with a cozy towel or blanket to soak up any accidents and to keep your dog comfortable.
- Provide one chewy or fuzzy toy that has no sharp edges or rips.
- Write your dog's name on the front of the crate so the staff can call your dog by his name.
- Affix the address and phone number of your destination to the crate.
- The ASPCA recommends adhering a photo of your dog to the crate in case he is separated from it. Carry an extra photo of your dog with you on the airplane.
- Tell anyone and everyone that you can that your dog is on the plane: ticket and boarding agents, pilots, and stewards.
- Wait to board the plane until you see your dog being boarded and the cargo hatch closed.
- Always book a direct flight.
- During warm weather, travel in the evening or early morning.
- Reconsider flying brachycephalic (short-nosed) dogs such as Pugs and Bulldogs or other dogs with respiratory difficulties. Short-nosed dogs are prone to breathing difficulties, which can be exacerbated when flying in cargo.

Travel Hints for Flying with Dogs

When any dog travels by airline, there are a few requirements. Contact your airline and ask about any rules or requirements be-fore buying your ticket. Keep in mind that not all airlines fly dogs, and those that do will probably charge for a dog traveling in cargo and may charge for a dog traveling in the cabin as well. Some airlines limit the number of dogs on a particular flight, so book your flight early.

Airlines require each dog to have a travel certificate from a vet, so make sure that your dog's vaccinations are up to date. Have a travel certificate filled out by your vet no more than 10 days before the trip. If your trip will last longer than 10 days, make sure that you ask your airline whether you will need another health certificate for your return flight.

Have your dog relieve himself before putting him into his carrier. At the airport, try to find a grassy spot for last-minute needs. Always pack a snack or two, water, a watertight bowl, and a favorite soft or chewy toy for nourishment as well as comfort before and after the flight. Out of respect for your fellow passengers, do not take your dog out of his carrier when flying in-cabin. Good flying etiquette by all pet owners will help ensure that small pets can continue to fly in the airline cabin with their people.

Lodging

Although assistance dogs, covered by the ADA, are legally entitled to stay in any hotel in the country, many lodging establishments are also reaching out to pet dogs. It depends on the region of the country, but in some areas there are now many establishments available to a person traveling with their dog.

To find a dog-friendly hotel or motel, you can surf the Web, visit a library or book-store, or phone facilities. The Web makes it

As of July 2004, dogs and other pets traveling among countries in the European Union must be fitted with microchips or have tattoos for identification. Pets must also carry passports with proof of rabies vaccinations and health exams to show when traveling between countries. A passport photograph is optional.

Be respectful when staying in dog-friendly hotels. Keep your animal off the furniture, or cover it in sheets brought from home before allowing your dog to jump up.

especially easy to find a good canine stopping spot—with Web sites devoted to just this purpose. There are also many books—usually regional—that provide information on where your dog will be welcome overnight. Make use of these books; you could end up without a bed if you play it by ear. No matter where you're going, it's good to have a backup plan before you get there. Although you may come across Pets Welcome signs, you may not always be pleased with the accommodations. Many hotels set aside rooms for customers with pets. Sometimes this works out well, other times it guarantees you the worst room in the inn.

Most hotels either require a pet deposit or have a special pet room rate—usually $15 to $50 above the usual rate. Although some hotels welcome dogs of all sizes and shapes, many have restrictions on size, accepting only dogs who are 20 pounds or lighter. Be sure that you are clear on the hotel's pet policy before booking a room.

Hints for Lodging with a Dog

Make sure your dog is flea free before departing on your trip. And aggressive or otherwise uncontrolled dogs should not be taken to hotels or motels. Any bad behavior an establishment experiences with one dog will be held against all dogs.

Try not to allow your dog on the bed or furniture in a hotel. If your dog can't stand to sleep away from you or insists on being on the couch, bring a sheet or blanket from home to cover the area where he will lie. Make sure your dog is house-trained before bringing him inside. Even if your dog has been reliable and has not had an accident in years, staying in a hotel is a new and sometimes unsettling experience, which can lead to accidents. Many dogs are reluctant to drink water or relieve themselves during a car trip or outside an airport, but once they arrive at a destination and relax, they cut loose. Take your dog for a couple of walks upon arrival and before settling down for the evening.

If you plan to leave your dog in the hotel while you are out, bring a crate. This will keep

Camping may be a good alternative if you cannot find pet-friendly lodging. State and national parks require that dogs be leashed at all times.

him safe and secure, eliminate the chance of his inflicting damage, and allow the housekeeping staff to come in while you're gone. If you don't use a crate, find a hotel that offers a dog-sitting service. This is unusual but not unheard of, especially in large cities such as New York or San Francisco. Some hotels pride themselves on being pet friendly and even offer pet packages with everything from keepsake food bowls to dog treat cookbooks to daily walks.

Another option is to stay in a guest rental. Many resort areas offer private homes for rent. This can be an ideal option for a dog owner, but again, check the pet policy before you book. If traveling to a rural area, camping facilities are usually dog friendly as long as the dogs are kept leashed. Ask about park policies when reserving a campsite.

Eating Out

Eating out can be a fun thing to do with your dog—that is, if you keep your expectations low, pack a warm coat, or travel in summer. Unless you have an assistance dog, your dog will not be allowed inside any restaurant. It's against health violations in almost every city in the United States. Some taverns that do not serve food allow dogs inside, but it's rare and generally limited to a few regulars.

Seek out dog-friendly sightseeing destinations on your vacation; you may be surprised by what you discover.

In most cases, eating out with your dog means finding a restaurant that has an outdoor patio and is pet friendly. There are good guides for most cities and regions, which you can consult. If you haven't planned ahead, the hotel concierge should be able to recommend a couple of places. You can also call a local animal shelter, which may have lists of pet-friendly destinations, or contact local pet supply shops. Upscale pet boutiques and pet bakeries will probably have advice on destinations that are both good and welcoming to dogs.

For the most part, dog-friendly restaurants are casual, although you may be able to convince some restaurants with outdoor patios to welcome your dog on uncrowded days. It's always a good idea to travel with your dog during off-peak times. Hotels, restaurants, cabs, and others who make their living off of tourists are more accommodating when they aren't busy.

If you bring your dog with you to a restaurant, he must be under your control at all

Top 10 Dog-Friendly Cities
1. San Diego, California
2. Long Beach, California
3. Carmel, California
4. Portland, Oregon
5. Seattle, Washington
6. Chicago, Illinois
7. New York, New York
8. Orlando, Florida
9. Colorado Springs, Colorado
10. Austin, Texas

Source: Dog Fancy *magazine, 2007. Order is based on the number and quality of dog-friendly places to stay and things to do with dogs.*

Atlanta—Civil War Self-Guided Tour and Centennial Olympic Park

Chicago—the Lakefront Trail along Lake Michigan

Orange County—Disneyland (There are on-premises kennels—afterward, take them to the almost mile-long Huntington Beach Dog Beach.)

New York—Central Park

Philadelphia—Independence Mall

San Francisco—Fisherman's Wharf

Washington, D.C.—the National Mall (Dogs are allowed, leashed, along the entire 2-mile mall. They are not permitted in covered or enclosed areas or on the memorial sites.)

times and must be completely dog and people friendly. Aggressive behavior such as snarling, growling, or snapping will not ingratiate you to restaurateurs. A dog who jumps up on people, relieves himself on the restaurant grounds, or snatches food is equally unacceptable. Dogs who aren't under complete control or completely trustworthy around all other living things have no place at a restaurant.

When waiting for your table, ask your dog to sit nicely so that other patrons do not become uncomfortable. Once at the table, your dog should be in a down-stay position under the table throughout the meal. It's not a problem if other patrons or staff members ask whether they can pet your dog. Just request that they squat next to him rather than encourage him to stand up. If your dog can't control his excitement when being petted, ask if they'll wait until you take him for a potty break. The less bother your dog makes, the more accommodating a restaurant will be the next time someone requests permission to bring a dog.

Many restaurants will supply your dog with a water bowl and perhaps even a treat. Don't expect this, though. Bring a supply of snacks and a bottle of water as well as a watertight bowl. This should keep your pup satisfied while you enjoy your meal. There are also restaurants that cater exclusively to canines and their people; these establishments include dog palatable items on the menu.

Dog Camps

Do you want to take a fun vacation with your dog, improve your skills, explore new activities? Then a dog camp may be just the place for you and your dog. Camp programs run for a weekend, a few days, or a week. Although a dog doesn't need to be highly trained to go to a camp, he should be under your voice control and not be aggressive toward other dogs or people.

You can choose among a wide variety of camps that offer either specific canine activities or a combination of activities such as agility, tracking, lure coursing, carting, herding, and disc catching. Some camps are focused on the serious canine competitor, while others are focused on providing a fun experience for dogs and owners. Most camps also offer workshops on such topics as canine nutrition, clicker training, behavior, and holistic dog care.

To find a dog camp, talk to your veterinarian or a dog trainer in your area, peruse dog magazines and other publications, or contact the organization representing the sport in which you are interested.

If you can't find a pet-friendly restaurant, don't despair. This can be an opportunity to explore some areas that you usually wouldn't discover when visiting a city. Ask a local for directions to the closest park, where dogs and people are equally welcome. Then stop at a deli and get some of your favorite take-out foods—a loaf of bread, cheese, fruit, and bottles of juice or water—and you're set. Your dog will get a nice workout while you relax. You may even meet some fellow dog lovers who can give you tips on other dog-friendly spots to visit in town.

Make an effort to strike up a conversation with fellow dog walkers; you'll likely get some excellent tips and receive an insider's view of your vacation spot.

Shopping

In Europe, dogs are a common sight in stores. Shopping with dogs hasn't caught on as thoroughly in the United States, but it's making headway. Visit any urban shopping, area and there's a good chance you'll find at least a few pet-friendly stores.

Your first stop should be the local pet boutique—de rigueur for trendy hot spots. There, you and your dog can browse the dog-theme and dog-product selections. If your dog is lucky, he might even be offered a homemade doggy treat—an increasingly common amenity. In fact, many metropolitan and resort areas in the United States even boast doggy bakeries. The local dog boutique is the perfect place to get the lowdown on dog shopping—which shops welcome dogs with a smile and biscuit and which shops are canid non grata. One sure sign of an uber dog-friendly establishment is the presence of a designer doggy water bowl at the front door.

When unsure, poke your head into the store and ask the nearest staff member if you can bring your dog in. Some dog owners

argue that it's more successful to just barge in, but in the name of dog etiquette, ask first. As retail business has slowed, stores have become increasingly accommodating of unusual requests, including allowing dogs inside.

Shopping is one of the many vacation activities you can share with your dog. Outdoor flea markets and bazaars can prove especially fun.

Some retail stores even allow dogs in the dressing room with you. Small boutiques remain the most accommodating of dogs, but many of the chain stores also welcome canine shoppers.

Shopping areas are also fun places for your dog to socialize with the locals—sniff a few Dalmatians here and there—and help you explore. When you're ready for a respite, make a beeline for a coffee bar. Cafes are some of the most dog-friendly places in town, although because of health regulations, you'll have to sit outside.

Dog-Friendly Sightseeing

Almost every city has a few dog-friendly spots. Public parks, beaches, or outdoor landmarks are all good destinations when your dog is in tow. You'll be surprised by how much you can see when you stay outside. Many cities offer tours—group or self-guided—of their distinctive architecture and landmarks. This can be great fun with your dog. Other good dog spots are outdoor shopping malls, pedestrian streets, shopping districts with small boutiques and outdoor cafes, parks, and waterfronts.

Public transportation in some cities can be surprisingly welcoming to dogs. In San Francisco, for example, muzzled, leashed dogs are allowed on all public transportation during off-peak hours. You must pay an individual adult fare for your dog. In Seattle, leashed dogs are allowed on Metro buses. Many taxicabs allow dogs as well. Ask pet-friendly businesses for advice on additional canine sightseeing.

World Travelers

Travel to the United Kingdom is finally available for American dogs. With the new laws in the United Kingdom, Americans and their pets can now travel together almost anywhere abroad. Savvy travelers, however, recommend against bringing dogs to any destination that has not historically valued dogs—such as some areas in the Middle East—or to areas where canine disease is rampant, for example in Southeast Asia. Dogs and other pets traveling among countries in the European Union must be fitted with microchips for identification purposes. Globe-trotting pets must also carry passports with proof of up-to-date rabies vaccinations and health exams. A passport photograph is optional.

Top 10 Dog-Friendly Beaches

1. Fort DeSoto Beach, Florida
2. Dog Beach, San Diego, California
3. St. George Island, Florida
4. Carmel City Beach, California
5. Cape San Blas, Florida
6. Hunting Island, South Carolina
7. Fort Funston State Park, California
8. Pistol River State Scenic Viewpoint, Oregon
9. Ft. Fisher State Recreation Area, North Carolina
10. Jekyll Island, Georgia

Source: America's Best Online

Antarctica Bans Dogs

Dogs were brought to Antarctica by polar explorers to act as sled dogs. They were banned in April 1994 because there were concerns they could spread distemper to seals and because they aren't native to the continent.

CHAPTER 16

Activities You Can Do with Your Dog

An abundance of dog activities await you and your dog. Some are only for certain breeds, while others are universal. Whether your dog is clumsy or graceful, thick or thin, big or small, there's a great activity just waiting for him.

Healthy Fun

As fun as dog sports are, participating in them can result in injury. Injuries can range from tendonitis and muscle strains to broken bones and sprains. Out-of-shape dogs or dogs with undetected illnesses can even suffer respiratory problems or heart attacks. To keep injuries at a minimum, your dog should be in good physical shape before getting started. Have your dog checked for any illness or injury that could be exacerbated by the activity. Older and out-of-shape dogs are at special risk. Once your dog gets a clean bill of health, there are still safety precautions you should take for all doggy activities.

Visit Your Vet

Before embarking on any new or rigorous activity, take your dog for a visit to the vet. She will do a general physical and baseline blood work, looking for any abnormalities or signs of lameness. Older dogs who are starting new training programs may undergo an electrocardiogram, to determine the heart's health, and lung X-rays. If the veterinarian finds signs of arthritis or joint disorders, she may recom-

Don't be a weekend warrior. Dogs need regular exercise programs and should always build up to strenuous activities.

mend that you keep your dog's exercise level fairly low, and she may prescribe joint supplements such as glucosamine or a canine non-steroidal anti-inflammatory drug such as Rimadyl, Metacam, or Etogesic.

Your vet will also look at your dog's weight and may recommend that he lose several pounds before participating in an activity or advise you to start slowly to avoid putting undo stress on your pet's bones, joints, heart, and lungs. Morbidly obese dogs require a veterinarian-approved diet and exercise regimen before beginning any activity.

Dog booties can protect canine feet on long hikes and are especially useful when hiking over rough terrain. They also help protect a paw that has been injured. Booties come in a variety of materials, including leather, neoprene, polar fleece, and nylon.

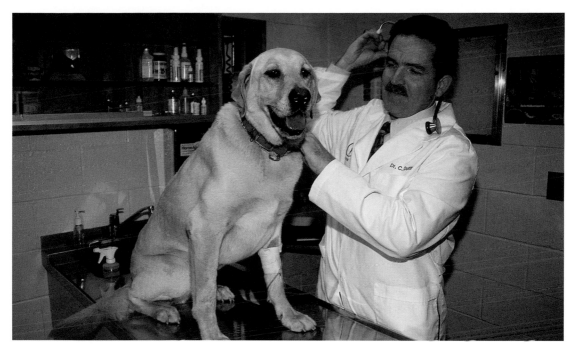

Owners are well advised to bring their adult dogs to the vet for an examination prior to beginning any new or rigorous activity regimen. A diet and a modest exercise plan could be the vet's sincere recommendation.

Weekend Warriors

Whether your dog's daily fitness regimen is as simple as a brisk walk or as intense as agility practice coupled with a 5-mile run followed by a swim, don't let your dog be a weekend warrior. Dogs who are sedentary all week and agility superstars on the weekends are subject to injuries. Establish a daily exercise program before starting any rigorous activity. If your goal is to go on a 5-mile run every day but your dog is used to five-minute walks, take it slow. Start with a ½-mile walk, and then gradually increase the distance. Once your dog is comfortable with a 5-mile walk, you can start running. Begin with running 1 mile the first day, and gradually increase distance as your dog becomes conditioned.

Safety Precautions

You may be eager to begin activities with your dog, but there are still safety precautions you

Heatstroke is common in dogs. Always supply plenty of fresh water and shade when exercising with your pet. Many dogs appreciate having a wading pool to immerse themselves in.

A study published in 2005 in the *Medical Journal of Australia* concluded that walking a dog daily can improve human health to a degree comparable with quitting smoking. Dog owners walked 18 minutes more per week than nondog owners did, and those who walked their dogs for at least an hour a week were more likely to meet the amount of physical activity required for significant health benefits.

Dogs are much more susceptible to heat than we are. Every year, many dogs become ill or even die as a result of overheating. To prevent heatstroke during warm weather, never leave your dog in a car, always exercise him during the early morning or evening when temperatures are cooler, and always provide plenty of fresh water. If your dog is outside during the day, be sure the doghouse or other shelter is comfortably cool during the hottest part of the day. Signs of heatstroke include:

- Anxious expression
- Collapse
- High fever (104°F or higher)
- Loud panting
- Rapid breathing
- Rapid heartbeat
- Refusal to obey commands
- Staggering
- Staring
- Vomiting
- Warm, dry skin

If you suspect heatstroke, call the closest emergency veterinarian to let the staff know you are on the way. Immediately lower your dog's body temperature by getting him to a cool, ventilated location and applying towels or sponges soaked in cool water to his body; or douse him with a hose and then wrap him in a cool, damp blanket. Offer him a small amount of water, but don't force him to drink because he may choke.

need to take. Heat can be an issue with any sport. Dogs regulate their body temperature through their tongues; their temperature can rise rapidly when they are overexerting themselves on a warm day. Provide your dog with plenty of rest in the shade. Dogs will go until

Just as the human athlete must warm up and cool down before and after vigorous exercise to avoid injury, so should the canine competitor. If your dog is involved in sports or another physically demanding activity, be sure to give him time to warm up and cool down.

they drop, so sometimes you may need to enforce relaxation. Always have a good supply of clean water available.

The opposite of overheating is frostbite. It is rare but can occur if a dog gets chunks of snow in his paws, is outside for too long in very cold weather, or has a thin coat. Thin-coated dogs need to wear a sweater or coat if outside in the cold for long periods without being active. Dog booties are also helpful if snow is icy or if the dog is walking on streets or sidewalks covered with salt or de-icing chemicals. Don't let your dog eat snow when out on long snow hikes because doing so will lower his body temperature. Instead, always carry a thermos of warm water, a bowl, and a portable stove to melt snow for drinking.

Another danger is bloat. Bloat, or gastric torsion, is caused when the stomach fills with gas and then twists. Although the definitive cause of bloat is unknown, veterinarians recommend that food be withheld from dogs an hour before and after rigorous activity. If your dog gulps a lot of water after exercising, place ice cubes in his water bowl to slow him down.

Don't forget the importance of stretching. Most handlers don't consider their dogs' need to warm up and stretch prior to rigorous exercise, but dogs need to stretch as much as we do. Start with a few stretches. Ask your dog to sit and then lie down several times. Then ask him to jump up and stretch his body against yours. This is an

To remove sticky substances from feet, try rubbing the area with margarine or shortening to soften the substance. Then you can use your fingers to gently work it out of the coat. Soaking the foot in a mixture of warm salt water and olive oil or mineral oil can work in much the same way. If chewing gum is stuck in the coat, rub it with ice to make it brittle or peanut butter to soften it. Then break it off or work it out of the coat.

excellent all-over body stretch. Finally, ask your dog to bow for you—the play bow is a good stretch and easy to teach. When your dog play bows on his own, stretches out on his front legs while leaving his rump in the air, reward him and say, "good play bow!" After a few weeks, he'll catch on and do it on command. Check with your vet first, however, to make sure this activity is right for your breed. Finally, warm up with a brisk ½-mile walk or a 15-minute game of fetch. This will get your dog's heart pumping.

Agility

Agility can be fun for any dog. It consists of a course with obstacles and jumps that the dog must go over, through, or under. In competition, the course is timed and dogs can be disqualified for various faults. The goal is to complete the course in the shortest time with the fewest faults. Successful agility dogs have a combination of speed, agility, and intelligence. Competitively, herding breeds especially excel; Border Collies lead the pack when it comes to championships. Besides being a fun competitive sport, agility has also become a spectator sport, with coverage on TV's Animal Planet and even ESPN. There is something exhilarating about watching dogs weave, run, and jump at breakneck speed.

Because agility is an individual sport, however, slower dogs can participate. Yorkshire Terriers to Saint Bernards can enjoy agility as much as any other dog. It is enjoyable even for elderly dogs, provided precautions are taken to keep it safe and upbeat. And because agility requires a handler to work closely with her dog, it's a great way to reinforce the dog-human bond. Any dog can participate and compete in agility, regardless of breed or age, although there are restrictions on mixed breeds competing in the AKC. Elderly dogs may qualify for

Agility has become very popular. It is an excellent activity for high-energy, intelligent dogs.

With their speed, smarts, and quick thinking, Border Collies really shine on the agility course.

NADAC and USDAA are open to all breeds and breed mixes. Each organization has different rules governing competition and classes.

The AKC offers five jump heights ranging from 8 to 24 inches, and dogs compete for titles in various levels of classes. UKC competitors jump up to 20 inches and compete in three classes with progressively more difficult jumps. USDAA has the most stringent rules for competition and the most challenging jumps, with the maximum jump height of 26 inches. The organization also offers games such as Gamblers, Snooker Agility, Relay, and Jumpers. The NADAC with its fast courses emphasizes speed. It offers five standard division jump heights from 8 to over 20 inches and an optional jump height of 24 inches. In addition to regular classes, games such as Touch 'N' Go, Weavers, Tunnelers, and Gamblers are offered.

Equipment

All dogs compete on the same type of equipment, which can be rearranged to vary the course. Jumps, or hurdles, consist of horizontal bars with two side posts. The height of the hurdle is based on the height of the dog: there are 8-, 12-, 16-, and 24-inch hurdles. There are several types of hurdles, including single, double, and triple-bar jumps; wing jumps with barriers on each side of the jump; long jumps, which are horizontal rather than vertical; and a tire jump. The weave poles require a dog to zigzag (weave) through 5 to 12 poles (depending on the organization and the dog's skill level) placed in a line, without missing one. Then there is the pause table or box. This is difficult for a revved-up dog because he must jump on a small table or enter a box and then hold a sit-stay or down-stay for five seconds. Continuing the fun are the two types of tunnel: one consists of an open, flexible tube, the other is a closed tunnel, or chute, made of a short, rigid tube connected to collapsible fabric through which the dog must run.

lowered jump heights and less stringent time requirements.

Agility was developed in 1977 by U.K. dog-fancier Peter Meanwell and made its debut in 1978 as intermission entertainment at the annual Crufts Dog Show. The sport quickly caught on and is popular throughout Europe, the United States, and Canada. There are four U.S. organizations that sanction agility: the AKC, the UKC, the North American Dog Agility Council (NADAC), and the United States Dog Agility Association (USDAA).

Just about all dog breeds and mixed breeds compete in agility, but some of the most popular breeds in the sport include Border Collies, Shetland Sheepdogs, Golden Retrievers, Labrador Retrievers, Papillons, Cocker Spaniels, Welsh Corgis, and Belgian Tervurens.

There are a number of contact obstacles that the dog must actually climb. The dog walk consists of a long, narrow walkway connected by two sloping ramps. The dog must ascend the first ramp, traverse the walkway, and descend the second ramp to the ground. This is slightly different from the A-frame, which consists of two wide ramps formed into the shape of an A. The dog must ascend one side and then descend the other. The teeter, another contact obstacle, essentially is a seesaw, or teeter-totter. The dog must ascend one side, tip the teeter, and then descend to the ground. Each of these obstacles has a contact zone, which the dog is required to touch with at least two feet before completely leaving the obstacle. Touching the contact zone is important for the safety of the dog, ensuring he does not jump off an obstacle from an unsafe height or angle. Missing the contact zone triggers an automatic disqualification, or DQ.

In agility, dogs are at risk of muscle strains and collision with their handlers or equipment. A good trainer will instruct you on the proper use of the equipment and will always stress safety before speed.

Flyball

In flyball, there are four dogs on each team and four hurdles placed 10 feet apart from one another. Each dog leaves the start/finish line; jumps each hurdle; hits the spring-loaded ball box, which shoots a tennis ball out; catches the ball; and returns over the four hurdles to the finish line. The next dog is released as soon as the first dog crosses the line. The object is for the dogs to complete the relay in the fastest time possible.

Although flyball can be just for fun, it is a team sport, so each dog is relied upon to help the team win. Serious competitors pay close

Flyball is a team sport on which many dogs thrive.

attention to the size, speed, and drive of the dogs who participate. Because the level of hurdles is based on the smallest dog in a four-dog team, keen attention is paid to finding speedy, small dogs. Some terriers are prized in flyball because they are fast, have a high drive, and are small enough to lower the height of the hurdles substantially. Muscle and ligament pulls can plague flyball dogs because they are running full-force while jumping hurdles, so these dogs should be warmed up prior to racing.

Because the relays are set up alongside each other, dogs face other dogs while running. There's the danger of collisions and dog combatting, so flyball participants cannot be overly aggressive. The dogs must have the drive to reach the ball box, get the ball, and bring it back to their handlers. Most handlers reward their dogs by playing a vigorous game of tug or fetch once the ball is brought over the start/finish line. Some handlers also play tug to get dogs revved up to go.

Flyball was developed in the 1970s in California. It is now popular throughout the United States, and its popularity continues to grow. Competitions are overseen by the North American Flyball Association (NAFA).

Equipment

The equipment for flyball is relatively simple: hurdles, four for each team; spring-loaded ball boxes, one for each team; and tennis balls. Most handlers use some sort of toy to stimulate the dogs before the run and to reward them following the run.

Earthdog Trials

Earthdog trials are popular in the United Kingdom, Canada, and across the United States. Trials in the United States are overseen by the American Working Terrier Association, which was established in 1971, and the AKC, which began sanctioning earthdog trials in 1994. The sport of earthdog trials is based on the terrier's hunting background. Some earthdog events are exclusive to a few specific breeds, but the majority of them are open to most terriers and Dachshunds. The companion terriers, such as the Yorkshire Terrier, are rarely allowed to participate.

Earthdog trials simulate the job most terriers were bred for: digging and burrowing into tunnels and then hunting prey through the narrow shafts. Earthdog tunnels can be dug below the ground or simulated with tunnels created on top of the ground. The goal is for the terrier to pick up the scent of the prey and track it through the tunnel to the cage, which holds the animal or animal scent. Once the dog reaches the source of the scent, he must work the quarry, meaning he must bark, scratch, growl, lunge, or otherwise indicate interest in the quarry.

Earthdog trials are set up in increasingly difficult levels to test a dog's hunting aptitude. Each level, described as Introduction to Quarry, Junior Earthdog, Senior Earthdog, and Master Earthdog tests, feature increasingly difficult tunnels with a set amount of time to complete each part of the test, including finding the den hole, finding the quarry, and working the quarry.

Bred to go to ground, many terriers excel in earthdog trials.

The popular term for what earthdogs do, in essence what terriers do, is *go to ground*. Terriers were developed in England to hunt small prey. They were bred and trained to pursue small animals such as foxes, rabbits, and even rats into their burrows and then kill them by shaking them furiously to break their necks. In many terriers, you can see the legacy of this breeding, from their habitual prey-shaking—watch a terrier with a stuffed toy—to the coarse fur that protects their skin against the rough sides of a burrow. In fact, even their short, stubby tails serve a hunting purpose: these were developed, through breed selection and docking, so that handlers could pull the dogs out of tunnels by their backsides.

Equipment

Essentially, the equipment needed to go to ground is a tunnel and prey. This is not as simple as it sounds. Modern terrier owners rarely allow their terriers to hunt in real burrows or tunnels because of the risk of a cave-in. To avoid this danger, earthdog events use aboveground or well-buttressed inground tunnels for competition. The tunnels can be hay bales arranged to form a tunnel, or they can be prefabricated and inground. Some tunnels even have a transparent plastic side so that the competitors can be viewed.

Few terrier owners still allow their dogs to hunt and kill prey. Instead, the competitors place a prey animal, such as a rabbit or rat, in a secure crate at the end of the tunnel. The dog must find the crate and work the quarry for a sustained period. Some organizations do not use live animals at all, opting instead to use animal urine.

Sledding

Although sled dogs are still used for transportation in some remote areas of the world, they are mostly used by racing competitors and hobbyists. There are many levels of participation in the dog sledding world, from the competitors who race in the 1,000-mile-plus Iditarod to handlers who run two or four dogs once a month for fun.

The sport of dog sledding consists of a handler, a team of dogs, and a sled. Dogs can be run in teams as small as two and as large as 24. Dog sledding was once restricted to the northern regions of the world, including northern Europe, Siberia, Alaska, and Canada, but the sport has now expanded into southern mountainous regions. There are even sled teams in California. While the use of dog sleds for transportation has dramatically decreased since the beginning of the twentieth century, when the advent of railroads and airplanes largely replaced them, recreational dog sledding has increased. Today, there are many

Although people in northern climes once depended upon dog sledding for transportation, it is now done almost exclusively for fun and competition.

weekend warriors who participate in the sport on a hobby level.

Sled dogs are usually northern breeds such as Siberian Huskies or Alaskan Huskies. In competition, Alaskan Malamutes are generally considered too big and slow to be competitive, but they, and other nontraditional sled dogs, are used for recreational teams. In fact, even Labrador Retrievers and Golden Retrievers can enjoy low-stress pulling.

U.S. sled dog teams compete under the International Federation of Sleddog Sports (IFSS), the International Sled Dog Racing Association (ISDRA), and a number of regional organizations. Although there are few mushers that make a living off sledding, most competitions offer prize money. Hobbyists point out that even if they win often, the cash prizes rarely cover even a fraction of the cost of housing, feeding, and training a team of four to 24 dogs.

Equipment

Dog sledding is an equipment-heavy sport. It also requires living in a region where it is snowy and cold enough to maintain a snow pack and, if you run a team larger than two dogs, rural enough to keep multiple animals on your property. Sled dogs are usually kept outdoors tethered to individual weather-resistant doghouses. The dogs also require an additional exercise area. During the off season, all-terrain vehicles

Sledding can be enjoyed on a recreational or competitive level. Many of the northern breeds are especially well suited to this sport.

A conditioned skijoring dog can pull consistently at 15 miles per hour or faster. Any healthy adult dog who weighs 35 pounds or more can learn to skijor. Exceptions are brachycephalic (short-faced) dogs such as Bulldogs, who aren't really built to pull and may have respiratory difficulties.

(ATVs) are used to train and exercise dogs. The harness is hooked up to the ATV, much as it is hooked up to a sled.

There are two common types of sled: toboggan and basket sled. Toboggans are generally used for recreational and long-distance sledding. They are heavier and sturdier than basket sleds, which are used for competition. All sleds are long in front with runners coming out the back. Baggage or other loads can be carried in front on the sled, while the musher stands on the runners.

Four standard pieces of equipment attach a dog to a sled. The first is the towline, a long line that attaches the sled or ATV to the dogs. The dogs run on either side of the towline. The towline attaches to the second piece of equipment, the tuglines, which are then attached to each dog's harness. The third piece of equipment is the neckline, which attaches each dog's collar to the towline. The neckline is not used for pulling but rather to keep the dog close to the towline. The fourth is the harness, which may be either an X-back harness or a freighting harness. X-back harnesses are used for racing, while freighting harnesses are used for heavy loads and pulling toboggans recreationally.

Sleds are equipped with a brake that is operated by the musher's foot. This brake may slow the team, but it will not stop it if the musher steps off the runners. To keep a team in place, an emergency brake, called a snow hook, is used. It acts something like an anchor in the snow. Mushers also are equipped with a sled bag that can be used to drag equipment or an injured dog behind the sled.

Skijoring

Skijoring is essentially an adaptation of dog sledding. Instead of a sled, mushers are on skis, and the team consists of only one to three dogs. Skijoring is basically cross-country skiing with a dog. Because the dog takes up some of the skier's weight, skijoring takes less effort than cross-country skiing does, and ski-

Skijoring developed in Norway, where cross-country skiing is common. Its rise in popularity has led to better equipment and organized competition.

jorers are able to cover more ground. Enthusiasts claim that skijoring requires less preparation and provides better exercise than dog sledding does. Skijoring can be as simple as a pair of skis, a towline, you, and your dog. It's extremely popular in northern climates, and if you're lucky enough to live in a rural, snowy area, you can skijor right out your front door.

Although skijoring is especially popular with owners of the Nordic dogs who live to pull, such as Siberian Huskies and Alaskan Malamutes, it's fun for high-energy dogs of all breeds. Gun dogs are popular skijoring dogs in Norway and are commonly used in racing. Even diminutive Corgis have been known to excel in skijoring. Although the Nordic breeds rarely develop the hard packs of ice that catch in the hair between toe pads and often cause frostbite, it is common for most other breeds, so be sure these dogs always wear snow booties when running. Wearing booties is also a good precaution for all dogs covering long distances or when the snow is icy. If your dog is not wearing booties, check his pads occasionally and remove any built-up snow or ice.

Although skijoring has been popular in Norway for centuries and in Alaska since the early 1900s, it only recently found its way to the continental United States. While most skijorers are strictly recreational, there are races and contests that are gaining in popularity. The North American Skijoring and Ski Pulk Association oversees skijoring competitions. A pulk is a small sled loaded with equipment sometimes used to handicap competitors in a skijoring event.

> The Westminster Kennel Club Dog Show is the second oldest continuous sporting event in the United States. Only the Kentucky Derby is older. Since its inception in 1877, Westminster has gone on in the face of world wars, power shortages, severe weather, and even the Great Depression.

Equipment

Skijoring equipment is fairly basic, although a few manufacturers are now taking advantage of the budding sport. New equipment is safer for both handler and dog than is the older, makeshift equipment skijorers once used.

Standard cross-country skis are used for recreational skijoring; skate skis are the preferred choice for racing. Skis cannot have metal edges because the edges can seriously cut a dog if he comes into contact with them. A harness, which is worn by both person and dog, is also used in this sport. Dogs generally use an X-back or H-back harness. The handler wears either a climbing harness, which attaches around the legs and buttocks, or a waist belt. The belt is padded to minimize impact on the spine. The handler's belt or harness is attached to the towline. The first few feet of the line is usually some sort of bungee or flexible line so that stops and starts are not jarring for handler or dog. The towline can attach directly to the dog collar or to a tugline. Tuglines are used when more than one dog is skijoring. They can accommodate up to three dogs. The tugline or towline attaches directly to the dog's harness. As with all cross-country skiing, poles are used. They help maintain balance and move the skier along.

Weight Pulling and Carting

Weight pulling is a sport for the big dogs. It basically consists of a dog pulling a heavy weight on a cart as far as he can. In competition, the winner is the dog who pulls the heaviest weight the farthest. It has gained recognition as an alternative to sledding and skijoring for northern breeds that live in warmer climes and for traditional hauling dogs such as the Saint Bernard. It's also a fun sport for both the guardian dogs and the powerful terriers such as the American Staffordshire Terrier. There are even organizations that promote weight pulling as an alternative to dog fighting in inner cities. Some of the

Large dogs often enjoy drafting activities such as carting or weight pulling.

dogs traditionally used in fighting seem to enjoy weight pulling. In the United States, both the International Weight Pull Association (IWPA) and the UKC sponsor weight pulling competitions and events.

Carting is another weight-pulling activity. Dogs are harnessed to carts and pull either people or loads. Although there are no national sanctioning organizations, several breed organizations, such as the Greater Swiss Mountain Dog Club of America, conduct draft tests (drafting includes any of the weight-bearing activities, including carting, weight pulling, and sledding).

Whether practicing at home or in competition, the dog's safety comes first in weight pulling.

In both weight pulling and carting, the dog's health and safety must be foremost because these activities can easily injure a dog. Without the use of properly fitted freighting harnesses or when pulling more weight than they are capable of, dogs risk serious injury, ranging from muscle strains or tears to ruptured disks or spinal injuries. Always use proper equipment and increase weight gradually. Puppies should never participate in weight pulling.

Equipment

A well-fitting freighting harness, towline, and a cart, with or without weight, are all necessary pieces of equipment for weight pulling and carting. For safety, many handlers use spreader bars at the back of the harness, which help distribute weight evenly.

Conformation Shows

Conformation shows, also known as dog shows, got their start in the United Kingdom in the nineteenth century; the first dog show in the United States was held in 1877. Although restricted for the most part to purebreds, con-

Junior handlers learn to groom, train, and show dogs through 4-H programs.

formation shows are the best known of dog activities. It is a popular participant and spectator activity due to the acclaim of dog shows like the Westminster Kennel Club Dog Show held each year at Madison Square Garden, in New York City, and the Crufts Dog Show, held annually in England. Conformation shows are also big business; some people spend a large amount of money on quality show dogs.

It's rare for a champion show dog to live with his owner. In most cases, a top show dog lives with a handler who cares for him and handles him in conformation shows. The handler is often the groomer as well. Show dogs sometimes require rigorous daily physical conditioning such as running on a treadmill, as well as meticulous grooming. Some may even wear protective clothing to keep fine hair from fraying.

Show dogs are campaigned all year, competing in local and regional shows as they seek entrance into Westminster or Crufts, and vying to make it into the top standing of their own breed. An award of Best in Show at Crufts or Westminster guarantees a comfortable living for the dog once he or she retires to a breeding career.

Conformation shows, however, are not just for wealthy fanciers. There are many levels of dog showing. Even children can participate in junior dog handling through 4-H. Many adults also participate in conformation shows as a hobby, competing at the local and regional breed levels and reveling in the successes of their dogs.

The world's largest annual dog show is Crufts, founded in 1891 by a British traveling salesman named Charles Cruft. It is held each year at the National Exhibition Centre in Birmingham, England.

There are several organizations that oversee conformation competitions and/or register dogs, including the AKC, the UKC, and the American Rare Breed Association (ARBA). Outside of the United States are the Kennel Club, in Britain; the Canadian Kennel Club; and the FCI, which recognizes hundreds of breeds seldom seen in North America and organizes shows overseas.

Equipment

Serious conformation showing involves a multitude of paraphernalia, from metal crates for safe transportation and enclosure of dogs to various brushes, combs, hair dryers, clippers, and grooming products to different show leads to enticing squeaky toys and edible bait to excite the dog in the ring and have him show enthusiastically and attentively. Of course, if you begin to show around the country, you'll want to invest in a comfortable van or RV for your travels.

Obedience Trials

Obedience training can be the tricks and commands you teach your dog in your home, but obedience trials are a popular sport with dogs competing on the regional and national levels. Obedience training is the building block for all other dog activities and sports. It requires a symbiotic relationship between dog and handler and tests how well the dog understands and responds to the handler's commands. The backbone of obedience training are the basic commands: *come, sit, down, stay,* and *heel.* The training continues with long down, long sit, heel on and off leash, figure eight, and more.

As an organized sport in the United States, obedience trials are under the oversight of the AKC, the UKC, and the American Mixed Breed

Scent discrimination is just one part of obedience events.

Over a five-year period, a residential home for elderly people that also houses dogs, cats, and birds had a mortality rate that was 15 percent lower than that of traditional nursing homes. The home in New York state participates in The Eden Alternative, a program that alleviates boredom and depression among the elderly by having them care for animals and plants.

Obedience Registration. The AKC and UKC both offer obedience titles, but dogs must be purebred to participate in obedience trials sponsored by either club. Dogs are judged on their ability to follow commands and their skill in scent discrimination and directed jumping.

A new derivative of obedience trials is rally obedience. It is designed to shake up obedience a bit, using a more relaxed judging style and changing obedience courses. It's currently overseen by the Association of Pet Dog Trainers (APDT), which allows dogs of any breed or breed mix to participate. The AKC also offers rally obedience trials.

Equipment

Hurdles and dumbbells are the equipment used in obedience trials. Hurdles are used for jumping, while the dumbbells are used for scent discrimination exercises. In scent discrimination, the dog must choose the dumbbell with his handler's scent on it.

Canine Freestyle

Canine freestyle is a relatively new sport in the dog world. Also known as dancing with dogs or canine dressage, it consists of a dog and his handler performing a routine choreographed to music. Although small-dog fanciers were the first to embrace freestyle, its popularity has spread to large dogs as well. In fact, some accomplished freestyle dogs are Dobermans and even Rottweilers.

In many ways, freestyle is a combination of agility, obedience, conformation, and dance. The handler uses her body as the

Canine dressage, combining choreographed movement with a spectator sport, certainly livens up the average outdoor dog show.

Organizations in the United States that hold herding dog trials include the Australian Shepherd Club of America, Inc. (ASCA), the American Herding Breed Association (AHBA), the United States Border Collie Handler's Association (USBCHA), and the American Kennel Club (AKC). The objective of the ASCA is to promote and maintain the Australian Shepherd's natural working instinct, but it also titles other breeds. Dogs work three classes of stock to earn titles, including cattle, sheep, and ducks. Competition is open to all herding breeds.

The AHBA offers trial classes and a herding test program. The AHBA is open to all herding breeds. Sheep, goats, ducks, geese, and cattle may be used as stock.

The USBCHA is the sanctioning body for Border Collie herding trials in the United States and Canada. The organization holds national championship trials each year in sheep and cattle herding.

AKC herding trials are open to all registered purebreds. The organization offers certificates recognizing various achievement levels.

agility equipment, asking the dog to jump over or climb up an outstretched leg. The dog must be able to lie still, come to the handler, or go away from the handler when directed. For a good team, the dog and the handler must communicate well.

Canine freestyle, or "dancing with dogs," is quite a production, with music, choreography, costumes, and fun.

Freestyle was developed in 1989 by Val Culpa. Since then, it has gained popularity throughout the world but especially in Europe, Canada, and the United States. Freestyle competitions are overseen by the World Canine Freestyle Organization. Dogs of any breed or breed mix can participate. There is no equipment required to do freestyle, but many participants like to use scarves or other visual accompaniments. You will also need a portable tape or CD player and music.

Therapy

Therapy qualifies as both work and play. It can be a great activity for a well-trained, gentle dog, but it really is more than a hobby. Taken seriously by participants and those in the health care world, dogs serve as both emotional and physical catalysts for people suffering with illness or injury or struggling with learning or emotional problems.

As important as the dog's job is, it is still possible to participate in therapy with your pet dog on a casual level. There are several requirements, though. First, your dog must be well trained—able to sit, down, come, and stay without coaxing. He must be completely reliable with strangers and have no history of aggression toward people or other animals. Second, he must complete both obedience training and

Trained therapy dogs work wonders for the people they visit, providing comfort and lifting spirits.

certification by an accredited therapy dog program, such as the Delta Society or Therapy Dogs International. Finally, therapy work is a commitment. It's not the type of activity that you can skip one week because you're not feeling well. People are depending on you. Before starting, be sure you can commit to weekly, biweekly, or monthly sessions for at least a year.

Field Trials and Hunt Tests

The first field trials and tests were held in the mid-nineteenth century in the United Kingdom, but their popularity now extends throughout Europe, Canada, and the United States. There are several governing bodies for both hunt tests and field trials within the United States, including the AKC, the UKC, the North American Versatile Hunting Dog Association, and the North American Hunting Retriever Association.

Both field trials and hunt tests test a dog's hunting skills. In field trials, different types of hunting dogs compete against one another, separated into two groups: gun dogs and hounds. Gun dogs include retrievers, spaniels, and pointing breeds; hounds include Beagles, Dachshunds, and Basset Hounds.

In hunt tests, dogs are evaluated individually based on their abilities in various hunting skills such as pointing, flushing, and retrieving. They do not compete against one another. Instead, they compete against the standard, receiving a qualifying or nonqualifying score for their performance in the test. They are awarded various levels of titles, with each title requiring a more advanced performance.

Although live prey is sometimes used, field trials and hunt tests generally use plastic decoys or dead prey called cold game. Some handlers who participate in trials and tests choose not to hunt wildlife or have no opportunity to hunt. Others are hunters who wish to test their dogs' mettle. Some owners simply want the opportunity to see their dogs' natural hunting instincts at work.

Herding

Many farmers and ranchers still use their herding dogs for day-to-day work, but herd-

Hunting events are good opportunities for field enthusiasts to hone their dogs' instinctive skills.

ing isn't restricted to just working dogs. Even urban owners of herding dog breeds are turning to herding competitions, which are held worldwide but are especially popular in the United Kingdom, United States, and Canada. Competitive herding can be a positive experience for a dog bred to herd, but there is no limit to the breeds that participate. The most common are Border Collies, Australian Cattle Dogs, Australian Kelpies, and Australian Shepherds. Although working herding dogs may herd cattle or sheep or llamas, most competitions use sheep. Some competitions have the dogs herd ducks, which takes a gentle touch.

Dog and handler must work together when herding. Dogs learn to watch their handlers for hand and eye signals and to listen for verbal commands such as *come by* and *away to me.* Some handlers also use whistles. The dogs must be able to take orders from their handlers but think on their own as well.

Many classes are available to people interested in introducing their dogs to herding, ranging from one-day seminars to weekly sessions. U.S. dogs can compete in herding under the AKC, UKC, American Herding Breed Association, and the National Stock Dog Registry. In addition, the North American Sheepdog Society and the Australian Shepherd Club of America, Inc., sanction events open to all breeds. The Canadian Kennel Club also sponsors herding events for all breeds.

Equipment
The equipment for herding is minimal: handlers carry a crook or sometimes a rake to guide dogs as they herd the livestock. Serious competitors may invest in sheep of their own to keep their dogs at peak performance.

Frisbee or Canine Disc
Although you probably play Frisbee in the backyard with your dog, you may not realize

Many city-dwelling herding dog owners have discovered the fun of recreational and competitive herding. Testing your dog's natural herding instincts can be inspirational.

that Frisbee is also an organized sport nationally and internationally. The experts call it canine disc, and Frisbee-loving dogs are known as disc dogs. Dogs who excel in canine disc are the herding dogs and gun dogs, who love the chase and the agility that canine disc entails. Border Collies and Labrador Retrievers both make excellent canine disc dogs, but canine disc competitions are open to dogs of all breeds and breed mixes.

Although playing Frisbee on a recreational level is a stress-free way to spend a day with your pooch, competitive canine disc combines a number of elements that recreational Frisbee does not. For example, dogs are scored on the number of Frisbees they catch versus those they miss, the number of Frisbee catches made in a given time period, and the

Disc dogs elevate the game of Frisbee to a high art.

tance, the dogs are given two tries to make the longest catches.

Canine disc events are sponsored by the International Disc Dog Handlers' Association (IDDHA), Skyhoundz, and other organizations. There are several national competitions held each year, including the Alpo Canine Frisbee Disc Championship and the Quadruped. Professional Frisbee teams tour the country giving exhibitions at fairs and dog shows.

Lure Coursing

Lure coursing is a sport created specifically for the runners of the canine kingdom: the sighthounds.

The American Sighthound Field Association (ASFA) began the first trials in 1972. Essentially, lure coursing is dog racing with a simulated rabbit or other prey animal used as a lure. Generally, the lure is a white plastic bag or a strip of rabbit fur, which is pulled by a rope-and-pulley system. Amateur lure coursing is popular with owners of Salukis, retired racing Greyhounds, and Afghan Hounds. You can train your sighthound for lure coursing using almost anything that attracts his attention. There are also local organizations that have open practices for lure coursing.

complication of the move. Handlers throw the Frisbee under their legs or behind their backs, or even throw more than one Frisbee at one time to raise the level of competition.

There are several formats of competition, including the catch and retrieve, in which a dog must catch and retrieve one Frisbee as many times as possible within a timed period, usually one minute. There is also freestyle, sometimes called free flight, when a routine is performed to music. In this format, accuracy is what the judges are looking for. In long dis-

Lure coursing competitors wear different colored vests and are scored on speed, endurance, and the ability to follow the lure (usually a white plastic bag). This trio of Afghan Hounds abounds with the desired enthusiasm.

In the United States, both the AKC and the ASFA sanction lure coursing trials. The Saluki Club of America also hosts trials, as does the CKC.

Because sighthounds lose all common sense when chasing prey, it's important that you take precautions to keep your lure courser safe. Be sure the field is clear of gopher holes and any other hazards that may trip and injure your dog. Lure coursers are also at risk of being entangled in the rope-and-pulley mechanism that pulls the lure. Be sure the operator is experienced and takes full safety precautions. Lure coursers can also pull or strain muscles or even break bones by overexerting themselves, so always warm up your dog before participation.

Schutzhund

Schutzhund, or Vielseitigkeitspruefung für Gebrauchshunde (VPG), meaning versatility test for working dogs, is essentially a way to test the abilities of working dogs. However, over the years it has come to be a sport in itself. Schutzhund tests dogs on three areas of skill: tracking, obedience, and protection. Although Schutzhund has been a popular sport in Germany since the turn of the twentieth century, it has existed in the United States only since 1969, when the now-defunct North American Schutzhund Association was established. Although Schutzhund is best known for its protection work, proponents of the sport say that all three areas are equally important.

In tracking, dogs must track a trail left by their owner or a stranger through a series of small, human-made items. In obedience, the dog must be able to heel through a crowd of people, as well as do a stay, sit, and recall. Dogs are also tested on their resistance to gunshot noise. In the protection phase, the dog must find and hold a decoy suspect and protect his handler when the decoy simulates attacking the handler with a stick or whip. The dog must

Protection training is the best known of the Schutzhund disciplines, but the sport also tests obedience and tracking.

show courage but not viciousness. Dogs are awarded Schutzhund I, II, and III certification. Each test is increasingly difficult.

In Germany, the most common dogs to participate in the sport are German Shepherds, Rottweilers, and Doberman Pinschers. In the United States, the sport has followers, but there is still some skepticism of the sport stemming from the perceived risks of training pet dogs for bite work. U.S. sanctioning organizations are LV/DVG America and United Schutzhund Clubs of America.

Equipment

Equipment varies for each section. Schutzhund obedience requires the same dumbbells and hurdles used in regular obedience. The tracking discipline requires the use of scent articles. In protection training, a bite sleeve and stick or whip are required. In addition, trials utilize a start gun or other device to simulate gunfire.

Tracking

Tracking is essentially a competitive form of search and rescue. In fact, a number of dogs who participate in tracking trials are also real-life search and rescue dogs. Dogs gain titles for their ability to track trails by scent that have aged from half an hour to three to five hours. The trails are from 440 to 1,000 yards long. The dogs must also track over variable surfaces and through a mixture of urban and wilderness terrain. The AKC oversees national competitions, so participants must be pure-bred. There are also local clubs that conduct regional trials, although most also require a dog to be purebred to participate. Mixed breeds can participate in tracking through the American Mixed Breed Obedience Registration (AMBOR) and the Mixed Breed Dog Clubs of America (MBDCA).

Dogs may title in tracking as a Tracking Dog (TD) for following a trail that is half an hour to two hours old and 440 to 550 yards long over open field and consistent cover; a Tracking Dog Excellent (TDX) for following a trail that is three to five hours old and 800 to 1,000 yards long over variable cover and

---

Signs of heat exhaustion and heatstroke include panting excessively, fatigue, dizziness, nausea, and loss of consciousness. Cool a pet with heat exhaustion by pouring water on the coat and working it into the hair. Loss of consciousness is an emergency situation and requires immediate veterinary care.

terrain; and a Variable Surface Tracking (VST) for following a trail that is three to five hours old and 600 to 800 yards long over variable terrain, including at least two surfaces with no vegetation. The completion of the three titles earns a dog the title of Tracking Championship (TCH).

Equipment

The only equipment necessary are a long line, usually 30 feet, so the dog can range out in search of scent, and a scent article.

Dock Diving

It was only a matter of time before people went from enjoying watching their dogs jump off docks into the water to competing to see whose dog could jump the farthest or make the biggest splash. Dock diving or dock jumping competitions take place around the country and are even televised on Animal Planet and

Puppies and older dogs tire more easily than do adult dogs in their prime. Signs of exhaustion include heavy panting, a swollen tongue, or refusing to continue. Always be aware of your dog's condition, and stop for a break and a drink of water if he appears to be tired or hot.

ESPN. Any dog can play this fast-growing sport as long as he loves having fun in the water, but of course the masters at it are the retrievers.

Competition categories include Big Air, equivalent to the long jump in track and field events; Speed Retrieve, in which dogs race against the clock to bring back an object at the end of the pool; and Extreme Vertical, a high jump contest. In Big Air, elite jumpers can achieve distances of more than 23 feet. The current world record holder is a Greyhound mix named Country who jumped 28 feet, 10 inches.

In tracking, dogs learn to follow a scent trail over all types of terrain.

In dock diving events, spectators watch water-loving dogs catch "big air."

Competitions are governed by Dock Dogs, which establishes rules and tracks and records results. Dogs must be six months or older to compete, but there are no other restrictions on age or breed. Another organization, Splash Dogs, promotes dock diving events in the western United States.

Everyday Recreation

Some of the best activities a person and dog can do together are unorganized. There are many games you and your dog can participate in without leaving your neighborhood or buying anything other than the basic equipment available at any pet supply store. Fetch, tug-of-war, Frisbee, and chase (coupled with coming upon command) are wonderful ways to get both you and your dog's heart pumping in your own backyard. Outside of the home, you can both benefit from taking long walks (either leisurely or briskly), running, visiting a dog park, in-line skating, swimming, biking, and hiking. As with any strenuous activity, however, there a few safety precautions you should take.

Running

Even with stretching, running can lead to strained muscles and ligaments as well as footpad injuries and heatstroke. Keep your dog on leash to avoid traffic injuries, and don't overdo it. Asphalt can be hard on a dog's pads. If your dog isn't used to running on asphalt, he may incur foot pad injuries. Check foot pads sporadically during your run. Running on asphalt exposes your dog to melted chewing gum, tar, and other sticky substances as well as chemicals and road salt. Always check your dog's footpads after a run or walk.

Hiking

Hiking is a wonderful way to enjoy the outdoors with your dog. Start with short hikes of half a mile to a mile during puppyhood. Because of the rough or uneven terrain, hiking is harder on the body than walking, so gradually work up to longer distances. Depending on the breed, a puppy's skeletal development may not be complete until he's 18 to 24 months old. Heavy exercise before he's ready can lead to orthopedic problems such as hip dysplasia.

When you hit the trail, be sure you have plenty of water for yourself and your dog. There are lots of canine canteens and folding nylon water dishes that can make it easy for you to give your dog a drink when he's thirsty. A small supply of food is important, too, in case your return is delayed.

Many dogs are heat sensitive, so plan hikes for cool mornings or stick to trails with plenty of shade. A frozen bandana around his neck can also help keep him cool. Temperatures above 80 degrees are generally considered too hot for most dogs to engage in this type of strenuous exercise.

Biking

If you're a biking enthusiast and want to bike with your dog, take the same precautions as you would when running your dog. Use a chest

With the proper precautions and equipment, biking with your dog can be fun for both of you.

Starting a Dog Park

Looking to start a dog park? Here are some tips:

- **Strength in numbers:** Form a group with other dog owners. Establish the group as a non-profit corporation to demonstrate your commitment.

- **Get help:** Don't reinvent the wheel. Many other people have started a dog park in their city. Get in touch with other groups for guidance and support.

- **Get informed:** Contact city officials and the local parks department for guidance on starting a park.

- **Site selection:** Identify potential locations, preferably sites that are not heavily used and that have parking nearby. Your local parks department may be able to help you with this.

- **Education:** Work to educate dog owners and others in your area about the benefits of a dog park for both humans and dogs. Hold community meetings to discuss the park and answer questions. Emphasize benefits such as an increased feeling of community, more exercise opportunities, fewer unleashed dogs in other parks, and a positive financial impact for local businesses near dog parks. Dogs who are exercised regularly and socialized with people and other dogs are happier and often experience fewer behavioral problems.

- **Public relations:** Good public relations keep the community on your side. Organize events that demonstrate the group's commitment to responsible dog ownership. These can be behavior and training workshops, adoption fairs, low-cost vaccine clinics, or educational events encouraging spaying and neutering. Be a good neighbor now, and you may fend off opposition later.

- **Play politics:** Get to know your city councilperson and other local government officials. Find someone sympathetic to your cause in city government.

- **Plan:** A good plan considers the type of fencing and surfacing to be used, waste disposal, and how the park will be maintained. Include a budget and plans for fundraising. Determine whether the city will help with funds to build the park or if all funds will be acquired through private means.

- **Rules and regulations:** Create rules for users of the dog park, and have a plan to enforce them once the park is up and running. Organize a dog park advisory board to address issues as they arise. Find volunteers to monitor the park and advise visitors on the rules.

- **Stay involved:** Your work isn't over after the ground is broken. Demonstrate your commitment to the park by keeping up on rule enforcement, cleanup, and maintenance. Many cities initiate new dog parks with a trial period; use this time to prove your good intentions to the community. Meet regularly with city leaders on management of the park. Organize ongoing fundraising campaigns to keep the park running smoothly and to finance any new projects.

harness so that your dog is not using his neck to pull. A specially made bike attachment that can be mounted to the side of a bicycle is a must. It keeps the dog from becoming entangled with the bicycle. These are available online and through specialty dog supply stores. Never bicycle with your dog in traffic.

Swimming and Boating

Dogs love water, and there are many ways they can enjoy it with their people. There is swimming in a backyard pool, frolicking in the waves at the beach, the sport of dock diving, and going boating in vessels ranging in size from canoes to yachts. Here are a few tips on getting wet with your dog.

Swimming is one of a dog's favorite activities, but if a dog isn't prepared, it can be deadly. Although it seems as if dogs are born to paddle, they aren't born knowing how to swim. Let your dog explore the shallow end of the pool or wade at the edge of a creek, pond, or lake with a gentle slope. As he gains confidence, he can venture farther out. Encourage him by throwing a ball or water toy for him to fetch. He'll be swimming before he knows it.

If you have a pool, be sure your dog knows where the steps are and how to use them to get out. It's also a good idea to equip your pool (or boat) with a product such as a Skamper-Ramp. It's white and angles down into the water, so it's easy for the dog to see when he's looking for a way out.

Be familiar with water conditions. Dogs cannot always handle currents or rough water. Do not allow your dog to swim in fast-moving rivers or in heavy ocean currents. Water can be deceiving, so before allowing your dog to swim in an unknown body of water, consult locals about riptides and strong currents. A gentle-looking river can be

Not all dogs are born to swim, but some can't get enough of the water.

Venomous Animals

The effects of toxins from venomous snakes, toads, spiders, and scorpions can be mild to life-threatening. The toxicity of a venomous snake bite is determined by the size of the dog, the type of snake, the intensity and depth of the snake's bite, the amount of venom injected, the snake's age, and the bite's location. Dogs are more likely to be bitten by a rattlesnake than other snakes because we've encroached upon its habitat. Water moccasins and copperheads inflict pain, but their bites are not usually fatal. The bite of a coral snake, even a small one, can kill a small dog. Coral snakes rarely bite dogs, though. The reason for this may be that these snakes have relatively small heads and it is difficult for them to open their mouths wide enough to bite and poison a dog.

If your dog is bitten by a snake, make a note of its size and coloration. This will be helpful in identifying it so that the correct type of antivenin can be administered. Antivenin is expensive, as much as $1,500 for two vials. Severe bites can require as many as 10 vials, so prevention—in the form of keeping your dog on leash—is highly recommended.

A rattlesnake vaccine is available for dogs, but it's unclear how effective it is. Dogs can react to the vaccine, and the vaccine does not protect against the bite of every species of rattlesnake. Dogs who have received the vaccine still need immediate emergency treatment, but they may not need as much antivenin.

While most toads are not toxic, some toads, such as the giant toad (also called marine or cane toad) and the Colorado River toad are so venomous that if a dog ingests or even licks one, he could die unless he receives quick treatment.

Black widow venom is a toxin that affects the nervous system. One bite is enough to severely injure or even kill a small dog. The bite of a brown recluse, another venomous spider found in the United States, is not as severe as that of a black widow. This spider's venom damages tissue surrounding the bite, may cause fever and nausea, and often takes several weeks to heal even with veterinary treatment. The sting of most scorpions is not deadly, except to insects, their favorite food. However, their bite can cause extreme pain in humans.

Protect your dog from venomous animals by keeping him on a leash when in wilderness areas and never allowing him to harass wildlife or root in holes or under rocks. If you live in an area where venomous animals are common, survey your yard before letting your dog out unsupervised.

If your dog has been bitten by a snake or other venomous animal, or if you think he may have eaten a toad, do not attempt to treat him yourself. If treated with an antivenin, chances are your dog will survive, but time is of the essence. If possible, note the type of animal that your dog came in contact with and then get him to an emergency veterinarian immediately.

---

deadly. Wave-riding dogs face other hazards. They can injure their legs, especially the knees. The jarring force of the waves is hard on the ligaments. And don't let your dog drink sea water. It can make him sick and in large amounts can be deadly.

Beware of blue-green algae. Taking a dog to the lake is a time-honored tradition, but both of you should stay out of the water if it looks like pea soup, smells swampy, or has a sheen like a paint slick on the surface. Toxic blue-green algae can cause nausea, skin irritation, and even convulsions and death.

Whether your dog has been swimming in a backyard pool or open ocean, give him a thorough freshwater rinse when the day is done. Chlorine and salt can dry and irritate the skin. Towel dry him thoroughly, right down to the skin, and don't miss getting inside any skin folds. Trapped moisture can cause skin infections. Protect ears—especially droopy ones—from infection by cleaning them after every swim. Use a mild acidic solution from your veterinarian or a pet supply store.

Boating is a super way to spend time on the water with your dog. Before inviting Bailey on board, however, be sure your boat is appropriate for him. It should be large enough for your dog to move around, with sides high enough to keep him securely on board. For a dog the size of a Golden Retriever, for instance, appropriate boats range from a small, center-console outboard such as a Boston Whaler to midsize or larger sailboats or cabin cruisers. A well-behaved dog of that size can go for short outings in canoes, kayaks, or rowboats without capsizing them, but small sailboats such as Sunfish or Lasers, or personal watercraft such as JetSkis or Seadoos, are probably not the best choice.

To accustom your dog to boating, start with short trips in nice weather. This is a good way to accustom him to the sounds and vibrations that come with being on a boat. He may be hesitant at first about walking on a gangplank or jumping from the dock into the boat. Be encouraging, and whatever you do, don't drag or force him on board. There is no quicker way to ensure that he hates boating. If you have

Curly-coated water dogs, like this Irish Water Spaniel, are born boaters, relishing any activity on, near, or in the water.

Dog goggles don't just look cute, they actually have some benefits. They can protect a dog's eyes from dryness or flying debris on windy days or when the boat is traveling at high speeds. The best ones have shatterproof lenses that block 100 percent of UV light, wraparound frames, and adjustable elastic straps.

another boat-experienced dog who can show him the ropes, so much the better.

A canine personal flotation device (PFD) is a must for boating safety. At some point, your dog is going to fall off the boat. A PFD will help keep him afloat until you can haul him back on board. Choose one in bright red, yellow, or orange so it is easy to see. A well-made PFD should fit your dog snugly but comfortably, permitting unrestricted motion of his front legs. Adjustable chest and belly straps should provide firm support and have easy-release buckles. Look for one with a sturdy handle on top to make it easier to grab and lift the dog out of the water. PFDs made for dogs are not subject to certification by the U.S. Coast Guard, so inspect them thoroughly for high-quality stitching and other manufacturing details. A PFD should not be used as a replacement for your personal supervision.

Fair Warning

In almost any activity, organized or not, your dog is going to be exposed to things he's never encountered before. He is subject to any doggy diseases that other dogs may be carrying, including parvovirus, distemper, and kennel cough. Hiking and swimming in the wilderness can expose your dog to a number of pests, including ticks. Ticks are dangerous because they can carry Lyme disease and Rocky Mountain spotted fever. Make sure your dog's immunizations are up to date, you're giving your dog preventive tick medicine if necessary, and that you socialize your dog as a pup so he can be a happy participant as an adult.

CHAPTER 17

End of Life

When you first bring home that bouncy puppy, it's hard to imagine that only 10 or 12 years later you will have to say good-bye. Dogs are so full of life, the inevitable end is hard to imagine.

Your Senior Dog

Dogs approach old age at different times, depending on their size and breed. While a Great Dane is considered elderly at 7, a Miniature Poodle doesn't hit old age until about 10 or 11. Some dogs are still running agility courses at 13. The oldest dog recorded lived to be 29.

As your dog ages, you will notice that he begins to slow down. He may have a harder time getting up or jumping into your car or onto furniture. The fur on his muzzle and around his eyes will become gray or white, and his coat may start to lose some of its shine. Mentally, your dog may slow down a little as well. He may even have moments of confusion or forgetfulness. His personality may change, and he may become fearful or aggressive, or he may have more anxiety than he used to.

Providing a supportive bed to cushion his achy bones, a ramp to a piece of furniture or to help him into the car, and regular veterinary treatment will ameliorate his discomfort. Your veterinarian can help determine the best route to take in treating age-related confusion and physical ailments.

Your elderly dog may also require special food and may receive some pain relief from nutritional supplements such as glucosamine and essential fatty acids. A senior diet may

Gray on the muzzle is one of the first visible signs of a dog's aging.

Dog Years Versus Human Years

People commonly think that each year of a dog's life is equal to 7 human years. If this were true, it would mean that a 1-year-old dog, who is able to reproduce, is the equivalent of a 7-year-old child. It would also mean that a 15-year-old dog, which is not an unusual age for a dog, is the equivalent of a 105-year-old person, which is an unusual age for a person.

A more accurate comparison between human and dog years has been devised. A 3-month-old puppy is 5 years old in human years (equivalent to a young child). A 1-year-old dog is a teenager of 15, and a 2-year-old is 24. After that, aging slows, and 4 human years are added for every dog year. At 3 a dog is 28, at 5 he is 36, at 10 he is 56, and at 15, he is 76. Sources differ on the exact age equivalents in the later years, but a dog who reaches 20 is considered to be 91 to 96 in human years.

help sedentary dogs keep off the pounds, and diets prescribed by your veterinarian can help manage kidney disease and other ailments. After your dog reaches about the age of 7, your veterinarian will likely recommend twice-yearly physicals to check for any age-related conditions. Use these visits to discuss nutritional and exercise needs, as well as physical symptoms.

Just because your dog is elderly doesn't mean he no longer enjoys life. While he may not be up to a 5-mile run, he will cherish a

A peaceful death can be one of the greatest gifts we give our canine companions.

leisurely walk, a car ride, and even a visit to the dog park. You may find that your bond strengthens as your dog ages—now that he is not busy chasing every squirrel he sees, there is more time for cuddling on the couch. He may begin to look to you for more companionship than he did as a rough-and-tumble youngster. Your dog's senior years provide you an opportunity to return all the gifts your dog has given you over the years. Pamper him; he deserves it.

Saying Good-Bye

These days, because of medical and nutritional advances, dogs are healthier than ever. We are able to keep our geriatric dogs living well into their senior years. Because we have the means to cure or temper many of the ills of old age, our dogs can live long lives, and we are often put in the position of deciding when it's time for our beloved friends to go. Sometimes, because of illness or injury, even relatively young dogs may need to be put to sleep.

When to put your dog to sleep is a personal decision. Some feel that it is most humane to put their dog to sleep before he ever suffers; others let their dog die naturally. Most people feel that their dog lets them know when he is ready: he loses interest in activities that once delighted him, may refuse to eat or drink, and seems depressed or in discomfort or pain more often than not. Whatever you decide to do, your veterinarian should support your decision and provide you with the information you need.

Today there are more options than there were in the past when it comes to ending your dog's life. Instead of going to the veterinarian, many have now implemented home visits for euthanasia. If your veterinarian doesn't do this, she can probably put you in touch with a veterinarian who does. There are even mobile veterinarians who specialize in this end-of-life care. Allowing your dog to pass away in the safety and comfort of his own home is a great gift to him and may be a comfort to you. To ensure that this is a possibility, it's a good idea to ask your veterinarian about her policy far before you need this service. Euthanasia at home can be a continuation of a relatively new concept in end-of-life care for pets, hospice care. Hospice care provides you the opportunity to keep your terminally ill dog comfortable in your home until the very end. Talk to your veterinarian about hospice care options.

Nearly 60 percent of owners bury their pets on family property when they die; 25 percent have them cremated, according to the 2002 American Animal Hospital Association.

Your senior dog deserves your special attention. Slow-paced walks, massages, cuddles, and one-on-one time are especially appreciated now.

Euthanasia

Whether you decide to put your dog to sleep at home or in your veterinarian's office, there are a few basic procedures. If possible, make arrangements for payment and body transportation and final disposition before putting your dog to sleep. This is a traumatic event for you, and you shouldn't need to deal with the mundanities of finding your checkbook or deciphering bills at this time. A good veterinarian will be happy to bill you or have you pay beforehand. If done at a clinic, your vet should be willing to euthanize first thing in the morning or at the end of the day when there are fewer patients waiting, and you should be allowed to wait in an exam room rather than in the waiting room.

Your vet should give you the option of being in the room with your dog as he dies.

Although it is a personal decision, many people who opt not to be in the room later regret the decision. Most people find comfort in seeing that as their dog dies, he feels no pain and simply slips away.

If you opt to have your dog euthanized at home, you can allow him to choose a location to lie down or lay him in a location of your choice. If he loved to sleep on the sofa or bed, he may feel most comfortable here. His

The first public pet cemetery, called the Cimitière des Chiens, was established at Asnieres near Paris in 1899 and still exists today. Founded by feminist Marguerite Durand, the pet cemetery lies on a forested river islet. It offered a sliding scale burial fee to accommodate the pets of both the wealthy and the poor.

Many dogs retain their fun-loving personalities well into their senior years.

favorite snoozing spot under a shady tree can also be soothing to both of you. If you are indoors, place an old blanket under your dog. Do not be alarmed if your dog seems to perk up when the veterinarian arrives; this is very normal and it does not mean that he has recovered or that you are doing the wrong thing.

Before putting your dog to sleep, your vet will probably administer a sedative. Your dog will become sleepy and lie down. This is a good time to say your last good-byes—give a last kiss and head rub. Then your veterinarian will administer a lethal dose of sodium pentobarbital. Your dog will rapidly lose consciousness and soon after, his heart will stop. Let your veterinarian know if you would like to spend time with your dog following his passing. A good veterinarian will accommodate your wishes.

Grieving

Losing a pet can be as difficult as losing any other family member. There is nothing wrong with grieving for your dog. You have shared many years together, living through both good and bad times. Unfortunately, our society doesn't provide as much support for grieving the loss of an animal companion as it does for grieving the loss of a human friend or relative.

Let your friends and family know what you are going through. They may be more supportive than you expected. If you do not have someone to turn to, seek support from a therapist, clergyperson, or other professional.

Some people grieve the loss of their dog for a long time and choose never to bring another animal into their lives. Others feel ready to adopt a new companion within a couple of weeks. There is nothing wrong with either, it's simply a matter of what makes you most comfortable. Do not assume, though, that a new dog can replace the one you lost; dogs are individuals.

Memorializing Your Dog

Many people feel that it is important to memorialize their dog. It helps them deal with their grief and honors the dog who has been by their sides for such a significant time. Memorializing your dog can be done in a number ways. Some people hold memorials or wakes for a departed companion. Bringing together a group of friends who share a thought about your dog and provide a shoulder to cry on can bring solace. Others feel that grieving for their dog is personal and choose to honor him by scattering his ashes in a special place, placing his ashes in an urn with a special photo next to it, or burying his body or ashes on their property so that their dog can remain close. Planting a tree or bush on the site can be symbolic and comforting.

Consider making a donation in your dog's name to a companion animal–related charity. If your dog died of cancer or another common disease, you may wish to donate to scien-

Place extra bowls of water around the house if you have an elderly dog. He may not feel like walking to get water, but it is important that he stay hydrated.

Dogs are our beloved family members, so it's no wonder that we put so much thought into their welfare at all stages of life.

tific research in this area. Some people even memorialize their dog by getting a tattoo in the dog's image or of his name. Others clip a lock of hair or make a paw print before leaving the body. The way you grieve and memorialize your dog is intensely personal. Make your decision based on what you and your family feel will bring the most comfort, not on what society expects of you. As much pain as you feel, remember, it is only relative to the joy that your dog brought you.

Getting a New Dog

While many people find that adopting a new dog helps heal the loss of a pet, others feel reluctant, even guilty, about acquiring another dog. Do not rush into buying a new dog. Take at least several weeks to allow yourself to grieve for your cherished pet. Buying a new dog too quickly can lead to feelings of guilt or even resentment over the new dog not being as good as or like your old dog. Other pets or children in the household might find the quick introduction of a new pet into the household confusing and disturbing.

Adopting another dog is a very personal decision. If you decide to adopt a new pet within a few weeks, then that's what's right for you. Or you may find that you are not ready for many months or even years.

If your dog's death left another pet the only dog in the house, consider his needs before buying or adopting another dog. Some dogs do very well after the death of a companion; others suffer immensely. Take the time to make the best decision for your existing dog.

Breeds

Although all dogs are of one species, there are more than 400 different breeds. In the canine family, there is everything from the giant Great Dane to the tiny Yorkshire Terrier.

All of the breeds were bred for performing a specific task, whether hunting, herding, or being a companion. Some breeds were developed for very particular jobs, such as retrieving lines from fishing boats or to power turnspits. Although most of the dogs in our lives are pets, we continue to breed dogs for both the looks and personalities of their ancestors.

Before buying or adopting a dog, it's important to learn as much as you can about the breeds and to find the one that fits best into your life. Even breed mixes reflect their ancestry in both looks and personality.

CHAPTER 18

The Breeds

Most dog breeds are recognized by a national registry in their homelands. Some breeds have become popular around the world and are recognized by more than one registry. In the United States, the largest and oldest registry is the American Kennel Club (AKC). The United Kennel Club (UKC), also located in the United States, registers many breeds from around the world in addition to those that are popular in this country. In England, the national dog registry is called The Kennel Club. European breeds are recognized by the Federation Cynologique Internationale (FCI). Some registries specialize in a particular breed or types of breeds. They include the Australian Shepherd Club of America and the Cavalier King Charles Spaniel Club, USA. All of these organizations record pedigrees, sanction dog shows, and set rules for conformation showing, field trials, and other canine events.

The breed descriptions that follow are based on a variety of sources, including individual breed clubs; registries such as the AKC, the UKC, the FCI, and the American Rare Breed Association (ARBA); and a number of dog publications and periodicals. Each breed description includes information on the history, physical description, temperament, possible health problems, and best living situation for the breed. The physical description is based on breed standards devised by the AKC or other registries. Unless you hope to show your dog in conformation, a slight variation in coloring, ear carriage, eye color, or height or weight will not affect the years of affection your companion will provide. In addition, not all breed standards are alike;

standards devised by registries in different countries or by breed clubs with differing goals for a breed may be different.

In many breeds, conformation and working bloodlines of dogs have diverged over time, with separate breed clubs that may look for very different characteristics in a dog. Although some breed standards indicate that a dog should have cropped ears or a docked tail, these procedures are not legal in every country. In addition, many U.S. pet owners refrain from docking or cropping their dogs for humane reasons. Unless your dog is competing in conformation, this is a personal choice.

Not all breed descriptions include possible health problems. This does not mean that these breeds do not have health concerns; rather, the breed is too few in number or is too new to have been studied extensively. All dogs are subject to health problems. Some breed descriptions do not have weight or height standards. In this case, dogs are either bred for a use in which size is not considered imperative, or the dog's weight is expected to

Breed looks may change over time, depending on new laws and fads.

correspond with its height. Some breeds are known by more than one name. We used the name a dog is most commonly associated with in the United States, with alternative names under the common name. The index includes both the common and alternative names for those breeds. Here, the breeds are listed in alphabetical order.

Although we have categorized dogs as appropriate for city, suburban, or rural life, these aren't absolutes. Many dogs categorized as best for suburban or rural homes will also do very well in a residential city neighborhood, depending on whether there is a fenced yard and local parks for exercise.

The breed descriptions may include some terms that are unfamiliar to readers; please refer to the glossaries in the back of the book.

Affenpinscher

Alternative Names: Monkey Dog
Group: Companion, UKC; Toy, AKC
Country of Origin: Germany
History: The Affenpinscher was known in Europe as far back as the seventeenth century. Originally, it was used to control rodents in stables and businesses but was eventually bred down to serve as a companion and to keep mice out of the home. The Affenpinscher is similar in looks to the Brussels Griffon, which descended from the breed, as did the Miniature Schnauzer. The Affenpinscher is named for its monkeylike looks; *Affenpinscher* means "monkey terrier." The Affenpinscher is one of the oldest toy dogs. It is somewhat rare in the United States.
Physical Description: The Affenpinscher is a small, well-balanced, compact, and sturdy

---

The Affenpinscher is known to walk on its back legs and to sit on the base of its spine with tail tucked underneath and back legs extended forward.

Affenpinscher

dog. It is square in proportion and has a distinctive monkeylike expression. Its head is carried confidently, its chin is prominent, and the skull is round and domed. The ears may be natural, erect, semi-erect, drop, or cropped erect. The tail is naturally long and curves over the back or is docked and carried erect. The short coat is dense and rough, shaggier and less harsh on the neck, chest, stomach, and legs. It has longer hair on its head, its eyebrows, and beard. The coat may be black, silver, gray, black and tan, or red. There is sometimes white on its chest.
Height: 9 to 11.5 inches
Weight: 7 to 10 pounds
Temperament: This is an alert and inquisitive dog that is loyal and affectionate toward its family. Although it is usually quiet, it may react to provocation and is sometimes dog aggressive. It can be bold and courageous, stubborn and mischievous.
Activity Level: Moderate
Best Owner: This breed does best with a firm owner. It adapts well to city life.
Special Needs: Grooming, socialization, training
Possible Health Concerns: Eye problems, hip dysplasia, Legg-Perthes disease, luxating patellas, patent ductus arteriosus

Afghan Hound

Country of Origin: Afghanistan

Group: Sighthound, UKC; Hound, AKC

History: The history of the Afghan Hound is uncertain, although it is believed to have been used for hunting by tribal chiefs. It was developed to course prey with a hunter on horseback. Because these tribes were isolated, the breed was kept very pure and was unknown to outsiders until the nineteenth century. Some even believe that the Afghan Hound is the original sighthound. It was first brought to England by British officers in the early twentieth century and arrived in the United States by the 1920s.

Physical Description: The Afghan is a large, powerful, squarely built, and agile dog. It is elegant looking with a long, refined head and neck and long, tapered muzzle. It has a black nose; dark, triangular eyes; and long, pendant ears. It has very large feet, promi-nent pelvic bones, and a long, ringed or curved tail. The coat is long and silky except on the face and back, where the hair is short. The ears and feet are feathered, and there is a long, silky topknot on the head. It can be any color.

Height: 25 to 27 inches

Weight: 50 to 60 pounds

Temperament: The Afghan Hound is a strong-willed and dignified dog. It is aloof with strangers but playful and affectionate with family. Because of its independent nature, it can be difficult to train. If socialized, it does well with children but is never trustworthy with small animals, as it has a strong prey drive.

Activity Level: Moderate

Best Owner: The Afghan Hound requires a patient, active family in the suburbs or country.

Special Needs: Exercise, fenced yard, grooming, leashed, socialization

Possible Health Concerns: Eye problems, hip dysplasia

Afghan Hound

Ainu

Alternative Names: Hokkaido-ken, Hokkaido-inu, Hokkaido, Ainu-ken

Country of Origin: Japan

Group: Northern, UKC

History: The Ainu was bred by the indigenous people of Hokkaido, the Ainu, to hunt bears and deer. Most of the dogs are now kept simply as companions. The breed was designated a natural monument by the Japanese in 1937.

Physical Description: The Ainu is a strong, medium-size dog with a body that is slightly longer than it is tall. It has small, triangular, dark brown eyes; a black nose; and small, erect ears. There are often black spots on the tongue. The chest is wide and deep, and the tail is carried over the back. The double

Ainu

Airedale Terrier

coat is short and thick; it comes in red, white, black, gray, sesame, or brindle.

Height: 18 to 22 inches

Weight: 45 to 65 pounds

Temperament: The Ainu is a bold and powerful dog that can be headstrong. It is affectionate with its owner but wary with strangers. It is faithful and alert.

Activity Level: High

Best Owner: The Ainu requires an experienced, firm owner in the suburbs or country.

Special Needs: Exercise, fenced yard, socialization, training

Possible Health Concerns: None known

Airedale Terrier

Alternative Names: working, waterside, or Bingley terriers

Country of Origin: Great Britain

Group: Terrier, UKC/AKC

History: The largest of all the British terriers, the Airedale dates to the mid-1800s when the Otterhound was crossed with the now-extinct Black and Tan Terrier. It was used to hunt small game and later large game in Africa, India, and North America. The Airedale also was used for police and military work. It is sometimes called the king of terriers.

Physical Description: The Airedale is a large, square terrier with a long, flat skull that equals the muzzle in length. The eyes are dark and small with a distinctive terrier expression. The ears are V shaped and carried at the side of the head. The back is short and the chest is deep. The tail is carried high but not curled over the back. It is double-coated with a soft undercoat and a hard, dense, wiry outer coat that lies straight. Some hard hairs are slightly wavy or crinkled. The coat is tan and black, with the head and ears, lower part of legs, chest, and belly always tan. The sides and upper parts of the body are black or dark grizzle. There is sometimes red mixed with the black and a small, white blaze on the chest.

Height: 22 to 23 inches

Weight: 45 to 50 pounds

Temperament: The Airedale is an excellent

Airedale Terriers excel in police work and were one of the first breeds used on the beat in Great Britain and Germany.

guard, alert and protective but not aggressive. It is proud and courageous with a high prey drive. It is unreliable with small animals and should be supervised with young children because it is very exuberant.

Activity Level: High

Best Owner: An active family or individual in a rural or suburban home is best for this breed.

Special Needs: Exercise, grooming, socialization, training,

Possible Health Concerns: Hip dysplasia, hypothyroidism, skin diseases

Akbash Dog

Akbash Dog

Alternative Names: Akbas

Country of Origin: Turkey

Group: Guardian, UKC

History: This is an ancient breed that probably descends from both mastiffs and sighthounds. In Turkey, they were used to protect sheep from wolves and other large predators. They were first imported to the United States in the 1970s and continue to be used as livestock guardians in both countries.

Physical Description: The Akbash is a large, powerful, long-legged dog that is slightly longer than it is tall. It has a blunt, wedge-shaped head with dark eyes, nose, and lip pigment. The ears are pendant. The long tail is slightly curled when relaxed but curled over the back when alert. It has a double coat with a soft undercoat and a coarse, white outer coat that is medium or long in length.

Height: 27 to 32 inches

Weight: 75 to 140 pounds

Temperament: The Akbash Dog is an extremely loyal animal that is intelligent and independent. It can make a good pet if raised with humans and well socialized; however, working Akbash Dogs that have not been socialized are aggressive toward trespassers. The Akbash Dog is very protective of its family, flock, and property.

Activity Level: Low to moderate

Best Owner: To be kept as a pet, the Akbash Dog requires a very dog-experienced, firm, and consistent owner in a rural setting.

Special Needs: Fenced yard, leashed, socialization, training

Possible Health Concerns: Cardiomyopathy, entropion, hip dysplasia, hypothyroidism, seizures, umbilical hernias

Akita

Country of Origin: Japan

Group: Northern, UKC; Working, AKC

History: The Akita is the tallest of Japan's native breeds. It is believed to be about 300 years old and was developed as a fighting dog and hunter of large game, as well as a home guardian. In Japan, its image is often used to represent good health. Although the breed almost became extinct several times, Japan has placed an emphasis on maintaining the breed, and it is now one of seven breeds that Japan had designated as national monuments.

Physical Description: The Akita is a large, heavy, and well-balanced dog. Its body is

Akita

longer than it is tall, and the chest is deep. There is a triangular-shaped head with powerful, square jaws. The eyes are small, dark, and triangular, and the ears are small and naturally erect. The tail is long and full and carried over the back in a single or double curl. The double coat has a thick, soft undercoat and short, straight, harsh outer coat. It can be any color with a mask or blaze; white Akitas have no mask. Pintos have a white background with patches of color on the head and body.

Height: 24 to 28 inches

Weight: 70 to 130 pounds

Temperament: The Akita is a loyal and courageous companion that is affectionate and docile with its own family but alert and wary with strangers. It makes an excellent guard.

The Akita is held in high esteem in its native country of Japan. When a child is born, friends often send the family small statues of Akitas, representing good health, happiness, and a long life. During illness, Akita statues are sent as a wish for a quick recovery.

Although it is generally good-natured and quiet, it can be stubborn and requires socialization in order to get along with a range of people. This breed is often aggressive toward other dogs and can be territorial.

Activity Level: Moderate

Best Owner: The Akita requires an experienced, firm owner in a suburban or rural home.

Special Needs: Fenced yard, leashed, socialization, training

Possible Health Concerns: Autoimmune disorders, degenerative myelopathy, hip and elbow dysplasia, hypothyroidism, progressive retinal atrophy (PRA)

Alaskan Klee Kai

Alternative Names: AKK, Klee Kai

Country of Origin: United States

Group: Northern, UKC

History: The Alaskan Klee Kai was developed as a companion dog during the 1970s through crosses of Alaskan Husky, Siberian Husky, American Eskimo, and Schipperke

Physical Description: The Alaskan Klee Kai is a small dog that resembles a miniature Siberian Husky. It has a wedge-shaped head with a black or snow-colored nose and almond-shaped eyes of any color. The tail curls over the back. There is a double coat in gray and white or black and white; sometimes hints of red can be found. The markings are symmetrical, and there is a distinct mask.

Height (Toy): up to 13 inches

Height (Miniature): 13 to 15 inches

Height (Standard): 15 to 17 inches

Weight: Minimum 5 pounds

Temperament: The Alaskan Klee Kai is affectionate and loyal with its family but alert and wary with strangers. It is protective of its home and family, making an excellent watchdog. It requires socialization. This dog

Alaskan Klee Kai

Alaskan Malamute

may not get along with children, and it has a strong prey drive. It is often described as catlike in its fastidiousness.

Activity Level: High

Best Owner: The Alaskan Klee Kai requires an experienced, firm owner. It can adapt to apartment life if provided enough exercise.

Special Needs: Exercise, fenced yard, grooming, socialization, training

Possible Health Concerns: None known

Alaskan Malamute

Country of Origin: United States

Group: Northern, UKC; Working, AKC

History: The Alaskan Malamute is an Arctic sled dog breed developed by the Mahlemuts, an Inuit tribe in western Alaska. The Malamute was used to pull sleds and was bred to perform in inclement weather and to be capable of great endurance. It was a freighting dog rather than a sled racing dog. It is now usually kept as a companion.

Physical Description: The Malamute is a powerfully built, heavy-boned dog with a deep chest and well-muscled body. It has a broad, deep head with triangular, erect ears. The muzzle is broad and the almond-shaped eyes are brown. The nose is black, brown, or snow. The plumed tail is curled over the back. It is double coated with a thick, harsh outer coat that ranges in color from solid white to mixtures of gray, black, sable, and red, always with white markings and a facial mask.

Height: 23 to 25 inches

Weight: 75 to 85 pounds

Temperament: The Malamute is gentle, stoic, and playful, an excellent pet. Because it is intelligent and easily bored, training can be difficult. It can be stubborn. It gets along with almost everyone, including children and other dogs.

Activity Level: High

Best Owner: The Malamute requires an active owner in a suburban or country home, preferably in a cool climate.

Special Needs: Cool climate, exercise, grooming, training

Possible Health Concerns: Bloat (gastric torsion), chondrodysplasia, hip dysplasia, PRA, skin problems

Alpine Dachsbracke

Alternative Names: Alpenländische Dachsbracke

Country of Origin: Austria

Group: Scenthound, UKC

History: The Alpine Dachsbracke is believed to descend from an ancient hunting dog. It

Alpine Dachsbracke

was developed to track wounded game. It was a favorite of Austrian royalty in the late nineteenth century.

Physical Description: This is a muscular, short-legged dog that is longer than it is tall. It has a long, strong muzzle; black nose; brown eyes; and medium long, broad drop ears. It has a muscular neck and a long, thick tail. The double coat has a dense undercoat and thick, smooth outer coat. It is dark red with or without black ticking, or black with red markings on the chest, head, legs, feet, and underside of tail. There may be white markings on the chest.

Height: 12.5 to 17.5 inches

Weight: 27 to 48 pounds

Temperament: This is an intelligent and outgoing dog that is courageous and hardworking.

Activity Level: Moderate

Best Owner: It adapts to a country, suburban, or city home.

Special Needs: Exercise

Possible Health Concerns: None known

American Bulldog

Country of Origin: Great Britain

Group: Guardian, UKC

History: The Bulldog was originally a cattle drover and home and property guardian. Later, it was used for the blood sport of bull

The best known lines of American Bulldogs arising from breeding programs following World War II are the Johnson and Scott types. The Johnson dogs tend to be more aggressive and are larger and wider, with a broad head, short muzzle, and undershot jaw. The Scott dogs are more athletic and somewhat lighter and leggier.

baiting. In Great Britain, the bulldog dogs evolved into the modern companion Bulldog when bull baiting was made illegal. However, imports of the prototype Bulldog continued to be bred true in the United States. These dogs were used for a variety of work on farms and ranches but came close to extinction by World War II. A returning veteran worked to revive the breed, which is now called the American Bulldog. The breed continues to be used as a working dog as well as a companion.

Physical Description: The American Bulldog is large, powerful, and well boned. The head is large and broad with a wide muzzle, powerful jaws, and strong chin. The large nose can be of any color, and the ears are small to medium in size and can be drop, semi-erect, tulip, or cropped erect. It has large, round eyes; a muscular neck, and a tail that can be docked or left long. The short, smooth coat comes in any color, pattern, or combination of colors, such as red brindle, all other brindles, white, red, or fawn. The only colors not permitted are solid black, solid blue, and tricolor.

Height: 20 to 27 inches

Weight: 60 to 125 pounds

Temperament: The American Bulldog is an assertive dog that is gentle and loving with its family but aggressive toward intruders and fearless with bulls. It is intelligent, sensitive, and generally quite calm.

Activity Level: High

Best Owner: The American Bulldog requires a dog-experienced owner with time for

American Bulldog

American Eskimo Dog

training and socialization. This breed can be good with older children, if well socialized, but generally should be housed with only one dog of the opposite sex.

Special Needs: Attention, fenced yard, leashed, socialization, training

Possible Health Concerns: Eye problems, hip dysplasia, parvovirus, skin allergies

American Eskimo Dog

Alternative Names: Eskie, American Spitz

Country of Origin: Germany

Group: Northern, UKC; Non-Sporting, AKC

History: The American Eskimo Dog is descended from white spitz dogs that came to this country with German immigrants. It is probably also related to the Volpino Italiano and the Japanese Spitz. In addition to serving as a companion, it has been used as a watchdog as well as a circus performer.

Physical Description: The American Eskimo Dog is square with a strong, compact body. Its head is wedge shaped with erect, triangular ears. Its thick double coat is pure white or white with biscuit cream. It has a pronounced ruff around the neck, a plumed tail carried over the back, and longer hair on the rump and hind legs. It comes in three sizes: toy, miniature, and standard.

Height (Toy): 9 to 12 inches

Weight (Toy): no standard available

Height (Miniature): 11 to 15 inches

Weight (Miniature): no standard available

Height (Standard): 14 to 19 inches

Weight (Standard): no standard available

Temperament: The American Eskimo Dog is alert, energetic, and intelligent. It is loyal, outgoing, and eager to please with its friends and family but wary with strangers. This breed makes an excellent watchdog. It is clever and can be mischievous but gets along with both children and other animals.

Activity Level: Moderate

Best Owner: This breed is adaptable and can do well in an apartment as long as it receives ample exercise.

Despite its name and appearance, the American Eskimo dog is not from Alaska or a descendant of the husky. The American Eskimo is a member of the spitz family, which originated in Germany. It is often called The Dog Beautiful for its striking looks.

Special Needs: Attention, grooming, socialization, training

Possible Health Concerns: Elbow and knee degeneration, hip dysplasia, PRA, seizures

American Foxhound

Country of Origin: United States

Group: Scenthound, UKC; Hound, AKC

History: The American Foxhound was developed in Virginia and Maryland from foxhounds imported to the United States from Europe in the eighteenth century. It was bred to hunt fox singly and in packs and later to participate in field events and drag hunts.

Physical Description: This is a medium-size to large muscular dog. It has a long, broad head; medium-length drop ears; and large, brown eyes. The muzzle is straight and square. It has a long back, straight legs, and a long tail that is set high and curved. The close, coarse coat is of any color.

American Foxhound

Height: 21 to 25 inches

Weight: no standard available

Temperament: This is an energetic but easygoing and friendly dog that gets along with almost everyone, including children and dogs. It can be stubborn and independent, so training takes patience.

Activity Level: High

Best Owner: This breed does best with an activity family in a rural or suburban home.

Special Needs: Exercise, fenced yard, leashed

Possible Health Concerns: Ear problems, hip dysplasia

American Pit Bull Terrier

Alternative Names: pit bull, APBT

Country of Origin: United States

Group: Terrier, UKC

History: In the nineteenth century, the English began crossing Bulldogs and terriers. Immigrants brought the result of these crosses to the United States. The APBT was developed in the United States as a guard, cattle catcher, livestock driver, and companion. Its most notorious use, however, was pit fighting, the now-illegal practice for which it was named.

Physical Description: The APBT is a medium-size, solid, and muscular dog that is slightly longer than it is tall. The large, broad, powerful head is shaped like a wedge, and the muzzle is broad and deep, shorter than the length of skull. The lower jaw is well developed, and the nose is large and of any color. The eyes are medium in size and set low, any color except blue. The ears are cropped erect or naturally rose or semi-erect. The chest is deep and hindquarters are muscu-

American Pit Bull Terrier

lar. The tail is medium length. Its coat is short and smooth, of any color.

Height: 18 to 22 inches

Weight: 35 to 60 pounds

Temperament: The APBT is strong, confident, stoic, and fun loving. Its fans say it has a zest for life. It is very friendly toward people, especially children. However, its fighting background often makes it aggressive with other dogs, especially dogs of the same sex.

Activity Level: High

Best Owner: A dog-experienced individual or family is the best home for an APBT. Kids are fine, but other dogs should be of the opposite sex. It adapts to the city or the country.

Special Needs: Exercise, firm but positive training, job or activity, socialization

Possible Health Concerns: Allergies, cataracts, hip dysplasia

American Staffordshire Terrier

Alternative Names: Am Staff

Country of Origin: United States

Group: Terrier, UKC/AKC

History: Although it descends from the same line as the APBT, the American Staffordshire has been bred independently of the APBT for at least 60 years, when the AKC changed the breed name. A result of English crossing of Bulldogs and terriers, descendants of the breed were brought to the United States in the late 1800s and used as general-purpose farm dogs.

Physical Description: It is very much like the APBT: medium-size, compact, stocky, and muscular, with a broad skull, medium-length muzzle, and strong jaw. The eyes are dark and round, and the ears are cropped erect or naturally rose or semi-erect. Natural ears are preferred. The American Staffordshire Terrier has a broad, deep chest and muscular hindquarters. The natu-

American Staffordshire Terrier

rally short tail tapers to a point. The coat is short and stiff and of any color but all white.

Height: 17 to 19 inches.

Weight: 40 to 79 pounds.

Temperament: The American Staffordshire Terrier is gentle and friendly but also stoic and courageous. It is very friendly toward people, especially children, but often aggressive toward dogs, especially those of the same sex. Many Am Staffs will get along only with dogs of the opposite sex.

Activity Level: High

Best Owner: The best owner is an active, experienced family or individual either in the city or the country.

Special Needs: Exercise, fenced yard, leashed, socialization, training

Possible Health Concerns: Allergies, cancer, heart problems, hip dysplasia, thyroid problems

American Water Spaniel

Country of Origin: United States

Group: Gun Dog, UKC; Sporting, AKC

History: The American Water Spaniel was developed to hunt waterfowl and small game in the Wolf and Fox River Valley regions of Wisconsin in the late nineteenth century. Some believe this breed to be a descendant of crosses with the now-extinct English Water Spaniel, the Irish Water Spaniel, and the Curly-Coated Retriever. American Water Spaniels were bred to be small enough to fit into a small boat but sturdy enough to work in cold water. Although the American Water Spaniel is the state dog of Wisconsin, it is quite rare.

Physical Description: This is a small to medium-size compact dog with drop ears, a pronounced brow, and eyes that range in color from yellowish brown to dark brown. The plumed tail is long and slightly curved

American Water Spaniel

and acts as a rudder when the dog swims. The tightly curled, dense, weather-resistant coat is liver to brown colored and moderate in length. There may be white markings on the toes or chest.

Height: 15 to 18 inches

Weight: 25 to 45 pounds

Temperament: The American Water Spaniel is a busy, friendly dog. It is an excellent hunter and companion. Its intelligence and eagerness make it highly trainable, and it loves water. It is generally fine with children but may be food possessive.

Activity Level: High

Best Owner: Having a job is ideal. This breed does well in a rural or suburban home with an active, dog-experienced family with time for training and exercise.

Special Needs: Firm, positive training; grooming; job or activity

Possible Health Concerns: Alopecia, blindness, deafness, epilepsy, heart problems, hip dysplasia, luxating patellas, poor temperament, spinal or neck problems, thyroid problems

---

The American Water Spaniel was the first breed developed in the United States to be an all-around hunter that could retrieve from boats.

Anatolian Shepherd Dog

Alternative Names: Coban Köpeg (shepherd's dog)

Country of Origin: Turkey/Asia Minor

Group: Guardian, UKC; Working, AKC

History: The Anatolian is an ancient breed that is descended from mastiffs and sighthounds. It was developed to guard livestock against large predators, and it continues to be used as a livestock guardian as well as a companion.

Physical Description: This is a very large, powerful dog with a large head; broad muzzle; dark nose; and almond-shaped, brown eyes. The drop ears are of medium size. The chest is deep, and the long tail may curve at the end. The Anatolian is double coated with a short or rough coat, ranging from 1 to 4 inches in length. There is a thick undercoat. All colors are acceptable. Some have a dark mask.

Height: 27 to 29 inches minimum

Weight: 80 to 150 pounds

Temperament: This is a highly protective and territorial dog, reserved with strangers but affectionate with friends and family. It is intelligent, independent, and watchful, calm but alert.

Activity Level: Moderate

Anatolian Shepherd Dog

Best Owner: The Anatolian requires a dog-experienced owner who is consistent and firm, with the time for proper socialization and training. This breed can be good with children but should be supervised because of its large size.

Special Needs: Fenced yard, leashed, socialization, training

Possible Health Concerns: Hip dysplasia, sensitive to anesthesia

Appenzeller

Alternative Names: Appenzeller Sennenhund, Appenzell Mountain Dog

Country of Origin: Switzerland

Group: Guardian, UKC

History: The Appenzeller is one of four Swiss dogs believed to be descendants of local dogs crossed with the mastiff breeds brought to Switzerland by the Romans. It was used as a cattle drover and a home, property, and livestock guard. The Swiss have worked to preserve the breed since the late nineteenth century.

Physical Description: The Appenzeller is a large, powerful, square-built dog with a broad head; strong muzzle; small, brown eyes; a black nose; and small to medium-size drop ears. The tail is carried over the back. The short, smooth coat is tricolor with black or brown as the base and tan and white markings.

Height: 19 to 23 inches

Weight: 48 to 55 pounds

Temperament: This is a confident dog that is affectionate and playful with family but wary with strangers. It is cheerful and trainable.

Activity Level: High

Best Owner: It does best with an active individual or family in a rural or suburban home.

Special Needs: Exercise, job or organized activity, positive training, socialization

Appenzeller

Possible Health Concerns: Ectropion, entropion hip dysplasia

Ariégeois

Country of Origin: France

Group: Scenthound, UKC

History: The Ariégeois was developed to hunt rabbit, hare, and fox in the French region of Ariège. It was created from crosses of local hounds, Grand Bleu de Gascogne, and Grand Gascon-Saintongeois.

Physical Description: This is a medium-size, muscular dog with a wide, deep chest. It has a long, narrow head; a black nose; and brown eyes. The long drop ears are of fine leather. It has a long neck and hare feet. The long tail is tapered. The short, fine coat is white with black patches. The skin corresponds to the hair color.

Height: 20 to 24 inches

Weight: 66 pounds

Temperament: This is an even-tempered, hardworking dog. It is generally friendly and gets along well with most people and other dogs.

Activity Level: Moderate

Ariégeois

Best Owner: The Ariégeois does best with an active owner in a rural or suburban home.

Special Needs: Exercise

Possible Health Concerns: None known

Australian Cattle Dog

Alternative Names: Blue Heeler, Heeler, Queensland Heeler, Red Heeler

Country of Origin: Australia

Group: Herding, UKC/AKC

History: The Australian Cattle Dog was developed by Australian cattle ranchers who needed a cattle drover with the endurance to go long distances. The Cattle Dog's

The French highly regard the Ariégeois for its endurance, especially in comparison with other hounds of its size. The Ariégeois, introduced in 1912, is rarely seen outside of its native France.

Australian Cattle Dog

immediate ancestor was the Hall's Heeler, a dog developed from a cross of the dingo and the smooth-coated Scottish Collie. In about 1860, the Hall's Heeler was mixed with the Australian Kelpie and the Dalmatian to create the modern Australian Cattle Dog.

Physical Description: The Australian Cattle Dog is a medium-size, sturdy, and muscular dog that is longer than it is tall. It has a strong, broad head and a medium-length, tapering muzzle. The almond-shaped eyes are brown, and the large nose is black. The medium-size ears are naturally erect. This dog has a muscular neck, deep chest, and muscular hindquarters. The brush tail is long. The double coat has a dense undercoat and a smooth, hard outer coat. It is of medium length, longer at the thighs and the neck. It may be blue, mottled or speckled, with or without black, blue, or tan markings; or red speckled, with or without darker red markings.

Height: 17 to 20 inches

Weight: 33 to 55 pounds

Temperament: This is a loyal and protective dog that is wary with strangers but easygoing with those it is familiar with. It tends to be a one-person dog. The Cattle Dog is alert and watchful, with high drive, energy, and intelligence.

Activity Level: High

Best Owner: It does best with an active owner in a rural or suburban home.

Special Needs: Exercise, job or activity, socialization, training

Possible Health Concerns: Deafness, hip dysplasia, PRA

Australian Kelpie

Alternative Names: Kelpie, Barb

Country of Origin: Australia

Group: Herding, UKC

History: The Australian Kelpie originated around 1870 and is descended from British and Scottish Collies. Some believe dingoes and various breeds also played a role in its ancestry. It was bred to herd sheep; Australians say that the country was built on the back of the Kelpie because of the large role the breed played in the development of the sheep and wool industry. Most Australian Kelpies are still used as working dogs in Australia, Europe, and North America. However, they are becoming increasingly popular as companions, as well.

Physical Description: This is a muscular but agile, medium-size dog. It is longer than it is high with a rounded skull and tapered muzzle, which is equal in length or slightly

According to the *Guinness World Records 2004,* an Australian Cattle Dog named Bluey holds the record as the world's longest-lived dog. He herded cattle and sheep in Australia for almost 20 years before retiring. Bluey was 29 years and 5 months when he died in 1939.

shorter than the skull. It has gold to brown, almond-shaped eyes and large, widely spaced prick ears. There is a strong neck and deep chest. The long brush tail is slightly curved when at rest and raised when active. The double coat has a dense undercoat and a short, straight, weather-resistant outer coat. There is a ruff at the neck. It may be black, blue, or red, with or without tan markings, or all tan. There may be white on the chest and toes.

Height: 17 to 20 inches

Weight: 26 to 45 pounds

Temperament: This is a highly intelligent dog that makes distinct differentiation between work and rest. Active and intense at work, it is mild and easygoing at home. The Kelpie is friendly but rarely affectionate and tends to be a one-person dog that is devoted to its person.

Activity Level: High

Best Owner: The Australian Kelpie does best with an active owner and the opportunity to participate in a job or activity. A rural environment suits it best, but it is adaptable. It gets along well with other dogs.

Australian Kelpie

Special Needs: Exercise, job or activity, positive training

Possible Health Concerns: PRA

Australian Shepherd

Alternative Name: Aussie

Country of Origin: United States

Group: Herding, UKC/AKC

History: Although the Australian Shepherd is believed to have originated in the Basque regions of Spain and France, the breed was developed by U.S. farmers and ranchers in the early 1920s. The Aussie was used as a herding dog, all-purpose farm dog, and performance dog, especially in the American West. Aussies continue to serve as herding dogs and companions in the United States. This breed has two registries; one is affiliated with the AKC, while the other is devoted to the working Aussie.

Physical Description: The Australian Shepherd is a medium-size, athletic dog that is longer than it is tall. It has a strong head with a slightly rounded skull. The muzzle is equal in length or slightly shorter than the back skull. The almond-shaped eyes can be brown, blue, amber, or any combination, including flecks or marbling. Triangular drop ears are set high on the head; they

Australian Shepherd

break forward when the dog is at attention. The straight tail is naturally bobbed or docked and shouldn't exceed 4 inches. The medium-length double coat may be straight or slightly wavy. It is feathered at the backs of the legs, thighs, and neck. The coat can be blue merle, red merle, black, or red, with or without white markings and tan points.

Height: 18 to 23 inches

Weight: 35 to 75 pounds

Temperament: The Aussie is an intelligent dog with a strong work drive. It is highly trainable and loyal to its family. The Aussie makes a good watchdog because it is wary with strangers but never aggressive. Playful and fun loving, the Aussie is good with children and other dogs, although it may try to herd them. It has a strong prey drive and is not trustworthy with small animals.

Activity Level: High

Best Owner: The Aussie requires an active family in a suburban or rural home.

Special Needs: Exercise, job or activity

Possible Health Concerns: Collie eye anomaly, deafness, hip dysplasia, PRA

Australian Terrier

Country of Origin: Australia

Group: Terrier, UKC/AKC

History: One of the smallest working terriers, the Australian Terrier shares a common ancestry with Silky Terriers, being a mix of rough-coated terriers and other British terriers. It was the first Australian breed to be recognized and shown in Australia. It was originally bred to help control rodents and snakes, to serve as a watchdog, and to be a companion.

Australian Terriers are natural-born diggers and stop at nothing to catch snakes, rodents, and other creatures. Avid gardeners considering this breed should prepare to make the garden inaccessible to dogs.

Physical Description: This small, sturdy terrier is longer than it is tall. The skull is long and flat and the powerful muzzle is equal in length to the skull. It has a medium-size black nose and small dark brown or black eyes. The ears are small, erect, and pointed. The tail is docked to half its length and carried high but not over the back. It is double coated with a long, harsh, blue-and-tan or sandy-and-red outer coat. The hair is shorter on the ears, with a topknot. There is a ruff on the neck, and the legs are feathered.

Height: 10 to 11 inches

Weight: 14 pounds

Temperament: The Australian Terrier is a spirited, alert, and courageous dog. It is self-confident, and although it is friendly and affectionate with its family, it is wary with strangers. It is fine with children and other animals as long as it is well socialized.

Activity Level: High

Best Owner: This breed does well with an active family or individual in the city, suburbs, or country.

Special Needs: Exercise, grooming, socialization, training,

Australian Terriers

Possible Health Concerns: Cancer, diabetes mellitus, eye and ear problems, luxating patellas, skin allergies

Azawakh

Alternative Names: idii 'n illeli (sighthound of the free people), Tuareg sighthound

Country of Origin: Mali, Niger, Burkina Faso

Group: Sighthound, UKC

History: The Azawakh is from the arid regions of the Sahara and the Sub-Saharan Sahel. It is used as a guardian, hunter, and companion by the Tuareg people, who are descendants of the Berber. The tribe bred the dog for purity and beauty. The breed has become rare in both its homeland and elsewhere.

Physical Description: The Azawakh is a tall, slender dog that is taller than it is long, with hips that are higher than the shoulders. It has a narrow head with pendant ears and dark, almond-shaped eyes. It has a very deep chest, which rises abruptly to an extremely tucked up belly. The coat is short

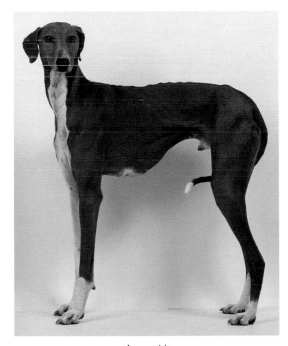

Azawakh

and fine and can be of sand to dark red, brindled, white, black, gray, blue grizzle, particolored, and all shades of brown, including chocolate.

Height: 23.5 to 29 inches

Weight: 35 to 55 pounds

Temperament: The Azawakh is gentle, affectionate, and playful with its family but wary, even aggressive, with strangers. It is intelligent and protective, making it a good watchdog.

Activity Level: Moderate

Best Owner: It does best with a firm owner in a rural or suburban home. It makes a poor kennel dog.

Special Needs: Close supervision with strangers, leashed, fenced yard, socialization, training

Possible Health Concerns: Bloat, cardiac problems, hip dysplasia, hypothyroidism, seizures, spondylosis

Barbet

Alternative Names: French Water Dog, Griffon d'Arrêt à Poil Laineux, Barbette (female)

Country of Origin: France

Group: Gun Dog, UKC

History: The Barbet is found in the ancestry of many popular breeds, including the Poodle, the Newfoundland, and the griffons. This is an old breed; its progenitors date to the fourteenth century. Barbets have served a variety of roles, from hunters to flock drovers to sailor's dogs, used to fetch lost items and lines at sea. Until the French Revolution, they were popular hunting companions for aristocracy. The breed is named for its beard. They are very rare in the United States.

Physical Description: The Barbet is a medium-size dog with a thick, woolly coat that covers the entire body. The head has especially long hair that covers the eyes and nose, with

Barbet

a mustache and a long beard. It has a square muzzle; dark brown eyes; a black or brown nose; and long, broad drop ears. The tail is long with a slight hook at the end. The coat may be black, gray, chestnut, tawny, sand, or white.

Height: 19.5 to 23.5 inches

Weight: 35 to 45 pounds

Temperament: This is a social, fun-loving dog with a passion for water. It is friendly toward almost everyone, including children and other animals. The Barbet is highly trainable.

Activity Level: Moderate

Best Owner: The Barbet is an adaptable dog that does well in a rural or city home, provided it receives regular exercise and attention. It does very well with a family.

Special Needs: Exercise, grooming

Possible Health Concerns: None known

Basenji

Alternative Names: Congo Dog, African Barkless Dog

Country of Origin: Zaire

Group: Pariah, UKC; Hound, AKC

History: The Basenji is a descendant of the earliest pariah dogs and was used as a hunting dog as long ago as 3600 B.C.E. Legend has it that early Basenjis were brought from Central Africa to Egyptian pharaohs as gifts. When the Egyptian civilization declined, the breed became rare, although it was maintained in a pure state in its native country of Zaire. The Basenji was first encountered by westerners in the early 1900s, and several were brought to England in 1936, where they were used as hunting dogs, pointing, retrieving, and bolting prey.

Physical Description: The Basenji is a medium-size, lightly built but muscular dog that is shorter than it is tall. It has a flat, wrinkled head and a muzzle that is shorter than the skull. The dark hazel to dark brown eyes are almond shaped and the nose is black. It has small, erect ears and an arched neck. The tail is high and curled and the feet are small and compact. The coat is short and

Basenji

fine, chestnut red, black, tricolor, or brindle. The feet, chest, and tail tip are white.

Height: 16 to 17 inches

Weight: 22 to 24 pounds

Temperament: The Basenji is an intelligent, alert, and independent dog. It is affectionate with its family but protective and wary with strangers. It is alert and curious with fastidious, catlike qualities. It yodels rather than barks.

Activity Level: High

Best Owner: The Basenji requires a dog-experienced family in a city, suburban, or country home

Special Needs: Activity or job, positive training, fenced yard

Possible Health Concerns: Anemia, hernias, hip dysplasia, PRA and other eye problems, renal problems, thyroid problems

Basset Artésien Normand

Alternative Names: BAN

Country of Origin: France

Group: Scenthound, UKC

History: The Basset Artésien Normand was created by French breeders in the late nineteenth century from a mix of bassets from Normandy and Artois. It was developed as a small game hound.

Physical Description: This is a small to medium-size sturdy but elegant dog that is markedly longer than it is tall. It has a narrow, domed skull and wide muzzle of medium length. The nose is broad and black, and the eyes are large and dark. The ears are set low, very long, and of fine leather; they are folded or corkscrewed. There is a long neck and large turned-out feet. The long tail is tapered. The short weather-resistant coat is typical hound tricolor or white with orange patches. The coat on the back may be grizzled.

Height: 10 to 14 inches

Weight: 33 pounds

Temperament: This is a good-natured, outgoing dog that makes a loving companion. It does well with families. It's very adaptable but will roam.

Activity Level: Moderate

Best Owner: This breed does well in a city, suburban, or rural home.

Basset Artésien Normand

Special Needs: Fenced yard, leashed

Possible Health Concerns: Disc disease

Basset Bleu de Gascogne

Country of Origin: France

Group: Scenthound, UKC

History: The Basset Bleu de Gascogne is descended from ancient scenthounds. It was developed from the Grand Bleu de Gascogne and the Basset Saintongeois in the late nineteenth century.

Physical Description: This is a medium-size, strong, sturdy dog that is longer than it is tall. It has a narrow, wedge-shaped head with a domed skull and long muzzle. The nose is large and black, and the eyes are dark brown with loose lower lids. It has very long, low-set ears that are of fine leather and fold, or curl, alongside the face. It has a deep chest, strong legs, and a long tail. The feet are large. The short coat is white with black ticking, giving a blue effect, and black patches.

Height: 12 to 15 inches

Weight: no standard available

Temperament: The Basset Bleu is an easy-going, friendly dog. It gets along with almost everyone, including other dogs.

Activity Level: Moderate

Best Owner: This breed does well with an active owner in a rural or suburban home.

Special Needs: Fenced yard, leashed

Possible Health Concerns: None known

Basset Fauve de Bretagne

Alternative Names: Fawn Brittany Basset

Country of Origin: France

Group: Scenthound, UKC

History: This dog was developed from the Griffon Fauve de Bretagne and was popular in the region of Brittany during the nineteenth century. In France during the late twentieth century, it gained national recognition as an excellent rabbit hunter.

Basset Bleu de Gascogne

Basset Fauve de Bretagne

Physical Description: The Basset Fauve de Bretagne is a medium-size, sturdy dog that is longer than it is tall. It has a long skull and rectangular, tapering muzzle. The large nose is dark brown or black, and the eyes are dark brown. It has very long ears, a short neck, and a long, sickle-shaped tail. The coat is medium-length and rough and fawn, from golden wheaten to rich red brown in color. There may be a small, white spot on the chest.

Height: 12.5 to 15 inches

Weight: no standard available

Temperament: This is a lively, fun-loving, and brave dog. It is both an excellent worker and companion. It gets along with almost everyone, including children, but can be stubborn.

Activity Level: Moderate

Best Owner: This breed does best with an active family in a rural or suburban home.

Special Needs: Fenced yard, leashed

Possible Health Concerns: None known

Basset Hound

Country of Origin: France

Group: Scenthound, UKC; Hound, AKC

History: The Basset Hound was developed in sixteenth-century France from a dwarf version of the Saint Hubert hound. It was developed to hunt small game with the hunter on foot. The breed was mostly kept by nobility but rose in popularity among commoners after the French Revolution. It continues to be used for hunting as well as as a companion. It is an especially popular companion in the United States.

Physical Description: This is a medium-size, short-legged, and heavy-boned dog. It has a large, wide head that is covered with loose, wrinkled skin. The very long, broad ears are

Basset Hound

set low, and the dark eyes have drooping lower eyelids. It has a deep muzzle and a dark nose with large nostrils. The coat is short and smooth in any hound color.

Height: 14 inches

Weight: 50 to 65 pounds

Temperament: The Basset is a friendly, mild, and easygoing dog. It gets along with almost everyone, including other dogs. This breed has a strong hunting instinct and will roam. It is vocal.

Activity Level: Low to moderate

Best Owner: It does well with an individual or family and is adaptable to different living situations, from city to country.

Special Needs: Eye and ear cleaning

Possible Health Concerns: Bloat, hip and elbow dysplasia, glaucoma, thrombopathia, thyroid problems, von Willebrand's disease

---

The Basset Hound has an extremely accurate nose; only the Bloodhound exceeds the breed in tracking ability.

Bavarian Mountain Dog

Alternative Names: Bayrischer Gebirgs-schweisshund

Country of Origin: Germany

Group: Scenthound, UKC

History: The Bavarian Mountain Dog is descended from the Bloodhound-like Hanoverian Schweisshunds and Bavarian Scenthounds and was developed in the late nineteenth century. It is the most popular and common scenthound kept in the Bavarian mountain region.

Physical Description: This is a medium-size, muscular, lightly built dog that is longer than it is tall. The skull and muzzle are broad. There is a black or dark red nose, brown eyes, and medium-length drop ears. The tail is medium length and set high. The thick, short coat is slightly longer and harsh on the belly, legs, and tail and finer on the ears and head. The coat is red, tan, fawn, or reddish gray, grizzled or brindled. There may be a lighter mark on the chest. The coat is darkest at the ears and muzzle.

Height: 21 inches

Weight: 53 to 80 pounds

Temperament: This is an easygoing, trainable dog, affectionate with its family but wary with strangers. It is generally calm and not shy.

Activity Level: High

Best Owner: This breed does well with an active family in either a suburban or a rural environment.

Special Needs: Exercise

Possible Health Concerns: None known

Beagle

Country of Origin: Great Britain

Group: Scenthound, UKC; Hound, AKC

History: Beagle-type dogs have existed for centuries, but the breed as we know it today was developed in Great Britain about 150 years ago. It has been one of the most popular breeds in North America for more than a quarter century.

Physical Description: This is a small, lean dog that is slightly longer than it is tall. It has a long skull and square muzzle. It has large, brown or hazel eyes and a black nose. The drop ears are long and broad, and the tail is set high. The short, hard coat is of any hound color.

Height: 10 to 15 inches

Weight: 20 to 30 pounds

Temperament: This is a good-natured but independent-minded dog. It is outgoing and friendly and gets along well with children and other animals as long as it is socialized. It will pursue scent.

Activity Level: Moderate

Best Owner: This breed does well with an active family and is adaptable to most living situations, country or city.

Special Needs: Fenced yard, leashed, socialization, training

Bavarian Mountain Dog

Beagle

Possible Health Concerns: Cleft palate, demodectic mange, dwarfism, epilepsy, eye problems, hip dysplasia, hypothyroidism, intervertebral disc disease, luxating patellas, reproductive disorders

Bearded Collie

Alternative Names: Beardie, Hairy Mou'ed Collie, Highland Collie, Loch Collie, Mountain Scotch Collie, Old Welsh Grey Sheepdog

Country of Origin: Scotland

Group: Herding, UKC/AKC

History: One of Great Britain's oldest dogs, the Bearded Collie is believed to be descended from European and British sheepherding dogs, particularly the Polish Lowland Sheepdog. This breed is a progenitor of both the Border Collie and the Old English Sheepdog. The dogs continue to be used as herding dogs and companions in Great Britain and the United States.

Physical Description: This is a medium-size dog with broad skull and full muzzle. It has medium-size drop ears; a large, square nose; and large eyes that are set wide apart. The nose and eye color complement the coat. There is a heavy double coat in black, blue, brown, or fawn, with or without white markings. With maturity, the coat may lighten. There is a heavy beard.

The Bearded Collie is one of Britain's oldest breeds, but it wasn't bred in the United States until 1967.

Bearded Collie

Height: 20 to 22 inches

Weight: 40 to 60 pounds

Temperament: This is a friendly, outgoing dog with strong herding instincts. It is very playful and devoted to family; getting along with almost everyone, including children.

Activity Level: Moderate

Best Owner: It does best with an active family in a rural or suburban home.

Special Needs: Attention, exercise, grooming

Possible Health Concerns: Allergies, autoimmune disease, hypothyroidism, skin problems

Beauceron

Alternative Names: Berger de Beauce

Country of Origin: France

Group: Herding, UKC/AKC

History: Although this is a very old breed, dating to the late sixteenth century, it was rarely known outside France. It is a cousin of the Briard, both being French livestock guardians. There was no distinction between the two breeds until the nineteenth century, when the shorthaired variety was renamed the Beauceron, and the longhaired variety remained the Briard. After the French Revolution, the breeds were used as herding dogs rather than guardians. They have recently gained popularity in other areas of Europe, as well as North America.

Physical Description: The Beauceron is a large, solid, and muscular dog, with a rectangular shape. It has a long head, dark eyes, and a black nose. The short ears are set high and are natural drop or cropped erect. It has a deep chest and a natural tail that is hooked at the end. The coat is double, with a dense gray undercoat and a rough, short outer coat. It is shortest at the head and may be black with rust markings, called bicolor or bas rouge (red stockings);

Beauceron

or gray, black, and rust, called harlequin.

Height: 24 to 27.5 inches

Weight: up to 110 pounds

Temperament: These are courageous and intelligent dogs that are highly trainable and eager to please. They are devoted to their owners, very versatile, and make excellent workers.

Activity Level: High

Best Owner: This dog requires an active, dog-experienced owner who can provide it with a job or organized activity. A rural or suburban home is best.

Special Needs: Attention, exercise, job or activity, socialization, training

Possible Health Concerns: Bloat, ectropion, entropion, hip dysplasia, PRA

Bedlington Terrier

Alternative Names: Rothbury Terrier

Country of Origin: Great Britain

Group: Terrier, UKC/AKC

History: The Bedlington Terrier is believed to have been developed in the mid-nineteenth century in Cumberland County in northern England. First known as the Rothbury Terrier, it was renamed after a mining village, where it was used to battle vermin as well as hunt badgers, foxes, and otters.

Physical Description: This is a medium-size, graceful dog with a lamblike appearance. The head is narrow and rounded, and the skull is shorter than the muzzle. There is a profuse topknot at the crown of the head, which tapers down the muzzle. The nose is black or brown, depending on the color of the dog, and the eyes are small, dark, and shiny. The natural drop ears are long with thin leather and are covered with hair that forms a tassel at the end. Its body is lightly muscled with long, harelike feet and a long, sickle-shaped tail. The coat is curly and short, a mix of hard and soft hair. It is blue, blue and tan, sandy, sandy and tan, liver, or liver and tan.

Height: 15.5 to 16.5 inches

Weight: 17 to 23 pounds

Temperament: This breed is generally mild and gentle, but when alert it is courageous and full of energy. It is friendly toward people and sensitive to human emotions; however, it can be wary of other dogs. It is independent and adept at entertaining itself.

Activity Level: Moderate

Best Owner: This breed is adaptable to city or country life and does well with families or individuals. It does best with a dog of the opposite sex.

Special Needs: Exercise, grooming, training, socialization

Possible Health Concerns: Copper toxicosis, juvenile cataracts, kidney disease, PRA

Belgian Shepherd Dog (Belgian Malinois, Belgian Tervuren, Belgian Sheepdog, Belgian Laekenois)

Alternative Names: Chien de Berger Belge

Country of Origin: Belgium

Group: Herding, UKC/AKC

History: The Belgian Shepherd Dog is considered one breed with four variations in every country but the United States, where each type is considered a separate breed: the Belgian Malinois, the Belgian Tervuren, the Belgian Sheepdog (Groenendael), and the Belgian Laekenois. The Belgian Shepherds were developed in Belgium in the late nineteenth century as livestock guardians and herders. They were also used as police and military dogs. In 1891, a panel of dog

Bedlington Terrier

Belgian Laekenois

Belgian Malinois

Belgian Sheepdog

experts explored whether there was one Belgian Shepherd Dog that fit a particular standard. They determined that the Belgian Shepherd Dogs were similar in size and shape but differed in coat length, texture, and color. These four were given names based on the villages or regions in which each was developed.

Physical Description: The Belgian shepherd dogs are large, muscular, elegant, squarely built dogs. The head is strong with a muzzle that is moderately pointed and equal in length to the skull. They have dark brown, slightly almond-shaped eyes and large, triangular prick ears.

These deep-chested shepherds differ by coat color, length, and texture. The Belgian Malinois has a short, straight, hard coat that is fawn to mahogany, with black tips with a black mask and ears. The Belgian Tervuren has a long double coat and is fawn to mahogany with black tips. The Belgian Sheepdog (Groenendael) has a long black coat, and the Belgian Laekenois has a wiry fawn to mahogany coat with black overlay.

Belgian Tervuren

High-energy Belgian Malinois do not like to sit still. When confined, these dogs will run continually in sweeping circles to keep moving.

Height: 22 to 26 inches

Weight: 40 to 80 pounds

Temperament: These are intelligent, highly trainable dogs with a strong work drive. They are affectionate with their families but reserved with strangers, both protective and territorial. They are highly energetic and responsive but tend to be one-person dogs.

Activity Level: High

Best Owner: Belgian Shepherd Dogs do best with active, dog-experienced owners in rural or suburban homes.

Special Needs: Attention, job or activity, positive training, socialization

Possible Health Concerns: Anesthesia sensitivity, cancer, epilepsy, hip and elbow dysplasia, PRA, thyroid problems

Bergamasco

Alternative Names: Cane da Pastore Bergamasco

Country of Origin: Italy

Group: Herding, UKC

History: The Bergamasco is an ancient dog and believed to be related to the Maremma Sheepdog and the Briard. It's speculated that the breed descended from Asian herding dogs that came to Europe with nomadic shepherds or Phoenician traders. It was developed in the Alps as a sheepherding dog and was so valued by the shepherds who kept it that the bloodlines were kept secret. The breed came close to extinction following World War II, but Italian fanciers resurrected it.

Physical Description: The Bergamasco is a medium to large, heavy-boned, and muscular dog that is slightly longer than it is tall. It has a large, long head with a blunt muzzle; a large, black nose; and thin drop ears. The tail is long and thick and the long, heavy, rough coat forms matted "flocks" (like cords). The hair on the head is long, cover-

Bergamasco

ing the eyes. The coat ranges in color from silver gray to coal.

Height: 22 to 25 inches

Weight: 60 to 85 pounds

Temperament: These are courageous and intelligent dogs that are eager to please. They are not submissive and respond to firm, consistent training rather than harsh punishment. They are devoted to friends and family, especially children, but wary with strangers.

Activity Level: Moderate

Best Owner: The Bergamasco requires a confident, dog-experienced owner in a rural home.

Special Needs: Positive training, socialization

Possible Health Concerns: None known

Berger Picard

Alternative Names: Berger de Picard, Berger de Picardie, Picardy Sheepdog, Picardy Shepherd

Country of Origin: France

Group: Herding, UKC

History: This is a very old French sheepherding and livestock guarding dog that was developed in the Picardie region of northeastern France. It may be a descendant of Celtic or Asian dogs. Some believe the breed to be related to the Briard or Belgian Shepherd Dogs. The Berger Picard came close to extinction following both world wars and continues to be rare both in and outside France, where it is still used as a herding dog.

The Berger Picard uses a boundary, or tending, herding style, which developed from the French practice of grazing sheep in unenclosed areas that often adjoin land planted with crops. The dogs patrol the perimeter, keeping the sheep in the area and looking out for predators. This style contrasts with that of British herding dogs, who use a fetching style. In Britain, sheep spread out over land and hillsides in small flocks. Because Britain has few natural predators, the dogs' primary function is to fetch, or gather, the sheep to the shepherd.

Berger Picard

Physical Description: The Berger Picard is a medium-size, muscular, and rectangular-shaped dog. It has a broad head with a skull that is equal in length to the slightly tapered muzzle. It has a large, black nose, brown eyes, and large ears that are naturally erect. The long tail curves slightly at the tip. The double coat has a soft, dense undercoat and a medium-length, rough, terrier-like outer coat. It has eyebrows, a mustache, and a beard. The coat is gray of various shades. A slight white marking is permitted on the chest and toe tips.

Height: 21.5 to 25.5 inches

Weight: 50 to 70 pounds

Temperament: This is an active, friendly dog that enjoys children. It is intelligent and independent minded with a strong work drive. It tends to be vocal.

Activity Level: High

Best Owner: The Berger Picard does best with an active, dog-experienced owner in a rural home.

Special Needs: Exercise, grooming, positive training, socialization

Possible Health Concerns: Hip dysplasia, PRA

Berger des Pyrenees

Alternative Names: Berger, Labrit, Petit Berger, Pyr, Pyrenean Shepherd, Pyr Shep

Country of Origin: France

Group: Herding, UKC/AKC

History: The Berger des Pyrenees was developed as a herding dog in the Pyrenees Mountain valleys in France. It is believed to descend from the dogs kept by nomadic shepherds in the Pyrenees. It is traditionally worked together with the Great Pyrenees flock guardian dog. The Berger des Pyrenees was a military dog during World War I. It was first seen in the United States in the nineteenth century, and it is believed to have played a role in the development of the Australian Shepherd.

Physical Description: The Berger des Pyrenees is a small- to medium-size lean and muscular dog with a triangular-shaped head and a flat skull. The muzzle is wedge shaped and short. Because of an overlapping top lip, the dog appears to be smiling. It has large eyes, which are brown, blue, or partially blue. The nose is black and the ears are short and cropped straight across, or natural drop. The tail is completely docked, a natural bob, or naturally long and crook shaped. The slightly wavy, harsh coat is semi-long to long. It may be corded or brushed out. The coat may be fawn, gray, merle, brindle, black, or black with slight white markings.

There are smooth- and rough-faced Bergers; smooth-faced dogs have longer muzzles that are covered with fine short hair, and rough-faced dogs have a short chin with hair that lengthens up the muzzle and is swept back on the head. Smooth-faced dogs also have shorter hair on the body.

Height (Rough-faced): 15 to 19 inches

Height (Smooth-faced): 15.5 to 20.5 inches

Weight: 25 to 30 pounds (both)

Temperament: The Berger des Pyrenees is a very active dog that is full of nervous energy. It is wary with strangers, alert, and fearless. It may be mischievous. The smooth-faced tends to be less nervous.

Activity Level: High

Best Owner: The Berger des Pyrenees requires an active, dog-experienced owner in a rural home.

Special Needs: Grooming, exercise, a job or activity, socialization, training

Possible Health Concerns: Epilepsy, hip dysplasia, luxating patellas, PRA

Berger des Pyrenees

Bernese Mountain Dog

Alternative Names: Berner Sennenhund

Country of Origin: Switzerland

Group: Guardian, UKC; Working, AKC

History: The Bernese Mountain Dog is another of the four Swiss dogs descended from crosses of local dogs and Roman mastiffs. The breed was named for the canton of Bern and was developed as an all-purpose farm dog, pulling carts, driving cattle, and guarding. It was first brought to the United States in 1926.

Bernese Mountain Dog

Physical Description: The Bernese Mountain Dog is a large, powerful, squarely built dog with a large head; a flat, broad skull; and straight muzzle. The breed has dark brown eyes, a black nose, and medium-size, triangular drop ears that are set high. The chest is deep and the tail is long and bushy. The coat is long, shiny, and straight or slightly wavy, tricolor, with a black base and rust and white markings.

Height: 23 to 27.5 inches

Weight: 75 to 105 pounds

Temperament: This is an easygoing breed that is confident and gentle. Some may be aloof with strangers, but they generally get along with everyone, including children and other animals.

Activity Level: Moderate

Best Owner: The Bernese Mountain Dog does best with an active owner in a suburban or rural environment.

Special Needs: Grooming, socialization, training

Possible Health Concerns: Autoimmune disease, bloat, cancer, hip and elbow dysplasia,

The Bernese Mountain Dog is the only one of the Swiss Sennenhunds with a long, full coat.

eye disorders, skin and coat problems, subaortic stenosis, von Willebrand's disease, thyroid disorders

Bichon Frisé

Alternative Names: Tenerife Bichon

Country of Origin: France

Group: Companion, UKC; Non-Sporting, AKC

History: The Bichon Frisé has been documented since the fourteenth century, when French sailors brought examples home from Tenerife in the Canary Islands. It is thought to have arrived in Tenerife via Italian traders, who bartered the dogs for other goods. As with all bichon breeds, it was first developed in the Mediterranean region during the Middle Ages. Originally dubbed the Tenerife Bichon, it was a favorite of French nobility during the 1500s. By the 1800s, it had become a common dog in France and was often seen accompanying organ grinders or performing in circuses. It received its new name in the 1930s. It was first seen in the United States in the mid-twentieth century.

Bichon Frisé

Physical Description: The Bichon Frisé is a small, compact, and sturdy dog with a powder puff appearance. Its skull is rounded and the muzzle is shorter than the skull, with a strong lower jaw. The black or dark brown eyes are round with a dark halo around them. The drop ears are set high and forward on the head. A well-plumed, medium-length tail curls over the back. The coat is double with a soft, dense undercoat and a medium-length, cottony outer coat. There is profuse hair on the head, beard, mustache, ears, and tail. The coloring is usually white but can be buff, cream, or apricot around the ears or on the body.

Height: 9.5 to 11.5 inches

Weight: 10 to 14 pounds

Temperament: It is a gentle, affectionate, and playful dog with a jaunty, cheerful attitude.

Activity Level: Moderate

Best Owner: This breed does well with an individual or family in a city or suburban home.

Special Needs: Grooming, socialization, training

Possible Health Concerns: Autoimmune disease, bladder problems, cancer, eye disease, kidney problems, luxating patellas, skin allergies

Black and Tan Coonhound

Alternative Names: American Black and Tan Coonhound

Country of Origin: United States

Group: Scenthound, UKC; Hound, AKC

History: The Black and Tan Coonhound is believed to be descended from the Talbot Hound, an ancient breed found in Great Britain during the eleventh century, as well as crosses of Bloodhound, foxhound, and Virginia foxhound. It was bred for its coloring and its opossum and raccoon hunting abilities.

Black and Tan Coonhound

Physical Description: This is a large, well-muscled dog that is only slightly longer than it is tall. It has a large, oval head; a large, black nose; and hazel or brown eyes. The long ears are low-set and hang in folds. The long tail is sickle shaped. The black coat is short and dense, with tan markings above the eyes, on the muzzle, on the legs, and on the chest and black pencil marks on the toes.

Height: 23 to 27 inches

Weight: 40 to 75 pounds

Temperament: The Black and Tan Coonhound is an easygoing, friendly dog. It gets along with almost everyone, including children and other dogs. It tends to be vocal and is prone to stealing food. Many describe it as clownish, and it is not easily trained.

Activity Level: Moderate

Best Owner: This breed does very well with a family in a rural or suburban home. It gets along with children and other animals.

Special Needs: Ear cleaning, fenced yard, leashed

Possible Health Concerns: Eye problems, hip and elbow dysplasia

Black Russian Terrier

Alternative Names: Blackie, Russian Black Terrier

Black Russian Terrier

Country of Origin: Russia

Group: Guardian, UKC; Working, AKC

History: The Black Russian Terrier was first developed in 1930 by the Russian military from a cross of Rottweiler, Giant Schnauzer, and Airedale to serve as a multi-purpose worker. They have been used as guards, herders, and sled dogs.

Physical Description: This is a powerful, large-size, muscular dog that is only slightly longer than it is tall. The head is long with a flat skull and a powerful, wedge-shaped muzzle with a black nose. The eyes are small and dark, and the drop ears are short and triangular. The chest is deep. The double coat ranges from 1.5 to 4 inches in length and covers the entire body. There is a dense undercoat and wiry short or medium-length outer coat. Shorthaired dogs have straight hair, while medium-haired dogs have wiry hair with a beard, eyebrows, and mustache. The coat may be black or black with gray hairs.

Height: 26 to 30 inches

Weight: No standard available

Temperament: The Black Russian Terrier is an alert and energetic dog that is affectionate and gentle with family but protective and wary with strangers. It is stable and quite adaptable.

Activity Level: High

Best Owner: The Black Russian Terrier requires a dog-experienced owner. It is adaptable to city, suburban, or country life as long as it is provided ample exercise.

Special Needs: Attention, grooming, socialization, training

Possible Health Concerns: Eye problems, hip and elbow dysplasia

Bleu de Gascogne

Country of Origin: France

Group: Scenthound, UKC

History: There are four Bleu de Gascogne breeds: the Grand Bleu de Gascogne, the Petit Bleu de Gascogne, the Petit Griffon Bleu de Gascogne, and the Basset Bleu de Gascogne. The Grand Bleu de Gascogne is the progenitor of the other three breeds. It is believed to be descended from the large coursing hounds of the Middle East and was developed in the southern French region of Gascony to hunt large game. The other types were developed as hunters saw a need to pursue smaller game, such as rabbit and fox. The petits bleus were smaller than the grand, while the bassets were even smaller dwarfs. The final breed, the Petit Griffon Bleu was created by crossing the Bleu with rough-haired hounds.

Grand Bleu de Gascogne

It is estimated that the Bleu de Gascogne has contributed to at least 80 different dog breeds worldwide, including hound and gun dog breeds.

The first of the Bleus came to the United States in the eighteenth century as a gift from Lafayette to George Washington. The Petit Griffon Bleu de Gascogne is the only of the four not found in the United States and is the rarest in France, as well.

Physical Description: Except for the Griffon, all of the Bleu de Gascogne breeds have short, dense coats with a blue coloration created from a white background with black patches, speckling, and points. The Griffon has a wiry, harsh coat, also blue. All have deep chests and long, drop ears of fine leather that fold as they fall. The tail is long and sabrelike.

Height (Grand): 23.5 to 27.5 inches

Weight (Grand): 71 to 77 pounds

Height (Petit): 20 to 24 inches

Weight (Petit): 40 to 48 pounds

Height (Petit Griffon): 17 to 20 inches

Weight (Petit Griffon): 40 to 45 pounds

Temperament: These are easygoing and fun-loving dogs. They may be slightly reserved at first but warm up quickly. They are vocal and active. They get along with almost everyone and are friendly and outgoing. They are hard, intense workers in the field but calm and relaxed at home. They may be stubborn and will wander if on scent. They get along with children and other dogs.

Activity Level: Moderate

Best Owner: They do best with an active family in a suburban or rural home.

Special Needs: Exercise, fenced yard, leashed

Possible Health Concerns: Bloat, hip and elbow dysplasia

Bloodhound

Country of Origin: Great Britain

Group: Scenthound, UKC; Hound, AKC

History: The Bloodhound is believed to be an ancient dog. The early Bloodhounds were black or white; the blacks called Saint Huberts and the whites called Southern hounds. In the twelfth century, the Bloodhound became popular with Church dignitaries who kept the breed pure over the next several centuries. The Bloodhound was further developed when it arrived in the United States in the early nineteenth century. Although it does not commonly hunt today, it is widely used by law enforcement as a tracking dog. It is also kept as a companion.

Physical Description: The Bloodhound is a large, powerful dog with thin, loose skin that hangs in folds. It has a long, narrow head with a long, deep foreface. The hazel to yellow eyes are deeply sunk, with heavy lids. The very long, low-set ears fall in folds.

Bloodhound

This breed has a large nose, deep flews, and profuse wrinkles on the face and neck. It has a long neck with a large dewlap. The chest is deep and the long tail is sickle shaped. The feet are large and knuckled. The coat is short and hard in black and tan, liver and tan, or red. There may be a small amount of white on the chest, feet, or tail.

Height: 23 to 27 inches

Weight: 80 to 110 pounds

Temperament: The Bloodhound is a good-natured and outgoing dog. It is very affectionate and gets along with almost everyone, including children and other dogs. It can be somewhat shy and tends to be sensitive. It is vocal, often stubborn, and tends to slobber. It is difficult to train.

Activity Level: High

Best Owner: It does well with an active, patient owner in a rural or suburban home.

Special Needs: Attention, ear cleaning, exercise, fenced yard, leashed

Possible Health Concerns: Bloat, cardiac problems, ear infections, eye problems, hip and elbow dysplasia, luxating patellas, thyroid disorders

Bluetick Coonhound

Country of Origin: United States

Group: Scenthound, UKC

History: The Bluetick Coonhound is believed to be descended from English Foxhounds and big game French hounds.

Physical Description: This is a large, muscular dog with a long, broad head and deep, square muzzle. The low-set, medium-length drop ears fall in folds, and it has large, dark brown eyes. It is deep chested and the tail is long, set high, and sickle shaped. The short, smooth coat is dark blue and mottled. There are black spots on the back, ears, and sides.

UKC's Top 10 Breeds
1. Treeing Walker Coonhound
2. American Pit Bull Terrier
3. Bluetick Coonhound
4. English Coonhound
5. American Black and Tan Coonhound
6. Redbone Coonhound
7. Beagle
8. Labrador Retriever
9. Plott Hound
10. American Eskimo

Source: 2007 United Kennel Club registration figures

Height: 21 to 27 inches

Weight: 45 to 80 pounds

Temperament: The Bluetick Coonhound is a fun-loving, hardworking dog that gets along with almost everyone, but it can be dog aggressive and has a high prey drive. It is active and enthusiastic. It is vocal and will roam.

Activity Level: Moderate to high

Best Owner: This breed does best with an active owner in a rural or suburban home.

Special Needs: Exercise, socialization

Possible Health Concerns: None known

Bluetick Coonhound

Bolognese

Country of Origin: Italy

Group: Companion, UKC

History: The Bolognese is an Old World bichon, originally called an Italian bichon. Distant ancestors of the Bolognese may have been used on ships more than two thousand years ago to hunt rodents and serve as watchdogs. Over time, it became a popular companion for royalty: Catherine de Médicis; Catherine I, wife of Peter the Great; and Maria Theresa, Empress of Austria, were all Bolognese owners. The Bolognese appears in many medieval paintings.

Physical Description: The Bolognese is a toy breed with a sturdy body that is only slightly longer than it is tall. It has a medium-length head and muzzle with a black nose and lips. The eyes are dark and round with dark rims. It has drop ears and the tail is carried over the back. It has a long, cottony coat that covers the entire body. The Bolognese is all white, although it may have some champagne coloring on the ears or occasionally on the back.

Height: 9 to 12.5 inches

Weight: 8 to 14 pounds

Temperament: This is a sweet and affectionate dog that is eager to please and enjoys being with its people. It is very intelligent and is highly trainable. Quite playful, it gets along with children and other animals.

Activity Level: Low

Best Owner: This breed is adaptable to many situations and will do especially well in an apartment with a devoted owner.

Special Needs: Attention, grooming

Possible Health Concerns: None known

Border Collie

Country of Origin: Great Britain

Group: Herding, UKC/AKC

History: The Border Collie was developed in the Border country of Great Britain, bred to

Bolognese

Border Collie

herd sheep and work closely with its owner. It is known for its use of eye when herding. The breed continues to be used as a herding dog and companion in Great Britain and North America. It has gained recent popularity in canine sports, especially agility. As with many working breeds, there is controversy over its participation in con formation shows and the development of show and working lines.

Physical Description: The Border Collie is a medium-size, lithe, and muscular dog that is longer than it is tall. It has a broad skull and strong, tapered muzzle. The ears are erect or semi-erect, and the eyes are brown or blue or partially blue in merles. The rough or smooth double coat is usually black with a white blaze and ruff, although it can be any color except all white. The tail is naturally long and set low.

Height: 18 to 22 inches

Weight: 30 to 50 pounds

Temperament: This is an energetic, intelligent, and responsive dog. It is affectionate with friends and family but reserved with strangers. Although the Border Collie is friendly with children and other dogs, it may try to herd them and can be compulsive. This breed is hardworking and has a great ability to learn. It will chase livestock, cats, and other fast-moving animals.

Activity Level: High

Best Owner: The Border Collie requires an active owner in a suburban or rural home.

Special Needs: Exercise, fenced yard, job or activity, leashed, socialization, training

Possible Health Concerns: Osteochondritis dissecans (OCD), PRA

Border Terrier

Alternative Names: Coquetdale Terrier

Country of Origin: Great Britain

Group: Terrier, UKC/AKC

History: The Border Terrier was called the Coquetdale Terrier until 1880, when it was renamed after the region it is from. It is among Britain's oldest terriers and has been used in conjunction with Border foxhounds for many years. It was bred to be large enough to keep up with the horses but small enough to go to ground and bolt foxes. It was only rarely known outside Border country until the early 1900s.

Physical Description: This is a small, sturdy dog. The otterlike head is broad with a black nose. The eyes are dark hazel and fiery, and the small drop ears are V shaped. The body is deep and narrow. Its somewhat short, natural tail is tapered and held high. The Border Terrier has a double coat with a short, dense undercoat and a wiry and broken outer coat, with pronounced whiskers and beard on the face. It may be red, grizzle and tan, blue and tan, or wheaten. A small amount of white is allowed on the chest.

Height: 12 to 14 inches

Border Terrier

Weight: 11.5 to 15.5 pounds.

Temperament: It is alert, game, and active in the field but good natured and affectionate at home. It is good with children and other dogs, although it may view small animals as prey.

Activity Level: High

Best Owner: An active individual or family in the country or suburbs is best.

Special Needs: Exercise, fenced yard, grooming, job or activity, leashed, socialization, training

Possible Health Concerns: Cataracts, epilepsy, heart defects, hip dysplasia, luxating patellas, PRA, shunts

Borzoi

Alternative Names: Russian Wolfhound

Country of Origin: Russia

Group: Sighthound, UKC; Hound, AKC

History: Coursing hounds of this type have been known in Russia since the thirteenth century. It is probably a descendant of the bearhound of early Russia, the coursing hounds of the Tatars, and the ovcharkas, among others. It was used by the Russian aristocracy to hunt wolves and was rarely bought or sold, almost always given or received as a gift. The breed was almost wiped out during the Bolshevik Revolution

Borzoi

Today's Borzoi is largely unchanged from his Russian ancestors. The first standard for the breed—written in 1650—does not differ greatly from today's standard.

because it was associated with the ruling class. A few dogs were saved and exported to Great Britain and North America, where breeding programs were established.

Physical Description: The Borzoi is a large, slender dog that is graceful and strong. It has an arched, powerful neck; narrow forequarters; and a deep, narrow chest. The skull is domed and narrow with a Roman nose. The jaws are long and powerful and the eyes are large and dark. The nose is black and large and the ears are small and semi-erect. It has large hare feet and a long, feathered, curved tail. The coat is silky and long and can be flat, wavy, or curly, with a neck frill and feathering on the hindquarters and tail, chest, and the back of the forelegs. It can be any color or combination of colors.

Height: 26 to 32 inches

Weight: 55 to 105 pounds

Temperament: The Borzoi is affectionate with its family but is also stubborn and independent. It has a high prey drive and tends to be a runner. It gets along with children if socialized but is not trustworthy with small animals.

Activity Level: Moderate

Best Owner: The Borzoi requires a dog-experienced, active individual or family in a suburban or rural home.

Special Needs: Exercise, fenced yard, grooming, leashed, positive training, socialization

Possible Health Concerns: Bloat, hip and shoulder dysplasia, OCD, PRA

Boston Terrier

Alternative Names: Round-headed Bull and Terrier, Boston Bull, Bullethead

Boston Terrier

Country of Origin: United States

Group: Companion, UKC; Non-Sporting, AKC

History: The Boston Terrier is a downsized version of the bull and terrier types so popular in early America. There are differing versions of its history, disputing whether it is the descendant of the American Pit Bull Terrier, Boxer, Bull Terrier, French Bulldog, and English Bulldog or the descendant of an English Bulldog and white English terrier cross. Regardless, it was developed in the late 1800s and is one of the first breeds created in the United States. It was the first American breed recognized by the AKC.

Physical Description: The Boston Terrier is a small, compact, and muscular dog. Its body is short and square. It has a square skull and a short, wide muzzle that is about one-third the length of the skull. It has a wide, black nose and large, round, dark eyes that are set far apart. The small ears are natural or cropped erect. The tail is short and may be straight or screw. The coat is short and smooth and may be brindle, seal, or black, all with white markings.

Height: 15 to 17 inches

Weight: 15 to 25 pounds

Temperament: The Boston Terrier is lively, intelligent, and alert. It is determined and strong but with a kind, even-tempered disposition. It gets along with almost everyone, including children and other dogs.

Activity Level: Moderate

Best Owner: This breed does well with a family or individual in a city, suburban, or rural home.

Special Needs: Attention, training

Possible Health Concerns: Brachycephalic syndrome, cataracts, deafness, hypothyroidism, luxating patellas, mange

Bouvier des Flandres

Alternative Names: koe hond (cow dog), toucheur de boeuf (cattle drover), vuilbaard (dirty beard)

Country of Origin: Belgium

Group: Herding, UKC/AKC

History: The Bouvier des Flandres was developed in the Flanders area of Belgium as a cattle dog, used for both herding and driving. It is believed to be descended from Continental herding breeds, such as the schnauzer. Its use was antiquated when the automobile was invented and cattle began being transported by truck; however, breed fanciers worked to save the breed. Although it is no longer used for herding or driving, it has worked as a police and military dog, guide dog, and search and rescue dog.

Bouvier des Flandres

The breed was first introduced to the United States in the 1930s.

Physical Description: This is a large, powerful, squarely built, compact dog with a large head. The flat skull is long and broad with a broad muzzle. It has oval, brown eyes; a large, black nose; and small ears that are cropped erect or naturally drop. The neck is muscular and the chest is broad. The Bouvier des Flandres is naturally tailless, or the tail is docked to about 4 inches long and set high. The double coat has a fine, dense undercoat and rough, tousled outer coat with a thick mustache, beard, and eyebrows with erect hairs. The coat is short on the skull and upper part of the back. It may be fawn, gray, brindle, salt and pepper, or black. Some have a small, white star on the chest.

Height: 23.5 to 27.5

Weight: 65 to 100 pounds

Temperament: This is a versatile dog that is even-tempered and gentle. It is protective but capable of determining real from imagined threats. It is both courageous and intelligent and does fine with children.

Activity Level: High

Best Owner: An active, dog-experienced owner in a rural or suburban home is best.

Special Needs: Fenced yard, grooming, positive training, socialization

Boxer

Possible Health Concerns: Autoimmune disorders, cancer, glaucoma, hip and elbow dysplasia, hypothyroidism, subaortic stenosis

Boxer

Country of Origin: Germany

Group: Guardian, UKC; Working, AKC

History: Boxers have been found in Europe since the sixteenth century. Although they were originally hunting dogs, they are believed to be descendants of Tibetan fighting dogs and cousins of the Bulldogs. They were used for fighting and bull baiting until the practice was outlawed in Germany in the mid-nineteenth century. Boxers have also been used as police and military dogs, performance dogs, and all-purpose companions. They were rarely known in the United States until World War II, when U.S.

servicemen became interested in the breed. The name "Boxer" stems from their tendency to use their forelegs when fighting.

Physical Description: The Boxer is a medium-size, compact, muscular, and squarely built dog. There is a square, blunt, Bulldog-like muzzle with thick upper lips, an undershot jaw, dark brown eyes, a black nose, and drop ears that can be cropped erect or left natural. It has a deep chest, compact feet, and a docked tail that is carried high. The short, smooth coat is fawn or brindle with a black mask, sometimes there are white markings.

Height: 21 to 25 inches

Weight: 50 to 80 pounds

Temperament: The Boxer is a fun-loving and playful dog that is extremely loyal and affectionate with family. Some may be initially wary with strangers but are generally confident and make friends easily. The Boxer is excellent with children.

Activity Level: High

Best Owner: The Boxer does well with a family in the city, suburbs, or country.

Special Needs: Attention, exercise, training

Possible Health Concerns: Breathing problems, cardiac problems, hip dysplasia, thyroid disease

Boykin Spaniel

Country of Origin: United States

Group: Gun Dog, UKC

History: The Boykin Spaniel is a relatively new breed, dating from the turn of the twentieth century. The breed was developed from one stray dog, who was trained as a turkey and waterfowl dog. Breeds in its background include the Chesapeake Bay Retriever, Pointer, Springer Spaniel, Cocker Spaniel, and American Water Spaniel. The Boykin was bred to work from a boat and for flushing and retrieving. The Boykin Spaniel is the state dog of South Carolina.

Boykin Spaniel

Physical Description: These are medium-size, sturdy dogs that are square in shape. They have medium-size drop ears; yellow to brown eyes, depending on the coat color; and a short, docked tail. The short to medium-length coat may be flat or curly with light feathering and very curly ears. They range in color from liver to dark brown and may have white markings on the chest.

Height: 14 to 18 inches

Weight: 25 to 40 pounds

Temperament: The Boykin Spaniel is an intelligent, trainable dog. It loves to work and enjoys water. It is good-natured and affectionate with great endurance and versatility.

Activity Level: Moderate to high

Best Owner: It does best with an active family which includes the dog in outdoor activities, especially hunting trials and boating. A rural environment suits the Boykin best.

Special Needs: Exercise, grooming

Possible Health Concerns: Cataracts, hip dysplasia, poor temperament, skin allergies

Bracco Italiano

Alternative Names: Italian Pointer
Country of Origin: Italy
Group: Gun Dog, UKC
History: The Bracco Italiano is an old breed, believed to have originated in fourteenth-century Italy based on depictions of a similar-looking dog in frescoes of the era. It was developed as a pointer and retriever. There were originally two types, a white-and-orange dog from Piedmont and a white-and-brown dog from Lombardy, but the two types are now considered one breed.
Physical Description: This is a large, tall, square-shaped, and muscular dog with a narrow head with long, low-set ears and loose skin at the face and neck. The large eyes are brown and the large nose is pink to brown. The chest is broad and deep and the tail is long and tapered. The short, smooth, fine coat is brown and white or orange and white.
Height: 22 to 26.5 inches
Weight: 55 to 90 pounds
Temperament: The Bracco Italiano is an easygoing, affectionate dog. It makes a sharp distinction between work and play: intense in the field and docile at home. It is intelligent but can be stubborn and sensitive.
Activity Level: Moderate to high
Best Owner: The Bracco Italiano does best in rural or suburban homes with active, dog-experienced owners who can provide a job or activity.
Special Needs: Attention, job or activity, training
Possible Health Concerns: Bloat, entropion, hip dysplasia, kidney disease

Bracco Italiano

Braque du Bourbonnais

Alternative Names: Bourbonnais Pointer
Country of Origin: France
Group: Gun Dog, UKC
History: The Braque du Bourbonnais is an old breed that has existed since the sixteenth or seventeenth century. Developed as a versatile bird dog, it is probably related to the Braque Français. The breed was close to extinct following World War II but was revitalized by breeder Michel Comte. The Braque du Bourbonnais continues to be used as a hunting dog in both its native country and elsewhere and is quite rare.
Physical Description: This is a medium-size, muscular dog with elegant bearing. It has hazel or amber eyes and drop ears and is naturally tailless or has a bobtail. The short, coarse coat is peach or liver, called fleur de pecher or lie de vin—peach blossom or wine dregs—by the French.
Height: 19 to 22 inches

Weight: 35 to 55 pounds

Temperament: The Braque du Bourbonnais is a hardworking, highly trainable dog. It is gentle but playful and can be sensitive. The breed is versatile, making a good hunter and companion. It is affectionate with family.

Activity Level: High

Best Owner: It does best in a rural or suburban home where it is given a job or included in an organized activity. The Braque du Bourbonnais makes a poor kennel dog. A weekend hunter and weekday family situation is ideal.

Special Needs: Attention, job or activity

Possible Health Concerns: Ectropion, entropion, hip dysplasia

Braque Français

Alternative Names: French Pointer

Country of Origin: France

Group: Gun Dog, UKC

History: The Braque Français originates from southwest France and the Central Pyrenees. It is one of France's oldest pointing dogs, going as far back as the seventeenth century. There are two types: the Gascogne and the Pyrenean. The lighter, racier Pyrenean is more popular and considered to be closer to the original Braque Français.

Physical Description: This is a strong, medium-size dog with very loose skin. The eyes are yellow to brown, the nose is brown, and the ears are drop. The tail is naturally short or docked, although some Gascogne

Braque du Bourbonnais

Braque Français

types have a long tail. The short, thick coat is brown, brown and white, brown and white speckled, or brown and tan.

Height (Gascogne): 22 to 27 inches

Weight: 55 to 70 pounds

Height (Pyrenean): 18.5 to 23 inches

Weight: 39.5 to 55 pounds

Temperament: Both types are gentle, easy-going dogs. They enjoy working and are intelligent and eager to please. Because they are sensitive, positive training is best.

Activity Level: High

Best Owner: It does best with an active, outdoorsy family in a rural or suburban home.

Special Needs: Job or activity, training,

Possible Health Concerns: Ectropion, entropion, hip dysplasia

Braque Saint-Germain

Alternative Names: Saint-Germain Pointer, Compiègne Pointer

Country of Origin: France

Group: Gun Dog, UKC

History: The Braque Saint-Germain was developed in 1830 in the French royal kennels at Compiègne in Saint-Germain-en-Laye. The breed is the result of a cross between an English Pointer bitch and a French Braque and was developed for use on small game. The breed became a favorite of Parisian hunters. In the mid- to late-nineteenth century, they were popular show dogs.

Physical Description: This is a medium-size, muscular breed with golden yellow eyes and a dark pink nose. The drop ears are fawn-colored, and the tail is long and low. The short coat is orange or fawn and white.

Height: 21 to 23 inches

Weight: 40 to 55 pounds

Temperament: This is a gentle and sensitive dog that is equally adept as a hunting dog and family companion. It enjoys working

Braque Saint-Germain

and is highly trainable but also thrives on attention and affection.

Activity Level: High

Best Owner: A suburban or rural home with an active family is best. It should be included in a job or organized activity.

Special Needs: Job or activity, positive training

Possible Health Concerns: None known

Briard

Alternative Names: Chien Berger de Brie

Country of Origin: France

Group: Herding, UKC/AKC

History: The Briard is an ancient breed that is believed to date back to the eighth century. It was developed as a flock guardian and herding dog and was also used as a military dog in both World War I and World War II. Charlemagne and Napoleon are both reputed to have owned Briards. The first Briards in the United States are said to have arrived with Thomas Jefferson.

Physical Description: The Briard is a large, powerful dog with a large, broad head that is well-covered with hair. It has large, dark eyes that are set wide apart; a square, black nose; and natural drop or cropped erect ears. The tail is long and set low. It has a double coat with a coarse, shaggy outer coat that is any color except white.

Height: 22 to 27 inches

Weight: 70 to 90 pounds

Temperament: This is an intelligent, loyal, and obedient dog. It is affectionate and playful with its friends and family but wary with strangers. It has a strong herding instinct.

Activity Level: Moderate

Best Owner: The Briard does best with an active owner in a rural or suburban home.

Special Needs: Grooming, socialization, training

Possible Health Concerns: Bloat, eye problems, hip dysplasia

Briquet Griffon Vendéen

Alternative Names: Medium-size Griffon Vendéen

Country of Origin: France

Group: Scenthound, UKC

History: Although a number of breeds once had *briquet*, meaning "medium size," in their names, this is the last of them. It was bred to hunt large and small game in a pack, bred down from the Grand Griffon Vendéen at the beginning of the twentieth century. Although the breed came close to extinction during both world wars, it was revitalized in the late 1940s.

Physical Description: This is a medium-size, stocky dog with a lightly boned head and straight, short muzzle. It has a black or brown nose, eyes that are large and dark and thin, long drop ears. It has a long neck and short, straight body. The long, tapered tail is held high like a saber. The double coat has a thick undercoat and

Briard

Briquet Griffon Vendéen

long, bushy outer coat, with a heavy mustache and eyebrows. This breed is black with white markings, black with tan markings, fawn with white markings, fawn with black markings, or tricolor—fawn with black and white markings.

Height: 19 to 22 inches

Weight: No standard available

Temperament: This is an active, intense, and enthusiastic dog. It is single-minded when on scent.

Activity Level: High

Best Owner: This breed does best with an active owner in a rural or suburban home.

Special Needs: Exercise, fenced yard, leashed

Possible Health Concerns: None known

Brittany

Alternative Names: Épagneul Breton, Brittany Spaniel

Country of Origin: France

Group: Gun Dog, UKC; Sporting, AKC

History: The Brittany was developed in mid-nineteenth century France from a cross of French spaniels and English Setters. The breed became popular in the United States in the 1930s and has remained one of the country's most popular hunting dogs.

Physical Description: This medium-size, strong, leggy, and compact dog has dark, deep-set eyes and short, triangular drop ears that are set high. The nose is fawn, tan, brown, or deep pink but never black. It is naturally tailless or docked to about 4 inches. The soft, wavy coat is orange and white or liver and white. It is sometimes tricolor, although this is not preferred.

The Brittany was originally registered with the AKC as the Brittany Spaniel. The word *spaniel* was later dropped from the name because the breed works game by pointing like a setter. It also stands higher on its legs than the spaniels do. The UKC continues to call the breed the Brittany Spaniel.

Brittany

Height: 17.5 to 20.5 inches

Weight: 30 to 40 pounds

Temperament: This is a good-natured and lively dog that is trainable and intelligent, exuberant and active. It is friendly and loves outdoor activities.

Activity Level: High

Best Owner: This dog does best with an active owner in a rural or suburban home. A hunter or other outdoorsy person suits it best. It makes a good family dog but can be too exuberant for small children.

Special Needs: Exercise, job or activity, training

Possible Health Concerns: Epilepsy, heart defects, hip and elbow dysplasia, PRA, temperament problems

Brussels Griffon

Alternative Names: Griffon Bruxellois, Brabancon (Smooth-coated Brussels Griffon)

Country of Origin: Belgium

Group: Companion, UKC; Toy, AKC

History: The Brussels Griffon was named after the city of its origin. Originally used as a ratter on farms, it was developed to its current form in the nineteenth century through crosses with Affenpinschers, Pugs, and English Toy Spaniels. The addition of the English Toy Spaniel into the Griffon's heritage changed its facial characteristics, making it no longer suitable as a ratter. It has been a companion since.

Physical Description: The Brussels Griffon is a toy dog with a short, thick body. Its skull is large and round and its chin is undershot. It has large, black eyes that are set far apart. The eyelashes are long and black, and the black, turned-up nose is extremely short and set back between the eyes. The ears are naturally semi-erect, although sometimes cropped to a point. The tail is docked to one-third its length and held high. There are two coat types: rough and smooth. The rough coat is wiry and dense, with hair covering the head and forming a fringe, especially around the eyes, nose, cheeks, and chin. The smooth coat is made up of short, straight hair. The color can be reddish brown, black and reddish brown mixed, black with reddish brown markings, and solid black.

Height: 8 to 10 inches

Weight: 8 to 12 pounds

Temperament: This is an intelligent, alert, jaunty dog that is full of personality. It is self-important and confident and may be challenging to train. Some do not get along well with children or strangers.

Activity Level: Low

Best Owner: This breed does best in a suburban or city home.

Special Needs: Grooming, training, socialization, supervision with children

Possible Health Concerns: Brachycephalic syndrome, cleft palate, reproductive problems

Brussels Griffon

Bulldog

Alternative Names: English Bulldog

Country of Origin: Great Britain

Group: Companion, UKC; Non-Sporting, AKC

History: Today's Bulldog is quite different than the early version of the breed. It was originally developed to hold bulls for butchers and was later used for the blood sport of bull baiting. When this sport was outlawed in 1835, the need for the breed ceased. However, fanciers worked to keep the breed alive as a companion, placing

Bulldog

Temperament: The Bulldog is gentle, stable, and affectionate. Although it is courageous and capable of great power, it gets along with almost everyone. On the down side, it has a proclivity for snorting and drooling, as well as chronic flatulence. It is occasionally scrappy with other dogs.

Activity Level: Low

Best Owner: The Bulldog is adaptable and can do well in an apartment.

Special Needs: Protection from heat, socialization, training, wrinkle cleaning on face

Possible Health Concerns: Allergies, brachycephalic syndrome, eye problems, elongated soft palate, hip dysplasia, reproductive problems, small trachea

value on its gentle temperament and distinctive looks rather than its fighting skills.

Physical Description: The Bulldog is a medium-size but massive dog with a heavy, thick-set body. The head is very large, broad, and square. The forehead is flat and the face is very short with a short, upturned muzzle. The massive jaws are square, and the lower jaw is undershot with thick pendant chops. It has dark eyes, a black nose, and small rose ears. The chest is broad and deep with a short back. The naturally short tail is straight or screwed. The skin is soft and loose, especially at the head, neck, and shoulders. The coat is short and it may be brindle, white, red, fawn, yellow, or piebald.

Height: 12 to 16 inches

Weight: 40 to 50 pounds

Bullmastiff

Country of Origin: Great Britain

Group: Guardian, UKC; Working, AKC

History: The Bullmastiff was developed in 1860 from the Mastiff and the Bulldog. It was bred to catch and hold poachers with-

Bullmastiff

out hurting them. Breeders believed the cross created a dog that was fast but not aggressive. The breed standard states that the original mating was 60 percent Mastiff and 40 percent Bulldog.

Physical Description: The Bullmastiff is a large and powerful dog with a large, broad head and a short, blunt muzzle. When alert, the forehead wrinkles. The eyes are dark and nose is black. The medium-size, triangular drop ears are set wide apart. This dog has a broad, deep chest and muscular loins, with a long tail that may be curved or straight. The short, smooth coat is brindle, fawn, or red, with a dark muzzle and ears. There may be a small, white spot on the chest.

Height: 24 to 27 inches

Weight: 100 to 130 pounds

Temperament: This is a quiet, docile dog that is patient and gentle with friends and family, especially children. It will, however, be protective and territorial.

Activity Level: Low

Best Owner: The Bullmastiff does well with a family and can adjust to most living situations but may be too large for apartment life.

Special Needs: Socialization, training

Possible Health Concerns: Bloat, eye problems, cardiac disease, hip dysplasia, hypothyroidism, kidney problems, panosteitis, tumors

Bull Terrier

Alternative Names: Bull and Terrier

Country of Origin: Great Britain

Group: Terrier, UKC/AKC

History: The Bull Terrier was established in about 1835 by James Hinks, probably by mating the Bulldog to the now-extinct white English terrier, then by crossing this mix with a Spanish Pointer. It was originally known as a bull and terrier. It was used to bait bulls and engage in pit fights. Although it was known as a fierce dog fighter, it was not supposed to provoke a fight.

Physical Description: The Bull Terrier is a muscular, medium-size dog with a distinctive egg-shaped head. The nose is black and its dark eyes are small, triangular shaped, and sunken. The ears are close together, small, and naturally erect. The body is rounded with a deep, broad chest and well-boned legs. The tail is short and tapered. It has a short, smooth coat, and two color varieties are recognized: white (with or without occasional dark markings on the head) and colored, which is any color with or without white markings. In the colored variety, all things being equal, brindle is preferred.

Height: 21 to 22 inches

Weight: 45 to 65 pounds

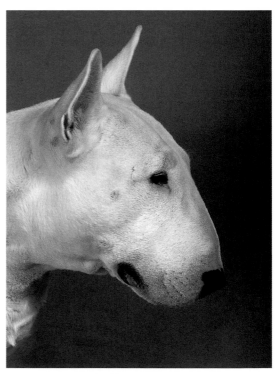

Bull Terrier, White

Bull Terrier, Colored

Temperament: The Bull Terrier is friendly, playful, and affectionate with humans. It is a good guard and very lively and busy. It may be aggressive toward other animals. If not well socialized, it can be food and toy possessive and reactive to provocation. Socialized Bull Terriers do fine with children and small animals, but two males generally will not get along.

Activity Level: High

Best Owner: The Bull Terrier does best with an experienced, active family or individual with time for it. It can adapt to a rural, suburban, or city home.

Special Needs: Firm training, inclusion in family activities, one-on-one exercise, socialization, supervision

Possible Health Concerns: Deafness, heart problems, renal problems, skin allergies, spinning disorder

Cairn Terrier

Country of Origin: Scotland

Group: Terrier, UKC/AKC

History: The Cairn Terrier is a descendant of the working terrier from the Isle of Skye that worked among the rocks and cliffs bolting otter, foxes, and vermin. The Cairn Terrier was grouped together with other Scotch terriers until 1873. In the late 1800s, Scottish Terrier breeders began to breed separate lines. The Cairn Terrier was first recognized as a distinct breed in 1912. In the early 1900s, it was often bred with the West Highland White Terrier.

Physical Description: This is a small, hardy, short-legged terrier that is longer than it is tall. The skull is broad, the muzzle is strong, and the nose is black. The hazel eyes are set wide apart and sunken with shaggy eyebrows. It has small, pointed, erect ears that are set wide apart on the head. The short tail is carried high but not over the back. It has a profuse double coat. The outer coat is hard and weather resistant but softer on the head. It is any color but white and is often dark on the ears, muzzle, and tail tip.

Cairn Terrier

The Cairn Terrier counts the Dandie Dinmont, Scottish, Skye, and West Highland White Terriers among its relations. The Cairn's conformation is probably the closest to that of their common ancestor, the Scotch terrier.

Height: 9.5 to 10 inches

Weight: 13 to 14 pounds

Temperament: The Cairn Terrier is lively and friendly. It is generally considered to be mellower than most terriers and some describe it as catlike. It is a good family dog that is eager to please and craves affection. It gets along with children and other animals.

Activity Level: Moderate to high

Best Owner: It does well with a family in the country, suburbs, or city.

Special Needs: Grooming, some exercise, training

Possible Health Concerns: Cataracts, CMO, globoid cell leukodystrophy, liver shunt, luxating patellas, skin allergies, Legg-Perthes

Canaan Dog

Alternative Names: Kelev K'naani

Country of Origin: Israel

Group: Pariah, UKC; Herding, AKC

History: This ancient breed is descended from a wild dog that has lived in the area that makes up Israel, the land of Canaan, for more than 4,000 years, where it was used as a herd and guard dog. When the Israelites were dispersed 2,000 years ago, most Canaan Dogs became feral, living as pariah dogs on the fringes of civilization; others followed the nomadic bedouins, who used them as flock and camp guardians. In the early twentieth century, the breed began to be domesticated again. During World War II, the Canaan Dog was used as a military dog in the Middle East, and it has been used by the Israeli military

Canaan Dog

as a mine detector, messenger, and search and rescue dog.

Physical Description: The Canaan Dog is a medium to large, strong, and squarely built dog. The head is wedge shaped and the skull is broad and equal in length to the muzzle. It has almond-shaped, dark eyes and a black nose. The ears are short, naturally prick, and set far apart; they are mobile and extremely sensitive to sound. The feet are catlike and the tail is a thick brush carried in a curl over the back. It is double coated with a profuse, soft undercoat and straight, harsh, medium-length outer coat. The neck has a ruff and the rump is feathered. It may be a solid color or spotted, between cream and red brown, gold, red, white, or black. Some have a black mask or white markings.

Height: 19 to 24 inches

Weight: 35 to 55 pounds

Temperament: The Canaan Dog is an alert and vigilant dog. It is devoted and affectionate with family but wary with strangers, both animal and human, including children. It reacts to provocation and is very protective. It matures slowly. It tends to be most active in the morning and evening.

Activity Level: Moderate

Best Owner: The Canaan Dog does best in a dog-experienced home, in the city, country, or suburbs.

Special Needs: Exercise, socialization, supervision with children and animals, training

Possible Health Concerns: Hip dysplasia

Canadian Eskimo Dog

Alternative Names: Canis Borealis, Qimmiq, Eskimo Dog

Country of Origin: Canada

Group: Northern, UKC

History: The Canadian Eskimo Dog is believed to be an ancient dog that has been used by the Inuit of Canada's Arctic region for at least 1,000 years as a hunting and sled dog. In the late nineteenth century, it became popular with western explorers who used Canadian Eskimo Dogs on expeditions to both the North and South Poles. It has come close to extinction several times during the past 100 years and continues to be rare.

Canadian Eskimo Dog

Physical Description: The Canadian Eskimo Dog is large and powerful. It has a broad, wedge-shaped head with small, triangular ears that are set wide apart. The muzzle tapers, and its small eyes can be of any color except blue. The heavily plumed tail is curled over the back. It is double coated and can be of any color or combination of colors.

Height: 23 to 27.5 inches

Weight: 60 to 105 pounds

Temperament: This is an intelligent and energetic dog that can be stubborn. It enjoys outdoor activities and a cool climate.

Activity Level: High

Best Owner: It does best with an active owner in a suburban or rural home.

Special Needs: Exercise, socialization, training

Possible Health Concerns: Vulnerable to transmittable diseases

Cane Corso

Country of Origin: Italy

Group: Guardian, UKC

History: This is an ancient breed descended from Roman mastiffs. It came close to extinction following World War II but has been revitalized by breeders. It was used as a hunter of large predators, a cattle drover, and a guard of home and livestock.

Physical Description: The Cane Corso is a large-size, muscular, and powerful dog that is longer than it is tall. It has a wide head with a short, broad muzzle, strong jaws, and a slightly undershot bite. The upper lips form an upside down V. The eyes are dark, the nose is black, and the medium-size drop or semi-erect ears are usually cropped erect. The tail is thick and docked. The thick skin does not wrinkle, and the coat is short and stiff, in black, gray, fawn or tubby (stripes of fawn and gray).

Cane Corso

Height: 23.5 to 27 inches

Weight: 88 to 110 pounds

Temperament: This is an even-tempered, trainable, and quiet dog that is loyal and affectionate with its family, including children, but extremely wary with strangers. It is very protective. It is intelligent and often aloof. It does fine with other animals as long as it is well socialized.

Activity Level: Moderate

Best Owner: This breed does best with a guardian dog–experienced owner in a rural or suburban home. It can adapt to apartment life if it receives enough exercise.

Special Needs: Fenced yard, leashed, socialization, training

Possible Health Concerns: Bloat, cherry eye, demodectic mange, ectropion, entropion, hip dysplasia

Cardigan Welsh Corgi

Country of Origin: Wales

Group: Herding, UKC/AKC

History: The Cardigan Welsh Corgi was developed in Cardiganshire, Wales, as a cattle

The Cardigan Welsh Corgi is adaptable to temperature extremes. It can adjust to temperatures from minus 20°F to 110°F.

herder and drover. It also served as a family companion and ratter. It is a cousin to the Dachshund, and it is believed to be descended from dogs brought to Wales by the Celts as long as 3,000 years ago. It is closely related to the Pembroke Welsh Corgi. It was first seen in the United States in the early 1930s and has gained popularity in recent years.

Physical Description: The Cardigan Welsh Corgi is a long, low, solidly built dog with a wedge-shaped head; large, erect ears; a black nose; and brown eyes. It has a deep chest and well-boned, bowed front legs. The long tail is bushy. The double coat has a soft undercoat and a medium-length outer coat in variety of colors and patterns, including

Cardigan Welsh Corgi

brindle, red, sable, blue merle, and black, with or without points. There may be white markings on the neck, chest, legs, muzzle, underbelly, tip of tail, and face. Some have black masks and ticking.

Height: 10.5 to 12.5 inches

Weight: 25 to 38 pounds

Temperament: The Cardigan is often described as a big dog in a small body; it is alert, intelligent, and hardworking. The Cardigan is playful and affectionate with friends and family but wary with strangers. It may herd small children and other animals.

Activity Level: Moderate

Best Owner: The Cardigan requires a dog-experienced, active owner and adapts to a suburban, rural, or city home.

Special Needs: Attention, exercise, job or activity, socialization, training

Possible Health Concerns: PRA

Carolina Dog

Alternative Names: American Dingo, Dixie Dingo, Indians' Dog

Country of Origin: United States

Group: Pariah, UKC

History: The Carolina Dog is native to the United States. Its descendants are believed by some to have crossed the Bering Land Bridge along with the Paleolithic people. Many Carolina Dogs continue to live as feral dogs throughout the southeast United States, although they are becoming increasingly popular as pets. It is not uncommon for Carolina Dogs to interbreed with domestic dogs.

Physical Description: The Carolina Dog is a medium-size, sturdy dog with a strong, broad skull and foxy look. The ears are large and naturally erect, the almond-shaped eyes are brown, and both the nose and lips are black. The brush tail is of medium length and hooked. Its forefeet may turn out, and it has a deep chest. It has

Carolina Dog

a short, profuse coat that is reddish in color, from cream with red hairs to a dingolike red. It is occasionally black and tan.

Height: 18 to 20 inches

Weight: 30 to 44 pounds

Some registries list size at 17 to 24 inches and 40 to 60 pounds.

Temperament: The Carolina Dog is a loyal, pack-oriented dog. It is devoted and affectionate with its family but wary with strangers. It is protective but will not bite unprovoked. Without socialization, it is often shy. It rarely roams.

Activity Level: Moderate

Best Owner: This breed is adaptable to most living situations as long as it is well socialized and receives adequate exercise.

Special Needs: Exercise, socialization, and training

Possible Health Concerns: None known

Caucasian Ovcharka

Alternative Names: Caucasian Mountain Dog, Russian Kavkazskaya Ovtcharka, Nagazi (Georgian Republic), Gampr (Armenia)

Caucasian Ovcharka

Country of Origin: Caucasus Mountain area in former USSR

Group: Guardian, UKC

History: The Caucasian Ovcharka is believed to have developed from Tibetan dogs who accompanied nomads who settled in the Caucasus Mountain area more than 2,000 years ago. Because the Ovcharka was isolated from other breeds and not subject to organized breed programs, it remained a pure but primitive dog. In the twentieth century, the USSR began a rigorous breeding program with the purpose of utilizing Ovcharkas as guard dogs.

Physical Description: The Caucasian Ovcharka is a very large, powerfully built dog that is slightly longer than it is tall. It has a large, broad, wedge-shaped head and high-set drop ears, which may be cropped. The muzzle is short and powerful, the almond eyes are deep set, and the nose is large and black. There is a double coat with a profuse ruff; it can be short, medium, or long. The coloring may be gray, white, cream, fawn, or tan, with or without white markings, as well as brindle, piebald, and white with gray patches. There is often a dark mask.

Height: Minimum 24.5 to 25.5 inches

Weight: No standard available

Temperament: The Ovcharka is an intelligent, bold, and even-tempered dog. Although protective, it is calm and loyal toward family.

Activity Level: Moderate

Best Owner: This breed requires an owner experienced with guardian dogs in a rural home where the dog is provided a job.

Special Needs: Grooming, job or activity, socialization, training

Possible Health Concerns: Hip and elbow dysplasia

Cavalier King Charles Spaniel

Country of Origin: Great Britain

Group: Companion, UKC; Toy, AKC

History: Small toy spaniels like this have been known in Europe since the sixteenth century; they were bred as companions and to hunt small game. In the seventeenth century, the toy spaniel became a special favorite of King Charles I and was popular with royalty throughout the reign of King Charles II. By the late seventeenth century, however, it had become rare and

Cavalier King Charles Spaniel

almost disappeared. The breed wasn't revived until the 1920s, when an American came to Britain looking for the breed he'd seen in old paintings. For five years, he offered money for the best old type spaniel at the Crufts Dog Show, stirring a revival of what was to become known as the Cavalier King Charles Spaniel. The breed has had a following in the United States and United Kingdom since, and it has become more popular than the original King Charles Spaniel (known as the English Toy Spaniel in North America).

Physical Description: The Cavalier King Charles Spaniel is small, well balanced, and graceful. The skull is slightly rounded but appears flat because of long, high-set drop ears. The full muzzle is slightly tapered and the eyes are round, large, and dark. The nose is black with large nostrils. The tail is naturally long; occasionally it is docked to two-thirds its length. The coat is moderately long, silky, and straight or slightly wavy, with feathering on the ears, feet, back of the legs, and tail. The coloring can be black and tan; rich red (ruby); white with chestnut markings (Blenheim); or black, white, and tan (tricolor).

Height: 12 to 13 inches

Weight: 13 to 18 pounds

Temperament: This is a gentle, friendly, and affectionate dog that is easygoing and gets along with almost everyone.

Activity Level: Low to moderate

Best Owner: This is an adaptable dog that does well with a family or individual, in the city or the suburbs.

Special Needs: Exercise, grooming, indoor lifestyle

Possible Health Concerns: Allergies, hip dysplasia, luxating patellas, mitral valve disease, syringomyelia

Central Asian Shepherd Dog

Alternative Names: Mid-Asian Shepherd

Country of Origin: Siberia, Mongolia, republics of the former USSR

Group: Guardian, UKC

History: The Central Asian Shepherd Dog is an ancient dog that is believed to descend from dogs kept by Central Asian nomads for several thousand years. They were used to guard against large predators, such as bear and wolves. The modern dog is believed to be similar to the original nomadic Central Asian Shepherd Dog, although there are up to ten new forms being developed in Russia. The breed continues to be used as a livestock guardian and is rare in the United States.

Physical Description: This is a very large, powerful dog that is slightly longer than it is tall. The broad head has a deep, blunt muzzle and a large, black nose. The ears are small

Central Asian Shepherd Dog

and drop, although they may be cropped close to the head. The tail can be naturally long or docked. The dog is double coated with a profuse undercoat and an outer coat that is white, black, gray, straw colored, red brown, gray brown, brindle, parti-colored, and ticked. The coat may be long or short.

Height: minimum 23.5 to 25.5 inches

Weight: 90 to 150 pounds

Temperament: It is an intelligent, protective dog that is wary with strangers but affectionate and loyal toward family. Some say it has catlike behaviors. It is often dog aggressive.

Activity Level: Moderate

Best Owner: This breed does best with a dog-experienced, firm owner in a rural home.

Special Needs: Fenced yard, leashed, socialization, training

Possible Health Concerns: None known

Cesky Fousek

Alternative Names: Bohemian Wirehaired Pointing Griffon, Ceska Fouska (female)

Country of Origin: Czech Republic

Group: Gun Dog, UKC

History: The Cesky Fousek was a widely used wirehaired pointing dog in the Czech and Slovakian Republics, but with the advent of World War I, the breed came close to extinction. The breed was revived in the 1930s with the help of German wirehaired and shorthaired pointers and is once again a popular hunting dog in its homeland.

Physical Description: This is a strong, medium-size dog with almond-shaped, brown eyes and drop ears. The tail is docked to three-fifths its length and carried horizontally. The coat is wiry with a soft, dense undercoat; a longer, coarse outer coat; and long, coarse guard hairs. The coat is longest at the thighs, chest, and shoulders, and there is feathering on the legs and facial hair, with a beard, mustache, and long

Cesky Fousek

eyebrows. Coloring is dark roan, with or without brown patches, or brown, with or without ticked markings.

Height: 23 to 26 inches

Weight: 60 to 75 pounds

Temperament: The Cesky Fousek is a hard-working, intelligent dog that is devoted to its family and highly trainable.

Activity Level: High

Best Owner: It does best with an active family in a rural or suburban environment.

Special Needs: Exercise, job or activity

Possible Health Concerns: Alopecia, hip dysplasia

Cesky Terrier

Alternative Names: Czech or Bohemian Terrier

Country of Origin: Czech Republic

Cesky Terrier

Group: Terrier, UKC

History: The Cesky Terrier is a relatively new breed that was created in 1949 by crossing Sealyham and Scottish Terriers with the goal of creating a dog that could both go to ground and hunt in open field.

Physical Description: This is a small dog that is muscular and slightly longer than it is tall. The Cesky Terrier's large head is blunt and long with a large nose that is black or liver. Its medium-size eyes are deep set. It has medium-size drop ears that are close to the head. The feet are large with arched toes, and it has a long tail. Its coat is thick and silky and may be blue gray or light coffee brown, with or without yellow, gray, or white markings. The skin is gray on blue-gray dogs and tan on brown dogs. The face is covered with hair, and the hair on neck is curly. The back, head, and neck are usually clipped short.

Height: 10.5 to 13.75 inches

Weight: 13 to 23 pounds

Temperament: The Cesky Terrier is an easy keeper; it is patient, gentle, and good with children. It is very mild for a terrier.

Activity Level: Moderate

Best Owner: This breed does well with an individual or family and is adaptable to apartment or rural life.

Special Needs: Grooming

Possible Health Concerns: None known

Chart Polski

Alternative Names: Polish Sighthound

Country of Origin: Poland

Group: Sighthound, UKC

Chart Polski

The Chart Polski has been referenced in hunting-related literature, paintings, and drawings since the thirteenth century. The illustrations show that the breed remained essentially unchanged until the end of the nineteenth century, when political and economic turmoil in Poland followed by the two World Wars almost led to the breed's demise. Only a few purebred Chart Polskis remained in Poland by 1974, when efforts to revive the breed began.

History: The Chart Polski is believed to have been in existence since the thirteenth century and probably descends from the Asian sighthounds. It was used as a hunting dog for hare, fox, deer, and wolf.

Physical Description: The Chart Polski is a large, muscular, and sturdy dog. It is less refined than the other sighthounds. It has a powerful jaw; folded ears; a large, dark nose; and amber eyes. The tail is long and thick, hooked at the end. The springy coat is of varying lengths and of any color. The eyelids and nose should complement the coat color.

Height:27 to 32 inches

Weight: No standard available

Temperament: The Chart Polski is a confident and courageous dog. It is wary of strangers and quite reserved.

Activity Level: Moderate

Best Owner: This breed requires a confident, experienced owner in a rural home.

Special Needs: Socialization, training

Possible Health Concerns: None known

Chesapeake Bay Retriever

Country of Origin: United States

Group: Gun Dog, UKC; Sporting, AKC

History: The Chesapeake Bay Retriever is descended from two Newfoundland-type puppies found in an English shipwreck off Maryland in 1807. The dogs, Sailor and Canton, were bred with other retrievers to create dogs who would work as duck retrievers in the Chesapeake Bay. The Chessie was recognized as a distinct breed by the end of the nineteenth century.

Physical Description: This is a strong, medium-size dog, slightly longer than it is tall. Some are taller at the loin than at the withers. It has small drop ears and yellow or amber eyes. The tail is long and hangs low, and the feet are large and webbed. The coat is short, oily,

Chesapeake Bay Retriever

and water-repellent, wavy on the body but straight on the head and legs. There is a dense undercoat, and there may be slight feathering on the rump and tail. Color may be any shade of brown, sedge, or dead grass.

Height: 21 to 26 inches

Weight: 55 to 80 pounds

Temperament: This breed is affectionate with family and friends but wary with strangers. A courageous, eager worker, it tends to be reserved and serious. It is intelligent and highly trainable. This breed is friendly with children but may react when provoked. It enjoys outdoor activities.

Activity Level: Moderate to high

Best Owner: It does well with an experienced, active owner in a rural or suburban home.

Special Needs: Exercise, socialization, training

Possible Health Concerns: Dwarfism, entropion, epilepsy, PRA

Chihuahua

Country of Origin: Mexico

Group: Companion, UKC; Toy, AKC

History: The history of the Chihuahua is vague. It is known that both the Toltec and Aztec cultures kept dogs, including a small breed called the Techichi, but it is uncertain

Chihuahua

whether these dogs were the ancestors of the Chihuahua. Some fanciers believe it is a descendant of dogs introduced by Chinese or Spanish explorers. It was first seen by North Americans in the mid-nineteenth century and brought to the United States shortly thereafter.

Physical Description: The Chihuahua is a very small dog that is slightly longer than it is tall. The skull is large and rounded, sometimes described as an apple head. The muzzle is short and slightly pointed, and the eyes are large and full. The ears are large and erect, with the tips pointing slightly outward. The tail is natural and moderately long, carried erect, horizontally, or in a loop over the back. There are two coat types: longhaired and smooth.

Archaeologists have found the remains of purported Chihuahua ancestors in human graves in Mexico and areas of the southwest United States. The breed, called Techichi, was kept as a companion and for religious purposes among the ancient Toltecs and Aztecs.

The longhaired type is soft, flat or slightly curly, usually with an undercoat. A large ruff on the neck and feathering on the tail, feet, and legs is highly desirable. The smooth variety has soft, glossy, straight hair. Any color is permitted; the coat can be solid, marked, or splashed. Common colors are red, sable, fawn, black and tan, tricolor, and brindle.

Height: 6 to 9 inches

Weight: 2 to 6 pounds

Temperament: The Chihuahua is an alert, sensitive dog. It tends to dislike dogs of other breeds and requires socialization to be comfortable with strangers and children.

Activity Level: Low

Best Owner: The Chihuahua makes an excellent apartment dog and companion for an elderly or sedentary adult.

Special Needs: Socialization, supervision with children and other animals

Possible Health Concerns: Collapsed trachea, heart problems, hydrocephalic, hypoglycemia, luxating patellas

Chinese Crested

Country of Origin: China

Group: Companion, UKC; Toy, AKC

History: Although there is little information on the origin of the Chinese Crested, it is believed to descend from African hairless dogs that were brought to Asia by traders and then bred down. It may be related to other hairless dogs. Chinese sailors often used the dogs on their ships as ratters because the lack of fur meant that they did not harbor fleas. In addition, the warm bodies of hairless dogs were believed to hold medicinal properties, and the dogs were often used in much the same way as a hot water bottle on sore spots. The breed was commonly found in port cities. It first arrived in the United States in the nineteenth century.

Chinese Crested

Physical Description: The Chinese Crested is a small, fine-boned dog. The color of its almond-shaped eyes and nose complement its coat. It has large, erect ears and a tapered muzzle. It comes in two varieties: the hairless and the powderpuff. The hairless variety has hair only on its head, feet, and tail. The powderpuff is completely covered in long hair. It comes in any color or combination of colors. The hairless usually has gray and pink skin.

Height: 11 to 13 inches

Weight: 10 to 14 pounds

Temperament: The Chinese Crested is an active, playful, inquisitive dog that is friendly to everyone. As long as it is socialized, it does well with children and other animals.

Activity Level: Moderate

Best Owner: This breed does best in a city or suburban home.

Special Needs: Attention, protection from sunburn, skin care, socialization

Possible Health Concerns: Dental problems, Legg-Perthes disease, liver shunts, PRA

Chinese Shar-Pei

Alternative Names: Shar-Pei

Country of Origin: China

Group: Northern, UKC; Non-Sporting, AKC

History: The Chinese Shar-Pei is believed to be an ancient breed that is thought to have originated in the region around the small village of Tai Li in the Guangdong Province during the Han Dynasty (c. 200 B.C.E.). Statues bearing a strong resemblance to the Shar-Pei have been dated to this period, and a Chinese manuscript from the thirteenth century refers to a wrinkled dog with characteristics much like those of the Shar-Pei. The Chinese Shar-Pei is thought to have been developed as an all-purpose dog. Although it has come close to extinction, it is now a popular companion dog.

Physical Description: The Chinese Shar-Pei is a medium-size, compact, and square dog. Its most distinctive feature is the loose skin that covers its head and body, creating a multitude of wrinkles. It has an oval-shaped muzzle, sometimes called a hippopotamus muzzle, small ears, and a

Chinese Shar-Pei

high-set tail. The tongue and lips are a bluish black. It comes in two coat types: a short and a longer coat, which should not exceed an inch in length. The coat can be any solid color or sable.

Height: 18 to 20 inches

Weight: 45 to 60 pounds

Temperament: The Chinese Shar-Pei is an alert, serious, and intelligent dog. It is affectionate and devoted to its family but wary with strangers. It prefers the company of humans to dogs and may be aloof.

Activity Level: Moderate

Best Owner: The best owner for this breed is an active person in a suburban or rural home.

Special Needs: Exercise, socialization, training, wrinkle cleaning

Possible Health Concerns: Amyloidosis, cancer, immune system problems, Shar-Pei fever

Chinook

Country of Origin: United States

Group: Northern, UKC

History: The Chinook is a northern breed derived from a single ancestor born in 1917, Chinook, the offspring of a Greenland Husky and a Saint Bernard mix. Chinook's offspring inherited his coloring, size, and intelligence. Chinook and over a dozen of his offspring hauled freight on Admiral Byrd's 1929 Antarctic Expedition, setting sledding records for distance, weight, and speed. Unfortunately, the senior Chinook lost his life on the expedition. The breed nearly died out in the 1980s, when there were only 11 breedable dogs left, but it has gained numbers in recent years.

Chinook

Physical Description: The Chinook is a medium- to large-size, powerful dog that is longer than it is tall. It has a broad skull; a tapered muzzle; brown, almond-shaped eyes; and ears that can be prick, drop, or semi-prick. It has a sabrelike tail and well-furred, webbed feet. The dense double coat is tawny with dark tawny to black markings on the ears and muzzle.

Height: 21 to 27 inches

Weight: 55 to 70 pounds

Temperament: The Chinook is a loyal, hard-working, and versatile dog. It is friendly and calm, reserved but not aggressive with strangers. It is intelligent, alert, and trainable but matures slowly. It gets along with children and other animals.

Activity Level: Moderate

Best Owner: The Chinook does best with an active family or individual in a rural or suburban home.

Special Needs: Exercise, fenced yard, grooming, indoor lifestyle, socialization, training

Possible Health Concerns: Cataracts, cryptorchidism, dysplasia, seizures, shyness, skin problems

Chow Chow

Alternative Names: lang gou (wolf dog), xiong gou (bear dog)

Country of Origin: China

Group: Northern, UKC; Non-Sporting, AKC

History: The Chow Chow originated in Asia, and it is believed that its ancestors can be traced to the Han Dynasty. Some believe it is the result of a cross between the old mastiff of Tibet and the Samoyed. It was first used as a hunting dog for pheasant and partridge. Its name is derived from the pidgin-English slang used by sailors to describe mixed cargo, chow-chow. Most theorize that the Chow Chow was brought to England as part of cargo and so was given that generic name. The breed became popular during the Victorian era in England and first appeared in the United States in 1890.

Physical Description: The Chow Chow is a medium-size, sturdy dog. It has a square body and large, broad head with a short muzzle. It has prick ears with rounded tips and a scowling expression. The eyes are dark brown, almond shaped, and deeply set, giving the dog limited peripheral vision. Its tongue is bluish black and its nose is large and black, except in blue Chows, when it is slate colored. The tail is set high and curled over the back. It is double coated and the outer coat can be smooth or rough. The smooth coat is short and dense. The rough coat is longer and abundant. It has a ruff around the head and neck and the tail is plumed. It may be red, black, blue, cinnamon, or cream.

Height: 17 to 20 inches

Weight: 45 to 70 pounds

Temperament: The Chow Chow is a dignified and aloof dog. It is intelligent but can be detached and is especially reserved with strangers. It is loyal to its family. With socialization and training it can be quite good with children but often does poorly with other animals.

Activity Level: Low to moderate

Best Owner: The Chow Chow requires a firm, experienced owner; it can adapt to a city, suburban, or rural home.

Special Needs: Grooming, socialization, training

Possible Health Concerns: Anesthesia sensitivity, cancer, entropion, heat sensitivity, hip dysplasia, knee problems

Chow Chow

Clumber Spaniel

Country of Origin: France/Great Britain

Group: Gun Dog, UKC; Sporting, AKC

Clumber Spaniel

One of the earliest depictions of the Clumber Spaniel is in the painting *Return from Shooting*, showing the second Duke of Newcastle and three of his Clumbers. It was painted by Francis Wheatley in 1788.

History: The Clumber Spaniel is believed to have been developed in France by the Duc de Noailles. When the French Revolution was imminent, he relocated his dogs to the kennels at the Duke of Newcastle's Clumber Park estate. There may be Alpine spaniel and Basset Hound in the Clumber's ancestry. The breed became popular among English nobility during the nineteenth century.

Physical Description: This is a long, low, solid dog with a rectangular shape. It has a massive head with long, broad ears; a short muzzle; and large, amber eyes. The nose is large and can be of various shades of brown, including beige, rose, or cherry. The tail is docked. The coat is silky and straight, with a neck frill and feathering on the ears. Color is white with lemon or orange markings.

Height: 17 to 20 inches

Weight: 55 to 85 pounds

Temperament: The Clumber Spaniel is a friendly, laidback dog that is affectionate with friends and family but somewhat reserved with strangers. It is quite playful but still dignified.

Activity Level: Moderate

Best Owner: This breed does best with an active family with time for it. It is best suited to a suburban or rural home.

Special Needs: Ear cleaning, grooming, positive training

Possible Health Concerns: Allergies, ear problems, ectropion, entropion, epilepsy, hip dysplasia, hypothyroidism, intervertebral disc disease

Cocker Spaniel

Alternative Names: American Cocker Spaniel, Cocking Spaniel

Country of Origin: United States

Group: Gun Dog, UKC; Sporting, AKC

History: The Cocker Spaniel is the smallest of the hunting dogs and was developed from early imports of the English Cocker Spaniel and bred as a woodcock hunter and companion. They are now popular show dogs and almost exclusively kept as companions.

Physical Description: This small, compact dog is square in shape with long drop ears, dark brown eyes, and a nose that is black or brown. The tail is docked. The silky, medium-length coat has a dense undercoat,

Cocker Spaniel

and there is feathering on the ears, chest, belly, and legs. The coat may be black, ASCOB (any solid color other than black), or parti-colored, with or without white markings at the chest and throat or tan points.

Height: 14 to 15 inches

Weight: 18 to 25 pounds

Temperament: The Cocker Spaniel is a lively, friendly dog with a strong work drive, intelligence, and a capacity for training.

Activity Level: Moderate

Best Owner: It adjusts well to city, suburban, or rural life and can be an ideal pet for an elderly person, as long as it is provided with daily walks.

Special Needs: Grooming, socialization

Possible Health Concerns: Cataracts, epilepsy, hypothyroidism, hip dysplasia, PRA, temperament problems, von Willebrand's disease

Collie

Alternative Names: Colley, Scotch Collie, Scottish Sheepdog,

Country of Origin: Scotland

Group: Herding, UKC/AKC

History: It was bred as a multipurpose farm dog, a herder, drover, guard, and companion. Its name comes from the Scottish word for a black sheep, *colley*. It later became popular with dog fanciers, including Queen Victoria, and became a popular companion dog in the early twentieth century. It was first shown in the United States in 1877.

Physical Description: The Collie is a large, strong, and lithe dog. It has a long, lean, wedge-shaped head with almond-shaped eyes that are brown or blue in merles, a black nose, and high, folded ears. The tail is moderately long. The Rough Collie has a long double coat, while the Smooth Collie has a short double coat. Both come in sable

Longest-Lived Dogs

1. Miniature Poodle
2. Miniature Dachshund, Toy Poodle
3. Tibetan Terrier, Bedlington Terrier, Whippet
4. Border Terrier
5. Jack Russell Terrier
6. Chow Chow
7. Shih Tzu
8. Beagle, Pekingese, Shetland Sheepdog
9. Cairn Terrier, Greyhound, mixed breed
10. Border Collie, Chihuahua, Dalmatian, English Springer Spaniel, Wire Fox Terrier
11. Bull Terrier, Irish Red and White Setter, Basset Hound, West Highland White Terrier, Yorkshire Terrier
12. Labrador Retriever, lurcher
13. Cocker Spaniel, Vizsla
14. Bearded Collie, German Shorthaired Pointer
15. Standard Dachshund, Rough Collie

Source: Caring for Your Dog *by Bruce Fogle, DVM*

Rough Collie

and white, tricolor (black, tan, and white), blue merle, or white with sable, tricolor, or blue merle markings.

Height: 22 to 26 inches

Weight: 55 to 80 pounds

Temperament: The Collie is an excellent family dog that gets along well with children. It is both active and intelligent. It is friendly and outgoing but will bark at intruders.

Activity Level: Moderate

Best Owner: The Collie does best with an active family in a suburban or rural home.

Special Needs: Grooming

Possible Health Concerns: Collie eye anomaly, PRA

Coton de Tuléar

Alternative Names: Royal Dog of Madagascar

Country of Origin: Madagascar

Group: Companion, UKC

History: The Coton de Tuléar is a member of the bichon family and has always been a companion. Its ancestors are believed to have been brought to Madagascar 400 to 500 years ago. The breed, named for the port city of Tuléar, was embraced by the Malagasy upper class and became known as the Royal Dog of Madagascar. Only members of the nobility could own the breed. In 1973, a North American doctor came across the breed and brought the first Cotons to the United States in 1974. Although it is the official dog of Madagascar, it is close to extinction there.

Physical Description: The Coton is a small, well-muscled dog. It has dark, round eyes and a large, black nose. There are triangular drop ears and a medium-length, low-set tail. It has a medium-length, soft, dense, cottonlike coat, for which it was named (*coton* is French for "cotton"). There are three color varieties: white, tricolor, and black and white. The white is the most common. Registries differ on whether the nonwhite cotons are permissible.

Height: 8.5 to 12.5 inches

Weight: 8 to 13 pounds

Temperament: The Coton is a cheerful, agreeable dog that gets along with almost everyone but is especially bonded with its family. It is friendly with children, strangers, and other animals. It is playful and sometimes even clownish.

Activity Level: Moderate

Best Owner: This breed is versatile and does well with a family in a city, suburban, or rural home.

Coton de Tuléar

Special Needs: Attention, grooming, and training

Possible Health Concerns: Eye problems, kidney disease, thyroid disease

Curly-Coated Retriever

Country of Origin: Great Britain

Group: Gun Dog, UKC; Sporting, AKC

History: The Curly-Coated Retriever was probably developed from the Saint John's Newfoundland, the Irish Water Spaniel, the Poodle, and the Old English Water Dog. It was bred to retrieve waterfowl and upland game birds. Although it is not popular in the United States, it is well known in Great Britain, Australia, and New Zealand.

Physical Description: This is a strong, medium- to large-size dog that is slightly longer than it is tall. The head is long and wedge shaped with dark, almond-shaped eyes and small drop ears. The chest is deep and the tail is long. The tightly curled water-resistant coat covers the entire body, even

Curly-Coated Retriever

the tail. The coat is short and straight only on the face, front of the forelegs, and feet. Its coloring may be black or liver.

Height: 23 to 27 inches

Weight: 65 to 85 pounds

Temperament: This breed is energetic and playful, adaptable to its owner's activity level. It is affectionate with its friends and family but reserved with strangers. It enjoys children.

Activity Level: Moderate to high

Best Owner: It does best with a family in a rural or suburban home.

Special Needs: Attention, training

Curs

The curs were developed in small pockets throughout rural America, especially in the southern United States. They were bred for their working ability, so a uniform appearance was not a priority; this led to disparate sizes and looks. They are all-purpose dogs, used for hunting game, as family companions, as watchdogs, and as livestock dogs. They are small to medium sized, square or rectangular shaped, short-haired dogs with a strong work drive. They are courageous and tenacious when on scent.

Curs are descended from European mongrels and terriers brought over by immigrants and adapted to the needs of rural America. Many are kept as companions as well as workers. Some are said to have been cross-bred with native American breeds as well. Most curs continue to work in their traditional jobs, in homes and small farms across rural America. A few of the better known curs are the Black Mouth Cur, Canadian Cur, Leopard Cur, Mountain Cur, Stephens' Stock, and Treeing Cur. Most of the curs are rare.

Possible Health Concerns: Alopecia, cancer, eye problems, hip and elbow dysplasia

Dachshund

Alternative Names: Teckel

Country of Origin: Germany

Group: Scenthound, UKC; Hound, AKC

History: It is believed that the Dachshund is a cousin of the Basset Hound and may go as far back as the sixteenth century. It was probably crossed with terriers. The breed was developed to hunt badgers and is still used as a hunting dog, as well as a companion. It first became popular in the United States during the 1930s and 1940s.

Physical Description: The Dachshund is a compact, muscular dog with a long body and short legs. It has a wedge-shaped head, long drop ears, a deep chest, and a long tail. There are two sizes, miniature and standard, and three coat varieties, smooth, longhaired, and wirehaired. The coat is short and smooth, long and silky with feathers, or long and wiry with bristly facial hair. It may be red or cream, or black, chocolate, blue, or fawn, with tan points. There is also a salt and pepper coloring called wild boar and a number of patterns, including dapple, brindle, and piebald.

Dalmatians are born with pure white coats and develop their distinctive black or liver spots during puppyhood.

Height (Standard): No standard available

Weight (Standard): 16 to 32 pounds

Height (Miniature): No standard available

Weight (Miniature): Under 11 pounds

Temperament: This is a friendly, good-natured, and fun-loving dog. It is intelligent, playful, and affectionate.

Activity Level: Moderate to high

Best Owner: The Dachshund is adaptable to many living situations, including city or rural life. The miniature is an ideal apartment dog.

Special Needs: Grooming

Possible Health Concerns: Bloat, epilepsy, hypothyroidism, intervertebral disc disease

Dalmatian

Alternative Names: English Coach Dog, Carriage Dog, Plum Pudding Dog, Fire House Dog, Spotted Dick

Country of Origin: Great Britain

Group: Companion, UKC; Non-Sporting, AKC

History: The complete history of the Dalmatian is unknown, but it takes its name from the place where it was first recorded as

Dachshunds

Dalmatian

existing, the Eastern European coastal area of Dalmatia, along the Adriatic Sea. The modern Dalmatian was most likely brought to Great Britain during the eighteenth century. There, it was developed as a coach dog. The Dalmatian's job was to guard passengers and property. Later, its affinity for horses made it well suited to following horse-drawn fire engines, leading to the perception of the Dalmatian as a firehouse dog. It is still sometimes used at fire stations as a mascot and for fire-awareness education programs. The Dalmatian has been in the United States since colonial times.

Physical Description: The Dalmatian is a large, muscular, and square dog. Its head is pear shaped from above, with the skull and muzzle parallel to one another. The skull is almost flat with a slight center groove. The nose is large, broad, and black. The eyes are medium size and brown or blue, or a combination. The ears are medium-size drop. It has a deep chest and compact, well-arched feet. The tail is naturally long and tapered and carried in a slight upward curve. The coat is short, glossy, and close-fitting, with a ground color of white and spots of black or liver.

Height: 19 to 24 inches

Weight: 45 to 65 pounds

Temperament: The Dalmatian is an active, lively dog that has an affinity for horses and running, especially with vehicles. It is wary with strangers but friendly and affectionate toward its friends. It makes an excellent watchdog. It has a strong work drive but can be stubborn.

Activity Level: High

Best Owner: The Dalmatian requires an experienced, active owner in a rural or suburban home.

Special Needs: Exercise, positive training, fenced yard, job or activity, socialization, leashed

Possible Health Concerns: Deafness, epilepsy, hip dysplasia, kidney and bladder stones, skin allergies

Dandie Dinmont Terrier

Alternative Names: Dandie Dinmont's Terrier
Country of Origin: Scotland
Group: Terrier, UKC/AKC

History: The Dandie Dinmont Terrier was bred from the Border region's native terriers to hunt otter and badger. It was first recorded as a distinct breed in 1700 and made famous in the book *Guy Mannering*, by Sir Walter Scott, which was published in 1814. In it, the character Dandie Dinmont keeps six of the dogs. King Louis Philippe of France owned a pair in 1845.

Physical Description: The Dandie Dinmont is a curvaceous terrier with no straight lines and a long back that is higher at the loins than at the shoulder. It has a large, domed head; the muzzle is about three-fifths the length of the skull. The large, bright eyes are deep hazel and the jaw is strong. It is a short dog with a deep chest, and its heavy-boned, crooked front legs have paws that point slightly outward. Its tail is natural and sickle shaped. It has a double coat that is about two inches long and made up of a dense, harsh overcoat and soft, woolly undercoat. This

Dandie Dinmont Terrier

intermingled coat is called a pily or pencil coat. The hair on the head is soft and silky, and it has feathers on its muzzle and forelegs. The coat is pepper or mustard and usually has some white on the chest.

Height: 8 to 11 inches

Weight: 18 to 24 pounds

Temperament: This is an independent and reserved dog that is both determined and intelligent. It is affectionate with its family.

Activity Level: Moderate

Best Owner: It is an adaptable dog that does as well with a family or individual, in the city or the country.

Special Needs: Grooming

Possible Health Concerns: Glaucoma, lens luxation, disk disease

Danish Broholmer

Alternative Names: Broholmer

Country of Origin: Denmark

Group: Guardian, UKC

History: Although they were once well known in Denmark, the Broholmer almost died out in the mid-nineteenth century and again in the mid-twentieth century. The breed was restored in the mid-1970s by the Danish Kennel Club. They are gaining popularity in both Denmark and abroad.

Danish Broholmer

The word *feisty* means lively and full of spirit, and it originated from *feist*, meaning "a small, snappish dog." The word *feist* comes from the obsolete *fist*, which means "to pass gas." There was a time when annoying dogs were called fisting hounds.

Physical Description: The Broholmer is a large, muscular, and powerful dog with a large, broad head and short drop ears. Its eyes are brown or black, and the lips are pendulous. The natural tail is curved, and the legs are powerful. The double coat has a short, harsh outer coat in fawn or black. There may be white markings on the chest and paws and a black mask.

Height: 27.5 to 29.5 inches

Weight: 90 to 130 pounds

Temperament: The Broholmer is calm, docile, and even tempered but can be dominant and protective when threatened.

Activity Level: Moderate

Best Owner: It does best in a rural home with a dog-experienced owner.

Possible Health Concerns: None known

Denmark Feist

Country of Origin: United States

Group: Scenthound, UKC

History: The Denmark Feist is descended from a small feist that was purchased by the Slade family in 1917. Bred as an all-purpose working dog, it is a silent trailer used to hunt boar, bobcats, and squirrel. It was established as a distinct breed in 1984.

Physical Description: This is a medium-size dog that is longer than it is tall. Its muzzle is slightly shorter than its skull, and the muzzle is broad with powerful jaws. The nose is black and eyes are dark with black rims. The ears are short and drop or semi-erect, placed at the outside of the head. It has a muscular neck and laid-back shoulders with a deep, wide chest. The feet are round and well-arched, and the thick tail is naturally long and tapered, a natural bob, or docked. The coat is short and dense and comes in red, yellow, or red and white spotted.

Height: 15 to 18 inches

Weight: 25 to 35 pounds

Temperament: This breed has two distinct personalities: tenacious at work and calm at home.

Activity Level: Moderate to high

Best Owner: One who can appreciate and enable this dog's hunting heritage; rural or working homes are best.

Special Needs: Attention, socialization, exercise

Possible Health Concerns: Allergies, luxating patellas, dental problems, demodectic mange

Deutscher Wachtelhund

Alternative Names: German Spaniel
Country of Origin: Germany

Deutscher Wachtelhund

Group: Gun Dog, UKC

History: The Deutscher Wachtelhund has a long history in Germany, where it is believed to have existed for centuries. In Germany, the Wachtelhund is classified as a stoberhund, which is similar to a spaniel in its flushing ability, but more versatile. The Wachtelhund nearly died out in the late nineteenth century, but it was revitalized by crossbreeding with other hunting dogs. In Germany, the breed continues to be used as a hunting dog on both large and small game and is rarely kept as a companion.

Physical Description: This is a muscular, medium-size dog that is longer than it is tall. The flat, broad head has a broad muzzle; large, dark nose; and dark eyes. It has long, broad ears, and the tail is docked to about one-third its length. The long, wavy coat is solid liver brown, white with ticking and large patches of brown, or red or liver roan.

Height: 18 to 22 inches

Weight: 44 to 66 pounds

Temperament: This breed is energetic and hardworking. It is intense in the field but friendly with family, both loyal and biddable.

Activity Level: Moderate to high

Best Owner: It does best in an active rural home where it has a job.

Special Needs: Exercise, job or activity

Possible Health Concerns: Hip dysplasia

Doberman Pinscher

Alternative Names: Dobermann
Country of Origin: Germany
Group: Guardian, UKC; Working, AKC
History: The Doberman Pinscher was developed in Germany in the late nineteenth century for use as a police, military, and guard dog. It is believed to have been bred by Louis Dobermann through a cross of the now-extinct old German Shepherd,

Doberman Pinscher

German Pinscher, Rottweiler, English Greyhound, Weimaraner, and black-and-tan Manchester Terrier, among others.

Physical Description: The Doberman is a large, squarely built, compact, and muscular dog. It has a long, blunt, wedge-shaped head with a long, tapered muzzle. The dark eyes are almond shaped, and the ears are cropped erect or medium size drop. The nose color complements the coat, which is smooth and short in black, red, blue, or fawn. There are rust markings above the eyes and on the muzzle, throat, chest, legs, feet, and below the tail. There may be a small, white spot on the chest. The tail is docked.

Height: 24 to 28 inches

Weight: 55 to 90 pounds

Temperament: The Doberman is loyal, active, and devoted to family. It makes an excellent watchdog, alert and fearless. It is intelligent and highly trainable and generally gets along well with children and other animals.

Activity Level: Moderate

Best Owner: The Doberman does well in a rural or suburban home with an active family or individual.

Special Needs: Exercise, fenced yard, socialization, training

Possible Health Concerns: Cardiomyopathy, hypothyroidism, osteosarcoma, wobbler syndrome (cervical vertebral instability), von Willebrand's disease

Dogo Argentino

Alternative Names: Argentine Dogo

Country of Origin: Argentina

Group: Guardian, UKC

History: The Dogo Argentino was developed in 1928 by an Argentinean doctor for use as a big game hound. Mastiffs, Bulldogs, Bull Terriers, and old fighting dogs of Cordoba all went into the mix. It was bred to track boar and then attack and hold the animal for the hunter. It continues to be used for hunting as well as a companion and in other jobs.

Physical Description: This is a large, muscular, and powerful dog that is slightly longer

Dogo Argentino

than it is tall. The large, broad head has a short, broad muzzle; the short drop ears are set wide and may be cropped into small erect triangles or left natural. There is a large, black nose that may have pink on it and almond-shaped, dark-brown to dark-hazel eyes. There is a deep chest, muscular hindquarters, and a natural tail. The short, smooth coat is white, although one dark marking is allowed on the head.

Height: 23.5 to 27 inches

Weight: 80 to 100 pounds

Temperament: The Dogo Argentino is a reliable dog that is affectionate with friends and family but wary with strangers. It is intelligent and likes to be the center of attention. It is highly trainable and generally enjoys children.

Activity Level: Moderate

Best Owner: This breed does best with an active, dog-experienced owner in a rural or suburban home. As long as it is socialized, it does well with children.

Special Needs: Positive training, socialization, sun protection

Possible Health Concerns: Deafness, hip dysplasia, sun sensitivity

Dogue de Bordeaux

Alternative Names: French Mastiff

Country of Origin: France

Group: Guardian, UKC; Working, AKC

History: This ancient breed was developed from Roman mastiffs. The Dogue de Bordeaux is one of France's oldest dogs and was originally considered three distinct breeds: the Bordeaux, Paris, and Toulouse. It was used by butchers and vintners to protect property as well as for blood sport entertainment, fighting large animals such as bear, jaguars, and wild boar. The breed came close to extinction after the French Revolution; many were killed because it was

Dogue de Bordeaux

considered to be a dog of the wealthy. It again came close to extinction after World War I. The breed was reinvigorated in the 1960s and 1970s, and it continues to be used as a guard dog and companion today. The breed was first imported to the United States in the 1980s.

Physical Description: This is a massively built dog, longer than it is tall, heavy boned, and broad. The head is large and broad with a short muzzle and undershot jaw. It has large, brown eyes and small drop ears. The forehead is heavily wrinkled, and there is a long, tapering tail. The short, smooth coat is any shade of fawn, ranging from mahogany to Isabella, with a black or self-colored mask.

Height: 22.5 to 26.5 inches

Weight: 80 to 100 pounds

Temperament: The Dogue de Bordeaux is affectionate and friendly with family but wary with strangers and often dog aggressive. It is good with children, if well socialized.

Activity Level: Moderate

Best Owner: This breed does best in the country or suburbs with an active, dog-experienced family or individual.

Special Needs: Socialization, training

Possible Health Concerns: Bloat, breathing problems, hip dysplasia, mange, thyroid problems

Drentse Patrijshond

Alternative Names: Dutch Partridge Dog, Drent

Country of Origin: The Netherlands

Group: Gun Dog, UKC

History: This breed is believed to have been bred in the sixteenth century from a Spanish dog, the spioenen. It was used to hunt partridge in the Drenthe province, in the eastern part of the Netherlands. The breed was officially recognized in the Netherlands in 1943.

Physical Description: This is a powerful, medium-size dog that is longer than it is tall. It has a broad head with a brown nose and amber eyes. The long tail is set high and curves upward, moving in a circle when excited. The medium-length coat is longest at the ears, tail, neck, feet, and legs. The coat is white with brown, orange, or tan patches or speckles.

Height: 22 to 25 inches

Weight: 50 pounds

Temperament: The Drentse Patrijshond is an enthusiastic and hardworking dog. It is highly trainable, loyal, and obedient but quite sensitive.

Activity Level: High

Best Owner: It does best with an active owner that includes it in outdoor activities. A rural or suburban home is most appropriate.

Special Needs: Attention, exercise, grooming

Possible Health Concerns: None known

Dunker

Country of Origin: Norway

Group: Scenthound, UKC

History: The Norwegian hounds, the Hygenhund and the Dunker, were considered one breed until 1934. The Dunker was imported to Norway by hunters during the eighteenth century and was bred for hunting rabbit. It is rare outside Norway.

Physical Description: The Dunker is a medium-size, strong, and rectangular-shaped dog. It has a long head with a pronounced

Drentse Patrijshond

Dunker

occipital bone. The large eyes are dark, sometimes blue. It has wide drop ears, the neck is short, and the chest is deep. The Dunker has small paws and a long tail that is carried horizontally. The coat is short and straight, black or merle with tan and white markings.

Height: 19 to 22.5 inches

Weight: 35 to 50 pounds

Temperament: This is a good-natured and gentle dog with strong hunting instincts. It is vocal.

Best Owner: This breed does best with an active owner in a rural environment.

Special Needs: Fenced yard, leashed

Possible Health Concerns: None known

English Cocker Spaniel

Alternative Names: Cocker Spaniel (outside the United States)

Country of Origin: England

Group: Gun Dog, UKC; Sporting, AKC

History: The English Cocker Spaniel was developed to hunt woodcock. It is descended from other Field Spaniels and is one of the oldest land spaniels. Until 1892, the English Cocker Spaniel and the Springer Spaniel were differentiated only by size; it was considered the same breed as the American Cocker Spaniel until 1936, when they were designated separate breeds.

Physical Description: This is a small to medium-size, powerful dog. There is a strong, softly contoured head with oval, brown eyes and long, low ears of fine leather. The tail is docked. The medium-length, silky coat is straight or wavy. The hair on the head is short, but the ears, tail, and legs are well-feathered. The coat may be solid colored, black, liver, or shades of red, with or without tan markings, or parti-colored with white appearing in combination with black, liver, or shades of red.

Height: 15 to 17 inches

English Cocker Spaniel

Weight: 26 to 34 pounds

Temperament: The English Cocker Spaniel is friendly, lively, and enthusiastic. It is a hard worker and makes a good hunter and companion. It is devoted to its family and very social. It gets along with older children.

Activity Level: Moderate

Best Owner: It does best with an active individual or family in a suburban or rural home.

Special Needs: Attention, exercise, fenced yard, grooming, leashed, training

Possible Health Concerns: Allergies, deafness, familial nephropathy, heart disease, hip dysplasia, luxating patellas, PRA, seizures

English Foxhound

Country of Origin: Great Britain

Group: Scenthound, UKC; Hound, AKC

History: This dog was developed in Great

English Foxhound

Britain for trailing red fox. It is believed to be a cross of Bloodhound types and Greyhounds or other scenthounds. It was first imported to the United States in the mid-eighteenth century, where it was quickly embraced. The American Foxhound was developed from the English Foxhound.

Physical Description: This is a medium to large-size, muscular dog with a strong head and pronounced brow. The muzzle is long and wide. The medium-size drop ears may be cropped smaller. It has a long neck, a deep chest, and straight legs. The short, glossy coat is of any hound color, black, tan, and white in any combination, as well as the various pied colors: white mixed with badger (a mixture of white, gray, brown, and black hairs), yellow, or tan.

Height: 21 to 25 inches

Weight: 65 to 70 pounds

Temperament: This is an energetic and enthusiastic dog with a strong prey drive. It

---

Of the four setters—English, Irish, Gordon, and Irish Red and White—the English setter is the smallest and most mild mannered.

---

gets along with almost everyone, including children and other dogs.

Activity Level: High

Best Owner: This breed does best with an active owner in a rural or suburban home.

Special Needs: Exercise, fenced yard, leashed

Possible Health Concerns: None known

English Setter

Country of Origin: Great Britain

Group: Gun Dog, UKC; Sporting, AKC

History: The English Setter is at least 400 years old. The breed is descended from various spaniels and possibly the Spanish Pointer. They are bred to find and point game in open country. Dogs have been developed along two lines: one for show and one for work, with the show dog being larger and heavier than the field dog.

Physical Description: The English Setter is a large, muscular dog with medium-length drop ears, a black or dark brown nose, and

English Setter

dark brown eyes. It has a long, lean head and long tail that is straight and tapers to a fine point. The long, straight coat has feathering on the legs, ears, chest, belly, and tail. The color can be orange belton (white and orange), blue belton (white with black markings), tricolor (blue belton with tan markings), lemon belton (lemon and white), and liver belton (liver and white). Belton is characterized by light or dark ticking or roaning.

The show dog is about 25 percent larger than the field dog, has a squarer muzzle, and carries the tail lower.

Height: 24 to 25 inches (show)

Weight: 50 to 70 pounds (show)

Temperament: Although both types are good-natured, mild, and friendly dogs, the field type is more active. Both love the outdoors and get along well with almost everyone, including children. The field type is especially well suited to hunting.

Activity Level: High

Best Owner: The English Setter does best with an active owner in a rural or suburban environment.

Special Needs: Attention, exercise, fenced yard, grooming, leashed

Possible Health Concerns: Allergies, deafness, hip and elbow dysplasia, hypothyroidism

English Shepherd

Alternative Names: Farm Collie, Farm Shepherd, Old Farm Collie

Country of Origin: United States

Group: Herding, UKC

History: The English Shepherd is a descendant of British herding dogs, such as the Collie

Although English Shepherds are born herders, they are also valued for their tracking, hunting, and treeing abilities. Advertising brochures of 40 years ago touted English Shepherds as being able to tree anything, including squirrels, raccoons, and possums.

English Shepherd

and Border Collie, which were brought to the colonies with early settlers. It was bred as a herding, hunting, and guard dog.

Physical Description: This is a medium-size dog with a slightly rounded, medium-size head and a broad muzzle that is equal in length to the skull. The broad ears are drop, the eyes are brown, and the nose is black. It is deep chested with a long or a natural bob tail. The double coat may be straight or curly, and the legs and tail are feathered. The coat is black and white, black and tan, tricolor (black, white, and tan), or sable and white.

Height: 18 to 23 inches

Weight: 40 to 60 pounds

Temperament: The English Shepherd is an intelligent and energetic dog. It is fearless and alert, devoted to its owner, and highly trainable. It is a good worker and companion.

Activity Level: High

Best Owner: The English Shepherd does best with an active, dog-experienced owner in a rural or suburban home.

Special Needs: Exercise, job or activity, socialization, training

Possible Health Concerns: Hip dysplasia

English Springer Spaniel

Country of Origin: Great Britain

English Springer Spaniel

Group: Gun Dog, UKC; Sporting, AKC

History: The English Springer Spaniel is the largest of the land spaniels and is closely related to the Cocker Spaniel. It was bred to find, flush, and retrieve game. The Springer was recognized as a distinct breed in Britain in 1902. The breed was first imported to the United States in the 1920s, and it continues to be used as a hunter as well as a companion.

Physical Description: This is a medium-size, muscular, and compact dog with long drop ears; dark, oval eyes; a liver or black nose; and a long, broad head. The medium-length tail is carried horizontally. The medium-length flat or wavy coat is feathered on the ears, chest, legs, and belly. It may be liver and white; black and white; blue or liver roan; or tricolor, black and white or liver and white with tan markings. The Springer may have freckles on the muzzle and legs.

Height: 19 to 20 inches

Weight: 40 to 50 pounds

Temperament: This is an outgoing and energetic dog that is hardworking and enthusias-tic. It is easygoing and friendly and affectionate with its family. It may be too exuberant for young children.

Activity Level: High

Best Owner: The Springer Spaniel adapts well to most living situations, even fitting into apartment life with enough exercise. It is best suited to rural or suburban life.

Special Needs: Exercise, grooming, training

Possible Health Concerns: Enzyme deficiencies, hip dysplasia, temperament problems

English Toy Spaniel

Alternative Names: King Charles Spaniel

Country of Origin: Great Britain

Group: Companion, UKC; Toy, AKC

History: The progenitor of the English Toy Spaniel probably came from Japan or China, but the breed has been known in England and Scotland since the sixteenth century. Mary, Queen of Scots, is said to have had one at her side when she was beheaded. It has been bred as a companion dog more than 500 years. The English Toy Spaniel may be one of four coat colors; until the early twentieth century, each coat color was considered a different breed.

Physical Description: The English Toy Spaniel is a small, compact, solid, and

English Toy Spaniel

square dog. It has a domed head, long drop ears, and a short, upturned nose. The round, dark eyes are prominent, and the muzzle is extremely short and wrinkled. The tail is docked or naturally short or screwed. The coat is medium length and silky, straight or wavy. It comes in four colors, with each color bearing its own name: The Blenheim is white with deep chestnut red markings; the Prince Charles is black, white, and tan tricolor; the King Charles is black and tan; and the ruby is a solid chestnut red.

Height: 9 to 11 inches

Weight: 8 to 14 pounds

Temperament: This is a friendly and affectionate dog. It is eager to please, intelligent, and laidback. It is friendly toward everyone, including children and other animals.

Activity Level: Low

Best Owner: The English Toy Spaniel makes an ideal apartment dog.

Special Needs: Grooming

Possible Health Concerns: Cataracts, heart defects, luxating patellas, umbilical hernia

Entlebucher

Alternative Names: Entlebuch Mountain Dog, Entlebucher Cattle Dog, Entlebucher Sennenhund

Country of Origin: Switzerland

Group: Guardian, UKC

History: The Entlebucher is the smallest of the four Swiss dogs developed from a cross of Roman mastiffs and local Swiss working dogs. It was developed as a cattle drover, herder, and guard dog.

Physical Description: This is a medium-size, rectangular-shaped dog with a flat skull; straight, strong muzzle; and small, dark brown eyes. The medium-size drop ears are triangular, and the nose is black. There is a deep chest and natural bob tail. The

Entlebucher

smooth, short coat is tricolor, with a black base and rust and white markings.

Height: 16 to 20 inches

Weight: 55 to 65 pounds

Temperament: This dog is easygoing, friendly, intelligent, and highly trainable.

Activity Level: Moderate

Best Owner: It does best with an experienced, active owner in a rural or suburban setting.

Possible Health Concerns: Eye problems, orthopedic problems

Épagneul Bleu de Picardie

Alternative Names: Blue Picardy Spaniel

Country of Origin: France

Group: Gun Dog, UKC

History: The Epagneul Bleu de Picardie is a pointing dog that was only classified as separate from the Epagneul Picard in the early twentieth century. The distinctive color was probably developed with an infusion of blue

Épagneul Bleu de Picardie

belton English Setters and possibly Gordon Setters. The breed was recognized in 1921 and is rare, even in its homeland.

Physical Description: This is a medium-size, square-bodied dog. It has an oval-shaped head and a long muzzle; large, dark eyes; and long drop ears. The medium-length tail is straight. The coat is straight or slightly wavy, with feathering on the legs, head, and ears. It is gray speckled with black patches, giving it a blue appearance.

Height: 22 to 24 inches

Weight: No standard available

Temperament: This is an easygoing and affectionate dog that is highly trainable and intelligent. It is devoted to family and gets along with children and other animals. It enjoys the water and the outdoors.

Activity Level: High

Best Owner: It does best with an active family in a rural or suburban environment.

Special Needs: Attention, exercise

Possible Health Concerns: None known

Épagneul Picard

Alternative Names: Picardy Spaniel

Country of Origin: France

Group: Gun Dog, UKC

History: This all-around hunting dog breed was developed in the French region of Picardy. It is related to the French Spaniel and was once considered a variety of that breed before being recognized in its own right in 1909. The Picardy fell out of favor in the nineteenth century but was revitalized by French hunters in the twentieth century.

Épagneul Picard

Physical Description: This is a medium-size, strong, broad dog. It has a wide head that slopes to the muzzle and the long tail curves in and then out at the tip. The eyes and nose are brown. It has low-set drop ears. The dense, slightly wavy coat is liver roan with brown patches and tan markings. There is feathering on the tail and feet.

Height: 22 to 24.5 inches

Weight: 44 pounds

Temperament: The Picardy Spaniel is an affectionate and devoted dog. It is enthusiastic in the field and highly trainable. It does well as a hunter, companion, or both.

Activity Level: High

Best Owner: It does best with an active family in a suburban or rural home.

Special Needs: Attention, exercise

Possible Health Concerns: None known

Épagneul Pont-Audemer

Alternative Names: Pont-Audemer Spaniel

Country of Origin: France

Group: Gun Dog, UKC

History: This pointer/retriever was developed in the nineteenth century, probably from Poodles and spaniels such as the Irish Water Spaniel, Picardy Spaniel, and Barbet. It was bred to point and retrieve duck. It is very rare, even in France.

Physical Description: This is a stocky, medium-size dog with a narrow head, brown nose, amber or hazel eyes, and long drop ears that are set away from the head. The medium-long tail is docked to one-third its length and carried straight, or left natural and curved. The curly, slightly rough coat is brown or brown and gray mottled. It has a topknot.

Height: 20 to 23 inches

Weight: 40 to 53 pounds

Temperament: The breed is enthusiastic, friendly, and adaptable, both a hard worker and an easygoing companion. It enjoys children and loves to swim.

Activity Level: High

Best Owner: It does best with an active family in the suburbs or country but can adjust to city life with enough exercise and attention.

Special Needs: Attention, exercise, grooming

Possible Health Concerns: None known

Estrela Mountain Dog

Alternative Names: Cão da Serra da Estrela, Portuguese Mountain Dog

Country of Origin: Portugal

Group: Guardian, UKC

History: The Estrela Mountain Dog is an ancient breed, reputed to be the oldest breed of the Iberian Peninsula. It was developed as a livestock guardian and drafting dog. It came close to extinction in the 1970s, but Portuguese breeders worked to revitalize it, and its numbers are rising.

Estrela Mountain Dog

Physical Description: This is a large, powerful, compact dog with a strong head; long, tapering muzzle; and a dark nose with wide nostrils. The amber eyes are oval in shape and the thin, round drop ears are laid back. It has a short, thick neck and sickle-shaped tail. The short, thick coat is fawn, brindle, gray, or yellow with white or self-colored markings.

Height: 24.5 to 28.5 inches

Weight: 66 to 110 pounds

Temperament: The Estrela Mountain Dog is affectionate with family but wary with strangers. It gets along with children and most animals. Although it can be stubborn, it makes a gentle and devoted companion.

Activity Level: Moderate

Best Owner: This is an adaptable dog that does well in both suburban and rural homes with an active or sedentary family or individual.

Special Needs: Socialization, training

Possible Health Concerns: None known

Eurasian

Alternative Names: Eurasier, Wolf-Chow

Country of Origin: Germany

Group: Northern, UKC

History: The Eurasian is a modern breed created in 1960 by crossing the Chow Chow, Wolfspitz, and Samoyed. It was bred as a guard dog.

Physical Description: The Eurasian is a medium-size, well-balanced dog that is longer than it is tall. It has a wedge-

Eurasian

shaped head, tapering muzzle, and strong jaw. The dark eyes are slightly slanted, and it has medium-size, triangular prick ears that are rounded at the tips. The thick, bushy tail is carried over the back. It has a double coat, with a thick undercoat and medium length, loose guard hair. The hair is short on the muzzle, face, ears, and fronts of legs but feathered on the backs of legs. It can be any color except white or liver.

Height: 19 to 24 inches

Weight: 40 to 70 pounds

Temperament: The Eurasian is a calm, self-confident dog. It is loyal and devoted to its family but wary with strangers. It makes an excellent watchdog, as it is watchful and alert. It does not like to be left alone.

Activity Level: Moderate

Best Owner: The Eurasian requires a dog-experienced, firm owner in a suburban or rural environment.

Special Needs: Can't be left alone for long periods, daily exercise, firm training, grooming, socialization

Possible Health Concerns: Eye disease, hip dysplasia, luxating patellas, temperament

Field Spaniel

Country of Origin: Great Britain

Group: Gun Dog, UKC; Sporting, AKC

History: The Field Spaniel and the Cocker Spaniel developed side by side until the twentieth century, with Fields being the larger in a litter. Poor breeding affected the breed adversely for many years, until fanciers refocused on maintaining effectiveness in the field. The breed was first imported to the United States in the late nineteenth century but never became popular. It remains rare.

Physical Description: This is a sturdy, medium-size dog that is longer than it is tall. The head is rectangular in shape with long, wide drop ears and almond-shaped brown eyes. There is a docked or natural tail. The glossy single coat has feathering on the chest, belly, back of the legs, and underside of the tail. It may

Field Spaniel

be black, liver, golden liver, roan, with or without tan points. A small amount of white on the chest and throat is allowed.

Height: 17 to 18 inches

Weight: 35 to 50 pounds

Temperament: The Field Spaniel is a lively, fun-loving, and vocal dog. It loves the water.

Activity Level: Moderate to high

Best Owner: It does best with an active owner in a rural or suburban home.

Special Needs: Exercise, job or activity

Possible Health Concerns: Hip dysplasia, ectropion, entropion, PRA, subaortic stenosis, thyroid disease

Fila Brasileiro

Country of Origin: Brazil

Group: Guardian, UKC

History: This breed is believed to result from crosses of mastiffs, Bloodhounds, and old Spanish Bulldogs. It is said to have been bred by Spanish conquistadors to track down escaped slaves.

Physical Description: This is a powerful dog with a massive head. There is a broad, deep muzzle with pendulous lips. The nose is wide and black, and the yellow to dark chestnut eyes are medium to large and almond shaped. The drop ears are large, V shaped, and broad. There is a strong neck; deep chest; and thick, natural tail. The skin is thick and loose, especially at the neck, and the coat is short and smooth. It is any solid color, except white, or brindle. There may be a dark mask.

Height: 23.5 to 29.5 inches

Weight: 125 to 180 pounds

Temperament: This is a courageous, stoic dog that is faithful and tolerant with its family, including children, but extremely wary with those it does not know. It is said to exhibit extreme distrust, or *ojeriza*, of strangers.

Activity Level: Moderate

Best Owner: This dog requires a very dog-experienced owner in a rural environment. Its home must have secure fencing. It dislikes strangers and will display aggression toward visitors.

Special Needs: Firm but positive training, leashed, securely fenced yard, socialization, supervision at all times

Possible Health Concerns: Bloat, hip dysplasia

Finnish Hound

Alternative Names: Suomenajokoira, Finsk Stövare

Country of Origin: Finland

Group: Scenthound, UKC

History: The Finnish Hound is believed to descend from European-type hounds found in Finland in the early nineteenth century. They were crossed with other dogs, including Harriers, Hamilton Hounds, and foxhounds, to create the modern Finnish Hound by the beginning of the twentieth century. The breed is still used to hunt hare and fox.

Physical Description: The Finnish Hound is a strong, medium-size dog that is longer than

Fila Brasileiro

Finnish Hound

it is tall. It has a deep chest. The skull and muzzle are equal in length. It has a large, black nose; curved upper lip; and dark brown eyes with black eyelids. The medium-length drop ears fall in folds. It has a low, long, tapering tail. The double coat has a straight, dense outer coat in black and tan with white markings.

Height: 20 to 24 inches

Weight: 45 to 55 pounds

Temperament: The Finnish Hound is a good-natured, energetic dog. It has a strong work drive but makes a good companion, as well. It gets along with almost everyone.

Activity Level: High

Best Owner: An active individual or family in a rural or suburban environment is best for this breed.

Special Needs: Exercise, training

Possible Health Concerns: None known

Finnish Lapphund/Swedish Lapphund

Alternative Names: (Finnish) Suomen-lapinkoira, Lapinkoira (Swedish) Svensk Lapphund

Country of Origin: Finland/Sweden

Finnish Lapphund

Swedish Lapphund

Group: Northern, UKC

History: Both the Finnish and Swedish Lapphunds are old breeds with common roots that are believed to be more than 9,000 years old. Their descendants may have accompanied humans to Scandinavia. They were developed by the native people of Scandinavia, the Sami (Laplanders). The Sami use the dogs for hunting and to herd reindeer. Both breeds continue to serve in these traditional roles but are also kept as companions.

Physical Description (Finnish): The Finnish Lapphund is a medium-size dog, compact, and square shaped with typical spitz looks. It has naturally prick ears and a tapered, foxy muzzle. It is double coated with a long, dense outer coat. It may be any color as long as one color predominates. It may have markings on the face, neck, stomach, and tail.

Height: 16 to 20.5 inches

Weight: No standard available

Physical Description (Swedish): The Swedish Lapphund is a medium-size, muscular, rectangular dog. It has typical spitz looks, with a rounded skull and a tapered muzzle that is about one-third the length of its skull. It has small, triangular prick ears. The double coat has a curly, dense undercoat and a long, straight outer coat. The coat is longest around the neck, at the back of the legs, and on the tail. It may be black, brown, or bear brown. It can have white on the paws, chest, and tail tip, but more white than that is undesirable.

Height: 16 to 20 inches

Weight: No standard available

Temperament: Both breeds are intelligent, trainable, and friendly. They can be stubborn and are known for vocalizing. They enjoy the outdoors and a cool climate.

Activity Level: Moderate to high

Best Owner: They do best in active homes in the suburbs or country.

Special Needs: Exercise, grooming, socialization, training

Possible Health Concerns: Epilepsy, hip dysplasia

Finnish Spitz

Alternative Names: Suomenpystykorva, Finnish Prick-Eared Dog, Finnish Cock-Eared Dog, Finnish Barking Bird Dog

Country of Origin: Finland

Finnish Spitz

Group: Northern, UKC; Non-Sporting, AKC

History: The Finnish Spitz is the national dog of Finland, where it is used as a hunting dog primarily on a large game bird called the capercaillie. It is trained to forge ahead of the hunter until it finds the capercaillie, then follow the bird until it sets in a tree. The dog keeps the bird's attention by swaying its tail and moving back and forth; meanwhile, it barks to alert the hunter to the location. This breed continues to be used as a hunting dog in Finland but is primarily a companion elsewhere.

Physical Description: The Finnish Spitz is a medium-size, foxlike dog that is square and well balanced. It has a pointed muzzle; small, mobile, erect ears; dark, almond-shaped eyes; and a black nose. It has a deep chest and a plumed, curled tail. The dense, red-gold double coat has a ruff at the neck. It may have white markings on the tip of toes and chest.

Height: 15.5 to 20 inches

Weight: 25 to 35 pounds

Temperament: The Finnish Spitz is a lively and friendly dog loyal to its family but somewhat cautious in new situations. It is intelligent and independent. It's often described as cat-like. It enjoys the outdoors.

Activity Level: High

Best Owner: It does best with an active owner in a suburban or rural home.

Special Needs: Fenced yard, leashed, socialization, training

Possible Health Concerns: Obesity, heart problems

Flat-Coated Retriever

Country of Origin: Great Britain

Group: Gun Dog, UKC; Sporting, AKC

History: The Flat-Coated Retriever was probably developed from a cross of Saint John's Newfoundlands, setters, sheepdogs, and

Flat-Coated Retrievers

water spaniels. Although the breed was heavily promoted by fanciers in the late nineteenth century, the dog never became as popular as the Golden Retriever, allowing it to retain more of its natural working ability.

Physical Description: This is a large, athletic dog. It has a flat, broad head, small drop ears, almond-shaped brown or hazel eyes, and a brown (on liver dogs) or black (on black dogs) nose. The tail is long and straight. The flat, medium-length coat is black or liver. The ears, chest, belly, legs, and tail are well feathered.

Height: 22 to 24.5 inches

Weight: 60 to 70 pounds

Temperament: The Flat-Coated Retriever is an enthusiastic, good-natured dog. It is playful and fun loving. It is a hard worker but also makes an excellent family companion, although its exuberance can overwhelm young children.

Activity Level: High

Best Owner: It does best with an active family in a city, suburban, or rural home.

Special Needs: Attention, exercise, positive training

Possible Health Concerns: Bloat, cancer, epilepsy, glaucoma, hip dysplasia, luxating patellas, thyroid problems,

Fox Terrier (Smooth Fox Terrier/Wire Fox Terrier)

Country of Origin: Great Britain

Group: Terrier, UKC/AKC

History: Until 1984, the Smooth and the Wire Fox Terrier were considered the same breed and were commonly bred together, although they are believed to originate from different sources. Except for the coat, they are virtually indistinguishable. They were both bred to drive foxes from holes and are longer legged than most terriers. The fox terriers' ancestors include the smooth-coated Black-and-Tan Terrier, the Bull Terrier, the Greyhound, and the Beagle. The Fox Terrier was first documented in 1790.

Physical Description: The Fox Terrier is a small, strong dog with a short back and square build. The skull is flat and narrow, and the foreface gradually tapers from eyes to muzzle. The muzzle is equal in length to the skull, with a strong jaw and a black nose. The small, deep-set eyes are dark. The small, V-shaped button ears are semi-erect, with the tops folding forward. The tail is held erect. The Smooth Fox Terrier has a short, hard coat and is mostly white. The Wire Fox Terrier has a broken coat with hairs that twist and an undercoat of

Wire Fox Terrier

fine, soft hair. The hair on the face is long. Like the Smooth Fox Terrier, it is mostly white.

Height: 14 to 15.5 inches

Weight: 15 to 19 pounds

Temperament: The Fox Terrier is a friendly, alert, and intelligent dog. It is very bold and active with a tendency to dig. It is not good with small animals, which it often sees as prey. It can be too exuberant for small children.

Activity Level: High

Best Owner: The Fox Terrier does best in a rural or suburban home.

Special Needs: Exercise, fenced yard, leashed, socialization, supervision with other animals, training

Possible Health Concerns: Cushing's disease, deafness, hip dysplasia, Legg-Perthes disease, luxating patellas, skin allergies

French Bulldog

Alternative Names: Bouledogue Français

Country of Origin: France

Group: Companion, UKC; Non-Sporting, AKC

History: The French Bulldog was developed as a companion dog from the miniature Bulldogs that English lace workers brought to France with them when they emigrated in search of better jobs. The

French Bulldog

The French Bulldog is distinguished by its bat ears, but originally the breed could also have rose ears. American fanciers drove the effort to develop the bat ear we see today.

English dogs mated with local breeds and soon became popular in fashionable circles.

Physical Description: The French Bulldog is a muscular, compact, and heavily boned dog. Its head is large and square with an upturned nose and short, heavily wrinkled muzzle. The large, naturally erect, rounded ears are often described as batlike. The skin is soft and forms wrinkles at the head, neck, and shoulders. The tail is naturally short and can be straight or screw. The short, fine coat may be brindle, fawn, white, or brindle and white.

Height: 10 to 12 inches

Weight: 18 to 28 pounds

Temperament: This is an affectionate, stable, and intelligent dog that can be stubborn. It gets along with most people, including strangers, children, and other animals. It tends to be a one-person dog.

Activity Level: Low

Best Owner: This breed does well in a city or suburban home and makes a good companion for an elderly or sedentary person.

Special Needs: Protection from heatstroke, supervision around water

Possible Health Concerns: Atopy, back problems, brachycephalic syndrome, elongated soft palate, heatstroke

French Spaniel

Alternative Names: Épagneul Français

Country of Origin: France

Group: Gun Dog, UKC

History: This pointing and retrieving breed was first described in the fourteenth century by Gaston Phebus, a well-known hunter of

French Spaniel

the era. It has changed very little since then. Related to the Drentse Patrijshond and the Small Munsterlander, this dog is passionate about work. It was first imported to North America in the 1970s but remains rare outside France.

Physical Description: This is a medium-size, muscular, and elegant dog that resembles the English Setters, although the body is slightly heavier and more rectangular. It has dark amber eyes and long drop ears. The tail is natural and sabrelike. The short, dense, water-resistant coat is in white and liver. The backs of the front legs and the tail are feathered.

Height: 21 to 24 inches

Weight: 45 to 55 pounds

Temperament: It is intelligent, biddable, eager to please, hardworking, and easily trained. Friendly and calm, the breed gets along well with children and enjoys outdoor activities.

Activity Level: Moderate

Best Owner: It does best with an active family in a rural or suburban setting.

Special Needs: Attention, exercise

Possible Health Concerns: None known

German Longhaired Pointer

Alternative Names: German Longhaired Pointing Dog, Deutsch Langhaariger Vorstehhund

Country of Origin: Germany

Group: Gun Dog, UKC

History: This all-around gun dog was developed at the end of the nineteenth century by hunters who wanted a dog that was faster than the German wirehaired or shorthaired pointers. They achieved this by crossing the breed with pointers and setters from England. The breed was first exhibited at a dog show in Germany in 1879.

Physical Description: This medium-size dog is powerfully built yet elegant. The muzzle and skull are equal in length, with the top of the head being slightly rounded. There is a brown nose, dark brown eyes, and drop ears. The double coat has a dense undercoat and a close-fitting smooth or slightly wavy outer coat, which is longest at the neck, chest, and belly. The ears, legs, and tail are well feathered. The coat may be brown, brown with white or speckled markings, brown roan with brown patches of various sizes, or trout-

German Longhaired Pointer

colored roan, with numerous small brown patches on a white background and a brown head with a white blaze or star.

Height: 23 to 26 inches

Weight: 66 pounds

Temperament: This is a friendly, active, and even-tempered dog that enjoys working and is highly trainable. It loves water and is friendly with children.

Activity Level: High

Best Owner: It does well with an active family in a rural or suburban environment.

Special Needs: Exercise, grooming

Possible Health Concerns: Hip dysplasia

German Pinscher

Alternative Names: Pinscher, Standard Pinscher, Smooth-haired Pinscher

Country of Origin: Germany

Group: Terrier, UKC; Working, AKC

History: The German Pinscher is an old breed dating to the 1700s. It is a forefather of both the Doberman Pinscher and the Miniature Pinscher. It was bred to find and kill vermin, as well as to guard. The breed came close to extinction following both world wars and was rebuilt through the offspring of one dog. It continues to be used as a hunting dog today but is usually kept as a companion.

Physical Description: The German Pinscher is a medium-size, strong, square dog. It has a long, wedge-shaped head; medium-size, dark eyes; and drop ears that are cropped erect or left naturally drop. Its tail is usually docked. It is short coated and black and tan, black with rust, solid red, stag red, fawn, or blue.

Height: 17 to 20 inches

Weight: No standard available

Temperament: The German Pinscher is intelligent, assertive, fearless, and sometimes manipulative. It makes a wonderful companion but can be possessive of its owner and belongings and is territorial. It

German Pinscher

is playful and exuberant well into adult-hood. It is OK with older children.

Activity Level: High

Best Owner: A suburban or rural home is best, but it can adapt to apartment life as long as it receives sufficient exercise.

Special Needs: Exercise, firm but gentle discipline, socialization, supervision with children, training

Possible Health Concerns: Eye problems, hip dysplasia

German Shepherd Dog

Alternate Names: Alsatian, Deutscher Schaferhund

Country of Origin: Germany

Group: Herding, UKC/AKC

History: The German Shepherd Dog is descended from old farm and herding dogs. A fairly new breed, it was developed in the early part of the twentieth century for herding and police and military use. It has been used as a guide and search and rescue

Top Breeds in Canada
1. Labrador Retriever
2. Golden Retriever
3. German Shepherd Dog
4. Poodle
5. Shetland Sheepdog
6. Yorkshire Terrier
7. Miniature Schnauzer
8. Boxer
9. Shih Tzu
10. Bernese Mountain Dog
11. Beagle
12. Pomeranian
13. Bichon Frisé
14. English Springer Spaniel
15. Pug
16. Bulldog
17. Siberian Husky
18. Havanese
19. West Highland White Terrier
20. Chihuahua

Source: 2007 registrations in the Canadian Kennel Club

dog and is a popular companion in the United States and elsewhere.

Physical Description: The GSD is a large, muscular dog that is longer than it is tall. It has large prick ears; a black nose; and dark, almond-shaped eyes. The neck is long and strong and the back slopes to the tail. The tail is set low and curves up slightly. The double coat has a short, dense undercoat and a straight, full outer coat, which may be slightly wavy. There is longer hair at the neck and thighs. The coat comes in a variety of colors, but strong, rich colors are preferred, the most commonly seen being black and tan, black and red, solid black, and sables of various shades. Although whites have been produced since the breed's beginnings, this

German Shepherd Dog

color is not accepted in the show ring by some registries.

Height: 22 to 26 inches

Weight: 60 to 90 pounds

Temperament: The GSD is a self-confident, even-tempered dog. It is affectionate and playful with its friends and family but reserved with strangers, although it warms up quickly. It is intelligent and highly trainable. The GSD is good with children and most animals.

Activity Level: High

Best Owner: The GSD can adapt to city, suburban, or rural life. It does best with an active family or individual who will provide it with ample exercise.

Special Needs: Exercise, socialization, and training

Possible Health Concerns: Bloat, epilepsy, exocrine pancreatic insufficiency, hip and elbow dysplasia, panostetis

German Shorthaired Pointer

Alternative Names: Deutscher Kurzhaariger Vorstehhund

Country of Origin: Germany

Group: Gun Dog, UKC; Sporting, AKC

History: The German Shorthaired Pointer was developed in the nineteenth century from the German bird dog, a pointer-type breed probably descended from Spanish Pointers, local scenthounds, and English Pointers. The breed was first developed as an all-around dog that could point, trail at night, and retrieve on land or in water. The dog first arrived in the United States in the 1920s and quickly became popular as a hunter and companion.

Physical Description: This is a medium- to large-size, muscular, square or rectangular-shaped dog that is well-balanced and symmetrical. The square-shaped head has drop ears and a long muzzle. It has almond-

German Shorthaired Pointer

shaped, amber eyes and a brown nose. The tail is docked to about two-fifths its natural length. The double coat has a short, smooth outer coat in liver or liver and white, which can be ticked, patched, or roaned.

Height: 21 to 26 inches

Weight: 45 to 70 pounds

Temperament: The German Shorthaired Pointer is intense and enthusiastic. It is very friendly, especially with children, and hardworking. It is trainable but exuberant.

Activity Level: High

Best Owner: This breed requires an active, dog-experienced owner in a rural or suburban home. It is not suitable for apartment life.

Special Needs: Exercise, fenced yard, job or activity, leashed, training

Possible Health Concerns: Hip dysplasia

German Wirehaired Pointer

Alternative Names: Deutscher Drahthaariger Vorstehhund

Country of Origin: Germany

Group: Gun Dog, UKC; Sporting, AKC

History: The German Wirehaired Pointer was developed from the Griffon, Stichelhaar, German Shorthair, and Pudelpointer breeds. The breed works on land and water,

German Wirehaired Pointer

both pointing and retrieving. The breed has been recognized in Germany since 1870.

Physical Description: This is a medium-size, muscular dog that is nearly square in shape. It has a distinctive wiry coat and facial furnishings; brown eyes; a dark brown nose; and rounded, medium-size drop ears. The tail is docked to two-fifths its length. The wiry outer coat is weather-resistant and lies over a dense, insulating undercoat; it has a wiry beard, whiskers, and eyebrows. The coloring is liver and white, which can be spotted, roaned or ticked.

Height: 22 to 26 inches

Weight: 45 to 70 pounds

Temperament: The German Wirehaired Pointer is aloof with strangers but loyal and affectionate with family. It has a strong work and prey drive and can be sharp. It is somewhat terrier-like in looks and personality. If well socialized, it is fine with children and other dogs.

Activity Level: High

Best Owner: It requires an active owner in a rural or suburban home.

Special Needs: Attention, exercise, fenced yard, grooming, socialization, training

Possible Health Concerns: Hip dysplasia, orthopedic problems, von Willebrand's disease

Giant Schnauzer

Alternative Names: Reisenschnauzer, Munchener

Country of Origin: Germany

Group: Guardian, UKC; Working, AKC

History: The Giant Schnauzer originated in the Württemberg and Bavaria regions of Germany, where cattlemen wanted a larger version of the Standard Schnauzer to use for driving cattle. It was created by crossing Standard Schnauzers with Great Danes, rough-haired sheepdogs, and Bouviers des Flandres. It was later used as a guard dog at breweries and stockyards, as well as a police dog and, in World War I, a military dog. The breed was threatened during World War II but was revitalized by fanciers.

Physical Description: The Giant Schnauzer is a large, powerful, squarely built dog. It resembles the Standard Schnauzer except in size. It has a long, strong head, dark brown eyes, and a black nose. The ears are cropped erect or naturally button. The tail is docked

Giant Schnauzer

short and carried high. It has a wiry, dense double coat, with a beard and heavy eyebrows, which is salt and pepper or black.

Height: 23.5 to 27.5 inches

Weight: 55 to 80 pounds

Temperament: The Giant Schnauzer is a brave, even-tempered, and intelligent dog. It is alert and protective. Although it is playful and gentle with friends and family, it can react if provoked. This dog should be supervised with children and other animals.

Activity Level: Moderate

Best Owner: The Giant Schnauzer does well with an active family in a rural or suburban home.

Special Needs: Exercise, positive training, professional grooming, socialization

Possible Health Concerns: Albinism, epilepsy, eye problems, hip and elbow dysplasia, hypothyroidism, renal problems

Glen of Imaal Terrier

Country of Origin: Ireland

Group: Terrier, UKC/AKC

History: This terrier is from the Glen of Imaal in the county of Wicklow. It was bred for hunting vermin, badger, and fox and used as a turnspit dog. Celebrated in Irish literature, it has been bred for at least several hundred years but was virtually unknown outside its hometown until the late 1800s.

Glen of Imaal Terrier

The Glen of Imaal Terrier has a big, deep bark that belies its small size.

Physical Description: This is a short but powerful dog with strength and substance. It is longer than it is tall. Its head is large and strong with a powerful foreface and black nose. Its round, dark eyes are set wide apart, and its ears are rose or half prick. The short, bowed, well-boned forelegs are distinctive. It has a wide chest and muscular hindquarters, and its docked tail is carried up. It is double coated with a soft undercoat and medium-length, harsh outer coat that is blue, wheaten, or brindle.

Height: 12.5 to 14 inches

Weight: 35 pounds

Temperament: The Glen of Imaal Terrier is a hardy, stoic, and spirited dog. It is an excellent companion and worker, gentle and docile at home and courageous at work. It is intelligent, highly trainable, and generally less excitable than most terriers. It tends to dig and is territorial. It's good with cats and with children, although it may have some dog aggression.

Activity Level: Low to moderate

Best Owner: This breed adapts well to the city, suburbs, or country with an active or sedentary family or individual.

Special Needs: Socialization, training

Possible Health Concerns: Allergies, PRA

Golden Retriever

Country of Origin: Great Britain

Group: Gun Dog, UKC; Sporting, AKC

History: The Golden Retriever was developed in the late nineteenth century from a cross of Flat- and Wavy-Coated Retrievers, Tweed Water Spaniels, and Red Setters. It was bred by British aristocrats as a retriever and companion. The Golden Retriever is one of the

Golden Retriever

most popular companion dogs but is also used for a variety of work, including hunting, search and rescue, and assistance work.

Physical Description: The Golden Retriever is a medium to large-size, athletic dog. It has a broad head with small drop ears, brown eyes, and a black or brownish black nose. The double coat has a soft, dense undercoat and a thick, straight or wavy outer coat in various shades of gold. There is a ruff around the neck and feathering at the legs, chest, belly, and tail. The coat is shortest at the head, ears, paws, and front of legs.

Height: 21.5 to 24 inches

Weight: 55 to 75 pounds

The most complete history of the Golden Retriever's development is in record books kept by gamekeepers at the estate of Lord Tweedmouth at Invernesshire, Scotland. Lord Tweedmouth developed some of the early golden, or yellow, retrievers. The books date from 1835 until about 1890.

Temperament: The Golden Retriever is very outgoing, friendly, playful, and even-tempered. It gets along with almost everyone, including children and other dogs.

Activity Level: Moderate to high

Best Owner: It does best with an active family in a suburban or rural home.

Special Needs: Exercise, grooming

Possible Health Concerns: Cataracts, ectropion, entropion, heart disease, hip dysplasia, PRA, cancer

Gordon Setter

Country of Origin: Scotland

Group: Gun Dog, UKC; Sporting, AKC

History: Similar dogs are believed to have been in the British Isles as long ago as the seventeenth century. The modern Gordon Setter, however, was not created until the 1820s, when the Duke of Gordon bred it as a bird dog. This was the only gun dog developed in Scotland. First imported to the United States in 1842, it continues to be used for hunting, although most are now companions.

Physical Description: This is a medium to large-size, sturdy, muscular dog with a heavy, deep, chiseled head and long muzzle. It has dark brown eyes; a broad, black

Gordon Setter

nose; and drop ears that are set low on the head. The long tail is held horizontally. The straight or slightly wavy coat is black with tan markings. There is feathering on the tail, ears, undercarriage, and backs of legs.

Height: 23 to 27 inches

Weight: 45 to 80 pounds

Temperament: The Gordon Setter is enthusiastic, intelligent, fun-loving, loyal, and affectionate. It does well with children if it is well socialized.

Activity Level: High

Best Owner: The Gordon Setter does best with an active family in a rural or suburban home.

Special Needs: Exercise, socialization, training

Possible Health Concerns: Bloat, eye problems, hip dysplasia

Grand Anglo-Français

Alternative Names: Large English-French Hound

Country of Origin: France

Group: Scenthound, UKC

History: This French hunting dog was developed in the 1800s for large game. There are three Grand Anglo-Français breeds: the blanc et noir (white and black), the blanc et orange (white and orange), and the tricolor. They are, as the names indicate, differentiated by coat color.

Physical Description: This is a large, powerful dog with a short, broad head and square muzzle. The nose is black or orange brown, the drop ears medium in length, and the eyes large and dark brown. The tail is long. The short, straight coat is in one of three colors: white and orange, black and orange, or tricolor.

Height: 24 to 27 inches

Weight: 60 to 80 pounds

Temperament: It is an easygoing and energetic dog.

Grand Anglo-Français

Activity Level: Moderate

Best Owner: The Grand Anglo-Français does best with an active owner in a rural or suburban environment.

Special Needs: Exercise

Possible Health Concerns: None known

Grand Basset Griffon Vendéen

Country of Origin: France

Group: Scenthound, UKC

History: The Grand Basset Griffon Vendéen was developed from the Grand Griffon at the end of the nineteenth century, when fanciers were looking for a straight-legged basset to be used on small game and deer. It is an accomplished hunter on larger game, as well.

Physical Description: This is a medium-size dog that is longer than it is tall but without the

Grand Basset Griffon Vendéen

extreme proportions of most bassets. It has a long, strong head and a square muzzle that is longer than the skull. It has a black or brown nose and large, dark eyes that show no white. It has a long, muscular neck; a thick, long tail; and straight legs. The coat is medium in length and hard, with longer hair at the ears and eyebrows. It is white and black, black and tan, white and orange, or tricolor.

Height: 15 to 17 inches

Weight: No standard available

Temperament: This is an intense, fun-loving, and hardworking dog. It is very energetic and vocal. It can be a bit stubborn but is generally friendly and good-natured. It gets along well with children.

Activity Level: Moderate

Best Owner: The Grand Basset Griffon Vendéen does well with an active family in a suburban or rural home.

Special Needs: Ear cleaning, fenced yard, leashed

Possible Health Concerns: Ear infections

Grand Gascon-Saintongeois/Petit Gascon-Saintongeois

Country of Origin: France

Group: Scenthound, UKC

History: The Grand Gascon-Saintongeois was created by breeding the now-extinct Saintongeois and Grand Bleu de Gascognes in the years following the French Revolution. The Petit Gascon-Saintongeois is a reduction of the Grand Gascon-Saintongeois, which is believed to be crossed with Ariégeois and other briquet hounds.

Physical Description: The Grand Gascon-Saintongeois is a large, muscular dog. It has a long, strong head with wrinkling at the cheeks. The lips are pendulous, the eyes are deep-set and brown with visible eyelids, and the nose is black. It has long, thin, low-set ears that twist inward as they fall. It is deep chested with a long, tapered tail. The coat is short, hard, and smooth, white and black, with tan to red points. The skin corresponds with the coat color. The Petit is almost identical in appearance except for size.

Height (Grand): 23 to 27 inches

Weight (Grand): 60 to 71 pounds

Height (Petit): 18 to 22 inches

Weight (Petit): 50 to 62 pounds

Temperament: These are hardworking, enthusiastic dogs. They are good-natured and friendly toward everyone but may be somewhat reserved when they are meeting strangers. They get along well with other dogs.

Activity Level: Moderate to high

Best Owner: Both breeds do best in active, rural homes.

Special Needs: Exercise, fenced yard, job or activity, leashed

Possible Health Concerns: None known

Great Dane

Alternative Names: Deutsche Dogge

Country of Origin: Germany

Group: Guardian, UKC; Working, AKC

History: This dog breed was developed as a boar hound in the sixteenth century and is believed to be a cross of the Mastiff and the

Great Dane

Irish Wolfhound. The Great Dane was proclaimed the national breed of Germany in 1876.

Physical Description: The Great Dane is a very large, muscular, and squarely built dog with a big, rectangular head and drop ears that can be cropped erect or left natural. The dog's dark eyes are almond shaped, and its tail is long and tapered. The breed's short, smooth coat is fawn, blue, black, harlequin, brindle, or a mantle pattern (black with a white collar and chest, a white muzzle, and white on all or part of the legs).

Height: 28 to 32 inches minimum

Weight: 100 to 130 pounds

Temperament: This is a friendly and playful dog that is extremely good-natured and affectionate.

Activity Level: Moderate

Best Owner: The Great Dane does best in a rural or suburban home but can adapt to city life.

Special Needs: Fenced yard, socialization, training

Possible Health Concerns: Bloat, hip dysplasia, osteosarcoma, wobbler syndrome

Great Pyrenees

Alternative Names: Pyrenean Mountain Dog, le Chien de Montagne des Pyrenees, le Chien des Pyrenees

Country of Origin: France

Group: Guardian, UKC; Working, AKC

History: The Great Pyrenees was developed as a flock guardian in the Pyrenees Mountains. It is believed to be related to the other flock guardians from Asia and Europe, including the Akbash and Maremma sheepdogs. In the seventeenth century, it became a popular companion of French nobility. The breed was first brought to the United States in 1824.

Great Pyrenees

Dog Breeds with Reported Congenital Deafness

Congenital deafness, meaning deafness that is present at birth, may be either inherited or the direct result of toxic or viral damage to a puppy fetus. In dogs, congenital deafness is linked to white or merle-colored coats. Here we present a partial list of breeds affected by congenital deafness, although some breeds, such as the Cocker Spaniel, that were once known to have congenital deafness, suffer less commonly from the disease due to improved, more selective breeding practices.

Akita
American Staffordshire Terrier
Australian Cattle Dog
Australian Shepherd (merle)
Beagle
Border Collie
Boston Terrier
Boxer
Bulldog
Bull Terrier (white)
Collie (merle)
Dachshund (dappled coat pattern)
Dalmatian
Doberman Pinscher (Isabella/white)
Dogo Argentino
English Setter

Foxhound
Fox Terrier
Great Dane
Great Pyrenees
Louisiana Catahoula Leopard Dog
Maltese
Old English Sheepdog
Papillon
Pointer
Miniature Poodle
Rhodesian Ridgeback
Scottish Terrier
Sealyham Terrier
Shetland Sheepdog (merle)
Treeing Walker Coonhound
West Highland White Terrier

Physical Description: The Great Pyrenees is a large, powerful dog that is slightly longer than it is tall. The wedge-shaped head has almond-shaped, dark brown eyes and a black nose and lips. The ears are small, V shaped, and drop. The long, well-plumed tail is carried low or over the back. There is a profuse, medium-length coat that is white or white with badger, gray, or tan markings.

Height: 25 to 32 inches

Weight: 90 to 125 pounds

Temperament: This is a stable, loyal, and confident breed, affectionate and gentle with its family but protective and territorial. It tends to be somewhat nocturnal, resting during the day and guarding at night.

Activity Level: Moderate

The Greater Swiss Mountain Dog is naturally protective of its family and property.

Best Owner: This breed does quite well with a family that lives in a rural or suburban setting.

Special Needs: Fenced yard, leashed, training, socialization

Possible Health Concerns: Bloat, entropion, hip dysplasia, luxating patellas

Greater Swiss Mountain Dog

Alternative Names: Grosser Schweizer Sennenhund

Country of Origin: Switzerland

Group: Guardian, UKC; Working, AKC

History: The Greater Swiss Mountain Dog is believed to be the oldest of the Swiss breeds created from crosses of Roman mastiffs and local Swiss dogs. This breed may be a progenitor of the Saint Bernard. It was used as an all-purpose guard and draft dog by farmers and merchants but dwindled in numbers after the invention of the car. It served as a military dog during World War II, but following the war the breed came close to

Greater Swiss Mountain Dog

extinction. It first arrived in the United States in 1968 and has gained popularity since.

Physical Description: The Greater Swiss Mountain Dog is a large, muscular dog that is slightly longer than it is tall. It has a large head with a flat, broad skull; a broad, strong muzzle; and medium-size, triangular drop ears. The almond-shaped eyes are dark brown, and the nose is black. The tail is long and tapered. The double coat has a thick undercoat and short, dense outer coat. The coat is tricolored with a black base and white and rust markings.

Height: 23.5 to 28.5 inches

Weight: 85 to 140 pounds

Temperament: This is a faithful, devoted, and stable dog that is territorial, alert, and watchful but never aggressive.

Activity Level: Moderate

Best Owner: It does best with an active dog-experienced owner in a rural or suburban home.

Special Needs: Exercise, socialization, training

Possible Health Concerns: Bloat, epilepsy, hip and elbow dysplasia, OCD

Greenland Dog

Alternative Names: Grønlandshund

Country of Origin: Greenland/Denmark

Group: Northern, UKC

History: The Greenland Dog is believed to be one of the world's oldest breeds and is used by the indigenous people of Greenland as a sled dog and to hunt seal and polar bears.

Physical Description: It is a strong, compact, rectangular dog with a broad, arched head and a large nose. The dark eyes are slanted, and the nose is black or liver, sometimes turning pink during the winter. There is a wedge-shaped muzzle, strong jaw, and small, triangular, erect ears. The feet are large and round, and its bushy tail curls over the back. It is double coated with a thick, soft undercoat and a coarse, straight outer coat that can be any color.

Height: 22 to 25 inches

Weight: 66 to 70 pounds

Temperament: This is a strong, energetic dog, friendly to everyone, including strangers, children, and other dogs. It tends to be independent, although it will bond with at least one family member. Like many sled dogs, it has a tendency to roam

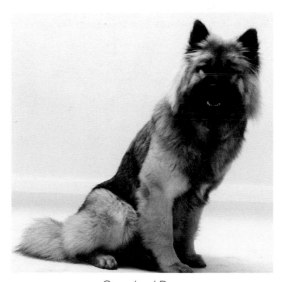

Greenland Dog

and can be difficult to train. It is not trustworthy with small animals because of its strong prey instincts.

Activity Level: High

Best Owner: It does best with an active rural family.

Special Needs: Exercise, fenced yard, grooming, job or activity, leashed, training

Possible Health Concerns: Albinism, bloat, cryptorchidism, hip dysplasia, hypothyroidism

Greyhound

Alternative Names: English Greyhound

Country of Origin: Great Britain

Group: Sighthound, UKC; Hound, AKC

History: The Greyhound is an ancient dog that has existed in its present state for almost 2,000 years. Its exact origins are unknown, but similar dogs can be traced back at least 5,000 years. The ancestor of the modern Greyhound was found in ancient Egypt and Greece. By the tenth century, it was imported to Great Britain, where it became popular among both commoners and royalty. In the eleventh century, commoners were forbidden from owning the breed; this law was reversed by Queen Elizabeth I more than 500 years later. By the eighteenth century, the breed had regained its popularity, and a number of coursing clubs were established. A greyhound-type dog is believed to have arrived in the United States in the sixteenth century with Spanish explorers. Over time, it was developed as a coursing and racing dog; commercial Greyhound racing was introduced in the 1920s. The majority of U.S. non-AKC Greyhounds are part of this controversial industry.

Physical Description: The Greyhound is a large, muscular, and sleek dog. It is powerful and built for speed, being long-limbed and narrow. It has a long, lean head and neck; deep chest; and powerful hindquarters. The small, fine ears are folded, and it has dark eyes. The long tail tapers to an upward curve. It has a short, smooth coat that may be of any color.

Weight: 60 to 70 pounds

Height: 27 to 30 inches

Temperament: The Greyhound gets along with almost everyone, including children and other dogs. It has a strong prey drive and may be untrustworthy with small animals. It is affectionate, gentle, intelligent, and playful. It is a couch potato at home and a runner in the field. Because most Greyhounds available as pets are retired racers, many need patience and training to adapt to home life.

Activity Level: Low to moderate

Best Owner: Greyhounds adapt to almost any situation, city or country, family or individual.

Special Needs: Attention, fenced yard, leashed, socialization, training

Possible Health Concerns: Anesthesia sensitivity, bloat, osteosarcoma

Greyhound

Griffon Fauve de Bretagne

Alternative Names: Fawn Brittany Griffon

Country of Origin: France

Group: Scenthound, UKC

Griffon Fauve de Bretagne

History: This is one of the oldest French scenthounds. It is believed to date to the fourteenth century and was popularly used to hunt wolves until the nineteenth century, when wolf populations declined substantially. It became rare but was revived in the late 1940s and again in the 1980s. It is an ancestor of the Basset Fauve de Bretagne.

Physical Description: This is a medium-size, bony, and muscular dog with a long head and a pronounced occipital peak. The nose is black or brown and the muzzle tapers. The lips cover the lower jaw. The eyes are dark brown, and the long, thin-leathered ears curl inward as they fall. It has a short neck and long, sickle-shaped tail. It has a rough, short coat with a slight mustache. It is fawn colored, sometimes with a small, white spot on the chest.

During the French Revolution, the ancestors of the Griffon Nivernais were severely diminished and scattered. Later, a renewed interest in this type of rough-coated rustic dog precipitated development of the modern Griffon Nivernais.

Height: 19 to 22 inches
Weight: 33 pounds
Temperament: The Griffon Fauve de Bretagne is intense and versatile in the field but easygoing and affectionate at home. It gets along with almost everyone and is outgoing and good-natured.
Activity Level: Moderate
Best Owner: This breed does well with an active owner in a rural or suburban home. Most are kept in packs in kennels but will be happy in a family home.
Special Needs: Exercise, fenced yard, leashed
Possible Health Concerns: None known

Griffon Nivernais

Country of Origin: France
Group: Scenthound, UKC
History: The Griffon Nivernais is at least several centuries old. It was developed in central France and used for hunting wild boar and other large game. It was specially developed for life in a cold climate.

Griffon Nivernais

Physical Description: The Griffon Nivernais is a large, well-boned, muscular dog with a long, rectangular body. It has a long head; long drop ears; and a large, black nose. It is deep chested with a long, saberlike tail. The thick, rough coat is dark charcoal with light charcoal and fawn markings.

Height: 21 to 23.5 inches

Weight: No standard available

Temperament: This is a courageous and hard-working dog. It is an enthusiastic hunter and is vocal and independent.

Activity Level: High

Best Owner: This breed does best with an active owner in a rural environment; it thrives in a cold climate.

Possible Health Concerns: None known

Hamiltonstövare

Alternative Names: Swedish Hound, Hamilton Hound

Country of Origin: Sweden

Group: Scenthound, UKC

History: The Hamiltonstövare was developed in the nineteenth century by Count A. P. Hamilton, founder of the Swedish Kennel Club. The breed is believed to be a mix of Harrier, foxhound, and German and Swiss hounds.

Hamiltonstövare

Physical Description: This is a medium-size dog with rectangular proportions. It has a long head; broad skull; and long, straight, rectangular muzzle. The nose is black and the lips are tight. It has dark brown eyes and medium-size drop ears. It has a deep chest and long, tapered tail. The coat is medium length, straight, and harsh. It is longest at the back of thighs and under the tail and smooth at the legs, ears, and head. The breed is tricolor, with a black, tan, and white coat.

Height: 18 to 23.5 inches

Weight: No standard available

Temperament: This is a friendly and outgoing dog that gets along with almost everyone, including children and other dogs. It is even-tempered and reliable, although it is quite active and playful. It will roam if it catches scent.

Activity Level: Moderate to high

Best Owner: The Hamiltonstövare does best with an active family in a rural or suburban home.

Special Needs: Exercise, fenced yard

Possible Health Concerns: None known

Harrier

Country of Origin: Great Britain

Group: Scenthound, UKC; Hound, AKC

History: The Harrier has been known for several centuries in its modern form and is believed to be descended from ancient scenthounds. It is used to hunt hare in packs, with the hunter on foot or horseback. In Great Britain, it is almost exclusively a hunting dog, but in North America it is found in other jobs, including companion.

Physical Description: This is a medium-size, solid, muscular dog that is slightly longer

Harrier

than it is tall. It has a square muzzle and wide nose. The eyes are brown or yellow, and the drop ears are low set and medium length. The feet turn inward. The short, smooth coat is usually tricolor in black, tan, and white, or red and white.

Height: 19 to 21 inches

Weight: 45 to 55 pounds

Temperament: The Harrier is an enthusiastic and friendly dog. It is very outgoing and gets along with almost everyone, including dogs and children. It is intelligent, independent minded, and curious.

Activity Level: Moderate to high

Best Owner: The Harrier does best with a dog-experienced, active person in a rural or suburban home.

Special Needs: Exercise, fenced yard, leashed, training

Possible Health Concerns: Epilepsy, hip dysplasia, temperament problems

Havanese

Alternative Names: Bichon Havanais, Bichon Habanero, Havana Silk Dog

Country of Origin: Cuba

Group: Companion, UKC; Toy, AKC

History: The Havanese is believed to be descended from Old World bichons, such as the Bolognese and Maltese. Interest in bichons developed throughout the port cities of the Spanish empire, including Havana. The Havanese is the bichon of Cuba and was developed sometime in the eighteenth century. It was kept as a companion by aristocracy, but it soon became popular with Cuba's middle class. The Havanese was brought to the United States with Cuban refugees who left the country after the revolution in 1959.

Physical Description: The Havanese is a small, sturdy dog that is longer than it is tall. The head is wedge shaped and slightly broad, and the skull is slightly rounded. The muzzle is equal in length to the skull. The eyes and nose are dark and the ears are drop. The plumed tail is carried over the back. The double coat has a long, soft outer coat. The hair on the forehead forms a curtain over the eyes in some dogs. In the United States, the coat may be brushed out or left to cord, hanging in tassels. Unlike

Havanese

other members of the bichon family, which are typically white, the Havanese comes in a rainbow of colors, from black, blue, and chocolate to various shades of gold as well as parti-colors (white overall with colored markings).

Height: 8 to 11 inches

Weight: 7 to 14 pounds

Temperament: The Havanese is a highly trainable, intelligent, and attentive dog. It is quiet and gentle but still playful. It is especially affectionate with its owner but is friendly with most everyone, including children, other animals, and strangers.

Activity Level: Moderate

Best Owner: This breed does well with a family in the city or suburbs.

Special Needs: Attention, grooming

Possible Health Concerns: Chondrodysplasia, deafness, hip dysplasia, juvenile cataracts, liver shunts, luxating patellas, skin conditions

Hovawart

Hovawart

Country of Origin: Germany

Group: Guardian, UKC

History: The Hovawart is an old working dog; its name comes from the Middle High German for "night watchman." The breed is believed to date to the fourteenth century but lost popularity following the medieval period. Until 1922, it was commonly mixed with German Shepherd Dog, Newfoundland, and Leonberger. It came close to extinction during World War II, but fanciers worked to revitalize the breed. It is currently used as a guard dog and a search and rescue dog, as well as a companion.

Physical Description: The Hovawart is a medium to large, powerful, rectangular-shaped dog. It has a broad head with a strong muzzle that is equal in length to the skull. It has a black or snow nose; dark to medium brown, oval eyes; and triangular, medium-length drop ears. The long, bushy tail curls over the back when the dog is active or alert but hangs down when relaxed. The double coat has a sparse undercoat and dense, long, and slightly wavy outer coat, which is black and gold, black, or blonde. Single white spots on the chest, toes, or tail tip are permissible.

Height: 23 to 28 inches

Weight: No standard available

Temperament: This is a self-confident, loyal, even-tempered dog that is gentle and affectionate with family but protective and territorial. The Hovawart is active with an independent streak.

Activity Level: High

Best Owner: It does well with an active family in a rural or suburban environment.

Special Needs: Attention, exercise, grooming, socialization, training

Possible Health Concerns: Eye problems, hip and elbow dysplasia, thyroid disorders

Ibizan Hound

Alternative Names: Podenco Ibicenco, Ca Eivissenc

Country of Origin: Spain

Group: Sighthound, UKC; Hound, AKC

History: The Ibizan Hound was considered to be an ancient breed for many years, but new research shows that it is likely a re-creation of an ancient breed. On the island of Ibiza, from which it takes its name, and the southern coast of Spain, the breed was kept by Spanish farmers and hunters and used to hunt small game, including rabbit.

Physical Description: The Ibizan Hound is a large, muscular dog with a deerlike look. It is slightly longer than it is tall, with a deep chest and a long, arched neck. It has a long, narrow head and muzzle. The nose is large and flesh colored, as are the lips. The small eyes range in color from amber to caramel.

Ibizan Hounds

The ears are large, naturally erect, and very mobile. The long tail is carried in a sickle, ring, or saber position. The Ibizan has two coat types: smooth and wirehaired. The smooth coat is hard and short, especially on the head and ears. It is longest at the rump. The wirehaired coat is 1 to 3 inches long. Colors for both coat varieties are white or red, either solid or in combination.

Height: 22.5 to 27.5 inches

Weight: 42 to 50 pounds

Temperament: The Ibizan Hound is an active, affectionate, and loyal dog. It is versatile and trainable and makes an excellent family pet. It is catlike in its fastidiousness. The Ibizan is playful with its friends and family but somewhat wary with strangers. It gets along very well with other dogs and children. It matures slowly.

Activity Level: Moderate to high

Best Owner: The Ibizan Hound does best with an active, dog-experienced owner in a suburban or rural home.

Special Needs: Exercise, fenced yard, leashed, positive training

Possible Health Concerns: Axonal dystrophy, sensitive to anesthesia and other drugs and pesticides

Iceland Dog

Alternative Names: Icelandic Sheepdog, Iceland Spitz, Friaar Dog

Country of Origin: Iceland

Group: Northern, UKC

History: The Iceland Dog is Iceland's only native breed. It is believed to have been brought to the island by Viking settlers in the late ninth or early tenth century. It was used to herd livestock and was considered a vital tool for farmers and ranchers. Although it has been on the brink of extinction several times, its numbers have increased during the past few decades.

Iceland Dog

Physical Description: The Iceland Dog is a small- to medium-size dog that is longer than it is tall, with a deep chest. It has a strong, triangular-shaped head with a muzzle that is shorter than the skull. The medium-size prick ears are triangular with slightly rounded tips. The tail is carried over its back. There is a medium-length and a longer coat type; both coats are dense and weather resistant with a thick undercoat. The coat is longest at the neck, back of legs, and the tail. It may be tan, gray, brown, or black with white markings.

Height: 16 to 20 inches

Weight: 25 to 35 pounds

Temperament: This is a gentle and cheerful dog that gets along well with people, including children. It is confident and enthusiastic in its work and playful and gentle at home.

Activity Level: Moderate to high

Best Owner: It does best with an active family in the country.

Special Needs: Exercise, grooming, job or organized activity, socialization, training

Possible Health Concerns: Hip dysplasia

Irish Setter

Country of Origin: Ireland

Group: Gun Dog, UKC; Sporting, AKC

History: The Irish setter was probably created from English Setters, spaniels, pointers, and Gordon Setters during the eighteenth century to hunt upland game birds. Both red and white and solid red dogs were produced; Irish Red and White Setters are now considered a separate breed by many registries.

Physical Description: The Irish Setter is a medium to large-size, lean dog that is slightly longer than it is tall. It has a long, lean head; almond-shaped, brown eyes; long drop ears; and a black nose. The tail tapers to a fine point. The moderately long, flat coat has silky feathering on the ears, the back of the forelegs and thighs, the tail, the belly, and the chest. It comes in a mahogany or rich chestnut red and may have white markings on the chest, toes, and throat.

Height: 25 to 27 inches

Weight: 60 to 70 pounds

Irish Setter

Temperament: The Irish Setter is very out-going, friendly, and lively. It is never hostile and gets along with children and other dogs. It is active and playful throughout its adulthood.

Activity Level: High

Best Owner: It does best with an active family in a rural or suburban home.

Special Needs: Attention, exercise, fenced yard, grooming, leashed

Possible Health Concerns: Eye problems, hip dysplasia, hypothyroidism, osteosarcoma

Irish Red and White Setter

Country of Origin: Ireland

Group: Gun Dog, UKC; Sporting, AKC

History: The Irish Red and White Setter was once recognized as the same breed as the Irish Setter and is still considered the same breed by some registries today. According to some fanciers, it may actually be older than the Irish red setter. The earliest records of the breed date to the seventeenth century, but paintings from a century earlier depict dogs that resemble the Red and White. The breed almost became extinct in the 1920s and then again in the 1970s, but it was revived by fanciers.

Physical Description: This is a medium to large-size, lean, muscular dog. It has a strong head with a long, square, tapered muzzle; round, hazel or dark brown eyes; a black or dark brown nose; and medium-length drop ears. The tail is long, carried level with or below the back. The straight, medium-length coat is silky, with feathering on the back of legs, chest and throat, feet, tail, and upper part of the ears. The coat is parti-colored, with a white base and red patches; some dogs have freckling on the face and feet.

Height: 22 to 26 inches

Weight: 40 to 70 pounds

Irish Red and White Setter

Temperament: This is a lively, friendly, and outgoing dog. It is intelligent and trainable but can be mischievous. It gets along with children if socialized.

Activity Level: High

Best Owner: It does best with an active family in a rural or suburban home.

Special Needs: Exercise, fenced yard, grooming, leashed, socialization

Possible Health Concerns: Cataracts

Irish Terrier

Alternative Names: Irish Red Terrier

Country of Origin: Ireland

Group: Terrier, UKC/AKC

History: This is probably the oldest native terrier in Ireland. Bred to work small game and to control vermin, it is also a good retriever and will retrieve from both water and land. It has been used to hunt big game, and it served as a military dog during World War I. A dog of the working class, it was only at the turn of the twentieth century that the breed was standardized.

Physical Description: This is a medium-size dog that is powerful but agile. Its head is long and the skull is flat and narrow and free of wrinkles. The skull and muzzle are equal in length, and the jaw is strong. The small, dark brown eyes are often described as fiery. It has a black nose and small, V-shaped ears that are semi-erect, folding forward. The tail is docked by about a quarter of its length and held high. It has a soft undercoat and a wiry, broken, medium-short outer coat that fits close to body. The face has a beard and whiskers. The coat can be bright red, golden red, red wheaten, or wheaten.

Height: 18 inches

Weight: 25 to 27 pounds

Temperament: This is a good-tempered, spirited dog that is affectionate and loyal to its family but fiery and courageous in the field. It is very protective, sometimes overprotective, making an excellent guard. It is somewhat difficult to train as it can be mischievous.

Activity Level: Moderate

Best Owner: This breed adapts well to the city or country. A dog-experienced owner is best.

Special Needs: Fenced yard, grooming, leashed, moderate exercise, socialization, training

Possible Health Concerns: Bladder stones

Irish Water Spaniel

Alternative Names: Rat Tail Spaniel, Rat Tails, Whip Tail

Country of Origin: Ireland

Group: Gun Dog, UKC; Sporting, AKC

History: The Irish Water Spaniel is descended from ancient water spaniels. The breed was developed in the 1850s from the South Country water spaniel and the North Country water spaniel. The Irish Water Spaniel was recognized as a distinct breed in 1859. The breed was first imported to the United States in the 1870s.

Physical Description: This is a medium-size, muscular, slightly rectangular dog. It has long drop ears, a long muzzle, and a strong head. The eyes are dark hazel. There is a smooth rat tail, a deep chest, and large,

Irish Terrier

Irish Water Spaniel

wide feet. The coat is crisp and curly or wavy. There are a few inches of curls at the bottom of the tail, and the feet are well-furnished. The coat is shortest at the face, tail, and throat, with a curly topknot at the top of the head. It may have a beard and sideburns as well. The coat is liver brown.

Height: 21 to 24 inches

Weight: 45 to 65 pounds

Temperament: The Irish Water Spaniel is active, intense, intelligent, and bold. It can be reserved and may be sharp or shy with strangers or in new situations.

Activity Level: High

Best Owner: It does best with an active owner in a rural or suburban home. It requires socialization throughout its life.

Special Needs: Exercise, grooming, socialization, training

Possible Health Concerns: Food allergies, hip and elbow dysplasia, thyroid problems, sensitive to sulfa drugs

Irish Wolfhound

Country of Origin: Ireland

Group: Sighthound, UKC; Hound, AKC

History: The original Irish Wolfhound is believed to be an ancient breed, dating from as far back as 339 B.C.E. It was first written about in Rome, when the Roman consul Quintus Aurelius received seven of these dogs as a gift. In Ireland it was used as a guardian and military dog and to hunt wolf. When wolves disappeared from Ireland in the late 1700s, so nearly did the Irish Wolfhound. It was revived by fanciers in the 1840s.

Physical Description: The Irish Wolfhound is a large, tall dog that is Greyhound-like but

The Irish Wolfhound can reach the height of 34 inches at the shoulders, making it the tallest of all dogs.

Irish Wolfhound

rough coated. It is muscular but graceful with a long head that is carried high and a long, pointed muzzle. The nose and eyes are dark, and the small ears are folded. It has a strong, long, arched neck with a deep chest, large feet, and a long, curved tail. It is double coated with a short, dense undercoat and medium-length, rough outer coat, which is especially wiry around the eyes and under the chin. It may be gray, brindle, red, black, white, or fawn.

Height: 30 to 32 inches

Weight: 105 to 120 pounds

Temperament: The Irish Wolfhound is a dignified, calm, and intelligent dog. It gets along well with people, especially children. It makes a poor guard. It is fun loving and active but calm in the home.

Activity Level: Moderate

Best Owner: This breed does best with an active family or individual in a suburban or rural home.

Special Needs: Exercise, fenced yard, grooming, training

Possible Health Concerns: Bloat, cancer, eye problems, heart disease, hip and elbow dysplasia, hypothyroidism, seizures, von Willebrand's disease

Italian Greyhound

Alternative Names: Piccolo Levriero Italiano

Country of Origin: Italy

Group: Companion, UKC; Toy, AKC

History: The Italian Greyhound is descended from dogs that are believed to have existed over 2,000 years ago, throughout Southern Europe during the Middle Ages. It became popular in Italy during the sixteenth century and in England during the seventeenth century. It was a favorite of royalty, including Catherine the Great of Russia and Princess Anne of Denmark. It has almost always been kept as a companion, although it may have originally been bred to hunt small prey. It was imported to the United States in the mid- to late-nineteenth century.

Physical Description: The Italian Greyhound is a small, slender, and finely boned dog. It is similar to the large greyhound; it is smaller and finer but with the same long, narrow head, folded ears, deep chest, and tapering, curved tail. It has a short, smooth coat that may be of any color. Brindle markings or tan points are not acceptable. Blue, fawn, red, seal, and white are the most common colors.

Height: 13 to 15 inches

Weight: 7 to 15 pounds

Temperament: The Italian Greyhound is an affectionate, playful, and somewhat needy dog. It is devoted to its owner but often aloof with strangers. It is intelligent and trainable but can be stubborn. It does well with older children.

Activity Level: Low

Best Owner: The Italian Greyhound does well with a family or individual in a city or suburban home.

Special Needs: Attention, fenced yard, leashed, socialization, protection from the cold

Possible Health Concerns: Autoimmune disease, hypothyroidism, Legg-Perthes disease, luxating patellas

Italian Greyhound

Jack Russell Terrier

Alternative Names: Parson Russell Terrier (AKC)

Country of Origin: Great Britain

Group: Terrier, UKC/AKC

History: The Jack Russell Terrier takes it name from the Reverend John Russell, who bred a strain of terriers for working fox in Devonshire, England in the mid- to late 1800s. The Jack Russell Terrier today is very much the same as the original terrier John Russell bred.

This breed has been the subject of debate among fanciers, with two breed clubs forming to promote differing philosophies. It is now called the Parson Russell Terrier by the

Jack Russell Terrier

AKC and its parent club, the Parson Russell Terrier Association of America (PRTAA), which favor the longer-legged dogs. The other breed club, the Jack Russell Terrier Club of America (JRTCA), associated with the UKC, continues to refer to the breed as the Jack Russell Terrier. The UKC also recognizes the Russell Terrier, which is a shorter, stockier dog.

Physical Description: The Jack Russell Terrier is a small to medium-size, sturdy, and muscular dog. It has a flat skull and black nose. The almond-shaped eyes are dark, and the small, V-shaped ears fold forward. It is well-balanced with a small chest and straight legs. Its short tail is carried erect. There is a short, smooth, or broken coat. There is always a minimum of 51 percent white on the body, with tan, black, and brown markings.

Height: 10 to 15 inches (PRTAA: 12 to 14 inches)

Weight: No standard available (PRTAA: 13 to 17 pounds)

Temperament: This is a very assertive, loyal, keen, and active dog with a great deal of intelligence and a strong work drive. It is often called a big dog in a small body.

Activity Level: High

Best Owner: The Jack Russell requires a terrier-experienced owner with an active, outdoor lifestyle. It does poorly in apartments and is better suited to suburban or rural life.

Special Needs: Attention, exercise, job or activity, socialization, training

Possible Health Concerns: Eye problems, deafness, Legg-Perthes disease, luxating patellas

Jagdterrier

Alternative Names: German Hunt Terrier, German Jagdterrier, Deutscher Jagdterrier

Country of Origin: Germany

Group: Terrier, UKC

History: This is a young breed that was developed at the turn of the twentieth century. It is

Jagdterrier

used as a hunting dog on a variety of game, including wild boar, badger, fox, and weasel. In North America, it has been used as a treeing dog on raccoon and squirrel. It is often hunted with hounds and used to bolt prey.

Physical Description: The Jagdterrier is a medium-size, narrow, square dog. The muzzle is shorter than the somewhat flat skull. It has a powerful muzzle and strong lower jaw. The eyes are small, dark, and deep set with a black or brown nose. The V-shaped drop ears are of medium size. It has a narrow chest and a docked tail. The coat is smooth or harsh and abundant, black, black and gray, or brown with lighter markings on the eyebrows, chest, legs, and under the tail.

Height: 13 to 16 inches

Weight: 16 to 22 pounds

Temperament: This is a clever, tough, and fearless dog with a strong work drive. Although it is affable with its family, it is wary of strangers and highly protective. Some believe that the Jagdterrier is too aggressive to be kept as anything but a working dog; others disagree.

Activity Level: High

Best Owner: This dog requires an experienced, active owner in a rural or suburban home. It does best where it can hunt.

Special Needs: Exercise, job or activity, socialization, training,

Possible Health Concerns: None known

Japanese Chin

Alternative Names: Japanese Spaniel

Country of Origin: Japan

Group: Companion, UKC; Toy, AKC

History: It is believed that the Japanese Chin originated in China and was brought to Japan as a gift from a Chinese emperor. In Japan, the breed became popular among nobility, and shoguns

Japanese Chin

bred different types, with a range of coat types and sizes. It was first seen outside Asia when the country opened to western trade in 1853, and several were brought to the United Kingdom.

Physical Description: The Japanese Chin is a small, well-balanced, square dog. It has a large, round head with large, dark eyes. It has a short, broad muzzle; a short nose with open nostrils; and small, triangular drop ears. The tail is carried over the back. It has a profuse, silky, straight, single coat that forms a ruff at the neck. The tail and thighs are heavily feathered. It comes in black and white, red and white, or black and white with tan points.

Height: 8 to 11 inches

Weight: 4 to 11 pounds

Temperament: The Japanese Chin is a sensitive, mild-mannered, and intelligent dog. It has strong likes and dislikes and an excellent memory. Some say it is cat-like in its habits. The Japanese Chin gets along with almost everyone, including strangers, other animals, and children.

Activity Level: Low

Best Owner: This breed does equally well in the city, suburbs, or country.

Special Needs: Grooming
Possible Health Concerns: Back problems, cataracts, heart problems, luxating patellas

Jindo

Country of Origin: Korea

Group: Northern, UKC

History: The Jindo is believed to have resulted from crosses between indigenous Korean dogs and dogs brought by the Mongols during the thirteenth-century invasion of Korea. Although the Korean king surrendered, part of the army withdrew to Jindo Island and brought their dogs with them. As a result of this isolation, a very pure breed resulted. The Jindo has been used as a guard and hunter of both small and large mammals. In 1938 ,the Korean government designated the Jindo a national treasure.

Physical Description: The Jindo is a sturdy medium-size dog with an octagonal-shaped head and small prick ears, which are slightly rounded at the tips. It has small, dark, almond-shaped eyes. The tail is thick and curled over the back. The Jindo has a medium-length double coat. The outer coat is harsh and straight, heavier at the neck and chest. The hairs on the cheek stand out, giving the head its peculiar shape. It may be white, fawn, gray, black and tan, or brindle. The Jindo has one of two body shapes: Tonggol (Gyupgae) or Hudu (Heutgae). The Tonggol type is very muscular and square with a deep chest. The Hudu type is more slender and longer than it is tall.

Height: 18.5 to 21 inches

Weight: 30 to 45 pounds

Temperament: The Jindo is a hard worker with a strong prey drive. Although it is wary with strangers, it is affectionate and loyal with its family. It is fastidious, even catlike. This is an intelligent and independent dog that does best with positive training. It may try to be dominant and can be aggressive toward other dogs.

Activity Level: High

Best Owner: The Jindo requires an active and dog-experienced owner in the suburbs or country.

Special Needs: Exercise, fenced yard, job or activity, leashed, positive training, socialization

Possible Health Concerns: Hip dysplasia, hypothyroidism, skin allergies, temperament problems

Kai

Alternative Names: Kai Tora-Ken, Tora (tiger), Kai-Ken

Country of Origin: Japan

Group: Northern, UKC

History: The Kai is an ancient Japanese breed that was developed as a hunting

Jindo

The Kai was once thought to be too primitive to serve as a family pet. But although Kais may be reserved with strangers, they are loyal and devoted to their families.

Kai

dog on the island of Honshu in the province of Kai. There, it was used as a hunter of deer and boar. The breed was kept pure due to its isolation. It was not recognized in Japan until 1934 and is still quite rare.

Physical Description: The Kai is a sturdy, medium-size dog that is similar looking to other Japanese spitz dogs. It has a broad, wedge-shaped head; black nose; and small, triangular, dark brown eyes. The large prick ears are triangular, and the tail curls over the back. It is double coated with a thick, soft undercoat and a harsh, straight outer coat. It can be black brindle, red brindle, or dark brindle. It sometimes has white on the legs, chest, and belly.

Height: 17.5 to 22 inches

Weight: 25 to 55 pounds

Temperament: The Kai is a courageous hunter with a strong prey drive but is gentle and devoted with its family. It's wary of strangers but not aggressive and gets along well with other dogs. It is known for its ability to climb trees.

Activity Level: High

Best Owner: The Kai requires an experienced active owner in the suburbs or country.

Special Needs: Exercise, fenced yard, leashed, socialization, training

Possible Health Concerns: None known

Kangal Dog

Country of Origin: Turkey

Group: Guardian, UKC

History: The Kangal is an ancient flock guardian from the Kangal district of the Sivas Province in Turkey. It was kept by villagers in the area but was especially associated with the large, land-holding Aga family. The Kangal is considered the national dog of Turkey and is often depicted wearing a spiked collar. It is believed to descend from early mastiffs.

Physical Description: The Kangal Dog is a large, powerful, heavy dog that is slightly longer than it is tall. The large head has a deep, blunt muzzle that is shorter than the skull. There is a distinctive furrow that runs from the skull to the muzzle. The nose is large and black and the eyes range from deep brown to amber. The medium-size drop ears are rounded and can be cropped erect or left natural; they are carried higher

Kangal Dog

when the dog is alert. The long, bushy tail curls and the feet are large. It has a double coat with a short dense outer coat that ranges in color from gray to dun, with a black mask and ears. There may be white on the feet, chest, and tail.

Height: 28 to 32 inches

Weight: 90 to 145 pounds

Temperament: The Kangal Dog is strong and courageous, affectionate with family but wary with strangers. It is naturally calm but will fight if necessary. It is intelligent and trainable.

Activity Level: High

Best Owner: The Kangal Dog does best in a rural or suburban home with the opportunity to work. Its owners should be dog-experienced and active. Children and other animals are fine as long as the dog is well socialized and interaction between them is supervised; however, most Kangals will react to provocation.

Special Needs: Exercise, fenced yard, leashed, socialization, supervision with children and other animals, training

Possible Health Concerns: Hip dysplasia

Karelian Bear Dog

Alternative Names: Karjalankarhukoira

Country of Origin: Finland

Group: Northern, UKC

History: The Karelian Bear Dog is believed to be descended from indigenous northern European dogs and was developed to hunt bear and elk, working alone rather than in packs. It is closely related to the Russo-European Laika. It is bred to harass the prey. It was nearly extinct after World War II, but the Finnish Kennel Club worked to restore the breed. Recently, the Karelian Bear Dog has been used in programs designed to deter bears from entering developed suburbs.

Karelian Bear Dog

Physical Description: The Karelian Bear Dog is medium-large and sturdy, slightly longer than it is tall. It has a large, triangular-shaped head, and its muzzle is short and thick. It has a large, black nose and small, brown eyes. The prick ears are medium sized and triangular. The tail is a natural bob or long and carried loosely over the back. It is double coated with harsh, medium-length, straight hair that is longest at the neck, back, and rump. The coat is black and white.

Height: 19.25 to 23.5 inches

Weight: No standard available

Temperament: It is often aggressive with other dogs and is not typically considered a suitable housepet.

Activity Level: High

Best Owner: The Karelian requires an experienced, active owner in a rural home.

Special Needs: Fenced yard, firm training, leashed, outdoor activities, socialization

Possible Health Concerns: None known

Keeshond

Alternative Names: Dutch Barge Dog

Country of Origin: Holland

Group: Northern, UKC; Non-Sporting, AKC

History: The Keeshond dates as far back as the sixteenth century in Holland and is believed to be a descendant of the German Wolfspitz. It was used as a watchdog on boats and farms during the seventeenth and eighteenth centuries and came to represent the Dutch Patriotic Party during the political unrest following the French Revolution. It was first imported to the United Kingdom in 1905 and to the United States in 1928, where it is a popular companion.

Physical Description: The Keeshond is a well-balanced, sturdy, medium-size dog. It has a foxy, wedge-shaped head; small, erect ears; and dark brown eyes. The plumed tail curls over the back. Its heavy coat stands out and is a mixture of silver gray, cream, and black. The coat is very thick around the neck, shoulders, rump, hind legs, and chest, forming a lionlike mane. There are distinctive spectacle-like markings around the eyes, with a line going to each ear.

Height: 17 to 18 inches

Weight: 30 to 45 pounds

Temperament: The Keeshond is a fun-loving breed with a gentle nature. It is friendly toward almost everyone, including children and other animals. It is intelligent and eager to learn, making it a highly trainable dog.

Activity Level: Moderate

Best Owner: This breed is adaptable and does well with a family in a city, suburban, or rural home.

Keeshond

Special Needs: Grooming
Possible Health Concerns: Cardiac disease, epilepsy, hip dysplasia, hypothyroidism

Kerry Blue Terrier

Country of Origin: Ireland

Group: Terrier, UKC/AKC

History: The Kerry Blue Terrier is one of three long-legged Irish Terriers. Although it was first noted in Ireland's County Kerry, for which it was named, little is known about its early history. It was first documented as a distinct breed in the late 1800s and was used to hunt small game and birds, retrieving from both land and water. It was also used to herd sheep and cattle. Later, it served as a police dog. The breed did not arrive in the United States until after World War I.

Kerry Blue Terrier

Physical Description: This is a medium-size, muscular dog that is long legged and slightly longer than it is tall. Its head is long, and it has a flat skull; the muzzle is equal in length to the skull. The nose is large and black, and the eyes are small and dark. It has V-shaped ears that are set high and folded forward. It has a deep chest and a straight tail of moderate length that is carried erect. It has a soft, dense, and wavy coat that is blue gray of any shade but with darker or black hair on the muzzle, head, ears, tail, and feet.

Height: 17.5 to 19. 5 inches

Weight: 30 to 40 pounds

Temperament: The Kerry Blue Terrier is a spirited, game, alert dog. It thrives on human companionship but is strong willed and often challenges leadership. It is fine with most dogs but has a high prey drive and shouldn't be kept with small animals.

Activity Level: High

Best Owner: This breed requires an experienced, active owner in a suburban or rural home. A fenced yard is a must. It is fine with children as long as it is socialized.

Special Needs: Exercise, fenced yard, firm training, grooming, leashed, socialization

Possible Health Concerns: Autoimmune diseases, cancer, eye problems, hip dysplasia, hypothyroidism, luxating patellas, progressive neuronal abiotrophy, skin cysts

Komondor

Country of Origin: Hungary

Group: Guardian, UKC; Working, AKC

History: The Komondor is believed to be descended from Tibetan dogs that came from Asia to Hungary with the nomadic Magyars around AD 900. It was developed as a flock guardian and continues to do this work today. It is also kept as a companion.

Komondor

Physical Description: This is a large, muscular, well-boned dog with a broad head and almond-shaped, dark brown eyes. The nose is usually black, although a dark brown or gray nose is acceptable. The drop ears are medium sized, the chest is deep, and the tail is long and curved. The double coat has a dense, woolly undercoat and heavily corded, white outer coat. The skin is gray.

Height: 25.5 to 30 inches

Weight: 80 to 120 pounds

Temperament: It is calm, alert, and protective. It is devoted to family but wary with strangers. Although it is an independent breed, it rarely roams.

Activity Level: Moderate

Best Owner: The Komondor requires a firm, dog-experienced owner in a rural home.

Special Needs: Fenced yard, grooming, leashed, socialization, training

The densely corded Komondor is the largest of the Hungarian livestock guarding dogs.

Possible Health Concerns: Bloat, hip dysplasia, skin allergies

Kooikerhondje

Alternative Names: Kooiker Dog, Dutch Decoy Spaniel, Dutch Decoy Dog

Country of Origin: The Netherlands

Group: Gun Dog, UKC

History: The Kooikerhondje is an old Dutch breed that is believed to have been developed in the sixteenth century. It was bred as a tolling dog, luring ducks into nets. The breed fell out of use as the result of a dwindling duck population and was almost extinct by the end of World War II. The Kooikerhondje was resurrected by fanciers and thrives in Holland, although the breed is still rare elsewhere in the world.

Physical Description: This is a small dog that is slightly longer than it is tall. It has a broad head with brown, almond-shaped eyes; a black nose; and long drop ears. The skull is equal in length to the muzzle. The

Kooikerhondje

double coat has a sleek, medium-length outer coat that is straight or slightly wavy, with a white base with orange-red patches and a white blaze on an orange-red face. The ears are well feathered with black tips, called earrings by fanciers. The long tail is feathered.

Height: 14 to 16 inches

Weight: 20 to 24 pounds

Temperament: The Kooikerhondje is friendly and active, although often noisy. It is devoted and affectionate with family, but it is wary of strangers. It is fine with older children.

Activity Level: Moderate to high

Best Owner: It does well with an active owner in a rural or suburban environment.

Special Needs: Positive training, socialization, supervision with children

Possible Health Concerns: Cataracts, epilepsy, hereditary necrotizing myclopathy, luxating patellas, von Willebrand's disease

Kraški Ovčar

Alternative Names: Karst Shepherd Dog, Illyrian Shepherd, Istrian Sheepdog

Country of Origin: Slovenia

Group: Guardian, UKC

History: The Kraški ovčar is a flock guardian that is believed to have followed Illyrian migration to the region that is now Slovenia. The breed was first documented in the seventeenth century but was known as the Illyrian Shepherd until 1968.

Physical Description: The Kraški Ovčar is a medium-size, muscular dog that is slightly longer than it is tall. The skull is slightly longer than the muzzle, and it has a large, black nose and almond-shaped, brown eyes. The medium-size drop ears are high set, and the chest is well developed. The medium length, bushy tail is saber shaped with a slight hook. The double coat has a

Kraški Ovčar

thick undercoat and a long, harsh outer coat that is gray with a dark mask.

Height: 22 to 24 inches

Weight: 55 to 88 pounds

Temperament: This is a playful dog that is affectionate with friends and family but wary with strangers. It can be sharp and tends to make friends slowly.

Activity Level: Moderate

Best Owner: It requires an experienced dog owner in a rural or suburban home.

Special Needs: Exercise, grooming, job or organized activity, socialization, training

Possible Health Concerns: None known

Kuvasz

Country of Origin: Hungary

Group: Guardian, UKC; Working, AKC

History: The Kuvasz is an ancient breed that is believed to have arrived in Hungary from Tibet during the thirteenth century. The breed was developed as a hunter, flock guardian, and companion and became popular with nobility. King Matthias I is said to have kept Kuvaszok (the plural of Kuvasz) as bodyguards. The breed's name means "armed guard of nobility" in Turkish and "archer" in Arabic. It continues to be used as a working dog in Hungary and elsewhere.

Physical Description: This is a large, muscular, rectangular dog. The long head has a sloping forehead and slanted dark brown eyes. The nose is large and black, and the V-shaped drop ears are small. The neck, shoulders, and hindquarters are muscular, and the chest is deep. The long tail is set low. There is a double coat with a woolly undercoat and long, coarse outer coat. It may be wavy or straight but is shorter on the ears, muzzle, lower legs, and feet. There is a ruff at the neck and feathers on the back of the legs and tail. The coat is white.

Height: 26 to 30 inches

Weight: 70 to 115 pounds

Temperament: The Kuvasz is a spirited, sensitive breed, gentle and devoted to family and wary but polite with strangers. It is intelligent and curious and can be independent.

Top 20 Breeds in the UK
1. Labrador Retriever
2. Cocker Spaniel
3. English Springer Spaniel
4. German Shepherd Dog (Alsatian)
5. Staffordshire Bull Terrier
6. Cavalier King Charles Spaniel
7. Golden Retriever
8. West Highland White Terrier
9. Boxer
10. Border Terrier
11. Rottweiler
12. Shih Tzu
13. Miniature Schnauzer
14. Lhasa Apso
15. Yorkshire Terrier
16. Bulldog
17. Dobermann
18. Bull Terrier
19. Weimaraner
20. Pug

Source: 2007 registration in The Kennel Club

Kuvasz

Usually good with children, it is protective and can misinterpret benign interactions such as rough play between friends.

Activity Level: High

Best Owner: The Kuvasz does best with an active, dog-experienced family in a rural or suburban home.

Special Needs: Exercise, fenced yard, grooming, leashed, positive training, socialization, supervision with children

Possible Health Concerns: Deafness, eye disorders, hip dysplasia and other orthopedic problems, thyroid problems, von Willebrand's disease

Labrador Retriever

Country of Origin: Newfoundland (Canada)

Group: Gun Dog, UKC; Sporting, AKC

Labrador Retrievers

History: Bred as a hunter and water retriever, the Labrador Retriever was developed from Saint John's Newfoundlands and other gun dogs in the early nineteenth century. It was a distinct breed by the mid-nineteenth century. The Lab is the most popular breed in the United States and is still used for hunting as well as for a number of other jobs, including search and rescue, detection, and service work.

Physical Description: This is a medium to large-size, muscular dog. It has a broad head with a black or brown nose (black on black and yellow Labs, brown on chocolate Labs); brown or hazel eyes; and short, triangular drop ears. The otter tail is long and thick. The double coat has a short, dense undercoat and short, straight, water-resistant outer coat in black, yellow, or chocolate. There may be a white spot on the chest.

Height: 21.5 to 24.5 inches

Weight: 55 to 80 pounds

Temperament: The Labrador Retriever is enthusiastic, social, and biddable. It is even-tempered and friendly with almost everyone, including children and other dogs. It loves the water and carrying objects in its mouth.

Activity Level: High

Best Owner: It does well with an active family in a rural or suburban environment but can adapt to city life with sufficient exercise.

Special Needs: Exercise, training

Possible Health Concerns: Arthritis, hip dysplasia, PRA

Lakeland Terrier

Country of Origin: Great Britain

Group: Terrier, UKC/AKC

History: The Lakeland Terrier is among the oldest working terrier breeds known today. It was bred in Cumberland County in the Lake District of England by farmers who hunted fox by working hounds and terriers together. The Lakeland Terrier was specifically bred for its gameness. It became known outside the area in the early 1900s. Interest in the breed decreased during World War I but was revived after the war was over.

Lakeland Terrier

Physical Description: This is a small, square, and sturdy dog with a deep, narrow body. Its skull is flat and broad, and the muzzle is strong and straight. The head is rectangular, with the length of the skull equaling the length of the muzzle. The nose is usually black but sometimes winter or liver in liver-coated dogs. The eyes are small, oval, and brown or hazel, depending on the color of the dog, and the small, V-shaped ears fold forward. The tail is docked and carried erect. It is double coated with a soft undercoat and wiry outer coat; the head is usually trimmed. The coat is blue, black, liver, wheaten, or red, with or without saddle marks.

Height: 14 to 15 inches

Weight: 15 to 17 pounds

Temperament: This is an alert, confident, bold dog. It is wary with strangers, although not aggressive, and friendly with those it knows. It tends to get along well with other dogs.

Activity Level: High

Best Owner: This breed would do well with an active individual or family, preferably in the suburbs or country. It is fine with children, other animals, and other dogs.

Special Needs: Fenced yard, grooming, leashed, socialization, training

Possible Health Concerns: Legg-Perthes disease

Large Münsterländer

Alternative Names: Grosser Münsterländer Vorstehhund

Country of Origin: Germany

Group: Gun Dog, UKC

History: The Large Münsterländer is a cross of pointers, Wachtelhunds, and Stoberhunds, all believed to be descended from the bird and hawk dogs used in the Middle Ages. The breed was developed in West Münsterland,

Large Münsterländer

Germany, and is a cousin of the Small Münsterländer and German Longhaired Pointer. It became a separate breed only in the early twentieth century and is differentiated from the German Longhaired Pointer by its black and white coloring.

Physical Description: This is a medium to large-size, muscular, and square-shaped dog. It has a long head with a black nose and dark eyes. The drop ears are broad and set high, and the tail is long. The medium-length, sleek coat is white with black patches or blue roan, with feathering on the legs, tail, and ears.

Height: 23 to 26 inches

Weight: 50 to 65 pounds

Temperament: The Large Münsterländer is active and easygoing. It is friendly with almost everyone, including children and other animals, and is highly trainable. It tends to vocalize.

Activity Level: High

Best Owner: It does best with an active family in a rural or suburban environment.

Special Needs: Exercise, grooming

Possible Health Concerns: Hip dysplasia

Leonberger

Country of Origin: Germany

Group: Guardian, UKC

History: The Leonberger is from Leonberg, Germany, where it has been bred since 1846. The breed was developed from crosses of Landseer Newfoundlands, Saint Bernards, and Great Pyrenees in an effort to produce a dog that resembled the town's lion crest. The Leonberger was

Leonberger

always a companion rather than a working dog. It almost became extinct following World War I, but the breed was revitalized by fanciers.

Physical Description: The Leonberger is a strong, powerful dog that is well proportioned, with a powerful head that is deeper than it is wide. The end of its deep muzzle is black, and it has medium-size drop ears and brown eyes. The tail is long and bushy. The double coat has a dense undercoat and a long, weather-resistant outer coat. It may be coarse or soft and is wavy, longest at the neck and chest and the tail. Color ranges from gold to reddish brown with a dark or black mask. The hair may have black tips, and there may be small, white markings on the chest and toe tips.

Height: 25.5 to 31.5 inches

Weight: 105 to 132 pounds

Temperament: Bred as a companion, the Leonberger makes an excellent family dog: affectionate, playful, and very good with children. It is protective of family and home.

Activity Level: High

Best Owner: It does best with an active family in a rural or suburban home.

After their development in the mid-nineteenth century, Leonbergers were often acquired as status symbols. Royalty who owned them included Empress Elizabeth of Austria, German Chancellor Prince Otto von Bismarck, and Italian King Umberto I.

Special Needs: Attention, grooming, socialization, training

Possible Health Concerns: Addison's disease, bloat, cancer, ectropion, entropion, hip and elbow dysplasia, hypothyroidism, OCD

Lhasa Apso

Alternative Names: Abso Seng Kye (bark lion sentinel dog)

Country of Origin: Tibet

Group: Companion, UKC; Non-Sporting, AKC

History: The Lhasa Apso is one of three companion breeds native to Tibet. Dogs of this type were known in Tibet for hundreds of years, where they gave warning of intruders at monasteries and temples. The first Lhasa Apsos came to the United States in 1933 as gifts from the Dalai Lama to an American naturalist who was visiting Tibet.

Physical Description: The Lhasa Apso is a small but hardy dog that is longer than it is tall. It has a medium-length muzzle that is about one-third the length of the head. The eyes are dark brown and the nose is black. The ears are pendant and the feet are cat-like. The tail is carried over its back and has a kink at the end. The coat, which may be

any color, is heavy, straight, and long. Abundant hair on the head falls over the eyes, and there are whiskers and a beard. There is heavy feathering on the legs, neck, and tail. The hair is parted down the middle from the nose to the tail.

Height: 10 to 11 inches

Weight: 14 to 15 pounds

Temperament: The Lhasa Apso is an intelligent and watchful dog. It is affectionate with friends but wary with strangers. It can be uncomfortable with children.

Activity Level: Low

Best Owner: This breed does well as an apartment dog.

Special Needs: Attention, grooming, socialization, training

Possible Health Concerns: Cherry eye, kidney disease, skin conditions

Louisiana Catahoula Leopard Dog

Alternative Names: Catahoula, Catahoula Cur, Catahoula Hog Dog, Catahoula Leopard Dog

Country of Origin: United States

Group: Herding, UKC

History: The exact origin of this breed is unknown; however, it is believed to be descended from crosses between Native American dogs, red wolves, and European dogs such as mastiffs and sighthounds brought to the continent by Spanish explor-

Lhasa Apso

Louisiana Catahoula Leopard Dog

ers. Some believe that Beaucerons were added to the mix by French settlers. Native Americans used the Catahoula to hunt large game; European settlers used it for hunting as well as herding livestock. The name is believed to come from a corruption of the word for the Choctaw Native American tribe.

Physical Description: The Catahoula is a medium-size, muscular, rectangular-shaped dog. It has a large, broad head with medium-size drop ears and a skull and muzzle of equal length. The muzzle is strong and slightly tapered. The eyes may be any color or combination of colors, including blue. It has a muscular neck and a long, slightly curved tail. The single coat is straight and of short to medium length, of any pattern or color, including leopard, patched, and brindle.

Height: 22 to 24 inches

Weight: 50 to 95 pounds

Temperament: Although the Catahoula is affectionate and playful with its family, it is protective and wary with strangers. It is often dog aggressive. It is very dominant and must be supervised with strangers, children, and other animals.

Activity Level: Moderate to high

Best Owner: This breed requires a firm dog-experienced owner in a rural or possibly suburban home.

Special Needs: Exercise, training, socialization, supervision

Possible Health Concerns: Eye problems, deafness, hip dysplasia

Löwchen

Alternative Names: Little Lion Dog, Lion Dog, Little Lion

Country of Origin: Germany

Group: Companion, UKC; Non-Sporting, AKC

History: The Löwchen is referred to as far back as the mid-fifteenth century. It may originally be from Germany, although some theories place its origins in the Mediterranean. It has been a distinct breed for at least four hundred years. It nearly disappeared in the nineteenth century but was resuscitated by a Belgian breeder. The name, which means "little lion," comes from its traditional lion cut. This breed has always served as a companion and is believed to have been a favorite among noblewomen during the European Renaissance.

Löwchen

Physical Description: The Löwchen is a small, square dog. It has a large, broad skull and muzzle that are equal in length. The eyes are deep set, large, and round. The eyes and nose are dark. The ears are medium sized and pendant. The tail is of medium length and carried curled over the back. The long coat is slightly wavy, dense, and soft. It is generally cut in a lion clip, shaved at the back and natural in the front. It can be of any color.

Height: 12 to 14 inches

Weight: proportionate to height

Temperament: The Löwchen is an alert and intelligent dog. This breed makes a good companion, being outgoing and affectionate. It gets along with most people, including children and other animals. It may fight dogs of the same sex.

Activity Level: Low

Best Owner: This is an adaptable dog that does fine in an apartment.

Special Needs: Grooming, socialization, and training

Possible Health Concerns: Luxating patellas

Lundehund

Alternative Names: Norsk Lundehund, Norwegian Puffin Dog, Puffin Dog

Country of Origin: Norway

Group: Northern, UKC

History: The Lundehund is believed to be an ancient dog that was originally used to hunt puffin, which nest along rocky cliff faces. It was developed specifically for this task: it is very flexible, has the ability to fold its ears tightly shut, and has six toes, which allow it to grip cliff walls. In the 1940s, a distemper epidemic destroyed most of the remaining Lundehunds, but breeders brought the breed back with the few breedable dogs that remained, some say as few as six. The breed is also able to throw out its arm at the foreshoul-

The Lundehund has the same type of jaw as the Varanger Dog, whose fossilized remains dating back 5,000 years were found in Russia. Each has one tooth fewer on either side of the jaw than other dogs have.

der joint and to turn its head upside down. It has a unique jaw that some believe can be traced to the ur dog before the Ice Age.

Physical Description: The Lundehund is a small-size dog that is longer than it is tall. It has a wedge-shaped head; slanted, brown eyes; and erect, triangular ears. It is double coated with a tail that is carried over its back or hanging. It is sable and white with a white ruff around its neck and additional white markings on the legs, belly, and face.

Height: 12.5 to 15 inches

Weight: 13.5 to 15.5 pounds

Temperament: The Lundehund is a cheerful and lively dog. It is devoted to family but wary of strangers. It gets along with most

Lundehund

dogs but is unreliable with small animals. This breed is independent and strong minded, so training can be difficult. It will sometimes revert to primitive behaviors such as hunting and eliminating in the home.

Activity Level: Moderate

Best Owner: It is adaptable but will do best in a rural or suburban home. Its owner should be financially prepared for the dog's health problems.

Special Needs: Activities, exercise, medical care, socialization, training

Possible Health Concerns: Protein-losing enteropathy (Lundehund syndrome or PLE) and gastrointestinal disease. The Lundehund is subject to a serious disease called intestinal enteropathy, which substantially reduces the life of most dogs. Up to 90 percent of Lundehunds are diagnosed with the disease, also called Lundehund syndrome.

Maltese

Country of Origin: Malta

Group: Companion, UKC; Toy, AKC

History: The Maltese is one of the many bichon breeds found in areas around the Mediterranean. It is believed to be at least 2,000 years old and was kept as a companion by nobility. Ancient authors often remarked on the beauty of the Maltese; the Greeks were so enamored with the breed that they even erected tombs for them. English travelers during the sixteenth and seventeenth centuries brought examples home with them, but the breed was not seen in the United States until the late nineteenth century.

Physical Description: The Maltese is a small dog with a compact body that is equal in height and length. It has a medium-length head with a slightly rounded skull and a firm jaw. The nose is small and black. The

At the first Westminster show in 1877, a white Maltese was listed as a Maltese lion dog. At Westminster in 1879, a colored Maltese was exhibited as a Maltese Skye terrier. The Maltese has also been called the Maltese terrier. In 1888, the American Kennel Club accepted the breed for registration as the Maltese.

eyes are dark and round, and the drop ears are set low. The long plume of a tail is carried arched over the back. The single coat is silky and flat. It hangs to either side of the body from a center part. The long hair on the head is usually tied into a topknot. It is usually pure white but may have some light tan or lemon on the ears, although this isn't desirable.

Height: 5 to 8 inches

Weight: 4 to 7 pounds

Temperament: The Maltese is a fearless dog that is trusting and gentle with friends but somewhat wary of strangers. It is affectionate and playful, although it may be prone to some anxiety.

Maltese

Activity Level: Low

Best Owner: This breed makes a good pet for a family or individual in a city or suburban home. It does well in an apartment.

Special Needs: Attention, grooming, socialization

Possible Health Concerns: Collapsing trachea, liver shunt, hypoglycemia, skin allergies, white shaker dog syndrome

Manchester Terrier

Alternative Names: English Toy Terrier

Country of Origin: Great Britain

Group: Terrier, UKC/AKC

History: The Manchester Terrier is believed to be a cross between the Whippet and Black-and-Tan Terrier. It was used in many parts of England, including Manchester, as a ratter. The Toy and the Standard varieties were considered two breeds until 1959.

Physical Description: The Manchester Terrier is a small, smooth, short-bodied, and muscular dog with the appearance of a miniature Doberman Pinscher. Its wedge-shaped head is long and narrow with a black nose and small, dark eyes that slant upward. The Toy Manchester Terrier has naturally erect and thin ears, while the Standard has naturally erect ears, cropped ears, or button ears. Its fairly short tail tapers to a point. It has a short, smooth, glossy black coat with mahogany markings on the eyebrows, muzzle, forelegs, under the tail, on the chest, and inside the ears. The toes have black pencil marks.

Height (Standard): 15 to 16 inches

Weight (Standard): 12 to 22 pounds

Height (Toy): 10 to 12 inches

Weight (Toy): under 12 pounds

Temperament: This is an alert dog that is usually less active than the typical terrier. Although it is affectionate with its family, it is wary with strangers, making it an excellent watchdog. It exhibits some typical terrier behaviors, being a digger, vocal, possessive, and untrustworthy with small animals.

Activity Level: Moderate

Best Owner: This breed adapts well to most living situations, city or country, active or sedentary.

Special Needs: Socialization, training

Possible Health Concerns: Glaucoma, skin problems, von Willebrand's disease

Maremma Sheepdog

Alternative Names: Maremmano-Abruzzese Sheepdog

Country of Origin: Italy

Group: Guardian, UKC

History: This is an ancient breed of dog, developed to protect livestock from predators, particularly wolves. Its white coat helped farmers distinguish it from these predators. It is believed to descend from dogs brought to Italy from the Middle East and continues to be used as a livestock guardian in Italy and in North and South America.

Physical Description: This is a large, heavy

Manchester Terrier

Maremma Sheepdog

dog that is longer than it is tall. It has a large, flat, wide head with a muzzle that is slightly shorter than the skull. The medium-size, almond-shaped eyes are dark; the nose is black; and the lips are black. It has natural drop ears that are set high. The long natural tail is set low. It is double coated, with a long, straight outer coat. It is shortest at the muzzle, ears, front of legs, and head. It is always white, sometimes with shades of ivory, lemon, or pale orange.

Height: 25 to 30 inches

Weight: 70 to 100 pounds

Temperament: This is a courageous, independent, and stoic dog that is extremely protective of its flock. It bonds tightly with livestock and is almost never aggressive to them. It is affectionate and gentle with family but wary with strangers. It can misinterpret benign situations.

Activity Level: Moderate

Best Owner: The Maremma does best when allowed to work as a livestock guardian. It is rarely kept as a pet.

Special Needs: Fenced yard, job or activity, leashed, ongoing socialization, training

Possible Health Concerns: Bloat, hip dysplasia, sensitivity to anesthesia

Mastiff

Alternative Names: Old English Mastiff

Country of Origin: Great Britain

Group: Guardian, UKC; Working, AKC

History: The Mastiff is an ancient dog that is believed to descend from the Tibetan Mastiff. It was developed as a guarding, fighting, and companion dog. Although its history is cloudy, the breed may have existed in Great Britain for more than 2,000 years.

Physical Description: The Mastiff is a large, powerful, heavily boned dog with a broad, rectangular-shaped head; a short muzzle; and small, V-shaped drop ears. It has a broad, dark nose and brown eyes. The chest is deep and wide, and the long tail tapers. The short, smooth coat is fawn, apricot, or brindle with fawn or apricot as the background color, with a dark mask.

Height: 27.5 to 30 inches

Weight: No standard available

Temperament: This is a patient, stoic, calm, and loyal breed. It makes an affectionate family dog.

Activity Level: Low

Mastiff

Best Owner: The Mastiff is adaptable to most living situations, equally suited to city, suburban, or country life. It may be too large for a small apartment.

Special Needs: Attention, financial ability to provide giant-size needs, socialization

Possible Health Concerns: Hip dysplasia

Miniature Bull Terrier

Country of Origin: Great Britain

Group: Terrier, UKC/AKC

History: Until 1913 there was no distinction between the Bull Terrier sizes. Like Standard Bull Terriers, the Miniature Bull Terrier was bred as a cross of Bulldogs and terriers. The Miniature worked primarily as a ratter.

Physical Description: The Miniature Bull Terrier is a small, strong, and well-muscled dog. It has a short, tight-fitting coat and the egg-shaped Bull Terrier head, with small, sunken, dark eyes; a dark nose; and small erect ears. It has a short, low-set, tapered tail. The Mini comes in a variety of colors: white, brindle and white, red and white, tricolor, and occasionally black and white.

Height: 10 to 14 inches

Weight: 25 to 35 pounds

Temperament: The Miniature Bull Terrier is extremely social and outgoing. It is a cheer-ful dog that is stable, amenable, fearless, and fun loving. It is very attached to its human companions. It does well with children and other animals if well socialized.

Activity Level: Moderate

Best Owner: This breed does well with a patient owner in a city, suburban, or rural home.

Special Needs: Attention, socialization, supervision around water, training

Possible Health Concerns: Deafness

Miniature Pinscher

Country of Origin: Germany

Group: Companion, UKC; Toy, AKC

History: The Miniature Pinscher is hundreds of years old, older than the Doberman (to which it is not related). It is believed to have been developed as a small ratter by breeding German Pinschers to Dachshunds or Italian Greyhounds. The breed was developed to its current form around 1895. Although World War I halted its development, fanciers outside of Germany took up

Miniature Bull Terrier

Miniature Pinscher

its cause after the war. It was first seen in the United States in the 1920s.

Physical Description: The Min-Pin is a small, sturdy, compact dog. Its muscular body is wedge shaped. It has a narrow, tapering head with a flat skull, which is parallel to the strong muzzle. The eyes are oval, almost black, and bright. The ears may be cropped or natural. The tail is docked and held erect. The coat is short, smooth, and straight; it comes in red, stag red (red with an intermingling of black hairs), black with rust markings, or chocolate with rust markings.

Height: 10 to 12 inches

Weight: 8 to 10 pounds

Temperament: The Miniature Pinscher is an alert dog with vigor and spirit. It is fearless and self-confident. It is wary with strangers and sometimes aggressive with other dogs. It will react to provocation.

Activity Level: Moderate to high

Best Owner: It does well with an active, patient owner in a city or suburban home.

Special Needs: Exercise, socialization, supervision with children, training

Possible Health Concerns: Cardiac problems, cervical (dry) disc, epilepsy, hip dysplasia, Legg-Perthes disease, luxating patellas, thyroid problems

Miniature Schnauzer

Country of Origin: Germany

Group: Terrier, UKC/AKC

History: The Miniature Schnauzer was developed from the Standard Schnauzer in the late nineteenth century, perhaps through the mixing of Affenpinschers and Poodles. It was used as a small farm dog, mostly as a ratter. Because it was not bred to go to ground, it has a temperament that is somewhat different from other terriers'. It is one of the few terriers not originating in Great Britain.

Physical Description: The Miniature Schnauzer is a small, sturdy, square dog that resembles the Standard Schnauzer. The head is strong and rectangular, and the muzzle is equal in length to the skull and blunt. Its eyes are small, brown, and deep set, and its ears are V shaped, small, and naturally folded, or cropped erect. The tail is docked, set high, and carried erect. It is double coated with a short undercoat and a hard, wiry outer coat, which is salt and pepper, black, or black and silver. The dog's heavy arched eyebrows, beard, and whiskers are distinctive.

Height: 12 to 14 inches

Weight: 14 to 18 pounds

Temperament: The Miniature Schnauzer is an alert, spirited, and intelligent dog. It is eager to please and loyal to its family, rarely roaming. It gets along with most people and other dogs. It is reactive to sounds and movement, so it makes a good watchdog and is not trustworthy with small prey animals. It is a one-person dog.

Activity Level: Moderate

Best Owner: The Miniature Schnauzer is adaptable to most living situations, rural, suburban, or city, active or sedentary.

Special Needs: Grooming, indoor lifestyle, socialization

Miniature Schnauzer

Possible Health Concerns: Allergies, diabetes, eye problems including cataracts and PRA, melanoma, myotonia congenita, urinary stones

Mudi

Alternative Names: Hajtókutya
Country of Origin: Hungary
Group: Herding, UKC
History: The Mudi was originally used to herd large or difficult stock but has also been used as a guard and companion. It was classified with the Pumi and the Puli until the 1930s, when it was reclassified as an individual breed. It is very rare.

Mudi

Physical Description: This is a square-shaped, medium-size dog. It has a wedge-shaped head with a tapered muzzle; narrow, dark eyes; and natural prick ears. The medium-length coat is wavy to curly. The head and legs are covered with a shorter, smoother coat. The backline slopes to the tail. It is usually black but can also be white with black patches.
Height: 14 to 20 inches
Weight: 18 to 29 pounds
Temperament: This is a courageous, versatile dog that is highly trainable. It is independent and tends to be a one-person dog. It is very active and has a strong work drive. It enjoys outdoor activities.
Activity Level: High
Best Owner: This breed does best with an active, outdoorsy owner in a rural or suburban home.
Special Needs: Exercise, socialization
Possible Health Concerns: Hip dysplasia

Mullins Feist

Country of Origin: United States
Group: Scenthound, UKC
History: The Mullins Feist was developed in the 1970s by Tennessean Jody Mullins from three Treeing Feists. It is used to tree raccoons and squirrels and to hunt boar and opossum. It is also used as a watchdog.
Physical Description: The Mullins Feist is a small to medium-size dog that is slightly longer than it is tall. It has a broad, flat head and muscular jaws, and the strong muzzle is slightly shorter than the skull. The nose is black, eyes are dark, and the drop ears are placed at the outside edges of the skull. It has a clean, muscular neck; wide, deep chest; and long legs. The hindquarters are strong and muscular, and it has round, well-arched feet. The tail is cropped, a natural bob, or naturally long and tapered with an

upward curve. The coat is short and dense and comes in yellow, yellow-red, or black, with or without white points.

Height: 14 to 18 inches

Weight: 16 to 35 pounds

Temperament: This is a courageous and bold dog that is tenacious in the field. It is good with people as long as it receives sufficient socialization. It is an intelligent, active dog with a strong working drive and does best in a home where it receives firm training, socialization, and has a job or activity.

Activity Level: High

Best Owner: One who can appreciate and enable this dog's hunting heritage; rural or working homes are best.

Special Needs: Attention, socialization, exercise

Possible Health Concerns: Allergies, luxating patellas, dental problems, demodectic mange

Neapolitan Mastiff

Alternative Names: Mastino Napoletano, Italian Mastiff

Country of Origin: Italy

Group: Guardian, UKC; Working, AKC

History: The Neapolitan Mastiff is a descendant of the ancient mastiff war dogs used in the Middle East and by the Romans. It was developed as a versatile working dog, used as a herder, flock guardian, drafting dog, hunter, guard, and companion. Despite the breed's antiquity, it has only been officially recognized since after World War II; Neapolitan Mastiffs didn't reach other parts of Europe and North America until the 1970s.

Physical Description: The Neapolitan Mastiff is a large, strong, powerful dog that is longer than it is tall. It has a massive, flat head that is covered with wrinkles, and the muzzle is wide and deep with heavy lips, causing the front of the mouth to look like an inverted V. It has deep-set eyes and a

Neapolitan Mastiff

large nose. The small, triangular-shaped drop ears are cropped erect or left natural. The thick tail is docked to about two-thirds its length. The skin is loose, especially on the head, and the coat is smooth and short. It may be gray (blue), black, mahogany, tawny, or any of these colors with brindling (stripes). There may be small, white patches on the chest or toes. The Neo has a distinctive lumbering, bearlike gait.

Height: 23.5 to 29.5 inches

Weight: 110 to 154 pounds

Temperament: This is a strong, protective dog that is loyal to family. It is calm, but it is independent minded.

Activity Level: Low

Best Owner: It does best in a rural or suburban home with a dog-experienced owner who isn't fastidious.

Special Needs: Financial ability to meet giant-size needs, protection from hot weather, socialization, supervision with children, training

Possible Health Concerns: Cherry eye, heart problems, hip dysplasia, hypothyroidism, immune system disorders, sensitivity to heat

Newfoundland

Country of Origin: Canada

Group: Guardian, UKC; Working, AKC

The Newfoundland has been called the Saint Bernard of the water; tales of its lifesaving exploits in the water abound. In 1919, one heroic Newfoundland pulled a lifeboat containing 20 shipwrecked people to safety.

History: Although the Newfoundland's history is cloudy, some believe the breed is descended from Great Pyrenees brought to Canada by fishermen. It was developed as a drafting and general working dog on the island of Newfoundland, off the coast of eastern Canada. The dogs were used to tow lines and nets and for water rescue.

Physical Description: The Newfoundland is a large, powerful dog with a broad head and muzzle, pendulous lips, and dark eyes. The ears are naturally drop, and the long tail hangs when relaxed. The thick double coat is black, brown, or gray, with or without white markings. Landseer-type Newfoundlands are white with black markings.

Newfoundland

Height: 26 to 28 inches

Weight: 100 to 150 pounds

Temperament: The Newfoundland is a gentle dog that is excellent with children. It loves the water and is known for attempting to rescue swimmers, whether or not they are in trouble.

Activity Level: Moderate

Best Owner: The Newfoundland does best in a rural or suburban home with an easy-going owner who is not fastidious.

Special Needs: Financial ability to meet giant-size needs, grooming, supervision around water so they don't inadvertently hurt swimmers, training

Possible Health Concerns: Skin allergies, hip and elbow dysplasia, hypothyroidism

New Guinea Singing Dog

Alternative Names: *Canis Hallstromi*, Singer, Hallstrom's Dog

Country of Origin: New Guinea

Group: Pariah, UKC

History: The New Guinea Singing Dog is an ancient wild dog from New Guinea. It was traditionally used as a hunting dog by native New Guineans. Some experts believe that the breed is actually a separate species from other domestic dogs. It is probably most similar to the Australian dingo. It was first exported from New Guinea in the mid-twentieth century, when several were brought to an Australian zoo; until 1989, the only Singing Dogs outside New Guinea were confined to zoos. Although this breed is rare both in and out of captivity, it is becoming somewhat better known in the United States.

Physical Description: The New Guinea Singing Dog is a medium-size, solid dog. It has a wedge-shaped head with wide cheekbones and a tapering muzzle. It has small prick ears that face away from one another

New Guinea Singing Dog

and triangular, brown eyes. The tail is brushlike and the round feet turn out. It has a double coat with a thick undercoat during the winter and a thick, straight outer coat that is red sable with white markings on the face, chest, feet, and tail tip. It is occasionally black and tan.

Height: 14 to 18 inches

Weight: 17 to 30 pounds

Temperament: The New Guinea Singing Dog is an intelligent, independent-minded dog that is friendly and gentle with people as long as it is well socialized. It has a high prey drive and may be dog aggressive. It is often described as catlike in its mannerisms and personality. It is inquisitive and tends to roam. A sensitive breed, it responds poorly to anger or harsh punishment. It howls rather than barks.

Activity Level: Moderate

Best Owner: This is an adaptable dog and does well with a dog-experienced owner in a city, suburban, or rural home.

Special Needs: Attention, job or activity, leashed, securely fenced yard

Possible Health Concerns: Monorchidism

Norfolk Terrier

Country of Origin: Great Britain

Group: Terrier, UKC/AKC

History: The Norfolk Terrier was not recognized as a separate breed from the Norwich Terrier until 1964. The main difference between the two is that the Norfolk has a drop ear and the Norwich a prick ear. It is one of the smallest of the working terriers and was originally bred in the nineteenth century to control rats and hunt foxes.

Physical Description: This is a small dog with substance and bone. Its head is wide and slightly rounded with a strong, wedge-shaped muzzle. The small, dark, oval eyes are placed well apart. It has small drop ears that are V shaped and slightly rounded at the tips. The chest is moderately wide and deep and the legs are short and strong. The tail is docked

Norfolk Terriers

and held erect. The double coat has a soft undercoat and a hard, wiry outer coat that is 1.5 to 2 inches long. There is a ruff at the neck, slight eyebrows, and whiskers. The coat comes in red, wheaten, black and tan, and grizzle, sometimes with dark points.

Height: 9 to 10 inches

Weight: 11 to 12 pounds

Temperament: The Norfolk Terrier is a good natured, friendly, and affectionate dog. It is fearless and game in the field but loyal and trainable with its owner. It is fine with children and cats as long as it is socialized, but the Norfolk is not trustworthy with small prey animals.

Activity Level: Moderate

Best Owner: This breed is adaptable to most living situations, city or country, active or sedentary.

Special Needs: Activity, exercise, fenced yard, grooming, leashed, socialization, training

Possible Health Concerns: Mitral valve disease and other cardiac problems, skin problems

Norwegian Buhund

Alternative Names: Norsk Buhund

Country of Origin: Norway

Group: Northern UKC; Herding, AKC

History: A Norwegian Buhund–like dog is believed to have been in existence since the Middle Ages, used as an all-purpose farm dog, both guarding and herding. When sheep farming became common on the west coast of Norway at the turn of the twentieth century, the best specimens of the old farm spitz farm dogs were collected, and a breeding program was created in order to breed the best herding dog possible. The Norwegian Buhund was the result.

Physical Description: The Norwegian Buhund is a medium-size, squarely built, deep-chested dog. The head is wedge shaped

Norwegian Buhund

with large prick ears and dark eyes and nose. Like most spitz, it has a foxy look. There is a double coat with a thick, soft undercoat and short, harsh outer coat. It is wheaten colored, with or without black tips, or black with minimal bronzing. Some may have a white blaze or spot on the chest or a white collar. A mask is permitted.

Height: 16 to 18.5 inches

Weight: 28 to 38 pounds

Temperament: The Buhund is a lively, agile, sometimes noisy dog. It is very intelligent with a strong work drive. This breed enjoys cool climates.

Activity level: Moderate to high

Best Owner: It does best with an active family in the country or suburbs.

Norwegian Elkhounds

Special Needs: Exercise, job or activity, training

Possible Health Concerns: Cataracts, epilepsy, hip dysplasia

Norwegian Elkhound

Alternative Names: Norsk Elghund Grå, Norsk Elghund Sort

Country of Origin: Norway

Group: Northern, UKC; Hound, AKC

History: The Norwegian Elkhound is believed to be an ancient breed, in existence since the Vikings. It was originally a hunter of large game, especially moose and bear. It was first brought to the United Kingdom after World War I and to the United States in 1928.

Physical Description: The Norwegian Elkhound is a medium-size, squarely built dog. It has a broad, wedge-shaped head with dark brown eyes; small, prick ears; and a foxy face. The tail is tightly curled over the back. It is double coated with a thick, coarse outer coat in gray, silver, and black, with a black saddle.

Height: 19.5 to 20.5 inches

Weight: 45 to 55 pounds

Temperament: A loyal and friendly dog, it can be independent and stubborn, too. It is bold, courageous, and alert, a good watchdog. It gets along well with older children.

Activity Level: Moderate

Best Owner: The Elkhound does best with an active individual or family in the suburbs or country.

Special Needs: Exercise, grooming

Possible Health Concerns: Hypothyroidism, PRA, renal problems, sebaceous cysts

Norwich Terrier

Country of Origin: Great Britain

Group: Terrier, UKC/AKC

History: This was considered to be the same breed as the Norfolk Terrier until 1964,

Norwich Terrier

with the main difference between the two being the Norwich Terrier's prick ears. From East Anglia, England, the Norwich was developed in the 1880s as a small ratting terrier.

Physical Description: It is very similar to the Norfolk but different in its prick ears and foxy expression.

Temperament: Like the Norfolk, it is game but affectionate, alert, and agreeable.

Activity Level: Moderate

Best Owner: This breed is adapts well to most living situations.

Special Needs: Exercise, fenced yard, grooming, leashed, socialization, training,

Possible Health Concerns: Eye conditions, heart disease, hip dysplasia

Nova Scotia Duck Tolling Retriever

Alternative Names: Little River Duck Dog, Yarmouth Toller, Duck Toller

Country of Origin: Canada

Group: Gun Dog, UKC; Sporting, AKC

History: The Toller was developed in Yarmouth County, Nova Scotia, in the early nineteenth century. Although the history is cloudy, the breed is believed to descend from the red decoy dogs brought with early European settlers. These dogs are believed to have been crossed with spaniels, retrievers, setters, and Collies to develop the Duck Toller. This is a multipurpose water retriever, guard, companion, and decoy dog. The breed has recently gained popularity outside of Canada.

Physical Description: This is a medium-size, compact, and muscular dog. It has a broad skull and short muzzle. The almond-shaped eyes blend with the coat, the broad nose is black or complements the coat, and the medium-length drop ears are set high. The

Nova Scotia Duck Tolling Retriever

tail is long. The double coat is red with lighter feathering underneath the tail, as well as white markings on the feet, chest, blaze, and tip of tail. It has a soft undercoat; medium-length, soft outer coat; and whiskers on the face.

Height: 18 to 21 inches

Weight: 37 to 51 pounds

Temperament: The Toller is outgoing, playful, and alert. It is intelligent, biddable, and friendly toward almost everyone, including children. It may be reserved in new situations.

Activity Level: High

Best Owner: It does best with an active owner in a rural or suburban home.

Special Needs: Attention, exercise, socialization, training

Possible Health Concerns: Eye problems, hip dysplasia

Old Danish Pointing Dog

Alternative Names: Gammel Dansk Hønsehond, Old Danish Bird Dog, Gamle Danske Hønsehund

Country of Origin: Denmark

Group: Gun Dog, UKC

History: The Old Danish Pointing Dog is believed to be a descendant of crosses between Italian and Spanish pointers and local Bloodhound-type farm dogs in Glenstrup, Denmark. The breed is traced back to the seventeenth century; the dogs were originally used as retrievers but also point and set. Today, they are used as hunting dogs and companions, and they are also trained for bomb detection. The breed continues to be popular in its native country.

Physical Description: This is a strong, medium-size, rectangular-shaped dog. It has a broad, domed skull, and a wide muzzle. The fleshy nose ranges from light to dark liver and the medium-size eyes are dark brown. The low-set, broad drop ears are rounded at the ends. The long, tapered tail droops, and the skin is loose fitting on the head. The short, hard coat is white with brown markings.

Height: 19 to 23 inches

Weight: 40 to 55 pounds

Temperament: This breed is active, easygoing, gentle, and affectionate with family. In the field, it is brave and tenacious.

Activity Level: High

Best Owner: This breed does best with an active individual or family in a rural or suburban environment.

Special Needs: Ear cleaning, exercise, and grooming

Possible Health Concerns: Ear problems, ectropion, entropion

The popularity of Old English Sheepdogs swelled in the 1950s, 1960s, and 1970s, following the release of movies such as *The Shaggy Dog* and *Please Don't Eat the Daisies*, which featured the breed. But once people realized that the Old English had high grooming and exercise needs, interest in the breed declined.

Old English Sheepdog

Alternative Names: Bobtail

Country of Origin: Great Britain

Group: Herding, UKC/AKC

History: The Old English Sheepdog was developed in the late nineteenth century as a herder and drover as well as a livestock guardian. It is believed to descend from the Bearded Collie and Russian Ovcharkas. The tail was originally docked to exempt the breed from the tax levied on dogs kept as companions rather than as workers.

Physical Description: This is a large, strong, compact dog with square proportions. It is taller at the loins than the withers. It has a square-shaped head with a muzzle and skull that are equal in length. The eyes are brown or blue, or one of each, and the medium-size ears are drop. It has a black nose. The tail is a natural bob or docked. The long, hard, profuse coat is gray and white with facial hair that covers its eyes.

Old English Sheepdog

Height: 21 inches and up

Weight: 60 to 100 pounds

Temperament: The Old English Sheepdog is a spirited, active dog that is friendly with almost everyone. It is highly intelligent, adapts easily, and is good with children and other animals. This breed makes an excellent house dog but does shed heavily.

Activity Level: Moderate

Best Owner: It does well with an active family in a rural or suburban home.

Special Needs: Attention, grooming

Possible Health Concerns: Ataxia, autoimmune disorders, epilepsy, eye problems, hip dysplasia, OCD

Otterhound

Country of Origin: Great Britain

Group: Scenthound, UKC; Hound, AKC

History: This breed is believed to descend from dogs that date to the fourteenth century and is probably related to the Bloodhound. It was originally developed for

Otterhound

hunting otter, although this practice is now illegal. It was first imported to the United States in 1900.

Physical Description: This is a large, powerful, straight-limbed dog. It has a large, narrow head. The muzzle and skull are approximately the same length, and the nose is broad. It has dark, deep-set eyes and long drop ears that fold as they fall. It has a deep chest and long, high-set, tapered tail. The feet are large, well knuckled, and webbed. It has a double coat with a woolly, oily undercoat; a medium-length, rough, broken outer coat; and a mustache and beard. It may be any hound color or combination of colors, including solid-colored grizzle, sand, red, wheaten, or blue, with or without white markings.

Height: 23 to 27 inches

Weight: 80 to 115 pounds

Temperament: This is a good-natured, active, boisterous, and enthusiastic dog. It gets along with almost everyone, including children and other dogs. It is vocal and may roam.

Activity Level: High

Best Owner: This breed does very well with an active family in a rural or suburban home.

Special Needs: Exercise, fenced yard, grooming, leashed

Possible Health Concerns: Bloat, bleeding disorders, hip dysplasia, seizures

Owczarek Podhalanski

Alternative Names: Polish Tatra Sheepdog, Polish Mountain Dog

Country of Origin: Poland

Group: Guardian, UKC

Owczarek Podhalanski

History: The Owczarek Podhalanski is from the region of Podhale in the Tatra Range of the Carpathian Mountains, located in southern Poland. The breed was developed as a flock guardian, drafting dog, herding dog, military and police dog, and personal guard and companion. It came close to extinction following World War II. Although the Owczarek Podhalanski was revitalized, it continues to be rare.

Physical Description: This is a large, powerful, and rectangular-shaped dog. The lean head has a slightly domed skull that is shorter than the broad, tapered muzzle. The dark brown eyes are slightly slanted. The nose is black and the triangular drop ears are medium sized. The feet are large and the long tail is held low. The double coat has a thick undercoat and a long, rough, straight or wavy, white outer coat. The coat is shorter on the head, muzzle, and the front of the legs and is longer on the neck and chest, tail, thighs, and feet.

Height: 23.5 to 27.5 inches

Weight: 100 to 150 pounds

Temperament: This is a calm, sober dog that is affectionate with its family but wary with strangers. It may react when provoked and is both intelligent and independent minded. It is especially alert at night.

Activity Level: Moderate

Best Owner: It does best in a northern climate with a dog-experienced owner. Suburban or rural life suits it well.

Special Needs: Fenced yard, grooming leashed, socialization, training

Possible Health Concerns: Allergies, bloat, cataracts, epilepsy, hip dysplasia

Papillon

Alternative Names: Continental Toy Spaniel, Épagneul Nain (dwarf spaniel), Phalene (drop ear version)

Country of Origin: France/Belgium

Group: Companion, UKC; Toy, AKC

History: The Papillon probably originated in Western Europe as a bred-down version of larger spaniels. Its type is believed to date to at least 1500. The Papillon was

Papillon

popular with noblewomen. Madame Pompadour and Marie Antoinette both had pet Papillons.

Physical Description: The Papillon is a small, fine-boned dog. It is slightly longer than it is tall. Its head is small with a thin, tapered muzzle, which is about a third of the length of the head. The nose is small and black and the eyes are round and dark. The large ears are naturally erect, resembling the spread wings of a butterfly, from which the breed takes its name, and are well fringed. Except for their drooping position, the ears of the Phalene are similar. The Papillon has thin, harelike feet. Its long, plumed tail is carried arched over the back. It is single coated, with long, silky, straight hair. The backs of the forelegs are feathered, and the chest has a profuse frill. It is parti-colored but the nose, eye rims, and lips are always black.

Height: 8 to 11 inches

Weight: 3 to 9 pounds

Temperament: The Papillon is an alert dog that is friendly toward almost everyone, including children and other animals.

Activity Level: Moderate to high

Best Owner: It does well in most environments but makes an especially good pet for an apartment dweller or a person who enjoys dog sports but must have a small dog.

Special Needs: Grooming, socialization

Possible Health Concerns: Liver shunt, luxating patellas, PRA

Patterdale Terrier

Alternative Names: Black Fell Terrier

Country of Origin: Great Britain

Group: Terrier, UKC

History: The Patterdale Terrier was developed in the 1920s to hunt fox and badger in the Patterdale region of the Lake District in England. It was bred from a cross of Lakeland terriers and small Staffordshire

Patterdale Terrier

Bull Terriers. Originally, it was considered a type of terrier rather than a distinct breed, and emphasis was placed on its value as a working dog.

Physical Description: The Patterdale Terrier is a small, muscular, and compact dog. It has a strong head and muzzle and ears that fold forward. The tail is docked to one-fourth its length and set high. It has a smooth or broken coat in black, red, liver, grizzle, bronze, and black and tan. Some white on the chest and feet is acceptable.

Height: 10 to 13 inches

Weight: 10 to 17 pounds

Temperament: The Patterdale Terrier is tractable and even tempered. It is a hard-working, confident dog and is not dog aggressive. It enjoys outdoor activities.

Activity Level: Moderate to high

Best Owner: This breed does best in a rural home with an active, outdoorsy person but can adapt to the suburbs or city if given adequate exercise.

Pekingese

Alternative Names: Lion Dog, Sun Dog, Sleeve Dog

Country of Origin: China

Group: Companion, UKC; Toy, AKC

History: Pekingese-type dogs have been known in China since the Tang Dynasty in the eighth century. Its ownership was limited to nobility; the theft of a Pekingese was punishable by death. It was known by three names: lion dog (for its heavy mane), sun dog (for its golden red color), and sleeve dog (for its tiny size, allowing it to be carried inside an owner's deep sleeve). It was first introduced to the Western world in 1860, when the Imperial Palace was looted by the British, and five of the dogs were stolen and taken to England, where one was given to Queen Victoria. The breed first came to the United States in the early twentieth century.

Physical Description: The Pekingese is a small, stocky dog with a heavy front and light rear, giving it a lionlike appearance. Its head is broad and the wrinkled muzzle is very short

Pekingese

Use this memory device to remember the difference between the Pembroke and the Cardigan Welsh Corgis. The Pembroke has a "broke" tail; the Cardigan has a long tail like the sleeves of a cardigan sweater.

and broad, with a strong jaw. The nose is short, flat, and black. The round eyes are large, prominent, and dark. The drop ears are heart shaped. It has a very short neck; flat feet that are often turned outward; and short, bowed legs. The tail is set high and curled over the back. It is double coated with a thick undercoat and a long, flat, soft outer coat. It has long feathers on its thighs, legs, tail, toes, and ears and a profuse mane. It can be any color, including red, fawn, black, black and tan, or white. It often has a spectacle-like mask on its face.

Height: 8 to 9 inches

Weight: 8 to 14 pounds

Temperament: The Pekingese is an independent and regal dog that is dignified and stubborn. It is not always friendly with children or with other dogs, but it is good tempered and playful with those it's familiar with. Its stubbornness makes it somewhat difficult to train.

Activity Level: Low

Best Owner: This breed does well in an apartment with adults and older children.

Special Needs: Grooming, protection from heat, socialization, supervision with small children, training

Possible Health Concerns: Anesthesia and heat sensitivity, brachycephalic syndrome, corneal ulceration, intervertebral disk disease, stenotic nares, umbilical hernia

Pembroke Welsh Corgi

Country of Origin: Wales

Group: Herding, UKC/AKC

History: The Pembroke was developed in Pembrokeshire, Wales, as an all-purpose

Pembroke Welsh Corgi

farm dog that herded cattle and drove geese. It is believed to descend from spitz-type ancestors brought to Wales by Flemish weavers. It is rarely used as a herding dog today. It is closely related to the Cardigan Welsh Corgi.

Physical Description: The Pembroke is a long, low, solidly built dog with short, well-boned legs. It has a foxy head with large, erect ears; oval, brown eyes; and a black nose. It is deep chested and naturally tailless. The medium-length coat is red, sable, fawn, or black and tan, with or without white markings.

Height: 10 to 12 inches

Weight: 25 to 30 pounds

Temperament: Like the Cardigan, the Pembroke is a big dog in a small package. It is an active, intelligent, and fun-loving dog and gets along with almost everyone. The Pembroke does well with children but should be supervised. It is devoted to its family but can be headstrong.

Activity Level: Moderate

Best Owner: The Pembroke does well with an active family in a rural or suburban home.

Special Needs: Grooming, socialization, training

Possible Health Concerns: Bladder stones, hip dysplasia, intervertebral disc protrusion, PRA

Perdigueiro Português

Alternative Names: Portuguese Pointer

Country of Origin: Portugal

Group: Gun Dog, UKC

History: This breed is believed to date back to the thirteenth century; paintings from that era portray dogs that look much like the modern Portuguese Pointer, and books describe a similar hound being used for hawking. The modern Portuguese Pointer was developed as a partridge dog and may be an ancestor of the English Pointer.

Physical Description: This is a medium-size dog that is equal in length and height. The square-shaped head has medium-length drop ears and slightly pendant lips. The nose may be brown or black, depending on coat color. The eyes are large and brown, and the tail is docked and carried below the back. The short, straight coat is

Perdigueiro Português

coarse on the body but silky on the head and ears. It is yellow or brown with white markings on the neck, legs, belly, and muzzle.

Height: 20 to 22 inches

Weight: 35 to 59 pounds

Temperament: The Portuguese Pointer is active, tenacious, and intense with strong hunting instincts. It is affectionate and submissive with family.

Activity Level: High

Best Owner: It does best with an active family or individual in a suburban or rural home.

Special Needs: Attention, exercise

Possible Health Concerns: Albinism

Perdiguero de Burgos

Alternative Names: Burgos Pointing Dog, Spanish Pointer

Country of Origin: Spain

Group: Gun Dog, UKC

History: The Perdiguero de Burgos is believed to have been in existence since the seventeenth century. Fanciers speculate that it was created by crossing Spanish breeds, perhaps the Perdiguero Navarro and the Sabueso Español. The breed may be an ancestor of some of the English Pointers. It was developed as a bird and game dog, in the field and the water. The breed came close to extinction at the turn of the twentieth century but is now popular in Spain.

Physical Description: This is a large, strong, but compact dog that is slightly rectangular. It has a strong, broad head; long, folded ears; and a brown nose. The almond-shaped eyes are dark hazel, and the lips are pendulous. The chest is deep and the tail is docked to half its length. The skin is pink and fine, and the short coat is liver and white with ticking.

Height: 26 to 30 inches

Weight: 55 to 70 pounds

Temperament: This even-tempered, easygoing dog is intelligent and eager to please, making it highly trainable. It gets along with almost everyone, including children. It may roam.

Activity Level: High

Best Owner: It does best with an active family in a rural or suburban home.

Special Needs: Exercise

Possible Health Concerns: Albinism

Perdiguero Navarro

Alternative Names: Old Spanish Pointer, Navarro Pointer, Pachon de Victoria

Country of Origin: Spain

Group: Gun Dog, UKC

History: The Perdiguero Navarro is believed to have been developed as early as the twelfth century. It may be the ancestor of other pointers. Although the breed has come close to extinction several times over the centuries, it was kept alive in rural Spain. Originally used to hunt elk, it is now used as a partridge dog, capable of hunting, pointing, and retrieving birds.

Perdiguero de Burgos

Physical Description: This is a medium- to large-size dog. It has a large head; long, rounded drop ears; pendant flews; and large, chestnut brown eyes. The split nose is a distinctive characteristic. The tail is long and curved, and the dense coat may be short or long and smooth. It is liver and white or orange and white, with or without ticking.

Height: 20 to 24 inches

Weight: 55 to 66 pounds

Temperament: The Perdiguero Navarro is an enthusiastic and active dog that loves to work and has great endurance.

Activity Level: High

Best Owner: It does best with an active individual or family in a rural or suburban home.

Special Needs: Exercise

Possible Health Concerns: None known

Peruvian Inca Orchid

Alternative Names: Perro Sin Pelo del Peru, Peruvian Hairless Dog, Moonflower Dog, Perro Flora, Inca Hairless Dog

Country of Origin: Peru

Group: Companion, UKC

History: Although there are many theories about the origin of the Peruvian Inca Orchid, everyone agrees that it is an old breed. The hairless dog may have arrived in South America by way of Africa or China, brought there by sailors or immigrants. There are two varieties of Peruvian Inca Orchids: hairless and coated. The coated were used as hunters, while the hairless were kept by the nobility as pets and bed warmers. It is said that when the Spanish conquered Peru, they discovered the dogs among the orchid flowers and thus called them flower dogs.

Physical Description: The Peruvian Inca Orchid is a medium-size dog that is well balanced and muscular. It has prick or rose

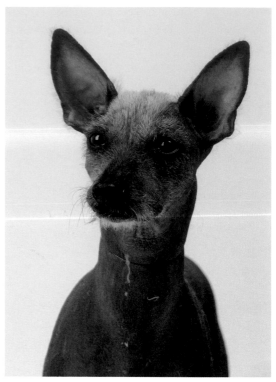

Peruvian Inca Orchid

ears and almond-shaped eyes, which complement the coat color. It has a long, tapering tail and webbed feet. There are two varieties, the coated (powderpuff) and the hairless. The powderpuff may have a short, medium, or long coat, which can be any color or color combination, including white with black, tan, blue, or red markings. Sometimes the coat is red or blue with lighter markings. The hairless's skin color ranges from black with spots of white, cream, pink, mahogany, blue, or red to pink, cream, white, mahogany, or red with spots of another color.

Height: 17 to 23 inches

Weight: 30 to 40 pounds

Temperament: This is a gentle, quiet, and fastidious dog. It is intelligent, easily trained, and outgoing. It gets along with almost everyone as long as it is socialized.

Activity Level: Moderate

Best Owner: This breed does well in the suburbs or city and makes an excellent apartment dog.

Special Needs: Protection from sun and cold, skin care, socialization

Possible Health Concerns: Dental problems, sun sensitivity

Petit Basset Griffon Vendéen

Alternative Names: PBGV

Country of Origin: France

Group: Scenthound UKC; Hound, AKC

History: The PBGV was developed as a trailing scenthound in the La Vendée district of France. This is the most common of four Griffon Vendéen breeds and is believed to have originated as long ago as the sixteenth century. It has gained popularity as a companion dog, especially in the United States.

Physical Description: This is a medium-size, sturdy, rectangular-shaped dog. The head is twice as long as it is wide. It has large, dark eyes with long eyebrows and a black nose. The long drop ears fold inward as they fall. The neck is long, the chest deep, and the legs short. The long, tapered tail is held like a saber. It is double coated with a long, rough outer coat and a beard and mustache. It is white

Petit Basset Griffon Vendéen

with lemon, orange, black, tricolor, or grizzled markings.

Height: 13 to 15 inches

Weight: 25 to 40 pounds

Temperament: The PBGV is a very outgoing, fun-loving, and enthusiastic dog. It is intelligent and eager to please, active, and energetic and can be a barker. It gets along with almost everyone, including children and other dogs.

Activity Level: High

Best Owner: This breed does best with an active family in a rural or suburban home.

Special Needs: Exercise, fenced yard, grooming, leashed

Possible Health Concerns: Aseptic meningitis, epilepsy, eye problems, heart murmur, hip dysplasia, luxating patellas

Pharaoh Hound

Alternative Names: Kelb Tal-Fenek

Country of Origin: Malta

Group: Sighthound, UKC; Hound, AKC

History: Dogs that resemble the Pharaoh Hound are common in ancient Egyptian art. Until recently, the Pharaoh Hound was believed to be a direct descendant of those dogs, but new research shows that it's more likely that this breed is a modern re-creation. It was first imported to Great Britain from its Mediterranean homeland of Malta in the 1930s. The first litter was born in the United States in 1970.

Physical Description: The Pharaoh Hound is a large, muscular, and graceful dog. It is slightly longer than it is tall, with a long, whiplike tail. It has a long, chiseled head

The Pharaoh Hound is known in Malta as the *Kelb Tal-fenek*, or rabbit dog. It was named the national dog of Malta, and a silver coin bearing the likeness of a Pharaoh Hound was minted in 1977.

Pharaoh Hound

with a wedge-shaped foreface and large, erect ears. The nose, lips, and eye rims are flesh colored. The eyes are amber, blending with the coat of tan or chestnut. A white tip on the tail is desirable, as is a white star on the chest. White on the toes or a slim white snip on the centerline of the face is permissible, but any other white markings are undesirable. The coat is short and smooth.

Height: 21 to 25 inches

Weight: no standard available

Temperament: The Pharaoh Hound is an intelligent, highly trainable dog that is always eager to please. It is affectionate and playful with its family but sometimes wary with strangers. It is often described as discriminating and catlike in its mannerisms. This breed is said to be capable of blushing and smiling. It gets along with children as long as it is socialized with them, but it is not trustworthy with small animals.

Activity Level: Moderate to high

Best Owner: This breed does well with an active family in a suburban or rural home.

Special Needs: Exercise, fenced yard, leashed, socialization, training,

Possible Health Concerns: Allergies, anesthesia sensitivity, hip dysplasia

Plott Hound

Alternative Names: Plott

Country of Origin: Germany/ United States

Group: Scenthound, UKC; Hound, AKC

History: The Plott Hound is the only one of the coonhounds that is not descended from the foxhound. It is, instead, a descendant of the Hanoverian Hound. It was originally from Germany and was used for boar hunting. Its descendants were imported to the United States in 1750 by Jonathon Plott, who settled in western North Carolina and bred the hounds to hunt bear. The modern Plott Hound is believed to descend directly from these dogs, with some outcrossings of other local hounds, including the Blevins Hound.

Physical Description: This is a large, powerful dog with a wide head that is carried proudly. It has brown or hazel eyes and

Plott Hound

medium-length drop ears of fine leather that fold as they fall. When at attention, the ears rise and there are wrinkles at the brow. The muzzle is moderately long with moderate flews. The chest is deep and the long, heavy tail tapers. It has solid, well-knuckled feet. The short to medium-length glossy coat is yellow, red, tan, brown, black, gray brindle, or blue.

Height: 21 to 25 inches

Weight: 40 to 60 pounds

Temperament: The Plott Hound is active, brave, and enthusiastic. It is intense in the field and highly trainable. It is gentle with its friends and family and gets along well with children.

Activity Level: High

Best Owner: This breed does best with an active family in a suburban or rural home.

Special Needs: Exercise, fenced yard, leashed, outdoor activities

Possible Health Concerns: Bloat

Polish Lowland Sheepdog

Alternative Names: Polski Owczarek Nizinny (PON)

Country of Origin: Poland

Group: Herding, UKC/AKC

History: The Polish Lowland Sheepdog is likely descended from a cross between the Hun herding dog and the Puli that dates to the thirteenth century. It was developed over several centuries to be an independent, adaptable sheep herder. Several examples were brought to Scotland in 1514 and are believed to be the ancestors of the Bearded Collie. The breed was close to extinction after both world wars, with only eight breedable dogs left after World War II. It was redeveloped by breed fanciers and is mostly a companion dog today.

Physical Description: The Polish Lowland Sheepdog is a heavily boned, medium-size

Polish Lowland Sheepdog

dog with a broad, domed head and a short muzzle. Its eyes are brown, the large nose is black or brown, and it has medium-size drop ears. It is double coated with a long, thick outer coat and soft undercoat and can be any color. The tail is naturally short or docked.

Height: 16 to 20 inches

Weight: 30 to 50 pounds

Temperament: This is an intelligent and independent-minded dog that is affectionate and devoted with its family but wary of strangers.

Activity Level: Moderate to high

Best Owner: The Polish Lowland Sheepdog requires an active, dog-experienced owner in a rural or suburban home.

Special Needs: Exercise, grooming, socialization, training

Possible Health Concerns: Patent ductus arteriosus

Pointer

Alternative Names: English Pointer

Country of Origin: Great Britain

Group: Gun Dog, UKC; Sporting, AKC

Pointer

History: The Pointer was developed in the late seventeenth century in England to be used when hunting with the slow-loading flintlock gun. Hunters needed a dog that could stay on point until they were ready to shoot. It is unclear whether the Pointer was originally developed in Spain, Britain, or elsewhere. Some believe it was developed at the same time in several countries. The breed is probably a cross of foxhounds, Greyhounds, and Bloodhounds. Its working ability rather than looks are most important to fanciers.

Physical Description: The Pointer is a large, muscular, square-shaped dog. The long, well-chiseled head is rectangular with a long muzzle that is equal in length to the width of the skull. It has a brown or black nose (it can be lighter in lighter-colored dogs) and drop ears. The tail is naturally short and carried slightly higher than the topline. The short, smooth coat is liver, lemon, black, orange, or a combination of colors and/or white.

Height: 23 to 28 inches

Weight: 45 to 75 pounds

Temperament: It is friendly, even-tempered, hardworking, and enthusiastic. It gets along well with children and other dogs but likes to run and has a strong prey drive.

Activity Level: High

Best Owner: It does best in an active rural home where it is allowed to participate in a job or activity.

Special Needs: Exercise, fenced yard, job or activity, leashed

Possible Health Concerns: Deafness, eye disorders

Pomeranian

Alternative Names: Toy German Spitz

Country of Origin: Germany

Group: Companion/Northern, UKC; Toy, AKC

History: The Pomeranian is said to have come from Pomerania, a province in eastern Germany. It is generally believed that it descends from a larger German spitz dog that was used for pulling sleds and herding sheep. It was bred down to its current size in the nineteenth century and was highly favored by Queen Victoria. It first made its way to the United States in the late nineteenth century.

Physical Description: The Pomeranian is a small dog with a foxy appearance and small,

Pomeranian

erect ears. It has a wedge-shaped head; dark, almond-shaped eyes; and a short, tapered muzzle. Its tail curls over its back, and it has small, compact feet. It is double coated with a thick, soft undercoat and a profuse, straight outer coat. It has a pronounced neck ruff. The coat comes in all colors and patterns, some of the most common being red, orange, cream, sable, black, and black and tan.

Height: 8 to 11 inches

Weight: 3 to 7 pounds

Temperament: The Pomeranian is a spunky, outgoing dog that is intelligent and highly trainable. If not socialized, Poms may be unfriendly toward strangers or even those familiar to them. It is a very clean dog, sometimes described as catlike. It is protective and makes an excellent watchdog.

Activity Level: Moderate

Best Owner: Pomeranians adapt well to city life; some Poms do best in adult-only households.

Special Needs: Grooming, socialization, training

Possible Health Concerns: Dental problems, luxating patellas, patent ductus arteriosus, PRA, tracheal collapse

Poodle (Standard)

Alternative Names: Caniche, Pudel

Country of Origin: France

Group: Gun Dog, UKC; Non-Sporting, AKC

History: The Poodle is an old breed whose name comes from the German word pudel, meaning "to splash in water." The Poodle was originally used as a water retriever and was mostly developed in France, where the breed became very popular. The dogs were used as hunters in France, Germany, and Great Britain into the nineteenth century, but they later became popular performers and companion dogs. The Standard is the prototype Poodle, from which the Toy and Miniature were bred. They first came to the United States at the end of the nineteenth century.

Physical Description: The Poodle is a medium to large, muscular, square-shaped dog. It has a long skull and long drop ears. The oval eyes are dark, and the nose is black or liver colored, depending on the coat color. The tail is docked and held erect. The double coat has a curly, harsh outer coat that is apricot, black, blue, cream, gray, silver, brown, café au lait, or white. While the coat is typically clipped,

---

AKC's Top 25 Breeds

1. Labrador Retriever
2. Yorkshire Terrier
3. German Shepherd Dog
4. Golden Retriever
5. Beagle
6. Boxer
7. Dachshund
8. Bulldog
9. Poodle
10. Shih Tzu
11. Miniature Schnauzer
12. Chihuahua
13. Pomeranian
14. Rottweiler
15. Pug
16. German Shorthaired Pointer
17. Boston Terrier
18. Doberman Pinscher
19. Shetland Sheepdog
20. Maltese
21. Cocker Spaniel
22. Great Dane
23. Siberian Husky
24. Pembroke Welsh Corgi
25. Cavalier King Charles Spaniel

Source: American Kennel Club 2008 registration figures

and specific cuts are stipulated for the show ring, the coat may also be left to cord, hanging in ropes.

Height: Over 15 inches

Weight: 45 to 70 pounds

Temperament: This is an intelligent, highly trainable dog. It is affectionate with friends and family but can be aloof toward strangers. It gets along well with children.

Activity Level: High

Best Owner: It does best with an active family in a suburban or rural home.

Special Needs: Exercise, professional grooming, training

Possible Health Concerns: Addison's disease, bloat, epilepsy, hip dysplasia, luxating patellas, PRA, renal disease, skin disorders, sebaceous adenitis, thyroid problems

Poodle (Miniature and Toy)

Country of Origin: France

Group: Companion, UKC; Non-Sporting (Miniature) and Toy (Toy), AKC

History: Miniature and Toy Poodles were probably bred down from Standard Poodles, although the Toy Poodle may be distantly related to the Maltese. Unlike the Standard Poodle, which was developed as a hunting dog, the smaller Poodles were always companions. They were popular with European royalty, including France's Louis XVI and Queen Anne of England; both sizes were depicted in seventeenth-century paintings. They also performed in circuses in the eighteenth and nineteenth centuries. They were first brought to the United States at the end of the nineteenth century but did not become popular until

Poodles

after WW II. All three Poodles are almost identical except for size.

Physical Description: These small to medium-size square dogs are elegant looking. The fine muzzle is straight and equal in length to the skull. The nose is black or liver, and the eyes are oval and wide apart. They have long, wide drop ears that hang close to the head. The tail is docked and carried erect. The coat is harsh and curly and can be left to cord or else clipped. The coat is of a uniform color, including apricot, black, blue, cream, gray, silver, or white.

Height (Toy): Up to 10 inches

Weight (Toy): 5 to 7 pounds

Height (Miniature): 11 to 15 inches

Weight (Miniature): 14 to 16 pounds

Temperament: Poodles are intelligent and highly trainable. They may be wary of strangers but are affectionate with their families and enjoy human companionship. They make very poor kennel dogs. Most are good with children and other animals as long as they are socialized.

Activity Level: Moderate

Best Owner: They do well in an apartment or suburban home.

Special Needs: Attention, grooming, protection from predators and rough play, socialization, some exercise, training

Possible Health Concerns: Addison's disease, bloat, Cushing's disease, epilepsy, hip dysplasia, hypothyroidism, Legg-Perthes disease, luxating patellas, PRA, von Willebrand's disease

Porcelaine

Alternative Names: Chien de Franche-Comté, Chien Blanc du Roi

Country of Origin: France/Switzerland

Group: Scenthound, UKC

History: Although there is some confusion as to whether the Porcelaine is a French or Swiss breed, it is believed to be the oldest of the French scenthounds. It may have been developed from the English Harrier and Swiss Laufhunds. It was used to hunt small game and is rarely found outside France, Switzerland, and Italy.

Physical Description: This is a lean, fine-boned, medium-size dog with a finely chiseled head; large, black nose; and flat forehead. The eyes are dark and the drop ears are long. It has a long, tapered tail. The coat is very smooth, short, and fine, white with orange spots on the ears and often on the body as well. The pink and black mottled skin shows through the coat.

Height: 21 to 23 inches

Weight: 55 to 62 pounds

Temperament: Although it is a fierce and enthusiastic hunter, the Porcelaine is gentle and easygoing at home. It gets along with almost everyone, including children and other dogs. It is vocal and independent minded.

Activity Level: High

Best Owner: The Porcelaine does best with an active family in a rural home.

Porcelaine

Special Needs: Activity, exercise, fenced yard, leashed

Possible Health Concerns: None known

Portuguese Water Dog

Alternative Names: Cão de Agua, Portuguese Fishing Dog, Cão de Agua de Pelo Ondulado (longhaired), Cão de Agua de Pelo Encaradolado (curly coated)

Country of Origin: Portugal

Group: Gun Dog, UKC; Working, AKC

History: Portuguese Water Dogs have played an important part in the Portuguese fishing industry for centuries. The dogs were used to gather fish, retrieve lines, and deliver messages from boat to boat. With the decline of fishing in the beginning of the twentieth century, the breed came close to extinction but was saved by a wealthy fancier. It is now a popular companion throughout the world.

Physical Description: This is a sturdy, medium-size dog. It has a strong, broad head, the skull slightly longer than the muzzle. The eyes and broad nose are brown or black, and the drop ears are heart shaped. The feet are webbed and covered with hair, and the tail is medium length. The single coat may be wavy or curly and is kept in a lion clip, with hair on the forequarters left long and the rear quarters shaved. In the United States and Canada, an all-over-curly retriever clip is also permitted in the show ring. The coat may be black, white, brown, or a combination of these colors.

A major ongoing study into the genetics of the Portuguese Water Dog began in 1996 and involves more than 600 dogs. The study, called the Georgie Project in memory of a Portuguese Water Dog who died of an autoimmune disease, is a collaborative effort among owners, breeders, and scientists at the University of Utah.

Portuguese Water Dog

Height: 17 to 23 inches

Weight: 35 to 60 pounds

Temperament: The Portuguese Water Dog is biddable and intelligent. It is devoted to family and has great endurance. It is spirited and courageous. It loves the water and is an excellent swimmer.

Activity Level: High

Best Owner: It does well with an individual or family in a rural or suburban home.

Special Needs: Exercise, grooming, training

Possible Health Concerns: Addison's disease, cancer, cardiac problems, eye problems, gastrointestinal disease, hip dysplasia, skin allergies, renal disease

Presa Canario

Alternative Names: Perro de Presa Canario, Dogo Canario

Country of Origin: Canary Islands

Group: Guardian, UKC

Presa Canario

History: This dog is native to the Canary Islands, which include Tenerife and Gran Canaria. It is believed to descend from a cross of mastiffs and native cattle dogs. It was popular in its native land during the sixteenth and seventeenth centuries when it was used as a guard and for driving cattle.

Physical Description: The Presa Canario is a large, strong, and muscular dog that is longer than it is tall. It has a massive head that is covered with loose skin, creating wrinkles. It has a short muzzle and wide, black nose. The oval, medium-sized eyes are medium to dark chestnut. The medium-size ears are naturally drop or rose or cropped

Think of the Canary Islands and bright yellow birds may come to mind. But the islands were actually named for the large dogs who once roamed there. The dogs are known today as Presas Canarios, or canary dogs. When explorers saw the dogs on one of the islands, they named the island Canaria from the Latin word canis. Canary birds, who are native to the islands, obtained their name later.

erect. There is a wide chest and thick, natural, sabrelike tail. The skin is thick and loose, especially at the head, and covered with a short, flat single coat. It is brindle or fawn with a dark mask.

Height: 22 to 25.5 inches

Weight: 88 to 110 pounds

Temperament: This is a calm, attentive, confident, and even-keeled dog. It is gentle and affectionate with family, including children but wary with strangers. It is aloof. It generally gets along with submissive dogs of the opposite sex.

Activity Level: Moderate

Best Owner: The Presa Canario does well with a dog-experienced family or individual in a rural or suburban home.

Special Needs: Fenced yard, firm but positive training, leashed, socialization, supervision with other animals

Possible Health Concerns: Entropion, epilepsy, demodectic mange, hip and elbow dysplasia, hypothyroidism, OCD, luxating patellas, wobbler syndrome

Pudelpointer

Country of Origin: Germany

Group: Gun Dog, UKC

Top Dogs in New York City
1. Labrador Retriever
2. Yorkshire Terrier
3. Dachshund
4. Havanese
5. Poodle
6. Cavalier King Charles Spaniel
7. French Bulldog
8. Golden Retriever
9. Bulldog
10. Pug

Source: 2007 AKC registration figures

Pudelpointer

History: The Pudelpointer was developed in Germany during the nineteenth century as a multipurpose hunting dog. The breed was created from various pointers and Standard Poodles with the intent of producing the quintessential hunting dog.

Physical Description: This is a rectangular, well-muscled dog. The head is moderately long, and on the face is a rough beard and profuse eyebrows. The round eyes are yellow to yellow brown, and the drop ears are medium in length. The tail, covered with wiry hair, is docked and carried straight out. The harsh, wiry coat may be brown or the color of dried leaves.

Height: 24 to 26 inches

Weight: 55 to 70 pounds

Temperament: The Pudelpointer is good-natured and intelligent. It is loyal and highly trainable. It is friendly with almost everyone, including children and other dogs.

Activity Level: High

Best Owner: This breed does best with an active family in a rural home.

Special Needs: Attention, exercise, grooming

Possible Health Concerns: Hip dysplasia, skin allergies

Pug

Alternative Names: Lo-sze (China), Mops (Germany), Mopshond (Holland), Carlin (France).

Country of Origin: China

Group: Companion, UKC; Toy, AKC

History: The Pug's progenitors probably originated in China more than 2,000 years ago. From there the breed made its way to Tibet and Japan, probably as royal gifts or objects of barter, and eventually to Europe in the sixteenth or seventeenth century. It became extremely popular in Holland. It first came to the United States in the nineteenth century.

Physical Description: The Pug is a square, short, and stocky dog with straight legs. The head is large and round with a heavily wrinkled forehead. The muzzle is short and wide with an undershot bite. Its large, prominent eyes are dark and set wide apart, and its small, thin ears are rose or button. The tail is tightly curled. It has a short, single coat with smooth, glossy hair that may be silver, apricot fawn, or black, with a black mask and ears.

Height: 10 to 11 inches

Weight: 14 to 18 pounds

Temperament: The Pug is a loving, affectionate dog. It is eager to please and enjoys the company of children. It is also intelligent and can be stubborn. It tends to snore.

Activity Level: Low

Best Owner: The Pug is extremely adaptable, doing especially well in an apartment.

Special Needs: Avoid strenuous exercise, needs protection from heat, wrinkle cleaning

Pug

Possible Health Concerns: Deformities of the mouth and nose, eye and eyelid problems, heatstroke, hip dyplasia, Legg-Perthes disease, luxating patellas, Pug dog encephalitis

Puli

Country of Origin: Hungary

Group: Herding, UKC/AKC

History: The Puli is an ancient dog that is believed to be a descendant of the Tibetan Terrier, a breed that was brought to Hungary around the ninth century with the Huns. The Puli was embraced by Hungarian shepherds, who used it as a sheepherding dog for more than 1,000 years. In the sixteenth century, Hungary was again invaded and repopulated with Western Europeans, who brought their sheepdogs and terriers with them. These dogs mixed with the native Pulik, leading to the Pumi. The Puli and Pumi were crossed so often that they were almost identical until the twentieth century, when a breeder revitalized the original Puli. The Puli continues to be used in Hungary as a herding dog for sheep, cattle, and horses. It was first brought to the United States in the 1920s.

Physical Description: The Puli is a medium-size, powerful, squarely built dog. It has a broad skull and a straight muzzle that is about one-third the length of the head. It has a large, black nose; deep-set, almond-shaped, dark brown eyes; and V-shaped drop ears. The neck appears to merge with the body because it is covered with profuse hair. The medium-length natural tail blends into the hair on the body. The double coat has a woolly undercoat and a profuse outer coat that is wavy or curly, brushed out or forming cords. It is several shades of black, gray, or white. The skin is blue or gray.

Height: 15 to 18 inches

Weight: 30 pounds

Temperament: The Puli is an intelligent, active dog. It is fun loving and devoted to its family. Playful and affectionate with friends and family, it is wary with strangers. It is vocal.

Activity Level: High

Best Owner: The Puli requires an active family in a suburban or rural home.

Special Needs: Attention, grooming, protection from heat, supervision when swimming, training

Puli

Possible Health Concerns: Deafness, eye problems, hip dysplasia

Pumi

Country of Origin: Hungary

Group: Herding, UKC

History: The Pumi was developed by crossing the Hungarian Puli with the European dogs who accompanied Western Europeans to Hungary during the sixteenth, seventeenth, and eighteenth centuries. It and the Puli were indistinguishable until Puli fanciers worked to resurrect the original breed in the early twentieth century. It is a herding dog but is also used for hunting.

Physical Description: This is a medium-size, terrier-like, squarely built dog. It has a long, narrow head with a long muzzle and a narrow, black nose. The eyes are brown and the ears are naturally prick, with the top third folded over. It has a long natural tail that is carried high and curved. The double coat is wavy and forms tufts but is not corded. The outer coat is long and elastic in texture. The coat is gray, black, or fawn, with or without white markings, or white.

Pumi

Height: 13.5 to 17.5 inches

Weight: 18 to 30 pounds.

Temperament: The Pumi is terrier-like in its personality, noisy and constantly busy. It is very active and bold. It is cheerful and affectionate with family but wary with strangers and will react to provocation.

Activity Level: High

Best Owner: The Pumi does best with an active family in a rural or suburban environment.

Special Needs: Attention, exercise, job or activity, socialization, training

Possible Health Concerns: None known

Rat Terrier

Country of Origin: United States

Group: Terrier, UKC

History: The Rat Terrier was descended from terriers brought over by working-class English immigrants, dogs that including the Smooth Fox Terrier, Manchester Terrier, and now-extinct English white terrier. The Rat Terrier was bred to control rats as well as to provide entertainment in the blood sport of ratting. The Rat Terrier was later crossed with Whippets, Italian Greyhounds, and Beagles. The breed was popularized by Teddy Roosevelt, who often hunted with Rat Terriers.

Physical Description: The Rat Terrier is a small to medium-size muscular dog that is slightly longer than it is tall. It has a wedge-shaped head and the skull and muzzle are of equal length. The nose is black or self-colored and the eyes are prominent. The ears are button, tipped, or erect and V shaped.

Rat Terriers were common farm dogs in the United States in the early years of the twentieth century. Some farmers in the Midwest bred the terriers to Whippets, Italian Greyhounds, and other fast breeds to increase their speed and versatility in helping control jack rabbits.

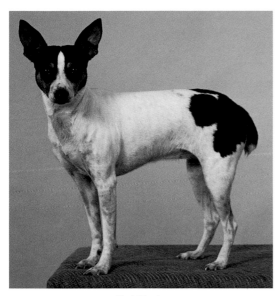

Rat Terrier

The tail may be docked, naturally long and curved upward, or a natural bob. Coat colors range from solid white to bicolor or tricolor, with white and black, tan, chocolate, blue, blue fawn, apricot, or lemon.

Height (Miniature): Under 13 inches

Height (Standard): 13 to 18 inches

Weight (Miniature): 4 to 8 pounds

Weight (Standard): 12 to 35 pounds

Note: The Rat Terrier description is somewhat convoluted, as different registrics have different standards: The UKC recognizes miniatures and standards as well as hairless Rat Terriers. The Rat Terrier Club of America recognizes miniatures and standards but not hairless, which they included under another breed, the American Hairless Terrier. The National Rat Terrier Association recognizes toy, miniature, and standards as well as two body types: Type A—square dog; Type B—longer than it is tall. The association also recognizes a larger variety called Decker Giants. Also see the Teddy Roosevelt Terrier.

Temperament: The Rat Terrier is an energetic, curious, and intelligent dog. It is game and tenacious when hunting but affable and affectionate at home. It gets along with children, other dogs, and cats.

Activity Level: Moderate

Best Owner: It adapts to most living situations: city or rural, active or sedentary.

Special Needs: Exercise, human companionship, socialization, sun protection, training

Possible Health Concerns: Allergies, bite problems, hip and elbow dysplasia, luxating patellas, mange

Redbone Coonhound

Country of Origin: United States

Group: Scenthound, UKC

History: The Redbone Coonhound is a descendant of the red foxhounds and red Irish foxhounds brought to the United States by Scottish and Irish immigrants in the eighteenth and nineteenth centuries. It was bred for intensity in treeing raccoons as well as for its red coloring. It is used for both trailing and treeing game, although treeing is its specialty.

Physical Description: This is a large, muscular dog that is square in shape. It has a broad head, square muzzle, and large, black nose. The oval eyes are hazel to dark brown, and the drop ears are long and finely leathered. There is a strong neck, deep chest, and sabrelike tail. The feet are catlike. The coat is short and smooth and solid red, although there may be a dark muzzle and white markings on the brisket and feet.

Height: 21 to 27 inches

Weight: 45 to 70 pounds

Ancestors of the Redbone Coonhound were called Saddlebacks because they were red with a black mark in the shape of a saddle. Through selective breeding, the saddle was bred out, and the solid red dogs became known as Redbone Coonhounds.

Redbone Coonhound

Temperament: This breed is intense and hard-working in the field but easygoing and gentle at home. It is intelligent and eager to please, making it more trainable than most hounds. It gets along with almost everyone.

Activity Level: High

Best Owner: The Redbone Coonhound does best with an active owner in a rural or suburban home.

Special Needs: Exercise, fenced yard, leashed

Possible Health Concerns: None known

Rhodesian Ridgeback

Alternative Names: Lion Dog, African Lion Hound

Country of Origin: South Africa

Group: Sighthound, UKC; Hound, AKC

History: The Rhodesian Ridgeback was developed in South Africa and Zimbabwe by European settlers. It is descended from the native dogs kept by the Khoikhoi people and was considered an all-purpose farm dog, used to herd, to guard, and to hunt African lion. It was first imported to the United States after World War II. It is a popular companion dog today.

Physical Description: The Ridgeback is a large, muscular dog that is slightly longer than it is tall. It has a powerful back and loins, a deep chest, and a long, tapering tail. The head is broad, with wrinkling on the forehead when the dog is alert. The drop ears are medium size, and the large eyes complement the coat coloring. It has a long, powerful muzzle and a large, black nose. The short, harsh coat comes in varying shades of wheaten red. There may be small, white markings on the chest or toes. It is distinguished by the ridge along the back, which is a result of two whorls of hair that grow in opposition to the rest of the coat.

Height: 24 to 27 inches

Weight: 70 to 85 pounds

Temperament: The Rhodesian Ridgeback is a good-natured, laidback dog. It is devoted to its family but intelligent and independent, so training can be a challenge. It has a high prey drive and is not trustworthy with small animals.

Activity Level: Moderate

Best Owner: The Ridgeback requires a consistent, firm, dog-experienced owner in the suburbs or country.

Rhodesian Ridgeback

Special Needs: Fenced yard, leashed, socialization, training

Possible Health Concerns: Dermoid sinus, hip dysplasia

Rottweiler

Country of Origin: Germany

Group: Guardian, UKC; Working, AKC

History: The Rottweiler was developed as an all-purpose working dog in the town of Rottweil. It is a descendant of Roman cattle dogs but has been used as a military and police dog, cattle drover, search and rescue dog, guard, and companion.

Physical Description: The Rottweiler is a large, powerful, muscular, and deep-chested dog that is slightly longer than it is tall. It has a broad head; short, broad muzzle; and short drop ears. The dark eyes are almond shaped and the nose is black. The tail is docked short and the short, smooth black coat has rust or mahogany markings

Height: 22 to 27 inches

Weight: 75 to 130 pounds

Rottweiler

Temperament: This is a calm, courageous, hardworking dog that is affectionate with family but wary with strangers.

Activity Level: Moderate

Best Owner: This breed does best with a dog-experienced owner in a rural or suburban home.

Special Needs: Socialization, training

Possible Health Concerns: Hip and elbow dysplasia, kidney problems, neurological disorders

Saint Bernard

Country of Origin: Switzerland

Group: Guardian, UKC; Working, AKC

History: The Saint Bernard was developed in the seventeenth century by Swiss monks at the Hospice of Saint Bernard, a refuge for travelers crossing the mountain passes between Switzerland and Italy. The dogs were used as drafting, guarding, turn-spit, and search and rescue dogs. Saint Bernards are believed to have saved over 2,000 lives through their work at the hospice. They were likely descended from

---

Boldest Dogs

Based on a study of 164 breeds conducted by Dr. Kenth Svartberg of Stockholm University from 1997 to 2000, the following breeds were found to be the boldest*:

1. Labrador Retriever
2. Flat-Coated Retriever
3. Belgian Malinois
4. Boxer
5. Rottweiler
6. German Shepherd Dog
7. Giant Schnauzer
8. Border Collie
9. American Staffordshire Terrier
10. Parson Russell Terrier (Jack Russell Terrier)

Boldest dogs combine measures of fearlessness, curiosity, sociability, and interest in chasing prey.

Roman mastiffs. The breed first came to the United States in the nineteenth century.

Physical Description: The Saint Bernard is a large, powerful, square-shaped dog with a large head with a deep furrow over the skull. The skull is twice as long as the short, blunt muzzle. When alert, the skin wrinkles under the diamond-shaped, dark brown eyes. The medium-size drop ears are set high and are shaped like rounded triangles. The nose is broad and black, and there are strongly developed flews. The feet are large and the tail is naturally long. The double coat has a dense undercoat and thick, straight outer coat that is short or long. It is red, brown, or brindle, with white markings at the chest, feet, tip of tail, nose band, and neck. Sometimes there are also markings at the collar, muzzle, between the eyes, belly, legs, and the lower half of the tail. There is generally a dark mask and ears.

Height: 25.5 to 30 inches

Weight: 120 to 180 pounds

Temperament: This is an affectionate, fun-loving, and playful dog that is equally friendly with strangers and family. It makes a poor guard dog but will bark at intruders. It is very good with children.

Activity Level: Moderate

Best Owner: The Saint Bernard does best in a home where neatness is not a concern. A rural or suburban home is preferred, although it can adapt to city life as long as it has enough room.

Special Needs: Protection from heat

Possible Health Concerns: Albinism, bloat, epilepsy, hip dysplasia, skin allergies, laryngeal paralysis, temperament problems

Saluki

Alternative Names: Saluqi, Persian Greyhound

Country of Origin: Middle East

Group: Sighthound, UKC; Hound, AKC

History: The Saluki is an ancient breed that descends from a hound that is believed to have existed in sixth century B.C.E. Mesopotamia. A skeleton of a similar hound was found in North Syria, dating to about 2500 B.C.E. The Saluki was bred by tribespeople for hunting game such as gazelle and hare. It continues to be used for this purpose in the Middle East but is primarily a companion in the United States.

Physical Description: The Saluki is a medium to large dog that is slender, muscular, and

Saint Bernard

Saluki

elegant. It has a long, narrow head; dark eyes; a black or liver nose; and long drop ears. It is deep chested with a long, curved tail. It has a smooth, silky coat with feathering at the ears, tail, legs, and thighs. There is also a smooth coat variety with no feathering. It comes in a variety of colors, from red, gold, fawn and cream to black-and-tan and various shades of grizzle.

Height: 23 to 28 inches

Weight: 45 pounds

Temperament: The Saluki is an intelligent, alert dog that can be sensitive. It loves to run but is calm and mild mannered in the home. It is affectionate with family and thrives on human companionship.

Activity Level: Moderate

Best Owner: The Saluki does well with an active family in the suburbs or country.

Special Needs: Attention, exercise, fenced yard, training, grooming (longhair)

Possible Health Concerns: Ehrlichiosis, epilepsy, hemangiosarcoma, hypothyroidism, sensitive to anesthesia

Samoyed

Country of Origin: Siberia

Group: Northern, UKC; Working, AKC

History: The Samoyed takes its name from the Samoyed people, a nomadic tribe from the Siberian tundra. The Samoyed used the dog as a hunter, reindeer herder, and sled dog. When western polar explorers came upon the dogs in the nineteenth century and early twentieth century, they brought examples home with them, where the breed soon became popular with the English aristocracy. Shortly thereafter, the first Samoyed was imported to the United States. It was also used in subsequent Arctic exploration. The Samoyed has become a popular pet in the United States.

Samoyed

Physical Description: This medium-size spitz has a wedge-shaped head, triangular prick ears, and dark, almond-shaped eyes. The corner of the mouth turns up slightly in a smile, and its nose is black, although brown, liver, or Dudley noses are not unusual. It is longer than it is tall, with a long tail that curls over the back or hangs down. It has a heavy double coat that is white or biscuit colored. The undercoat is dense and soft, while the outer coat is long and coarse. There is a heavy ruff on the neck, and the tail is plumed.

Height: 19 to 23.5 inches

Weight: 35 to 65 pounds

Temperament: The Samoyed is an affectionate, gentle dog that craves human interaction. It is intelligent and lively and can be mischievous. It gets along with almost everyone, including children and other dogs.

Activity Level: High

Best Owner: The Samoyed does well with an active family in the country or suburbs.

Special Needs: Attention, exercise, grooming, training

Possible Health Concerns: Bloat, cardiac problems eye problems, hip dysplasia, renal, skin allergies

Sarplaninac

Alternative Names: Yugoslavian Shepherd Dog, Illyrian Shepherd Dog

Country of Origin: Serbia and Macedonia

Group: Guardian, UKC

History: The Sarplaninac is believed to have developed from Tibetan shepherd dogs that were brought from Asia to the Balkans. The descendants of these dogs have worked as flock guardians in Sarplanina, the mountainous areas of Serbia and Macedonia, for more than 2,000 years. The isolation of their mountain homes kept the Sarplaninac pure. It is now kept as a flock guardian as well as a companion across Europe and in North America.

Physical Description: The Sarplaninac is a large, well-proportioned, and muscular dog with a body that is slightly longer than it is tall. It has a broad head with a large, black nose; dark, almond-shaped eyes; and V-shaped drop ears. The tail is long and sabrelike. The heavy, rough coat is self-colored, ranging from white to dark gray. Some have white markings on the chest and toes.

Sarplaninac

Height: 22.5 to 24 inches minimum

Weight: 66 to 99 pounds

Temperament: This breed is affectionate with family but wary of strangers. It makes an excellent guard and is courageous and intelligent. It is independent minded and can be dominant.

Activity Level: Moderate

Best Owner: This breed does best with a dog-experienced owner in a suburban or rural home.

Special Needs: Fenced yard, leashed, socialization, training

Possible Health Concerns: None known

Schapendoes

Alternative Names: Dutch Schapendoes, Dutch Sheepdog

Country of Origin: The Netherlands

Group: Herding, UKC

History: The Schapendoes was developed as a sheepherding dog. It was prized by Dutch shepherds for its strong work drive and intelligence and was widely used during the late nineteenth and early twentieth centuries. It came close to extinction following World War II but was rescued by a fancier. It is only rarely used as a herding dog today.

Physical Description: The Schapendoes is a large, agile dog with a large head with a wide skull and short, broad muzzle. It has large, round, brown eyes, and its ears are naturally drop and set high. It has a long natural tail. It is double coated with a clumpy, long, thick, slightly wavy outer coat. The head and tail are heavily furred, with long feathering on the ears.

Height: 16 to 20 inches

Weight: 33 pounds

Temperament: It is an intelligent and brave dog that is independent minded and can be stubborn. It is playful and affectionate with its friends and family.

Schapendoes

Activity Level: High

Best Owner: It does best with an active, dog-experienced owner in a rural or suburban home.

Special Needs: Attention, exercise, grooming, job or activity

Possible Health Concerns: Hip dysplasia

Schipperke

Alternative Names: Spits, Spitske

Country of Origin: Belgium

Group: Companion, UKC; Non-Sporting, AKC

History: The Schipperke is from the Flemish provinces of Belgium. It was bred down from the Leauvenaar, a large black sheepdog, and is traced as far back as 1690. It was originally called spits or spitske, but in 1888

According to legend, the Schipperke lost its tail because of a quarrel between two neighbors, one of whom was angry about repeated visits from the other's Schipperke. Out of vengeance, the angry neighbor cut off the dog's tail. Fanciers liked the new look and incorporated it into the breed standard.

Schipperke

Height: 9 to 13 inches

Weight: 7 to 18 pounds

Temperament: The Schipperke is a watchful, curious, and courageous dog. It is wary with strangers and makes an excellent watchdog. It's an adaptable dog that does well with most people as long as it is socialized.

Activity Level: Moderate to high

Best Owner: It adapts to most living situations and does well in the confines of a boat, making a good live-aboard companion.

Special Needs: Exercise, socialization, grooming

Possible Health Concerns: Hypothyroidism, Legg-Perthes disease

the name was changed to Schipperke, which means "little boatman," in honor of the canalboat-line owner who championed the breed. The breed was often seen on canal barges during this time but was also popular as a shop guard, a home companion, and even a hunter.

Physical Description: The Schipperke is a medium-size dog with a short, thick body that is heavier in front than back. Its wide head narrows at the eyes, giving it a foxy look. The muzzle is tapered and equal in length to its skull. The nose is small and black, and the eyes are small and dark brown. It has small, triangular, erect ears and a docked tail. It has a heavy, harsh double coat that is long on the neck and rump but shorter on the body. In the United States, it is always black; in Europe it can be fawn, cream, sable, and chocolate.

Scottish Deerhound

Alternative Names: Deerhound

Country of Origin: Scotland

Group: Sighthound, UKC; Hound, AKC

History: The history of the Scottish Deerhound is vague, but some believe it comes from the same ancestor as the Irish Wolfhound. It was bred to hunt stag and was known as the Deerhound during the sixteenth and seventeenth centuries. Only nobility was allowed to own the breed; these restrictions on its ownership

Scottish Deerhounds

almost led to its extinction. A breeding program was established in 1825, resuscitating the breed. They are still rare but gaining popularity, especially in the United States and United Kingdom.

Physical Description: The Scottish Deerhound is a large, heavy dog that is quite similar to the Greyhound. It has a long, narrow head with a tapered black muzzle and flat skull. It has dark eyes, a black nose, and small ears that are folded when it is relaxed and semi-erect when alert. It has a long neck and a deep chest. The long tail tapers and reaches almost to the ground. The thick, medium-length coat, mostly wiry, is soft on the chest and belly. The hair on the head is long and soft with a mustache and beard and sometimes silky, silvery hair at the tip of the black ears. The coat is generally a dark blue-gray; historically, shades of yellow, red, or fawn were prized but are seldom seen today. It may have a white chest, toes, and tail tip.

Height: 28 to 32 inches

Weight: 75 to 110 pounds

Temperament: The Scottish Deerhound is an intelligent and strong-willed dog that is very attached to its people. It is courageous and keen in the field but charming and gentle in the home.

Activity Level: Moderate

Best Owner: The Scottish Deerhound does best with an active family in a suburban or rural home.

Special Needs: Exercise, fenced yard, grooming, leashed, socialization

Possible Health Concerns: Allergies, anesthesia sensitivity, bloat, cardiomyopathy, osteosarcoma

Scottish Terrier

Alternative Names: Aberdeen Terrier

Country of Origin: Scotland

Group: Terrier, UKC/AKC

History: The Scottish Terrier was originally bred to go to ground after vermin such as foxes and badgers. It was expected to fight and kill whatever it encountered underground. It was first brought to the United States in the late nineteenth century. In the early twentieth century, the breed became a popular show dog and family pet in the United Kingdom and the United States.

Physical Description: The Scottish Terrier is a small but substantial, rectangular-shaped dog with short legs and a long head. It ears are small, prick, and high set. The tail is shaped like an inverted carrot and carried erect. The Scottie has a short, dense, soft undercoat and a harsh, wiry outer coat that is trimmed to follow the outline of the body and head, with longer furnishings on the face, legs, and underbelly. Scotties come in black, wheaten, and all shades of brindle.

Scottish Terrier

Height: 10 inches

Weight: 18 to 22 pounds

Temperament: The Scottie is brave, confident, and independent but can be stubborn and sensitive. It has a high pain tolerance and may be hot tempered. It is often dog aggressive but gets along with cats. It does fine with older children.

Activity Level: Moderate

Best Owner: The Scottie requires a confident, firm, reasonable owner. It's adaptable to most living situations and activity levels in a city, country, or suburban home.

Special Needs: Grooming, socialization, supervision with small children, training

Possible Health Concerns: Craniomandibular osteopathy, elbow dysplasia, intervertebral disc protrusion, Scottie cramp, von Willebrand's disease

Sealyham Terrier

Country of Origin: Wales

Group: Terrier, UKC/AKC

History: In the late nineteenth century, the Sealyham was developed to hunt otter, badger, and fox on the Sealyham estate in Pembrokeshire, Wales. Today, it is mostly used as a show dog and companion.

Physical Description: The Sealyham is a small but powerful dog. It is rectangular in shape with a rectangular head. It is heavily bearded and whiskered, with small, dark eyes and a large, black nose. The ears are folded level with the top of the head. The tail is docked short and erect. It is double coated with a dense undercoat and wiry outer coat that is all white or with lemon-, tan-, or badger-colored markings on the head and ears.

Height: 10.5 inches

Weight: 20 to 24 pounds

Temperament: The Sealyham is hardworking, robust, and resilient. It can be willful but is loyal to its family. It will chase small animals.

Activity Level: Moderate

Best Owner: This breed does best with a patient, terrier-experienced owner. It's adaptable to city, suburban, or country life.

Special Needs: Fenced yard, firm but positive training, grooming, leashed, socialization

Possible Health Concerns: Allergies, deafness, eye problems

Shetland Sheepdog

Country of Origin: Scotland

Group: Herding, UKC/AKC

History: The Shetland Sheepdog is an old breed that is descended from the dogs brought to the Shetland Islands off the Scottish coast by invading Vikings in the tenth century. These were spitz-type dogs that were similar to Vallhunds. The dogs were developed as herding dogs and kept isolated until the fifteenth century, when the Shetland Islands became part of Scotland and Scottish Collies were introduced to the islands. These dogs gave the Sheltie a more Collie-like look. The Sheltie is one of many compact animals bred by Shetland islanders.

Sealyham Terrier

The Shetland Sheepdog is often referred to as a "miniature Collie." The two breeds do bear a resemblance, and the Collie is an ancestor of the Shetland Sheepdog, but the two are separate and distinct breeds.

It was first brought to the United States in the early twentieth century.

Physical Description: The Sheltie is a small- to medium-size, muscular, rectangular-shaped dog. It looks like a miniature rough Collie. It has a narrow, wedge-shaped head with a skull and muzzle of equal length. The nose is black and the eyes are almond shaped and brown or blue or a combination of the two. The small ears are folded when at rest and semi-erect when alert. The thick, long tail is set low, and there is a double coat with a dense undercoat and a long, straight outer coat. The coat forms a mane at the neck and trousers at the thighs and may be black, blue merle, sable, sable merle, or mostly white, with or without tan or white markings.

Shetland Sheepdog

Height: 13 to 16 inches

Weight: 20 to 25 pounds

Temperament: This is an intelligent, hard-working, trainable dog. It is affectionate with its family but wary with strangers. It is responsive and prone to barking, making it a good watchdog.

Activity Level: High

Best Owner: The Sheltie does best with an active owner in a rural or suburban home.

Special Needs: Exercise, grooming, job or activity, socialization, training

Possible Health Concerns: Epilepsy, eye problems, hip dysplasia, Sheltie skin syndrome, thyroid problems, von Willebrand's disease

Shiba Inu

Alternative Names: Shiba Ken

Country of Origin: Japan

Group: Northern, UKC; Non-Sporting, AKC

History: The Shiba Inu is the smallest and oldest of Japan's native breeds. It was bred to flush birds and small game and was occasionally used to hunt wild boar. It has great cultural significance in Japan and is considered a natural monument. It came close to extinction after World War II. Most Shiba Inu are now kept as pets. The breed was first brought to the United States in 1954.

Physical Description: The Shiba Inu is a foxy, medium-size, compact, and well-muscled dog that is slightly longer than it is tall. It has a broad head with dark, upward-slanting eyes; a black nose; and small, erect ears. It is double coated with a dense outer coat in red, sesame (black-tipped hairs on a red background), or black with tan points. The undercoat is cream, buff, or gray.

Height: 13.5 to 16.5 inches

Weight: 15 to 25 pounds

Shiba Inu

Temperament: The Shiba Inu is an alert, curious, intelligent dog with a lively, fun-loving personality. It is independent and known to wander.

Activity Level: Moderate

Best Owner: This breed does well with an active owner in a city, suburban, or rural home.

Special Needs: Fenced yard, leashed, socialization, training

Possible Health Concerns: Eye problems, heart problems, hip dysplasia, luxating patellas

Shih Tzu

Alternative Names: Fo Dog, Chrysanthemum-faced Dog

Country of Origin: China

Group: Companion, UKC; Toy, AKC

History: The history of the Shih Tzu is somewhat cloudy. It may have existed in China as far back as the Tang Dynasty during the seventh century, or it may not have arrived in China until the tenth century. Regardless, it is well-documented in Chinese art, including carvings and embroideries. It was bred in the Forbidden City in Beijing and was probably developed to resemble the tame lion, or Fo Dog, which is sacred to Buddhists. It was kept only by royalty. Because it was associated with the ruling class, most were killed during the Chinese Revolution. Some were spared, and breeding was continued in England and the United States.

Physical Description: The Shih Tzu is a small, sturdy, well-balanced dog that is slightly longer than it is tall. It is compact but with substance and an arrogant carriage. Its head is round and broad with the eyes set wide apart. The unwrinkled snout is short and square, with a broad jaw. It has large drop ears. The tail is set high and curls over the back. The breed is double coated, with a dense, long, flowing outer coat. The long hair on the head is tied in a topknot. It can be of any color or color combination.

Height: 8 to 11 inches

Weight: 9 to 16 pounds

Temperament: The Shih Tzu is a friendly, trusting, companionable dog. It gets along with everyone, including children, strangers, and other animals. It is lively, alert, and affectionate.

Shih Tzu

Activity Level: Low

Best Owner: The Shih Tzu does very well living in an apartment with an attentive owner.

Special Needs: Attention, grooming

Possible Health Concerns: Allergies, cleft palate, eye problems, renal disease, von Willebrand's disease

Siberian Husky

Country of Origin: Siberia

Group: Northern, UKC; Working, AKC

History: The Siberian Husky is believed to have been developed by the Chukchi Indians, natives of the region now called Siberia, more than 3,000 years ago. The Siberian Husky was first used as a sled dog to pull small loads. Because of its isolation, the breed was kept very pure until the twentieth century, when Alaskans began importing the dogs to use for sled racing. Although largely replaced in dog sledding by the more-competitive Alaskan Husky, the Siberian Husky continues to be used as a recreational sled dog and companion. It also served as a sled dog with the U.S. military during World War II.

Physical Description: The Siberian Husky is a medium-size dog with a compact, muscular body. It is slightly longer than it is tall. It has medium-size, erect ears and almond-shaped eyes that can be brown, blue, one of each, or parti-colored. Depending on the color of the dog, the nose is black, liver, flesh-colored, or streaked with pink. It is double coated with a medium-length, straight outer coat and a dense undercoat. The tail is well-furred. It can be any color, ranging from black to white, with a variety of black or white markings.

Height: 20 to 23.5 inches

Weight: 35 to 60 pounds

Temperament: The Siberian Husky is an active, lively dog that is friendly and out-

Siberian Husky

going with almost everyone. It tends to be independent and is not a one person dog. It will roam and is known to be a consummate escape artist.

Activity Level: High

Best Owner: This breed does well with an active family in a suburban or rural home.

Special Needs: Exercise, fenced yard, job or organized activity, leashed, socialization, training

Possible Health Concerns: Cataracts, corneal dystrophy, hip dysplasia, PRA

Silky Terrier

Alternative Names: Australian Silky Terrier

Country of Origin: Australia

Group: Terrier, UKC; Toy, AKC

History: The Silky Terrier was developed from crossings of native Australian Terriers and Yorkshire Terriers, when Yorkies were brought to Australia at end of the 1800s. It is one of two native Australian terriers and has mostly been used as a companion.

Silky Terrier

Physical Description: The Silky Terrier is a small, lightly built dog that is slightly longer than it is tall. Its head is strong, long, and wedge shaped with a flat skull that is slightly longer than the muzzle. The nose is black and the eyes are small, dark, and almond shaped. The ears are naturally erect, small, and V shaped. The body is low set and the tail is docked and set high. It has small, cat-like feet. The coat is single, straight, and glossy. It has a topknot but no long hair on the face. The blue and tan coat is parted down the middle from head to tail.

Height: 9 to 10 inches

Weight: 8 to 10 pounds

Temperament: The Silky Terrier is a keen, friendly, and lively dog. It requires a great deal of attention and human interaction.

Activity Level: Moderate

Best Owner: This breed is adaptable to many living situations, making an excellent apartment dog.

Special Needs: Attention, socialization, grooming

Possible Health Concerns: Cancer and non-cancerous tumors, cataracts, Cushing's disease, epilepsy, hypothyroidism, Legg-Perthes disease, luxating patellas, pancreatic disease

Skye Terrier

Country of Origin: Scotland

Group: Terrier, UKC/AKC

History: The Skye Terrier is from the Isle of Skye, the largest island in the Inner Hebrides off the coast of Scotland. It is believed to have originated in the sixteenth century. Some say that the Waternish Terrier, an ancestor of the Cairn and Australian Terriers, was the original Skye Terrier.

Physical Description: The Skye Terrier is a long, low dog that is twice as long as it is tall. It is well boned and muscled. It may have either prick or drop ears and has brown eyes and a black nose. It is double coated with a soft, woolly undercoat and a profuse outer coat that falls straight to either side of the body. The coat is especially profuse on the head and covers the forehead and eyes. It may be a blend of various shades of black, blue, dark or light gray, silver platinum, fawn, or cream. It may have black points on the ears, muzzle, and tip of the long, feathered tail.

Height: 9 to 10 inches

Weight: 23 to 28 pounds

Temperament: The Skye Terrier is serious and dignified. It is calm indoors but fearless and active in the field. It is loyal and sensitive. It is wary of strangers and will react if pro-

In the nineteenth century, Skye Terriers with prick ears became more popular than those with drop ears, partly because of Queen Victoria's fondness for the variety. The prick-eared Skye Terrier became valued as a companion and show dog, and the drop-eared Skye Terrier was valued as a working dog.

Skye Terrier

voked. It does well with children as long as it is socialized.

Activity Level: Low

Best Owner: The Skye Terrier does best with a terrier-experienced owner and can adapt to a city, suburban, or rural home.

Special Needs: Fenced yard, grooming, leashed, socialization, positive but firm training

Possible Health Concerns: Copper toxicosis, hypothyroidism

Sloughi

Alternative Names: Arabian Greyhound, Slougui

Country of Origin: North Africa

Group: Sighthound, UKC

History: Although its history is cloudy, it is believed that the Sloughi is one of the descendants of the drop-eared sighthounds treasured by ancient Egyptians. It is the dog of the Berber people of Morocco, Tunisia, Algeria, and Libya and the bedouin people, who use it as a hunter on small and medium-size game. It is also used as a flock guardian. The breed almost became extinct at the turn of the twentieth century due to disease and political and social upheavals in North Africa. There has been renewed interest in the breed in North Africa, France, and the United States, but it is still quite rare. The Sloughi first came to the United States in 1973.

Physical Description: The Sloughi is a medium-size dog with a muscular, racy, square build. It has a long neck and triangular head with a tapering muzzle that is even in length with the skull. The head tends to be stronger than that of most sighthounds. It has triangular drop ears and brown eyes that are often lined with black. The short, smooth coat may be sand colored, black with tan or brindle markings, or brindle. It often has a black mask and other black markings and may have a white on the chest and on the tips of the toes. Among the Sloughis there are two types, a desert and a mountain type. The desert type is smaller and more lightly built.

Height: 24 to 29.5 inches

Weight: 40 to 63 pounds

Temperament: The Sloughi is affectionate and devoted to its family but wary with strangers. It gets along well with almost

Sloughi

everyone, including children and other dogs, if it has been properly socialized. It enjoys running but can be calm in the home. It is slow to mature and tends to be sensitive, reacting if provoked.

Activity Level: Moderate

Best Owner: Sloughis do very well with active, patient owners who have time for them. A suburban or rural home is best.

Special Needs: Exercise, fenced yard, leashed, socialization, training

Possible Health Concerns: Anesthesia sensitivity, atrophy of the jaw, heart murmur, PRA

Slovac Cuvac

Alternative Names: Slovensky Čuvač, Slovakian Chuvach, Tatransky Čuvač, Slovensky Kuvac

Country of Origin: Slovakia

Group: Guardian, UKC

History: The Slovac Cuvac is an old breed that has been used as a flock guardian and shepherd's companion for centuries. It came close to extinction after World War II but was revitalized by fanciers and the School of Veterinary Medicine in Brno, Czech Republic.

Physical Description: The Slovac Cuvac is a large, powerful dog. The skin is pink but black at the eye rims, neck, muzzle, and foot pads, with black mucous membranes. The oval eyes are dark brown. The double coat has a profuse outer coat that is longest at the neck, forming a ruff. It is shortest at the head and legs. The coat is white, sometimes with yellow at the ears.

Height: 23 to 28 inches

Weight: 70 to 110 pounds

Temperament: This is a loyal and courageous dog that is highly protective of home and family.

Activity Level: Moderate

Best Owner: The Slovak Cuvac does best with a dog-experienced owner in a suburban or rural home.

Special Needs: Fenced yard, leashed, socialization, training

Possible Health Concerns: None known

Small Münsterländer

Alternative Names: Small Münsterländ Pointer, Kleiner Münsterländer Vorstehhund

Country of Origin: Germany

Group: Gun Dog, UKC

History: The Small Münsterländer was developed in the Münster region of Germany, probably from crosses between German Longhaired Pointers and continental spaniels. The dogs are versatile hunters, used for pointing and retrieving both in the water and on land.

Physical Description: This is a medium-size, muscular dog. It has a slightly rounded head, brown nose; brown eyes; and broad drop ears that are set high and end in a point. The double coat has a sleek, slightly wavy outer coat of moderate length. There is

Slovac Cuvac

Small Münsterländer

feathering on the tail and legs. The medium-length tail is carried straight, although the last third may be lightly curved upward. The coat is brown and white or white ticked with brown (roan). Tan markings are permitted on the muzzle and eyes.

Height: 19 to 22 inches

Weight: 33 pounds

Temperament: The Small Münsterländer is an active, social dog. It is affectionate but can be stubborn and has a strong prey drive. Fanciers describe it as having a sweet and sassy personality. It loves water activities and gets along well with children and other dogs.

Activity Level: High

Best Owner: This breed does best with an active rural or suburban family.

Special Needs: Exercise, grooming, training

Possible Health Concerns: Hip dysplasia

Soft Coated Wheaten Terrier

Country of Origin: Ireland

Group: Terrier, UKC/AKC

History: The Soft Coated Wheaten Terrier is likely a descendant of the ancient dogs found in Ireland for thousands of years. It is believed to be related to the Irish Terrier and the Kerry Blue Terrier and may be a forefather of the Glen of Imaal terrier. It was used primarily as an all-purpose farm dog, family guardian, and companion, as well as a herding dog. It did not come to the United States until the 1940s.

Physical Description: It is a medium-size, square dog with a long, rectangular head and small drop ears that break forward. Its nose is large and black, and its eyes are almond shaped and reddish brown or brown. It has a deep chest and a docked tail that is held erect. Its single coat is soft and slightly wavy. The coat is profuse on its head, covering its eyes and forming a beard. It can be any shade of wheaten.

Height: 17 to 19 inches

Weight: 30 to 40 pounds

Temperament: The Soft Coated Wheaten Terrier is stubborn but playful. It is the quintessential self-confident terrier, although it may be less aggressive than some. It enjoys being with its family and hates to be left alone for long periods.

Activity Level: High

Best Owner: An active owner in a suburban or rural home is best.

Special Needs: Exercise, firm but positive training, grooming, socialization

Soft Coated Wheaten Terrier

Possible Health Concerns: Addison's disease, cancer, kidney problems, PRA, skin problems

South Russian Ovcharka

Alternative Names: Youzhnorusskaya Ovcharka, Youzhak

Country of Origin: Russia

Group: Guardian, UKC

History: The South Russian Ovcharka was developed in the early nineteenth century in the Crimean region of Askania Nova from a blend of Spanish and German sheepdogs and local dogs. It was developed to guard sheep from large predators. The breed went into a steep decline when a reduction of wolves and agricultural land during the mid-nineteenth century led to a reduced need for livestock guardians. By the end of the Russian Revolution, the breed was close to extinction. The breed was revitalized but again declined following World War II. Cross-breeding with Komondors was required to resurrect the breed. It continues to be rare and is again in decline.

Physical Description: This is a large, powerful, lean dog with a long, broad head and a

South Russian Ovcharka

large, black nose. The eyes are dark and the ears are small, triangular, and drop. The chest is deep and the long tail is curved. The double coat has a profuse undercoat and long, harsh outer coat. It is usually white but may be gray, beige, or white with gray markings.

Height: 24 to 26 inches minimum

Weight: No standard available

Temperament: This is a very independent dog that can be willful and dominant. It can be affectionate with family but also temperamental. It is very wary with strangers and should be allowed to approach rather than be approached.

Activity Level: Moderate

Best Owner: The South Russian Ovcharka requires a very dog-experienced owner in a rural home. It is not suitable as a pet in most circumstances.

Special Needs: Fenced yard, firm training, grooming, job or activity, leashed, moderate exercise, rigorous socialization

Possible Health Concerns: None known

Spanish Greyhound

Alternative Names: Galgo Español

Country of Origin: Spain

Group: Sighthound, UKC

History: The Spanish Greyhound is descended from Asian Greyhounds and was bred for coursing hare and other small game in the steppes and mountains of the Iberian Peninsula. It is believed that it originally arrived in Spain with Arabs and may be a descendant of the Sloughi or Ibizan Hound. It was exported to Ireland and England in the sixteenth, seventeenth, and eighteenth centuries and is often cited as the ancestor of the English Greyhound. It continues to be used for hunting and for Greyhound racing in its native Spain. As is true of other Greyhounds, the use of the

Spanish Greyhound

working Spanish Greyhound is controversial, with reports of cruel treatment by some racetrack owners and hunters.

Physical Description: The Spanish Greyhound is a large, rectangular, narrow dog with a deep chest. It is both muscular and elegant, with a long, narrow head and muzzle that is longer than the skull. It has a small, black nose and almond-shaped eyes. The natural, triangular ears are folded when at rest and semi-erect when alert or active. It has a long neck and a long, tapered, hooked tail. The coat may be short and smooth or longer and wiry. It can be any color but is usually black, flecked with black, burnt chestnut, fawn, brindle, yellow, red, white, or white with pied markings.

Height: 24 to 28 inches

Weight: No standard available

Temperament: The Spanish Greyhound makes an excellent pet; it is gentle with children and devoted to its family. It loves to play but tends to be sedentary in the home. It is sensitive and may be wary with strangers and aggressive toward small animals. Most Spanish Greyhounds kept as pets are retired racing Greyhounds or hunting dogs, so they require some basic training for their new roles.

Activity Level: Moderate

Best Owner: This breed adapts to almost any living situation but shouldn't be homed with small animals.

Special Needs: Moderate exercise, protection from the cold, training

Possible Health Concerns: None known

Spanish Hound

Alternative Names: Sabueso Español

Group: Scenthound, UKC

Country of Origin: Spain

History: The Spanish Hound is an old breed that is believed to date to the Middle Ages. It was popular with the Spanish aristocracy and intelligentsia. It hunted both big and small game and continues to be used for hunting today.

Physical Description: This is a medium-size dog that is much longer than it is tall. It has a long head with a rectangular muzzle. The large nose ranges in color from light to black. It has moderate flews and almond-shaped, hazel eyes. The long drop ears are finely leathered and fall in a corkscrew. The skin is loose on the strong neck, and the chest is deep. The long tail is sabrelike.

Spanish Hound

There is loose, elastic skin over the entire body and a short, smooth coat of white and orange.

Height: 19 to 22 inches

Weight: 44 to 55 pounds

Temperament: This is an even-tempered, active dog that is an intense hunter and can be stubborn. It is not easily trained.

Activity Level: High

Best Owner: This breed is only rarely kept as a companion animal but would do well with an active family in a rural home.

Special Needs: Exercise, fenced yard, leashed

Possible Health Concerns: Hearing problems, hip dysplasia

Spanish Water Dog

Alternative Names: Perro de Agua Español, Turco de Andaluz

Group: Gun Dog , UKC

Country of Origin: Spain

History: This curly-coated breed is probably an old variety of Barbet or other water dog. The dogs have been used to retrieve from water and to herd sheep. The dog is an amazing swimmer and can dive underwater! Over the centuries, similar dogs were kept by goat and sheepherders in southern Spain, but it wasn't until the 1970s that they were considered a distinct breed.

Physical Description: The Spanish Water Dog is strong, medium size, and deep chested. It is longer than it is tall. The curly coat has a woolly texture and forms cords when long. It can be white, black, or chestnut or white and black or white and chestnut (parti-color). The eye color can be hazel to chestnut, harmonizing with the color of the coat. If not a natural bobtail, the tail is docked.

Height: 17.3 to 19.7 inches

Weight: 30.9 to 48.5 pounds

Temperament: This is a fun-loving, active dog. It is faithful, obedient, and hardworking.

Activity Level: High

Best Owner: This breed does best with an active owner in a rural environment.

Special Needs: Exercise, grooming

Possible Health Concerns: Eye problems, hip dysplasia

Spinone Italiano

Alternative Names: Italian Spinone

Country of Origin: Italy

Group: Gun Dog, UKC; Sporting, AKC

History: The Spinone Italiano is descended from an ancient hunting dog in the Piedmont region of Italy. Although the breed is considered to be one of the oldest griffon types, it is actually an old-type pointer. The Spinone is valued for its great stamina and ability to work any terrain.

Physical Description: This is a large, muscular, and sturdy dog. It has a large head and square muzzle with yellow-brown eyes, a large nose that ranges from flesh to brown, and triangular, long drop ears.

Spanish Water Dog

Spinone Italiano fanciers say the breed surpasses all other Italian gun dogs for its efficiency as a worker.

Spinone Italiano

The chest is deep and broad. The harsh coat is medium length on the body but longer on the face, forming a beard, mustache, and eyebrows. It may be solid white, white and orange, orange roan with or without orange markings, white with brown markings, or brown roan with or without brown markings. The tail is docked and carried horizontally or down.

Height: 22 to 27 inches

Weight: 60 to 90 pounds

Temperament: The Spinone Italiano is enthusiastic and playful with a gentle, calm demeanor. It can be obstinate and is often wary with strangers and in new situations. It is hardworking and tends to be vocal.

Activity Level: Moderate

Best Owner: This dog requires an active family in a rural or suburban environment.

Special Needs: Attention, exercise, training, socializing

Possible Health Concerns: Cerebellar ataxia, eye problems, hip dysplasia, malocclusion of the teeth, visceral leishmaniasis

Stabyhoun

Alternative Names: Frisian Pointing Dog

Country of Origin: The Netherlands

Group: Gun Dog, UKC

History: This Dutch gun dog was developed in the Frisian woods in the province of Friesland during the nineteenth century. The breed is believed to be descended from spaniel-like hounds brought to the Netherlands by the Spanish. It is an all-purpose dog, used for hunting, guarding, drafting, and as a companion.

Physical Description: This strong, medium-size dog is longer than it is tall. It has medium-length drop ears that are set high and a long tail that curves upward. It has a broad skull with brown eyes and a black nose. The sleek coat is medium long and the head and body are of two different colors. The head is black, brown, or orange and the body is white with black, brown, or orange markings.

Height: 19.5 to 21 inches

Weight: 40 to 55 pounds

Stabyhoun

Temperament: The Stabyhoun is friendly, lively, and affectionate. It is very good natured and gets along well with children and other pets.

Activity Level: High

Best Owner: It does best with an active family in a rural or suburban home.

Special Needs: Exercise

Possible Health Concerns: Epilepsy, hip dysplasia

Staffordshire Bull Terrier

Country of Origin: Great Britain

Group: Terrier, UKC/AKC

History: The Staffordshire Bull Terrier is one of the bull-and-terrier crosses of the early nineteenth century. It was developed for dog fighting and was once known as the old pit Bull Terrier. After dog fighting was made illegal, it evolved into a companion. The Staffie arrived in the United States in the 1880s, where some lines were developed into today's American Staffordshire Terrier. In England, it is known as the nanny dog because of its innate love of children.

Physical Description: The Staffordshire Bull Terrier is a medium-size dog that gives the impression of great strength and power. It has a large, broad, wrinkled head with pronounced cheek muscles and a short foreface. The jaw is powerful and the nose is black. The eyes are dark and round. The medium-size ears are rose or semi-erect. Its straight, well-boned forelegs are set wide apart and the hindquarters are well muscled. The medium-length tapered tail is set low. The short, smooth coat comes in red, fawn, white, black, blue, or brindle, with or without white.

Height: 14 to 16 inches

Weight: 24 to 38 pounds

Temperament: The Staffie is a courageous, tenacious, and even-tempered dog. It is extremely affectionate to people, especially children. It is often aggressive toward other dogs and has a strong prey drive.

Activity Level: Moderate to high

Best Owner: The Staffie does best with an owner that is dog-experienced and has time for him. It is adaptable to the country or the city.

Special Needs: Attention, exercise, supervision around water, socialization, training

Possible Health Concerns: Cataracts, entropion

Staffordshire Bull Terrier

Standard Schnauzer

Alternative Names: Schnauzer

Country of Origin: Germany

Group: Guardian, UKC; Working, AKC

History: The Standard is the prototype of the three schnauzers; its ancestry dates to the fifteenth century. It is believed to be a cross between the black German Poodle, gray Wolfspitz, and Wirehaired Pinscher. It was developed as a farm dog, guard, and ratter but also served as a companion. It was often kept by farmers to guard their carts at market. It has also been used as a military dog. The Standard Schnauzer was not known in the United States until after World War I, but the breed has since become a popular companion dog.

Physical Description: A medium-size dog, the Standard Schnauzer is muscular and squarely built. It has a strong, rectangular head with brown, oval eyes, and an arched brow. The V-shaped button ears are cropped erect or left natural, and the large nose is black. It has a long neck and short body. The tail is docked short and carried erect. The double coat has a short, soft undercoat and harsh, wiry outer coat with long, wiry eyebrows, and whiskers. It is salt and pepper or black.

Height: 17 to 20 inches

Weight: 30 to 50 pounds

Temperament: This is an intelligent and highly trainable dog. It is very lively and playful, some say mischievous. It is affectionate and devoted to its family but territorial and wary of strangers, making it an excellent watchdog. It gets along with children but has a strong prey drive and isn't trustworthy with small animals.

Standard Schnauzers

Activity Level: High

Best Owner: This dog does best with an active, dog-experienced family. It adapts to city, rural, or suburban life with adequate exercise.

Special Needs: Exercise, grooming, socialization, training

Possible Health Concerns: Hip dysplasia

Stumpy Tail Cattle Dog

Country of Origin: Australia

Group: Herding, UKC

History: Although they are cousins, this is not the same breed as the Australian Cattle Dog. The Stumpy Tail is said to be a cross between a dingo and the Smithfield, the first type of cattle dog used by Australian ranchers. This original cross resulted in the Timmins Biter, which was crossed with the blue-merle, smooth-coated Collie. It lacks the Australian Kelpie cross found in the Australian Cattle Dog.

Physical Description: The Stumpy Tail Cattle Dog is leggier than the Australian Cattle Dog and has no tail. It is a muscular, square-shaped dog with a broad head, flat skull, and moderately long foreface. The eyes are dark brown and oval, and the nose is black. It has small prick ears. The chest is deep. The tail is a natural bob, no longer than four inches in length. The double coat has a soft undercoat and short, straight outer coat. There is a ruff around the neck. The coat is blue or blue mottled, with or without black markings; or red speckle, with or without darker red markings.

Height: 17 to 20 inches

Weight: No standard available

Temperament: It is a hard worker with great endurance and energy. It is a one-person dog and is naturally reserved but not unfriendly.

Activity Level: High

Best Owner: This breed does best with an active family in a rural home, especially on a ranch or farm.

Special Needs: Exercise, job or activity, socialization, training

Possible Health Concerns: Cleft palate, spina bifida and other vertebral problems

Sussex Spaniel

Country of Origin: Great Britain

Group: Gun Dog, UKC; Sporting, AKC

History: The Sussex Spaniel was developed in Sussex, England, as a field dog. It has been recognized as a distinct breed since the eighteenth century and was well known as a hunting dog on large estates during the nineteenth century.

Physical Description: This is a muscular, rectangular-shaped dog. It has a strong head with heavy eyebrows and a wide, long skull. The muzzle is square and the lips are pendulous. It has a liver-colored nose and large, hazel eyes. The long, wide drop ears are set low. The tail is docked. There is a profuse, flat or slightly wavy, golden liver coat that is heaviest at the ears, legs, and tail.

Height: 13 to 15 inches

Weight: 35 to 45 pounds

Temperament: The Sussex Spaniel is easygoing and friendly. It is a hard worker and protective of home and family. It tends to vocalize.

Activity Level: Moderate

Best Owner: It does best in a rural or suburban home.

Special Needs: Grooming, socialization, training

Possible Health Concerns: Cardiac problems, intervertebral disc syndrome, otitis externa

Swedish Vallhund

Alternative Names: Västgötaspets, Viking Dog, Swedish Cattle Dog

Country of Origin: Sweden

Group: Northern, UKC; Herding, AKC

Sussex Spaniel

Swedish Vallhund

History: The Swedish Vallhund is believed to an ancient dog, first developed as an all-purpose farm dog and cattle herder. It is believed to have been brought to Sweden with the Vikings and may be related to the Corgis. It was close to extinction until the mid-twentieth century, when a fancier revitalized the breed. The Vallhund is a herder of both cattle and sheep. It was first imported to England in the 1970s and to the United States in the 1980s.

Physical Description: This is a sturdy, small- or medium-size spitz-type dog with a rectangular shape. It has a wedge-shaped head, black nose, and prick ears. The tail is naturally long or bob, or it is docked. The double coat has a thick undercoat and coarse outer coat that is gray to red with harness markings and a facial mask.

Height: 12 to 14 inches

Weight: 25 to 35 pounds

Temperament: The Vallhund is an alert, bold, curious, and energetic dog. A hard worker, it is intelligent, trainable, and eager to please. It gets along with almost everyone, including children and other animals.

Activity Level: Moderate

Best Owner: The Vallhund requires an active owner. It can adapt to a city, suburban, or rural home, provided it receives enough exercise and attention.

Special Needs: Exercise

Possible Health Concerns: Cleft palate, cryptorchidism, hip dysplasia, luxating patellas, retinal dysplasia

Teddy Roosevelt Terrier

Alternative Names: Teddy, Bench Legged Feist, Feist, Rat Terrier Type B

Country of Origin: United States

Group: Terrier, UKC

History: The Teddy Roosevelt Terrier is essentially a Rat Terrier with short legs. It was developed from terriers brought over by English miners and other working-class immigrants; contributing breeds include crosses between the Smooth Fox Terrier, the Manchester Terrier, the Bull Terrier, the Beagle, the Whippet, the Italian Greyhound, and the now-extinct white English Terrier. Because they were used as ratters, they soon became known as Rat Terriers. Two types of Rat Terriers evolved, distinguished by leg length. The short-legged Rat Terrier developed its own following and was named in honor of President Teddy Roosevelt, who is believed to have owned these ratters.

Physical Description: The Teddy is a low-set, muscular, small dog, slightly longer than it is tall. Its ears may be button or erect and its tail docked, naturally bob, or naturally long and curved. It has a short, smooth coat found in several colors and patterns: solid white, tricolored (with patches of black and tan), and bicolored (any combination of black, tan, chocolate, red, orange, lemon, or blue with white), with or without tan or rust markings on the cheeks and over the eyes.

Height: 8 to 15 inches

Weight: Proportionate to height

Temperament: The Teddy is a lively, friendly, affectionate dog with its family. It is often a one-person dog. The Teddy gets along well with children and other pets if socialized with them. It may be aloof with strangers.

Activity Level: Moderate

Best Owner: The Teddy Roosevelt is a versatile breed and can fit into a city, suburban, or rural home as long as it receives ample attention and exercise.

Special Needs: Attention, socialization

Possible Health Concerns: Luxating patellas, mange

Thai Ridgeback

Country of Origin: Thailand

Group: Sighthound and Pariah, UKC

History: The Thai Ridgeback is believed to be at least 350 years old. It is most common in eastern Thailand, where it is used for hunting and guarding. It is a rare dog but is becoming more common in the United States.

While hunting and playing, Teddy Roosevelt Terriers are very vocal. The dogs demonstrate their exuberance and excitement by growling and snarling.

Thai Ridgeback

Physical Description: The Thai Ridgeback is a medium-size, muscular dog that is slightly longer than it is tall. It has a wedge-shaped muzzle; large, erect, triangular ears; and dark, almond-shaped eyes. It has a short, smooth coat with a ridge along the back that is formed by hair growing in the opposite direction. It may be chestnut, red, blue, fawn, or black.

Height: 20 to 25 inches

Weight: No standard available

Temperament: The Thai Ridgeback is a tough and protective dog. It is often dog aggressive.

Activity Level: Moderate to high

Best Owner: This breed does best with an experienced dog owner in a rural or suburban home.

Special Needs: Exercise, training, socialization, training

Possible Health Concerns: Dermoid sinus

Tibetan Mastiff

Country of Origin: Tibet

Group: Guardian, UKC; Working, AKC

History: The Tibetan Mastiff is an ancient breed that was used to guard livestock and property in Tibetan villages, although the breed may have originally come from China. This breed is believed to be the progenitor of all mastiffs, but it was not exported during modern times until 1847, when Queen Victoria received a Tibetan Mastiff as a gift. The first Tibetan Mastiff came to the United States as a gift to President Eisenhower.

Physical Description: This is a heavy, powerful dog that is longer than it is tall. The broad head is heavily wrinkled with a square muzzle and broad nose. The lips are moderately pendulous, and the eyes are brown and

Tibetan Mastiffs were bred to have a deep, booming bark to warn villagers when something was amiss. Today's Tibetan Mastiff still has the instinct to protect and the big bark to accompany it.

Tibetan Mastiff

slanted. The ears are drop. The long tail curls over the back. The double coat has a dense undercoat and a hard, straight outer coat. The neck, chest, tail, and hind legs are feathered. The coat may be black; black and tan; brown; gold; gray and blue; or gray, blue, and tan, with tan markings above the eyes, lower legs, under the tail, on the muzzle, and around the eyes. There may be white markings on the chest and feet.

Height: 24 to 30 inches

Weight: 75 to 160 pounds

Temperament: The Tibetan Mastiff is a reserved and independent-minded dog that is dominant and often stubborn, with what some call catlike behavior. It is very protective and makes a good guard. It should be supervised with children and other animals, as it can be overprotective and may misinterpret benign interactions.

Activity Level: Moderate

Best Owner: The Tibetan Mastiff does best with a firm, dog-experienced owner in a rural or suburban environment. It does not make a good fulltime livestock guardian.

Special Needs: Fenced yard, firm training, grooming, leashed, socialization

Possible Health Concerns: Ectropion, hip and elbow dysplasia, entropion, hypothyroidism

Tibetan Spaniel

Country of Origin: Tibet

Group: Companion, UKC; Non-Sporting, AKC

History: The Tibetan Spaniel is not actually a spaniel; instead, it is related to the Pekingese and the Japanese Chin. It was developed by Tibetan Buddhist lamas to resemble lions, or Fo Dogs, which are revered in Buddhist symbolism. It was commonly given as a gift to rulers in other Buddhist countries. In the monasteries, it served as a companion and guard, barking from the top of the monastery walls. The first of these dogs were brought to England in the late nineteenth century, but the breed did not make its way to the United States until 1965.

Physical Description: The Tibetan Spaniel is a small dog that is slightly longer than it is tall. Its head is small in proportion to its body and carried proudly. It has a medium-length muzzle that is blunt and wrinkle free. Its nose is black, dark eyes are medium size and oval, and ears are medium size and pendant. It has small hare feet and a well-feathered tail that is set high and carried curled over the back. It is double coated with silky, medium-length hair. There is a ruff around the neck and the ears; the back of the legs and rump are well feathered. The face and front of the legs are smooth. All colors and combinations are seen.

Height: 9 to 11 inches

Weight: 9 to 15 pounds

Temperament: The Tibetan Spaniel is an affectionate, family-oriented, and eager-to-please dog. It is wary with strangers, making it a good watchdog, but good with people and animals it knows. Some describe it as catlike.

Activity Level: Low to moderate

Best Owner: It is very adaptable, doing well in the country or city, with an individual or family.

Special Needs: Socialization, moderate grooming

Possible Health Concerns: Cataracts, PRA

Tibetan Spaniel

Tibetan Terrier

Country of Origin: Tibet

Group: Companion, UKC; Non-Sporting, AKC

History: The Tibetan Terrier is an ancient breed traced back 2,000 years. It was originally used to guard Tibetan monasteries in the Lost Valley as well as for herding and as a companion. Highly valued by the monks as a holy symbol, it was never sold, only given as a gift. Belying its name, it is not actually a terrier. It is likely the forefather of the Lhasa Apso. It first made his way to the West when an English doctor was given several Tibetan Terriers, which

Tibetan Terrier

she raised in India and, later, England. The first Tibetan Terrier was brought to the United States in 1956.

Physical Description: The Tibetan Terrier is a medium-size, powerful dog that is squarely built. Its skull and muzzle are equal in length. The ears are pendant and V shaped. It has distinctive feet: they are large, flat, and round, providing a snowshoe effect. The tail is of medium length. It is double coated, with a soft, woolly undercoat and a heavy, long, wavy or straight outer coat. It is heavily coated on the feet, tail, face, and ears. It can be any color or combination of colors.

Height: 14 to 17 inches

Weight: 18 to 30 pounds

Temperament: The Tibetan Terrier is wary and reserved with strangers but loyal and affectionate with family. It is both intelligent and good-natured and gets along with almost everyone it meets, including children and other animals.

Activity Level: Low to moderate

Tibetan Terriers were bred for good health and temperament rather than coat color. Today, Tibetan Terriers continue to come in a variety of colors, with no preferred colors or combinations.

Best Owner: This is an adaptable dog that does well in the city, suburbs, and country.

Special Needs: Attention, grooming, moderate exercise, positive training, socialization

Possible Health Concerns: Lens luxation, hip dysplasia, hypothyroidism, PRA

Tosa Ken

Alternative Names: Tosa Inu

Country of Origin: Japan

Group: Guardian, UKC

History: The Tosa Ken was developed only after Commodore Perry traveled to Japan in 1854, opening up trade between Japan and Western countries. Japanese breeders bred foreign dogs, such as Bulldogs, Mastiffs, Great Danes, and German Pointers, with native breeds, such as the indigenous Shikoku, to create the canine equivalent of a sumo wrestler. The dogs were and continue to be used in ceremonial dog fighting. The breed came close to extinction after World War II but was revitalized by fanciers.

Physical Description: The Tosa Ken is a large, powerful, and muscular dog that is longer than it is tall. It has a large, boxy head; pendulous lips; and a prominent dewlap. The head wrinkles when the dog is alert. The

Tosa Ken

skull is broad and the muzzle is broad and blunt with powerful jaws. The nose is black, and there may be black on the pink tongue. The high-set, medium-size ears are drop, and the eyes are small, almond shaped, and brown. The natural tail is long and tapered. The short, thick coat is any solid color, brindle, black with markings, or pied. All-red dogs are preferred. There may be a black mask and white on the chest and feet.

Height: 21.75 to 23.5 inches minimum

Weight: 90 to 240 pounds

Temperament: This is a quiet, reserved dog that is affectionate and friendly with family and aloof with strangers. It may be dog aggressive. It is devoted to its owner and highly trainable.

Activity Level: High

Best Owner: The Tosa Ken does best with a dog-experienced owner in a suburban or rural home. It is fine with children if supervised but does well only with animals with which it is raised.

Special Needs: Attention, socialization, and training

Possible Health Concerns: Bloat, eye problems, hip and elbow dysplasia

Toy Fox Terrier

Country of Origin: United States

Group: Terrier, UKC; Toy, AKC

History: This American Toy breed has been around for the better part of a century, primarily as little working dogs on farms, where they rid barns and granaries of rats and other small vermin. The Toy Fox Terrier was developed by breeding small Smooth Fox Terriers with toy breeds such as the Chihuahua and Manchester Terrier. After the initial crosses to set the size, later breedings involved only smaller Smooth Fox Terriers. The United Kennel Club registered its first Toy Fox Terrier in 1936, but

Toy Fox Terrier

the breed didn't gain American Kennel Club recognition until 2003.

Physical Description: The TFT is a well-balanced toy dog with an athletic, graceful appearance and agile movement. The body is square, with height being approximately equal to length. The head is elegant and balanced, with an intelligent, eager, alert expression. The nose is black, with the exception of chocolate-colored dogs, which have a self-colored nose. Eyes are clear, bright, and dark. Erect, pointed ears with an inverted V shape are set high and close together. The smooth, shiny coat has fine texture and comes in tricolor, white, chocolate and tan; white and tan; or white and black. The docked tail is set high and held erect.

Height: 8.5 to 11.5 inches (9 to 11 preferred)

Weight: 3.5 to 7 pounds

Temperament: Terrier exuberance and small size combine to create an active but lap-loving dog that loves to hunt, play fetch and spend lots of time with its people. The TFT can be noisy, but it's a super watchdog. It's smart and learns quickly but can also be stubborn. May be aggressive toward dogs it doesn't know, including large ones.

Activity Level: High

Best Owner: This is an adaptable dog that does well in any environment. It's suited to homes with older children and other pets, including cats.

Special Needs: Attention, plenty of playtime, positive training, socialization, protection from cool or cold temperatures.

Possible Health Concerns: Patellar luxation, congenital hypothyroidism with goiter, broken bones when daredevil puppies fly off the furniture.

Treeing Feist

Country of Origin: United States

Group: Scenthound, UKC

History: The Treeing Feist was developed in the American South to hunt small game, especially squirrel, and to rid homes and farms of vermin. It is also used to hunt raccoon, possum, and rabbit and to flush game birds. It is a very new breed.

Physical Description: The Treeing Feist is a small, agile dog that is slightly longer than it is tall. It has a blocky, broad head with a strong muzzle that is slightly shorter than the skull. The nose is black or self-colored, and the eyes are brown. The ears are set at the outside edges of skull and are erect or button. It has a clean, muscular neck; a moderately wide, deep chest; and round, well-arched feet. The tail is a natural bob or long and carried in an upward curve. The coat is short, dense, and smooth, of any color.

Height: 10 to 17 inches

Weight: 12 to 30 pounds

Temperament: The Treeing Feist is an alert,

Treeing Feist

tenacious, and courageous dog. It is a highly trainable working dog, although there are differing opinions as to its suitability as a pet. Some believe its gameness make it too aggressive to keep as a family companion; others contend that if socialized and trained, it makes an excellent house dog. Regardless, it will do best with an owner who is dog-experienced and who provides it a job or other organized activity.

Activity Level: High

Best Owner: One who can appreciate and enable this dog's hunting heritage; rural or working homes are best.

Special Needs: Attention, socialization, and exercise

Possible Health Concerns: Allergies, luxating patellas, dental problems, demodectic mange

Treeing Tennessee Brindle

Country of Origin: United States

Group: Scenthound, UKC

History: The history of this breed is cloudy, but it was probably developed in the state of Tennessee and surrounding region in the

American South, where it was used for trailing large game and treeing.

Physical Description: This is a medium-size, muscular dog with a flat, wide skull; heavy muzzle; and dark eyes. The drop ears can be short or medium and are set high. It has a deep chest, catlike feet, and a medium-length tail. The coat is short and smooth in brindle or black with brindle trim. This breed can have small, white markings on the chest or feet.

Height: 16 to 24 inches

Weight: 30 to 50 pounds

Temperament: This is a good-natured dog that is friendly with almost everyone, including other dogs. It is intelligent and alert with a strong work drive. It is vocal.

Activity Level: High

Best Owner: This breed would do well with an active family in either a rural or a suburban environment.

Special Needs: Exercise, fenced yard, leashed

Possible Health Concerns: None known

Treeing Walker Coonhound

Country of Origin: United States

Group: Scenthound, UKC

History: The Treeing Walker Coonhound was developed from English Walker Foxhounds, which were imported from England in 1742 and developed by Thomas Walker of Virginia. These dogs were crossed with foxhounds that George Washington imported from England several years earlier. This Virginia Hound cross was developed into Walker Hounds, which were later crossed with a foxhoundlike mongrel with an intense work drive, leading to the modern Treeing Walker Coonhound.

Physical Description: This is a medium-size dog that carries its head high. It has low-set, medium-length ears that fold as they fall. The eyes are dark and the muzzle is long

Treeing Walker Coonhound

and square. It has straight, well-boned legs; a deep chest; catlike feet; and a long, tapered, sabrelike tail. The tricolored coat is smooth and short. Some dogs are white with tan spots or white with black spots.

Height: 20 to 27 inches

Weight: 45 to 70 pounds

Temperament: This is an outgoing, energetic, and confident dog. It gets along well with almost everyone and is very gentle.

Activity Level: High

Best Owner: This breed does best with an active family in a rural or suburban home.

Special Needs: Exercise, fenced yard, leashed

Possible Health Concerns: None known

Vizsla

Alternative Names: Hungarian Vizsla, Magyar Vizsla

Country of Origin: Hungary

Group: Gun Dog, UKC; Sporting, AKC

History: According to depictions found in stone etches and fourteenth-century

The Treeing Walker Coonhound is named for his ability to tree quarry. If untrained, this dog even climbs trees to get prey. It is the most popular breed in UKC registrations.

Vizslas

manuscripts, dogs of the Vizsla type have been found in central Europe for as long as 1,000 years. The breed came close to extinction after World War I, but fanciers struggled to save it. The Vizsla was first imported to the United States in the 1950s and serves as both a hunting dog and companion.

Physical Description: The Vizsla is medium-size, lean, and muscular. It has a deep, tapering muzzle and the head is narrow and strong. The short, smooth coat is golden rust, and the eye color blends with the coat; the nose is brown. The long, thin ears are rounded at the ends. The tail is docked. It may have white markings on the chest or toes. There is also a wire-haired variety of Vizsla that is seen occasionally in North America but is more common in Europe.

Height: 21 to 24 inches

Weight: 50 to 65 pounds

Temperament: This is a lively and good natured dog. It makes an excellent hunter but is affectionate and gentle in the home. It can be sensitive.

Activity Level: High

Best Owner: The breed does best with an active owner in a rural or suburban home.

Special Needs: Attention, exercise, job or activity, positive training

Possible Health Concerns: Allergies, cancer, epilepsy, eye problems, hip dysplasia, thyroid disorders, von Willebrand's disease

Weimaraner

Country of Origin: Germany

Group: Gun Dog, UKC; Sporting, AKC

History: The Weimaraner was created by German aristocrats in the court of Weimar during the nineteenth century. The breed was originally used to hunt big game in the Thuringian forest but was later adapted to hunt birds. It continues to be used as a

Weimaraner

hunting dog and companion in Germany and the United States. The Weimaraner is nicknamed the "Gray Ghost" for its stealth in the field.

Physical Description: This is a medium to large, lean, muscular dog. It has a long, broad head; long drop ears that are slightly folded and set high; light amber, gray, or blue gray eyes; and a gray nose. The tail is docked. The short coat is sleek and gray, and there may be a small, white marking on the chest. Longhaired Weimaraners, disqualified from AKC shows, can be seen in Europe.

Height: 23 to 27 inches

Weight: 55 to 85 pounds

Temperament: The Weimaraner is intelligent, energetic, and fun-loving. It is a hard worker but will try to get its way.

Activity Level: High

Best Owner: This dog requires an active, dog-experienced owner in a rural or suburban home.

Special Needs: Exercise, job or activity, socialization, training

Possible Health Concerns: Bloat, dermoid cysts, dwarfism, eye problems, hip dysplasia, von Willebrand's disease, cancer

Welsh Springer Spaniel

Alternative Names: Starter, Tarfgi

Country of Origin: Wales

Group: Gun Dog, UKC; Sporting, AKC

History: Similar hunting spaniels have existed in Great Britain since the Middle Ages. In Wales, hunters kept packs of red and white spaniels for flushing game, but they were little known outside the region until the late nineteenth century. The breed suffered during the world wars, but fanciers kept the dogs alive. It was first imported to the United States following World War II.

Physical Description: The Welsh Springer Spaniel is a medium-size, muscular, rectangular-shaped dog. The head is in proportion and moderately wide. It has medium-length drop ears, brown eyes, and a brown or black nose. The tail is docked or can be natural. The smooth coat is of moderate length; there is feathering on his chest, ears, back of legs, feet, and belly. It is red and white with red freckles.

Height: 17 to 19 inches

Weight: 35 to 50 pounds

Temperament: This is a jovial, outgoing, and amenable dog. It is active, intelligent, and

Longhaired Weimaraner

Welsh Springer Spaniel

highly trainable when motivated. It is especially devoted to its family but gets along with almost everyone, including other dogs.

Activity Level: High

Best Owner: It does best with a family or individual in a rural or suburban home.

Special Needs: Attention, exercise

Possible Health Concerns: Cataracts, entropion, hip dysplasia, hypothyroidism, seizures

Welsh Terrier

Alternative Names: Old English Terrier, Black-and-Tan Wirehaired Terrier

Country of Origin: Wales

Group: Terrier, UKC/AKC

History: Originally used to hunt otter, fox, and badger, the Welsh Terrier is believed to be a very old breed. It is still used as a hunting dog as well as a companion, and it has changed little during its existence. It first appeared in the United States in the late nineteenth century.

Physical Description: The Welsh Terrier is a sturdy, compact, rugged, medium-size dog that is square in proportions. The head is rectangular. The muzzle is half the length of the entire head, strong and squared off with a black squared-off nose. It has small, almond-shaped, dark brown eyes. The small, V-shaped ears fold forward. The Welsh Terrier has a deep chest and muscular hindquarters. Its tail is docked very short and carried upright. It is double coated with a soft undercoat and a wiry, dense outer coat. It is black and tan, with a black jacket and tan base.

Height: 15 inches

Weight: 19 to 22 pounds

Temperament: It is game in the field but friendly and outgoing with people and other dogs. It is spirited, courageous, and intelligent.

Activity Level: Moderate

Welsh Terrier

Best Owner: The Welsh Terrier does best with a dog-experienced owner; it adapts to city, country, or suburban life as long as it receives enough exercise.

Special Needs: Exercise, firm but positive training, grooming, socialization

Possible Health Concerns: Epilepsy, glaucoma, skin allergies, thyroid problems

West Highland White Terrier

Alternative Names: Poltalloch Terrier, Roseneath Terrier

Country of Origin: Scotland

Group: Terrier, UKC/AKC

History: The Westie is believed to have been developed on the Poltalloch estate of the Malcolm family and the Roseneath estate of the Duke of Argyll. It was bred to be part of a working pack used to hunt fox, badger, and vermin. Evidence of the breed is seen in two paintings by Sir Edwin Landseer done in about 1839. Despite its hunting past, most Westies are now companions. In the early twentieth century, the Westie was often mixed with the Cairn Terrier, their color difference being the main distinction between the breeds today.

West Highland White Terrier

Why was the West Highland White Terrier bred to be white? Legend says that Colonel Edward Donald Malcolm, originator of the breed, kept a pack of terriers for hunting. The terriers ranged in color from black to red to cream to white. After one of his dogs was mistaken for a fox and shot, Malcolm decided to breed for only white dogs so they could be easily identified in the field.

Physical Description: The Westie is a small, well-balanced, and hardy dog with a compact body that is slightly taller than it is long. It has a broad skull and blunt muzzle; dark brown, almond-shaped eyes; a black nose; and small, naturally erect ears with pointed tips. Its tail is short and shaped like an inverted carrot. It is double coated with a hard, straight outer coat that is about two inches long. The coat is bristly around its face, giving its head a rounded appearance.

Height: 10 to 11 inches

Weight: 15 to 20 pounds

Temperament: The Westie is an alert, fun-loving, and friendly dog. It is stable, courageous, and self-reliant, with great self-esteem. Although it is independent, it is loyal to its family. Like most terriers, it tends to dig. It may not be suitable for all children.

Activity Level: High

Best Owner: This breed does well with a terrier-experienced owner; it is adaptable to city, suburban, or rural life.

Special Needs: Attention, exercise, grooming, firm but positive training, socialization

Possible Health Concerns: Atopy, cataracts, copper toxicosis, craniomandibular osteopathy, deafness, enzyme deficiency, inguinal hernia, Legg-Perthes disease

Whippet

Country of Origin: Great Britain

Group: Sighthound, UKC; Hound, AKC

Whippet

History: The Whippet was developed more than 100 years ago as a racing dog and ratter for the working class. It is believed to descend from a cross of various terriers, Greyhounds, Italian Greyhounds, and possibly Pharaoh Hounds.

Physical Description: The Whippet is a small to medium-size elegant and muscular dog. The Whippet's length is equal to or slightly longer than its height. It has a long, narrow head with a long, powerful muzzle. It has large, dark eyes; a black nose; and small rose ears. It has a long neck and a long, tapering tail. The short, smooth coat is of any color.

Height: 18 to 22 inches

Weight: 20 to 28 pounds

The Whippet is the fastest domestic animal of its size. It is capable of reaching speeds of up to 35 miles per hour.

Temperament: This is an amiable and friendly dog that likes almost everyone, including children and other dogs. It has a pronounced prey instinct and will chase and roam. It is intelligent and can be intense.

Activity Level: Moderate

Best Owner: This breed does well with an active family or individual and is adaptable to both the city and the country.

Special Needs: Attention, fenced yard, leashed, protection from the cold

Possible Health Concerns: Eye problems

Wirehaired Pointing Griffon

Alternative Names: Korthals Griffon, Griffon d'Arrêt à Poil du Korthals, Russian Setter

Country of Origin: France

Group: Gun Dog, UKC; Sporting, AKC

History: The Wirehaired Pointing Griffon was developed as a versatile hunting dog in the mid- to late nineteenth century by the son of a wealthy Dutch banker. Developed in France, it's believed that the German Shorthair, Barbet, Small Münsterländer, Otterhound, and Braque Français were crossed to create the breed. It was first introduced to the United States in 1887.

Physical Description: This is a medium-size dog that is slightly longer than it is tall. The head is square, and the skull and muzzle are

Wirehaired Pointing Griffon

equal in length. There is a profuse mustache and eyebrows. The large, round eyes are yellow to brown, the drop ears are medium size, and the nose is brown. The tail is docked one-half to one-third its length and is carried straight or slightly raised. There is a downy undercoat and a rough, straight, or wiry outer coat. The color can be gray with brown markings; chestnut brown; roan, brown, and white; or orange and white.

Height: 20 to 24 inches

Weight: 45 to 60 pounds

Temperament: The Wirehaired Pointing Griffon is intelligent, good-natured, and eager to please. It gets bored easily and can be manipulative.

Activity Level: High

Best Owner: It does well with an active, dog-experienced owner in a rural or suburban home.

Special Needs: Firm training, job or activity, socialization

Possible Health Concerns: Hip dysplasia

Xoloitzcuintli

Alternative Names: Mexican Hairless Dog

Country of Origin: Mexico

Group: Companion, UKC

History: The Xoloitzcuintli is believed to date back 3,000 years, preceding the Aztec Empire. It was held in great esteem by both the Mayan and Toltec cultures, who believed it to be a manifestation of the god Xolotl. It was later used as a sort of tonic by the Aztecs, who believed that contact with the skin or eating the meat of the dog could cure illness. When the Aztec were defeated by the Spanish, the breed quickly dwindled but was kept extant by native Indians. Interest in the breed was revived in the mid-twentieth century.

Physical Description: This is a small- to medium-size dog that is slightly taller than it

Xoloitzcuintli

is long. It resembles a combination of a terrier and sighthound and has a range of varieties, including toy, miniature, and standard, as well as hairless and coated. It has a broad head with forehead wrinkles when it is alert. The muzzle is longer than the skull with a strong chin. It has almond eyes that range from yellow to dark brown and a nose that may be black, brown, or spotted. Its large ears are carried to the side when relaxed but erect when alert. It has hare feet and a long, low tail. Coated dogs have a short, flat coat, while hairless dogs have no hair except on the lower portion of the tail, the forehead, and the nape.

Height (Toy): up to 13 inches

Weight (Toy): 9 to 18 pounds

Height (Miniature): 13 to 18 inches

Weight (Miniature): 13 to 22 pounds

Height (Standard): 18 to 23 inches

Weight (Standard): 20 to 31 pounds

Temperament: The Xolo is a faithful and affectionate pet but wary with strangers. It is intelligent and active, with a happy, calm demeanor. It gets along with children and other animals as long as it is socialized.

Activity Level: High

Best Owner: The Xolo does best with an active family or individual in a suburban or city home.

Special Needs: Attention, socialization, sun protection and skin care for hairless type

Possible Health Concerns: Acne, missing teeth, skin and food allergies, skin infections

Yorkshire Terrier

Country of Origin: Great Britain

Group: Companion, UKC; Toy, AKC

History: The Yorkie was originally bred to control rats in cotton mills and mines in Yorkshire, England. It was popular among the working class, especially weavers. Later, it became a fashionable pet during the Victorian age. Originally called a broken-haired Scotch terrier, the breed was renamed the Yorkshire Terrier by 1870. It is a descendant of the Waterside Terrier, Old English Black-and-Tan Terrier, rough-coated English Terrier, Paisley Terrier, and Clydesdale Terrier. It first came to the United States in the 1870s.

Physical Description: The Yorkie is a very small, well-balanced dog with square proportions and a high head carriage. Its skull is small and flat; the muzzle is tapered with a small, black, button nose. The naturally erect ears are small and V shaped. The tail is docked to medium length and carried slightly higher than the back. The distinctive coat is long, silky, and glossy, parted down the center of the back and hanging straight to the floor. The long hair on the head is parted or tied into a bow. The hair on the muzzle is long and blends into the chest hair.

A Yorkshire Terrier named Big Boss holds the Guinness World Records' title for world's smallest dog. Given the title in 1995, the Yorkie was just 4.7 inches tall and 5.1 inches long on his first birthday.

Yorkshire Terrier

Puppies are born black and tan but by about two years old develop their adult steel blue and tan coloring.

Height: 7 to 9 inches

Weight: 3 to 7 pounds

Temperament: The scrappy Yorkie is a true terrier. Despite its small size, it is courageous and assertive. It tends to get along well with most animals and children, but can become demanding and nippy if not socialized and trained.

Activity Level: Moderate

Best Owner: This is an adaptable dog that does well in a city or suburban home. It makes a good apartment dog.

Special Needs: Dental care, grooming, socialization, supervision with children and larger animals, training

Possible Health Concerns: Dental problems, hypoglycemia, Legg-Perthes disease, liver shunt, luxating patellas

CHAPTER 19

Mixes and Designer Dogs

It's no secret that many of today's purebred dogs were created by mixing two or more breeds and then breeding the resulting puppies that had the desired characteristics, such as a particular color, temperament, or ability. When those traits can be consistently reproduced, the dogs are said to breed true. A dog is generally considered a breed when a true-breeding population has been bred only within itself for at least seven generations. Simply crossing the same breeds over and over again does not a breed make. Among the breeds that were developed this way are the Doberman Pinscher, Whippet, Yorkshire Terrier, and German Shepherd Dog.

In addition to the hundreds of breeds found throughout the world, there are an infinite number of combinations of breeds. We refer to them affectionately as mixes, mutts, and Heinz 57s. Also falling into this category are cross-breeds, the results of a deliberate mating between two individual breeds, usually in an attempt to produce a dog with the best characteristics of each parent. Sometimes called designer breeds because they're produced to cater to society's love of the unique, cross-breeds are the latest incarnation of the human desire to create the perfect dog.

If you want a one-of-a-kind dog, the best place to start is your local animal shelter. There you can find every kind of mix, from large to small, longhaired to shorthaired, laidback to active. Sometimes it's easy to tell from a dog's looks what its probable background is, but often it's a mystery. Still, there are usually some clues that you can go by to determine what your potential new best friend will be like. Here's a guide to what you can expect from various types of mixes. Whether you are adopting your mix from a shelter or rescue organization, always ask a volunteer or staff member to help you determine the breeds in the dogs you are interested in and how that combination will fit into your life.

Herding Breed Mixes

There are many herding breed mixes available through rescues and shelters, especially in rural areas. Herding dog mixes are especially common in areas where there is a large sheep or cattle industry. However, urban shelters are also seeing more herding dog mixes and purebreds, especially Australian Shepherds and Border Collies. An increase in the popularity of those breeds has led to a greater number of irresponsible and unethical breeders.

Herding mixes often find their way into shelters when a pet store or backyard breeder sells an adorable puppy to a busy family without explaining his high energy level. The family finds itself overwhelmed by the demands of the dog and relegates him to the backyard, where he becomes increasingly hyperactive and desperate for attention. Finally, they bring the dog to a shelter. Most of these dogs make excellent pets; they simply need obedience training and a daily exercise regimen.

Most of these mixes retain their high-energy demands and intelligence and will do very well in organized activities, such as agility and herding trials. They do require a lot of exercise and attention. Formal training and

Australian Shepherd mix

participation in a canine sport such as agility, herding, or flyball will keep their minds and bodies stimulated and fulfilled. They tend to get along with almost everyone, although they have strong herding tendencies and can unintentionally injure or frighten small children or other animals.

Shepherd mixes are among the most common mixes in the United States. They can be of almost every variety, from Lab shepherd mixes to Corgi-shepherd mixes. They tend to be medium to large in size, with prick, semi-prick, or rose ears. Most have long, tapered muzzles, and many have the black and tan coat that some German Shepherd Dogs display. Some may even have one ear up and one down. Like purebred GSDs, they need daily exercise and obedience training. Depending on their mix and parentage, they may or may not have protective tendencies.

Although herding dogs tend not to be highly aggressive, they are energetic, intelligent, and prey driven, so a dog-experienced owner is best. Most herding dogs do best in a rural or suburban home where their high exercise needs can be met.

Companion Dog Mixes

Among the companion mixes, the most common must be the Poodle mixes, which are so well established that many are actually given names. The cockapoo is a blend of Cocker

A German Shepherd mix named Shadow was awarded the 21st National Hero Dog Award by the Los Angeles SPCA. He saved his owner's life by scuffling with an adult grizzly bear who was charging. The award recognizes heroic efforts by dogs who are companion animals and not formally trained for rescue or law enforcement.

Chihuahua/Pug cross

Spaniel and Miniature Poodle, while the peekapoo is a cross between the Pekingese and the Miniature Poodle.

Because most companion dogs are small, so are their mixes. But that doesn't mean they will necessarily have the personality of the companion breed in the mix. Companions are often mixed with terriers, which generally have tougher, feistier personalities than companions do. Like the companions, many of their mixes have special grooming needs and can be somewhat nippy with strangers or children if not well

Ever wanted to know just what breeds contribute to your Heinz 57? Thanks to advances in canine genetics, you can find out through a simple blood test. The sample is sent to a laboratory, which responds within two or three weeks with a full report, including the breeds detected, a behavioral profile of those breeds, and insights about their physical traits. The test is capable of recognizing more than 130 different breeds.

socialized. On the positive side, many make excellent pets for apartment dwellers or others with sedentary lifestyles.

Terrier cross

Irresponsibly bred Dalmatians were increasingly common after the success of the *101 Dalmatians* movies, leading to an increase in their mixes as well. Whether a Dalmatian is mixed with a Lab or a shepherd, it will often maintain its high-energy needs as well as its protective nature. Although there tend to be fewer small companion mixes available in animal shelters, many regions have rescues devoted to these types of dogs. Work with your shelter or rescue group to find the right companion mix for you.

Northern Breed Mixes

There are many types of northern breed mixes available through most shelters and many rescue organizations. The Chow Chow has shown up in shelters disproportionately in recent years. Often mixed with Lab or German Shepherd Dog, Chow mixes may exhibit the fluffy coat or tell-tale blue-black tongue of their progenitor. Siberian Husky and Akita mixes are also fairly commonly found in shelters.

It's always difficult to say what personality traits will predominate in a mix, but it's a good idea to be aware of the breeds that make up a dog before adopting. A Chow Chow or Akita mix, for example, may display some of the dog aggressive or aloof behaviors of the purebred, while a husky mix may well become a roamer unless provided very secure fencing.

The most popular sled dog currently used in recreational and competitive sled racing is the Alaskan Husky, which is a northern breed mix. The Alaskan Husky is a blend of breeds and individual dogs chosen to create the fastest sled dog. Alaskan Huskies are frequently husky/sighthound crosses. In areas where sledding is common, these mixes are more common than purebreds and have

Alaskan Husky puppies

Chow mix

largely replaced Siberian Huskies as the sled dog of choice.

In general, the northern breeds are high-energy, independent dogs that will enjoy living in a cool climate and being engaged in outdoor activities.

Gun Dog Mixes

Gun dogs are arguably the most common mixes found in shelters across the United States. Labs can be found in a variety of mixes: there are Lab/Rotts, Lab/Chows, Lab/shepherds, and Lab/Mastiffs and even Lab/Chihuahuas, Lab/Poodles (known as Labradoodles) as well as Lab/Dachshunds. Golden Retrievers are also commonly found in mixes. In fact, Golden/Lab mixes have proven so popular that service dog breeders are intentionally crossing the two to create

service dogs. That said, unless you are adopting a change-of-career service dog from a reputable agency, don't buy that Golden/Lab mix from the classifieds in your newspaper or on Craigslist. Backyard breeders do not have the best interests of their dogs in mind. Instead, visit your local shelter or contact a rescue, where you will find a variety of gun dog mixes available for adoption.

As with all the gun dogs, the mixes are high-energy dogs that often exhibit hunting instincts, meaning they may not be reliable with small animals and tend to roam. They need a lot of exercise and formal training to be good members of the family. Most gun dogs do quite well with other dogs and are wonderful playmates for youngsters, although some individuals may be too exuberant for very small children.

In appearance, these mixes will range from almost purebred Lab, Golden, or Pointer looks to prick-eared black-and-tan shepherd/Lab crosses. It's always difficult to say what exact breeds are in a mix and which of them will dominate. A reputable rescue or shelter can help you to pick the individual mix that will fit into your life best.

Pointer cross

Golden Retriever cross

Rottweiler/Chow cross

Beagle/Corgi cross

Guardian Breed Mixes

These dogs have developed a poor reputation in recent years. Indiscriminate breeding and the intentional breeding of aggressive dogs to large Mastiff mixes have led to concern about their dangerous potential and even legislation banning so-called dangerous breeds. Unfortunately, this has allowed many wonderful guardian mixes to languish in rescues and shelters. Rottweiler mixes are some of the most common dogs found in shelters, and many make wonderful companions. There are also many Mastiff, Saint Bernard, Great Dane, Great Pyrenees, and Newfoundland mixes that are gentle giants and truly round out an active family.

The guardian mixes, like all of the guardians, do require extensive socialization with both people and animals. Their large size is also an issue when it comes to space and economics: big dogs require room and cost more than smaller dogs do for grooming, boarding, food, and veterinary care. They may also have the pendant lips that cause Mastiffs, Newfoundlands, and Saint Bernards to drool. It is difficult to maintain a very neat home with a large guardian breed living in it.

The mixes also require the same conscientious care when it comes to making sure their bones and joints stay healthy. The excess weight they carry can affect their hips and elbows, so owners must keep this in mind when making decisions regarding their dogs' nutrition and exercise needs.

Guardians and their mixes are large, dominant dogs; keep this in mind when considering adopting one. Work with your shelter or rescue to determine whether you have the right lifestyle for a dog like this.

Hound Mixes

There are a number of hound mixes found in shelters and rescues, especially in rural areas of the United States. They may be either leggy or of the short-legged dwarf variety; long drop ears are the rule. Hound mixes can make exceptional companion dogs and fit very well into a family situation, even one with multiple children and dogs.

Hound mixes do very well in rural environments because they love the outdoors, and nothing will make them happier than a

Coonhound cross

romp in the woods with their favorite canine and human friends. Still, even a mix may retain the resolute scent trailing of most hounds, so leashing and fencing is important. They are often quite vocal, so few will do well in an apartment home.

Consider whether your lifestyle can adapt to a dog who is vocal and may roam. For all the scenthounds' excellent qualities, they often require a lot of work and time commitment from their people. Some of the smaller hound mixes, for example Beagle and Basset Hound mixes, may fit better into the life of a more sedentary person. However, even these dogs may be vocal and more interested in chasing down critters than hanging out with you on the couch.

There are a not a great number of sighthound mixes available in the United States, probably because of the relative rarity of most of the breeds. In Great Britain, however, the lurcher, which is a cross of any sighthound—often a Greyhound—and another breed, such as a terrier, retriever, or herding dog, is common.

Although there are few Greyhound mixes in the United States, it is worth mentioning that most pet Greyhounds are retired racing dogs that are adopted out through a host of rescue agencies. Many Greyhounds are euthanized when their working days are over, but the fortunate few are made available through these rescue organizations. Although these dogs often must learn some basic tricks to surviving the average suburban tract home, such as using stairs and navigating slippery linoleum, they can make excellent pets.

Carolina Dog

Terrier/hound cross

Terrier cross

Sighthound mixes will often display the racy build and sensitive temperament of the purebreds. They tend to run, so they should be kept in a fenced yard or on leash at all times. They may also be sensitive to anesthesia.

Pariah Dog Mixes

In theory, most pariah dogs are mixes; only a few of them are registered breeds, and most are undomesticated dogs living at the peripheries of civilization. The Carolina Dog, for example, is clearly interbred with other feral or domestic dogs. The breed was discovered only after researchers noticed a number of similar feral dogs being captured by Southern animal control agencies. They are often found in shelters in the American South.

Terrier Mixes

Terrier mixes are quite common in shelters and rescues. As with the purebred terriers,

there are two types: the traditional terriers and the bull and terrier type. In many urban areas, bull and terrier–type mixes—often referred to generically as pit bulls—make up the bulk of the dogs in shelters. Although bull and terrier types are generally very stoic, calm, and gentle dogs, irresponsible breeding has led to an increase of aggressive dogs. Although dog fighting is illegal, it continues throughout the United States. Dogs who come from irresponsible or unethical breeders may have been bred or trained to fight and can be unpredictable. That said, the majority of bull and terrier mixes bear the same even-keeled disposition of their ancestors and are ideal family pets.

Pit Bulls may be mixed with a variety of other breeds, including German Shepherd Dogs, Labs, and Chow Chows. They tend to have the strong head and jaws of the APBT and Staffie, along with rose ears, warm brown eyes, and a short coat. Brindle coats are not uncommon. They are strong dogs with high energy, so socialization, training, and ample exercise are requirements.

When adopting a pit bull mix, work with your shelter or rescue worker to find the right dog for you. An experienced dog person with the time and patience for extensive training may do fine with one dog, while an active family with less time for organized activities will do better with another. Pit bull mixes have a range of personalities, so take the time to find the right one for you.

They vary in size but are generally small to medium-size dogs. Don't let their small size fool you, however; they require train-ing, socialization, attention, and exercise. They usually have prick or folded ears, facial whiskers, and compact bodies. As with pit bull mixes, there is a range of personali-ties found in the traditional terrier mixes. Most are lively and spirited, but whether this translates to nippiness and possessive-ness or playful and fun-loving depends on the individual dog. Work with your shelter or rescue representative to ensure that you choose a dog suited to your lifestyle and level of dog experience.

Designer Dogs

Ever hear of a floppy-faced Jujitsu? How about a King Daley Shepherd? A Germox Retriever? Those are just a few of the

Yorkiepoo

monikers that clever dog owners have come up with to distinguish their all-American dogs—mutts, to people with less imagination and pride in their one-of-a-kind dogs.

What's behind the desire to have a dog "be" something? Everybody wants something unique. People who seek out the dog du jour—which these days is a cross-breed or hybrid such as a Maltipoo (Maltese/Poodle) or Goldendoodle (Golden Retriever/Poodle)—like the idea of having a dog that not very many people have. Some people pay a thousand dollars or more for one of these crosses, even though the very same dogs are often available at animal shelters throughout the country.

Sometimes it's because they are attracted by claims that hybrids are hypoallergenic or have fewer health problems or will carry the best traits of each breed. That's just not the way genetics work, however. Genetic characteristics sort out randomly, so there's no guarantee you'll get the best of each breed. In fact, you may end up with the worst traits of each! No matter what his breed or mix, whether he's deliberately bred from two specific breeds or a jumble of many, an individ-

Goldendoodle

ual dog may be more or less allergenic or intelligent or healthy.

Just like any other dog, purebred or not, designer dogs require obedience training, house-training, grooming, and exercise. Many of them have high-maintenance coats that are not allergy friendly, no matter what your neighbor, your sister, or the dog's breeder tells you.

Cross-breeds and mixes have a reputation for being healthier than purebreds, but that's not necessarily the case. Mixed breeds as a class have more inherited diseases than any single pure breed has because of their broader gene pool, but the frequency of any given disease is likely to be lower because the population is more diverse. And because designer dogs are purposely bred from dogs of specific types or breeds, they may have a higher incidence of certain diseases, such as breathing difficulties, cancer, or hip dysplasia, depending on the breeds used to create them.

Puggle

Labradoodle

Health

Your dog's health care starts from day one. His mother is the first to look out for his health, providing him with infection-fighting colostrum from breast milk and protecting him from dominant litter-mates and other dangers. After you bring him home, you continue to provide the preventive health care your dog requires and ensure that he gets the veterinary care he needs throughout his life. Your job is to protect your puppy from disease and injury and provide him with adequate nutrition to build sound muscles and bones. His veterinarian helps by vaccinating him against infectious diseases, treating him for worms and other intestinal parasites, and altering him.

Because every part of a dog's body, from the tip of his nose to the tip of his tail, needs its own special care, it's important to understand what each part of a dog's body does and to know what to look out for in case of a problem. A good veterinarian, regular preventive health care, and vigilant attention to signs of injury and illness all go a long way toward a full and healthy life for your dog.

CHAPTER 20

Establishing a Health-Care Regimen

When choosing a health-care regimen for our dogs, we have many decisions to make, including which veterinarian to choose; what type of health care, holistic or conventional, is best for our dogs; when to seek help; and when to look for a specialist.

Choosing a Veterinarian

Your veterinarian is your number one partner in dog care, so finding one isn't a task to be taken lightly. Choose a veterinarian before you need one. If there's an emergency, you don't want to have to rely on someone with whom you're not familiar. Lining up a veterinarian for your dog in advance is especially important if you prefer a holistic approach to canine health, choose not to vaccinate annually, or have a dog with special needs. Finding the right veterinarian can involve both referrals and personal interviews.

Word of mouth is a good way to get veterinary referrals. A referral from someone you trust is the best place to start. If you're moving to a new city, your own veterinarian may be able to refer you to a colleague there. Or ask friends, neighbors, and co-workers about their veterinarians, including what they like about the hospital, and even what they don't like. If a personal referral isn't possible, contact the American Animal Hospital Association for the names of AAHA-certified veterinarians in your area.

Did you know that there are veterinarians who will come to you? Contact the American Association of Housecall and Mobile Veterinarians, a member organization of the American Veterinary Medical Association, for veterinarians throughout the country who make house calls: www.housecallvets.org.

These practitioners must meet certain standards for cleanliness, pain management, quality of care, diagnostic and pharmacy services, and more, and hospitals must be inspected regularly to maintain their accreditation.

What you look for in a hospital depends on what is most important to you. Look for one that suits your needs, provides the level of care you want, has friendly and knowledgeable lay staff, and has a veterinarian who provides the type of care you're looking for. Some questions to ask are: Is this a high-tech clinic or a family practice? Will I get referrals for specialty care if needed? Is emergency care available?

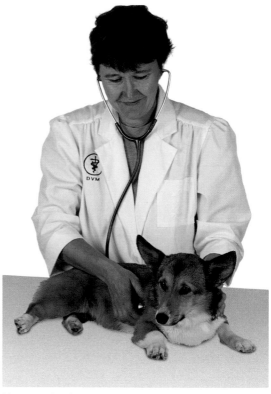

Your veterinarian will be a lifelong partner in maintaining your dog's health. Choose her carefully.

Finding a Veterinarian

Your veterinarian will be a critical person in your dog's life, so it is important for you to choose a veterinary professional you feel comfortable with, while also taking into account such things as convenience and cost. Here are a few tips for finding a veterinarian:

- Ask people you trust for referrals.
- Contact the American Animal Hospital Association for recommendations.
- Ask for a tour of the clinics you're considering.
- Look to see if the clinic is clean and organized.
- Check that the lighting is good and the equipment is up to date.
- Choose a veterinarian you are comfortable with.
- Choose a veterinarian who is willing to answer your questions and who is gentle with your dog.
- The veterinarian's credentials should include graduation from an accredited veterinary school and board certifications.
- The clinic staff should be friendly and attentive.
- The hours, location, and parking should be convenient for you.
- Consider the importance of same-day appointments and walk-ins.
- Some emergency services should be available.
- The office should be able to handle serious medical problems requiring overnight hospitalization.
- There should be an attendant on duty during the night and when the hospital is closed.
- Dogs and cats should be kept in separate areas.
- The fees should fit your budget.
- Ask if the clinic offers senior citizen, multipet, or other discounts.

When you have the names of a few veterinarians, set up appointments to meet them and tour their hospitals. Interview several veterinarians and ask about their philosophy on things that are important to you, such as how they feel about raw or homemade diets or annual vaccinations. The hospital tour and a meeting with the veterinarian and staff will help you make the right decision. Not every hospital—even if it's a good one—is going to be right for everyone.

Ask if the veterinarian is affiliated with a professional organization such as the American Animal Hospital Association (AAHA) or a holistic or homeopathic veterinary medical association. The AAHA, for instance, has a set of standards that veterinarians must meet in such areas as surgery, anesthesia, dentistry, and recordkeeping. Hospitals must be inspected regularly to maintain their accreditation.

There may be a time when you will want a second opinion or need to have your dog seen by a specialist. You may like your veterinarian very much but simply want another perspective. There's nothing wrong with that. It's OK to ask your own veterinarian for a referral. A good vet will be happy to refer you to a specialist and may do so automatically in the case of a serious diagnosis. Another option is to ask for a referral from a friend or colleague who has a pet with a similar problem.

Complementary Therapies/ Holistic Medicine

Also known as alternative therapies, complementary therapies include acupuncture, chiropractic, herbal medicine, homeopathy, massage therapy, nutraceuticals, physical therapy, and trigger point therapy. During the past decade, these treatments have gained more and more credence not only among dog owners but also among veterinarians. Some conventional practitioners use herbs and acupuncture along with surgery and antibiotics. Veterinarians who don't use complementary therapies themselves may refer clients to colleagues who practice these therapies.

Sometimes the use of complementary therapies is described as holistic medicine, which is a comprehensive approach to health care that employs alternative and conventional diagnostic and therapeutic techniques. Holistic veterinary medicine incorporates but is not limited to the principles of acupuncture and other forms of acutherapy, chiropractic, herbal medicine, homeopathy, massage therapy, nutraceuticals, physical therapy, and trigger point therapy as well as conventional medicine, surgery, and dentistry.

Acupuncture

Practiced in China for thousands of years, acupuncture is the stimulation of certain points, or what practitioners call meridians, in the body. According to Chinese medical theory, energy flows through the meridians, and acupuncture corrects excesses or deficiencies in the body's energy flow. Needles are most commonly associated with acupuncture, but related techniques include applying pressure with the fingers (acupressure), burning an herb near the appropriate meridian (moxibustion), and injecting various solutions into the point (aquapuncture). The area may also be stimulated with ultrasound or lasers.

Conditions that are most responsive to acupuncture include musculoskeletal problems such as arthritis and hip dysplasia; partial tears of the cruciate ligament; postsurgical recovery; skin diseases and allergic dermatitis; and chronic diarrhea or vomiting. Veterinarians who use acupuncture find that it works best for pain relief. Sometimes acupuncture shows immediate results, but it's not always a quick fix, and its benefits can be subtle. You must commit

Acupuncture is an alternative therapy that is often used in conjunction with traditional Western medicine.

Finding Holistic Vets

To find veterinarians with a natural bent, visit www.altvetmed.com, which lists the directories of a number of associations for complementary and alternative veterinary medicine, including the Academy of Veterinary Homeopathy, the American Academy of Veterinary Acupuncture, the American Holistic Veterinary Medical Association, the American Veterinary Chiropractic Association, and the International Veterinary Acupuncture Society.

to regular treatments to see results. Acupuncture is often used in conjunction with nutraceuticals, foods or food ingredients that are believed to have health benefits.

Acupuncture isn't appropriate for every ailment. Practitioners advise against using it to treat cancer. Performing acupuncture near or into a tumor or along a meridian line that goes through the tumor can increase its size. Acupuncture is not recommended in conjunction with homeopathy, a system of medical practice that treats a disease with tiny doses of a remedy that in a healthy animal would produce signs of the disease being treated. The two forms of medicine can interfere with each other.

Chiropractic

Chiropractic is a therapy that is based on the belief that disease results from abnormal nerve function, which can be treated through the manipulation and adjustment of body structures such as the spinal column. Chiropractors carefully manipulate vertebrae to restore correct body alignment, which is believed to improve nerve function through the spinal column. Chiropractic can be used for various reasons, from easing the pain of spinal arthritis (spondylosis) to giving athletic dogs an edge by helping keep their bodies tuned. Although little research has been done on the benefits of veterinary chiropractic, clinical and anecdotal evidence suggests that it can be beneficial. For some dogs, the benefits of chiropractic are immediate and visible.

Ideally, chiropractic is performed by licensed veterinarians. If a veterinarian skilled in chiropractic is unavailable, look for a licensed chiropractor who works with a veterinarian or is educated in veterinary chiropractic. The chiropractor should have earned a DC (doctor of chiropractic) or be certified through the American Veterinary Chiropractic Association.

Western and Chinese medicine can complement one another in keeping your dog healthy and balanced.

Herbal Medicine

Herbal, or botanical, medicine is the use of plants and plant products as therapeutic agents. The leaves, roots, and flowers of herbs and other plants have been used in healing for thousands of years. A number of modern medications are compounded from herbs, but herbalists believe that the plant in its pure state has stronger and more effective properties. Herbs in their natural state contain a number of chemicals that work together. While an herb might contain one main chemical that gives a certain effect, tiny amounts of other chemicals may play a role in reducing side effects or otherwise assisting the action of the primary chemical.

Herbs work by detoxifying the body—eliminating troublesome substances from it—

When used properly under the supervision of a practitioner educated in their use, plants can be our dogs' friends when it comes to homeopathic treatments.

Remedies and essences made from flowers can be used to treat both medical and behavioral/emotional issues.

or by acting as a tonic to invigorate or build up the system. They also contain efficacious blends of vitamins and minerals. Some herbs have antimicrobial properties, whereas others are believed to boost the immune system. While herbs cannot be used to act directly on individual cells—for instance, an herb can't make T cells increase—they have been shown to speed healing. Other immune system–enhancing effects of herbs include stimulating natural killer cells, which detect and eliminate infected cells, and inhibiting tumor growth. Sometimes herbs fill in where there is no pharmaceutical drug available. One of the best examples of this is milk thistle, which is used in the treatment of liver disease.

Herbs can be divided into two types: Chinese and Western. Chinese herbal remedies combine 15 to 20 different herbs. In essence, they're recipes that have been passed down for hundreds or even thousands of years. Western herbal medicine tends to make use of a single herb at a time. Is one better than the other? Not necessarily. They're just different.

While herbs have many health benefits, they are powerful medicines and should not be given casually. Just because herbs are natural doesn't mean they're nontoxic. Herbal medicines should be prescribed or approved by a veterinarian trained in the uses of herbs. That's because a veterinarian can both diagnose a problem and has enough medical information to be aware of other conditions that might have similar signs. The veterinarian also knows how an herbal medication reacts with other medications.

Herbs can be used in conjunction with pharmaceutical drugs, but it's important to know the effects of each and whether they are compatible. An example of a medication that doesn't work well with herbs is cortisone, a hormonal drug that is used to decrease inflammation. As a rule, cortisone and herbal medicines fight against each other, the result being that neither does much good.

Herbal medicines usually are manufactured as a liquid or a powder in capsule or tablet form. Be wary of any herbal medicines that are bought over the counter rather than prescribed by a veterinarian. The effectiveness of an herb depends on the type of soil in which it was grown, the type of fertilizer used, the health of the plant, and when and how the plant was harvested. There are no quality control standards for herbal medicines, so it's important to choose one from a company that researches and grows its herbs carefully. Reputable companies adjust their formulas to compensate for increased or decreased

Your veterinarian should be willing to refer you to practitioners of alternative therapies even if she does not practice them herself.

potency, so look for a product whose label explains how the herbs are prepared. An expiration date is a must.

Popular herbal medications include echinacea, goldenseal, and ginseng. Commonly used by people to ward off colds, echinacea is purported to break down immune complexes and possibly neutralize viruses. Holistic veterinarians may use it for direct antibacterial effect or to stimulate the gums to resolve gingivitis. Although the latest research shows no benefit from echinacea, including it in your dog's diet is not known to be harmful.

Goldenseal has a reputation for relieving pain, healing wounds, stopping bleeding, and fighting off bacteria. It is more powerful than echinacea and must be used carefully since it can be toxic in high doses, and long-term use can damage the liver. Goldenseal contains alkaloids—complex organic bases—which can be both helpful and harmful, depending on how they're used. The alkaloids in goldenseal, hydrastine and berberine, are believed to reduce inflammation of mucous membranes, work against bacteria and fungi, and stimulate the immune system. Signs of goldenseal overdose include nausea, vomiting, and a decrease in the white blood cell count.

The root of the ginseng plant has played a major role in Chinese medicine for thousands of years. One of its benefits is that it strengthens the immune system by increasing resistance to stress. Ginseng is also believed to aid metabolism, improve skin and muscle tone, and protect against cancer. Like most herbs, however, ginseng is not a quick fix. It may take weeks or even months to work.

Another example of botanical medicine is the use of Bach flower essences. These are extracts of about 30 different kinds of flowers. They were developed in England in the early twentieth century to address particular characteristics or emotional states in a natural

Shark Cartilage—Salvation or Snake Oil?

Shark skeletons are composed of cartilage rather than bone and are said to have special qualities that fight against arthritis, cancer, and other diseases. So far, studies do not support this claim, but shark cartilage still has the reputation of being a cure-all, which is bad news for the shark.

The estimated world catch of sharks is between 30 and 70 million each year. Few if any controls exist to regulate shark fishing, and many species are now endangered, not only because of the high catch rate but also because sharks are slow to mature and don't reproduce in large numbers. Before you decide to try shark cartilage, ask yourself whether another product would serve just as well.

way. They include the well-known Rescue Remedy, which is a commercial product that contains five different flower essences and is useful for pets (and people) with anxiety. Other Bach flower essences are less commonly used on dogs but are used on humans for such emotions or behaviors as fear of unknown things, lack of confidence, and exhaustion following physical or mental effort. Some of these might be good for search and rescue dogs, for instance.

Other natural tranquilizers include products containing valerian root, kava kava, and St. John's wort, which are believed to have a relaxing effect on animals. Melatonin, a hormone, is another natural substance that appears to have calming properties. Neither Bach essences nor other natural products have a true sedative effect like that resulting from conventional drugs, but they can still relieve anxiety, fear, and stress. Another benefit is that they are easy to keep on hand because they can be bought over the counter and don't require a prescription. Herbs, however, can be dangerous in large doses, in animals with allergies, and when combined with a drug that is contraindicated. Consult your veterinarian before using any herb or supplement.

Homeopathy

Homeopathy involves treating conditions by administering substances that would produce signs in healthy animals similar to those of the disease being treated. For instance, if a dog is vomiting and has diarrhea, a homeopathic veterinarian would prescribe a drug that in a larger dose would produce vomiting and diarrhea. The homeopathic drug is made up of an infinitesimally small dose of the appropriate substance.

The key phrase in homeopathy is "like cures like," meaning that what a homeopathic drug causes in a healthy person will stimulate correction in an ill person. It's important in homeopathy to match the substance to the dog's symptoms. For instance, the homeopathic remedy for 12 puppies brought into a clinic with parvovirus would be based on each puppy's signs, and the remedy could be different for each puppy.

Homeopathic drugs are created in FDA-regulated laboratories and registered with the FDA, just as conventional drugs are, and there are well-established ways of applying the remedies. Research in veterinary homeopathy is limited, but clinical and anecdotal evidence indicate that it may be beneficial.

Massage Therapy

Massage therapy is the application of a scientific system of activity to the muscular structure of the body by means of stroking, kneading, tapping, and vibrating with the hands for the purpose of improving muscle

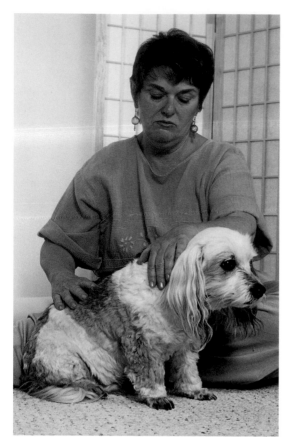

Massage therapy can help relieve aches and pains for canine athletes and dogs suffering from arthritis and other musculoskeletal disorders.

tone and circulation. Massage also helps induce relaxation and gives comfort.

In massage therapy, balance is key. Simply massaging the affected area isn't enough. It's important to treat the opposite end as well. For instance, if a dog is painful in the rear, he's usually putting excess strain on his front end, and vice versa. A good massage therapist will treat the whole animal.

Massage therapy can be performed by a licensed veterinarian with education in massage therapy or by a graduate of an accredited massage school who has been educated in animal massage therapy. Some massage schools teach classes in animal massage. As with humans, massage should not be used on dogs with fractured or sprained limbs, ruptured vertebral disks, cancer, fever, or shock.

Nutraceuticals

The word *nutraceutical*—coined by combining nutrition and pharmaceutical—refers to a food or food ingredient that is believed to have health benefits. Nutraceuticals are naturally occurring compounds that come from animal and vegetable sources and include amino acids, essential fatty acids (EFAs), herbs, antioxidants, vitamins, and minerals. Nutraceutical medicine is the use of micronutrients, macronutrients, and other nutritional supplements as therapeutic agents. Nutraceuticals are popular because they rarely cause side effects.

Nutraceuticals such as EFAs are often used to help with skin problems. Joint pain can be helped by the nutraceuticals chondroitin sulfate, glucosamine, and methyl sulfonyl methane—better known as MSM—as well as the antioxidant vitamins C and E and herbs such as yucca or certain Chinese herbal combinations. These nutraceuticals affect the joint fluid, so they're most likely to have an effect in big joints such as the hips and knees.

Glycosaminoglycans (GAGs) are popular nutraceuticals for joint pain. They are

Tellington TTouch Massage Method

Tellington TTouch is a massage method that stimulates circulation and releases tension through specific exercises involving touch, lift, and movement. Developed by animal trainer Linda Tellington-Jones, Tellington TTouch helps trainers, behaviorists, owners, and veterinarians with a variety of physical, emotional, and behavioral problems in dogs. Tellington TTouch is used to help curb aggressive behavior, fear, and shyness; calm excitable and nervous dogs; relieve aging-related problems such as arthritis and stiffness; relieve car sickness; promote improved gait and balance; and help other problems as well.

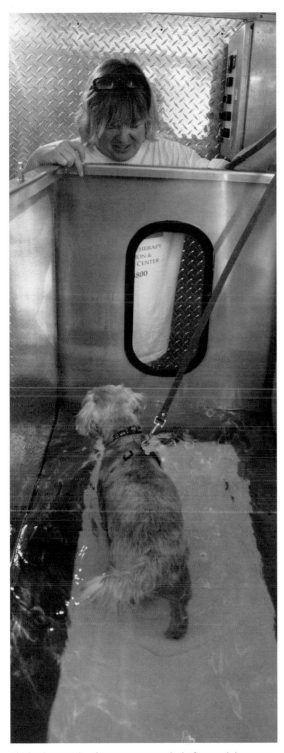

the building blocks of many types of body tissues, including cartilage. The body uses glucosamine to synthesize, or create, GAGs. Products that contain GAGs are termed chondroprotective nutraceuticals and usually come from animal tissues such as cartilage. For instance, the primary ingredient in one nutraceutical product is *Perna canaliculus*, the green-lipped mussel, a rich source of GAGs. Researchers once thought that cartilage couldn't be rebuilt once it degenerated. Now, however, they believe that glucosamine supplements can help the body repair cartilage.

Physical Therapy

This is the use of noninvasive techniques other than veterinary chiropractic for animals recovering from orthopedic or neurologic surgery, the rehabilitation of joint or soft tissue injuries, and treatment of chronic pain. These techniques include stretching; massage; stimulation by use of low-level lasers, electrical sources, magnetic fields, and ultrasound; rehabilitative exercises; hydrotherapy; and applications of heat and cold. Veterinary physical therapy should be performed by a licensed veterinarian; or if allowed by state law by a licensed, certified, or registered veterinary or animal health technician educated in veterinary physical therapy; or by a licensed physical therapist educated in animal anatomy and physiology.

Trigger Point Therapy

Trigger points are hyperirritable tender spots in muscles that trigger pain in other muscles. An active trigger point results in tight muscles, restricted blood flow, and compressed nerves. The object of the therapy is to release the trigger point so that it stops causing pain. Trigger points can be released through acupuncture, chiropractic, and massage therapy.

Hydrotherapy is often recommended after an injury or as part of a treatment plan for chronic conditions like arthritis, benefiting the affected areas without stressing the bones and joints.

CHAPTER 21

Infectious Diseases and Immunization

The first health care decision you will make for your dog is establishing a vaccination schedule. Fortunately, many of the infectious canine diseases that ran rampant in the past can now be prevented with vaccinations or treated with medication. Infectious diseases are transmitted by viruses, bacteria, fungi, and internal parasites.

Vaccination

Annual vaccinations used to be the norm, but veterinarians now believe that too-frequent vaccinations can be linked to health problems. New vaccination recommendations include spacing out vaccinations and giving them less frequently.

What Is a Vaccine?

Vaccines contain substances called antigens that stimulate a response in the immune system, protecting the dog against future exposure to a disease. The process of injecting a vaccine into a dog is called vaccination.

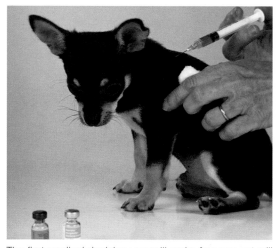

The first medical decision you will make for your pet will concern vaccinations.

Dogs receive vaccines that protect against distemper, viral hepatitis or adenovirus, leptospirosis, parainfluenza, parvovirus, rabies, and coronavirus. They used to receive one combination vaccine against all of those diseases called DHLPPC or DALPPC. Now, because of concerns that too many vaccines at once can overload the immune system and be harmful, some owners and veterinarians are choosing to spread them out, giving only one or two at a time.

Most experts agree that so-called core vaccines—distemper, adenovirus, parvovirus, and rabies—are essential for all dogs. The administration of other vaccines such as those for leptospirosis, coronavirus, giardia, bordetella, parainfluenza, and Lyme disease should be limited to dogs who are realistically at risk of exposure to the specific infectious agent. In the case of Lyme disease, for instance, tick control is more effective than vaccination. For a time, many veterinarians stopped giving the leptospirosis vaccine because a number of dogs had reactions to it, but a new vaccine has been developed that is expected to reduce these problems.

Vaccination Pros and Cons

While vaccinations are generally safe, they're not without risk. Possible adverse effects include allergic reactions and, in rare cases, seizures. Among the breeds that have been reported to be at increased risk of such reactions are Miniature Dachshunds, West Highland White Terriers, Old English Sheepdogs, Akitas, Weimaraners, and dogs with coat color dilutions such as double dilute Shetland Sheepdogs or harlequin Great Danes.

Vaccination Timeline

The following are general vaccination recommendations for adult dogs from the American Animal Hospital Association Canine Vaccine Task Force. However, the best vaccination schedule for your dog should be based on lifestyle and area of the country; talk to your dog's veterinarian.

- Bordetella (bacterial illness commonly called kennel cough): optional, but recommended annually or more often for dogs at risk for infection
- Borrelia burgdorferi (Lyme disease): optional, but recommended annually prior to start of tick season for dogs in high exposure areas
- Canine adenovirus-2 (virus seen in combination with other agents causing upper respiratory infection): booster at one year, revaccinate every three years; also guards against canine adenovirus-1
- Canine distemper (severe multisystemic viral disease): booster at one year, revaccinate every three years
- Canine parvovirus (virus seen mostly in puppies that attacks the lining of the digestive system): booster at one year, revaccinate every three years
- Leptospirosis (bacteria causing acute infection that can lead to kidney or liver disease): optional, but can revaccinate every six months in high-risk situations, discontinuing booster schedule when exposure ceases
- Parainfluenza virus (viral disease, but less severe than distemper; also a type of kennel cough): booster at one year, revaccinate every three years
- Rabies (virus affecting the brain and spinal cord): booster at one year, revaccinate every three years depending on state mandates

Instead of choosing not to vaccinate your dog at all, you may want to avoid unnecessary vaccines and consider going to a triennial (every three year) vaccination schedule after your dog is one year old.

How frequently vaccinations should be boosted after the first series is currently a matter of discussion in the veterinary community. Veterinary schools and the American Animal Hospital Association now recommend a two- or three-shot series of the core vaccinations for puppies, spaced three to four weeks apart, followed by a booster at one year of age, and boosters every three years or longer thereafter. Some pet owners and veterinarians prefer to do titers (a type of blood test) to determine whether a booster shot is necessary. A titer measures the concentration of an antibody in blood serum. Other veterinarians advise against further vaccinations after one year of age, with the exception of rabies vaccines as required by law. Some areas of the country have a higher incidence of certain infectious diseases, such as distemper and parvovirus, than others do. Your veterinarian can advise you on the vaccination schedule that is appropriate for your area.

Vaccines stimulate the immune system to produce antibodies against a particular virus as well as memory cells, which produce more antibodies if the same virus attacks the dog later in its life. The presence of antibodies at any level—as determined by a titer—indicates that memory cells are still functioning. Titers can help breeders and new puppy owners determine whether a recently given vaccine took effect.

Puppies and Vaccination

It's important to understand that no vaccine is 100 percent effective all the time. Factors that

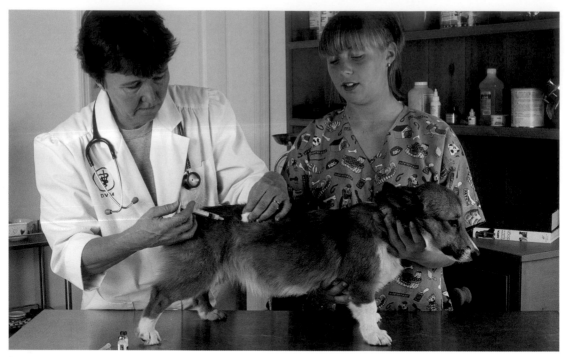

Many infectious diseases can be prevented through vaccination. Discuss the pros and cons with your veterinarian.

can affect immune response in a puppy include his health and the level of maternal antibodies still circulating in his system. And if a puppy is exposed to a virus shortly before or at approximately the same time a vaccination is given, the vaccine is likely to fail. This occurs for any number of reasons. Some puppies simply don't have adequate immune function. Stress, poor nutrition, and other factors can interfere with immunity for short periods of time as well.

Young puppies have some degree of natural immunity to disease, which they receive from the rich colostral milk their mother produces the first two or three days of a pup's life. The colostrum contains antibodies to disease, which provide the pups with limited protection during the first few weeks of life. Called passive immunity, or sometimes maternal immunity, this protection gradually decreases and may diminish by as much as 75 percent by the time a pup is 2 weeks old. Most puppies completely

lose passive immunity by the time they're 14 to 16 weeks old.

Until it reaches a low threshold, passive immunity can interfere with immunization; the maternal antibodies destroy vaccine viruses. For this reason, puppies are given a series of vaccinations to ensure that the immune system responds to the vaccine. Otherwise, a virus can sneak in during the window of opportunity that arises when the level of maternal antibodies is low enough to make a pup susceptible to infection, yet high enough to interfere with immunization. Veterinarians generally recommend that puppies be immunized at three- to four-week intervals, beginning at 8 weeks of age and ending around 18 weeks of age. The final vaccine is the most important of the immunization series.

How frequently vaccinations should be boosted after the first series is currently a matter of discussion in the veterinary and dog-owning communities. Many veterinary schools now recommend a booster vaccine at one year of age, followed by additional boosters every three years thereafter, instead of previous recommendations of annual boosters. Some areas of the country have a higher incidence of certain infectious diseases, such as distemper and parvovirus, than others. Your veterinarian can advise you on the vaccination schedule that is appropriate for your area.

Infectious Diseases

Distemper

This potentially fatal disease is caused by a virus. Distemper is highly contagious and is usually transmitted through contact with mucous and watery secretions discharged from the eyes and noses of infected dogs as well as through contact with their urine or fecal matter. The virus may also be airborne or carried on inanimate objects such as shoes. A healthy dog can contract distemper without ever coming in physical contact with an infected animal.

A dog with distemper appears to have a bad cold. He may sneeze and have a runny nose and runny eyes. Other signs to watch for are squinting, weight loss, coughing, vomiting, and diarrhea. A dog with distemper is usually listless and has a diminished appetite. As distemper progresses, it can attack the nervous system, causing a dog to become partially or completely paralyzed. The dog may twitch or have seizures.

Distemper is spread mainly from sick to susceptible dogs. Puppies and young adult dogs are most susceptible to infection by the distemper virus, but the disease also infrequently strikes older dogs. Most cases of distemper occur in puppies 8 to 16

The majority of infectious diseases strike the most vulnerable dogs: the very young, the elderly, and the immunocompromised.

weeks old. Distemper is more severe in younger pups.

Distemper is not always easy to diagnose. Lab tests such as blood chemistry and blood cell counts aren't of much value in pinning down distemper. The veterinarian may need to run more sophisticated tests to determine whether the virus is present. Because the signs of distemper can be varied, treatment is often delayed. To be on the safe side, take any sick young dog to the veterinarian for a definite diagnosis.

The only treatment for the distemper virus is good supportive care and control of neurological symptoms such as seizures. Nursing care involves keeping the eyes and nose dry and encouraging the dog to eat and drink. Dogs who survive the initial infection may develop retinal damage, corneal discoloration, or extreme hardness of the nose leather or foot pads.

Infectious Canine Hepatitis (ICH)

This is a highly contagious viral disease. Often confused with distemper, ICH begins in the tonsils and spreads to lymph nodes and the bloodstream. The virus is shed in urine, stool, and saliva, and a dog who has recovered remains infective for up to nine months.

The effects of ICH range from mild to rapidly fatal. Signs of a mild infection include loss of appetite and lethargy. The fatal cases develop suddenly, with bloody diarrhea, collapse, and death within hours.

Recovered dogs may develop a cloudy cornea in one or both eyes, referred to as blue eye, but this usually disappears in a few days. Fortunately, the disease is rare and is

The average body temperature of a dog is 99.5°F–102.5°F. The average pulse rate is 60–120 beats per minute.

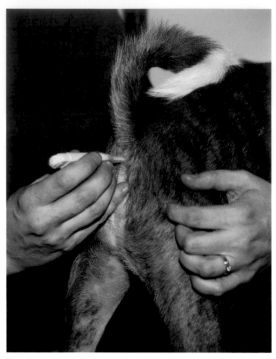

An elevated temperature may indicate that your dog is suffering from an illness.

seen mainly in wild dogs or unvaccinated dogs younger than one year of age.

Canine Influenza

You may be aware of the appearance of a new canine influenza virus. The highly contagious virus causes a cough, runny nose, and low-grade fever for ten to twenty-one days. Dogs with severe cases may develop pneumonia, a high fever, and secondary bacterial infections. While all dogs are susceptible to infection, the fatality rate is only 1 to 5 percent so far, and cases are limited geographically. Dogs most at risk are the very young, the very old, or those already in poor health.

Despite the stories you may read on the Internet, experts say the new form of influenza isn't as deadly as people make it out to be. It's safe to walk your dog on the street or take him to the dog park. Use common sense about taking your dog out in public if he has or has recently recovered from a respiratory infection. Call your veterinarian for advice if your dog shows signs of respiratory illness.

Parvovirus

A highly contagious viral disease, parvovirus first appeared in the 1970s. It's most common in young puppies but can affect dogs of any age. Doberman Pinschers, Labrador Retrievers, Rottweilers, American Pit Bull Terriers, and pit bull–types seem to be unusually prone to parvovirus and may suffer a more severe case than other breeds. One form of parvovirus affects the heart and is rapidly fatal. Parvovirus is shed in feces and transmitted by oral contact with infected feces. Signs of parvovirus start with depression, vomiting, and diarrhea. Some dogs develop a high fever.

Your puppy needs special protection during his formative months. Although he must be socialized, do not let him interact with unvaccinated dogs or sniff around canine potty areas until he has received his puppy shots.

Let's discuss some of the diseases that create the need for vaccination in the first place. Following are the major canine infectious diseases and a simple explanation of each.

Rabies: A devastating viral disease that can be fatal in dogs and people. In fact, vaccination of dogs and cats is an important public-health measure to create a resistant animal buffer population to protect people from contracting the disease. Vaccination schedules are determined on a government level and are not optional for pet owners; rabies vaccination is required by law in all 50 states.

Parvovirus: A severe, potentially life-threatening disease that is easily transmitted between dogs. There are four strains of the virus, but it is believed that there is significant "cross-protection" between strains that may be included in individual vaccines.

Distemper: A potentially severe and life-threatening disease with a relatively high risk of exposure, especially in certain regions. In very high-risk distemper environments, young pups may be vaccinated with human measles vaccine, a related virus that offers cross-protection when administered at four to ten weeks of age.

Hepatitis: Caused by canine adenovirus type 1 (CAV-1), but since vaccination with the causative virus has a higher rate of adverse effects, cross-protection is derived from the use of adenovirus type 2 (CAV-2), a cause of respiratory disease and one of the potential causes of canine cough. Vaccination with CAV-2 provides long-term immunity against hepatitis, but relatively less protection against respiratory infection.

Canine cough: Also called tracheobronchitis, actually a fairly complicated result of viral and bacterial offenders; therefore, even with vaccination, protection is incomplete. Wherever dogs congregate, canine cough will likely be spread among them. Intranasal vaccination with Bordetella and parainfluenza is the best safeguard, but the duration of immunity does not appear to be very long, typically a year at most. These are non-core vaccines, but vaccination is sometimes mandated by boarding kennels, obedience classes, dog shows, and other places where dogs congregate to try to minimize spread of infection.

Leptospirosis: A potentially fatal disease that is more common in some geographic regions. It is capable of being spread to humans. The disease varies with the individual "serovar," or strain, of Leptospira involved. Since there does not appear to be much cross-protection between serovars, protection is only as good as the likelihood that the serovar in the vaccine is the same as the one in the pet's local environment. Problems with Leptospira vaccines are that protection does not last very long, side effects are not uncommon, and a large percentage of dogs (perhaps 30%) may not respond to vaccination.

Borrelia burgdorferi: The cause of Lyme disease, the risk of which varies with the geographic area in which the pet lives and travels. Lyme disease is spread by deer ticks in the eastern United States and western black-legged ticks in the western part of the country, and the risk of exposure is high in some regions. Lameness, fever, and inappetence are most commonly seen in affected dogs. The extent of protection from the vaccine has not been conclusively demonstrated.

Coronavirus: This disease has a high risk of exposure, especially in areas where dogs congregate, but it typically causes only mild to moderate digestive upset (diarrhea, vomiting, etc.). Vaccines are available, but the duration of protection is believed to be relatively short and the effectiveness of the vaccine in preventing infection is considered low.

There are many other vaccinations available, including those for Giardia and canine adenovirus-1. While there may be some specific indications for their use, and local risk factors to be considered, they are not widely recommended for most dogs.

Suspect parvo any time vomiting and bloody diarrhea develop suddenly in a puppy. The veterinarian can diagnose the disease with an in-office blood test.

Dogs with parvo almost always require hospitalization so they can receive intravenous fluids and medications. There is no cure for parvovirus, so this supportive treatment is all that can be done. Antibiotics can be administered to help prevent bacterial infections. Recovery, which can take one to two weeks, depends on how quickly the dog was diagnosed and treated as well as the strength of his immune system. Puppies who receive good, early veterinary care usually recover without ill effects.

Rabies

This fatal disease is caused by a virus that enters the body through the bite or scratch of an infected animal. Because the virus is transmitted through saliva, an infected animal can transmit the disease even if the saliva only touches an open wound. The rabies virus travels to the brain, causing inflammation. Dogs can be vaccinated against rabies, but there's no treatment once the disease takes hold.

Changes in behavior are common in rabid animals. A normally friendly dog with rabies might become unusually aggressive or attack people or other animals without warning. Shy dogs can become uncharacteristically affectionate. The classic sign of rabies is frenzied, vicious behavior. Because the dog is unable to swallow, he drools or foams at the mouth. Paralysis develops in later stages.

If a rabies-vaccinated dog is bitten by a rabid or potentially rabid animal, the dog should be revaccinated immediately, preferably within 72 hours. The dog must then be quarantined according to local or state ordinances—generally between 30 and 90 days. If an unvaccinated dog is bitten, he must either be euthanized or quarantined for six months without human or animal contact. If he shows no signs of developing rabies, he must be vaccinated one month before release from quarantine.

CHAPTER 22

Basic Health Care

Living with a dog entails a certain ability to provide care at home, both for maintenance of good health and in case of emergencies. To keep your dog in the pink, you must provide dental hygiene, parasite prevention, and medication. There may also be times when you will need to provide your dog with first aid and emergency care.

Dental Care

To ensure good dental health, a dog's teeth need to be brushed daily using a special toothbrush and toothpaste made for dogs. This regimen should start when your puppy is six to eight months of age, once the adult teeth are in. For dogs who aren't willing to have their teeth brushed but have a problem with rapid tartar buildup, some veterinarians recommend feeding a special dental diet that's designed to have a crosshatch effect on teeth, scrubbing them all the way to the gum line. Other dry foods and biscuits can help crack off tartar but don't affect the gum line area.

Other preventive measures include providing dogs with toys and treats that have a tartar-removing effect. These include hard rubber chew toys with hollow interiors that can be stuffed with treats as well as rope or sheepskin toys, which have fibers that help keep teeth clean.

Periodontal Disease

If a dog's teeth aren't cared for, the result is sure to be periodontal disease, the most common dental condition affecting dogs. Periodontal disease is the inflammation and infection of the gums and supporting tissues of the teeth. It begins when bacteria-laden plaque and tartar

(calculus) build up on teeth, especially below the gum line, Pockets form under the gum line, and food lodges in the pockets. These bits of food that remain on teeth are breeding grounds for bacteria. The resulting infection causes bad breath, bleeding and inflammation of the gums, receding gums, loosening of teeth, and eventual tooth loss.

According to the American Veterinary Dental Society, more than 80 percent of dogs over the age of three years develop gum or periodontal disease. Any dog can develop

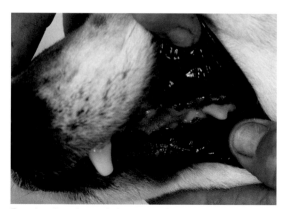

Regular dental care is important for your dog. Tartar can build up quickly and may lead to periodontal disease.

periodontal disease, but it's seen most commonly in Toy breeds. They have the same number of teeth (42) as larger dogs do, but the teeth are crowded into a smaller area. Regular brushing is the best way to get rid of food residue so it doesn't harden and form the ugly brown deposits known as tartar.

Routine periodontal treatment performed by a veterinarian typically includes ultrasonic scaling, subgingival manual scaling, and polishing. For advanced cases of periodontal disease, some dental specialists use antibiotic therapy, which involves cleaning and polishing the teeth, regular home brushing, and administering antibiotics for the first five days of every month. This regimen decreases the progression of the disease. Another new treatment is Doxyrobe, a gel placed inside the socket to sterilize it. This sustained-release form of doxycycline is used in periodontal pockets to increase attachment. A relatively new treatment is a sealant called OraVet, a gel that can be applied weekly to help prevent the formation of plaque and tartar. If the dog's teeth are in really bad shape, periodontal surgery such as bone grafting and guided tissue regeneration can be performed. For the most severe cases, extraction is the only option. Dogs can still eat well and enjoy chewing their toys, even if they're missing a few—or even a lot of—teeth, and their mouths will be healthier.

Endodontic Conditions

Broken or abscessed teeth may require root canals or extractions. Endodontic problems are most common in large dogs, especially shepherd and retriever breeds. These dogs chew a lot on such things as fences, cow hooves, and bones, wearing their teeth down and sometimes breaking them. Even chewing on ice cubes can cause teeth to fracture.

Your veterinarian may suggest having your dog's teeth professionally cleaned, but this is not a replacement for regular brushing.

Signs of Dental Problems

Odor: If your dog's breath smells like the inside of a garbage can, something's wrong. Normal dog breath smells good.

Lack of appetite: Dogs with dental problems have trouble eating. They may pick up food and then drop it or stop eating altogether. Check your dog's water dish for bits of food.

Pawing at the mouth or drooling excessively: This can be a sign that the area is painful or that something is stuck inside. Take your dog to the veterinarian.

Dental fractures are common in dogs, and treatment is a must if the pulp, the soft tissue that fills the center of a tooth, is exposed. This is not only painful but can also lead to tissue death and abscess. A root canal is the preferred method of treatment for such cases, although occasionally extraction may be the best choice.

Don't ignore a broken tooth, even if it doesn't seem to bother your dog. The majority of dogs are happier and more active once a tooth repair is made.

Oral Surgery

Oral surgery is usually done to remove teeth or repair fractured jaws. Thanks to new pain relief techniques and drugs, extractions can be performed with minimal pain and discomfort, and jaw fractures can be repaired using new techniques that minimize damage to teeth and ensure a rapid return to normal function.

Dogs may also need oral surgery when they're diagnosed with tumors of the mouth and throat, which are common in dogs. Radiotherapy and recently developed surgical techniques for removing oral tumors are now available. These techniques often give excellent results, both in terms of cosmetic appearance and prognosis, provided they are performed at an early stage of the disease.

Examine your dog's mouth monthly. Oral tumors can go unnoticed until they've reached an advanced stage of development, making successful treatment more difficult. Bring any suspicious swellings or persistent sores to the attention of your veterinarian. Besides oral tumors, dogs can also develop noncancerous masses and swellings such as gingival hyperplasia, an overgrowth of the gums.

External Parasites

Parasites are organisms that survive by living off other life forms. Among the external parasites that can infest dogs are fleas, ticks, and mites. Internal parasites include roundworms, tapeworms, hookworms, whipworms, and heartworms. Parasites can spread disease and even help transmit other parasites. For instance, fleas are instrumental in spreading tapeworms. Keeping your dog free of parasites is an essential part of good health care.

Fleas

Fleas may well be the most aggravating external parasite a dog will encounter. Only dogs who live in extreme locales—sunny, arid climes or excessively cold environments—are likely to escape the exasperating itch-scratch cycle brought on by flea bites. Some dogs are so sensitive to flea saliva—the substance that causes the itch—a single bite can send them into a fit of biting and scratching at the itchy area. This extreme sensitivity is called flea allergy dermatitis.

Fleas don't actually live on dogs—they just hop on for a blood meal when they want to feed—so a little detective work is necessary to establish their presence. Stand your dog on a white towel or piece of paper, and run a brush or comb through his coat. If small black flecks fall onto the white area, wet them to see if they turn red. Any flecks that turn red are so-called flea dirt. In other words, it's the blood the flea excretes after feeding on your dog.

Flea Control on the Dog

To rid your dog of fleas, talk to your veterinarian. There are so many good flea control products available now that there's really no need for any dog to suffer the agony of flea bites. These products can be topical (applied to the dog's skin) or given in pill form. Some of the products control ticks and other parasites as well. The best product for your dog depends on both the climate in your area and the lifestyle of your dog. A dog who spends a lot of time outdoors or playing in water may need a different product than that used for a dog who spends most of his time in the home or show ring.

Some of the flea control products available include Program, Frontline, and Advantage. Program contains a chemical called lufenuron. Lufenuron, given in pill form, works by sterilizing female fleas that bite the dog, thus preventing their eggs from hatching and breaking the

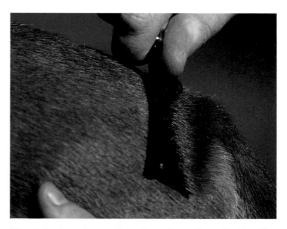

Check for fleas by combing just above the tail with a flea comb. Black peppery flakes that turn red when wetted are flea dirt and indicate that your dog has fleas.

There are more than 2,000 known species and subspecies of flea in the world. One flea species, however, accounts for almost all the fleas found on dogs and cats in the United States. It is known as the cat flea.

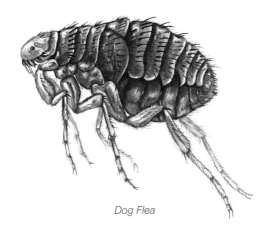

Dog Flea

Ingesting fleas is the main cause of tapeworm in dogs and cats. Some animals eat 50–90 percent of the fleas on their body.

flea life cycle usually within two months of use. Program is safe, effective, and easy to give, but its drawback is that the flea must bite the dog to be affected.

Frontline, which contains a chemical called fipronil, is applied topically between the dog's shoulder blades and kills fleas for up to three months. It's safe for use on puppies as young as 10 weeks and dogs who are taking other medications. Fipronil works by collecting in the skin's oil-producing glands and wicking back out with the coat. It's a good choice for dogs who are bathed frequently or otherwise spend a lot of time in the water.

The active ingredient in Advantage is called imidacloprid. Applied to the skin over the back, it kills adult fleas on contact and is effective for up to a month. Like Frontline, it's safe for use on puppies as young as 10 weeks and dogs who are taking other medications.

Never use topical flea control made for dogs on cats.

Environmental Flea Control

To eradicate fleas from the home, you need to treat the dog, the indoor living areas, and the yard at the same time using appropriate products for each. For instance, never use a premise spray meant for use around the house on your dog. And check with your vet-erinarian to make sure you aren't using chemicals that could be toxic when combined.

Treat the home and yard, being sure to apply the flea-control product in such areas as along the baseboards, around the perimeter of the yard and home, and under and around decks and patios. Clear the yard of leaves and other debris. If you use an exterminator, make sure the product employed is safe for use around pets. Don't forget to treat the inside of the car and the doghouse and kennel area.

Generally, the least toxic products for use on pets or in the home and yard are those containing pyrethrins or pyrethroids, which are fast acting but don't remain long in the environment. Products that are more powerful, more long-lasting, and more toxic include those containing chemicals called cholinesterase inhibitors, sold under such names as carbaryl, diazinon, Sevin, Dursban, fenthion, and malathion. Use them sparingly, if at all. Look for premise sprays that contain not only an insecticide to kill adult fleas but also an insect growth regulator (IGR). These chemicals, which go by the names methoprene or pyriproxyfen, work by preventing flea eggs from hatching and larval fleas from reaching adulthood. Premise sprays are more effective than foggers are because they can be directed toward specific areas. Foggers simply dissipate in the room and don't provide good penetration.

Undisturbed, a flea can live on a dog for more than 100 days.

Fighting Fleas in Your Home

If you've seen fleas on your dog, chances are there are more in your house. To help eradicate fleas in the home and yard, try these tips:

- Eliminate fleas on your dog through grooming and medical treatment.

- Vacuum at least once a week. Be especially thorough in areas and rooms that your dog frequents. Vacuum upholstery and area rugs and in crevices, cracks, and baseboards. If possible, use a vacuum cleaner with a beater bar, a metal cylinder with thick bristles that combs the carpet and can suck up fleas, their larvae, and their eggs. Remove the vacuum bag after each use, seal it, and throw it in an outdoor garbage container.

- Wash your dog's bedding weekly. If your dog sleeps on a bed that is difficult to wash, keep the bed covered with a sheet or blanket, and wash that once a week. Roll the sheet or blanket up as you remove it, so fleas and eggs are contained. Regularly wash your dog's collar and plush toys.

- Keep floors free of clutter. Don't give fleas places to hide from your attempts to get rid of them.

- Consider keeping some rooms off limits to your dog to reduce problem areas.

- Treat severe infestations with flea control products. If your house is severely infested with fleas, you may need to apply a spray or powder directly to carpets, rugs, and upholstered items. Ask your veterinarian about the best and safest products to use. In severe cases, you may need to call in a professional exterminator.

- For nontoxic flea control in the home, use diatomaceous earth. This natural product tears up a flea's exoskeleton and absorbs its body fluids, causing it to dehydrate and die. Diatomaceous earth can be sprinkled on floors and furniture and swept into cracks and crevices. Be sure to use food (or garden) grade and not pool grade. Pool grade diatomaceous earth is treated with chemicals and should not be used for pest control.

- Rid your yard of fleas. Concentrate mostly on shady areas because fleas don't like sunlight. Remove wet leaves, grass clippings, and other moist vegetation, which is where fleas live.

- Spray your yard with a commercial insecticide. (Limit your dog's access to the yard for 24 hours after spraying.) If you prefer a more natural route, you can release nematodes into your yard. Nematodes are microscopic worms that kill flea larvae. They are available at most pet and garden supply stores. Ladybugs, which can also be purchased at garden supply stores, are another natural flea predator.

Bathe the dog with a good flea-control shampoo made for dogs. Leave it on for at least 10 minutes before rinsing. Shampoos that contain a natural insecticide called d-limonene are safe and effective for puppies and older dogs. After bathing, apply the topical product recommended by your veterinarian. Avoid using flea collars, which are ineffective and may cause allergic reactions or other side effects.

Ticks are not insects; they are actually arachnids, as are spiders. The bodies of some ticks can expand 20–100 times as they feed.

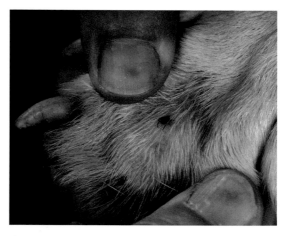

Common in many areas of the United States, ticks are small external parasites that can carry serious disease.

Deer Tick

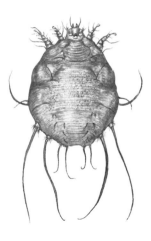

Sarcoptes Mite

Ticks

Just as nasty as fleas are ticks. Ticks belong to the arachnid family and are related to spiders. They have brown or black tear-shaped bodies with eight legs. An adult female tick is about the size of a poppy seed or a sesame seed, although ticks that are fat with blood can be bigger, up to the size of a pencil eraser. The two ticks most

Keeping your dog free of external and internal parasites will help him stay happy and healthy.

It may be more difficult to find fleas and ticks on long-haired dogs. Be sure to keep up to date on monthly preventives.

commonly found on dogs are the brown dog tick and the American dog tick, but the deer tick and the western black-legged tick also feed on dogs.

Using their sharp mouthpieces, ticks attach themselves to a dog's skin, usually around the head, neck, ears, or feet, and make a meal of the dog's blood. That's bad enough, but certain ticks also transmit Lyme disease and Rocky Mountain spotted fever. A large number of ticks feeding off a single dog can cause severe anemia or tick paralysis.

Tick season is spring and summer, but any time your dog is outdoors or in a heavily wooded area, you should examine him for these nasty creatures. Don't touch the tick with your bare hands. The spirochete that causes Lyme disease can enter through the skin. Wear gloves and part the dog's coat to look down close to the skin. Ticks can be easy to miss, especially on dark-colored dogs.

In late 2003, the U.S. Congress passed the Animal Drug User Fee Act, designed to speed U.S. Food and Drug Administration review of new drugs for improving animal health.

To remove a tick, grasp it at the head with tweezers or forceps. Pull slowly but firmly to dislodge it without leaving any part of it behind. After the tick is removed, clean the bite site with rubbing alcohol, and apply a topical antibiotic ointment. Do not hold a lit match to the tick or attempt to smother the tick with nail polish, petroleum jelly, kerosene, or gasoline.

Many products help kill or repel ticks, and a dog can be vaccinated for Lyme disease if your veterinarian thinks the risk of infection warrants it. Usually, the vaccine is recommended if there is a high incidence of Lyme disease in the area or if a dog's lifestyle puts him at risk. For instance, hunting dogs in the forests of northern Michigan would be much more likely to require vaccination than those in New Mexico, a state that has few if any cases of Lyme disease.

Mites

Mites are also members of the arachnid family. Dogs can become infested with several mite species: *Demodex canis*, or mange; *Sarcoptes scabei var. canis*, or scabies; and *Cheyletiella*, or walking dandruff. There is also a type of mite that affects only the ears, *Otodectes cynotis*, or ear mites.

Mange

Demodex mites, which are recognizable microscopically by their distinctive cigar shape, usually live peacefully on dogs, inhabiting the hair follicles of the skin. The presence of *Demodex* mites is determined through skin scrapings or biopsies. Problems begin when the *Demodex* population grows uncontrollably, resulting in a condition called demodicosis, or demodectic mange. Demodicosis, which is not contagious, can occur in only a single area (localized), or it can spread over the entire body of the dog (generalized). Fortunately, the much milder localized demodicosis is more common.

Dogs with demodicosis usually have patchy hair loss and scaly red skin, especially around the face, eyes, corners of the mouth, and on the front legs. If demodicosis affects the entire body, the signs are usually more severe, with the skin becoming darker and thicker as a result of chronic inflammation.

Demodicosis is most commonly seen in dogs younger than one year, but adults can also be affected. Generalized demodicosis in puppies is probably hereditary, so young dogs who have this condition should be spayed or neutered so they don't pass on the tendency.

Cases of localized demodicosis usually disappear without treatment, but your veterinarian can prescribe an ointment that will kill the mites. Dogs with widespread demodicosis must be dipped once or twice a week in a miticide (solution that kills mites) until the problem is resolved. Dogs with long or heavy coats may need to be clipped so the solution can work more effectively. Antibiotics are prescribed to treat the bacterial skin infections that often accompany demodicosis. Whirlpool soaks and frequent baths with a shampoo containing benzoyl peroxide may also be helpful. Generalized demodicosis can be difficult to treat effectively, especially if the dog is not young.

Scabies

Sarcoptes mites cause a condition called scabies, or sarcoptic mange. Unlike demodicosis, canine scabies is highly contagious between dogs and can sometimes spread to people and cats. Dogs with scabies suffer intense itching, triggered when the small, oval, white *Sarcoptes* mite burrows beneath the dog's skin. Other signs of scabies are crusty sores and hair loss. Because the dog constantly bites and scratches at the itchy spots, wounds and bacterial skin infections can also occur. Scabies is diagnosed through skin scrapings and clinical signs.

Isolate dogs with scabies from other pets and family members until the condition is resolved. Shampoos and dips prescribed by the veterinarian will kill the mites over a period of a month. Most dogs need to be dipped at least six times, once every five to seven days. Corticosteroids can help control severe itching. Treat other dogs who have been in contact with the infested dog, even if they don't show signs. Talk to a dermatological specialist about additional treatments, both topical and systemic.

Cheyletiella Mites

Cheyletiella mites look like small white specks and can sometimes be seen with the naked eye moving on the affected dog's skin or coat. Infestation with *Cheyletiella* mites causes a mild but itchy skin disease that's indicated by dandruff along the back; hence, the common nickname of walking dandruff. *Cheyletiella* mites can be passed on to other animals and to people. The presence of these mites can be confirmed with a skin scraping. Like other mite infestations, treatment involves a series of medicated baths and dips. Other dogs and cats in the household should also be treated. Clean the house thoroughly to make sure no mites remain. *Cheyletiella* infestation isn't common, and when it does occur it's usually in puppies or adolescent dogs. A good flea-control program usually prevents infestation.

Internal Parasites

Many parasites can take up residence inside a dog—usually in the gut—but the ones that most commonly cause problems are roundworms, hookworms, whipworms, tapeworms, and heartworms. Left uncontrolled, these parasites do their dirty work by consuming nutrients a dog needs or preventing

Because puppies are especially susceptible to internal parasites, they should be dewormed before being placed into their new homes.

the dog's body from properly absorbing those nutrients; destroying red blood cells, causing anemia; damaging or killing tissues and cells as they move through the body; and transmitting disease. If the infection is severe, some internal parasites, such as heartworms, can even kill a dog. For your dog's good health, take steps to prevent internal parasites, which are easily con-

---

The first published description of heartworm in dogs appeared in 1847 in *The Western Journal of Medicine and Surgery*.

---

trolled through regular medication. Certain heartworm and flea-control medications also control most other internal parasites.

Roundworms

Roundworms are so common that most dogs are born with them, unless the mother was treated for worms during and after her pregnancy. Whether or not they show signs of infection, puppies should be dewormed every two weeks until they are eight weeks old. Then they can be started on preventive medication. Treat roundworms with a dewormer prescribed by the veterinarian.

Over-the-counter dewormers usually aren't effective.

While roundworms don't usually cause serious problems in adult dogs, they can be big trouble for puppies, especially if there are a lot of them. Puppies with roundworms look thin and scrawny, except for their distinctive potbelly, and they may vomit frequently or have diarrhea. A rough, dull coat is another sign of roundworm infestation. Pups with a heavy load of roundworms may develop a cough or even pneumonia.

Although it's rare, roundworms can be passed from dogs to people. Usually this occurs when young children put their hands in their mouths after touching egg-laden feces or playing in dirt or grassy areas where roundworm eggs have been deposited. Prevent roundworm infection by picking up and disposing of dog feces daily. Adult dogs should have an annual fecal exam so they can be treated for any worms that may be present.

Talk to your veterinarian about preventive care to protect against external and internal parasites. There are many excellent products now on the market.

Hookworms

These parasites are most common in warm, humid climates and thrive in warm, damp, sandy soil. Microscopically small hookworm larvae penetrate the skin, usually through the feet, or are transmitted to pups through their mother's milk. They can also be ingested from the environment, off a blade of grass for instance. Once inside the dog, hookworms migrate through the body to the small intestine, where they latch onto the intestinal wall with their goblet-shaped mouths (lined with three sets of teeth) and suck blood from it, causing anemia in severe cases. Signs of hookworm infection include diarrhea, weakness, and weight loss. A fecal exam can confirm the presence of hookworms. Medication can be given to kill the worms; keeping feces picked up will help prevent reinfection. Hookworms can be passed to people.

Whipworms

Whipworms are acquired when a dog eats something that has been in contact with contaminated soil or infective larvae. Whipworms live in the large intestine and feed on blood. Mild infections usually don't cause a problem, but heavy loads of the worms can cause anemia, diarrhea, and weight loss. Because dogs pass whipworm eggs only occasionally, these parasites can be difficult to diagnose. It may take several fecal exams to confirm their presence. The veterinarian can prescribe medication to kill the worms. Prevent reinfection by picking up feces daily.

Tapeworms

Tapeworms look like long, flat ribbons. They use hooks or suckers on their heads to attach themselves to their host. The most common type of tapeworm found in dogs is called *Dipylidium caninum*, which is spread by fleas. Tapeworm segments, which look like white rice, can sometimes be seen with the naked eye, crawling on a dog's rear end or in his bedding or stool. Medication prescribed by the veterinarian will rid a dog of tapeworms, and good flea-control measures will help keep them away.

Heartworm Disease

This serious and potentially fatal condition is caused by the parasite *Dirofilaria immitis*, commonly known as a heartworm because it takes up residence in the heart and major blood vessels of dogs, cats, and other species of

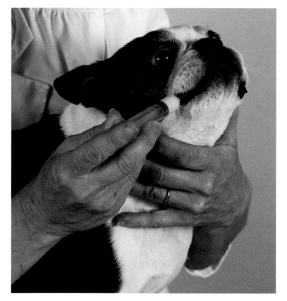

Some medications can be administered in liquid form. Discuss this with your veterinarian.

mammals. Heartworm larvae enter a dog's body through the bite of a mosquito, grow to maturity, and begin to reproduce, all in a period of six to seven months.

Heartworms used to be considered a regional problem of the southern United States, but the infection has been found in all 50 states. The highest infection rates occur in dogs who don't receive heartworm preventive.

Signs of heartworm disease vary, depending on the load of worms the dog is carrying. Dogs with few worms may not show any physical signs, but if the infection is heavy, the dog may be lethargic, lose weight, cough during exercise, or even pass out after exertion. Dogs with severe cases may suffer congestive heart failure.

Heartworm disease is diagnosed through blood-concentration tests and radiographs (X-rays). Radiographs of the heart and lungs are the best way to evaluate the severity of the heartworm infection. Antigen tests can detect specific antigens from adult female heartworms, but these tests aren't useful for detecting infections of five months or less.

Heartworm disease is treated by using drugs to poison the adult worms and eliminate them from the dog's system. The dog must be hospitalized during treatment so he can be monitored for possible complications such as obstruction of arteries by dead worms. A new

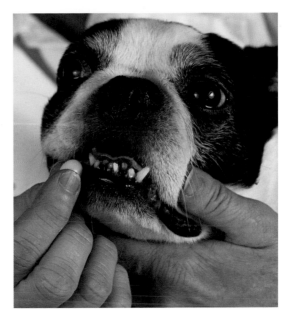

It is important that your dog receive his medication in the dosage prescribed by the veterinarian.

drug, Immiticide, is available for treating heartworm disease that is safer and more effective than the medication previously used. After the adult worms are eliminated, the dog can be treated to kill the microfilariae, or baby worms. This treatment usually takes place three to six weeks later and requires that the dog be hospitalized for eight hours to ensure that he doesn't suffer any adverse reactions.

Prevention is far better than treatment. It's not only safer for the dog, it's also much more cost-effective. Four types of medications are available for the prevention of heartworm disease. Diethylcarbamazine (DEC) must be given daily and is effective only against heartworms. Heartgard Plus and Interceptor are given monthly and also control other internal parasites such as hookworms, roundworms, and whipworms. Sentinel is a monthly tablet that's effective against heartworms and fleas. Revolution is applied to the skin. In addition to preventing heartworms, Revolution is effective against fleas, ear mites, sarcoptic mange, and American dog ticks. Proheart 6, an injectable preventive, was removed from the market in 2004 following adverse reactions, including deaths. The FDA permitted its reintroduction in 2008 on a limited basis, with warnings against giving it within one month of vaccinations and advice to use it with caution in dogs with allergies or who are sick or debilitated. Veterinarians must complete an online seminar before they can prescribe the drug. Reactions can range from mild muscle pain and fever to severe pain and high fever. Adverse reactions to this product should be reported by your veterinarian to the Food & Drug Administration and to Fort Dodge Animal Health.

Medication

At some point, every dog will need to take medication of some kind. Knowing the basics of how different drugs work can help make the process more successful.

Some medications must be given under certain conditions; for instance, with food or on an empty stomach. While it's often easier to give a pill if it's wrapped in dog food, cheese, or some other treat, you may need to use another method if the medication requires an empty stomach.

Check with your veterinarian before pulverizing a pill and sprinkling the powder on the dog's food. Powdered pills can have an unpleasant taste that makes the dog reluctant to eat the food, let alone the pill. Some pills have a protective coating that plays a role in the delayed release of the medication in the dog's system. If the coating is destroyed, the drug won't be as effective.

Dose and Dosage

The amount of medication a dog should take at one time is called a dose. A dose varies depending on the drug and the size of the dog. For one antibiotic, the dose might be 8 mg per pound of body weight, while for another it might be 25 mg per pound. A dose is determined by weighing the dog, dividing the total daily dose into equal parts, and giving them at prescribed intervals. There are other factors the veterinarian considers in determining a dose because they can affect whether a drug is helpful or harmful. These include the severity of the infection or disease, the dog's age and physical condition, and whether the dog is taking other drugs as well.

Some drugs counteract each other's effects or cause adverse effects if they're used together. If you are giving your dog any kind of herbal or homeopathic remedy, for instance, you should let your veterinarian know. It's also a good idea to ask if the medication being prescribed is safe for use with dogs taking heartworm pills or systemic flea control products.

The strength of a medication is its concentration or weight; for example, 50 mg, 100 mg, or 200 mg. How much is a milligram? There are 464,000 milligrams in a pound. The fact that most drugs are measured in milligrams indicates that sometimes tiny amounts

Canine First Aid Kit

Be prepared for emergencies by purchasing a ready-made first aid kit, or assemble one from common household items. Include in the kit the veterinarian's phone number, as well as the phone number of and directions to the nearest emergency clinic. Store the kit in an accessible area such as under the bathroom sink. Replace items as necessary. Ask your veterinarian about appropriate uses and doses before giving any medication. A well-stocked first aid kit includes the following items:

- Activated charcoal (available at drugstores) for absorbing poisons
- Adhesive tape to secure bandages
- Antibacterial ointment or powder for cleaning wounds
- Artificial tears for flushing eyes
- Benadryl, for allergic reactions, as directed by the veterinarian
- Blunt-tipped scissors to trim hair from wounds and cut bandaging material
- Chlorhexidine for cleaning wounds
- Cloths or sanitary napkins to help stem blood flow
- Cotton balls
- Cotton swabs
- Disinfectant solution
- Eye dropper, turkey baster, or syringe to flush wounds
- Gauze pads and rolls to make bandages and a muzzle
- Hydrogen peroxide (3 percent) to induce vomiting as instructed (Do so only on veterinary instruction. Do not induce vomiting unless the vet advises you to; in some cases of poisoning, throwing up can make the situation worse.)
- Kaopectate (ask your veterinarian what amount is appropriate to control your dog's diarrhea)
- K-Y Brand Jelly or petroleum jelly to lubricate a thermometer
- Needleless syringe for giving liquid medications
- Needle-nose pliers to remove obstructions from the mouth or throat
- Plaster splint for broken limbs
- Rectal thermometer
- Towels
- Tweezers

Insect Bites and Stings

While most insect bites and stings are not dangerous to dogs, they can be irritating and painful. Aloe vera, either in a store-bought gel or fresh from the plant, can help soothe irritation caused by bites and stings. Or try a commercial product from a pet supply store specifically for insect bites. Other compounds that help include a mixture of baking soda and water, using just enough water to make a paste, applied several times a day; milk of magnesia; calamine lotion; and hydrocortisone cream or spray. An oatmeal soak also can help if your dog is uncomfortable all over. Colloidal oatmeal is best, but regular oatmeal can be substituted.

If your dog is stung by a bee, hornet, or wasp, remove the stinger first. Locate the stinger, using a magnifying glass if necessary, and carefully pull it out with tweezers or your fingers. After removing the stinger, bathe the area with a weak solution of baking soda mixed with water (one part baking soda to several parts water). Then apply a cold compress or ice pack for several minutes to reduce the pain and swelling. Repeat this periodically for several minutes at a time.

To help discourage biting insects, spray on Avon's Skin-So-Soft Original Bath Oil mixed with water. Use a small percentage of the product so your dog doesn't get greasy.

Some dogs will need immediate veterinary attention because they are allergic to bites and stings. If a dog is bitten or stung on the face, severe swelling can interfere with breathing. If the affected area swells up quickly or if your dog is having trouble breathing or seems disoriented, take him to a veterinarian immediately. In emergency situations when you cannot reach a veterinarian, give your dog Benadryl. Ask your veterinarian before an emergency occurs about the proper dosage for your dog. This should slow the allergic reaction. If you suspect a venomous spider bit your dog, he will need immediate veterinary attention. Try to describe the spider as best you can to the veterinarian to facilitate proper treatment.

---

of a substance can be very powerful. Follow the veterinarian's label instructions carefully.

A drug can have a wide or narrow margin of safety, depending on such things as the health of the dog's liver or kidneys or the dog's physical maturity. Dogs with impaired liver or kidney function don't process and excrete drugs as efficiently as dogs without those problems do. Puppies need a lower dose per pound of body weight simply because their liver and kidneys are still immature.

When too much of a drug is given—an overdose—the symptoms may be far advanced before they're discovered, and the results can be serious. They include damage to the otic (ear) nerves, jaundice and liver failure, kidney failure, anemia, and impaired immunity. Never assume that more of a drug will be better or work faster.

The dosage—as opposed to the dose—is the amount of medication to take over a period of time. This is noted on the prescription bottle, which might read "Two capsules every 8 hours until gone." The dosage is important because many medications must reach a certain level in the bloodstream before they become effective. The length of time between doses of medication is determined by studies of the absorption, distribution, and metabolism of the drug in the body. If a drug isn't given, say, every 8 hours, then effective levels can't be maintained over a 24-hour period.

Giving medication on such a strict schedule can be difficult, however, for working dog-owners, who may face irregular office hours or unexpected traffic tie-ups. If this is a

---

Just as people donate blood to help save the lives of other people, dogs donate blood to help fellow canines. There are four veterinary blood banks in the United States.

potential problem, consider asking a neighbor or pet sitter to step in when you can't be there. Or explain your situation to the veterinarian. Sometimes a different schedule can be worked out.

Don't stop giving medication just because your dog's condition improves. Antibiotics commonly fail because they're not given often enough or because they're given for too short a time. Besides leading to a possible recurrence of an infection, giving too little of an antibiotic can result in the development of bacterial strains that are resistant to a particular drug, making the bacteria more difficult to control.

Side Effects

In addition to the desired effect of treating a disease, a drug can also cause conditions other than the one intended. These are known as side effects. For instance, many antihistamines, in addition to counteracting some allergic reactions, cause drowsiness. The drowsiness is a side effect of the antihistamine. Steroids can have the side effect of increased appetite. Side effects can be as minor as drowsiness or as serious as liver damage or even sudden death.

Other reactions to medications can include vomiting, fever, diarrhea, or rashes. These can be the result of an allergic reaction or of the disease being treated. Let your veterinarian know right away if your dog experiences such signs. It may be necessary to switch to a different drug.

If your veterinarian doesn't discuss side effects when he or she prescribes a drug, ask what they are so you'll know what to look for. Ask when you should expect to see improvement in the dog's condition as well. Pay attention to how well your dog eats, the color and consistency of his stool, and frequency of urination. These observations will help the veterinarian know how well the drug is working.

Emergency/First Aid

Knowledge of first aid is a must for dog owners. Emergencies may require not only that you treat the problem on the spot but also that you stabilize the dog until he can be treated by a veterinarian. Situations that require emergency first aid include allergic reactions, bleeding, burns, choking, fractures, frostbite, heat exhaustion or heatstroke, poisoning, puncture wounds, shock, and spinal injuries.

Allergic Reactions

Allergic reactions from insect bites and stings can cause swelling, hives (raised circular areas on the skin), rashes, itching and scratching, or watery eyes. A bite or sting on the face or neck can cause dangerous swelling that closes off the dog's airway. Take your dog to the veterinarian right away if he's having difficulty breathing. For less severe reactions, relieve itching by applying calamine lotion or a paste made of baking soda and water. An ice pack can help reduce pain and swelling.

Bleeding

A wound with bright red blood gushing from it indicates that an artery (a main highway for blood flow) is involved. Blood loss can be rapid, so apply firm pressure on the wound immediately, using a clean cloth if possible, but use whatever's available if necessary. The blood from a vein looks dark red and has a slower, more even flow. Again, apply and maintain direct pressure on the wound. Secure a pad or have someone hold it in place, and get the dog to a veterinarian immediately. Do not use a tourniquet to stop bleeding. Direct pressure is more effective, and an improperly used tourniquet can injure the dog.

To deal with less serious bleeding such as from a scratch or scrape, clean the wound with Nolvasan (chlorhexidine), which is available in any drugstore. When the wound stops bleeding, apply antibiotic ointment.

Burns

Burns can be caused by heat (fires, stoves, the sun), chemicals, or electricity. Bathe heat burns with cool water or apply a cool compress using gauze or cloth. Never cover a burn with butter or ointment, and don't apply ice to it. Butter and ointments hold the heat in, and ice can damage the skin. If the burn is caused by battery acid or some other chemical, such as toilet bowl cleaner, rinse the area with cool water. Wear gloves to protect your hands.

Chewing on electrical cords can cause burns on a corner of the mouth or on the tongue and palate. Dogs who suffer electrical shock may convulse or lose consciousness. Their respiration may slow, and a severe shock can cause the heart to stop

Soothe your dog's sunburn by misting it with cool water from a squirt bottle every half hour. If your dog doesn't like the spray, try a cool compress. Other soothing remedies include witch hazel, aloe vera, a cool bath with colloidal oatmeal, and over-the-counter human sprays like Solarcaine.

beating. Never touch the dog until the electrical source has been switched off. Don't perform CPR unless the heart has stopped.

In any of these situations, get veterinary help immediately, especially if a large area of the dog's body is burned or if the dog has suffered serious electrical shock.

Choking

Dogs use their mouths to explore, and frequently they swallow what they find. If it doesn't go down correctly, the dog can

Home health care for your pet is an important part of his recovery. Keep your pup warm and subdued as much as possible while he is on the mend.

choke. Bones, rocks, bottle caps, small balls, and tinsel are just a few of the things a dog might swallow that could cause him to choke.

Signs of choking include coughing, gagging, or pawing at the mouth. To check for a foreign object, open the mouth by pressing the thumb and forefingers into the upper cheeks, and then sweep a finger through the mouth. Gently try to remove any obstruction with the fingers or a pair of needle-nose pliers. If the item won't budge, perform the Heimlich maneuver by standing behind the dog, encircling his abdomen with the arms just beneath or behind the rib cage, and compressing the chest. Repeat until the object is coughed up. If the object still does not come out, get the dog to a veterinarian immediately.

Fractures

A fracture is a broken bone. Dogs can get broken bones from a bad fall, being hit by a car, or some other traumatic injury. Broken bones aren't limited to active, outdoorsy dogs; Toy dogs with delicate bones such as Italian Greyhounds can break a leg just by jumping off the sofa.

Types of bone breaks include simple fractures and compound fractures. A simple fracture is one in which the broken bone doesn't pierce the skin. A compound fracture is obvious because the bone sticks out through the skin. If the lower jaw is hanging open and the dog is drooling, the jaw may be fractured. A dizzy or unconscious dog, or one with a bloody nose, may have a skull fracture.

If your dog breaks a bone, keep him still and try to avoid moving the limb and injuring it further. For a fractured jaw, tie a scarf or bandage underneath the chin and fasten it behind the ears. To help ward off shock, control any bleeding and keep the dog warm by wrapping him in a blanket. It's a good idea to muzzle an

---

Fashioning an Emergency Splint

To quickly make a splint, roll up newspaper, a magazine, or a towel, and slip it on top of the injured leg. Use masking tape or another strong tape to hold the splint in place. The splint should extend one joint above the fracture and one joint below or cover the length of the dog's leg.

Be sure that the splint is not so tight that it constricts blood flow. If you have cotton padding available, wrap the leg in the cotton first, and then place the splint over it, or wrap an Ace bandage around the cotton padding and secure.

---

injured dog before touching him. Dogs in pain will bite, no matter how well they know you. Seek veterinary help as soon as possible.

Frostbite

This painful condition results from prolonged exposure to very cold temperatures and usually

Your pet can be injured when playing outdoors or when overdoing exercise. Frostbite can affect dogs exposed to very cold weather.

Dogs with very short coats can get chilled easily and should not be outside in cold weather for long periods without adequate protection.

affects the extremities: a dog's ear tips, footpads, and tail. It's most serious in very young, very old, or sick dogs.

Signs of frostbite are pale skin that later reddens and becomes hot and painful to the touch; swelling; and peeling skin. Keep a frostbitten dog warm, and thaw frostbitten areas slowly, using warm, moist towels. Don't massage the skin or apply hot compresses; this can worsen the damage. When the skin regains its normal color, stop warming it. Wrap the dog in a blanket to help prevent shock, and get him to a vet.

Heat Exhaustion/Heatstroke

Most dogs have few sweat glands to cool them, so they control their body temperature by panting. As the dog pants, the body loses heat through evaporation from the mouth. If the body can't disperse heat quickly enough, the dog's temperature can rise to a dangerous level.

Heat exhaustion is associated with too much exercise on hot days, but the dog's tem-

Panting is a dog's normal mechanism for cooling himself. Be aware of the signs of overheating, though, as it can be dangerous if a dog's body temperature remains elevated.

perature doesn't necessarily rise to dangerous levels. A dog with heat exhaustion may collapse, vomit, or have muscle cramps.

Heatstroke can develop in only a few minutes, with the body temperature rising to 108°F or higher. A dog with heatstroke can die if he is not cared for immediately. Wet the body with cool, not cold, water, and get him to a veterinarian.

Poisoning

Common household items such as cleansers, rat poisons, and yard treatments can cause poisoning in dogs. Also toxic are seasonal plants such as Easter lilies; common household, yard, and garden plants such as azalea, caladium, dieffenbachia (dumb cane), English ivy (berries and leaves), ficus (leaves), holly, mistletoe (berries), oleander, and philodendron; and bulbs such as amaryllis, daffodil, iris, and tulip. Signs of poisoning include drooling, vomiting, convulsing, muscle weakness, diarrhea, or collapse. The eyes, mouth, or skin may become irritated.

If the poison is known, call a veterinarian or the National Animal Poison Control Center (NAPCC) for advice. If the poison is on the skin, put on rubber gloves and wash the affected area with warm water. If the dog has been poisoned by something he ate, give activated charcoal tablets to help absorb the poison, binding it to the surface of the charcoal so it doesn't spread through the bloodstream. Do not induce vomiting unless advised to by the NAPCC or your veterinarian. Take the dog to your veterinarian as soon as possible. Bring the package containing the suspected poison and a sample of anything the dog has vomited.

Puncture Wounds

Types of puncture wounds include penetration of the body by a sharp object (stepping on a nail, for instance) or a bite from another animal. Untreated puncture wounds can become infected or abscessed. Signs of infection include swelling, redness, warmth, and pain.

To cleanse a bite or puncture wound, flush the area with a mild disinfectant such as povidone-iodine or 0.05 percent chlorhexidine. A course of antibiotics prescribed by the veterinarian can help ward off infection. A tetanus shot isn't usually necessary as long as the wound is treated promptly.

Shock

Shock is a common result of serious injury such as being hit by a car, poisoning, or severe fluid loss from vomiting or diarrhea. It can be fatal if not dealt with rapidly. When a dog

---

Inducing Vomiting

If your dog has ingested a poisonous substance and you can't get to help quickly, you may need to induce vomiting. Call your veterinarian or a poison hotline first, though. Vomiting after the ingestion of some substances can be harmful to your dog. Never induce vomiting in a dog who has swallowed a caustic substance such as kerosene or drain cleaner because they burn as they come up. Do not use syrup of ipecac, a common vomit-inducing substance, because it may be ineffective and even harmful.

To induce vomiting, give your dog about 1 tablespoon of hydrogen peroxide solution (3 percent hydrogen peroxide and 97 percent water) for every 10 pounds of weight. It can be squirted down his throat using a syringe or meat baster. Your dog should vomit within about 5 minutes; if he doesn't, try again after 10 minutes.

that vital organs such as the brain, heart, and lungs don't get enough blood supply, causing them to fail.

Signs of shock include a weak, rapid pulse; dry gums; lips that are pale or gray; shallow, rapid breathing; a low body temperature; and weakness or lethargy. Control any bleeding, keep the dog immobilized, warm him with blankets, and seek immediate veterinary treatment.

Spinal Injuries

Suspect a spinal injury if a dog is paralyzed; his legs are rigid, stiff, or limp; or his head is thrust backward. Move the dog as little and as carefully as possible. Improvise a stretcher using a board large enough to support the dog's back. Tape or otherwise secure the dog to the board so he won't roll off or move around. If a board isn't available, use a blanket pulled taut. If possible, slide the dog onto the stretcher instead of lifting him. Treat for shock as needed, and try to keep the dog as still as possible during the ride to the veterinary hospital.

goes into shock, the body is unable to maintain adequate blood pressure. This means

Large-breed dogs, like the Leonberger, may be susceptible to a variety of health problems. Owners of all giant dogs should seek veterinary services from professionals with experience with super-size canines.

Long-backed dogs, like Welsh Corgis and Dachshunds, are prone to back injuries and should not be encouraged to jump, walk on their hind legs, or exercise on stairs.

CHAPTER 23

The Dog Body and Health Care

Part of taking good care of a dog is understanding how his body works and what can go wrong. The skin and coat, ears, eyes, paws, and all the other components that make up a dog have a role to play in health and activity. The cardiovascular system, respiratory system, digestive system, musculoskeletal system, urinary system, nervous system, and immune system are each body systems that keep your dog running, barking, eating, scratching, sniffing, and fetching. Let's start with the outside—the skin and coat—and move on to learn all about your dog's body.

Skin and Coat

Skin is formed in two layers; and while we might not think of it as such, skin is the dog's largest organ. It forms a protective barrier against germs and helps the dog maintain body temperature. The epidermis is the outer layer of skin that covers a dog. It ranges from the thin skin covering the body to the thick, tough skin that protects the nose and paw pads. Beneath the epidermis lies the dermis, which contains hair follicles, sebaceous glands (which produce oil that coats each hair, allowing it to shed water), toenails, and sweat glands. Skin color ranges from pink to brown. Sometimes it has patches of black. This dark pigment is called melanin.

Covering the skin is a protective layer of hair. Hair is a dead structure; it is a complex, compact, three-dimensional layer of many kinds of proteins. The upper, visible portion of hair is called the shaft. The shaft has three layers: the cuticle (outside), cortex (middle), and medulla (bottom). Each shaft is anchored by a root to the skin.

Hair is produced by living cells beneath the epidermis called hair follicles. A follicle consists of a hair bulb—where the hair originates—and a follicular sheath through which the hair passes before emerging at the skin's surface.

Dogs have compound hair follicles, which produce bundles of 7 to 15 hairs. The number of hairs in a follicle varies by dog and breed. Usually each compound follicle contains a single large, long, stiff guard hair along with finer underhairs. The type of coat a dog has depends on variations in the size and number of guard hairs and underhairs within compound follicles.

Among the different types of dog coats are the wiry covering seen on many terriers and some sporting breeds; the profuse double coat of the Nordic breeds, which range from the Pomeranian to the Alaskan Malamute; the long, silky coats seen on such breeds as Maltese and Yorkshire Terriers; the curly or corded coat of the Poodle, Puli, or Komondor; and the short- or medium-length double coat of such breeds as German Shepherds, Labrador Retrievers, Beagles, and Pugs. Short coats can be coarse, like that of the Rottweiler, or fine, like that of the Boxer.

The hair coat protects the dog's skin from cuts, scrapes, and sunburn and serves as insulation from heat and cold. Hair becomes damaged by sun, air pollutants, dryness, and the normal wear and tear of being scratched and lain on. So periodically the body replaces the hair coat with new hairs. The dogs whom we tend to think of as shedding breeds are both longhaired dogs and dogs who have a dense undercoat. But all of the hairs on all dogs are shed; it's just that it's more obvious on longhaired dogs.

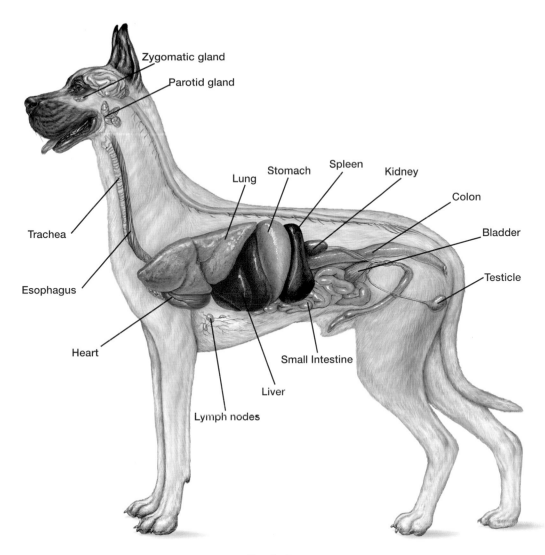

Dog Anatomy

Labels: Zygomatic gland, Parotid gland, Lung, Stomach, Spleen, Kidney, Colon, Bladder, Testicle, Trachea, Esophagus, Heart, Lymph nodes, Liver, Small Intestine

Growth Cycle and Shedding

Hairs grow to genetically programmed lengths, which may vary on different parts of the body. Once they reach their maximum length, dogs' hairs rest for various periods of time. Eventually, new hair pushes out the old hair, a phenomenon known as shedding, or blowing coat.

Shedding is seasonal, with hair growth and loss taking its cue from the hours of daylight to which it's exposed. As the days grow shorter—fall into winter—the hair grows thick. As the days grow longer—spring into summer—hair begins to drop off. But domestication has changed this seasonal cycle to an extent. House dogs, who are exposed to long hours of artificial light, tend to shed small amounts year-round.

Surges of hormones can also induce shedding. Intact females usually shed twice a year, coinciding with their heat cycles. Females in the same household often cycle and shed at the same time. Some males blow coat after they breed, while others stay in coat year-round. Spayed females usually come into a fuller coat, and they have a tendency to shed year-round, although some shed seasonally as well.

Poodles and Bichons Frisé, breeds with a reputation for not shedding, actually have a longer growth cycle to their hair than other breeds do. That's why they need to be clipped so often. Their hair doesn't go into a resting stage as often as that of other dogs. Although they require more frequent grooming—the clipping of the still-growing hair—they don't shed as much.

Of all the coat types, dogs with short hair shed the most. Other heavy shedders include dogs with double coats and those with certain hormonal diseases. Dogs with double coats consisting of a harsh, protective outer coat and a soft, insulating undercoat shed the undercoat heavily, and at times their fur can look patchy. This is normal, unless the patches have no fur at all. Hypothyroidism or other hormonal diseases can lead to excessive or altered shedding, and many hereditary diseases can cause abnormal shedding. Hair loss caused by stress or illness usually occurs in specific areas, such as the rear or flanks, where hair grows fastest.

Regular grooming helps keep the skin and coat healthy. Brushing distributes skin oils and removes dead hairs. Even dogs without hair, such as the Chinese Crested, require grooming care, including bathing and moisturizing the skin and protecting it from sun damage.

Skin Disease

Skin disease is a common problem in dogs. Abscesses and cysts, various forms of dermatitis such as atopy and flea allergy dermatitis, hot spots, lick granulomas, and pyoderma are among the skin problems that can affect dogs. Following are descriptions of just a few of these skin conditions.

Abscesses and Cysts

An abscess is a collection of pus lying in a cavity beneath the skin. Abscesses can develop from bites or other wounds, often on the head or neck area. They must be drained, and the accompanying infection must be treated with antibiotics.

A cyst is a simple saclike cavity that develops under the skin and usually contains fluid or a semisolid cheesy or doughy substance. Cysts are usually harmless, although they can become infected, requiring surgical removal.

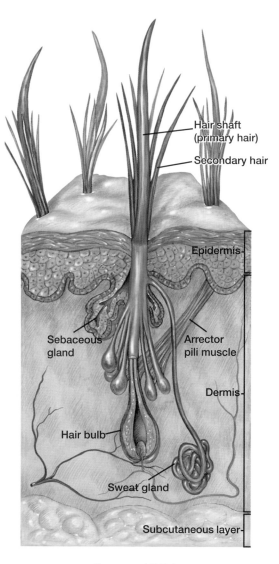

Compound Follicle

Atopic Dermatitis

Atopic dermatitis, also known as canine atopy, is a common allergic skin disease and is believed to affect about 10 percent of dogs. Breeds susceptible to atopy include Golden and Labrador Retrievers, Lhasa Apsos, Wire Fox Terriers, West Highland White Terriers, Dalmatians, Poodles, English and Irish Setters, Boxers, and Bulldogs. Atopy usually appears when the dog is between one and three years of age.

The itch-scratch cycle seen in atopy is triggered first by pollens, with the dog eventually reacting to all kinds of allergens, including wool, dust, feathers, and molds. The constant itching and scratching leads to hair loss and scabbing, and the skin becomes thick and flaky. Secondary bacterial infections are common, as are frequent ear infections.

Atopy is difficult to treat and first requires a thorough diagnosis. This may involve skin scrapings, intradermal skin testing (injecting tiny amounts of known allergens and observing the skin reaction), bacterial and fungal cultures, and a trial on a hypoallergenic diet (food containing ingredients to which the dog has never been exposed) to help discover if the dog has food allergies. Flea control is important as well, because flea allergy dermatitis can complicate the situation.

Treatment involves changing the dog's environment where possible, antihistamines to control itching and scratching, essential fatty acid (EFA) supplements, and medicated shampoos. Corticosteroids used intermittently in low doses for short periods can also help control itching. If all else fails, allergy shots (hyposensitization) can be given. This involves intradermal skin testing to identify specific allergens and then desensitizing the dog to these irritants through a series of antigen injections. Dietary changes may also be beneficial. For instance, some dogs are allergic to wheat or corn.

Flea Allergy Dermatitis

Flea allergy dermatitis (FAD), which can erupt from the bite of a single flea, is the most common allergy in dogs. Many dogs are highly sensitive to certain substances in flea saliva, and the allergic reaction caused by the bite results in severe itching, inflamed skin, and red bumps on the skin, even long after the fleas have been eliminated. While FAD is at its worst in high summer during flea season, it can last year-round if fleas aren't controlled in the home.

Good flea control is the only real treatment for FAD. Itching can be relieved with antihistamines and short-term doses of corticosteroids. If the dog chews at the bites so much that the skin becomes infected, topical and oral antibiotics will be necessary.

Hot Spots

Hot spots are warm, painful, swollen patches of skin. They ooze pus and smell bad. Like so many skin problems, they develop in response to flea bites, allergies, other skin diseases, and lack of grooming. Hot spots are especially common in thick-coated dogs with dead hair trapped next to the skin (that's why thorough brushing down to the skin is so important).

Hot spots are treated by clipping away the hair and cleansing the skin. Because this is painful, the dog may need to be sedated or anesthetized. Then a topical antibiotic is applied for up to two weeks. Oral corticosteroids may be necessary to control severe itching, and an Elizabethan collar (a plastic cone or a more comfortable soft foam collar that fits around a dog's neck) can help keep the dog from gnawing at the spot. The veterinarian will also treat the underlying skin problems that led to the hot spots in the first place.

Lick Granulomas

Lick granulomas, formally known as acral pruritic dermatitis, are open sores, usually on the

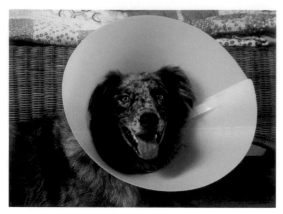

An Elizabethan collar may be necessary to keep your dog from licking hot spots.

dog's wrist (located on the foreleg) or ankle (located on the hind leg). They're common in many large dogs, including Doberman Pinschers, Labrador Retrievers, and Great Danes.

The licking and chewing brought on by itchy skin diseases such as atopy, demodectic mange, or bacterial or fungal infections is believed to be what precipitates a lick granuloma. As the dog licks at the itchy area, the hair comes off and the skin becomes red and eventually thickens.

If the underlying cause is determined and treated, the itching will go away, but it's still necessary to break the dog's habit of licking the area. This can be done by putting an Elizabethan collar on the dog so he can't reach the spot to lick or covering the spot with Bitter Apple (a widely used commercial chewing deterrent that comes in spray or paste form) or a similar bad-tasting substance. Providing the dog with extra companionship and playtime can take his mind off licking. In extreme cases, the short-term use of behavior-modification drugs such as Prozac or Valium helps break the cycle.

Pyoderma

Pyoderma is a bacterial infection of the skin that develops when the skin becomes dam-aged by chewing, rubbing, or scratching. It usually develops as a result of a primary itchy skin disease such as atopy or FAD. One type of pyoderma develops in skin folds, where moist skin surfaces rub together and become inflamed. Skin fold pyodermas are common in fleshy, wrinkly dogs such as Chinese Shar-Pei; Pekingese (face fold pyodermas); spaniels and Saint Bernards (lip fold pyodermas); and Bulldogs, Boston Terriers, and Pugs (tail fold pyodermas). Pyodermas are treated with topical and oral antibiotics.

Ears and Hearing

The ear has three main components: the outer ear, the middle ear, and the inner ear. The pinna is the flap that forms the outer section of the ear. It initiates the hearing process by trapping sound waves. The pinna also takes on the shape and movement of the ear. Some dogs have prick ears, which stand erect all the time; some have floppy ears; and still others have ears that fold down most of the time but perk up when the dog is surprised or alert.

The middle ear processes sound and consists of the tympanic cavity, the section of the middle ear that is located behind the eardrum; the eardrum (the tympanic membrane); and the auditory

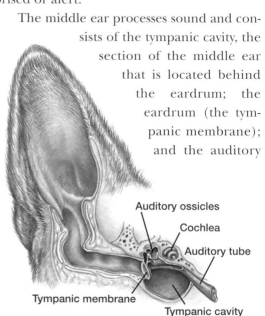

Auditory ossicles
Cochlea
Auditory tube
Tympanic membrane
Tympanic cavity

The Dog Ear

result can be an ear infection. The outer ear is most likely to be injured or infected because it's exposed to dirt and foreign objects. Otitis externa, infection of the outer ear, is one of the most common problems seen in dogs. Causes of these infections include excessive moistness in the ears, the presence of mites or bacteria, and skin allergies. Dogs with ear infections frequently scratch at their ears, shake their heads, or rub their ears on the floor. The inside of the ear may be red, with a bad-smelling discharge oozing out.

Dogs prone to ear infections include those with moist ears and those prone to skin allergies. Heredity, anatomy, and trauma can also predispose dogs to ear infections. Dogs with a weak or insufficient immune system may suffer frequent ear infections as well.

ossicles, a series of tiny bones known as the hammer (malleus), anvil (incus), and stirrup (stapes). Sound waves travel down the ear canal to the eardrum, where they are transmitted across the middle ear by the auditory ossicles to the inner ear.

Deep within the skull is the inner ear. Small, fluid-filled tubes, or canals, make up part of the inner ear. Tiny hairs inside the tubes record movement of the fluid and changes in the dog's posture and position. This information, when passed along the auditory nerve to the brain, governs the dog's sense of balance. The rest of the inner ear consists of the cochlea, a snail-shaped tube that converts sound vibrations into messages, and the auditory nerve, which carries the messages to the brain, where they are translated into meaningful sounds.

Ear Infections

Normal ears contain bacteria and yeast in an appropriate amount and ratio, but when the yeast or bacteria get out of proportion, the

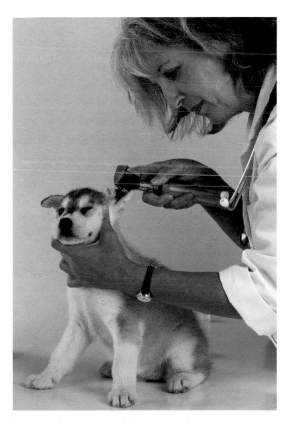

Your veterinarian should check your dog's ears regularly. Signs of infection include shaking and scratching the head and ears, a bad odor, and discolored wax.

Almost any dog with long, droopy ears seems to be prone to ear problems because the hanging ear holds in moisture. Basset Hounds head the list, with English Springer Spaniels, Cocker Spaniels, and Chinese Shar-Pei following close behind. Sometimes dogs whose ears contain a great deal of hair, such as Poodles, Schnauzers, and Old English Sheepdogs, have recurring ear problems as well. Water-loving dogs often develop swimmer's ear, an ear infection caused from moisture retained in the ear canal.

It's often claimed that prick-eared dogs have fewer infections, and this seems to be true, possibly because the prick ears get aired out. Exceptions are prick-eared dogs with faulty immune systems, skin allergies, or higher than normal amounts of oil-secreting glands in the ears.

Other ear infections are linked to generalized skin diseases such as seborrhea, which can cause changes in the lining of the ear canal. Ear infections can also indicate food allergies. Sometimes the only clinical sign of food allergies is chronic ear problems. Unless the underlying disorder is diagnosed and treated, these ear infections can't be eliminated successfully.

Diagnosis and Treatment

Veterinarians diagnose ear infections by examining the ear with an instrument called an otoscope, which allows them to see inside the ear canal to check for foreign bodies, inflammation, mites, and other abnormalities. If a foreign body is the problem, the veterinarian may try to remove it with long, narrow alligator forceps. The veterinarian may also take a sample of discharge from the ear and examine it under a microscope for evidence of bacteria, yeast, or parasites.

When something other than a foreign body is the cause of an ear infection, the first

Ear medication can be tricky. To avoid a mess, massage the medication into the ear before releasing your dog.

step is to clean the ear with a cotton ball and ear cleanser to remove debris that can shelter organisms from topical treatment. But avoid using cotton-tipped applicators to clean the inside of the ear canal. They can push debris farther into the ear and block the passage. To maximize cleanliness, many vets suggest trimming excess hair rather than plucking it (which has the added benefit of being less painful for the dog). Some believe that plucking hair from within the ears can contribute to or initiate inflammation that will set up the environment for infection to begin or continue. Plus the hair pores ooze a serum that can be a good medium for bacterial growth. Many groomers, however, promote plucking rather than clipping. You should discuss your options with your groomer and veterinarian.

To help clear up the infection, the veterinarian will prescribe a topical antibacterial or antifungal agent. If mites are an issue, the veterinarian will prescribe a medication aimed specifically at killing them.

To apply ear medication, hold the dog's head firmly with one hand (ear flap raised if he's a floppy-eared dog) and use the other hand to squeeze the medication—usually in the form of an ointment or drops—into the ear. Then gently massage the cartilage at the base of the ear. This helps get the medication down into the ear canal. That way, when your dog finally shakes his head, the medication won't go flying everywhere.

Give all the medication prescribed, even if the ear appears to be better. If the dog doesn't get the full treatment, the infection can pop right back up again. Expect to take the dog in for at least one follow-up exam so that the veterinarian can make sure the treatment is working.

When infections are complicated by deep soft-tissue involvement, oral antibiotics may be necessary. Underlying allergies require appropriate treatment as well. Often, treatment is intense for initial control, and regular treatment is needed for the rest of the dog's life to avoid recurrences.

In chronic cases, cultures may be necessary to determine the exact type of bacteria or fungus that's causing the problem so the veterinarian can choose the most effective medication. It may also be necessary to seek a second opinion from a veterinary dermatologist or to investigate potential underlying causes, such as allergies (especially food allergies), thyroid disease, immune deficiencies, or adrenal diseases. If these problems are diagnosed and treated, the ear infections often clear up as well.

Serious Infections

Persistent or severe infections sometimes require more drastic measures. In up to 25 percent of cases, the dog may need to be anesthetized several times so the ear canal can be flushed and debris removed.

If ear canals become thickened and narrowed after many infections, surgery to remove part or all of the outer ear canal may be the best option for humane management. A dog's ear canals are L shaped, so moisture and foreign bodies can easily get trapped. Opening up the ear canal makes treatment more effective and improves air circulation. This surgery can be painful, and the dog will need nursing care and pain medications while healing. However, the results can be wonderful.

Ear Infection Prevention

To help prevent ear infections, check your dog's ears weekly. Dogs who spend a lot of time playing outdoors are sure to pick up foreign bodies in their ears at some point. Grass seeds, burrs, and foxtails are the most common irritants that can get stuck in the ear. Besides being painful, foxtails and other foreign bodies can cause infection. If foxtails or other plants with seeds are common in your area, examine your dog's ears several times a week. If you can see something stuck in your dog's ear, try to remove it with blunt-nosed tweezers, being careful not to push it deeper into the ear canal. Foreign objects that fall deep into the ear canal should be removed by a veterinarian.

Clean the ears with a cleansing solution recommended by your veterinarian. Many over-the-counter remedies for ear infections contain alcohol. Besides causing painful stinging, the alcohol can cause inflammation that doesn't promote healing. And while some types of ear infections respond well to drying agents, others are worsened by drying. Do not use a drying agent without the advice of your veterinarian.

Trim excess hair. Depending on the individual dog, ear hair should be trimmed every one to three months. And it can't hurt to pull back a floppy-eared dog's ears once or twice a week to let them air out. Use tape or a child's soft headband to hold the ears in place for about 10 minutes at a time.

Ear infections sometimes flare up in warm weather. This can be related to trapped moisture from swimming or playing in sprinklers; hot spots that develop during hot, humid weather; or flea allergies. If swimming seems to be the trigger, your veterinarian may recommend using a drying agent after your dog plays in water. Use a good flea-control program to help keep hot spots and flea allergies under control.

Many ear infections are chronic and can only be managed, not cured. Regular preventive care is much more cost effective than treating out-of-control flare-ups. Each flare-up causes thickening and narrowing of the ear canals. The eventual result is that treatment becomes less effective.

If an ear infection recurs, don't assume that the medication used for the previous infection will work again. The organisms and ear environment can change from one infection to another, so see the veterinarian for a definitive diagnosis.

Ear Mites

Ear mites are tiny, spiderlike creatures that invade the ear canal and feed on skin debris. They prefer cats as their hosts, but dogs aren't immune to infestation. Signs of ear mites include head shaking and ear scratching, as well as a discharge that looks reddish brown or black and waxy. The veterinarian can diagnose a case of ear mites by studying the discharge under a microscope. These parasites are most common in puppies and young dogs.

Once mites have been diagnosed, the veterinarian will clean the ears and prescribe a mite-killing medication. Keep ears clean and continue the medication until there are no further signs of mites. This usually takes at least one month. Mites are contagious to other dogs and to cats, so it's a good idea to treat all animals in the home, even if only one shows signs. Severe ear mite infestations can block

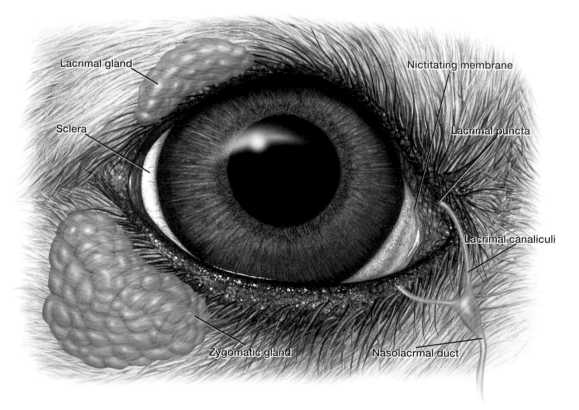

Lacrimal gland

Sclera

Nictitating membrane

Lacrimal puncta

Lacrimal canaliculi

Zygomatic gland

Nasolacrmal duct

The Dog Eye

Eye exams should be a routine part of your dog's preventive care.

the ear canal and cause serious yeast or bacterial infections, so don't wait to treat them.

Eyes and Vision

The canine eye is uniquely adapted to a dog's needs. Dogs have excellent night vision, good depth perception, and a total visual field of 250 degrees, all of which are important for an animal that evolved as a predator. The spherical eyes, set in bony sockets and cushioned by a layer of fat, are placed on the front of the face, rather than to the side as on some animals. This allows the dog's field of vision to overlap and increases his ability to judge depth and perceive detail.

The eye's components begin with the cornea, the transparent outer coating. Surrounding the cornea is a white area of connective tissue called the sclera, which supports the eyeball, or globe. Covering the white of the eye is a pinkish membrane called the conjunctiva, which contains blood vessels and nerve endings. At the center of the eye is a dark, round opening called the pupil, which is the central opening of the iris through which light enters the interior of the eye. Behind the cornea is the iris, a circular pigmented (colored) structure that widens and narrows to regulate the amount of light

that enters the eye. It's also what gives the eye its color. The retina is a sensitive inner lining with an abundance of rod cells to detect light and a smaller number of cone cells to distinguish among colors. It converts incoming light into electrical impulses and transmits them to the brain via the optic nerve. The brain then translates these impulses into a visual image.

Supporting the front of the eye are tight folds of skin, the eyelids. Unlike people, dogs have a third eyelid, the nictitating membrane, at the inner corner of the eye. This membrane normally stays retracted, but if necessary it can cover the eye for protection. When this happens, it looks as if the eyes have rolled back into the head.

Tears, secreted by the lachrymal glands, keep the cornea moist and contain immune

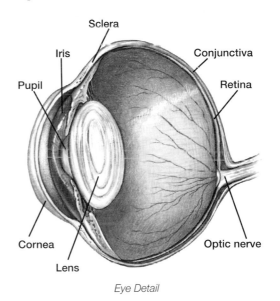

Eye Detail

Therapeutic soft contact lenses are used in dogs to treat corneal injuries caused by cat scratches, infections, foreign bodies in the eye, and other trauma. A contact lens gives the eye time to heal and relieves pain by keeping the eyelids from rubbing over the injured surface of the eye. The lens is usually worn for several days.

Tearing, squinting, and light sensitivity are all signs of eye pain. Visit your veterinarian if your dog exhibits these symptoms.

body if your dog is pawing at an eye, the eye is tearing, or the dog is blinking frequently or squinting. To remove foreign material from the surface of the eye, hold the eyelid open and flush the eye with sterile saline solution (the kind used by contact lens wearers) or cool water if saline solution isn't available. This can be done by soaking a cotton ball and dripping the solution into the eye. If the dog continues to demonstrate pain after 10 or 15 minutes, or if the object is stuck behind the third eyelid, seek veterinary help. It is better to be proactive than to risk permanent injury to the eye.

Entropion and Ectropion

Entropion is a condition in which the eyelids roll inward, causing eyelashes to come in contact with the surface of the eye. This abnormality causes irritation that results in tearing, squinting, and corneal injuries. Entropion is considered to be an inherited condition in some breeds of dogs, especially those breeds with large heads and loose facial skin such as Chinese Shar-Pei, Chow Chows, Great Danes, Bloodhounds, Saint Bernards, Great Pyrenees, and Bulldogs. Entropion can be corrected surgically.

With ectropion, the lower eyelid rolls out from the surface of the eye, exposing the eye to irritants and resulting in chronic conjunctivitis and corneal injury. Like entropion, ectropion occurs in dogs with loose facial skin. To correct the condition, the eyelids can be tightened surgically.

Conjunctivitis

The conjunctival membrane covers the back of the eyelids and the surface of the eyeball up to the cornea. When it becomes inflamed, the result is conjunctivitis (commonly referred to as pink eye in humans). A dog with conjunctivitis has a red eye with a dis-

substances that help fight infections. Tears collect at the corner of the eye and are then carried along the nasolacrimal ducts into the nasal cavity. When tears aren't carried away, they can stain the fur beneath a dog's eyes.

Signs of eye problems include tearing, squinting, and sensitivity to light, all of which indicate pain; a teary or mucous discharge; a filmy or cloudy eye; swelling, crusting, or itching; and a bulging or sunken eye. A number of eye problems can affect dogs. These include trapped foreign bodies such as seeds, dirt, or other debris; entropion and ectropion; conjunctivitis; dry eye (keratoconjunctivitis sicca); corneal abrasions or ulcers; cataracts; glaucoma; and progressive retinal atrophy.

Foreign Objects

Foreign objects can get stuck in the eye especially when a dog hangs his head out the window of a fast-moving car or runs through tall or dense brush. Suspect a trapped foreign

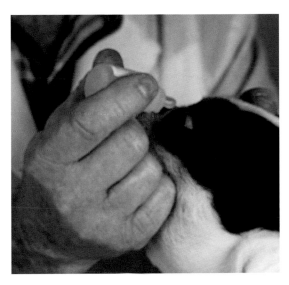
Medication may be required to relieve eye symptoms.

charge that can be clear, mucuslike, or pus-like. If the discharge is clear, simply flush the eye several times daily with a sterile saline solution. If it is mucuslike or puslike, seek veterinary attention. The mucus or pus will need to be removed from the eye and the condition treated with antibiotics. Conjunctivitis isn't painful, but it can cause the eye to feel itchy. If the eye appears painful, see the veterinarian; the problem could be more serious than conjunctivitis.

Dry Eye

Eyes must stay lubricated to be healthy. If tear production malfunctions, the cornea can become dry. Insufficient tear production is called keratoconjunctivitis sicca, or dry eye. Dry eye produces a discharge that's thick, stringy, and mucuslike, and the eye looks dull. Left untreated, dry eye can eventually result in blindness. Certain breeds, including Bulldogs, Cocker Spaniels, Lhasa Apsos, and West Highland White Terriers, are predisposed to dry eye. The veterinarian diagnoses dry eye by measuring the volume of the dog's tears. The condition can be treated by apply-ing cyclosporin ointment, artificial tears, and topical antibiotics to the affected eye until the problem resolves. However, sometimes dry eye can't be cured. In this case, the dog will need lifelong care to keep the condition under control.

Corneal Injuries

While the cornea is covered by a protective layer of epithelial cells, it can be easily damaged by a scratch or debris in the eye. At the first sign of pain, such as squinting, tearing, or the protective raising of the third eyelid, take your dog to the veterinarian to have his eye checked and treated with topical antibiotics to prevent infection.

A corneal injury can degenerate into a corneal ulcer if the condition is not treated. An ulcer goes deeper into the cornea of the eye and is very painful. Most corneal ulcers result from an injury to the eye, but ulcers can also develop in response to dry eye, diabetes, hypothyroidism, and other diseases. Treatment for corneal ulcers can involve the injection of antibiotics directly into the eye. Another option is surgery. The veterinarian will suture the third eyelid or a flap of conjunctiva over the eye until the eye heals. This serves to cover the surface of the eye and protect the cornea while it heals.

Cataracts

A cataract is an opaque spot on the lens of the eye. The lens is a normally transparent structure that focuses images upon the retina. Cataracts can be inherited or acquired as a consequence of aging or other diseases such as diabetes. They eventually lead to loss of vision. Many dogs, especially seniors, get around just fine with reduced vision, but if necessary the cataract can be removed through a surgical procedure called phacoemulsification. This involves fragmenting the lens with ultrasonic vibrations and then replacing it with a clear plastic intraocular lens.

Glaucoma

When fluid in the eye is produced more quickly than it can be removed, the result is a sustained increase in pressure within the eye. The high eye pressure damages the optic nerve and the retina and leads to pain and blindness if left untreated. This condition is known as glaucoma. Two types of glaucoma affect dogs: primary and secondary. Primary glaucoma is hereditary and is seen in Beagles, Cocker Spaniels, Basset Hounds, and Samoyeds as well as other dogs. Secondary glaucoma accompanies other eye problems such as uveitis (inflammation of the uvea, the cellular layer of the eye that contains blood vessels, the iris, ciliary body, and choroid), injury, or displacement of the lens. Signs of glaucoma include tearing and squinting, which indicate pain. The eye may appear red. Glaucoma is diagnosed with an eye exam and the measurement of intraocular pressure. Glaucoma can't be cured, but it is treatable with eye drops and sometimes surgery.

Progressive Retinal Atrophy

Reluctance to go out in the dark and eventually obvious night blindness are signs of progressive retinal atrophy (PRA), an inherited degeneration of the retina that's recognized in more than 86 breeds. PRA can take several different forms but all end up destroying the retinal cells in both eyes, resulting in reduced vision or blindness. Unfortunately, there's no cure or treatment for PRA, although genetic research holds promise for the future. The best way to prevent PRA is by breeding only dogs who are certified free of PRA and analyzing pedigrees to ensure that those dogs are unlikely to carry and transmit the gene for PRA.

Keeping your dog's nails clipped can help reduce the chance of foot disorders.

Paws and Nails

The canine foot is a marvel of engineering. Thick, leathery skin protects the bottom of the paw. The fatty inner layer acts as a shock absorber when feet touch down on the ground and contains the eccrine glands, which allow the dog to lose heat, or sweat, through his paws. Tough toenails provide traction and permit digging.

Most dogs are born with five toes on the front feet and four toes on the back feet. One of the front toes, the dewclaw, is located on the leg and doesn't touch the

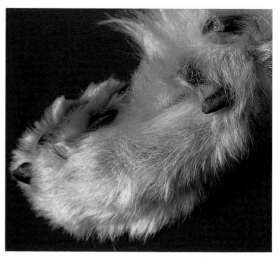

The canine foot is specially made to support a dog through his daily travels.

ground. It is sometimes removed during a puppy's first week or two of life. Some breed standards require dogs to have dewclaws. The Briard is unusual in that it has double dewclaws on each hind leg.

Foot Care

Routine foot care keeps a dog in good running order. All that's required is nail trimming, toe hair trimming if needed, and regular inspection for wounds or other problems.

Ideally, toenails should barely touch the ground as a dog walks. Nails that are too long can become snagged on carpet or other ground cover and tear or cause the feet to spread out improperly.

Foot Disorders

Common foot problems are caused by puncture wounds, allergies, and irritation from salt or chemicals used on icy streets and sidewalks. Dogs can also develop lick granulomas and interdigital cysts on their feet. Interdigital cysts are swellings or abscesses between the toes that are caused by infec-

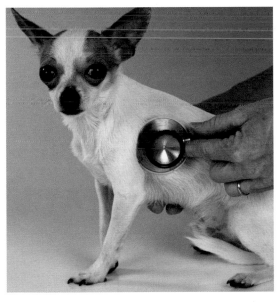

An irregular heartbeat or murmur can indicate a problem with the cardiovascular system.

tions of the eccrine glands. The infection caused by an interdigital cyst must be treated with antibiotics.

Cardiovascular System

The cardiovascular system is made up of the heart and the vasculature, or blood vessels, which include the arteries, arterioles, capillaries, venules, and veins. The heart's job is to pump blood through the blood vessels. The cardiovascular system plus the cellular and fluid components of blood, red blood cells, white blood cells, platelets, water, proteins, electrolytes, and salts make up what is called the circulatory system.

With its pumplike action, the heart is the engine that powers the body's circulatory system. The heart is divided into four chambers—the right atrium and right ventricle and the left atrium and left ventricle. The two sides of the heart are separated by a muscular wall. The heart also has four valves that work to keep blood flowing in one direction. The valves open and close, letting blood in and then pumping it out. The sound a normal heartbeat makes is lup-dup, lup-dup. That lup-dup sound is created from the movement of the valves and the flowing of the blood.

The job of the circulatory system is to deliver inhaled oxygen from the lungs to the mitochondria, which are specialized structures within body cells that produce energy. The circulatory system then removes carbon dioxide—a cellular waste product—from the cells to the lungs, where it is exhaled when the dog breathes out. In addition, the circulatory system moves blood through the kidneys and liver and transports hormones, glucose, electrolytes, and other compounds throughout the body.

The heart is prone to a number of diseases and defects. These include dilated cardiomyopathy, heart murmurs, mitral valve disease (MVD), patent ductus arteriosis (PDA), and pulmonary stenosis.

Dilated Cardiomyopathy

Dilated cardiomyopathy occurs when the heart chambers become enlarged and the walls of the ventricles become thin. This causes the heart muscle to weaken and eventually fail. It's the most common reason for congestive heart failure in large and giant-size dogs, and it primarily affects male dogs. Some of the breeds that are prone to dilated cardiomyopathy include Boxers, Doberman Pinschers, Springer Spaniels, and Cocker Spaniels.

Signs of the disease usually appear when the dog is between two and five years of age. They include rapid weight loss; lack of energy; rapid breathing; and frequent coughing, sometimes bringing up blood. The condition is diagnosed through electrocardiogram, chest X-ray, and echocardiogram.

New advances in cardiac veterinary care are promising; however, as dogs live longer the incidence of heart disease increases.

Dilated cardiomyopathy can be treated for a time with medication, rest, diet, and careful monitoring by the veterinarian. Some dogs given good treatment can live for a year or more after diagnosis.

Heart Murmurs

When heart valves become diseased or worn, they may fail to close completely with each heart-

Secondhand smoke causes structural and functional cardiac changes in dogs, including high blood pressure and an enlarged heart muscle. A research study performed in 2006 at the University of Saskatchewan showed measurable changes in the heart and blood vessels of dogs who lived in homes where they were exposed to secondhand smoke. The study included blood tests and electrocardiograms to determine the dogs' condition.

beat, resulting in a backwash of blood. The effect is an abnormal sound called a heart murmur.

The sound a murmur makes depends on when it occurs in the cardiac cycle. A murmur that occurs when the ventricles are beating is called a systolic murmur. A murmur that occurs when the ventricles are relaxed, a period called cardiac diastole, is called a diastolic murmur. Instead of going lup-dup, lup-dup, the heart with a systolic murmur goes lup-shh-dup; one with a diastolic murmur makes the sound lup-dup-shh.

Severity of Murmurs

Murmurs are graded in severity from 1 to 6, with 1 being the quietest murmur that can be heard and 6 being loud enough that it's evident before the stethoscope even touches the chest. Murmurs graded at 4 to 6 can often be felt if the hand is placed at the right spot on the chest. Heart murmurs can result from a birth defect or a congenital malformation. Congenital heart murmurs are typically seen in young dogs and are hereditary in nature.

Most murmurs are diagnosed by auscultation, which simply means that the veterinarian listens to the heart with a stethoscope. While auscultation can indicate the presence of a murmur, further tests are needed to determine its cause and severity. The veterinarian is likely to make a referral to a veterinary cardiologist for these tests. Depending on the breed, age, and predisposition of the dog, the cardiologist will want to take thoracic radiographs (chest X-rays) if the referring veterinarian hasn't taken them and run an electrocardiogram and an echocardiogram (ultrasound).

The radiographs indicate overall heart size and enable the cardiologist to see the pulmonary vessels in the lung. This allows her to judge the degree of normality or abnormality resulting from the heart disease. An electrocardiogram shows the heart's rate and rhythm and is useful if abnormal rhythms are detected through auscultation. An echocardiogram provides a precise measure of the thickness of the various chamber walls of the heart as well as a look at each of the cardiac valves. This test allows the cardiologist to determine the state of the valves, calculate overall cardiac performance, and help decide whether therapy is necessary. Follow-up echocardiograms indicate whether the prescribed therapy is working.

The cardiologist may also check the dog's kidney function. Renal disease is the most frequent cause of high blood pressure (hypertension) in dogs and cats. The presence of renal disease adds a greater workload onto the heart and can make some cardiac conditions much worse much quicker unless the hypertension is brought under control. The veterinarian may screen the blood for buildup of waste products (BUN/creatinine), perform a urinalysis, and check enzymes that are associated with liver disease and congestion that sometimes develop as the heart fails.

The seriousness of a heart murmur depends on factors such as the dog's age and whether the breed in question is prone to heart disease. Some dogs with murmurs can go for years without showing any signs of heart disease. What's most important is an accurate diagnosis of the murmur's cause and the underlying problems associated with it. Once the cause is known, adjustments can be made based on the dog's lifestyle and the severity of the condition.

Causes of Murmurs

Some cardiac murmurs, especially in puppies, are innocent, or benign, meaning they eventually disappear. It's often not possible to determine whether a murmur is innocent until the dog reaches maturity at two or three years of age. To avoid passing on genetic defects to another generation, it's important to refrain from breeding a dog until he has been cleared of any problems. A dog with a hereditary heart problem, even one that has been repaired, should not be bred.

Other murmurs are caused by anemia. Anemia thins the blood, making it more prone to turbulence. As the heart contracts, blood is ejected into the vessels with great velocity. Severe anemia causes a rapid pulse and breathing rate, and overexertion can cause the dog to pass out. Heart disease and severe anemia have similar signs and can sometimes be confused.

The presence of internal parasites such as whipworms or hookworms can cause anemia.

If the murmur is caused by anemia, the veterinarian will determine what's causing the anemia. If it's something as simple as worms, ridding the body of the worms puts an end to the heart murmur.

Mitral Valve Disease

Sometimes referred to as mitral regurgitation, mitral valve disease is one of the most common conditions associated with heart murmurs. MVD occurs when the valve degenerates and begins to leak. MVD can also result from an infection of the valves (endocarditis), from a valve that's malformed at birth, or in response to dilated cardiomyopathy.

Valvular degeneration is most often seen in small dogs, especially as they age. Cavalier King Charles Spaniels are particularly prone to MVD, which often appears earlier in that breed than in others. Other dogs in which it tends to occur include Chihuahuas, Miniature Poodles, Miniature Pinschers, Fox Terriers, Boston Terriers, and Miniature Schnauzers. It's more often seen in males than in females.

When mitral regurgitation occurs, blood leaks back from the left ventricle into the left atrium. In response, the left atrium enlarges to make room for the extra blood, and the left ventricle also increases in size so it can pump more blood to make up for the leak. Severe cases lead to congestive heart failure, which is indicated by fluid accumulation in the lungs (pulmonary edema). Signs of MVD are exercise intolerance and coughing or wheezing.

When a dog with MVD has difficulty breathing and chest X-rays show a buildup of fluid in the lungs, diuretics—drugs that promote urination—may be prescribed to relieve the congestion and fluid. For the same reason, a low-sodium diet is sometimes prescribed to reduce fluid in the body. Dietary therapy isn't always beneficial, however, and

Brachycephalic Dogs and Heat

Brachycephalic dogs (dogs with short noses), such as the Pug, Bulldog, and Pekingese, are particularly susceptible to high temperatures and heatstroke. Dogs do not perspire through the skin the way people do; instead, they cool themselves by panting. Short-muzzled dogs have narrowed and abbreviated respiratory tracts. They have a hard time increasing their rate of panting, so they are more likely than other dogs to suffer from respiratory distress in hot weather. While care should be taken with all dogs during hot weather, brachycephalic dogs need extra consideration and should always be kept in a cool location, preferably in an air-conditioned house, during the hottest part of the day. In warm weather, they should not be exercised during the day, and plenty of water should always be available. They (and all other dogs) should never be left in a hot car, not even for a few minutes.

It's also generally considered unsafe to fly brachycephalic dogs in the cargo compartment of an airplane. Anxiety, increased altitude, and extreme temperatures can contribute to their breathing difficulties. Many airlines will no longer accept these dogs as cargo, particularly during summer, because they face an increased risk of mortality during the flight. If you can't take your brachycephalic dog in the cabin with you, consider some other means of transporting him.

---

its effectiveness depends on the precise condition. A number of studies suggest that severe salt restriction early on in the course of heart disease may do more harm than good.

Other medications that may be prescribed for dogs with heart disease in general are afterload reducers, which lower blood pressure, decreasing the workload on the heart. One of the most popular drugs now for that use is called an angiotensin converting enzyme (ACE) inhibitor. Enalapril is the only drug of this kind approved for veterinary use.

Drugs that strengthen heart contractions may also be prescribed. One such drug in this category is digitalis, an extract of foxglove, which has been well known as a heart tonic for centuries. Digitalis is usually prescribed when the heart's contractions begin to weaken, which is determined by an echocardiogram.

When a dog with MVD should begin taking medication is a matter of some debate among vets. It's not clear that early administration has any advantage, and there are side effects to consider, such as changes in urination, decreased appetite, vomiting, sudden lethargy, or weakness. Some cardiologists start dogs on medication when the resting heart rate is consistently more than 100 beats per minute. The normal canine resting heart rate is 80 to 100 bpm. When the heart rate goes up and remains high over a long period, the heart's workload increases and the heart can become damaged.

Patent Ductus Arteriosus (PDA)

This is a common congenital heart defect, meaning the dog is born with the condition. PDA is seen most commonly in Miniature Poodles and German Shepherd Dogs. It occurs when the ductus arteriosus—a vessel in fetuses that allows blood to bypass the as-yet nonfunctional lungs—remains open after birth. The result is a leak from the aorta through the open ductus into the pulmonary side of the heart. This causes the left ventricle to work harder to maintain normal blood flow. PDA is usually recognized when a veteri-

---

Dogs with weak hearts are getting a new lease on life with donated pacemakers. After a pacemaker has been used by a person, it cannot be used by anyone else; but it can be used by a dog. Some people will their pacemakers to veterinary schools.

> Death from heart disease appears to be increasing among pets as animals live longer. The most common cause of heart disease in dogs is related to the heart valves. The valves thicken and then leak when the heart pumps.

narian listening to the heart detects a continuous heart murmur—one that is present during both the systolic and diastolic cycles of the heartbeat. Chest X-rays and an echocardiogram can confirm the diagnosis. Left untreated, PDA leads to heart failure, but the condition can be repaired surgically.

Pulmonic Stenosis

Another common congenital heart defect, pulmonic stenosis is a narrowing of the connection between the right ventricle and the pulmonary artery, which increases the resistance to blood flow and makes it more difficult for the right ventricle to pump blood. In response, the right ventricle enlarges and thickens, just as any muscle does when it's worked. This defect is usually seen in small dogs.

A systolic murmur is usually the first hint of pulmonic stenosis, a diagnosis that is confirmed with chest X-rays and an electrocardiogram. In severe cases, pulmonic stenosis can be treated with a balloon valvuloplasty, a procedure with a success rate of about 70 percent. A balloon valvuloplasty involves inserting a catheter into the heart through a peripheral blood vessel. Attached to the catheter is a large, stiff balloon. The catheter is placed across the narrowed connection, and the balloon is inflated to widen the connection.

Respiratory System

The respiratory system has two parts: the upper respiratory system and the lower respiratory tract. Comprising the upper respiratory system are the nasal passages, throat, larynx, and trachea. The bronchi, air passages that lead from the trachea to the lungs, and the lungs make up the lower respiratory tract. The bronchi branch off and become smaller, eventually opening into the air sacs, or alveoli, in the lungs. Together, the bronchi, air sacs, and blood vessels make up the lungs. The ribs and muscles of the chest work the lungs, moving air in and out of them. The average dog takes 10 to 30 breaths per minute when at rest.

Signs of problems in the respiratory system include abnormal or obstructed breathing, which can sound rapid, labored, shallow, noisy, or wheezy (sort of a whistling sound). Some of the respiratory conditions that can affect dogs are brachycephalic syndrome, elongated soft palate, coughing, collapsed trachea, and reverse sneezing.

Brachycephalic Syndrome

Brachycephalic syndrome affects short-nosed dogs such as Bulldogs, Pugs, and Pekingese. Dogs with this problem snort, snore, and breathe through their mouths. They become overheated easily and tire rapidly from exercise. Sometimes surgery to enlarge the nasal openings can help.

Elongated Soft Palate

The palate is the roof of the mouth that separates the mouth from the nasal cavity. An elongated soft palate is closely related to brachycephalic syndrome. A long soft palate can block part of the airway into the lungs, causing breathing difficulty. To determine whether the palate is too long, the dog must be anesthetized and examined by a veterinarian. The problem can be corrected surgically with great success, especially if the dog is less than a year old. Surgery allows the dog to breathe easier and relieves the strain on the heart and lungs.

Coughing

Irritations in the airways trigger coughing, a reflex action that is the body's attempt to remove an irritant. Too much coughing dries out mucous membranes, which irritates the breathing tubes and makes coughing worse. A chronic cough could signal any number of problems, including kennel cough, pneumonia, heart disease, or a collapsed trachea. Take the dog in for a veterinary exam.

Collapsed Trachea

A collapsed trachea is a common structural defect seen mostly in toy dogs. The trachea, also known as the windpipe, is tubular and lined with cartilage. If this cartilage is weaker or softer than normal, it can be damaged by external or internal pressure. Dogs can be born with collapsed tracheas, or the problem can develop with age. It's sometimes brought on by pressure from a collar or too much excitement that causes a sudden intake of breath. Suspect a collapsed trachea if your dog has a honking cough or makes a high-pitched breathing sound. The dog may also breathe through his mouth or cough or gag when the throat is rubbed.

To prevent coughing episodes, relieve pressure on the neck by switching from a collar to a chest harness or head halter and limiting exuberant play or exposure to things that excite the dog. Keeping the dog's weight under control helps, and a cool-mist humidifier can make breathing easier. The veterinarian may also recommend a cough suppressant, a bronchodilator—a type of drug that keeps bronchial tubes open—or antibiotics in case of a bacterial infection. Glucosamine supplements may help build cartilage and heal damaged connective tissue. If these measures don't help, surgery may be nec-

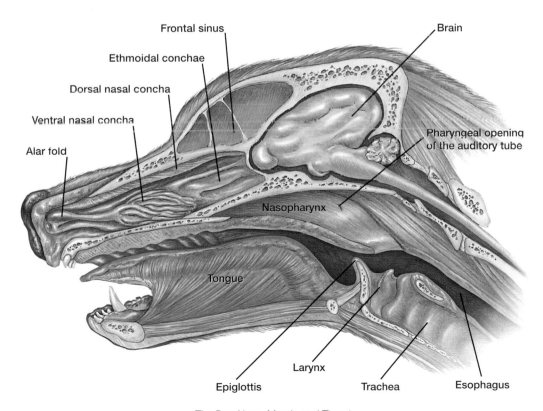

The Dog Nose, Mouth, and Throat

Canine Orthodontia

The goal of orthodontia for dogs is to correct abnormal bites, or malocclusion, relieving pain and preventing serious problems like periodontal disease, damage to the mouth's soft tissue, and excessive wear on the teeth. Both genetics and external factors that cause the teeth to move out of correct position can cause bite problems. Retained deciduous (baby) teeth, base narrow canines, overbites, under bites, and cross bites are some of the more commonly treated orthodontic problems.

- Retained deciduous teeth—normally, baby teeth fall out when incoming adult teeth put pressure on the baby teeth, causing the roots to be reabsorbed. When this process fails and a baby tooth does not fall out, the adult tooth is pushed to the side and the two teeth overcrowd the area. Soft tissue, tooth, and periodontal problems can result unless the baby tooth is extracted.

- Base narrow canines—this means that the lower canines protrude inward. It is caused by retained baby teeth or an overly narrow lower jaw and can damage the roof of the mouth. Treatment involves extraction of the baby teeth, or in the case of an overly narrow jaw, the use of an orthodontic device that pushes the teeth into the correct position called for.

- Overbite—overbite means that the lower jaw is shorter than the upper jaw. Overbites can cause problems because the lower canines can strike the upper canines or the palate. In young dogs, the teeth interfering with jaw growth are removed. For dogs with permanent teeth in place, crown removal and capping may be necessary if the teeth are causing problems.

- Under bite—an under bite occurs when the teeth in the lower jaw protrude in front of the teeth in the upper jaw. It is common in Boxers, Bulldogs, and other short-nosed breeds. It is not normal in dogs with longer muzzles. Under bites can cause periodontal disease, tooth loss, lip trauma, and uneven wear on the teeth. In young dogs, the teeth interfering with jaw growth are extracted. For dogs with permanent teeth in place, crown removal and capping may be used if the teeth are causing trauma to the lips.

- Cross bite—there are two types of cross bites: anterior and posterior. In an anterior cross bite, the upper incisors are positioned behind the lower incisors. It can be caused by several things, including playing too many tug games and impacted roots. It is not an inherited problem. Orthodontic devices that adjust the position of the teeth can correct the problem. In a posterior cross bite, the lower jaw premolars overlap teeth in the upper jaw. This is a rare condition that occurs most often in Collies and other long-nosed breeds. The teeth function properly, and treatment is not necessary for most dogs. It is a difficult bite to correct.

essary, but it's not always successful. Left untreated, fluid builds up in the lungs and causes the airways to further shut down.

Reverse Sneezing

Pulling on the leash, eating or drinking too quickly, or just plain excitement can cause a dog to go into a fit of snorting, honking, or wheezing. Reverse sneezing, or pharyngeal spasms, is usually attributed to an elongated soft palate, which is believed to temporarily become misaligned. It's common in Toy dogs, perhaps because their miniaturized form has brought about organs that aren't always proportionally correct.

Whatever the reason, and whatever the size of the dog, reverse sneezing looks and sounds frightening, but it's far from being an emergency. The episode may last for a few seconds or a few minutes and usually ends when the dog swallows a couple of times or is distracted by something else. Some dog owners successfully end reverse sneezing events by gently rubbing the throat or closing off their dogs' nostrils with their fingers, forcing them to breathe through their mouths and inducing swallowing.

Nose, Mouth, and Throat

If dogs could communicate their favorite anatomical components, they might well choose the nose, mouth, and throat. Their noses helps them sniff out good things to eat, and the mouth and throat—well, we know where those good things to eat go.

The nose is formed by the nostrils (sometimes called nares) and the nasal cavity. The nasal cavity, which is lined with a mucous membrane rich in blood vessels, nerves, and tiny hairlike structures called cilia, is divided into two passages, one for each nostril. These passages open into the throat behind the soft palate. The lining of the nasal cavity helps protect the dog against infection by trapping bacteria and irritants, which are then swept to the back of the throat by the cilia. There, the troublesome particles are trapped in mucus and coughed out or swallowed.

But what about that famous sense of smell? A dog's nasal cavity contains turbinates, bony plates of specialized cells that continuously feed sensory information about odors to the olfactory nerve. This nerve connects to the olfactory center in the dog's brain, where odor information is processed. Inside the nose, dogs have an olfactory membrane, specialized tissue that contains smell-receptor nerve cells, of up to 22 square inches. Compare that with the measly 1 square inch in a human nose.

Covering the exterior of the nose is a layer of thick, leatherlike skin, usually dark in color, although some dogs have a brown, pink, or spotted nose. And forget that old wives' tale about a dog's nose indicating his level of health. The nose is usually cool and moist to the touch, but a number of factors such as tem-

The canine tongue has more responsibilities than any other part of a dog's anatomy, except for the brain. It is used to communicate, conduct heat, register tastes and textures, convey food, lap water, and heal wounds. To perform its diverse duties, the dog's tongue has eight pairs of muscles and five pairs of cranial nerves that come directly from the brain through tiny openings in the dog's skull.

perature, activity level, and state of hydration can cause it to be warm and dry.

Signs of nasal irritation include discharge, sneezing, and breathing through the mouth. These might indicate allergies, trapped foreign bodies, infections, or blocked nasal passages. Dogs don't get colds, but they can suffer respiratory illnesses that produce coldlike symptoms. Other nasal problems that can affect dogs include collapsed nostrils (stenotic nares), which usually affect short nosed dogs such as Pugs and Bulldogs; crusty dermatitis that affects many herding dogs, hence its nickname of Collie nose; and plastic dish nasal dermatitis, easily solved by feeding dogs out of metal or ceramic dishes. Surgery is required to reopen the nostrils of dogs with stenotic nares, and Collie nose can be prevented by regularly applying sunscreen and limiting exposure to the sun.

The mouth and throat are made up of the lips and cheeks; the hard palate (roof of the mouth) and soft palate; the tongue; the salivary glands, which secrete an alkaline fluid that lubricates food and helps digestion; the larynx (the voice box and gateway to the respiratory system) and pharynx (the area extending from the back of the mouth and nasal passages to the larynx and esophagus); and the epiglottis, a flaplike valve that keeps food from entering the respiratory tract. Living inside the mouth are good bacteria that drive out harmful bacteria, reducing the incidence of mouth infections in dogs. The antibacterial enzymes in canine saliva serve the same purpose.

Dogs can suffer many discomforts and disorders of the digestive system. Some, such as vomiting and flatulence, can be benign, while others, such as bloat, can be very serious.

Common problems of the mouth and throat include lip fold pyoderma; lacerations of the lips, gums, and tongue; burns from chewing on electrical cords or licking corrosive chemicals; foreign objects stuck in the mouth or throat; and periodontal disease. Dogs can also suffer from incorrect bites, which interfere with their ability to hold and chew food. Incorrect bites can be overshot, with the upper jaw protruding beyond the lower jaw, or undershot, which is just the reverse. An undershot bite is correct for some dogs such as Bulldogs and Pugs. Another type of incorrect bite is called wry mouth, in which one side of the jaw grows faster than the other, twisting the mouth. Sometimes bite problems can be corrected orthodontically, although these dogs should not be bred and cannot be shown. There is no good treatment for wry mouth. Teeth may have to be pulled to keep the mouth aligned reasonably well.

Cancers of the mouth are rare in dogs. Sometimes they might develop a benign growth in the mouth called an epulis, which forms in response to gum inflammation. Boxers and Bulldogs frequently develop these tumors. An epulis can be removed surgically.

Certain terriers and sometimes other dogs can develop a condition called craniomandibular osteopathy, which is essentially a swollen jaw. It's most often seen in West Highland White Terriers, Scottish Terriers, and Cairn Terriers, but has also occurred in Boston Terriers, Boxers, Labrador Retrievers, Great Danes, and Doberman Pinschers. Dogs with this painful condition, which usually develops at 4 to 10 months of age, have excess bone deposited along the underside of the lower jaw as well as on other parts of the jaw and skull. Signs include drooling, reluctance to eat, and fever. Unfortunately, no effective treatment exists, but the excess bone sometimes regresses as the dog matures. Aspirin in amounts prescribed by a veterinarian can be used to control the pain.

Digestive System

Dogs have a digestive system much like our own. The gastrointestinal tract starts at the mouth, runs through the body, and ends at the anus, where waste is eliminated. In between the two ends are the various areas where food is swallowed, digested (processed), and absorbed for use by the body.

Swallowing is initiated at the pharynx and is a reflex action, meaning it's not under the dog's control. Once swallowed, the food then passes through the esophagus, a muscular tube that extends from the pharynx to the stomach. It enters the stomach at a sharp angle, which is why food generally doesn't back up into it.

Once the food reaches the stomach, secretions called hydrochloric acid and proteolytic enzymes (protein bashers) break it down. This can take up to eight hours. Then the pyloric sphincter, a ring of muscle located between the stomach and duodenum, goes into action, moving the stomach's contents into the duodenum, the first part of the small intestine. In the intestinal tract, more enzymes secreted by the pancreas and the intestinal mucosa—the inner surface lining of the intestine—as well as bile secreted by the liver continue the digestive process, turning the food into usable carbohydrates, amino acids, and fatty acids. These end products are absorbed and carried to the liver, where they're converted to energy and stored.

Anything left over, such as fiber or undigested food, moves on to the colon, or large intestine. Here, water is removed and the remaining waste material is stored until it's eliminated in the form of feces.

From one end to the other, any number of things can go wrong with the digestive system. They include trouble swallowing, vomiting and diarrhea, bloat, intestinal obstructions, anal sac problems, constipation, colitis, and flatulence (passing gas). Many other gastrointestinal problems can affect dogs, but these are among the most common.

Difficulty Swallowing

Dogs who have trouble swallowing may have a partial blockage of the esophagus caused by a foreign object that's stuck or a tumor that's blocking the passage. Another possibility is a condition called megaesophagus in which the esophagus becomes enlarged and is no longer able to push food into the stomach. Megaesophagus can be congenital or it can develop later in life, usually for unknown reasons. Megaesophagus can be managed by raising the dog's food and water dishes off the floor to facilitate swallowing. Some surgical techniques have been tried, with variable success.

When foreign bodies become stuck in the esophagus, it's an emergency. Take your dog to the vet right away for X-rays and removal.

Vomiting and Diarrhea

Vomiting and diarrhea are common problems in dogs. The brain actually has a vomiting center, and the dog's center is highly developed, making it easy for a dog to vomit. The usual suspects behind vomiting are indigestible substances, eating too fast and then being too active, anxiety or excitement, and infectious or chronic diseases.

Should you be concerned about vomiting? That depends on certain factors such as how often your dog vomits, whether the vomiting is violent (projectile), and whether the vomited matter contains blood, worms, or other foreign matter. If your dog is healthy and the vomitus doesn't appear abnormal, simply withhold food and water for 12 hours to give the stomach a rest. Then give a small, bland meal of rice and boiled hamburger meat, cottage cheese, or chicken and rice soup. Feeding your dog one or two tablespoons of this diet every few hours is enough. If he is able to keep the food down, you can gradually return him to his regular diet.

Take your dog to the vet right away if vomiting continues even though your dog hasn't eaten for several hours, the vomitus contains blood, or the dog seems weak and listless. Diarrhea is another warning sign. A dog who's vomiting and has diarrhea can quickly become dehydrated.

Loose or liquid stools characterize diarrhea. Most often, diarrhea occurs when a dog eats something indigestible that irritates the stomach or bowel. Other times the irritant is a food to which the dog is sensitive, such as certain meats, spices, fats, milk products, and grains. Each dog is different, so it's hard to say exactly what might cause a bout of diarrhea. Intestinal parasites, anxiety, or excitement can also cause diarrhea. The reason the stool is runny or liquid is because the food passes rapidly through the bowel before it has time to remove the water.

If diarrhea is a problem, be prepared to tell your veterinarian its color (yellow, greenish, black, bloody, light, or gray), consistency (watery, foamy, mucuslike), and odor (foodlike or rancid). Mild cases of diarrhea can be treated at home by withholding food for 24 hours while still giving the dog plenty of water to drink. Take the dog to the veterinarian if diarrhea continues for more than 24 hours, the stool looks bloody or black and tarry, the dog is also vomiting, or the dog seems weak or has a fever.

Bloat

Also known as gastric torsion or gastric dilatation volvulus, bloat is a life-threatening emergency that occurs when the stomach distends with gas and fluid (gastric dilatation) and then twists (volvulus), trapping gas and fluids in the stomach. Any dog can suffer bloat, but it's most common in large dogs with deep chests such as Bloodhounds, Boxers, Doberman Pinschers, Great Danes, German Shepherd Dogs, Great Pyrenees, Irish Setters, Irish Wolfhounds,

Labrador Retrievers, Old English Sheepdogs, and Standard Poodles.

A dog in the early stages of bloat may pace restlessly or appear sluggish, gag, or make unsuccessful attempts to vomit, producing only excess saliva. Other early indicators include shallow breathing and a dull, vacant, or pained expression. The abdomen may look distended, sounding hollow if thumped. In later stages, dogs with bloat may retch or salivate, their pulse weakens, their gums look pale, and they become unable to stand. A dog with bloat is unable to belch or vomit; he is in obvious physical distress.

If you believe your dog has bloat, take him to the veterinarian or emergency clinic immediately, even if it's the middle of the night. The earlier bloat is caught, the more likely the dog is to survive.

In simple cases, bloat is relieved when the veterinarian passes a long rubber or plastic tube through the mouth and into the stomach, allowing air and fluid to escape. Abdominal X-rays can confirm whether the stomach is twisted, a condition that requires emergency surgery. Surgery involves returning the stomach and spleen to their correct positions and then suturing the wall of the stomach to the abdominal wall, which helps prevent bloat from recurring.

You can take steps at home to prevent bloat from occurring or recurring by dividing the amount of food your dog gets into three meals daily instead of one or two meals; restricting access to water for an hour before and after meals; enforcing a rest period after meals; and ensuring that your dog doesn't drink a large amount of water all at once.

Intestinal Obstruction

Swallowing something such as a ball, toy, rawhide, piece of string, tea towel, or other cloth is the most common cause of an intestinal obstruction. The list of things that dogs will put in their mouths and swallow could go on and on. When a foreign object isn't the problem, the next most likely cause is a condition called intussusception, in which the bowel sort of turns itself inside out. This is most common in puppies.

If the intestinal obstruction is partial, the dog may suffer vomiting and diarrhea over several weeks or until the problem is recognized. If the blockage is complete, the dog is unable to defecate. Intestinal obstructions are determined through abdominal X-rays and must be corrected surgically.

Anal Glands

Dogs have two glands called anal sacs on either side of the anus—usually at the five o'clock and seven o'clock positions. The anal sacs are scent glands that serve to identify the dog and help mark his territory when he eliminates. As the stool passes out of the anus, the pressure empties the anal sacs. When this doesn't occur, however, the sacs can become impacted. Infection and abscess can follow if the impaction isn't relieved by manually emptying the anal glands, a technique your veterinarian can show you how to do at home. You may, however, prefer to have it done by a groomer or veterinary technician. Impacted anal glands are most common in small dogs and are indicated by the dog scooting on the ground or licking and biting at his rear.

Constipation

A dog with constipation strains while defecating, defecates less often than usual (normal is one or two stools daily), or doesn't defecate at all. While fewer or no canine stools might be nice for an owner to deal with, it's not at all comfortable for the dog. Constipation is usually a problem of advanced age and is also seen when dogs

Incontinence

Incontinence is the involuntary passing of urine. It can occur for different reasons related to the bladder, urethra, or abnormalities in the parts of the brain and spinal cord responsible for controlling bladder function. Before diagnosing incontinence, rule out medications and diseases such as diabetes, Cushing's disease, and kidney failure, which can increase urine production and cause a dog to involuntarily urinate. Some causes of incontinence include:

- Aging—incontinence related to aging is quite common and can be caused by the weakening of bladder muscles, senility, or diseases common to older dogs.

- Birth defects—the most common birth defect that can cause incontinence is an ectopic ureter, which may cause puppies to drip urine. The ureters carry urine from the kidney to the bladder, but if defective one or both ureters may bypass the bladder and connect to an abnormal location. The condition is most common in females and in certain breeds such as Siberian Huskies, Miniature Poodles, Labrador Retrievers, Collies, Welsh Corgis, Wire Fox Terriers, and West Highland White Terriers.

- Partial blockage of the urethra—a stone or tumor partially blocking the urethra can cause an animal to become incontinent. If urine flow becomes totally blocked, the animal can die within a few days.

- Bladder infections—though not true incontinence, bladder infections can cause a strong urge to urinate leading to inappropriate elimination. Veterinarians commonly evaluate incontinent animals for bladder infections.

- Brain or spinal cord diseases—a dog dribbling urine may have a brain or spinal cord disease, but other signs of nervous system disease are usually present as well.

- Hormone-responsive incontinence—this occurs most often in spayed female dogs, although it can occur in neutered male dogs, too. The dog leaks urine while resting.

Depending upon what's causing the incontinence, surgery or treatment of an underlying disease may be necessary. When no specific reason can be found, drugs may be prescribed to help increase muscle tone in the bladder. These drugs include phenylpropanolamine, estrogen, and ephedrine. Use of l-deprenyl (Anapryl), which can reverse some of the behavioral changes related to aging, may help remedy incontinence in older dogs. Dogs can wear specially made diapers, which are available at pet supply stores, to help manage the incontinence.

---

don't drink enough water. Indigestible materials such as bone chips, grass, or other items can become compacted with feces, causing a hard mass that's difficult to pass. Constipation can also be a side effect of certain medications.

If your dog is constipated, don't just assume that giving him a laxative will solve the problem. Constipation and colitis (inflammation of the colon) are similar in nature, so it's best to let your veterinarian make the call. If the problem is indeed constipation, he or she can advise you about the appropriate laxative to give and suggest ways to prevent recurrence, such as adding fiber to the diet.

Colitis

This inflammation of the colon is usually caused by a form of inflammatory bowel disease or an infestation of whipworms. Signs of colitis are painful defecation or straining to defecate; flatulence; or small stools that contain blood or mucus. Dogs with chronic diarrhea should also be checked for colitis. Both a colonoscopy and a colon biopsy are necessary to diagnose colitis. Treatment involves correcting the underlying condition, and it can range from feeding the dog a hypoallergenic diet to the use of antibiotics and corticosteroids.

Flatulence

Less serious, but not very pleasant for those with a sensitive nose, is flatulence, or passing gas. Dogs who emit stinky fumes often do so because they've swallowed large amounts of air while wolfing their food. Dogs can also be prone to flatulence if they eat foods such as beans, cauliflower, cabbage, and soybeans. A medical cause of flatulence is malabsorption syndrome, in which the dog isn't able to completely digest carbohydrates.

To reduce the incidence of flatulence, try feeding your dog a highly digestible low-fiber diet, and try feeding him two or three small meals a day instead of one large meal. If that doesn't help, your veterinarian may recommend giving your dog a dose of simethicone, available over the counter in drugstores, to absorb intestinal gas.

Urinary System

The kidneys, ureters, bladder, and urethra make up the urinary system. The bean-shaped kidneys filter waste products from the blood. They also produce a hormone called erythropoietin that stimulates the production of red blood cells, and they maintain the body's water and electrolyte balance. The kidneys also funnel filtered waste material—in the form of urine—into a ureter, where it's transported to the bladder and then eliminated through the urethra, a hollow tube leading from the bladder out of the body.

Signs of urinary tract trouble include painful urination, bloody urine, excessive urination, and incontinence. Dogs can suffer bladder infections (cystitis), and bladder and urethral stones.

Bladder Infections

Frequent, painful urination signals a bladder infection (cystitis), one of the most common problems in dogs. The urine may look cloudy or smell funny because of the bacteria and blood cells in it. Some of the conditions that can trigger cystitis include urethral infections, diabetes, or simply increasing age. Letting a bladder infection go without treatment can lead to kidney infection, so seek veterinary advice if a dog shows these signs. Cystitis is treated with oral antibiotics, and it's a good idea to have a follow-up urinalysis to ensure that the infection is gone.

Stones

Stones, or uroliths, are rocklike collections of minerals that form in the bladder or urethra. Most such stones are formed of magnesium ammonium phosphate and are called struvites. Other stones are made of calcium oxalate or cystine. Uric acid stones form in an alkaline urine and often result from a bladder infection. Dogs can have a single large stone or many small stones. Bladder stones are common in dogs, but some dogs have a greater incidence of them, including Dalmatians, Dachshunds, Bulldogs, Miniature Schnauzers, and Shih Tzu. Signs of stones are painful urination and bloody urine. Sometimes stones can be felt by the veterinarian when examining the abdomen by hand, but in most cases diagnosis is made with X-rays. Stones are treated by resolving a bladder infection if present and feeding the dog a special diet that helps dissolve the stones. If stones are blocking the urethra or if bladder stones fail to dissolve, surgery is the best treatment.

Musculoskeletal System

Bones, joints, muscles, ligaments, and tendons support and protect the body, as well as allow it to move. Together, these components form what is known as the musculoskeletal system.

Dogs have 319 bones altogether. A specialized type of connective tissue called cartilage is the foundation of bone. In the womb, a puppy's bones form when an underlying matrix of cartilage mineralizes, or hardens. Bone is a living tissue with blood vessels and nerves. As such, it's continually renewing itself. Besides being the framework upon which the body is built, bones store minerals such as calcium, magnesium, phosphorus, and fluoride. Minerals are important in building bone and maintaining the body's acid-base, electrolyte, and fluid balances. When the body's mineral level is out of whack, the results include skeletal abnormalities, muscular weakness, and poor growth. Bone marrow, found in the heart of the long bones, such as the leg bones, produces the red and white blood cells the body needs to function.

Joints are what connect the bones and permit movement. Synovial joints such as the hips and elbows are enclosed in a joint capsule. They're lubricated by synovial fluid, which allows cartilage surfaces to move against one another without the resistance caused by friction. Sesamoid joints such as the knee (or patella, as your veterinarian may refer to it) protect the tendons (fibrous tissues that connect muscle to bone) as they move over the surfaces of bone near the bone ends. Fibrous joints hold the skull bones together and root teeth in their sockets. Ligaments are bands of fibrous tissue that support and stabilize the joint structures.

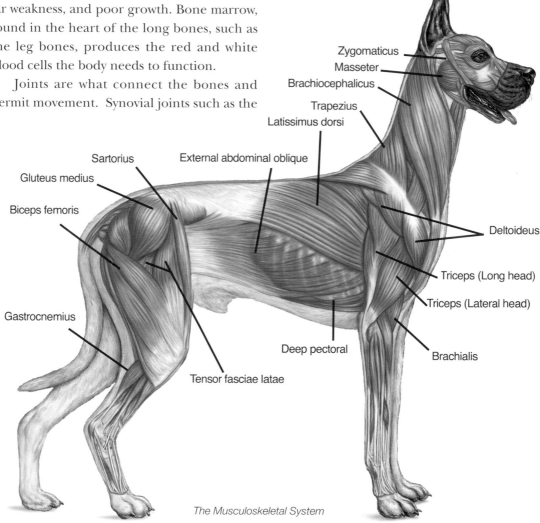

Zygomaticus
Masseter
Brachiocephalicus
Trapezius
Latissimus dorsi
Sartorius
Gluteus medius
Biceps femoris
External abdominal oblique
Deltoideus
Triceps (Long head)
Triceps (Lateral head)
Gastrocnemius
Deep pectoral
Brachialis
Tensor fasciae latae

The Musculoskeletal System

Tendons are fibrous tissues that attach muscle to bone.

Muscles are body tissues that consist of long cells. When these cells are stimulated, they contract and produce motion. Each type of muscle performs a different job. Skeletal muscle is involved in the dog's movement. Smooth muscle is found in the walls of blood vessels and in the major internal organs. The heart is made up of cardiac muscle. When the cardiac muscle contracts, the heart beats.

Musculoskeletal problems are common in dogs. Dogs can suffer stiffness or lameness in joints such as hips, elbows, and knees. Joint pain can be a consequence of injury, disease, or old age. Among the conditions that cause joint pain in dogs are hip dysplasia, osteoarthritis, and old fractures. Some of these conditions are developmental, while others are hereditary. Dogs with joint pain move stiffly, limp, struggle to get to their feet in the morning, or cry out in pain if they move the wrong way. Listed are just a few of the orthopedic problems that can affect dogs.

Hip and Elbow Dysplasia

Hip dysplasia, a hereditary developmental disease, is one in which the hip joint fails to develop properly. In dogs with hip dysplasia, the head of the thigh bone (femur) does not fit into its socket in the hip. This imperfect fit causes the joint to become loose and unstable, eventually leading to osteoarthritis.

Although hip dysplasia is a hereditary condition, environmental factors such as excessive weight gain during puppyhood can also play a role in its development. Any dog can develop hip dysplasia, but the condition is most common in large and giant dogs such as Saint Bernards, Newfoundlands, Rottweilers, Golden Retrievers, and German Shepherd Dogs.

Signs of hip dysplasia are lameness, reluctance to exercise, and muscle atrophy. It's confirmed with an X-ray of the hips and pelvis. Dogs with mild hip dysplasia can often get along well with the help of nutraceuticals and pain-relieving medications. In the case of dogs with severe hip dysplasia, total hip replacement is the treatment of choice. Other hip surgeries may be recommended depending on the dog's specific condition.

Owners of young dogs with excessively loose hip joints may be interested in a new surgical technique called juvenile pubic symphysiodesis. In this procedure, the surgeon burns away tissue with an electric cur-

An exuberant dog can break a bone or sprain a joint or muscle in the course of heavy play.

The first total hip replacement in a dog occurred in 1974; since then, thousands of dogs have undergone the procedure to restore mobility and relieve pain.

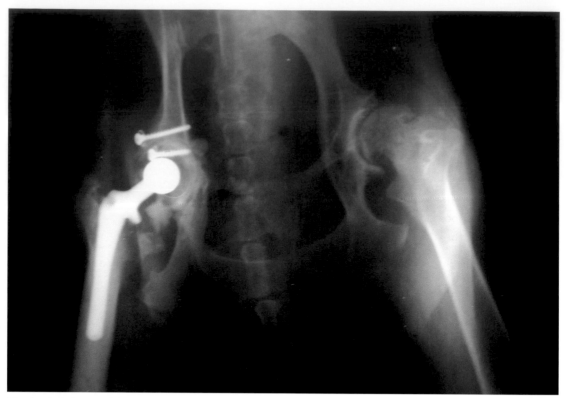

Hip dysplasia is one of the most common disorders afflicting the musculoskeletal system. Fortunately, this common disorder is now treatable through surgery.

rent to close the pubic symphysis, the area between the two halves of the pelvis. As the pup grows, the closed pubic symphysis forces the hip socket to rotate into normal alignment. The surgery can be performed only before a puppy is five months old, so he must be evaluated for loose hips by three months of age.

Elbow dysplasia occurs when the bones involving the elbow of the foreleg fail to unite and move properly. It can also result from bone fragments within the joint. Elbow dysplasia is a common cause of front-leg lameness in dogs. Dogs who are predisposed to elbow dysplasia include Golden and Labrador Retrievers, English Springer Spaniels, Rottweilers, German Shepherd Dogs, Bernese Mountain Dogs, Newfoundlands, and Bloodhounds.

Osteoarthritis

Osteoarthritis is caused by the inflammation, breakdown, and eventual loss of a layer of protein called articular cartilage. This cartilage layer covers the ends of the bones in a joint, acting as a shock absorber, or cushion, to keep bones from rubbing against each other as joints bend and flex. With normal aging, the water content of the cartilage increases, and the protein makeup of cartilage degenerates. Repetitive use of the joints over the years irritates and inflames the cartilage, causing mild to severe joint pain and swelling. Eventually the cartilage begins to degenerate by forming flakes and tiny crevices. In advanced cases there is a total loss of this articular cartilage, leaving the ends of the bones stripped bare of their protective cushion. At this point the bones rub together, causing further damage to the joint and leading to severe pain and the growth of bone spurs. Osteoarthritis can also develop as a result of hip or elbow dysplasia. Although any joint can develop osteoarthritis, the hip and elbow are the most commonly affected.

Physical therapy, the use of pain relievers such as carprofen and etodolac, and supplementation with nutraceuticals such as chondroitin and glucosamine can help relieve achy joints. For severe cases, total hip replacement is the only surgical intervention available and is very successful. Elbow replacements are not yet available, so arthritis is usually treated medically.

Osteochondritis Dissecans (OCD)

This is a problem of cartilage development. It usually affects the shoulder joints but can also strike the elbow, hock, and knee joints. Signs include gradual lameness and pain when the joint is flexed or extended. A definitive diagnosis requires X-rays. OCD can be treated with rest and nutraceuticals such as Adequan that protect cartilage and help prevent pain, inflammation, and further degeneration. If the shoulder and elbow are the joints that are affected, surgery can be performed to scrape away defective cartilage or remove cartilage flaps that are loose in the joint.

Patellar Luxation

This term simply means that the kneecap (patella) slips (luxates) out of place. It's usually an inherited defect and is common in small dogs. Sometimes it occurs in large dogs, appearing during puppyhood usually at five to six months of age.

Patellar luxation is diagnosed during a range of motion test. The veterinarian will try to push the patella out of its groove and see how easily it pops back into place. If the patella becomes dislocated easily, surgery can be performed to deepen the groove in which it rests and repair any ligaments that are loose or torn.

Small dogs are especially prone to patellar luxation, but if your dog has two parents with healthy knees, perhaps he, too, will dance through life with no problems.

Sprains and Strains

Signs of swelling and lameness indicate a joint or muscle sprain or strain. Swelling can be related to injury, immune-mediated diseases, or growth abnormalities. It can also be caused by an accumulation of fluids in soft tissues, chronic changes in the joint capsule, or arthritis. Swelling due to exercise usually occurs when very young, old, or out-of-shape dogs overexert themselves in an attempt to keep up with their people. Muscle sprains occur when the muscle fibers become torn through overuse.

The joints most likely to suffer a sprain or strain are the stifles (knees), hocks (ankles), elbows, and carpus (wrist joint). Swelling can occur in the shoulder and hips, but swelling in these areas is difficult to locate except by veterinarians, who are trained to feel for and rotate the joint.

Swollen joints are usually painful and often feel hot to the touch.

A dog who is stiff or limping mildly for 24 to 48 hours should be examined by a veterinarian. Take your dog to the vet immediately if the joint is misaligned, if your dog has acute pain, or if there's any break in the skin. An X-ray or a joint tap (draining off and analyzing fluid from a painful joint) may be necessary to determine the problem. Sprains and strains can be treated with physical therapy, massage, warm and cold compresses, rest, and nonsteroidal anti-inflammatory drugs (NSAIDs).

Preventing Joint Problems

Just a few simple steps can help prevent or ease joint problems. They include easing young dogs into exercise, dietary control, supplements, and various forms of physical therapy such as massage, swimming, or the application of heat or ice.

Even though puppies have oodles of energy, they shouldn't be allowed to run or jump excessively until they reach full physical maturity, which is at 18 months to 2 years of age. Be aware that large-breed dogs mature more slowly than small-breed dogs do. Your 3- or 4-month-old Golden Retriever puppy may look big enough to go jogging, but his skeletal system is still developing. The pounding it takes from jogging can damage skeletal development and lead to joint problems. The same holds true for jumping, carrying or pulling heavy loads, and engaging in activity on uneven or slippery surfaces. Help your puppy avoid risky behaviors such as jumping off furniture, turning flips in pursuit of a flying disc, or going over high jumps in agility or obedience training. Avoid repetitive jumping as well.

A 14-year study of Labrador Retrievers proved what veterinarians had long believed: a good diet plays an important role in bone and joint health. The study showed that dogs kept lean for life developed osteoarthritis later in life than did other dogs, and their pain was less severe.

Be aware that large-breed puppies need a different balance of nutrients for growth than small-breed puppies do. Look for a diet created especially for large-breed dogs to reduce the risk of your pup developing skeletal defects such as OCD and hip and elbow dysplasia. Too much weight on a dog of any age can stress joints as well.

For dogs who already have orthopedic problems, joint pain can be relieved by pharmaceuticals such as aspirin, corticosteroids, and nonsteroidal anti-inflammatory drugs such as carprofen; or through the use of nutraceuticals such as glycosaminoglycans, including chondroitin and glucosamine, methyl sulfonyl methane (MSM), the antioxidant vitamins C and E, which help speed healing and relieve inflammation, and herbs such as yucca or various Chinese herbal combinations. Other beneficial treatments include massage, applying warmth to the painful area, swimming, and physical therapy. Every dog who is slated to be bred should first be screened for orthopedic problems by the Orthopedic Foundation for Animals (OFA). If problems are detected, the dog should not be bred so these devastating genetic problems aren't passed on to the next generation.

Nervous System

The nervous system allows dogs to receive and use information about their environment. It's made up of the central nervous system (CNS)—the brain and spinal cord—and the peripheral nervous system (PNS)—the nerves.

The brain consists of the cerebrum, cerebellum, hypothalamus, and brain stem. The cerebrum, located in the front part of the brain, is the largest area and directs conscious thought, awareness of surroundings, sight, hearing, taste, smell, touch, learning, decision making, and voluntary movement. The cerebellum, known as the little brain, coordinates movement. Appetite, thirst, and other bodily functions such as temperature and sleep cycles are controlled by the hypothalamus. It also produces hormones that affect growth, thyroid function, reproductive cycles, and stress responses. The brain stem contains areas that control heart rate, respiratory rate and pattern, and level of consciousness. It's also the home of sensory and motor nerve fibers, as well as the cranial nerves that control facial muscles, sight, smell, and hearing.

Sensory information travels to the brain and motor impulses travel from the brain to the muscles along the spinal cord, which connects the PNS with the brain through nerve fibers. Protecting the spinal cord are the blocklike bones of the spinal column called vertebrae. The vertebrae are cushioned against the stress of motion by intervertebral disks.

When the nervous system receives information, the dog responds with reflexes that may be automatic and involuntary, or conscious and voluntary. An example of an involuntary response is pulling a paw away after stepping on something sharp. A voluntary reflex involves recognizing a signal and then taking action. For instance, chasing and retrieving a thrown ball is a voluntary response.

Neurological diseases that can affect dogs include deafness and ruptured disks.

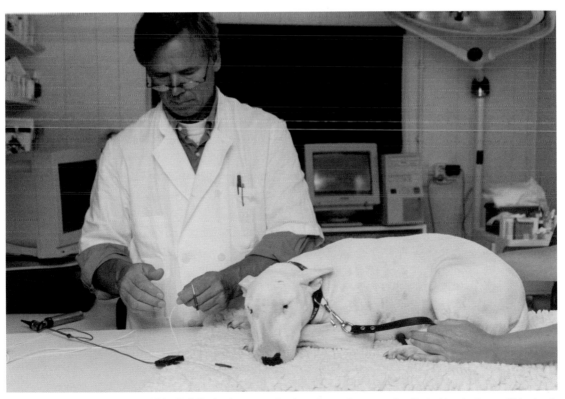

The Bull Terrier, especially the White Bull Terrier, is among the breeds most commonly affected by deafness. This dog is undergoing BAER testing, in which probes measure the brain's response to audio stimulation.

Disk disease can cause paralysis in hind legs. A number of owners are now finding ways to help their dogs live with paralysis rather than euthanizing them, as was done in the past.

Deafness

While deafness sometimes accompanies old age or results from recurring ear infections, some dogs are congenitally deaf, meaning they're born with little or no hearing. Congenital deafness occurs when the sound receptor cells in the ear fail to form. Deafness is hereditary in many breeds, including Australian Shepherds, Boxers, Bull Terriers, Collies, Dalmatians, and Shetland Sheepdogs. Hearing loss is confirmed by a test called a Brainstem Auditory Evoked Response (BAER) test. Deaf dogs can be trained by teaching them to respond to hand signals rather than verbal commands.

Ruptured Disk

When an intervertebral disk that cushions the vertebrae degenerates or ruptures, the result is severe neck and back pain. This condition is referred to as a herniated disk, a slipped disk, or intervertebral disk disease. Dachshunds and Beagles disproportionately suffer from this condition.

Disk disease can develop gradually, brought on by repetitive stress such as jumping off furniture, or it can occur suddenly. Dogs with a ruptured disk act as if their back is hurting them, limping or walking hunched over. Severe disk disease can cause paralysis of the hind legs. If a neck disk is affected, the dog may carry his head rigidly or be unable to lower his head to eat. These dogs may cry out if patted on the head.

Rest and anti-inflammatory medications can help ease the pain and reduce swelling caused by a ruptured disk. Sometimes hospitalization is required to keep the dog quiet and still. Disks may heal or at least improve over time, but some do not. In some cases, surgery is the only answer.

Immune System

The immune system is one of the wonders of the body. Using specialized white blood cells called T lymphocytes (T cells) and B lymphocytes (B cells), the immune system wields a multipronged defense when the body is invaded by unfriendly bacteria or viruses, known as antigens. An antigen is any substance that's alien to the body. When the immune system recognizes that an antigen is present, it develops antibodies that bind the antigen and prevent it from harming the dog or causing infectious disease such as distemper or parvovirus. An antibody is a protein substance produced by the immune system to disable the effects of an antigen.

The T cells, which are manufactured in the bone marrow, circulate throughout the body. Their job is to track down and kill dangerous foreign bodies. The B cells produce antibodies that help disable or destroy antigens and then stay behind on guard, ready to go to work again should the same antigen attack later. A check and balance system ensures that the immune system gears up when it's needed and winds back down when the battle is over.

Problems of the immune system include allergies and autoimmune diseases such as lupus or immune-mediated arthritis.

Allergies

An allergy is a reaction of the immune system caused by exposure to an allergen. An allergen is any substance capable of causing an allergic reaction. Common allergens that affect dogs are drugs, insect toxins, pollens, molds, and foods.

Dogs in general are prone to a variety of types of allergies, including food aller-

In the United States, from 10 to 15 percent of dogs are afflicted with allergies. Allergies are always uncomfortable and sometimes even life threatening. Dogs can be allergic to fleas, types of food, airborne substances, or dust mites and molds, among other things. Some dogs suffer from multiple allergies. Scratching, chewing, biting, face rubbing, redness in the ears, rash, and hair loss are all signs of an allergic reaction.

For more severe allergies, your veterinarian may recommend allergy shots. Less severe cases may be controlled by reducing or eliminating the source of the allergies. To eliminate fleas from your dog, home, and yard, vacuum and dust several times weekly; wash dog bedding weekly; use HEPA (high-efficiency particulate air) filters in the home to reduce irritation from dander and pollens; and keep dogs indoors during peak pollen periods, such as early mornings and evenings during the spring and summer.

To help soothe itchy skin, soak your dog in cool water for 10 minutes. To relieve itchy feet, soak his feet in Epsom salts. Because Epsom salts can act as a laxative, be sure your dog doesn't drink the water. Fatty acid supplements, available from your veterinarian or pet supply store, also help itchy skin. Ask your veterinarian about the appropriate dosage for your dog.

Dogs, just like humans, can be affected by many allergens that are found outdoors.

can range from avoidance (staying away from certain foods or insects, for instance) to desensitization injections to corticosteroids.

Autoimmune Diseases

Autoimmune diseases are a result of the body attacking itself. For some reason, the immune system develops antibodies against a normal part of the body. This misguided missile is called an autoantibody. Often, the skin is the target of these autoantibodies. Examples of autoimmune skin diseases are pemphigus, in which the autoantibody attacks the wall of the skin cell; lupus erythematosus, which affects not only the skin but also other organs; immune-mediated arthritis; and autoimmune hemolytic anemia. Autoimmune skin diseases are usually characterized by red skin patches on the face and ears; the formation of pustules and blisters; crusting, oozing skin; and hair loss.

There's no cure for autoimmune diseases, but they can usually be managed with corticosteroids, which have an anti-inflammatory effect. The course of various autoimmune diseases can range from mild to fatal. Some can

gies, flea allergy dermatitis, and atopic dermatitis. Allergies can be hereditary or acquired. Some breeds seem to be more prone to allergies than others, but any dog can suffer from allergies. Allergy treatments

be managed or will go into remission, while others cause death fairly rapidly.

Immune-Mediated Arthritis

Immune-mediated arthritis occurs when antibodies attack the body's connective tissue. One form of immune-mediated arthritis (nonerosive) causes inflammation, while the other (rheumatoid arthritis) destroys cartilage and joint surfaces. Rheumatoid arthritis is usually seen in toy breeds and other small dogs. Signs include morning stiffness, transitory lameness, and swelling of small joints such as the wrists and hocks. Nonerosive arthritis has similar signs but usually occurs in medium-size and large dogs. Both conditions can be helped by anti-inflammatory medications such as corticosteroids.

Autoimmune Hemolytic Anemia

Autoimmune hemolytic anemia (AIHA) is the destruction of red blood cells by autoantibodies—antibodies directed against the body's own tissues. It's not known why this condition develops. It can occur in any dog but is frequently seen in Cocker Spaniels, English Springer Spaniels, Poodles, Old English Sheepdogs, West Highland White Terriers, and Irish Setters. AIHA is diagnosed through blood work, chest radiographs, abdominal ultrasound, and lymph node and bone marrow aspirates. Corticosteroids and immunosuppressants can help block further red cell destruction. Dogs with severe cases may need blood transfusions. Even with treatment, the mortality rate is more than 40 percent.

Canine Genetics and Heredity

A gene is a unit of hereditary information in cells that is passed down from parents to offspring. It controls the transmission and manifestation of one or more traits. Once in a while, genes mutate, which may give rise to

Responsible breeders have appropriate health checks done on their breeding animals and breed only from dogs who test free of genetic disorders, thus giving the pups the best chance at good health.

genetic diseases. Genetic diseases can affect all areas of the body.

Scientists are working to understand the underlying causes of hereditary canine diseases, including a determination of the genetic mutations that actually cause the diseases. With this information, scientists can develop diagnostic tests so breeders can reduce or eliminate the incidence of hereditary disease in dogs. It's very important that dogs with hereditary conditions such as mitral valve disease, hip dysplasia, and epilepsy are kept from producing puppies who will continue to pass on these serious problems.

This work has already brought results, including the discovery of three inherited diseases that affect the retina for which genetic tests have been developed. Thus far, more than 20 tests for inheritable canine diseases have been developed, and some researchers believe that tests for all known canine genetic diseases could be developed within the next 10 years. Eventually, gene therapy for dogs will be used to treat genetic diseases. Currently, genetic testing can help breeders plan breedings that will avoid these canine diseases.

CHAPTER 24

A Lifetime of Good Health

There are a number of times in a dog's life when he is vulnerable and requires special care. Newborn puppies, pregnant mamas, and geriatric dogs are all at special risk and require special health considerations.

Sex and Reproduction

Not all dogs should be mated. Unless you are a serious breeder with a dog of excellent health and personality, and you have a commitment to placing every one of the puppies in a responsible and loving home, do not breed your pet. For females, pregnancy and whelping can have long-term negative effects on her personality, threaten her health, and even lead to her death. Unless a dog is a superb example of his or her breed and has health, temperament, and conformation qualities that should be passed on, he or she should be spayed or neutered.

Reproductive Organs

The female reproductive organs begin with the vulva; the entrance to the vagina, which is made up of external lips and folds (labia); and the clitoris. The vagina is the genital canal that extends from the cervix outward to the vulva. Connecting the vagina to the uterus is the cervix. The Y-shaped hollow uterus is where the fertilized eggs implant and the fetuses develop. Uterine horns branch off to the fallopian tubes, where egg and sperm meet for fertilization. The ovaries, which resemble lima beans in shape, are responsible for egg production. At birth, a female puppy's ovaries contain approximately 700,000 eggs.

During estrus, more commonly known as heat, the ovaries release an indeterminate amount of eggs, and the female becomes receptive to the advances of a male dog. Most females experience estrus twice a year, or every six to seven months. Sexual maturity usually takes place at 6 to 10 months of age, although some breeds may not reach it until 18 to 24 months of age.

The male reproductive organs include a penis, two testicles, a scrotum (the pouch of skin that holds the testicles), and the prostate gland, which is important in the production of seminal fluid. The penis is used to deposit semen into

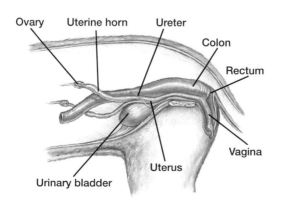

The Female Dog Reproductive System

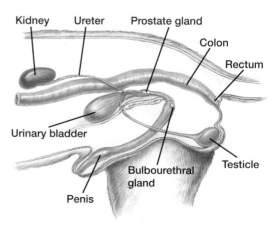

The Male Dog Reproductive System

the female. The testicles produce sperm, which fertilize the female's eggs.

Mating

Dogs should be at least two years old before they're bred. At that age, they've reached full physical and emotional maturity, and most potential health problems will have shown up. Before breeding, both bitch and stud should undergo an extensive health exam. They should be free of genetic defects that could be passed on to puppies such as orthopedic conditions, eye disease, heart problems, deafness, bleeding diseases, and poor temperament (such as shyness or aggression). Vaccination and deworming of the bitch two to four weeks before breeding helps ensure that puppies are protected from disease and parasite infestation. She should also be checked for dental infections so she doesn't transmit bacteria to puppies when she bites their umbilical cords.

The bitch and stud should also be tested for brucellosis, a sexually transmitted disease in dogs. It can cause a litter to be aborted or pups to be born dead. Other consequences of brucellosis are infertility, inflammatory diseases of the testicles or prostate gland, and inflammation of the intervertebral disks in the lower back. All dogs should be tested for brucellosis a month before a breeding takes place. Repeat tests are necessary for females before every breeding. Males should be tested every 6 to 12 months, depending on how frequently they're used at stud.

Bitches go into estrus, or heat, twice a year. Breeding usually takes place 10 to 14 days after the female goes into estrus, although the time of readiness can vary. Signs that a bitch is ready for breeding include a pinkish discharge and flirtatious behavior toward the male such as lifting her tail or presenting her vulva to him. Depending on the dogs and their level of experience, the mating process may require

Both mom and pups require special health care before and after a birth.

some human assistance such as physically guiding the male as he mounts his partner or holding the female still. Once the penis enters the vagina, it's held inside by powerful vaginal contractions. Called a tie, this union can last for 30 to 45 minutes. The bitch may flail and scream in discomfort or indignation during the tie; she should be held so she doesn't injure herself. Separation can be painful, so be careful not to get bitten.

The mating records kept by the stud owner (bitches are always sent to studs when breeding) can help determine when puppies will be due.

Pregnancy

A canine pregnancy lasts 57 to 63 days. Signs of pregnancy include enlarged nipples, a slightly swollen vulva, increased appetite, and a cranky or demanding personality. At five weeks, she may begin to show.

During pregnancy, bitches have increased nutritional needs.

Ultrasound can confirm a pregnancy as early as 18 to 25 days. If ultrasound is unavailable, a blood test conducted at 25 to 37 days can indicate pregnancy. Radiographs, or X-rays, can be done after about 45 days to confirm pregnancy and indicate the number of puppies. Litter sizes vary depending on the size of the dog. A toy dog might carry 1 to 4 pups, while a large dog might produce 17 or more.

Exercise during the pregnancy helps keep the bitch in optimum shape for giving birth. She'll need good muscle tone, especially if she's delivering a large number of puppies. Long walks are beneficial in the early part of the pregnancy. As she gets larger, limit walks to a few turns around the yard every day. She'll begin resting for longer periods of time as the pregnancy progresses.

A pregnant bitch needs a high-protein puppy diet during the last six weeks of the pregnancy. This helps ensure that she does not become malnourished as the puppies grow inside her and that she can produce milk for them after giving birth. Try not to let the bitch get too fat. Do not give bone meal or calcium supplements since they can cause development problems in the puppies.

Schedule at least two prenatal exams, one that is two to three weeks after mating and one that is two weeks before the due date. During the pregnancy, the bitch should not be treated with flea-control products or deworming medications, but heartworm pills are safe to give. If she becomes ill, remind the veterinarian that she's pregnant so any treatment can be modified for her condition.

For the last 7 to 10 days of the pregnancy, take the bitch's temperature twice a day. When her temperature drops below 99°F, she will probably whelp (give birth) the litter within 24 hours. Make sure your veterinarian will be available in case of emergency, or have an alternate vet lined up in case your regular vet can't assist.

Have a whelping box ready, placed in a warm, dry area where the bitch won't be disturbed. The size varies depending on the size of the dog, but the sides should be high enough to keep puppies from crawling out, yet low enough that the bitch can easily step out. Line it with newspapers, and cover the papers with towels or some other easily washable bedding that provides good traction. As labor approaches, the bitch will become restless and start exhibiting nesting behavior. Show her the whelping box a week or two before the expected delivery date so she can become accustomed to it. If she ends up giving birth elsewhere, move the bitch and pups to the whelping box later.

Involuntary contractions that last for 6 to 12 hours indicate the beginning of the whelping process. As contractions become stronger, the puppies are pushed out one at a time. During this period, the bitch may pant, seem anxious, or throw up. This is normal. Bitches may deliver puppies while lying down, standing, or squatting. As each puppy is born, the mother should break the surrounding water bag (amniotic sac) with her teeth if it didn't break during delivery. She then licks the puppy to clean him and severs the umbilical cord by biting it. Often, new mothers don't know what to do after puppies are born. Be prepared to tear open the amniotic sac, wipe away mucus from the mouth and nose, and cut the umbilical cord yourself. Disinfect the stump of the cord with iodine to prevent infection. After each puppy has been born and cleaned up, place him in a warm spot where he won't get rolled on. Most puppies are born at intervals ranging from 15 minutes to 2 hours. Between births, let the puppies nurse.

Difficult births can involve puppies who are too large to fit through the vaginal canal or puppies who are positioned incorrectly—rump or hind feet first instead of head first. Both conditions require veterinary assistance and possibly a caesarean section. Call the veterinarian if the bitch strains for up to an hour without giving birth; if more than four hours go by between births; if labor is weak and goes on for two hours without producing a puppy; if there's a puslike or bloody discharge from the vagina; or if the bitch produces a dark green or bloody fluid before giving birth to the first puppy.

Be aware that breeding dogs isn't all fun and games. If whelping goes wrong, the mother may require a caesarean section or she may even die during the process. Sometimes she doesn't produce milk and the pups must be hand-fed or a foster mother must be found.

Spaying and Neutering

To spay a dog, the veterinarian surgically removes the ovaries and uterus. This is also known as an ovariohysterectomy. Neutering is the surgical removal of both testicles. The term *altering* is used to refer to both procedures. Altering does not affect instincts such as retrieving, herding, and guarding, and it often has beneficial health effects, such as a great reduction in the incidence of mammary cancer in females and testicular cancer in males.

Typically, veterinarians recommend that dogs be altered at approximately six months of age, before a female experiences her first estrus period and a male reaches full adoles-

The Alliance for Contraception in Cats & Dogs (ACCD) is researching nonsurgical technologies for the humane control of dog and cat populations. The Alliance is composed of veterinarians, members of humane organizations, and others interested in fighting animal overpopulation.

cence. Early spaying and neutering—before six months of age and often as early as eight weeks of age—has become increasingly common in recent years. Most animal shelters and rescue groups alter dogs before releasing them to their new homes. Early spay and neuter programs have been extremely effective in reducing the pet overpopulation problem in the United States, and there's little or no disagreement that it's appropriate for dogs coming from shelter situations.

For some breeds, however, some studies show that later spay or neuter surgery, after the dog reaches full growth at 12 to 14 months of age, may be more advantageous when it comes to preventing certain orthopedic problems, diseases, and negative behaviors. For instance, giant breeds that are altered before puberty appear to be more at risk for osteosarcoma. And Akitas, German Shepherds, Golden and Labrador Retrievers, Newfoundlands, Poodles, and Saint Bernards that are altered early are among the breeds at higher risk for cranial cruciate ligament (CCL) ruptures. Females that are spayed early in life are more prone to urinary incontinence, although this condition is easily controllable with daily medication.

A study of several thousand dogs conducted by Deborah L. Duffy, PhD, and James A. Serpell, PhD, at the University of Pennsylvania School of Veterinary Medicine concluded that with a few exceptions, spaying and neutering was associated with worse behavior, although those effects were often specific to certain breeds and depended on the age at which the dog was altered. Benefits were a lower energy level and less urine marking.

For most dogs, however, the risks of spay and neuter surgery don't outweigh the benefits, which include a greatly reduced rate of mammary cancer and no chance of uterine infections later in life, prevention of unwanted litters, no

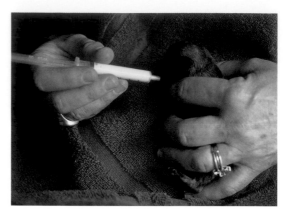

Newborn pups need to eat almost constantly to gain an adequate amount of weight to survive. If a pup isn't receiving enough milk from his mother, he may need supplements.

messy twice-yearly estrus cycles in females, and less likelihood of a pet being relinquished to an animal shelter. Spayed and neutered dogs also have longer life spans. Consult your veterinarian about the appropriate age for your dog to be spayed or neutered, based on such factors as age, size, the level of risk for certain diseases, your lifestyle, and your plans for the dog, such as competing in certain sports.

Newborns

Puppies are born with their eyes and ears shut tightly against the world. They spend all their time eating and sleeping. They nurse about every one to two hours during their first five or six days of life and double their birth weight within a couple weeks. The colostral milk they receive from their mother during their first two or three days of life provides them with passive immunity that protects them from disease until they receive their first immunizations.

It's important that newborns gain weight; if their mother can't provide them with sufficient calories, they will need to be bottle fed. Your veterinarian can help you with this. A pup can also fail to thrive as a result of infection or disease. If a puppy is not actively nursing and/or gaining weight, consult your veterinarian.

Puppies begin to open their eyes and explore their environment by the time they are about two weeks old. They can begin to eat gruel, along with mama's milk, by about three weeks of age and can be completely weaned by seven or eight weeks. Most puppies continue to eat four or more times a day until they are eight or nine weeks old, when they can be switched to three regular meals.

Although pups should be handled as little as possible during the first two weeks of life, socialization with humans must begin shortly thereafter. Three-week-old pups can be held and cuddled and should be introduced to as many people as possible.

Geriatrics

As dogs age, their veterinary and nutritional needs change, and they benefit from specialized care, health testing, and dietary changes. With good care, dogs can live from 8 to 18 years. Large dogs usually have the shortest life span, small dogs the longest. Some of the factors that can increase the length of a dog's life include a good diet, regular exercise, neutering or spaying, good grooming (even dogs feel good when they look good), and regular veterinary care. There are many ways you can keep your dog in good condition as he ages.

Seven years marks the age at which dogs are considered to be senior citizens, even if they still look and act young. This is a good time to schedule a baseline geriatric exam to screen for stiffness, heart murmurs, bad breath, skin lesions, and other typical signs of aging. Blood work to evaluate liver, kidney, and bone marrow function is important as well. Many problems of old age can be easily treated if they're caught early.

Signs of age include a graying muzzle, stiff joints, dental problems (which can be indi-

According to the American Veterinary Medical Association, dogs are generally considered senior citizens by the age of seven. Size, breed, and overall health of the dog can affect this determination, however. Nearly 40 percent of dogs in the United States have reached senior status.

cated by bad breath or a picky appetite), a thinning coat, nuclear sclerosis (a bluish haze in the lens that doesn't interfere with vision), hearing loss, a gain or loss in weight, excessive thirst, and less tolerance for temperature extremes. Report any of these signs to the veterinarian at your dog's annual exam so he or she can keep tabs on your dog's condition. Even small changes in appearance or behavior can be important.

Diseases and Conditions

Even with the best care, the infirmities of age are unavoidable. Among the age-related problems that can affect dogs are cancer, cognitive dysfunction syndrome, hearing or vision loss, arthritis, congestive heart failure, dental disease, and kidney failure. We will discuss some of these problems here.

Cancer

The risk of cancer increases with age. Because dogs are now living longer than ever before, cancer is one of the most common problems of older animals. A diagnosis of cancer used to be considered a death sentence, but these days if it's caught early, cancer is one of the most treatable chronic diseases that dogs face. Any time you notice a lump or bump on your dog, don't wait to see whether it changes or disappears; take your dog in for a veterinary exam. Such growths are usually harmless, but they should always be checked out. Be concerned if the tumor increases in size or changes color or texture.

Senior dogs face a number of physical changes and often have age-related health conditions, such as kidney failure, hearing loss, and dementia.

Cognitive Dysfunction Syndrome

Cognitive dysfunction syndrome (CDS) is caused by the degeneration of the dog's brain and nervous system. It's the diagnosis for any age-related mental decline that can't be attributed to an illness. It is roughly comparable to Alzheimer's disease suffered by people. Signs of CDS are disorientation or confusion such as aimless wandering or staring into space; fewer or less animated interactions with family members; changes in sleep and activity habits such as sleeping more than usual during the day or pacing the house and howling in the middle of the night; and forgetting their house-training. If your dog shows signs of CDS, talk to your veterinarian about prescribing medication that can help. An ongoing study at the University of California, Berkeley, shows that 62 percent of dogs between ages 11 and 16 demonstrate one or more signs of the syndrome; the percentage goes up as dogs get older.

Congestive Heart Failure

Another disease of old dogs is congestive heart failure. If your dog is coughing, has trouble breathing, is restless at night, or tires easily even after mild exercise, take him to the veterinarian. Like so many diseases of old age, congestive heart failure has no cure, but it can be managed for a time with diet, medication, and rest. Congestive heart failure is worsened by obesity, so an appropriate diet and weight loss plan if needed can also help.

Hearing Loss

Dogs are often accused of having selective hearing, but they aren't always ignoring you when they don't respond to your commands. As they get older, their ability to hear really does diminish. To determine if your dog's sense of hearing has declined, walk up behind him and clap your hands. If he does not respond, he may have hearing loss.

Just as people may develop memory problems as they age, so do dogs. You can help keep your dog's mind alert by offering him puzzles, such as Kong toys or Buster Cubes filled with food, and by playing games such as hide-and-seek with treats. Memory-improving medication may also be of benefit, so talk to your veterinarian.

Deafness can result from a history of ear infections or simply from degeneration of the sound receptors in the ear. Take your dog in for a veterinary exam to make sure the problem isn't related to an ear infection or neurological disease.

Deaf dogs usually get along without any problems, adjusting to their condition by making better use of their other senses. You can communicate with a deaf dog by using hand signals instead of verbal commands. When you approach the dog, be sure he sees you or feels the vibrations from your footsteps so he isn't startled.

Eye Problems

One of the most obvious signs of aging in dogs is nuclear sclerosis, a condition in which the nucleus, or center, of the lens changes density, causing the eye to become a hazy gray color. Nuclear sclerosis eventually occurs in all old dogs, but it doesn't noticeably affect their vision.

Cataracts, a clouding that obstructs light within the lens of the eye, are also associated with old age. Every case is different, but sometimes cataracts can be removed surgically by a veterinary ophthalmologist. If that's not possible

or cost effective, be aware that most dogs learn to adapt to sightlessness without much problem, especially if they're in a familiar environment. Rearranging the furniture might cause a slight problem, but dogs are masters at using their sense of smell to navigate. You can help your dog learn a new arrangement by guiding him around the room. Another tip is to mark the furniture at the dog's nose level with a fragrance so he can use the smell as a map. Some visually impaired dogs may be fearful of going down stairs so it may be necessary to keep them on the ground floor or to carry them downstairs.

Kidney Failure

As dogs age, their kidneys become less able to remove waste from blood. Kidney failure is the loss of 65 percent or more of functional tissue in both kidneys. The early signs of kidney failure are subtle, so regular testing can help the veterinarian keep tabs on a dog's condition, and treatment can start before the problem gets serious. In the latter stages of the disease, dogs may drink and urinate much more than usual. They may begin to have accidents in the house or be unable to hold their urine through the night. Chronic kidney failure can be managed with a special diet that can help slow the progression of the disease.

Kidney disease is one condition in which early detection can mean years rather than months of additional life for a dog. In the past, kidney dysfunction didn't show up in blood tests until 75 percent of the kidney's function was destroyed. Now a new test called the E.R.D.-HealthScreen Canine Urine Test catches kidney dysfunction earlier than the blood test by detecting microscopic levels of albumin in the urine. When albumin, a protein, shows up, it's a clear indication of damage to the kidneys' filtration units. The test allows veterinarians to change a dog's diet earlier than in the past, which can have a substantial effect on the dog's longevity.

Keeping Your Older Dog Comfortable

There are many ways to keep a dog comfortable in old age. Cushion achy bones by providing a cozy bed in a warm spot. The bladder is a little weaker in old age, so take your dog out to eliminate more often. If you aren't home during the day, put down papers for him to eliminate on, or leave him in a room where the floor can be easily cleaned. Tartar-encrusted teeth can be painful, and dogs whose mouths hurt won't want to eat, so provide good dental care, including annual cleanings. Offer your dog opportunities to enjoy the outdoors. Even if an old dog can't walk as far as he used to, the exercise and stimulation of a short walk is still good for him.

CHAPTER 25

Chronic Diseases and Conditions

Chronic diseases persist over a long period. They have no cure, but they can be treated with medication. Some of the most common chronic diseases in dogs are diabetes, epilepsy, hypothyroidism, and cancer. Pain also can be a chronic condition.

Diabetes Mellitus

Diabetes is a condition that occurs when the pancreas doesn't produce enough insulin. Insulin is what allows glucose to enter into cells, and glucose is used to produce energy for the body. When cells can't take in glucose, it remains in the blood, causing hyperglycemia, better known as high blood sugar. The sugar in the blood spills over into the urine, causing the dog to urinate frequently and in large volume. This frequent urination leads to dehydration, which the dog tries to compensate for by drinking large amounts of water, causing more urination. It's a vicious cycle. Compounding the problem is the fact that the dog doesn't metabolize enough sugar, so he develops a ravenous appetite. If the condition continues untreated, appetite decreases and the dog becomes malnourished and loses weight. Most pet owners first notice this dangerous cycle when their dog's house-training manners begin to regress.

Evidence now suggests that canine diabetes may be an immune-mediated phenomenon, just as it is in humans with Type 1 diabetes. It may also have a genetic component, researchers are finding. Compounding factors that can accelerate its development include obesity.

Diabetes can't be cured, but it can be managed with daily insulin injections and good dietary control. The amount of insulin needed varies with each dog and must be established through a series of blood sugar tests designed to see when the levels of glucose in the blood reach highs and lows. Insulin injections are easily given at home. Your veterinarian can demonstrate how to give the subcutaneous (beneath the skin) injection.

One breakthrough has been the ability of owners to check a pet's blood glucose level at home using a blood glucose meter. That makes it a lot easier to ensure that a dog is receiving the right amount of insulin without subjecting him to a stressful overnight stay at the veterinary clinic. And many experienced owners of diabetic dogs can tell if the insulin level needs adjusting just by how their dog looks and acts.

Diet can help manage the disease in dogs so they may need less insulin, but there is no diet or supplement that will reverse diabetes in dogs. It's important for dogs with diabetes to eat a diet with moderate amounts of carbohydrates and increased levels of fiber. They also need to eat specific amounts at specific times to help minimize fluctuations in blood sugar levels. It's important to keep the amount of food constant to ensure that the dog doesn't get too much or too little insulin. Too much insulin leads to hypoglycemia, or low blood sugar.

Dogs with hypoglycemia may appear confused, tired, or shaky. Sometimes they collapse or have seizures. To treat hypoglycemia, give your dog corn syrup or honey. If there's no improvement within half an hour, take the dog to the veterinarian. If the dog is unconscious, rub the syrup or honey on the gums so it will be absorbed through the tissues, and take the dog to the veterinarian for further treatment.

Epilepsy

Epilepsy is a brain disorder marked by bursts of abnormal electrical activity in the brain, which usually results in recurrent seizures. Seizures may last for only a few seconds or a few minutes. In rare cases, they can last for an hour or more. A dog having a seizure may jerk or become rigid, appear anxious or hysterical, salivate, lose control of his bowels or bladder, or lose consciousness. Seizures are not life-threatening except when they recur rapidly and frequently or continue without stopping. It's a good idea to keep a log of seizures, noting frequency, length of seizure, and the dog's behavior during the seizure. This can help your veterinarian with diagnosis. Do not put your hands in your dog's mouth while he is having a seizure. Unlike human seizure victims, dogs do not swallow their tongues.

Epilepsy is one of the most common neurological diseases in dogs. While it can be acquired through brain injuries or infectious diseases such as distemper, it is also hereditary. Inherited epilepsy is referred to as idiopathic, meaning the cause is unknown. Mild forms of epilepsy can be treated with medication to control the seizures. Dogs who have seizures that last for more than five minutes or occur one after the other within a short period of time don't have a good prognosis. There's no surgery or other medical treatment that can help.

Dogs prone to idiopathic epilepsy include Beagles, Belgian Sheepdogs, Belgian Tervuren, Cocker Spaniels, German Shepherd Dogs, Golden Retrievers, Irish Setters, Keeshonden, Labrador Retrievers, Poodles, Saint Bernards, and Vizslas. There is no screening test for epilepsy, and it often doesn't appear until a dog is older, which means that the dog may have already been bred and has passed on the disease to his offspring. The good news is that the

Some chronic conditions can be genetic, appearing in family lines or being prevalent in certain breeds.

incidence of epilepsy can be reduced through selective breeding.

Hypothyroidism

Hypothyroidism is a common hormonal disorder in many middle-aged dogs. Golden Retrievers, Irish Setters, and Cocker Spaniels are the dogs known to have a genetic predisposition for the disease.

The thyroid gland secretes two hormones that regulate the metabolism of most cells in the body. When thyroid hormone production slows or stops because the thyroid gland becomes inflamed, atrophies, or is destroyed by cancer, the result is a deficiency that causes such signs as mental dullness, lack of energy, unwillingness to exercise, and weight gain. Poor skin condition—hair loss; a dull, dry coat; scaliness—is another sign.

The disease is diagnosed through physical examination, medical history, and blood tests for thyroid hormone concentrations. A daily dose of synthetic thyroid hormone given for the rest of the dog's life usually stabilizes the dog.

Cancer

Cancer is another type of chronic disease that can occur in dogs. It comes in many forms and can attack many areas of the body, but in general cancer can be described as the uncontrolled growth of cells on or inside the body. Normal cells die and are replaced over and over again, but mutant cells reproduce at a high rate and form masses (tumors) that crowd out normal cells. If left to grow unchecked, the cancer takes over the organ, spreads throughout the body, and eventually kills the dog. Cancer is not a curable disease, but patients can be in remission without recurrence of the disease for long periods of time, even throughout their lives. Treatments for cancer in dogs include surgery, chemotherapy, and radiation.

Signs of Cancer

- Unusual swellings that continue to grow, especially in the lymph nodes
- Sores that don't heal
- Bleeding or other discharge from the mouth, nose, urinary tract, vagina, or rectum
- Bad odor
- Difficulty eating or swallowing
- Difficulty breathing
- Difficulty urinating or defecating
- Lack of energy
- Loss of appetite
- Unexplained weight loss
- Persistent lameness or stiffness
- Lumps in the breast area
- Abnormality or difference in size of testicles

Cancer is common in dogs, especially as they age. It's estimated that almost half of the dogs over 10 years old will die of cancer. Common types of cancer seen in dogs are skin tumors, including breast cancer, testicular cancer, and melanoma; mouth or nasal cancer; cancers of the lymph nodes and other blood-forming organs; bone cancer; and hemangiosarcomas.

Skin Tumors/Skin Cancer

Skin tumors in dogs can be benign (harmless) or malignant (harmful). Small tumors can be removed entirely for study by a pathologist. Larger tumors require biopsies, meaning a tissue sample is removed by the veterinarian for examination.

A melanoma is a tumor of the skin cells that produces melanin (pigment). It appears as brown or black nodules on darkly pigmented areas of the skin and is especially common on the eyelids. It can also occur on the lips, in the mouth, on the body or legs, and in the nail bed. Skin melanomas are usually benign, but those in the mouth are highly malignant. Melanomas can be removed surgically, but they often recur. Boston Terriers, Boxers, Cocker Spaniels, and Scottish Terriers are especially prone to melanomas. A vaccine against melanoma has been developed and is showing great promise in treating this disease.

Mammary Cancer

The most common tumors seen in dogs are those of the mammary (breast) glands. They usually affect older female dogs. The main sign of a mammary tumor is a painless lump, usually in the area closest to the groin. Frequently these lumps are benign, but they should always be checked by a veterinarian, who will perform a biopsy to determine whether the mass is cancerous. Once a dog reaches six years of age, examine her for mammary lumps every month. It's also a good idea to check younger females regularly.

Whether benign or malignant, it's best if mammary tumors are removed surgically. The prognosis often depends on the size of the tumor. Dogs with very small tumors usually recover well, but dogs with large, aggressive tumors have a less favorable prognosis. The risk of mammary cancer can be greatly reduced by spaying a female before her first heat cycle.

Testicular Tumors

Testicular tumors are common in dogs. Dogs with retained testicles may be especially prone to them. Testicular tumors are removed surgically and can be prevented altogether by having your dog neutered.

Mouth Cancer

Signs of mouth cancer are a mass on the gums, bleeding gums, bad breath, or difficulty eating. Bleeding from the nose, difficulty breathing, or facial swelling may indicate nasal cancer. Early, aggressive treatment is important for these types of cancer, so don't delay a veterinary visit if your dog

shows these signs. Mouth cancers can be benign or malignant. Treatment ranges from radiation to hyperthermy (a type of treatment in which body tissue is exposed to high temperatures to damage and kill cancer cells or to make cancer cells more sensitive to the effects of radiation and certain anticancer drugs) to radical surgery.

Lymphoma

Lymphoma is characterized by enlargement of one or more lymph nodes. Lymph nodes are small specialized structures that help the body filter out foreign material so it can be destroyed by the immune system. They are found throughout the body. This type of cancer is usually treated with chemotherapy, which has a good rate of effectiveness. The prognosis varies depending on such factors as the age of the dog and the extent of the cancer.

A diet has been developed that appears to help improve quality and length of life for some dogs with lymphoma that hasn't yet reached an advanced stage. The diet, which is available commercially from veterinarians, contains moderate amounts of fat and protein and low levels of carbohydrates. Recipes for homemade versions of the diet can be

If you suspect your dog has a medical condition, visit the veterinarian for a full workup.

obtained in consultation with a veterinary nutritionist or oncologist.

Osteosarcoma

Osteosarcoma is the most common bone cancer seen in dogs. It's seen most often in large and giant-breed dogs and usually affects the front or hind legs, although it can also occur in the flat bones of the ribs or in the jaw. Limping for no reason is a possible early sign of bone cancer, which is followed by a swelling of the leg or a bone mass. Osteosarcoma is diagnosed with X-rays and biopsy. It can be treated with surgery and chemotherapy. Dogs can be expected to live for eight months to two years after treatment.

Hemangiosarcomas

Hemangiosarcomas are tumors of blood vessels and associated tissues such as the heart. Diagnosed by echocardiogram, they're usually found on the right atrium of the heart and are highly malignant. No treatment is available, and the prognosis is poor.

Transitional Cell Carcinomas

This malignant tumor makes up only 1 to 2 percent of all the cancers that affect dogs, but it is the most common cancer of the urinary bladder in dogs. The disease can also develop in the kidneys, ureters, prostate, and urethra and can spread to other areas of the body.

The incidence is greatest for certain terrier breeds: Scottish Terriers, West Highland White Terriers, and Wire Fox Terriers. Shetland Sheepdogs and Beagles are also affected at a higher than normal rate. It's suspected that TCC develops from a combination of genetic predisposition and environmental factors, specifically exposure to lawns treated with herbicides or insecticides. Dogs at risk should be kept away from lawns or parks treated with these types of products. Weight and gender also factors. Dogs at highest risk are obese females.

If your dog is at risk for TCC, be sure he eats his vegetables. One case-controlled study showed that the risk of bladder cancer was reduced in dogs who ate vegetables at least three days each week.

The tumor develops when the transitional epithelial cells that line the bladder invade the deeper layers of the bladder wall. Signs of TCC resemble those of urinary tract infections and include blood in the urine, straining to urinate, and frequently recurring urinary tract infections. A tissue biopsy is required for an accurate diagnosis. If TCC is diagnosed, radiographs of the thorax and abdomen can indicate whether the cancer has spread as well as uncover the size and location of the tumor.

Treatment depends on whether the tumor is limited to the bladder and where in the bladder it's located. Options include surgical removal or chemotherapy to either shrink the tumor or prevent it from enlarging. Complete diagnosis and treatment can cost from $1,000 to more than $5,000.

Adenocarcinomas

Adenocarcinomas are malignant tumors that affect organs such as the stomach or intestinal tract. They account for approximately 2 percent of canine cancers. Common signs include a large gastric mass, chronic vomiting, weight loss, and lack of appetite. Some types of adenocarcinomas also cause diarrhea. Commonly, gastric adenocarcinomas, which are the most common tumors of the stomach in dogs, are not diagnosed until they are far advanced; and in the case of malignant tumors, the prognosis is generally poor. On the plus side, dogs with benign gastric tumors have an excellent survival rate.

Risk Factors

While age is the most important risk factor for the development of cancer in dogs, some cancers are hereditary, commonly seen in certain breeds. For instance, skin cancers (malignant melanomas) are common in Boxers and Scottish Terriers, and certain families of Saint Bernards are at increased risk for osteosarcoma. Bernese Mountain Dogs have a high incidence of cancers affecting all body systems. These are just a few of the breeds that are susceptible to different types of cancers.

Diagnosis and Treatment

Most forms of cancer are diagnosed through a biopsy, the removal and examination of a section of tissue. Blood tests, X-rays, and physical signs can also indicate cancer. Once a diagnosis is confirmed, the appropriate treatment can be determined.

Fortunately, the treatment of cancer is an area of veterinary care where great strides have been made, not only in the understanding of the disease but also in the tools used to fight it. For many types of cancer, veterinarians can now use radiation therapy, cryotherapy (the use of liquid nitrogen to destroy tissue), chemotherapy (drugs), or a combination of these techniques. With a technique called polymerase chain reaction (PCR), veterinarians can better evaluate tumors and predict the behaviors of different types of cancers. With PCR, scientists are able to quickly reproduce a particular piece of DNA in a test tube, allowing them to make virtually unlimited copies of a single DNA molecule for study.

Surgery is used to treat many types of cancers. It's fast, effective, safe, and less expensive than other forms of treatment. Skin tumors and tumors in other parts of the body can be removed surgically. For instance, testicular tumors are usually resolved by neutering the dog. In cases of osteosarcoma (bone cancer), amputation of the limb is often required. Surgery may be followed by chemotherapy or radiation therapy to make sure all the cancer cells are eliminated.

Chemotherapy is the use of drugs to kill cancer cells. It's usually used to treat dogs with cancer that's widespread throughout the body. It might be used after amputation due to osteosarcoma or in the case of lymph tumors. Dogs must undergo several courses of treatment and have their condition monitored with blood tests. Although they don't suffer nausea or hair loss, chemotherapy can leave dogs feeling tired or weak for several days.

Radiation therapy involves targeting a tumor with a concentrated beam of radiation. Dogs undergoing this type of therapy usually need a series of 10 or more treatments. Each treatment lasts only a few minutes. Types of cancer that might call for radiation therapy include tumors of the mouth and nasal passages. Another form of radiation therapy is the use of radioisotopes (radioactive elements) to treat thyroid gland tumors. Side effects usually involve the sloughing off of dead tissue.

Lasers are used to remove tumors and to irradiate tumors. Surgeons irradiate tumors by first injecting a drug that's sensitized to the effect of light. After 24 to 48 hours, the tumor is irradiated with light. This activates the drug, which then destroys the tumor tissue. This therapy has been used successfully to treat oral squamous cell carcinomas (mouth tumors) and bladder tumors. It's most effective when tumors are very small. A drawback is that it's not yet widely available.

Natural Treatment

Natural treatments alone cannot be used to treat cancer. Their primary benefit is to improve the dog's quality of life. Homeopathic treatments for dogs with cancer have not been well evaluated scientifically, so there is no evidence that they can help. One alternative therapy that can be helpful for a dog with cancer is a natural homemade diet containing high-quality protein and cancer-fighting vegetables such as broccoli, cabbage, brussels sprouts, cauliflower, bok choy, kale, radishes, tomatoes, red peppers, and carrots.

Researchers at Colorado State University have developed a diet that appears to be supportive for dogs with lymphoma. The diet contains moderate amounts of protein and fat and low levels of carbohydrates. It is available commercially and can be prescribed by a veterinarian if appropriate for the type of cancer a dog has. Homemade versions are available in consultation with a veterinary nutritionist.

Other foods or supplements that may benefit dogs with cancer are fish oils or other omega 3 fatty acids, vitamins C and E, and coenzyme Q10.

Cancer Research

Promising cancer research and discoveries include a way to limit tumor size through reducing the amount of copper available in the body, mapping and characterizing cancer susceptibility genes, and confirming that tumor suppressor genes have an important role in not only canine melanoma but also other forms of cancer.

Tumors grow as new blood vessels develop, a process called angiogenesis, which requires high levels of copper. A new approach to combating this is treating cancer with tetrathiomolybdate (TM), a substance that inhibits angiogenesis. TM binds to copper and carries it out of the body. This treatment has worked in mice, humans, and now dogs.

The mapping and characterization of cancer susceptibility genes is also valuable. Of the 364 known genetic disorders in dogs, 46 percent occur either predominantly or exclusively in a single breed or only a few breeds. The theory, then, is that the quickest way to identify the locations of disease-causing genes is through the analysis of several unrelated breeds in which a similar but not necessarily identical disease expresses itself.

Researchers have confirmed an important role for several tumor suppressor genes in canine melanoma. They have also begun to establish the role of these and other genes in canine lymphoma, osteosarcoma, and hemangiosarcoma. Results from these studies have begun to provide tools that may be useful in predicting prognosis and designing new treatments. Eventually, it's hoped that by understanding the genetics of cancer and the use of genetic agents, researchers will be able to create the opportunity for the dog's immune system to kill its own cancer or even to find linkages that will allow them to prevent cancers altogether.

Pain

Pain management is needed for any condition that interferes with a dog's normal activity, appetite, interaction with others, and ability to have a good day. How pain is managed depends on the type and cause of the pain. Some pain can be cured, while other types of pain can only be managed.

Pain is physical suffering that's associated with disease or injury. Two types of pain can affect dogs: acute pain and chronic pain. Acute pain is a sharp, severe pain that usually appears suddenly. Common causes of acute pain include underlying problems such as fractures, bowel obstructions, stones in the bladder, or gastroenteritis (stomach ache). Pain from minor injuries such as muscle strains can be acute as well. Veterinarians frequently choose to deal with acute pain surgically.

Chronic pain is a pain that lasts over a long period of time. Rather than being cured, chronic pain can only be managed. Chronic pain is usually caused by inflammatory disease, often brought on by arthritis or old injuries or fractures. The most effective treatments are those that relieve inflammation. Although they don't directly eliminate the dog's chronic pain, they can decrease it by treating the inflammation.

Signs of pain include changes in behavior such as eating less, failing to greet owners at the door, flinching or yelping when being groomed, or crying out when picked up or touched. Dogs who develop osteoarthritis in their spine or pelvic joints often don't want to be petted anymore. They may yelp or get grumpy if touched in a sensitive area. These changes are significant and suggest that a visit to the veterinarian is in order.

Veterinarians diagnose pain by palpating the dog's body, examining him by hand to check the condition of the organs and search for painful lumps or bumps. They put pressure on the trigger points along the spine and take the dog's legs through a range of motion, extending and flexing the joints, looking for evidence of discomfort.

Pain Management

Managing pain in dogs has always been a challenge because they can't say where or how much they hurt. Up until 10 or 15 years ago, little was known about how animals experienced pain, and few drugs were available that could help. Of course, dogs have always received anesthesia for surgeries, but beyond that not much was done about recognizing or treating any pain they might be feeling. But because of increased owner concern about pain and anxiety, plus veterinarians' own interest in animals, this situation has begun to change. New anesthesia techniques and medications are available to help dogs feel better and recover more quickly.

With their increased knowledge, veterinarians are beginning to use pain relief in new ways. These include epidurals, constant rate infusion, regional blocks and soaker catheters.

An epidural is an injection into the epidural space of the spine. Epidurals help prevent pain in the abdomen and lower part of the body, so they're especially beneficial for dogs undergoing orthopedic procedures.

A technique called constant rate infusion (CRI) involves an ongoing, constant-flow delivery of pain-relieving drugs into the circulation over a period of time. The CRI drugs target pain receptors in the spinal cord and brain, preventing pain signals from reaching the cortex, the brain's central processing center. Each drug works on different receptors, producing a complementary effect. These very small doses, trickled into the body, block pain but don't block physiologic functions such as breathing and heart activity.

Regional blocks, also known as nerve blocks or local blocks, obstruct the nerves that would otherwise carry pain signals to the brain, making them an important means of preventing pain in dogs having surgery. Examples include the injection of local anesthetic along an incision line prior to surgery and facial blocks during dental procedures.

Soaker catheters deliver local anesthetic to the surgical site to reduce pain after surgery. Placed during surgery along an incision area, the pain-numbing medication usually is delivered through a tiny tube, allowing even distribution of the drug over a wide area. Soaker catheters have been used for canine surgeries ranging from total ear canal ablation to amputations.

Nonsteroidal Anti-Inflammatory Drugs

Avoid giving your dog nonsteroidal anti-inflammatory drugs (NSAIDs) designed for humans

Chronic pain can often be managed with medication, exercise, and alternative therapies such as massage and acupuncture.

such as acetaminophen (Tylenol) or ibuprofen (Advil). Even a small amount can be toxic. Instead, your veterinarian may prescribe a canine NSAID such as carprofen (Rimadyl), Tramadol, or etodolac (EtoGesic) or a combination of an NSAID and nutraceuticals.

While these drugs have helped many dogs remain mobile and pain free, long-term use of canine NSAIDs can have serious side effects, including potential liver damage. Some retrievers are so sensitive to carprofen that they can die suddenly after taking it. Etodolac's potential side effects include gastrointestinal signs, such as vomiting and diarrhea, and renal and liver damage. Dogs at highest risk for side effects are usually old or have a history of liver or kidney disease, inflammatory bowel disease, or other chronic conditions. These potential side effects are something to be concerned about. The veterinarian will probably want to test your dog's blood about every three months to check liver and kidney values. Know the potential side effects of any drug you give your dog, and watch for any sign of them.

Natural Pain Relief

A number of natural treatments are also available for pain that results from injuries or orthopedic problems. These include massage, Tellington TTouch, warmth application, swimming, physical therapy, acupuncture, and nutraceuticals.

Nutraceuticals such as glucosamine and chondroitin sulfate are desirable because they rarely have side effects. They're not a quick fix, though. It can take up to two months to see results. Occasionally, a dog given nutraceuticals may vomit or have diarrhea. If this happens, reduce the dose slightly. Glucosamine can cause a dog to drink more water than usual and sometimes prolongs bleeding time, which means blood doesn't clot as well. These effects are unusual.

CHAPTER 26

Diagnostic Tests and Techniques

Besides hands-on examination and looking at a dog's medical history, veterinarians use laboratory tests, diagnostic imaging, and other techniques as some of the many ways of diagnosing a dog who is sick or in pain. In recent years, diagnostic tests have become increasingly advanced, with many veterinary clinics using the same state-of-the-art equipment as found in laboratories and hospitals for humans.

Advances in Diagnostics and Treatments

When Rex, a yellow Labrador Retriever belonging to Tour de France winner Lance Armstrong, underwent heart valve replacement surgery in 2005, he was at the forefront of veterinary medical breakthroughs, which have accelerated rapidly in recent years. In addition to the option of open-heart surgery, which once was considered impossible in dogs, pet owners now have access to advanced treatments for cancer, improved surgical techniques for orthopedic conditions such as anterior cruciate ligament (ACL) tears, nutritional management of osteoarthritis, and better options for anesthesia and pain relief, to name just a few.

By cracking open the textbooks of life through the sequencing of the canine genome, researchers have opened up new approaches to pet health and disease. They've begun to identify the genes responsible for certain inherited diseases and to create genetic tests to identify affected animals. These breakthroughs mean new hope for people whose dogs suffer from such diseases, as well as for breeders, who can use new techniques to screen for disease and prevent passing it on.

Some diseases are genetically complex, linked to more than one gene. In the past, that's been a difficult issue for breeders and researchers, especially if diseases don't occur until later in life. By the time the disease shows up, the animal may have offspring that also carry the genes for the disease. New genetic tests to identify carriers are helping breeders deal with this problem. And being able to evaluate the genetic contributions to diseases such as cancer is leading to advances as well. Veterinary cancer researchers are actively working to target certain cancers, in particular melanoma, with gene therapy. Their goal is to manipulate the genes of mutated cells to help the body's immune system fight the cancer.

Laboratory Tests

Veterinarians use lab tests to help them make diagnoses, especially when the problem isn't obvious from the dog's medical history and physical exam; to detect diseases; and to assess

Advances in diagnostics have allowed veterinarians to pinpoint and treat many conditions that were once a mystery.

the dog's overall health such as before anesthesia is administered. Lab tests are also recommended on a regular basis when animals start to age. When lab tests appear abnormal or don't seem to fit with other findings, repeating the test may be appropriate. Sometimes, for instance, drugs in the system or food in the stomach can influence the results of tests. Veterinarians also repeat tests to evaluate trends in the dog's condition.

The development of many specialized tests and techniques has made veterinary medicine more effective than ever before. Advances in diagnostic technology allow laboratories to run many different tests on a single blood sample. Such a series, called a screening test panel, can be done quickly and is more cost effective than ordering separate individual tests.

Types of lab tests include blood tests, chemistry panels, urinalyses, skin scrapings and biopsies as well as fecal exams and screenings for infectious agents such as bacteria, fungi, and viruses. Some lab tests can be performed in the veterinarian's office, while others must be sent out to specialized laboratories for evaluation.

Blood Tests

One of the most common routine screening tests is a complete blood count (CBC), or hemogram. It measures the amount of hemoglobin, the oxygen-carrying substance in red blood cells, and the number of red blood cells (RBCs), white blood cells (WBCs), and platelets that are circulating in the bloodstream. It gives the veterinarian a good picture of what's going on in a dog's body. For instance, a decrease in red blood cells indicates anemia, while an increase may be due to concentration of the blood caused by dehydration. Low numbers of neutrophils—a type of white blood cell that helps dogs fight infection—can indicate bone marrow disease or

A veterinarian may do his own diagnostics at his clinic or may send samples out to specialized laboratories for testing and evaluation.

certain viral diseases. High levels of neutrophils are common in dogs with an inflammation or infection.

Platelets are cells that help the blood clot. They're produced in the bone marrow and must be constantly replaced because they live for only a few weeks. A low platelet count can mean that the bone marrow is damaged or that the dog is suffering from a condition that's causing the platelets to die at a more rapid rate than usual. External signs of a low platelet count are bruising and blood in the urine or stool.

The chemistry panel is a blood test that measures the levels of certain proteins, enzymes, minerals, and other substances useful in evaluating organ function. Among the dozen or more substances measured are albumin, alkaline phosphatase, alanine aminotransferase, bile acids, and bilirubin, which indicate

A 2007 Gallup poll showed that 71 percent of Americans rate veterinarians high or very high with regard to honesty and ethical standards. Veterinarians placed below nurses and pharmacists but above physicians and dentists.

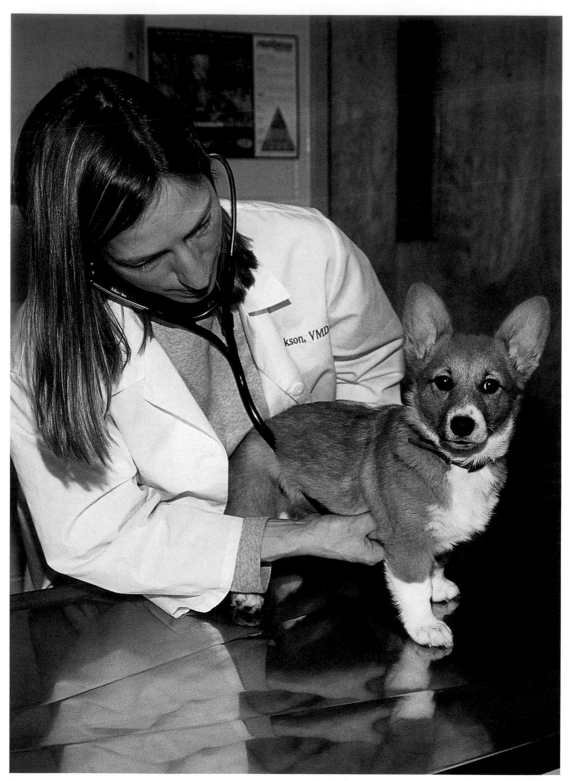

Regular veterinary exams starting in puppyhood will keep your veterinarian abreast of your dog's health and will enable her to catch any abnormalities early on.

liver function; amylase and lipase, which indicate pancreatic function; blood urea nitrogen (BUN) and creatinine, which indicate kidney function; calcium; phosphorus; cholesterol; glucose; and electrolytes such as sodium, potassium, and chloride.

An example of advances in diagnostic blood work is a test for early detection of heart disease and congestive heart failure in dogs. It measures levels of NT proBNP, molecules called natriuretic peptides that are secreted by the heart as a result of heart disease and can help identify heart disease or failure at an early stage, before outward signs are noticeable. When this type of test is available and accurate, it benefits dogs and people by making diagnosis less stressful and less costly.

Urinalysis

The blood isn't the only bodily substance that can tell a story about a dog's health. The state of the urine is crucial in evaluating the urinary system and kidney function. Urinalysis in conjunction with the BUN and creatinine levels help provide a complete evaluation of what's going on with the kidneys. In addition, urinalysis can indicate infection relative to the urinary tract and occasionally give clues to other diseases as well.

A urinalysis is usually called for when a dog shows such symptoms as increased thirst, increased frequency or volume of urination, reluctance or straining to urinate, or urine that has an unusual smell or color. The test can indicate the presence of sugar, protein, or blood in the urine, as well as its specific gravity—a measure of the level of concentration or dilution. Urine sediment—separated by a centrifuge—indicates whether the urine contains bacteria, white blood cells, or other evidence that the urinary tract is infected.

Most people catch a urine sample by holding a container beneath their dog when he urinates. This method works well for some tests and with some dogs. Sometimes, however, your veterinarian may need a clean sample that's uncontaminated by any external bacteria or other debris. And some dogs are shy and prefer to do their business without anyone nearby. In either of these situations, urine can be obtained by passing a catheter into the bladder or removing it by means of a small needle placed through the body into the bladder. These are simple procedures that can be performed without sedation in most cases. If your dog needs to undergo one of these procedures, make sure it's been a while since he has urinated so his bladder is full when you take him in to be tested.

Cytology and Histopathology

Cytology is another type of lab test. A cytological examination is the microscopic study of fresh cells obtained by aspiration, surgical biopsy, or scraping. An aspiration biopsy is when fluid or tissue is drawn out with a fine-gauge needle, whereas all or part of a tumor is removed with surgical biopsy. Biopsies are used to confirm whether a lump or bump is cancerous. They are also used to identify bacterial abscesses or benign cysts. Use of a local anesthetic makes the biopsy a painless procedure. The study of skin scrapings can identify the presence of tiny external parasites such as mites.

Other types of cytological exams include the study of bone marrow samples and analysis of fluids extracted either from the spinal canal or skull cavity (cerebrospinal fluid) or from the joint spaces (synovial fluid). Test results may reveal if there's too much fluid, abnormal consistency or color, or changes in certain chemical components of the fluid such as protein or glucose.

Histopathology is the study of thin sections of tissues or organs. Once placed on a slide, the sample is dyed or stained to enhance the detail. The slide is placed under a microscope, and the pathologist can get information about how the cells are organized within the tissue as well as their relationship to each other. This allows the pathologist to see changes or characteristics in a cell, including the degree or pattern of an infection or tumor or the disease process in the organ.

Molecular Diagnostics

With the breaking of the code for the canine genome, tests for many hereditary disorders have been developed using DNA-based polymerase chain reaction (PCR) techniques. They can be used to find, among other things, genetic markers for disease and to identify dogs that are carriers of a particular disease, even if they don't have it themselves. Molecular diagnostics can even be used for early, quick, and sensitive detection of DNA of cells shed by heartworms in dogs, enabling treatment to begin long before the worms cause serious problems. They also offer an improved method for detecting the presence of bacterial pathogens such as *E. coli* and *Salmonella*.

Other Tests

Microscopes are also used to examine fecal samples for the presence of intestinal parasites such as roundworms, tapeworms, and hookworms, which are generally invisible to the naked eye (tapeworm segments can be seen in fresh feces). This type of exam is called a fecal flotation. To gather a sample, simply place a plastic bag over your hand, scoop up the stool, and place it in a disposable plastic container for transport to the veterinary clinic. If you can't get there right away, refrigerate the sample until you leave.

Other types of microscopic exams include the study of blood, other bodily fluids, and tissue samples to identify various bacteria, fungi, viruses, and protozoa. The samples are placed in sterile containers and then stained or cultured so the organisms can be classified. In the case of a stubborn infection, the organisms can be tested further for their responses to various antibiotics. This allows the veterinarian to choose the most effective treatment.

Viruses are too tiny to be seen with an ordinary microscope, and certain protozoa and fungi are difficult to find as well. That's where serology comes in. This type of testing makes use of serum antibodies that are known to bind only to a particular virus or other disease agent. In some tests, enzymes or dyes bring the culprit to light, changing color when antibody binding occurs. This is called an antigen-antibody reaction. A serological test detects a specific disease agent or indicates high levels of antibodies, meaning that an immune response has occurred. Serological tests include those for parvovirus and heartworm disease.

The development of so many specialized tests and techniques has made veterinary medicine more effective than ever before. A lab test can speed diagnosis, saving precious time. The next time your dog needs a lab test, you'll be much better equipped to understand the purpose behind each one and how the results help determine the diagnosis.

Technology in Diagnostics

Other diagnostic techniques include various forms of imaging technology such as X-rays and ultrasounds. Imaging technology gives veterinarians a glimpse of what's inside a dog's body. They can see bone breaks, moving images of internal organs, and electrical impulses generated by the heart.

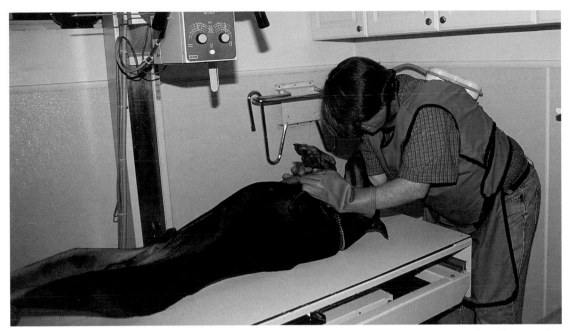

Many of the radiographic and other advanced diagnostic techniques available to humans are also available for evaluating the health of our dogs.

X-rays, also known as radiographs, produce black-and-white photographs that detail such anatomical changes as decreased organ size, bone abnormalities such as hip dysplasia, and masses such as tumors. Other types of radiological studies are angiography and myelography, which involve the injection of dyes into the dog's blood vessels or into the spinal canal.

Advances in diagnostic imaging include computerized axial tomography, or CAT scan; magnetic resonance imaging (MRI); and ultrasonography, or ultrasound. While these techniques may seem more at home in a human hospital, they're widely available now for pets at veterinary colleges and specialized animal hospitals. The advantage of these technologies is the great detail they offer, allowing improved understanding of a dog's condition as well as better accuracy for biopsies.

Veterinarians can also use endoscopy to see inside a dog's body. An endoscope is a flexible instrument that uses specialized light-ing and magnification techniques, permitting the veterinarian to examine such areas as the nasal cavity and gastrointestinal tract without the need for invasive surgery. Endoscopy is frequently used to obtain samples for biopsy, culture, or cytology.

Other noninvasive procedures are electrocardiograms (ECGs), electroencephalograms (EEGs), and electromyography (EMG). The ECG records the electrical impulses generated by the heart and is useful for studying heartbeat irregularities and monitoring dogs under anesthesia. EEGs and EMGs are used to evaluate electrical activity in the brain, nerves, and muscles, and they play a role in the diagnosis of neuromuscular disease. Veterinary ophthalmologists use electroretinography (ERG) to examine the dog's retina for possible abnormalities.

Many of these techniques can be expensive and aren't always widely available, but without them veterinary medicine wouldn't be where it is today.

Daily Care

To maintain good health, dogs need more than just regular veterinary care. They also need to be groomed and provided with adequate nutrition. Grooming keeps the skin and coat healthy, allows you to monitor your dog's physical condition, and reduces the occurrence of external parasites. Good nutrition keeps the body in motion, reduces the risk of disease, and maintains a dog's vital organs.

Whether you use professional groomers, feed an organic or raw food diet, or maintain healthy daily grooming and nutritional regimens, you're contributing to your dog's health and well-being.

CHAPTER 27

Grooming

Grooming, like regular health care and nutrition, is an essential part of caring for your dog. From a pedigreed Poodle to a lovable pound pup, all dogs require some level of grooming. Brushing and bathing your dog keeps his skin and coat healthy and makes him more pleasant to live with and to love. Daily teeth brushing and regular nail clipping prevent future health concerns such as periodontal disease and foot problems. For some dogs, professional grooming is almost a requirement; for others, a monthly bath and a weekly brushing is sufficient.

History of Dog Grooming

When humans first invited dogs to sit with them by a campfire over 10,000 years ago, dog grooming was probably not on their minds. In fact, evidence of dog grooming does not emerge until many thousands of years later, in Roman times. Patrician families in ancient Rome dressed their lapdogs in jewelry, a trend we still see today in rhinestone-bedecked collars and fancy hair ribbons. The high status of these dogs was indicated by the Roman practice of naming them after friends and family members. The most common pet dogs of the time were most likely a bichon-type white dog and another small breed of dog that was the forerunner of the modern Italian Greyhound.

Canine images carved on monuments and tombs during the reign of Emperor Augustus (27 B.C.E.–A.D. 14) feature Poodle-like dogs bearing the earliest examples of what is now called the lion clip. Left full on the chest and head but shaved from the rib cage to the tail, including the legs, these dogs were groomed to resemble the king of beasts.

Greek and Roman coins of the era bear similar depictions. It was European aristocracy, however, that truly brought dog grooming to popular culture some 1,500 years later.

From the fifteenth through the seventeenth centuries, dogs resembling today's spaniels, Bichons Frisés, Malteses, and Poodles appear in paintings and tapestries depicting European royalty and nobility as regularly as hounds of the hunt. German woodcuts portray a poodle ancestor, a curly-coated water dog, again trimmed to resemble a lion right down to the tuft at the end of the tail. This trim, however, was more for utility than style: a dog's legs and hindquarters were shaved to aid him in swimming while his bouffant front end and padded

Be sure you have all the tools you need to properly groom your dog.

joints kept him warm. Although Poodles today are rarely used for retrieving as they once were, two variations of the lion clip—the English saddle and the Continental—are the only acceptable trims for adult Poodles in the U.S. show ring.

Grooming in Europe

The art and occupation of pet grooming owes its existence to one particular dog: the Poodle. Although today's groomers must know how to execute clips on a vast variety of breeds and mixes, it was the Poodle's predecessor, an ancient water dog, which first had its coat trimmed for beauty and utility.

When discussing the art of dog grooming, all roads lead to the Poodle.

Later on, it was the beloved Poodles of French royalty that brought this highly developed skill into vogue and made it part of popular culture.

In the royal court of France's Louis XVI (1774–1792), the Toy Poodle was the official dog. Its elaborate styling became an art form and fashion statement. Using shears and hand-operated clippers, entrepreneurial women—the first professional groomers—carved amazingly intricate patterns into the coats of Poodles, and sometimes other pet dogs.

An 1820 engraving by the artist J. Chalon called *Les Tondeuses de Chien* shows women in voluminous aprons scissoring Poodles who lie across their laps with a long-suffering patience today's groomers would envy. Poodles of this time sported high pompadours like those of the ladies of the court and rakish moustaches and pointed beards like those of noble gentlemen. The dogs were perfumed, festooned with colored powders, and adorned with jeweled collars and anklets, as dandified as their human counterparts.

By the end of the nineteenth century, dogs had become a fashion accessory as well as a status symbol. In London, pampered pets of the wealthy were taken to fashionable salons such as the Dogs' Toilet Club, which had a menu of services that included egg yolk shampoos, colored powders, and the ministrations of a canine chiropodist. A Poodle's wardrobe might have included shirts, cloaks, dressing gowns, evening outfits, and even seaside wear. London's star groomer, R.W. Brown, traced monograms, family crests, and even pastoral themes and battle scenes into Poodle coats.

Grooming in the United States

During the same period in North America, dog conformation and sport hunting were

The phrase *hair of the dog that bit you* is said to have originated in the sixteenth century when the fear of rabies ran high. It was believed that if you plucked a hair from the dog that bit you and rubbed it on the wound, you would be OK. These days, the term commonly refers to having a drink to relieve a hangover.

being celebrated in in such publications as *The Sportsman's Companion* and *The American Turf Register*. The popularity of purebred dogs and purebred dog grooming began to blossom in earnest in 1884 with the formation of the American Kennel Club (AKC). Keeping dogs clean and beautiful enough to share one's lodgings and trimming them according to their breed standard usually fell to the breeders and handlers. Early grooming instructions appeared in *The American Book of the Dog* by G.O. Shields in 1891. Recommendations for grooming were also featured in Ashmont's *Kennel Secrets*, published in 1893.

By the 1930s, doggy barbershops—small, simple operations with a tub, a table, and a few cages— first appeared. The postwar population explosion brought with it a corresponding growth in dog ownership and the demand for dog grooming. No longer simply toys of the rich or four-legged farm hands, dogs were now part of the family.

Every Dog Needs Grooming

The healthiest dog is a groomed dog. Brushing and combing help remove dirt, burrs, tangles and parasites, and distributes oils to keep canine skin healthy. Nails must be clipped to prevent painful breakage or tearing. Overgrown nails can make walking difficult and, in extreme cases, even deform a dog's paws. Because dogs are prone to tartar buildup and gum infection, regular teeth brushing should be part of a grooming routine. Ideally, teeth should be brushed daily and nails trimmed monthly. Depending on his coat, your dog's grooming regimen may be as simple as a weekly brushing or as complex as daily combing, bi-weekly bathing, and monthly haircuts.

There are no downsides to regular grooming—it's all good. You can cuddle with your dog without the worry of offensive odor and excessive shed hair (though even groomed dogs shed), and you reduce dander (shedding skin) that causes allergies in some people. A dog with clean teeth has fresh breath, making him pleasant to be near, and short nails keep him from damaging carpets, furniture and you. Regular grooming keeps your dog feeling and looking great.

Grooming and Health

If you neglect grooming your dog, he can suffer. For example, the fur can mat and tangle so tightly that it needs to be shaved off. After such a matted pelt is removed, your dog may chew himself raw because his skin itches. Often, there are sores, parasites, or a skin condition underneath a dirty coat of matted hair. A dog whose teeth are never brushed or professionally cleaned by a veterinarian is a prime candidate for gum disease, which can contribute to infections of internal organs such as the heart and kidneys. If left untreated, dental problems often progress until the teeth fall out.

A monthly bath will keep your pooch looking and feeling his best.

Grooming is an opportunity to examine your dog from head to tail, to monitor his health and his appearance. You might notice signs of skin problems caused by injury, allergy, parasites, or infection while grooming. As you brush the coat, examine the skin to spot problems such as swelling caused by an insect bite, wound, or vaccination. A bump in the groin could be an umbilical hernia. Breeds such as the Pug, Bulldog, Boxer, and Chinese Shar-Pei can develop bacterial infections if their distinctive wrinkles are not cleaned regularly. Some dogs develop warts or fatty tumors as they age. Dogs are vulnerable to the same cancers as people are; cancer is the most common cause for concern with lumps and bumps. Early detection increases a dog's chance for survival.

Grooming should feel good to your dog, so pain during grooming is a sign that something isn't right. A dog who winces when you touch his muzzle may have dental problems. A dog who constantly shakes his head or paws at his ears may have ear problems, which can also be detected by a musty odor. Redness or

Condition your pup to being handled as soon you bring him home. It will make future grooming much easier.

swelling in the ear canal, tenderness, or discharge could indicate ear mites or an infection. A discharge from the eyes or genital area may also be a sign of infection. If your dog is limping, is acting touchier than usual about having his paw handled, or is licking a foot, examine his footpads for irritating dirt, debris, a sliver of glass, pad puncture, or broken nail. Sand, rock salt, and road tar can also adhere to a dog's pads and irritate his feet.

Fleas, ticks, and mites are some of the parasites that can plague your dog. The first sign of fleas is usually an itchy dog, or you may see flea eggs or feces, small particles that look like salt and pepper. Ticks look similar to spiders, and once they dig into the skin and become engorged with blood, they can swell to the size of a grape. Since ticks can carry disease,

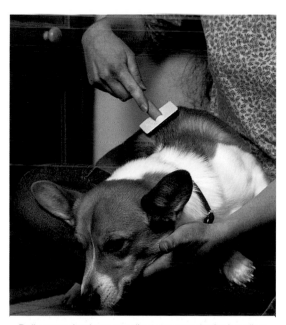

Daily grooming is an excellent opportunity for bonding.

Drool. Slobber. Salivate. Whatever you call it, all dogs do it. Some dogs, Newfoundlands, Saint Bernards, and Basset Hounds, drool more than others do because of anatomical characteristics such as excessive skin around the mouth. But dogs drool for a variety of reasons. They may drool when they are nervous, when excited, or when their salivary glands become stimulated thinking about their next meal. A little drooling is perfectly normal. Wiping your dog's mouth periodically or giving him chew toys that cause him to swallow may help reduce the mess. If your dog's fur gets damp from drool, tie a bandana around his neck with the triangular side covering the dog's chest.

When a dog who doesn't normally drool much starts slobbering excessively, it is time for a trip to the veterinarian. One of the most common causes of abnormal drooling is dental problems. Other causes include nausea, which is why dogs may drool when riding in a car; a foreign object lodged in the mouth; dietary distress; poisoning; and diseases such as rabies.

including Lyme disease and Rocky Mountain spotted fever, you should always wear gloves and use tweezers to remove ticks. Drop the tick into rubbing alcohol to kill it, swab the bite site on your dog with hydrogen peroxide, and then apply antibacterial ointment.

Grooming and the Human-Animal Bond

If you acquire a dog at seven or eight weeks of age, you have a perfect opportunity to accustom him to being groomed. Regular grooming at a young age builds trust and confidence between dog and owner and establishes a

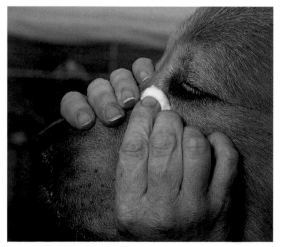

Clean tearstains and face folds to prevent permanent stains and dermatitis.

bond that will continue throughout your dog's life. Immediately after birth, your puppy received a "sponge bath" from his mother, who licked him clean. Now the job of keeping him clean is up to you—but no licking is required. It's important that your puppy becomes accustomed to, and accepting of, your touch.

Handling your puppy is the first step in familiarizing him with grooming. As soon as you bring your puppy home, touch his feet, tail, and ears—even tickle his tummy. These sessions can be performed as you sit on the floor or on a sofa with the puppy in your lap. At first your puppy may not take to this type of pregrooming session. He may resist because he is bored, assertive, afraid, or playful. You don't want to break his spirit, but it is important to assert your position of leadership. You are the top dog. Be sure to correct unacceptable behavior such as nipping and struggling by saying "No" firmly. When the puppy is still and cooperative, praise him.

If you plan to have your dog groomed professionally, his first visit should be between three and four months of age after he's received his vaccinations, or whenever your veterinarian gives the OK. Introducing an adult dog to grooming can be more difficult than introducing a puppy. An adult dog may resist grooming at first. He must learn to trust you and overcome any fears

Removing Ticks

Ticks are always looking for a free ride, especially during warm-weather months. This common parasite, which is actually a type of bloodsucking mite, prefers wooded, grassy, and damp areas but can be found just about anywhere. Always check dogs carefully after they have been outdoors, especially if they've romped through grassy fields, meadows, or woods.

If you find a tick on your dog, comb him with a flea comb or other fine-toothed comb to remove any other ticks that may still be loose. It is helpful to spray dogs with a tick insecticide prior to combing. Remove any embedded, feeding ticks as soon as possible to reduce the risk of disease transmission.

To remove embedded ticks, use tweezers to grab the tick as close to the head as possible, and gently pull it out, head and all. An alcohol swab rubbed around the tick may help loosen its grip. After removal, dab the affected area of the dog's skin with an antibiotic ointment or topical antiseptic. Place the tick in a jar of rubbing alcohol or insecticide to kill it. Don't throw a live tick in the toilet or trash because it may crawl back out. Never try to remove a tick with a match, cigarette lighter, or other lit object. This method does not work and could burn your dog.

Commercial tick removal kits are also available at pet supply stores. They offer specialized tweezers, magnifying glasses, antiseptic, information about Lyme disease, and bags for storage of the tick following removal.

he may have. Keep grooming sessions short and sweet with a lot of positive reinforcement: words ("Good boy!"), gentle petting, and tasty treats (liver flavor is always a favorite). Gradually increase the length of the grooming sessions.

If a puppy or adult dog really dislikes having his ears, face, or feet handled, do not give up. Be patient. Remember that your goal is bonding and acceptance, not irritation and exasperation. Continue handling his feet, for example, and combine the handling with something super positive such as irresistible food or a favorite toy. That way, in time the dog comes to associate the handling with the beloved toy or treat. The dog may never grow fond of having his feet handled, but he may accept it politely.

If you're beginning a grooming regimen on an adult dog, be aware that he may resist initial grooming sessions because he's not used to it. He needs to learn to trust you and overcome any fears he may have. Keep your initial grooming sessions short, and supply a lot of positive reinforcement, verbally and with gentle strokes and tasty treats. Gradually, you can increase the length of your sessions.

If a puppy or adult dog resists being handled on a particular spot such as his ears, face, or feet, focus your attention on the problem area until he becomes accustomed to your touch. Be lavish with your praise, and offer an

Grooming will help your pup stay free of external parasites.

occasional treat for his cooperation as you build that all-important lifelong connection.

Breeds and Grooming

Along with size, energy level, and exercise requirements, consider grooming requirements when choosing a dog. All dogs are appealing, especially when they are puppies, but you need to use your head as well as your heart when choosing the one who's right for you. Your companion may be the quintessential wash-and-go dog (such as a Labrador Retriever), or he may require extensive daily brushing (Maltese) or professional grooming (Poodle). Not all pet owners want to invest a large amount of time in home grooming, and professional grooming can be expensive. Think it over carefully.

Coat Types

Dogs have either a double or a single coat. The outer hair, or guard hair, of a double coat is relatively long and coarse, while the undercoat is softer and downier. Depending on many

To accustom your puppy to nail clipping, start by just clipping the very tip of the nail.

variables, including the breed's geographic origin, the undercoat may be either heavy or sparse. Dogs with a single coat have only guard hair. Coats of any length can be either double or single and come in a variety of textures.

Long coats are at least 3 inches long if allowed to grow. The Afghan Hound, Rough Collie, and Pekingese all have long coats. Medium coats are generally 2 to 3 inches long. The German Shepherd Dog, Golden Retriever, and Australian Shepherd have medium-length coats. Short coats are ½ to 2 inches long. The Labrador Retriever, Beagle, and Welsh Corgi have short coats. There are also smooth coats, which are shorter than a ½ inch. Breeds with smooth coats include the Doberman Pinscher, Boxer, and Greyhound.

Coat texture also varies among breeds. Some coats are silky, with fine, glossy hair; and others are wiry, with hair that is coarse and harsh. The Yorkshire Terrier and Silky Terrier are examples of dogs with silky hair; the Wirehaired Dachshund and Airedale are examples of dogs with wiry coats. A northern coat is a double coat that is thicker and denser than other coats. It can be long or short. Dogs with a northern coat include the Samoyed and the Chinese Shar-Pei. Curly coats fall into natural ringlets. Among the curly-coated breeds are the Poodle and the Bichon Frisé as well as the Komondor with its corded coat. Cording occurs when long hair curls around itself and forms coils. Then there are the hairless breeds. These dogs are almost completely hairless, although most have wisps of hair at the top of the head and sometimes on the feet and tail. The Chinese Crested is one example of a hairless breed.

Every breed has specific grooming requirements, which are based, in part, on the type of coat. Companion dogs are usually groomed for comfort and convenience, but conformation show dogs are groomed to spe-

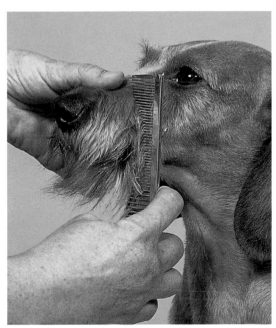
Use a wide-tooth comb to make sure facial hair looks spiffy.

cific guidelines that enhance how closely they conform to a particular breed standard (a breed standard is a written description of the perfect example of the breed set forth in detail by a national breed club). Professional groomers, breeders, and handlers must be aware of these particulars for show dogs, but grooming for the companion or mixed-breed dog is more about comfort than looks.

Home Grooming Fundamentals

Unless you desire the showy look of a precision-scissored Poodle, Bichon, or Portuguese Water Dog, it is not necessary for you to take your dog to a professional groomer. Home grooming is easy once you get the hang of it, and soon your dog will look forward to the attention he receives from you. Before you begin, however, you need some basic skills and the right equipment.

When it comes to grooming, the most important skill you can develop is patience. Of course, learning how to properly brush and bath your dog is essential. But without patience, you will be frustrated with your attempts at grooming and frustrated by your dog's squirming, reluctance, or fear of grooming. Be patient—with yourself and with your dog.

The floor or your lap is fine for initial experiences of getting your dog used to being touched, but it's best that your dog learns to stand on a table so you can reach every area of his body—and save your back in the process. Folding grooming tables can be purchased for approximately $100 from pet supply stores and catalogs. You'll also need a grooming post and a training noose to secure your dog while he's being groomed.

At first, leave the collar and leash on your dog while he is on the table to reinforce your control. If your dog is stressed and squirmy, ask a friend to assist you. Grooming time is not playtime, so don't allow your dog to bite at the brush or dance around the tabletop. Initially, grooming sessions should be brief, about 10 minutes. If your puppy is a bundle of energy, schedule grooming sessions after a walk or playtime so he's not as active. If he misbehaves, firmly say, "No," but praise him softly and quietly when he remains still and calm. End grooming sessions with an especially tasty treat. And *never* leave your dog on the table unattended.

Brushing and Combing

Brushing a dog's coat eliminates mats, burrs, and tangles, and it removes dead hair, distributes coat oils, and stimulates the blood supply to the skin. Severe matting can prevent the skin from doing its primary job of protecting and regulating a dog's body temperature.

Many dog owners mistakenly believe they have been doing a good job of brushing, when in reality they have been brushing only the coat's top layer, leaving a thick matted pelt underneath. Groomers sometimes can get these mats out, but it is time-consuming,

expensive, and an unpleasant experience for the dog. Such a job may take more than one visit. The only humane alternative is to clip off the coat. To avoid putting your dog through such an ordeal, brush and comb him regularly.

It can be confusing when you first venture into the world of grooming tools. Chances are your local pet supply store has an entire aisle devoted to them. Which tools are right for your dog, and how do you use them?

For all dogs except hairless or smooth single-coated breeds and their mixes, a slicker brush should be the first tool in your grooming kit. These come in different sizes and shapes, but all contain hundreds of short wires embedded in a firm rubber backing. The gentle slicker has softer wire bristles, either straight or curved, and works best on puppies and tiny breeds. The larger version is the workhorse of grooming; its curved bristles are made for pulling dead undercoat and packed fur from most breeds.

For a young puppy, you can use a human nail clipper.

Show dogs require special grooming. Some handlers even wrap the hair to ensure it is not damaged.

Grooming Expectations

The basics of grooming, bathing, brushing, ear care, and toenail trimming are about the same for every breed. But along with the basics are specific grooming requirements for breeds and coat types. When choosing a breed for your family, it's always wise to consider grooming requirements. Some coats, while strikingly handsome, are high maintenance and require a lot of effort and cost. Following are a few general categories of coat types with the grooming you might expect for breeds or mixed breeds that best fit within the category.

Wash and Go

Smooth, short (single or double) coats are an owner's best friend because they're so easy to groom. The Labrador Retriever, Beagle, Boxer, and Pug are examples of breeds that fit in this category. Shorthaired breeds can easily be groomed at home or, if desired, by a professional groomer, although it is not necessary. The best tools for short coats are a soft slicker and a grooming mitt. Weekly brushing to remove dead hair (short coats *do* shed) and dirt is sufficient, but more frequent brushing is fine. Although these breeds have short coats, they shed heavily, and brushing two or three times a week will help keep hair under control. A bath once a month will keep a dog with a short coat clean and sweet smelling. Ears should be checked and cleaned once a week and toenails trimmed once a month.

Long and Silky

The grooming requirements for dogs with long and silky coats are not nearly as simple as requirements for dogs with short coats. Long, silky coats, such as those of the Maltese, Silky Terrier, Lhasa Apso, and Afghan Hound, need frequent brushing and combing to remain tangle free; daily or every other day is best. Home grooming is fine for the owner who is motivated and skilled, but many owners of these breeds hire a professional groomer to help with coat upkeep. A metal comb, soft slicker, and pin brush are the best tools for these coats. Daily brushing, along with bathing in mild shampoo followed with conditioner every few weeks, is desirable. Detangle spray is helpful for brush outs. Ears should be checked and cleaned once a week and toenails trimmed once a month.

Long-coated breeds are shown with their coats long and gleaming.

The heavy undercoat of double-coated dogs should be kept groomed with a shedding blade or grooming rake.

Long but Fluffy

Long, fluffy coats, especially those with under-coats, need frequent brushing. Breeds with these coats include the Golden Retriever, Bernese Mountain Dog, Rough Collie, and English Springer Spaniel. Some breeds with long, fluffy coats require professional groom-ing; others can be groomed at home. Brushing several times a week is necessary. A metal comb, slicker, rake, and pin brush are appro-priate tools. Monthly bathing is sufficient. Ears should be checked and cleaned once a week and toenails trimmed once a month.

Terriers

The ideal terrier coat is wiry and coarse. Some terrier coats are short, such as that of the Border Terrier, and some coats are long, such as that of the Schnauzer. Brushing twice a week is sufficient, depending on the length of the coat. Professional grooming is necessary for most terriers unless owners are motivated to learn how to clip and scissor at home. Be aware that trimming with clippers tends to soften the terrier coat, which is why terrier

show enthusiasts "strip" coats with a metal blade instead of using clippers. A metal comb and a soft slicker brush are good tool choices. Trimming and bathing every six to eight weeks is sufficient. Ears should be checked and cleaned once a week and toenails trimmed once a month.

Low Shed

Allergy sufferers love breeds with minimal shedding such as the Poodle, Bichon Frisé, and Portuguese Water Dog. Minimal shed-ding has its cost, though. These coats require professional grooming unless an owner is motivated to learn how to trim at home. Show grooming for the Poodle or Bichon Frisé is a highly complex art form. A metal comb and a soft slicker are tools of choice for pet owners. Trimming and bathing every four to six weeks is necessary. Ears should be checked and cleaned once a week and toenails trimmed once a month.

Corded

The unusual corded coat is found on such breeds as the Puli and the Komondor. A corded coat is not for beginners. Professional

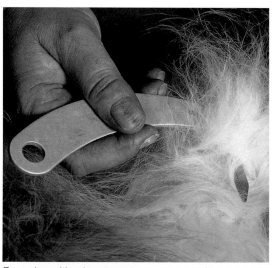

For a dog with a heavy coat, you may need to use a mat splitter to work through tangles.

help from a groomer or breeder is advised. While it might look like a tangled mess, it requires care. The corded coat is never brushed but instead is managed by hand, dampened with water, and cords are separated and twirled. The length of the corded coat is sometimes trimmed to keep it from collecting dust and dirt. Some coats are self-cording, although most are helped along by the process of separating the cords by hand when the adult coat comes in at one year of age. As the coat texture changes from puppy fluff to adult coat, the undercoat is packed into the interior of the outer coat tendril to form a feltlike structure. Bathing the corded coat frequently is not recommended. The corded coat collects food (around the face), urine, feces, eye matter, and burrs, so regular maintenance is essential. Ears should be checked and cleaned once a week and toenails trimmed once a month.

Northern

Northern breeds such as the Siberian Husky, Samoyed, and Shiba Inu have a naturally harsh outer coat with a thick undercoat designed for maximum warmth in cold environments. Home grooming is possible, although many owners opt to hire a professional groomer, especially during shedding season when fur begins to fly. A slicker brush, metal comb, and shedding rake are good tools for these coats. Frequent bathing is not necessary; every three months or so is suffi-

Even hairless dogs need grooming, including bathing, moisturizing, and sun protection.

cient. Ears should be checked and cleaned once a week and toenails trimmed once a month.

Hairless

Breeds with little or no fur include the Chinese Crested and the American Hairless Terrier. Skin care, rather than coat care, is what's necessary for hairless breeds. For those breeds with small tufts of hair, a soft, natural bristle brush is fine. Frequent bathing is needed to prevent acne; a bath once a week or every other week is advised. Follow a bath with an application of hypoallergenic or oil-free moisturizer. Sunscreen is necessary to prevent sunburn if these dogs go outdoors. Consult a veterinarian or the dog's breeder for specific skin care products. Ears should be checked and cleaned once a week and toenails trimmed monthly.

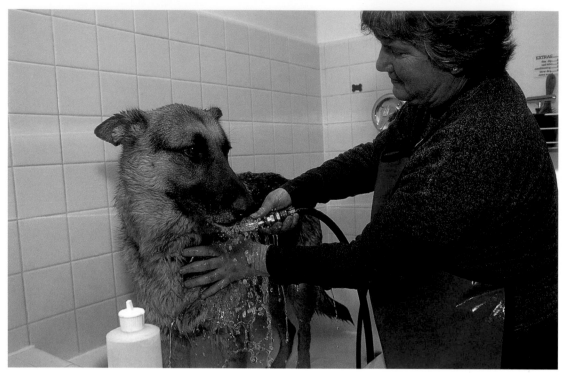

A professional groomer has all the tools to effectively bathe and groom your dog. To find a good groomer, ask the advice of dog-loving friends and professionals.

Bathing

Admittedly, bathing a dog is easier in a grooming salon than it is at home. Salons have tubs that are waist high and often equipped with a walk-in ramp and a collar and safety cables to keep the dog in place. Salons also have a variety of shampoos and conditioners, as well as high-velocity dryers to blow moisture from coats. But if you are well prepared, you can certainly give your dog a good bath at home. The kitchen sink can double as a tub for small dogs and puppies. The bathtub works just fine for larger dogs if you have a hand-held shampoo hose or shower massage attachment. Hosing down a dog in the driveway is never a good alternative. Dogs like an ice-cold shower about as much as we do. However, there are portable grooming tubs on the market with hot and cold plumbing designed for outdoor use.

There are hundreds of dog shampoos from which to choose. To make sure you are using a quality product, look for natural botanicals without harsh chemicals. Human hair products and household cleansers are not suitable alternatives. They do not have the appropriate pH balance for your dog's skin and could cause an allergic reaction. For most dogs, a tearless dog shampoo works well. While people may enjoy fresh and flowery fragrances, some sensitive dogs can tolerate only hypoallergenic, tearless, colorless, and odorless shampoos. For dogs with dry skin, a medicated shampoo soothes and heals. Your veterinarian may also recommend a special product for chronic skin problems. For hard, shiny coats, a protein-enhanced shampoo adds a glossy sheen. Texturizing shampoos are available for hard, wiry coats, and bluing shampoos brighten white coats. Aromatic deodorizing shampoos combat all kinds of smells, including doggy odor, and flea shampoos banish those pesky pests. Ask your groomer or vet to recommend a product that is right for your dog's coat.

Flea and tick products, as well as medicated shampoos, should be left on the dog for 15 minutes to do their job. Monitor your dog closely when using any product that contains chemical or botanical pesticides. If your dog appears lethargic or nauseous, drools or has trouble standing, immediately rinse the product from the coat and take him to your veterinarian. Just like people, dogs can have an allergic reaction to a medicinal product.

Conditioners or cream rinses made especially for dogs help combat static electricity while adding body and brushability to long or fluffy coats. Use a gallon jug to mix the cream rinse with water—finishing rinses are usually diluted at the rate of 1 cup per gallon of water.

Before the bath, brush all knots and tangles from your dog's coat. Knots and tangles that are wet multiply and are harder to untangle and rinse thoroughly. Gather towels, sham-

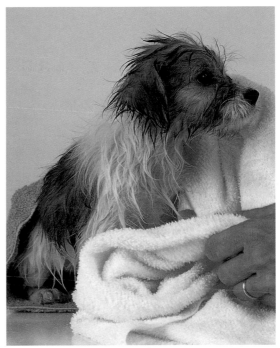

Dry your pooch thoroughly after bathing. You don't want him to catch a chill.

poo, cotton balls for the ears, drops to protect the eyes, and a nonskid rubber mat to help your dog keep his footing in the tub. Carefully put eyedrops (purchased from a veterinarian or pet supply store) in your dog's eyes. The eyedrops provide a coating that protects the eye from being irritated by shampoo. Place a cotton ball in each ear to keep water out.

Gently hose down your dog with warm water, starting with the hindquarters. Never spray directly into his eyes or ears. If your dog has a water-repellant coat, it's important to make sure he is soaked all the way to the skin. Work the shampoo into the coat, lathering the dog all over. Pay particular attention to

Toys and treats can make a bath a more pleasant experience for some dogs.

When grooming an older dog, be especially gentle. Senior dogs may suffer from arthritis in the hips, legs, or back. Have your dog lie down during grooming sessions. If he has a heart condition, keep the blow dryer set no higher than medium. Dogs with heart problems can overheat easily.

Even shorthaired dogs should be combed thoroughly.

frequently soiled areas such as the face, the feet, and the rear end. Lather long coats with the lay of the coat so you won't create tangles as you scrub. Do just the opposite on fluffy dogs, swirling against the grain to make the coat stand up during shampooing. Almost all dogs enjoy being lovingly massaged as they are being washed.

For a clean look, show dog handlers will shave the whiskers on the chins of some breeds.

Begin rinsing at the head, working your way down the body. Be sure to rinse thoroughly. Shampoo left in the coat results in an itchy dog. If you use a conditioner, repeat the process you used for shampooing, then rinse thoroughly. Gently squeeze moisture from the ears and legs of long-coated dogs before toweling. Wrap your dog in a soft towel, rubbing him as dry as you can. On curly breeds, patting dry rather than rubbing prevents matting.

After towel drying your dog, finish off with a quick blow dry. If you don't have a pet dryer (available through pet supply catalogs, pet supply stores, and online sites), you can use your own hand-held hair dryer. Turn on the heat setting to low. Be careful not to direct the airflow too long on one spot, which could cause a burn. Groomers cage- or crate-dry some breeds, using blow dryers mounted on the cage or using floor-standing models. Then they may table-dry a slightly damp dog to finish the process, brushing each section as the coat is blown dry. Shorthaired dogs can be air-dried in a warm, draft-free room. Do not use a blow dryer on curly-coated dogs, as their coats will become frizzy.

Don't let your dog outside to dry. Your squeaky-clean canine could become chilled or decide to take a roll in the dirt, in which case you'll have to start the entire process all over again.

Nail Trimming

It's important for you to keep your dog's nails trimmed. Overgrown nails can ruin a dog's appearance, permanently splay his toes, and even impede his ability to walk. Neglected toenails can curl all the way around to perforate the footpad, a situation that requires veterinary attention. Groomers offer nail trimming services, but you can do it yourself at home. If you have been handling your dog's feet, you have begun the desensitizing process. At first, just nip the tip of each nail on a weekly basis to get the dog used to the procedure. Later, your dog should receive monthly pedicures.

Nail clippers come in several sizes and types. Some resemble scissors, some look like pliers, and one is known as the guillotine style because it cuts with one blade. The pliers-type clipper is arguably the easiest to use and is available in sizes to suit every dog from a Chihuahua to a Saint Bernard. Regular nail clippers become dull over time, and once this happens they need to be replaced. Because short nails are a must in the show ring, many show dog breeders and handlers favor a power nail file that works some-

Some breeders and handlers opt to use a nail clipper that operates like a Dremel tool. Puppies must be accustomed to this tool very early.

thing like an electric sander to file down the nails. An electric grinder takes some getting used to, and not all dogs are comfortable with the process, which is why show dog breeders start using it soon after puppies are whelped.

Nail trimming is easiest with the dog on a grooming table. Face his rear end and use your body to support him while you lift each paw so you are looking down at the footpad, as if you were shoeing a horse. The nail is solid where it emerges from the paw but grows downward into a hollow, shell-like portion near the tip. This is the part that needs to be trimmed.

The tricky part about dog pedicures involves the vein within each nail known as the quick. If nicked, it will hurt and bleed—and your dog may yip because it hurts. Quicking a nail is not a major calamity though, and it happens to every dog now and then, especially those with black nails. On white nails, the pink vein is visible, removing the guesswork. A dab of styptic powder instantly stops the bleeding. This product is available in pet supply stores, grooming salons, and pet supply catalogs. In a pinch, a rub from a soft bar of soap or even a dab of flour is the next best thing. Keep pressure on the nail until the bleeding stops, and don't immerse the paw in water—that will only make it more difficult to stem the bleeding.

If the dog misbehaves while you are trimming his nails—and this is not unusual because many dogs dislike having their nails

Beyond Tomato Juice: Deskunking Your Dog

When it comes to home remedies for removing skunk odor from dogs, professional groomers have seen it all, from the ever-popular tomato juice and its many variations like spaghetti sauce or ketchup to lemon juice, mayonnaise, vinegar, and mouthwash. You name it; groomers have seen an unfortunate dog smeared with it. While the acidic content of some of these cure-alls does help wash away the stench by breaking down the oily skunk spray, none of them really works all that well.

Nowadays there are commercial products available from groomers, pet supply stores, and vets that do a far better job. Some are detergent-based shampoo products, while others are sponge-on enzymatic cleaners that actually digest the odor-causing bacteria. They come in liquid or powder form and are used at the grooming salon prior to a deodorizing bath. Dogs are usually soaked with one of these products for at least 15 minutes before being washed. If your dog was sprayed in his mouth, the smell will cling to the mucous membranes of the gums and tongue. Groomers spray the mouth with doggy breath spray to help alleviate this problem.

If you don't have any commercial deskunking products on hand, don't despair. Try this home remedy developed by chemists to treat the problem:

- 1 quart 3 percent hydrogen peroxide
- 1/4 cup baking soda
- 1 teaspoon liquid dish detergent

First, gently flush out your dog's eyes with plain water. When a dog takes a direct hit in the face, skunk spray stings and burns the eyes. Next, rub the solution into the dog's coat, penetrating all the way to the skin and taking care not to get it in his eyes. Thoroughly rinse the dog with lukewarm tap water, and then discard any leftover solution. (Warning: This product cannot be made up ahead of time, nor should you store any unused portion for future use. Because it produces oxygen, it is combustible and will explode if left in a closed container.) Follow up with a good shampoo to make the dog your welcome housemate once again.

---

clipped—firmly tell him, "No," and don't let go of the paw. If the dog wins this battle, it will only become increasingly difficult to trim the nails. If your dog is frightened and stressed, ask a friend to help hold the dog while you continue to cut his nails. Stay calm and positive while you trim the nails, and be sure to tell him what a good dog he is when he cooperates. Don't forget to clip the dewclaws, small thumblike nails that can be found on the side of the rear and the front feet.

Ear Cleaning

Keep your dog's ears clean by wiping them regularly with a cotton ball or soft tissue moistened with an over-the-counter ear cleanser made for dogs. The goal is to remove excess wax and dirt. Popular home remedies are a mixture of three-quarters vinegar and one-quarter alcohol, or mineral oil straight from the bottle (use sparingly—it's greasy). Ask your veterinarian to recommend an ear cleanser if you are unsure of what to use. Do not use cotton-tipped swabs because it's easy to poke too far into the ear with them, causing injury.

A small amount of honey-colored wax is normal in healthy dogs, but a dark discharge or the presence of yellow or green matter could indicate infection or ear mites, necessitating a trip to the vet. Check for foul odor, redness, or swelling. A dog who is shaking his head, pawing at his ears, or losing his equilibrium may be trying to tell you something is wrong with his ears.

Hair grows in the ear canal of many breeds of dogs. The hair should be trimmed because it can facilitate the growth of bacteria, leading to ear infections. Trimming the ear hair helps keep the ear dry and makes it less likely to become infected. It also allows you to keep the ear clean. How to trim the hair, however, is a source of controversy among groomers and veterinarians. Many experts believe that plucking is the best way to remove excess hair. Others say that plucking the hair creates an opening for bacteria to enter the skin and leads to irritation and itchiness that will cause the dog to scratch at his ear, which can also lead to infections. Before doing anything, speak to your veterinarian about the best method for removing hair from your dog's ears.

If you decide to pluck, use your fingers, tweezers or forceps (hemostats), the tool favored by professionals. Use a dab of ear powder, available from groomers or at pet supply stores. The powder makes it easier to grip the waxy hair before pulling it out. Pluck only a

Use cotton balls and a cleanser to clean canine ears thoroughly. Never use cotton-tipped swabs.

few hairs at a time, never yanking big clumps. Finish by swabbing out the powder with cleaning solution. If you use scissors or clippers, be careful around the cartilage in the ear. The ear is easy to cut if the dog jerks his head.

Dogs with drop ears, such as the Cocker Spaniel and Basset Hound, are especially susceptible to fungal and bacterial infections that can result from yeast or bacteria that thrive in the deep moist recesses of the ear canal. Infected ears may also signal skin allergies, often manifested first inside the ears or on the feet. Becoming well acquainted with the look and smell of your dog's normal healthy ears will help you determine when something is amiss.

To prevent infection in any breed, but especially for those prone to infection, wipe out the ear with cleanser after bathing, swimming, or any time the dog gets wet. Doing so restores the natural pH balance to the ear, lessening the likelihood of infection.

Brushing the Teeth

Dogs rarely get cavities, but they still require regular dental care. Like people, dogs develop gum disease brought on by tartar buildup. A chronic gum infection can spread to other organs and can result in heart or kidney damage.

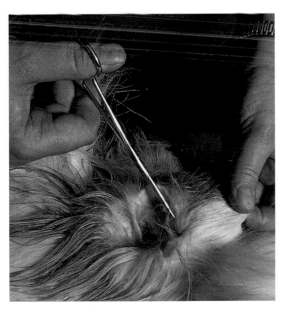

Vets and groomers may have differing opinions about the proper way to remove ear hair. Talk to your veterinarian for specific advice about your dog.

When you examine your dog's teeth, you will probably see some tartar buildup, a yellow or brownish crust where the teeth meet the gums. Signs of periodontal disease include chronic bad breath, drooling, pawing at the mouth, inflamed or bleeding gums, and loose teeth. Gum disease is preventable—if you brush your dog's teeth and if he recieves regular oral health checkups from the veterinarian.

If your dog is an adult, it's best to start with a professional cleaning. The vet usually does this while the dog is under anesthesia. You may opt to use a nonanesthesia dental cleaning service for your dog. Nonanesthetic cleaning services are generally provided by dental hygienists. Nonanesthetic dental cleaning may serve a purpose for dogs that are sensitive to anesthesia, such as some sighthounds and elderly dogs. However, most veterinarians recommend against it as a replacement for prophylactic dental cleaning under anesthesia. Hygienists conducting nonanesthetic dental cleanings are not able to clean under the gums and may not be qualified to diagnose serious periodontal problems. For this reason, many veterinarians recommend nonanesthetic dental cleaning only in addition to prophylactic cleaning.

If you have a puppy, buy a soft toothbrush and start brushing. Use toothpaste made specifically for dogs. People may like cool mint toothpaste, but dogs prefer beef or chicken flavor, and they can swallow it without getting sick.

Many groomers offer tooth brushing as an additional service, but to be most effective it should be done at home, ideally on a daily basis. Use a doggy toothbrush or a rubber finger brush. Gently lift the dog's lip and gently massage the teeth and gums. With a puppy, brush just a couple of teeth initially, gradually building up to a full treatment as he gets used to it.

Brush your dog's teeth daily to prevent tartar buildup and periodontal disease.

Anal Glands

One of the least pleasant jobs in grooming is expressing a dog's anal glands, also known as anal sacs. Located slightly below and to the sides of the anus, these two little glands are scent markers connected through small ducts to the anal area. The fluid they contain is usually released when the dog defecates, marking what the dog leaves behind with his own unique scent.

If the pungent fluid from the anal glands is not released, it can build up, causing the glands to swell and making the dog uncomfortable. When your dog scoots his behind along the floor or bites and licks his rectum, it usually means the anal glands are full and the dog is trying to relieve the pressure. If the condition persists, the glands can become painfully infected and abscessed.

Clogged anal glands must be emptied by expressing the fluid inside. If you do not wish to perform this chore, your veterinarian or groomer will do it for you. Groomers prefer to do this in the tub when the dog is being bathed because the expelled material smells foul. The odor from even a tiny drop will linger on the dog.

Expressing the anal glands is best done by standing the dog on a table or in a tub, lifting his tail with one hand, and placing a thumb and forefinger on each side of the anus. For sanitary reasons, wear disposable gloves. The glands may look swollen and feel like marbles. As you gently squeeze with an upward motion, the contents will be expelled, but be careful— sometimes the fluid forcefully squirts out when the pressure is relieved. If you cannot expel the fluid, the glands may be impacted, so do not persist. Instead, take your dog to the veterinarians immediately to prevent more serious complications.

Professional Pet Grooming

Our love for dogs, cats, and other household pets is evidenced by the amount of money we spend on them: $41.2 billion in 2007 and an estimated $43.4 billion in 2008, according to a recent survey by the American Pet Products Association, Inc. (APPA). The growth of professional grooming reflects this trend; almost 50 percent of our dogs go to the groomer. Even pet superstore chains have added grooming to their services. Yesterday's stereotype of the Poodle parlor is fading as owners realize that a clean well-groomed dog of any breed is a more enjoyable household companion.

Today's groomers have vastly improved equipment: electric tables, specially designed tubs, improved clippers, higher-quality precision shears, professional uniforms, safer dryers, and vacuum systems that whisk away hair as it's clipped. With the increasing trend toward holistic solutions for pest control, gone are the toxic dips of yesteryear. Additionally, air conditioning and ventilation make the grooming shop a safer and more comfortable place for dogs and groomers alike.

Not all groomers are alike, however; some are better than others. It's up to you to determine which one is right for you and your dog. Base your decision on factors such as professionalism, cleanliness, certification, training, and a good dose of gut instinct.

Unlike hairstylists for people, dog groomers are not required to be licensed. Groomer certification programs are the industry's own voluntary credential program. While not a replacement for vocational licensing, certification gives the groomer confidence and recognition. It also lets the dog owner know that the person working on her dog has completed an advanced level of training and has undergone performance testing to earn this distinction.

Certification is offered independently by four different professional organizations: the National Dog Groomers Association of America (NDGAA), World Wide Pet Industry Association (WWPIA), International Professional Groomers, Inc. (IPG), and Inter-national Society of Canine Cosmetologists (ISCC). Groomers become certified through both written and hands-on testing, which covers pet health, anatomy, first aid, breed expertise, and grooming of various breeds according to AKC standards.

Finding a Groomer

Finding a great groomer for your dog is a lot like finding the hairstylist of your dreams. It depends on your ability to communicate what you want as well as the groomer's ability to deliver. You may have to try a few groomers before you find the right one.

Cost is a consideration when shopping for a groomer, but it should not be the only determining factor when making a choice. Costs vary according to region, overhead, quality of products used, and the groomer's own experience and pride in her professionalism.

Upscale groomers may offer specialty services for your pet. Some even supply treats.

Today, groomers are located everywhere, from the storefront salon to the vet's office to the kennel to the pet supply superstore. You may even have a home-based groomer right in your neighborhood. There are mobile groomers who will bring their salon on wheels right into your driveway. Accomplished masters of the art can be found among the ranks of all these professionals.

Word of mouth is the pet care professional's best source of advertising. Referrals are a groomer's lifeblood. If you see a well-groomed dog in your neighborhood or at the park, don't be shy—ask where he was groomed. Most owners will be happy to tell you; after all, you are admiring their baby. You can also locate groomers in the Yellow Pages under pet grooming, or in newspaper ads.

Another option is to ask your veterinarian for a recommendation. You can also contact the Better Business Bureau to find out if the groomer you are considering has any unresolved health or safety issues on record.

Now it's time to scope out your prospects in person. For a groomer, time is money. If the shop is a one- or two-person operation, it may be wise to call and ask about the best time to visit. Groomers work on the clock and may not be able to talk at length with you while they are working on someone else's dog.

When you enter a salon, it should smell and look clean. There should not be loud music blasting from the radio or any other loud noises. Groomers should not be yelling at their four-legged customers. You're looking for a groomer who is friendly and willing to let you take a look at her grooming area. Caring professionals should have nothing to hide.

What about experience? Longevity counts for a lot when working with animals, but years alone are not enough to ensure the skills of a groomer. Some groomers may turn out the exact same type of styling they learned 25 years ago. Look for evidence of membership in a professional organization, framed certificates of advanced training, or photos of winning entries in grooming competitions. Groomers who constantly strive to improve their skills are still excited about their profession. If the groomer has spent the time and

Find a Groomer on the Internet

There are few Web sites on the Internet devoted to grooming. Check out www.petgroomer.com and www.findagroomer.com. The Groomers Lounge, www.groomers.com, has links to groomers throughout Canada and the United States. There is another directory at www.intergroom.com, home page of one of the largest international conventions and trade shows.

money to be certified, you will probably see it noted on the window and on business cards.

Attitude counts for a lot. The groomer should be willing to answer your questions, outline price structures (not giving exact quotes—groomers simply can't do that until they meet your dog), and be willing to work with you to accommodate any special needs your dog might have.

Your dog's safety is always a concern. To help you determine whether the salon you have chosen is a safe place, the first thing you can do is ask questions and observe. Is there a vet nearby in case of emergency? Do the groomers always use metal training collars when they take dogs out for a potty walk? Even if you do not usually use a training collar, this is an important safety measure for dogs in new situations. Dogs can bite through or slip out of a nylon collar in seconds. Animals should not be left unattended on grooming tables or in tubs. Cages and cubbies should be secure. The groomer should make sure dogs are up to date on their shots. And the facilities should look and smell sanitary. It's not a good sign if the groomers are wading around in knee-high dog hair.

If you come away from an exploratory visit with a good feeling, the final test will be how your dog is groomed when he has his first appointment. If any problems arise, your groomer should be willing to listen to your complaint and do what she can to remedy the situation—providing a medicated bath for a dog who itches due to an allergic reaction to a shampoo or paying for a vet visit for a dog who suffers from clipper burn. An ethical groomer is forthcoming about any injury that takes place, a nicked ear, a toenail cut too short, any kind of scratch or abrasion. Accidents happen, even in the best grooming shops.

If your dog leaves the groomer happy and beautiful with tail wagging a mile a minute, you'll know that your search was a success.

Grooming the Groomers

The professional groomer learns to execute the proper trim on all recognized AKC breeds and the mixes that resemble them. If you have ever viewed the glorious array of canine contenders parading around the ring at the Westminster Kennel Club Dog Show, you can appreciate the body of knowledge this involves. For professional groomers, it's a labor of love.

In the past, most groomers learned through on-the-job apprenticeships, but today's pet stylists are more likely to be graduates of grooming schools, typically requiring 600 to 1,000 hours of training and offering business management courses as well. Many budding dog stylists are drawn from the ranks of midlife career changers, weary of the rat race and looking to turn their passion for pets into a way of making a living.

Grooming Is Fundamental

Not all dogs have to be perfectly clipped, but all dogs do require a basic grooming regimen that keeps them clean and healthy. Whether you decide to groom your dog at home or pay for professional grooming, do your homework. Having the right equipment and socializing your dog to being handled will make your job a thousand times easier. Knowing what to look for in a groomer and preparing your dog to be handled by strangers will lead to a better looking dog and a less stressful time for both dog and groomer. For the sake of your dog's health, the cleanliness of your home, and your human-canine relationship, take steps to keep your dog looking and feeling his absolute best.

February is National Pet Dental Health Month. The Pets Need Dental Care Too campaign, which seeks to raise awareness about pet dental care, kicks off during this month.

CHAPTER 28

The Complete Guide to Feeding Your Dog

Feeding your dog is the most basic and effective way that you can care for him and keep him healthy. Good nutrition helps dogs fight disease, grow correctly, and age gracefully. Yet every dog has different nutritional needs. Size, breed type, coat type, skin sensitivity, digestive sensitivity, and many other factors impact an individual dog's ideal nutritional profile. Finding a formula that works well for your dog may take a little research and trial and error.

The market offers a dizzying array of dog foods, from canned to kibble to raw meat and bones to vegetables. You can choose from among so-called natural foods and special formulas designed for such nutritional issues as weight loss, digestive disorders, and the low-protein requirements of giant-breed puppies. You can even go with a homemade diet. To make the right decisions, it's important for you to know your dog's nutritional requirements and how to read dog food labels. Then you need to consider whether your dog should take vitamin, mineral, or herbal supplements. It's up to you to choose the food that is right for your dog.

Basic Food

If you are like most dog owners, you probably buy bags of kibble at the grocery store or the pet supply store, scoop the proper amount according to package directions into your dog's bowl once or twice a day, keep the water dish full, and consider that to be that. For some dogs, this nutritional strategy works. For others, it does not.

Not all dog food is the same. Are you sure the kibble or the canned or the semimoist food you chose is providing your dog with the nutrition he needs to function at his best? Is your dog food of choice complete and balanced? Does it meet your dog's special needs?

Maybe you also supplement your dog's food with table scraps. Does this improve or compromise your dog's health? You've probably heard from some sources that a good-quality commercial kibble is all your dog ever needs. Other sources say that a healthy homemade diet is best. With so much conflicting information, it can be hard to decide what type of food is reasonable, affordable, and best for your dog's health.

Dog owners typically spend more money on dog food than on any other pet-related expense. Knowing the basics of canine nutri-

Whether you choose to feed a commercial or homemade diet, make sure it meets basic nutritional requirements.

tion, how to read a dog food label, and what your dog really needs—and doesn't need—for good health will help you make sure that your investment in canine nutrition is wise, contributing to rather than compromising your dog's healthy life.

Fortunately, you don't have to do all the work on your own. Canine nutrition is a complicated subject, but it is also widely studied, and every dog owner has access to the experts. The reputable breeder, animal shelter, or rescue group from which you adopted your dog can give you a lot of information about what your dog has been eating and how to continue feeding him. Your veterinarian knows about canine nutrition and can recommend a food that matches your dog's needs. Some pet supply store employees also have been well trained in the merits of different brands of dog food and may have additional information, often in the form of take-home brochures from various product lines. A holistic pet store may have more information on natural foods, small stores may stick with the brand they have found to be superior, and larger chains may have a wide array of choices. Even the Internet has a lot of information about canine nutrition, although reputable Web sites from established authorities are likely to be the most reliable. (When in doubt, check with your veterinarian.)

Another important ally in the quest for information on sound canine nutrition is the Association of American Feed Control Officials (AAFCO). AAFCO is an organization that formulates regulations and enforcement strategies for the pet and livestock industries. State regulators may choose either to follow or not to follow AAFCO standards, but most pet food manufacturers choose to comply with AAFCO's regulations so they can sport the AAFCO wording "a complete and balanced diet" on the feed bag, meaning that the food is acceptable as a complete diet without any

other supplementation. The manufacturers of treats, by comparison, can't put the AAFCO wording on their bags because treats aren't made to stand alone as a complete diet. The AAFCO wording indicates that the food sustains the animal for which it was manufactured, for growth or maintenance (whichever is specified). Growth foods are puppy foods, and maintenance foods are adult foods. Some foods are acceptable for both.

Finally, keep in mind that no one source will necessarily give you all the information you need. Gather information from several sources to make the best and most informed decision about what to feed your dog.

Just as a good diet can help strengthen and invigorate your dog, a poor diet can cause him to become fatigued and suffer other symptoms of malnutrition.

The Price of Poor Nutrition

Without good nutrition, your dog can suffer from a number of problems, including allergies, malnutrition, skin and coat problems, and obesity. Nutrition-related problems can affect any dog, no matter the size.

While dogs can be allergic to many things, some have food allergies to different

Dogs may stop eating because of an upset stomach or a big change in their life such as moving to a new house. In general, a healthy dog can go without eating for three or four days. If your dog refuses to eat for longer than that, see a veterinarian.

meats, grains, dairy products, and artificial additives such as colorings, flavorings, and preservatives. Dogs with food allergies often develop skin problems such as rashes, hives, chronic itching, and hot spots (painful, warm infected areas of skin). Some dogs develop allergies to protein and carbohydrate sources after being exposed to them for a long time, so simply changing the protein and carbohydrate sources of your food—from beef and corn to turkey and rice, for example—may be enough to halt the allergic reaction. Many dogs with severe skin allergies finally find relief when their owners switch to feeding them a homemade diet.

Most pet dogs are more likely to become overweight than malnourished, but when a dog is fed a diet lacking in basic nutrients, he can become malnourished. Malnutrition can be caused by a diet that is not complete and unbalanced or by a limited diet (for example, meat only). Dogs who aren't fed enough, often due to neglect or other poor conditions, are likely to become malnourished.

On the other hand, too much protein may contribute to kidney disease in some dogs. Some dogs, especially the large and giant breeds, can develop bone problems if they were fed too much calcium as puppies. Some puppies, especially the toy breeds, need many small, frequent, nutrient-dense

---

In 2002, Nestlé Purina PetCare Company announced the results of a 14-year longevity study of dogs. Researchers fed one group of 24 Labrador Retrievers a nutritionally complete diet and fed another group of 24 Labs 25 percent less of the same diet. They were monitored throughout their lives. The dogs eating less lived an average of two years longer. The results indicate that a reduced diet increased the longevity of the dogs studied.

---

meals to avoid hypoglycemia. A lack of antioxidants like vitamins C and E could possibly contribute to an increased cancer risk (studies suggest this could be true for people), and inadequate fat can result in a dull, dry coat and itchy, sensitive skin. Some dogs are sensitive to too much copper or a deficiency of zinc in their diet.

Obesity

Probably the most significant nutrition-related problem in pet dogs is obesity, which is caused by too many calories and not enough exercise. It is estimated that 40 percent of dogs in America are overweight. Obesity can aggravate joint problems, arthritis, and heart disease in dogs. It could shorten your dog's life and will definitely decrease his quality of life.

Overweight dogs suffer from many of the same health problems as do overweight humans, including chronic pain and liver disease. They are likely to suffer from mobility

Too much of a good thing can be bad for your pet. An obese dog is not a healthy dog.

To easily and accurately weigh smaller dogs, first stand on a scale while holding your dog, then weigh yourself alone. Deduct your weight from the combined weight of you and your dog. The result is your dog's weight.

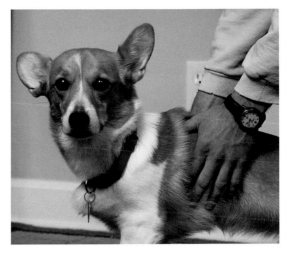

Monitor your dog's weight by regularly checking whether his ribs are prominent or difficult to feel and whether he has an hourglass shape or looks like a sausage.

problems and have a hard time catching their breath. One of the most healthful and humane things you can do for your dog is to keep him from becoming overweight by feeding him the correct amount of food, limiting treats, and providing plenty of exercise opportunities.

Dog food labels typically display charts that show consumers how much to feed dogs based on age and weight. However, these instructions are suggestions based on averages and may not apply to your dog. Some vets believe that a dog may not need as much as the dog food label suggests, especially if he doesn't get adequate exercise. A good rule of thumb is to start with the minimum amount listed on the package for your dog's weight. For example, the label on the food you choose says to feed 2¾ to 3½ cups of food to a dog who weighs 40 to 60 pounds. Your dog weighs 50 pounds. Begin by feeding 2¾ cups per day to your dog, preferably divided into two meals. In other words, feed your 50-pound dog a little less than 1½ cups in the morning and again at night.

If you think your dog is gaining weight, decrease the amount of food a little, say to 1 cup in the morning and 1 cup at night. If your dog begins to look too thin, up the amount slightly until your dog maintains a healthy weight, evident by sufficient energy, palpable but not prominent ribs, and a visible waistline.

Many dogs become overweight simply because they are fed too many treats in addition to their regular meals. Just a couple of extra treats each day can quickly turn a small dog into a small obese dog; larger dogs are equally susceptible to treat overload and excessive weight gain. Helping a dog lose weight is as easy as limiting portion size, cutting back on treats, and increasing the daily walk or adding an extra game of fetch in the yard every afternoon.

With some dogs, obesity is obvious. They tire easily and have rolls of fat around their necks; pendulous abdomens; and wide, barrel-shaped bodies. But every dog is different and every breed is different, so it is impossible to have a weight chart or quantitative determination of obesity. What is a healthy weight for a Labrador Retriever would be overweight for a Greyhound.

According to a 2005 study conducted by Purina, almost half of the people who owned overweight dogs did not believe their dogs were overweight.

Many dogs overeat if allowed unlimited access to food. This tendency may have its foundation in the gorging behavior of dogs' wild ancestors, who had to make one meal last several days.

Look at your dog. Does he have enough energy? Is he retaining his youthful waistline, or is he starting to look like a sausage? To determine if your dog is at a healthy weight, check the following:

Ribs: You should be able to feel your dog's ribs. If they protrude obviously, your dog may be underweight. If you can barely feel your dog's ribs, he may be overweight. It can be hard to feel the ribs on heavily coated dogs, though. And highly athletic dogs such as cattle-herding Border Collies or Siberian Huskies running the Iditarod may appear too thin but are actually in excellent shape. Some breeds such as Greyhounds and Whippets are naturally lean with a smooth coat that makes their ribs visible even at a healthy weight.

Waistline: Your dog should have a waistline when viewed from above. An extreme waist tuck with protruding hip bones may mean your dog is underweight. A sausage-shaped or barrel-shaped body from neck to tail base may mean your dog is overweight.

Breathing: Your dog should be able to move easily and run around the yard in temperate weather without losing his breath. (Breathlessness can be a symptom of other health conditions, too, so see your vet if you are concerned.) Some short-faced dogs such as Pugs, Pekingese, and Bulldogs are less tolerant of hot weather but should be able to exercise in cool weather without becoming distressed.

Abdomen: Your dog's abdomen, when viewed from the side, should tuck up

Although some human food is fine for dogs, never feed chocolate, caffeine, or alcohol.

slightly from the chest. A hanging belly is a sign of a weight problem.

It's important to monitor your dog's health and make sure weight gain isn't caused by something other than overeating. Sudden weight gain, as well as sudden weight loss, can be a sign of a medical problem. If you suspect your dog is overweight, schedule a visit with your vet for a professional opinion and advice on how to treat your dog's weight problem. For some dogs (as for some people), too much exercise too fast can cause injury. Your vet may advise you to start with a weight-loss formula and gradually incorporate more activity into your dog's schedule.

People Food: The Good, the Bad, and the Ugly

Not everyone agrees whether dogs should ever eat the food we eat. Because high-quality dog foods provide a dog with all the nutrients he needs in the correct proportions, many vets and dog experts advise never straying from that highly researched formula. Too many additional extras can throw off that perfect ratio of nutrients.

On the other hand, some people, particularly holistic veterinarians and other alternative

---

No more than 10 percent of a dog's daily calories should come from dog treats and snacks. If you are concerned about your dog's weight but enjoy enhancing the bond with your dog by giving him snacks, save some of the dry food from his bowl and feed it to him periodically throughout the day.

---

health care experts for instance, believe that because many of the original nutrients and enzymes in dog food are destroyed during processing, a strict diet of processed kibble isn't sufficient and is at best unnatural for dogs. They feel that the addition of healthful people food to a dog's diet won't hurt and may even provide the dog with fresher, more available nutrients than those in processed dog food. These people choose to feed their dogs a homemade diet of unprocessed fresh foods either as a supplement to a commercial food or as a complete diet.

An occasional healthy snack is probably fine for your dog in moderation, but certain foods humans eat are dangerous for dogs. Others, such as potato chips and ice cream, may not be toxic, but they can cause gastrointestinal upset, contribute to obesity, and provide no benefits. Avoid the following foods when giving your dog treats or a homemade diet:

Most dogs are eager for mealtime. A poor appetite can indicate a health problem—see your veterinarian.

As people in the United States gain girth, so do dogs. Recent studies show that 30 to 40 percent of all pets in the United States are overweight, making obesity one of the most common diseases afflicting pets today.

Chocolate: Chocolate contains two substances harmful to dogs: theobromine and caffeine. Both of these substances occur in only a small amount in milk chocolate but are much more concentrated in baker's chocolate. The darker and less sweet the chocolate, the more dangerous it is for dogs. Milk chocolate adulterated with sugar and other ingredients, such as M&Ms, may result in mild to severe diarrhea depending on the amount eaten. Dark chocolate, which more of us are eating and cooking with these days, affects the dog's nervous system and could cause hyperexcitability, restlessness, frequent urination, tremors, and vomiting. Severe cases can result in seizures and cardiac arrest, or even death.

Onions and garlic: In large quantities, onions and garlic can cause hemolytic anemia. Ingesting a small amount of garlic is harmless; it's an ingredient used in many dog treats. Onions are more potent. While your dog may tolerate eating bits of meat cooked in onion, don't actually feed your dog the cooked onion pieces or onion-infused broth.

Raisins and grapes: According to the ASPCA Animal Poison Control Center, grapes and raisins have caused numerous cases of poisoning when ingested by dogs for as yet unknown reasons. Dogs typically experience

Do most people share meals with their dogs? It appears so. In a 2001 Veterinary Information Network survey, almost 80 percent of respondents said that they feed their animals from their plates either all the time or sometimes.

Homemade Treats

Everyone enjoys delicious homemade treats and dogs are no exception. The trio of recipes that follow will have your dog licking his chops for more.

Cheddar Lover's Biscuits

2 cups unbleached white flour

½ cup low-fat cheddar cheese, shredded

1 teaspoon garlic powder (do not use fresh garlic)

¼ cup vegetable oil

¼ cup water

In a large bowl, mix all the ingredients. Knead the dough on a floured surface. Roll out the dough on a lightly floured surface to ½-inch thick. Cut out shapes with a cookie cutter. Place the biscuits on a baking sheet, ½ inch apart. Bake at 400 degrees for 15 to 20 minutes. When done, the biscuits should be firm to the touch. Turn the oven off, and leave the biscuits in for 1 to 2 hours to harden. Yields approximately 40 two-inch biscuits.

Apple Cinnamon Training Bits

4 cups whole wheat flour

½ cup cornmeal

1 egg

2 tablespoons vegetable oil

1 teaspoon cinnamon

1 small apple, grated

1⅓ cups water

In a bowl combine all ingredients except the apple and water. Grate apple into mixture and add water. Mix until it starts forming a dough. Turn out on a lightly floured surface. Knead well. Roll out to ¼- to ½-inch thick. Take a straight edge and score the dough horizontally then vertically to make a grid of ¾-inch squares. Be careful not to cut through the dough completely. Place the dough on a baking sheet that has been sprayed with a non-stick spray. Bake at 325°F for 1 hour. Break apart for storage.

Pooch Munchies

3 cups whole wheat flour

1 teaspoon garlic salt

½ cup soft bacon fat

1 cup shredded cheese

1 egg, beaten slightly

1 cup milk

Preheat oven to 400°F. Place flour and garlic salt in a large bowl. Stir in bacon fat. Add cheese and egg. Gradually add enough milk to form a dough. Knead dough and roll out to about 1-inch thick. Use a dog bone-shaped cookie cutter to cut out dough. Place dog bones on a greased cookie sheet and bake about 12 minutes or until they start to brown. Cool and serve.

Recipe courtesy of Cheryl Gianfrancesco, Doggy Desserts (BowTie Press)

Recipe courtesy of www.recipesource.com

Recipe courtesy of Three Dog Bakery

---

lethargy, vomiting, diarrhea, and eventually renal failure. While many dogs eat the occasional grape as a treat without a problem, keep dogs away from grape vines or from eating an entire bunch of grapes. Don't ever feed raisins to your dog; even small servings of raisins have been linked to toxic reactions, and raisins aren't good for canine dental health, either.

Alcohol: Dogs absorb alcohol quickly and are prone to toxic reactions such as inebria-tion, seizures, arrhythmias of the heart, low body temperature, kidney damage, and even coma or death. Never give any form of alcohol to your dog.

The Building Blocks of Canine Nutrition

Canine nutrition involves the same basic components as human nutrition. Every dog food designed to be a complete diet contains protein, fats, carbohydrates, fiber, vitamins, minerals, and water, although the sources and proportions of each may vary widely. Dogs may also benefit from antioxidants (some of which are also vitamins), nutraceuticals (components of food in supplement form such as glucosamine for joint health and probiotics for better digestion), and phytochemicals (nonnutritive but possibly medically beneficial components of plants).

Protein is an essential part of the canine diet. Dogs need protein to grow and develop properly; to heal from injury; and to maintain coat, nails, and connective tissue. The main function of cells is to assemble protein molecules, which consist of chains of amino acids. The sequence of amino acids in a protein plays a big role in determining the protein's function. The essential amino acids must come from food, which is part of why a nutritious diet is so important. Nonessential amino acids can be synthesized by the body if the dog gets adequate nutrition to remain healthy. Lean meat and eggs are excellent sources of complete protein, providing all the essential amino acids that dogs need.

When it comes to dog food, the protein picture gets even more complicated by each protein source's digestibility percentage. Dogs can digest most of the protein in muscle meat, but very little of the protein in other animal parts like hair, horns, or beaks. To find out a food's digestibility, contact the dog food manufacturer.

Fat also is important in a dog's nutritional profile. It delivers certain vitamins to a dog's system and is a dog's primary energy source. Fat also keeps a dog's coat healthy and shiny, and keeps his skin, paw pads, and nose resilient and flexible. Fats are made out of fatty acids, and different kinds of fatty acids are helpful to your dog in different ways. A dog can synthesize all types of fatty acids except omega-6 (also called linoleic acid), which he can get from muscle meat and vegetable oil, common ingre-

Keep your pup hydrated with a constant supply of fresh, clean water.

dients in dog foods. A small amount of omega-3 (found in fish oil) may decrease a dog's arthritis symptoms, but the amount of omega-3 must be in the correct proportion to omega-6 fatty acids (about 1:5) to be most effective.

Carbohydrates provide a dog with another form of energy, and they supply the cells of the body with glucose. Every cell in the body requires glucose for energy, so carbohydrates are an important part of a dog's diet. Carbohydrates come in two forms. The simple form (starches and sugars) is quickly converted to glucose in a dog's body. The complex form (whole grains, fruits, and

Do you have to work late but your dog is at home waiting for dinner? Remote-controlled pet feeders released by Japan-based NTT-ME Corp. and AOS Technologies allow owners to feed their pets by issuing commands via the Internet or a Web-enabled cell phone. It can dispense either a meal or a snack and uses a musical signal to indicate feeding time. Owners can monitor their dogs with the feeder's built-in camera.

Monitor your dog's eating and drinking habits. Changes can indicate problems.

vegetables) takes longer to digest and usually contains more fiber. Simple carbohydrates provide quick energy, while complex carbohydrates supply a slower, steadier stream of energy. Fiber promotes healthy digestion.

Fiber is nonnutritive bulk that helps a dog's digestive system run smoothly. Grain sources of fiber need to be cooked for them to be processed properly by the dog's digestive system. Many dog foods contain various components of rice, corn, oats, and other grains as well as parts of vegetables and fruits, both for their nutrient and for their fiber content.

The first commercially prepared food was a dog biscuit introduced in England around 1860.

The vitamins and minerals a dog needs may be required only in small dosages, but they are necessary for many complex chemical processes in the body. They deliver nutrition from food, regulate growth, and affect many of the thousands of nervous system processes. AAFCO-approved dog foods are formulated to contain all the right vitamins in the proper amount for your dog. Each vitamin plays many roles in maintaining healthy function, a few of which we've listed here:

Biotin: Aids in enzymatic processes
Choline: Helps maintain the nervous system
Folic acid: Works with vitamin B_{12} and helps form red blood cells
Vitamin A: Helps maintain vision, bone growth, tissue, and reproductive processes

Dry kibble and wet food have their pros and cons. Decide which works best for your dog.

Vitamin B_1 (Thiamin): Aids in normal growth, appetite, and energy production

Vitamin B_{12}: Helps synthesize DNA and aids intestinal function

Vitamin B_2 (Riboflavin): Aids in growth

Vitamin B_5 (Pantothenic acid): Helps produce energy and metabolize protein

Vitamin B_6 (Pyridoxine): Helps metabolize protein and form red blood cells

Vitamin C: Helps form tissue, heal skin, and maintain bones and teeth; may help support healthy joint function as well as immune function

Vitamin D: Helps use calcium and phosphorous to maintain bone and cartilage

Vitamin E: Important for muscle function and normal reproduction; protects muscle cells from damage due to oxidation in the body

Vitamin K: Facilitates proper blood clotting

Dogs also require some of the same minerals humans require. Calcium, magnesium, phosphorous, and sulfur are the most important of these minerals, in the correct amounts. For example, insufficient calcium (such as might result from an all-meat diet) can result in muscle, nerve, bone, and blood problems, but excess calcium can cause bones to grow too quickly and lead to future orthopedic disorders such as hip dysplasia. Calcium and phosphorous in the correct dosages work together to strengthen bone. Magnesium helps with cell action and nutrient metabolism, and sulfur helps the body synthesize protein and protects joints. Dogs also need trace minerals like iron, zinc, copper, cobalt, selenium, manganese, iodine, and cobalt. Mineral requirements differ slightly for different dog breeds. Check with a veterinarian to be sure the food you have chosen has the correct nutritional profile for your individual dog.

All living beings need water to survive, and dogs are no exception. An overheated dog or a dog who has been vomiting or having diarrhea can easily become dehydrated, but so can a perfectly healthy dog if you forget to refill the water dish. Be sure your dog always has easy access to a source of clean, fresh water.

In some areas, tap water is fine for dogs and people, but purified water may be a better option because it is subject to an additional level of filtering. Especially for very young, very old, very sensitive, and ill pets, purified water may help ensure hydration without any potential interference in growth, healing, and health maintenance.

Select a food bowl for your dog based on his physical characteristics. Puppies and short-nosed dogs eat most comfortably from shallow dishes. A deep bowl is the best choice for long-nosed dogs. Food and water bowls with steep sides prevent the ears of long-eared dogs from dipping into food or water.

Commercial Dog Food

Sorting out your dog food options can get confusing. Should you choose kibble or canned, dehydrated or frozen? Which brand should you choose? Most dog owners choose to feed their dogs a commercially prepared diet. But even a dog food labeled Premium or Super Premium is no guarantee that the manufacturer used only the highest-quality ingredients available. The dog food industry is regulated, but many terms often applied to dog food are not. The more you know about dog food and the better you understand what the dog food label really means, the more informed you can be when making your choice.

Nutritional choices of commercial dog food are kibble, canned, dehydrated, and frozen varieties. All contain protein, carbohydrates, vitamins, minerals, and fat. Kibble has the water removed through extrusion or baking, making the food hard and crunchy and giving it a longer shelf life. Canned food retains its original moisture content, so it must be sealed in a can to keep it fresh. Dehydration removes water from food and kills bacteria while leaving intact the enzymes, vitamins, and minerals that may be destroyed during a high-heat process. Frozen foods may be raw or cooked.

Each type of food has advantages and disadvantages. Some people like to mix them, giving their dog a little of each to provide variety. The following chart displays some differences and considerations when comparing types of food.

Kibble

Less expensive than canned
Lasts longer than canned once open
Doesn't require refrigeration
Higher in fiber than canned
Available in many different custom formulas
May help keep teeth cleaner than canned

Canned

Not extruded so may retain more vitamins and enzymes than kibble
Longer shelf life
Cans are easy to open
More palatable to picky eaters
Easier to chew
High moisture content helps hydrate dogs
Easy to store

Dehydrated

Long shelf life
Doesn't require refrigeration until rehydrated
Easy to prepare
Often uses ingredients described as human-grade or certified as organic
Easy to chew
Easy to store

Frozen

Instant-freeze techniques retain freshness and nutrient value
Easy to thaw in refrigerator
Easy to eat once thawed
Often uses ingredients described as human-grade or certified as organic
High moisture content helps hydration

Kibble doesn't look like chicken and rice, or beef and corn, or any of the other ingredients listed on dog food bags. The process of turning basic food ingredients into kibble is designed to best preserve the nutrients in the original ingredients while creating a food that won't spoil and which dogs find palatable.

Treats should make up no more than 10 percent of a dog's daily calories.

First, everything is separated into parts: muscle meat, animal parts according to their respective types, and grain parts (the germ, bran, and so on). In some cases, the meat, animal parts, and grains are rendered, a process in which all the oil is removed, making the meat or grain into meal such as chicken meal, animal by-product meal, and corn meal.

The dog food manufacturer then mixes the meat parts, grain parts, meals, and any other ingredients according to that food's formula and puts them into an extruder or bakes them. Extrusion is the most common manufacturing process for dry pet food. The extruder uses steam and pressure to mix and compress the food, then squeezes it out into long noodles of dog food, which are sliced into small kibble-shaped pieces. These pieces are then dried and allowed to cool.

Because the extrusion process uses high pressure and temperature, many of the vitamins and enzymes originally present in the meat and grains are gone by the end of this process. To replace what was lost, manufacturers spray the kibble with vitamin spray and fat to bring proportions up to recommended levels. Flavorings are also added to make the kibble taste better. The food is then packaged and shipped to pet supply stores, grocery stores, and other retailers. Canned food is mixed in a similar way, but because it is not extruded, it retains more moisture.

We all know that dogs are different from cats. But did you know that dogs and cats even drink differently? When a dog drinks, his tongue curls down, bringing the water under his tongue. A cat's tongue works the opposite way, scooping liquid back into his mouth. This difference even affects the sounds that dogs and cats make when drinking. Dogs are noisier because of the way their tongues work, causing them to gulp more while drinking.

Dehydration prevents the growth of bacteria, yeasts, and molds and suspends the action of enzymes until food is rehydrated with warm water. Rehydration with warm water takes 5 to 10 minutes. Dehydrated food can be mixed with additional raw or cooked meat or other ingredients as desired.

High-quality raw dog foods are flash-frozen to eliminate parasites. They must be thawed in the refrigerator before being fed. It's important to use good food-handling techniques when feeding a raw diet to prevent bacterial contamination. Always wash your hands thoroughly with soap and water after handling any raw meat.

How to Read a Dog Food Label

The dog food label can tell you a lot about the food inside the can or bag, including what is in the food, whether it is complete and balanced, what age, size, and condition of dog it's designed for, and whether the manufacturer has chosen to follow standards set by AAFCO.

Dog food labels must contain certain information, but many manufacturers choose to go above and beyond the basic requirements. Grab a bag or can of dog food and take a look.

On the front, the label should display the names of the food and manufacturer, and whether it is for puppies, adult maintenance, senior dogs, overweight dogs, or highly active/performance dogs. The label will probably have an appealing picture or logo: cute puppies, chunks of fresh meat, or dogs playing.

In smaller print, the label should list company contact information, a requirement on all pet food labels. Many also include a Web site address. Use that contact information if you have any questions about the food that aren't answered on the label, such as digestibility percentages.

Somewhere on the bag or can, probably on the back and possibly also on the side, you'll find text that describes the food. You may find long notes about wolves evolving into dogs and natural nutrition, or a short and succinct explanation of exactly what the food inside that bag or can is supposed to do. Keep in mind that this information, while it may be factual and can't legally be misleading, is an advertisement written to win you over.

If the manufacturer is following the standards set by AAFCO, you'll find that advertised on the bag or can. Typically, this statement contains AAFCO-approved wording about whether the food is 100 percent complete and balanced to meet the nutritional levels for all life stages and whether feeding trials were used to determine this. Puppy food may say the food meets the nutritional levels established by AAFCO for growth. Some foods state they meet the needs for growth and reproduction for use in breeding programs.

Although AAFCO doesn't regulate the use of terms *Premium* and *Super Premium*, it does regulate the use of the terms *proven* (companies must have the scientific proof), *100 percent*, and *new and improved*, and it prohibits misrepresentation on the label. The food must meet AAFCO standards to put any of these claims on the bag, but just about every dog food manufacturer voluntarily complies with the standards to earn the right to use the AAFCO statement. Manufacturers meet the claim by doing at least one of the following:

Meet nutrient requirements: Meet the nutrient requirements that AAFCO has established in its Dog Nutrient Profile. The Profile sets minimum and sometimes maximum percentages for amino acids, crude fat, linoleic acid, vitamins, and minerals, with separate percentages required for growth/reproduction formulas and for maintenance formulas. Although the AAFCO requirements are not listed on the bag or can (these requirements are in the AAFCO manual for manufacturers to follow), the percentages of the nutrients in each type of dog food are listed. For example, AAFCO requires a growth and reproduction formula to have a minimum of 22 percent crude protein, and an adult maintenance formula to have a minimum of 18 percent crude protein.

Run feeding trials: Successfully demonstrate the product's nutritional adequacy through animal feeding trials

Produce proven product: Come out with a new type of dog food that varies only slightly from another in the same product line, which has already been proved to meet the AAFCO standard. AAFCO has strict procedures for establishing this similarity.

The guaranteed analysis must list either the minimum or maximum (depending on the requirements of the AAFCO Dog Nutrient Profile) levels of crude protein, fat, fiber, and moisture. Some dog foods list other ingredients like fatty acids, although this isn't required. Keep in mind that the percentages listed aren't necessarily the exact percentages actually in the food; they are minimums and maximums. This analysis doesn't tell you how much of the protein is digestible or usable by a dog or what the sources of protein, fat, and fiber are in the food. You can guess by comparing the ingredients list with the percentages, but the label won't tell you what percentage of the protein comes from muscle meat and what percentage comes from animal by-products, meal, or grains.

When comparing kibble and canned food, the numbers look quite a bit different because the differences in moisture between them are not taken into account. If you were to remove all possible moisture from the same amount of kibble and canned food, you could compare them equally, but the guaranteed analysis doesn't do this for you.

If you want to compare the protein, fat, or fiber content of kibble to canned food, you have to estimate. Dry kibble is approximately 10 percent moisture, and canned food is approximately 75 percent moisture, so the trick is to calculate how much protein, fat, and fiber each food has in its dry-weight form. To do this, follow these steps:

1. Find the percentage of protein, fat, or fiber.
2. Find the moisture percentage.
3. Subtract the moisture percentage from 100 to get the dry-weight percentage.
4. Divide the protein, fat, or fiber percentage by the dry-weight percentage.
5. Multiply that number by 100. That is the dry-weight percentage. Do this for both canned and dry, and you can compare. You will probably find that canned food generally has higher protein content than dry, while dry food generally has more fiber. (More protein may or may not be desirable, depending on the dog's breed, size, age, and activity level.)

The feeding guidelines, often presented in chart form, are the manufacturer's recommendations for the amount of food to feed your dog; it is typically based on weight.

The phrase *dog in the manger* refers to a selfish person who keeps others from using something even though he is not using it himself. The allusion is to an Aesop's fable about a dog taking a nap in a manger. The dog would not allow the ox to come near the hay to eat, even though the dog did not want it himself.

Food and water bowls should be heavy enough that they won't tip or spill.

Remember that these guidelines may be on the high side, depending on a dog's activity level.

Food doesn't last forever, even unopened. Bags of dry dog food usually contain an expiration date that tells you how long the food will last unopened on the shelf. However, some brands use a code known only to the manufacturer. If you can't find an expiration date on a bag, contact the company with the label in hand to find out what it is. You want to be sure to buy food fresh and use it up well within the expiration date. If you can't use a new bag of dog food within a month, don't buy it. Once opened, kibble gets stale quickly, even if you keep the bag tightly shut.

Most dog food manufacturers guarantee your satisfaction and describe their guarantee on the label. If you have a problem with a food, don't hesitate to contact the manufacturer. Customer feedback helps manufacturers fine-tune products to provide people with what they want and need for their dogs.

Guide to Dog Food Ingredients

Although the amount of each ingredient is not listed, dog food manufacturers must list ingredients in descending order according to weight. If corn meal is listed first, the food contains more corn meal by weight than any other single ingredient. If chicken is the first ingredient, the food has more chicken by weight than any other single ingredient. Generally, because dogs require high-quality protein, they do better on a food that has one or two meat sources at the top of the list. Grain-based diets don't typically provide dogs with as much usable protein and may be harder to digest.

Sometimes the order of ingredients can be misleading because grains may be separated into different parts and listed separately. If, for example, the label lists chicken, cornmeal, ground corn, chicken by-product meal, and corn gluten meal, the food could be primarily corn-based, even though chicken was listed first. The order of ingredients can also be misleading when the first ingredient is fresh meat rather than meat meal. Fresh meat has a much higher percentage of moisture, therefore less protein, than does meat meal, which has its moisture removed before it is added to dog food. So the protein content in 1 pound of fresh meat is lower than it is in 1 pound of meat meal. Incidentally, some studies show that fresh meat does increase palatability.

AAFCO regulates ingredient definitions so that terms such as *poultry by-products* or *cornmeal* mean the same thing to all manufacturers. AAFCO doesn't define every ingredient, though. For instance, some dog foods contain blueberries or carrots, and AAFCO doesn't require these ingredients to be defined in any particular way. It does, however, formulate regulations for the use of words such as *fresh, dried, toasted,* and *rolled,* and it also categorizes certain ingredients such as roughage, which may take the form of various specified ingredients, including dried apple pomace, sunflower hulls, or rice mill by-product.

In addition to protecting consumers from false advertising, AAFCO protects dogs through regulations that prohibit the use of ingredients that haven't been shown to be safe for consumption and by making many specific designations about ingredients. For instance, if a meat in a dog food is from any animal other than cattle, swine, sheep, or goats, the label must specify what animal the meat is from and cannot just list it as meat or meat by-products.

According to the AAFCO feed ingredient definitions, meant to help standardize the industry, this is what some common dog food ingredient terms actually mean:

Animal by-product meal: The rendered tissue of animals, not including added hair, hooves, horns, hide trimmings, manure, stomachs, and rumen contents except as unavoidable in processing

Many puppies thrive on a special puppy diet. Large-breed puppies, however, may do best on a normal adult diet.

Animal digest: A material resulting from the chemical and/or enzymatic hydrolysis (decomposition by reaction with water) of clean, undecomposed animal tissue, not to include hair, horns, teeth, hooves, and feathers except as unavoidable in processing

Beef, chicken, and other animal fat: Fat obtained from mammal or poultry tissue during the process of rendering and extracting

Corn gluten meal: The dried residue from corn after starch, germ, and bran are removed

Grains: Whole, ground, cracked, flaked, kibbled, toasted, and heat processed grain, including corn, barley, wheat, rice, grain sorghum, oats, brewer's rice, brown rice, and any other grains

Ground corn: The entire corn kernel, ground or chopped

Meat by-products: The nonrendered clean parts of slaughtered mammals other than meat. This includes lungs, spleen, kidneys, brains, livers, blood, bones, fatty tissues, and content-free stomachs and intestines. It may not include hair, horns, teeth, and hooves.

Meat meal: The nonmeat rendered tissues of mammals, not including added blood, hair, hooves, horns, hide trimmings, manure, stomachs, and rumen contents except as unavoidable in processing

Meat or fresh meat: The clean flesh of mammals, including muscle, tongue, heart, diaphragm, and esophagus, with or without the attached fat; skin, sinew, nerve, and blood vessels

Poultry: The clean flesh and skin either with or without accompanying bone from whole carcasses of poultry, not to include feathers, heads, feet, and entrails

As dogs age, their metabolism slows down and their calorie requirements decrease by about 20 percent.

Poultry by-product meal: The ground, rendered, clean poultry parts such as necks, feet, undeveloped eggs, and intestines. This may not include feathers except as unavoidable in processing.

Poultry by-products: The nonrendered clean parts of slaughtered poultry, including heads, feet, and viscera free of fecal and foreign matter except as unavoidable in processing

Supplemental ingredients: Other ingredients added to pet foods may or may not provide a benefit to dogs with special needs such as digestion problems or joint pain. Common supplemental ingredients include probiotics as digestive aids like dried *Lactobacillus acidophilus* fermentation product and joint-supporting ingredients like glucosamine and chondroitin. Many supplemental ingredients such as glucosamine aren't actually approved feed additive ingredi-

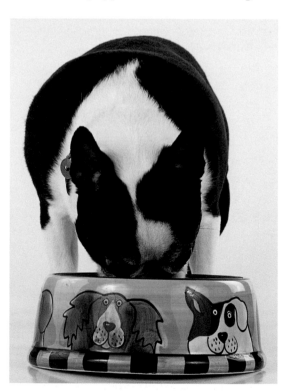

Small dogs need to eat more often than other dogs do. Small-breed puppies should be fed three to four times each day.

ents according to AAFCO, but many manufacturers choose to include them anyway because they are convinced of their safety and their value for companion animals.

Dog Food Safety

After contamination of more than 150 brands of pet food led to the deaths of approximately 2,200 dogs and prompted the largest pet food recall in U.S. history in March 2007, dog owners were understandably anxious about what went into their pets' mouths. The recall led to passage of federal legislation to require the Food & Drug Administration to set up an early warning system to identify contaminated pet food and outbreaks of illness associated with pet food. The legislation also required the FDA to establish pet food ingredient standards and definitions, processing standards, and updated labeling requirements for nutritional and ingredient information. It did not, however, provide the FDA with mandatory recall authority. That means that in future events the FDA cannot order foods to be removed from shelves; it can only encourage manufacturers to do so.

How can you know if the food you choose for your dog is safe? Pet food companies don't have any incentive to make foods that are harmful to dogs, but no pet food manufacturer is exempt from human error or bad luck. They can take steps to minimize risks, such as testing food before releasing it for sale, as some companies do, but that wouldn't have helped in the Menu Foods recall. The toxic substance in that case was not one that would normally be tested for because it wasn't supposed to be in food at all. Nonetheless, it doesn't hurt to pick up the phone, call the manufacturer's toll-free number listed on the bag or can, and ask whether food is always tested before it leaves the plant or only if a problem is suspected. The following informa-

Depending on his activity level, your senior dog may require a senior diet or just less of a regular adult diet.

tion can help you do your best to keep your dog safe from contaminated food.

• Expensive foods labeled "premium," "super premium" or "ultra premium" are no guarantee that a food will be safer or more nutritious for your dog, but the price difference may mean that their manufacturers use more expensive ingredients, have better quality control, do more research and analysis of their foods, or feed them to dogs in a controlled setting to ensure that the foods are nutritionally complete. Call and ask what's behind the price difference.

• Many pet foods are now labeled organic. That means the contents are made with ingredients that are free of pesticides or other chemicals, but it's not a guarantee against contamination. Some toxins occur naturally.

• Any time you open a bag or can of dog food, give it the sniff test. If it has an unusual odor or appearance, don't give it to your dog. Return it to the store for a refund, and contact the manufacturer with your concerns.

• If your dog becomes ill after eating a new food—or even after eating his usual

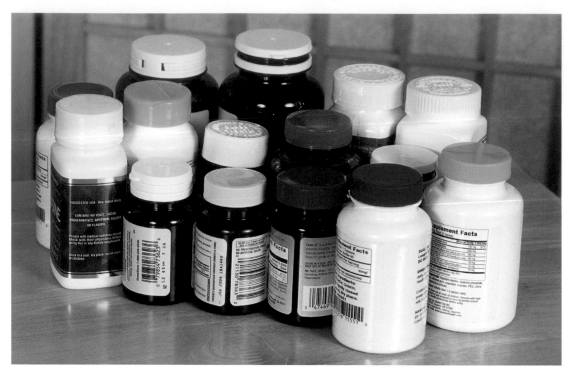

Many dog owners swear by supplements and vitamins. Discuss the supplement option with your veterinarian.

food—stop giving that food, and take your dog to the veterinarian.

Commercial Food for Special Needs

One of the interesting trends in dog food is specialization. Dog foods used to come in three basic types: puppy food, adult food, and senior food. Today, however, as scientists learn more about the specific nutritional needs of dogs, including special needs of different breeds, sizes, ages, and health conditions, manufacturers have responded by producing a variety of specialty foods.

In 2002, Chomp Inc. became the first U.S. company to stock dog treats alongside human snacks in vending machines. YipYap, a canine breath mint, and Sniffers, a chewy beef and cheese candy for dogs, can be purchased from vending machines at rest stops along Interstate 95 in Maine.

Puppy foods formulated for Toy dogs, medium dogs, large dogs, and giant dogs meet each of their unique needs. Senior formulas now often include supplemental ingredients to aid in digestion and promote joint health and supple skin. These are the same compounds many people use as natural remedies for joint pain and digestive problems. Weight-loss formulas typically include reduced calories and more fiber to help dogs feel full, with nutrient-dense formulas to keep dogs healthy.

Other specialty formulas offered include foods available through veterinarians that address specific medical conditions such as urinary problems, kidney disease, heart disease, food allergies, liver disease, copper storage issues, gastrointestinal problems, dental problems, orthopedic and growth problems, obesity, diabetes, and canine dementia. Therapeutic diets are made for use in helping treat a specific disease. That's why they are available only when prescribed by a veterinarian. They are not preventive in nature and should not be fed as a normal diet. Often they're needed for only short periods of time until the problem is resolved. Therapeutic diets can be expensive, but if they help, they're well worth the money.

Some people believe supplements should never be added to pet food and that they should be taken in supplement form instead, to ensure proper dosage and efficacy. However, many pet food companies include them anyway. Here are some of the common supplements you might see added to your dog's food:

Antioxidants: Vitamins such as C, E, and selenium and some nonnutritive phytochemicals (plant substances) may have anticancer properties, according to some studies. Research suggests that antioxidants may actually help fight the development or growth of cancer and generally support the immune system to help keep dogs healthier. As supplements, they are added to food above and beyond the vitamins naturally occurring in the food ingredients.

Fatty acids: May help keep dogs' skin supple and healthy, combating itching, allergies, and flea bite dermatitis. Omega-3 fatty acid found in fish oil and flax seed oil is one such fatty acid.

Glucosamine, chondroitin, MSM (methylsulfonylmethane), shark cartilage, blue-lipped mussel, and other joint-friendly ingredients: These supplements are thought to support and promote healthy, flexible joints and may even restore cartilage. They are common supplements for arthritic dogs, and many people also take these to help combat or prevent arthritis and other joint problems.

Probiotics: Intestinal-friendly, "good" bacteria that promote healthy digestion and even boost immune function, according to recent studies. These friendly bacteria also live in fermented products that people consume such as yogurt, kefir, and fermented cheeses.

Good Nutrition for Every Age and Stage

With the specialization of dog foods, manufacturers are providing more nutritional options for each stage of a dog's life than ever before. Most puppies grow to their full size in well under a year, so they require an appropriate high-protein and high-fat diet to grow into strong, healthy adult dogs. Dogs of different sizes, however, have different needs. For medium-size dogs, a high-quality puppy food is probably sufficient. But a breed-specific or size-specific puppy formula may be better suited to a very small or very large dog's needs.

Some dog owners feel a commercial diet is perfectly adequate; others believe in a homemade diet or BARF diet.

The puppies of large and giant-size dogs such as Great Danes, Irish Wolfhounds, and Saint Bernards grow at a phenomenal rate, some gaining 100 pounds in a matter of months. Such rapid growth can be taxing on the canine skeleton, and many large and giant-size dogs suffer from serious orthopedic problems like hip dysplasia and elbow dysplasia later in life.

Breeders used to believe that calcium supplements and a lot of calories fortified bones and helped large and giant breeds grow strong. Now, however, canine nutrition scientists have discovered that just the opposite is true. A lot of calories and calcium actually increase the growth rate in the puppies of large and giant-size dogs, and when bones grow too fast, they become less dense, more porous, weaker, and more vulnerable to degenerative conditions.

Most large and giant-breed dog breeders agree that regular puppy food isn't a good idea for the biggest breeds of dogs. Puppy food is too high in fat and, some say, protein and calcium, promoting growth that is too rapid. In fact, many breeders of large and giant breeds recommend never feeding these dogs puppy food. Adult maintenance foods, with their more moderate protein, fat, and calcium levels, may be all that puppies of large and giant-size dogs need, these breeders claim.

Other breeders prefer to feed a puppy food specifically formulated for large and giant breeds. These foods are widely available and vary according to the manufacturer. Most have lower fat levels than typical puppy food, but some have higher protein levels, while others are more moderate. Calcium levels vary also, and may or may not be listed on the bag, so talk to your vet about which, if any, large/giant-breed puppy food to feed your puppy. Again, supplementation is probably unnecessary for large and giant-size dogs.

The small-breed puppies have their own special nutritional needs, too. Yorkies, Chihuahuas, Papillons, and other small breeds may not get the energy they need to survive if they aren't fed often enough, due to their quick metabolisms and tiny stomachs. They need to eat often (and excrete often, part of the reason why small breeds can be more difficult to house-train) in small amounts. Small breeds should be fed three or four times a day for the first few months, then the feedings should gradually decrease, always dividing up the day's allowance of food among the number of meals. Most small dogs should eat at least twice a day rather than just once, even as adults. Small breeds are easy to overfeed, though, because just a few extra teaspoons of kibble can soon translate into excessive weight gain for a tiny dog.

Some manufacturers also offer special formulas designed for small breeds (some specify they are for "Toy breeds," a specific group of very small breeds according to certain breed registry organizations). These formulas are typically formed into much smaller kibble, which small dogs find easier to eat, and contain more concentrated nutrition so that every bite delivers maximum nutrition.

For the serious canine athlete or working dog, extra calories can provide much-needed energy. A highly active dog, whether he's a working farm dog, an agility star, a sled dog, or a daily jogging partner, may need a different food than a sedentary dog. Consider formulas custom-made for highly active canine athletes and working dogs. These formulas typically contain a high percentage of calories from protein, with highly digestible animal proteins as the primary ingredients, and high fat content for energy.

Overweight dogs may need nothing more than a little less of the food they love and a temporary moratorium on treats. But for dogs who gain weight easily and keep it on stubbornly, a special food formulated for overweight or obese dogs may be beneficial. These foods contain fewer calories, less fat, and higher fiber than do standard adult maintenance formulas while still providing dogs with a nutritionally complete diet. Some foods double as formulas for both senior and overweight dogs because senior dogs may get less exercise and require fewer calories. However, some senior formulas are not appropriate for weight loss.

Senior dogs don't necessarily need a senior diet if they stay active, maintain a healthy weight, and are free from serious health problems. In some cases, however, a senior dog does require a slight adjustment in diet. Arthritis, heart disease, and other age-related conditions could mean less exercise. While exercise is important for senior dogs to maintain their good health, not every senior dog is able to exercise as much as a younger dog. Less exercise means a lower calorie requirement, and if the amount of calories in the dog's diet isn't reduced, the result often is weight gain. Weight gain, in turn, can exacerbate age-related disorders such as arthritis and joint problems.

While most senior dogs with kidney problems need to limit protein intake, sufficient protein for healthy senior dogs is essential to help maintain muscle mass. Some senior-formulated dog foods contain low protein, so talk to your vet about whether such a formula is advisable for your senior dog. In many cases, reducing portion sizes and limiting treats is all that a less active senior dog needs.

Continually evaluate how your dog is doing as he ages. If you detect a shift in weight gain or loss, coat quality, mobility, or any other aspect of your dog's health, discuss a change in diet with your vet. A change in weight may also signify a medical condition, so always check with your vet if you notice that your dog experiences weight changes.

Vitamin, Mineral, and Herbal Supplements

If you pop a multivitamin every morning, should you be tossing your dog a canine supplement as well? Vitamins and minerals are essential components of a dog's diet. They govern many processes in the body, including regulation of heartbeat, ability of the circulatory system to deliver nutrients to the body, and neural activity. High-quality dog foods are specifically formulated to deliver all the nutrients dogs need to stay healthy. Why then do manufacturers produce so many different dog dietary supplements of vitamins, minerals, herbs, and other substances?

Some dogs have special needs such as a weakened immune system that make supplementation a smart choice. Many people claim that supplements have helped their dogs overcome chronic diseases or have alleviated their symptoms. Some dog owners may choose to use supplementation as a preventive measure against future health problems. But some vets advise against supplementation because dog foods are nutritionally complete and certain vitamins, minerals, and herbs given in large doses may be harmful to some dogs. Other vets worry that processed commercial dog food has lost much of the nutrition present in the original ingredients and that supplementation is an important safeguard against deficiencies, some of which

Make mealtime more interesting for a picky eater by warming up the food. Adding warm water to dry dog food softens it and creates appetizing gravy. Canned food can be put in a bowl and warmed slightly in the microwave. Be sure to test the temperature before feeding it to your dog to ensure that it's not too hot.

Instead of commercial treats, offer your overweight dog carrots or dried fruit.

instance, dogs store fat-soluble vitamins like vitamin D in their bodies. If they ingest too much of it, the vitamin can accumulate to the point of becoming toxic. Supplements of water-soluble vitamins like C and E probably are less likely to cause a toxic reaction in dogs because they are typically eliminated from the body daily, but any vitamin or mineral taken in megadoses could be potentially dangerous.

Although vets disagree on the importance of supplementing a dog's diet, most dogs remain in good health on a nutritionally complete and balanced dog food, and many may benefit from, or at least are not harmed by, certain supplements. For example, consider vitamin C. Unlike people, dogs can synthesize vitamin C in their bodies and may not benefit from a vitamin C supplement the way a person could. Some studies suggest, however, that vitamin C supplements may be useful to highly athletic and working dogs. Dogs who lack the ability to synthesize vitamin C could benefit from supplementation of this antioxidant vitamin. Some breeders believe that vitamin C supplementation helps maintain orthopedic health in giant breeds. When it comes to canine dietary supplements, dog owners and their veterinarians must consider many variables.

The best course of action is to talk to your vet about supplements and determine together if your dog is likely to have a particular deficiency, then supplement that deficiency specifically. Or, if you are interested in supplements to treat a chronic disorder like arthritis or allergies, be sure to tell your vet that you are considering this kind of addition to your dog's health regimen. Your vet may have new information about the safety and efficacy of supplements. For example, the FDA announced that certain substances previously available for dogs such as comfrey and kava kava may not be safe. Other supplements are touted as having the ability to reduce a dog's need for insulin. No diet, vita-

may be too minor to detect but which could eventually lead to chronic health problems. Supplementation, these vets argue, is a safety net and will not hurt dogs as long as their owners administer supplements according to package directions.

Supplement manufacturers and many holistic veterinarians argue that supplements aren't effective unless given in doses more exacting than those in dog foods; it can be difficult to determine how much of a supplement a dog actually receives from a bowl of kibble. In supplement form, vitamins, minerals, herbs, and other substances can be administered in the exact dosages appropriate for different ages, weights, and breeds of dogs.

According to regulatory agencies like the FDA, dog supplements fall into a gray area between food and medicine, and many of the ingredients in these supplements are unregulated. Proceed with caution and give them to your dog only under the guidance of a veterinarian who is knowledgeable on the subject. Even if herbs are legal and saleable, they aren't always safe for every dog in every situation.

Supplements that contain the same vitamins and minerals found in food may seem safe, but this isn't always so, either. For

min, or mineral can accomplish that, and using an untried supplement for such a reason can harm or even kill a dog. Because your vet may have access to dog health news you don't hear about, it pays to ask before giving your dog a new supplement.

Until supplements are more closely regulated, follow these safety precautions:

Look for quality: Buy supplements from reputable manufacturers.

Follow directions: Always follow package directions for dosage. Don't base an estimate of your dog's doseage on how much of the supplement you take.

Adhere to animal specifications: Never give your dog a supplement packaged for a human or for a different type of animal. For instance, don't give a cat supplement to a dog, and vice versa. Accurate dosage matters when it comes to small animals.

Always make diet switches slowly. Your dog may react to a sudden change with digestive upset.

Inform your vet: Always tell your vet if you are supplementing your dog's diet.

Herbs and supplements should be treated like any other medication or dietary change: if your dog experiences any sudden change in health or behavior, see your vet.

Dog Food and Holistic Health

Holistic health is an alternative mode of health care that considers the whole animal instead of isolating symptoms and disease, as is sometimes the case in conventional veterinary medicine. Rather than focusing on medications or symptom relief, holistic health care focuses on a dog's whole self: breed, age, size, condition, activity level, emotional health, and diet. Holistic vets may prescribe supplements, flower essences, homeopathic remedies, or chiropractic care, among other things. Many holistic vets concern themselves with a dog's diet because this is an easy-to-control aspect of daily care that has a potentially significant impact on a dog's health. What your dog eats or doesn't eat could result in chronic conditions or relief from conditions, holistic vets say.

Those who are moving toward a more natural diet and lifestyle in their own families may feel that including the dog in these changes makes sense. But dogs don't always tolerate these nutritional changes. Before changing your dog's diet, learn as much as you can about the holistic health diet you are considering, and talk to your vet about whether the change is safe for your dog.

Feeding your dog the wrong foods can cause illness, and many people believe that feeding the right foods can actually act like medicine. A diet rich in fatty food can lead to pancreatitis, obesity, and digestive problems, but can a diet rich in antioxidants cure cancer?

Research suggests that antioxidants may contain potent anticancer properties. Cancer is one of the leading causes of mortality in adult dogs, so dog owners may decide to include more antioxidants in their dogs' diets, either through prepared foods or supplementation with fruits and vegetables that contain antioxidant vitamins like C, E, and selenium. Vegetables and fruits also contain phytochemicals such as carotenoids (like beta carotene), indoles, isothiocyanates, lycopene, and hundreds of others, which have been linked to anticancer action.

Many studies support the notion that a diet rich in fruits, vegetables, and whole grains decreases the risk of many chronic diseases like heart disease and cancer in humans. Likewise, many veterinarians believe a diet rich in healthy, fresh foods free of chemical additives similarly decreases a dog's risk of developing chronic diseases. Even if the link between diet, health, and longevity is not confirmed scientifically, many dog owners believe that this inextricable relationship is a matter of common sense. However, feeding a dog a healthy natural diet with the possible potential for healing takes some forethought and planning.

As nutrition scientists continue to learn more about food and its healing properties, dog foods will evolve to encompass these properties; some dog food manufacturers have already taken the first steps by offering organic diets, vegetarian diets, frozen prepared raw meat diets, and BARF (bones and raw food) diets.

The world's largest recorded dog biscuit measured 7.7 feet long, 1.9 feet wide, and 1 inch thick. The People's Company Bakery in Minneapolis, Minnesota, produced the gargantuan biscuit on August 11, 1999.

Source: Guinness World Records, 2004

Organic and Natural Dog Food

What does it mean when dog food manufacturers state that their food is organic and/or natural? Regulating organizations have moved quickly to make sure these terms can't be misused. AAFCO has published guidelines for the use of the term *natural* in dog foods. According to these guidelines, any food that includes the word *natural* on the label should be derived only from plant and animal sources that are either unprocessed or processed physically by heat, rendering, purification, extraction, hydrolysis, enzymolysis, or fermentation but not made by or subjected to any chemically synthetic process. That said, a food with some "natural" ingredients may also contain ingredients that don't seem natural at all. The term *natural* is not regulated by the U. S. Department of Agriculture, which oversees pet food labeling, and use of the term does not guarantee any kind of official sanction or oversight of the production of foods with those ingredients. The term *holistic* and other related terms are largely unregulated in the dog food industry, so although a food can profess to be holistic, the claim can mean just about anything.

Foods labeled *organic* must be produced, handled, and labeled in compliance with the USDA standards for the term *organic*. These standards include requirements regarding how produce must be grown (for instance, pesticides cannot be used), and how livestock must be raised (for example, free from growth hormones and antibiotics).

Organic foods may be prepared in many different ways. They may be baked instead of extruded so they are subject to less intense heat. Some contain meats and grains acceptable for human consumption, instead of the parts left over from human food processing plants. Some organic foods are simply a base with which to mix raw meat while others con-

Homemade Food Guidelines

HEALTHY FOODS	FOODS TO AVOID
Raw or cooked lean cuts of boneless poultry(chicken or turkey), beef (ground or cubed), lamb, cod, and other whitefish, and fatty fish such as salmon and herring	Fatty meats; cured meat such as sausage, bacon, and hot dogs; fried chicken; raw pork
Finely chopped or ground raw vegetables, including carrots, broccoli florets, white potatoes, sweet potatoes, and leafy greens (collards, mustard greens, brussels sprouts, romaine lettuce)	French fries, onions in any form, fresh garlic (small amounts of garlic powder is OK), batter-dipped deep-fried vegetables
Cooked grains such as rice, barley, bulgur, polenta, oatmeal, and pasta	White bread, pastries, cookies, cakes, and other sugary baked goods and processed foods
Raw, scrambled, fried (in canola oil), hard-boiled, or poached eggs	Eggs fried in butter or vegetable oil
Plain yogurt, a small amount of grated hard cheese	Milk, cream, ice cream
Bits of fruit such as blueberries, blackberries, raspberries, strawberries, melons, apples, pears, and bananas	Grapes and raisins
Healthy people meals such as stew or soup with meat and vegetables (not onion soup or onion or garlic pieces), meatloaf, egg salad, and tuna salad	Junk food, frozen dinners, fast food, chocolate, and other sweets

tain fresh organic meat, frozen or dehydrated for easy preparation.

Some organic dry and canned foods contain a wider variety of ingredients, including organic fruits, vegetables, and grains, than is typically found in conventional dog food. This is an effort to duplicate the nutrition a dog would get in the wild by eating a whole animal, including the stomach contents of herbivores like rabbits and chickens. Natural and organic foods are also likely to contain supplements such as those discussed earlier in this chapter.

Foods with the regulated terms *organic* and/or *natural* may cost more than standard dog food, and no extensive studies have compared the long-term effects of organic foods (dog or human) with those that don't contain organic ingredients. But that hasn't stopped many people from making natural and organic food choices for themselves and their dogs.

The BARF Diet

Some people choose to feed their dogs the BARF (bones and raw food) diet. This diet consists of raw meat, raw bones, and finely ground raw vegetables and fruit. Proponents say the diet retains a high level of nutrients and enzymes, and it keeps dogs healthier. The diet is free of preservatives, and chewing on raw bones gives dogs a vigorous and engaging activity as well as a thorough dental cleaning. (Never feed your dog cooked bones, especially poultry bones, which can splinter and cause internal injury if swallowed.)

Some vets believe the BARF diet is a superior diet to commercially prepared dog food; others aren't sure the BARF diet is a good idea for pet dogs. While dogs do eat raw meat and bones in the wild, the raw meat available in our supermarkets is often contaminated with bacteria like *E. coli* and *Salmonella.* Many dogs are fairly resistant to these bacteria, but some can become very sick. Dogs can also get parasites from raw food, and so can the people who handle and prepare the food every day.

Another argument against the BARF diet asserts that domesticated dogs aren't necessarily the same as dogs raised in the wild, including the way their digestive systems have developed. Our pet dogs may be less immune to dangerous bacteria and parasites than is a dog raised in the wild.

Still, some dogs do very well on the BARF diet; many people claim their dogs have recovered from chronic diseases and behavioral problems as a result of switching to a BARF diet. Some dog food manufacturers have even developed more convenient forms of the BARF diet: frozen or dehydrated raw meat patties and raw bones ready for thawing or rehydrating. Talk to your vet to help you determine whether the BARF diet is an option for your dog, and consider whether you are willing to prepare it.

Pros of BARF Diet:
- More closely resembles a dog's natural diet; may resolve chronic problems such as allergies, digestive disorders, diarrhea
- Very palatable
- Raw bones keep dogs' teeth clean
- Free of preservatives and chemical additives
- Rewarding for owner if the dog thrives on the diet

Cons of BARF Diet:
- Time-consuming to prepare (although frozen and dehydrated options are much easier)
- Inconvenient, especially when traveling (dehydrated options work well for traveling)
- Dogs can react adversely to bacteria and/or parasites that could be present in raw meat;

If your dog is healthy and full of energy and has a shiny coat and bright eyes, his diet is working for him.

Homemade Diets

Many people feed their dogs commercial dog food; some people, for a variety of reasons, choose to feed their dogs a homemade diet. A successful homemade diet is well balanced, containing just the right mixture of food to provide a dog with essential nutrients. Here are two suggested homemade recipes that provide a full day's worth of necessary nutrients. Feed one cup by volume per day per 35 pounds of dog or 15 pounds of puppy (5 to 24 months old). Extremely active dogs will require more.

BASIC CANINE THREE-PART COMBO

- *¼ pound (½ cup) ground chicken, turkey, beef, or lamb (heart or muscle is OK; liver is OK but not more than once a week). Use one type of meat per meal, and vary the meat at least every three or four days.*

- *4 to 6 shredded slices whole grain natural bread; or cup whole grain cereal such as brown rice, oatmeal, buckwheat, wheat, quinoa, couscous*

- *1 cup whole milk (raw and nonhomogenized, if possible)*

- *2 large eggs*

- *¼ cup string beans or other vegetable (carrots, broccoli, leafy greens, beets)*

- *1 tablespoon vitamin/mineral powder*

- *1 tablespoon ghee, olive, or vegetable oil*

- *1½ teaspoons calcium, or softened eggshells from 2 large eggs (bake in toaster oven to soften)*

- *¼ teaspoon tamari, Braggs liquid amino acids, or a dash of iodized salt (optional)*

- *1 clove garlic, crushed or minced (optional)*

- *¼ teaspoon ginger, licorice, and/or cumin (optional)*

- *200 IU vitamin E*

Combine all ingredients; water can be added. Serve raw or shape and bake at 325°F until lightly browned (20 to 30 minutes).

CONTINENTAL CANINE

This is a quick and easy homemade meal containing the three basic food groups of raw meat, raw grated vegetables, and cooked grain.

- *2 cups water*

- *1 cup raw rolled oats*

- *3 eggs (shells crushed and baked at 350°F for 12 minutes)*

- *1 teaspoon calcium/magnesium powder (or eggshells)*

- *½ cup cottage cheese*

- *1 cup raw grated vegetable (any common vegetable is fine)*

- *½ cup raw chopped meat (chicken, turkey, or beef)*

- *1 tablespoon of brewer's or nutritional yeast, lecithin, and/or olive oil (optional)*

Bring 2 cups of water to a boil. Add the raw oats; cover, cook 2 minutes, turn off the heat, and let stand about 10 minutes. Stir in the rest of ingredients, mixing in brewer's or nutritional yeast, lecithin, and/or olive oil, if desired.

Recipes courtesy of William Pollak, DVM

for this reason, many vets advise against the BARF diet

- Preparation can be repugnant for some owners, and people must be careful when handling raw meat to avoid harmful bacteria (again, frozen and dehydrated options are easier and more pleasant to handle)
- Vegetables and fruits must be finely ground to be digestible

- Frozen and dehydrated options, while easier, can be more expensive and take up more storage space

Homemade Diets

Some people enjoy cooking for their dogs and believe that a homemade diet of meat, whole grains, vegetables, and fruits is superior to a commercially prepared diet. Processed dog food is a relatively new phenomenon, and nutrition scientists don't yet fully understand the subtle differences that may exist between the absorption of nutrients in fresh food and the absorption of nutrients cooked out of a food then sprayed back on.

Some people also believe that the extremely high heat and pressure that are used to produce extruded dog food may actually alter the protein structure in the meats used to make dry dog food. Again, scientists aren't yet sure whether such protein alteration has any adverse affect on the dog's body, and because dogs who are fed commercial dog food remain healthy during regulated feeding trials, most people feel confident that such a diet is adequate for maintaining their dogs' health.

In addition, many dog owners don't have the time, inclination, or knowledge to cook for their dogs. Others fear that if they don't feed their dog commercially prepared dog food, their dogs may end up deprived of certain key nutrients, eventually degrading their health. These fears are legitimate. Dogs fed all-meat diets will suffer serious nutritional imbalances, and dogs who eat only what people eat may also suffer deficiencies and the problems that can result from too much high-fat, high-sugar, or highly processed food. Feeding a homemade diet takes some work and adherence to a specially formulated diet, not just offering table scraps.

However, many dog owners who opt not to feed commercial foods and who are willing and able to learn about, prepare, and feed their dogs a homemade diet find it extremely rewarding, in the same way they are rewarded by cooking for their families. Seeing a dog relish a good home-cooked meal feels great, especially when the dog also enjoys improved health when fed such a diet. If you decide to prepare a homemade diet for your dog, research his nutritional needs as carefully as you would research any other aspect of his health and welfare.

Ask your veterinarian for guidance when developing a homemade diet for your dog. Every dog has unique nutritional needs.

A basic formula for a homemade diet is 50 percent protein such as beef, chicken, or turkey; 25 percent grain such as rice or oatmeal; and 25 percent vegetables, ground so your dog can digest them. This formula can comprise a large variety of foods. Most proponents of homemade diets also recommend using supplements of certain vitamins, minerals, and flaxseed or other oils rich in omega-3 fatty acids for healthy skin and coat. Your vet or a homemade diet reference book can help you decide what supplements to use and in what amounts.

The components of a homemade diet will be familiar to most people who cook for themselves. Some of the ingredients that should and should not be included in a healthy homemade diet are represented in the chart on page 573.

A homemade diet can be easy to cook, especially if you are already cooking meat, grains, and vegetables for your family. Consult a veterinarian-approved homemade diet resource before deciding on an actual menu and nutritional plan for your dog, especially regarding the necessary nutritional supplements to include in a homemade diet. A sample menu for a homemade diet for a moderately active 40-pound dog could look something like this (always have your vet approve any dietary change, as some pets don't do well on a homemade diet and your individual dog's nutritional needs may vary):

Breakfast:
  1 hard-boiled egg, mashed
  1 cup cooked oatmeal
  1 teaspoon eggshell powder
  1 tablespoon nutritional yeast
Dinner:
  1 cup cubed chicken
  ½ cup rice
  ½ cup finely chopped broccoli and carrots

  1 tablespoon flaxseed oil
  1 pinch of ground vitamin C

Remember to pay attention to how your dog responds when making any dietary switches. If he gains or loses too much weight or begins to suffer other health problems, you may need to make some adjustments. Every dog is different, and not all dogs thrive on a homemade diet. Some may have trouble adjusting, and some may not like the food you prepare or may suffer (usually temporary) digestive upset during the switch. Changing the diet very gradually can help mitigate digestive upset. Be sure to tell your vet that you are feeding your dog a homemade diet. She may have some suggestions to help you tailor the diet for your dog.

Feeding for Health and Happiness

Feeding your dog doesn't have to be a complicated process, but knowing what dogs need to stay healthy helps you make the right decisions about how to meet your dog's nutritional needs and keep him from suffering nutritional deficiencies or excess. Working with your vet as an ally, you can determine your dog's nutritional requirements. With the help of regulating organizations like the AAFCO and the FDA, you can choose a commercially prepared diet that meets those needs with the highest- quality ingredients. Using information from vets and other qualified professionals who have designed homemade diets that keep dogs healthy, you can decide to prepare your dog's diet at home. A well-balanced, nutritional diet should result in an energetic dog with a shiny coat and supple skin, free of digestive problems. If that sounds like your dog, you know you are feeding him exactly what he needs.

Training and Behavior

Dogs don't come into our lives knowing what we want them to do. Their natural instincts often run counter to what we consider appropriate behavior. What is normal to them such as protecting food, digging, and marking may be distasteful, be irritating, or even feel threatening to us. Before dogs can assimilate to our lifestyles, we must first understand why they do what they do, then teach them to live according to our expectations. Understanding canine behavior and how dogs communicate with us and each other is what helps us integrate our dogs into our homes.

To teach dogs how to fit into our human lives, training is a necessity. A trained dog is allowed more freedom and more opportunities for fun. If your dog has a reliable recall, you can allow him to run off leash in safe areas. A friendly attitude helps him gain entrance into dog parks and other canine-friendly facilities. Training your dog will pay off for both of you.

CHAPTER 29

Canine Communication

Communicating with your dog is an intrinsic part of training. We need to learn the canine language before we can train our dogs successfully. That doesn't mean we have to learn how to bark. Dogs rely more on body language than on anything else to communicate with each other. To understand this language, we need to understand the foundation of canine behaviors and social structure. Then we can start to learn how we can communicate with our dogs and train them to be the wonderful companions we know they can be.

A submissive dog may indicate his position by showing his belly. Dogs frequently try out the dominant and submissive roles during play.

Talking Dog

Dogs everywhere on earth share a common language, which includes certain sounds, postures, gestures, and actions. This canine form of communication is to some degree inherited, but it is also learned through contact with other dogs and then further refined through practice.

A puppy raised in isolation tends to be an awkward communicator when he first meets other dogs. It's important, then, for your puppy to have frequent contact with well-socialized dogs while he is still young so he can learn and prac-

Mama dogs teach puppies much about proper canine etiquette before they ever leave their whelping homes.

tice the communication skills necessary for getting along peacefully with other dogs. This social exposure is best done before your puppy reaches six months of age because adult dogs are far more tolerant of a young puppy's blunders than of those made by socially clumsy adolescents.

Social Hierarchy

Dogs are social creatures by nature. In the wild, they tend to live in packs consisting mainly of related individuals. The dog pack has some close parallels to a human family, with members sometimes cooperating for mutual benefit and other times competing with each other for valued resources. Parent dogs and other adults in a pack normally are patient and tolerant with puppies. They may willingly share their food and other resources with puppies, but that generosity usually ends when youngsters reach adolescence.

Within a dog pack is a power hierarchy; top-ranking individuals have better access to resources than lower-ranking members do. This is a relative hierarchy, not a static one. Rank can rise or fall as changes occur in a pack member's health, strength, or age. The hierarchy also changes when individuals join or leave the group.

Social Communication

A dog raised to at least eight weeks of age by an experienced mama dog learns a lot about

The dam and other adult dogs help puppies understand how to interact appropriately by disciplining them when they're too rough or impudent.

canine social manners from her and his litter siblings. Well-socialized puppies don't normally grow up to be aggressive because they learn good communication and social skills, which are needed for interacting with other dogs successfully. With dogs as with humans, adept social skills can dispel aggression and make physical fights unnecessary. Without resorting to combat, two well-socialized dogs can work out details about rank and turf ownership. They do this through a postural conversation. Once the dogs have determined where they rank relative to each other and whether they're compatible, they either diplomatically go separate ways or sniff and become friends.

Puppies who don't have opportunities to learn and practice canine social skills while young tend to be uncomfortable meeting new dogs. They often are nervous and self-protective, either starting fights or trying to escape. When a frightened dog can't flee, he shows his teeth, growls, and may dart forward in a self-protective attack. This kind of offensive action, even from a frightened dog, may generate an aggressive reaction from the other dog. If neither retreats, tension keeps building, and the standoff may escalate into a fight.

Some dogs enjoy being adoptive parents. They will provide foster care to another dog's puppies. Some dogs may even nurse and raise kittens or other animal species.

Aggression

Some dogs are aggressive toward strangers, even when owners welcome the people as guests. This reaction is often especially strong in dogs whose owners receive few visitors.

Small children are a fairly common trigger for aggression in dogs who haven't been raised around them. Their high-pitched voices and jerky movements are startlingly similar to those of prey animals, so it's not surprising that dogs sometimes react by chasing or nipping children. Young children's faces are at the same level as many dogs', increasing the danger of serious bites to the head.

With positive training methods, many dogs can be retrained to be more relaxed and polite around strangers or children, but it takes skill and experience owners often don't possess. If your dog is nervous and unfriendly around people, enlist help from a professional dog trainer or behaviorist.

If your dog is behaving in any of the following ways, have your veterinarian examine him to detect health problems that might be making him irritable or self-protective:

- Snapping at people, especially children
- Stiffening and growling or snapping when approached or handled
- Biting in defense of food, bed, or other resources
- Attacking other dogs

If there is no apparent medical cause for your dog's aggression, ask your veterinarian to recommend an experienced trainer or behaviorist who can help you solve the problem.

It's wise to choose the social situations you expose your puppy to so you can avoid run-ins with aggressive dogs. Sometimes it takes only one frightening incident to make a puppy aggressively self-protective. If the puppy's blustery display causes the other dog to leave him alone, the aggressive behavior is self-rewarding and may become the way he deals with all dogs he encounters.

Larger, dominant dogs may come across strong with smaller, more submissive dogs.

Dominance

Dominance is not the same as aggression, although the two terms are often mistakenly interchanged. Dominance is an attitude of self-confidence that shows in everything the dog does, while aggression involves confrontation. Dominance is a relative quality, depending on the situation and the company. A dog can be dominant over one individual yet subordinate to another.

A dominant dog doesn't necessarily need to use physical force to take and maintain control of resources or hold onto his high-ranking position in the group. Splitting up is an example of a diplomatic dominant behavior. A high-ranking dog interrupts conflict between lower-ranking dogs simply by moving between them. This display of take-charge dominance prevents arguments among pack members from escalating into dangerous aggression.

When a group of dogs meet, they size each other up by sniffing and exhibiting various body postures. Then they will either play or go their own ways.

Dog-Dog Relationships

Dogs' social etiquette is quite a bit different from our own, but it is just as nuanced. The need to establish hierarchies is well ingrained in dogs, so when two dogs first meet, they attempt to sort out who's the boss right away. Sometimes it's clear. For example, a normal puppy immediately acquiesces to an adult dog. He shows his submission by rolling on his back and showing his tummy, licking the mouth of the adult dog, and avoiding the adult dog's eyes.

The first thing dogs do when they meet another dog is size up one another. They sniff each other's anus to introduce themselves; get information about the other dog's age, sex, and sexual status and establish rank. Dogs have glands on either side of the anus. These anal glands release a smelly substance when a dog defecates, is frightened, or feels aggressive. When a dog sniffs another dog's behind, he is gaining information about the dog through these glands. Too often, well-meaning owners try to interrupt this process, but this is all part of being a dog. For dogs to get along, they must first figure out who is who. Once they establish their introductions, dogs sniff one another's face and other areas of interest. Finally, rank is established, and they can play or avoid one another.

While it seems awfully impolite to us, mounting is another important form of dog-to-dog interaction. As you probably know, even altered dogs and dogs of the same sex mount one another. Mounting may be an expression of dominance, or the dogs simply may be playing. Puppies use this type of play often.

Play is an extremely important part of the way dogs interact with one another and with the rest of the world. Even as they age, most dogs never lose the desire to play. Although rough play may sound quite alarming, with loud barks, yips, and growls, dogs have thick hair, which protects them. Unless the dogs are clearly fighting, there is no need to interfere.

Diplomatic Behavior

Many canine behaviors convey peaceful intent. Dogs use these behaviors to make friends and reduce tension between themselves and other dogs. They also use diplomatic behaviors when interacting with humans, although sometimes the messages don't get through to us quite as clearly as they would to another dog.

Dogs often wag their tails when trying to make friends or appease superiors, although a wagging tail does not always indicate a friendly dog. There are different types of tail wags: fast, slow, stiff, and relaxed. Each type conveys a different mood, so the way a dog moves his tail can tell you a lot about how he's feeling in a situation. A dog that is using his tail to indicate friendliness and confidence will exhibit a loose relaxed wag. The tail will neither be raised high nor held low between the legs. A less-assured dog may indicate his friendly submissiveness by wagging his tail quickly but holding it low and generally assuming a lower posture when meeting a dominant dog.

Licking is another way dogs show diplomacy. They lick to show affection and sometimes respect or deference.

The Senses

Along with sounds, postures, gestures, and actions, a dog's senses help him communicate with other dogs and with the rest of the world. Dogs use their ears, eyes, and noses to

A dog's senses are important in communicating with other dogs. His hearing, vision, and sense of smell help him decide whether a stranger is friend or foe.

learn about other dogs such as whether they are curious, excited, dominant, or interested in mating.

Dogs have a keen sense of hearing. They can hear sounds from a greater distance than we can, and they can hear pitches, especially at the high end, that we cannot hear at all. Dogs are also better than we are at pinpointing the source of a sound. When communicating, dogs growl, bark, whine, howl, even yodel. The tone and frequency of the sounds they make often have different meanings.

A dog's ears swivel independently of one another and can turn to catch sounds. Dogs with prick ears tend to have the best hearing because their ears act as cups, directing and amplifying sound. In the wild, canine hearing helps dogs track prey, and in our homes it helps dogs guard their families.

A dog's sense of vision is poor, though, compared with ours, and they live mostly in a world of grays with muted reds and greens. But they do have better peripheral vision than we do. They can best see moving objects, while stationary objects can be confusing. Dogs are also better able to see at night than are we. Although their night eyesight isn't even close to that of the night-stalking cats, they have a reflective tissue behind the retina that concentrates light. It is light reflecting off this tapetum lucidum that causes canine eyes to glow at night.

Dogs use vision to receive social clues from one another. Play bowing, exposing the belly, baring teeth, and posturing are all intended to convey messages that dogs assume are being seen and understood. Dogs with vision problems can have difficulty in canine social situations because of their inability to pick up visual cues.

One of a dog's most impressive senses is that of smell. It's no wonder since dogs live in a world of odors. They hunt, guard, and communicate with one another by using their sense of smell. Dogs emit odors, by releasing anal glands, defecating, and urinating, that indicate to other dogs whether they are dominant or submissive, male or female. Through odors, dogs also relate information about their sexual cycles and even their age. That's why scent marking is so important.

Dogs use their urine to mark their territory but also to tell neighborhood dogs who they are and how they are doing. Although your dog's continuous starts and stops along your daily walk might be irritating to you; in fact, he is just checking up on the neighborhood news and adding his own bits of information to the hodgepodge. He may even try to cover another dog's information with his own urine to show his sense of ownership over an area or simply to add his calling card to the pot. Male dogs mark more often because they tend to be more territorial than females are. But female dogs in heat also mark often. Dogs spread information through their paws, too, by scratching at the ground where they've eliminated in order to spread the scent.

The dog nose is made precisely for smelling. Its wet exterior traps and dissolves molecules of odor; it's long so it can house more olfactory cells, 150 to 250 million in all (compared with our 5 million); the nostrils are

Dogs mark territory through their urine and feces. They also leave information about themselves for the next dog to find.

covered with cilia, about 15 times the number we have; and it has specialized mucous membranes that are folded in such a way as to create the most possible surface area for trapping odors for the brain to interpret. Not only is the canine nose highly specialized but a larger portion of the canine brain, as compared with ours, is devoted to odors—dogs have 40 times more cells in the olfactory center than we do. A dog's sense of smell is so good that he can tell whether a person is nervous and fearful or confident and relaxed just by her odors. Dogs also have astute odor memory and are easily able to pick out and remember important odors. Once a dog has met someone, especially if that person has had an impact on him in some way, he will always remember that person's odor.

Vocalization

As we already know, dogs have a keen sense of hearing. So it would follow that vocalization plays an important part in their communications. The variety of vocalizations and the changes in inflection add to a dog's communication repertoire.

Barking is the main vocal expression of most dogs. It may be used to convey a threat, warn of an intruder, get attention, or express boredom. Almost all dogs bark when excited, but certain breeds tend to bark more than others do, and some individuals are more talkative than others are. Most herding dogs bark at livestock to get them moving and at intruders to keep them away. Toy dogs and terriers are excitable, and most are quick to bark at sudden sounds and anything that moves. Some breeds—the Basenji is the best known of these—don't bark at all but make other sounds such as yodeling instead. A certain amount of barking should be tolerated, but it can get out of control. Boredom barking is often a problem with dogs left alone for long periods.

Barking dogs are often just lonely or bored. Fence barking is a habit that can be discouraged by blocking a dog's view through the structure.

Whining is a familiar sound to most dog owners. Dogs whine for attention, when they are frightened or hurt, and when they are frustrated. They may also whine in an attempt to get something they want, whether a tidbit of food or a favorite toy that is out of reach. Some dogs also whine and bark when they are excited. Whining is typically a puppy behavior in wild canids but persists into adulthood with most companion dogs probably because it works well. Although heartrending, most dog whines have more to do with a desire for something rather than a reaction to an injury or scare.

Wild canids use howling for several purposes, including assembling the pack for hunting and for expressing pack identity. Although dogs howl less than wolves do, they do it for similar purposes. Instead of barking when they are left alone, some lonely dogs howl. Howling is often a group event, with one dog starting the song and others joining in the chorus. Most dogs howl when they hear another dog howling, and some can be encouraged by a person mimicking a howl. Many dogs howl when they hear sirens or wind instruments like flutes, bagpipes, or harmonicas.

When people began breeding dogs, they selected for useful qualities. The sound of howling carries a long way, so it was a good trait to breed into dogs who trailed game for great distances or over rough terrain with thick vegetation. Hunters could lose sight of the hounds but keep track of where they were by listening for their howling. When the sound stopped moving and the tone changed to one of greater excitement, hunters would know the dogs had cornered an animal. Hunters could then follow the sound of the dogs' persistent baying, catch up with the pack, and dispatch the quarry.

With pet dogs, howling is usually self-limiting and of short duration, so it seldom becomes a problem—unless you happen to live next to a fire station or your neighbor plays bagpipes in a marching band. If your dog howls when you're not home, a radio or television left on as background noise can help cover or scramble environmental sounds that may trigger howling.

Baying is similar in sound to howling but is practiced almost exclusively by hounds. When hunting, hounds bay when they are on scent; the sound of one dog baying attracts the rest of the hound pack to the trail. The baying sound also alerts the hunter that his hounds are on scent.

When scolded, some dogs grumble or bark back. The best response to this sassy back talk is to act as if you don't hear it. If your dog can't engage you in an argument or get you to respond, he will learn that back talking doesn't work, and he will quit doing it.

Dogs who get into frequent trouble and are scolded a lot are the most likely to engage in back talk. This may be a clue that you need to be more proactive with training and management so your dog will get into less trouble and receive more rewards for good behavior. Dogs may sometimes back talk to one another, as well. In a multidog household, a subordinate dog may grumble when a dominant dog takes the best bone or edges him off the couch.

To express irritation, fear, or anger, dogs growl to warn others to stop what they're doing. They also growl in play, but the tone of a play growl is generally distinctive from a serious growl. Growling serves an important function—it's a red flag that, when heeded, reduces the potential for sudden aggression. If his warning growl is ignored, however, the dog's behavior may escalate to snapping, biting, or a full attack.

Understand that if your dog growls, he feels stressed; don't push him any further right then, or you're likely to make the problem worse in the long run. Although punishment temporarily suppresses growling, it won't reduce the anxiety or irritation that caused the dog to growl. This can create a dangerous situation because when denied the chance to communicate that important back-off message, a dog may bite without warning. Instead, figure out what is triggering the growl. Once you know what makes your dog growl, teach him to accept that situation calmly. Without pushing him, gradually expose your dog to the situation a bit at a time to the point where he starts to growl. Over time, with supportive and positive training, a dog can learn to tolerate situations that formerly triggered growling.

When dogs play, they bark and growl, but these vocalizations have a different, less threatening tone than serious barking and growling does. They're generally higher pitched and have a singsong inflection.

Dogs practice canine life skills through play. They go through the same motions in play as they do in hunting, herding, and self-protection. They are just pretending, though, so they don't use the full force of their muscles or teeth. There's no reason to be concerned when your dog makes play sounds. He's only pretending to be fierce and will actually learn to control his emotions and actions better through play fighting.

Periodically during play, a dog yelps and play temporarily stops. A dog yelps when he is injured or startled, indicating pain or displeasure. Older dogs and littermates yelp when a puppy nips them too hard, which teaches the puppy to use a softer bite.

Reading Your Dog

One of the ways dogs express their moods is through their body language. Our interaction with a dog can be either positive or negative depending greatly on how we read his body language. It's up to us to learn how to interpret it.

In dog language, postures and movements express mood, rank, and intention. These messages, although understood clearly by dogs, can sometimes be confusing to people. For example, just because a dog wags his tail doesn't necessarily mean he's friendly or will welcome your approach. A wagging tail

Hounds were developed over hundreds of years to use a distinctive baying type of howl. This baying alerts hunters to the dogs' positions.

A friendly dog is relaxed and outgoing, with relaxed ears and a loose wag to his tail.

could also mean the dog is frightened and hopes you won't hurt him. Or it could mean he's gearing up for a confrontation and might bite you if you trespass on his turf. How can you know what the dog is really communicating? You need to look at all of the dog's body messages—those conveyed through facial expressions, the tail, and stance. Interpreting canine language can be even more difficult with a dog who has cropped ears or a docked tail, whose tail naturally curls over his back, or whose ears are floppy. Since many of these dogs will not exhibit all the classic signs of aggression or fear, you need to pay special attention to the body language you can interpret.

A happy, playful dog leans forward but in a less tense manner than he exhibits when alert or aggressive. His tail is relaxed, wagging at a leisurely pace if he's merely happy, or at a quick pace if he's excited and ready to play. He may

even show a canine grin, quite recognizable as different from a snarl—although the teeth may be exposed, the gums aren't, and the facial muscles are not tensed so there are fewer facial wrinkles. If playful and excited, he may jump, play bow, or bark and even growl excitedly. Both playful growls and barks are issued at a much higher pitch than those indicating aggression or irritation.

When frightened, dogs try to make themselves as small as possible. They may draw back and even crouch, and they avert their gaze. In general, the tail is down or even between the legs. They may lick their lips in a nervous manner, roll on their backs to show their bellies, or urinate.

Muscles tensed, ears forward, and slight wrinkles in the face are all signs of an alert dog. His tail may be up or out straight, and it may wag slowly from side to side. His hackles may also rise. A dog at attention may become aggressive quickly, or he may just be trying to figure out who is approaching. In contrast, a dog who is comfortable and at ease indicates this through a general relaxation of body posture and facial muscles. His mouth may be slightly open, and generally there is no facial wrinkling. The tail is relaxed.

Dogs show aggression in a variety of ways. As with all animals, a dog's instinct in the face of danger is to fight or flee. The role of the fight instinct in aggression is obvious; but curiously, the flee instinct is as likely or even more likely to incite an aggressive incident.

A good example of the aggressive potential of the flee instinct is this: A frightened dog approached by another dog wants to run away. If the frightened dog is on a leash, he cannot run away. He becomes more fearful and attacks the other dog. Although this may look aggressive to the casual observer, it is really more illustrative of fear-aggressive behavior. Fear-aggressive dogs are more likely to bite than dominant dogs are. Instead of fighting, some fear-aggressive dogs tuck their tail and cower back from the threat, while baring teeth and issuing a low, threatening growl.

Fearful or skittish dogs may crouch, put their tails between their legs, or avert their eyes. Not every fearful dog displays every sign, so be alert to the entire body language.

In general, dominant-aggressive dogs are likely to exhibit the fight instinct. They lean forward on their toes, trying to make themselves appear larger. They bare their teeth, and their body and face stiffen, exhibiting deep facial wrinkles. The ears move forward and the tail wags stiffly and slowly from side to side. And they stare.

The hackles are hairs that are raised along the back of a dog when the dog is feeling fearful or aggressive, making him appear larger than he actually is. Raised hackles are a clear sign that the dog is feeling some sort of anxiety, but it's not quite at the same level of aggression as bared teeth or a snarl. Dogs will, for example, raise their hackles when meeting strange dogs. You may notice this during the sniffing greeting between two dogs. Once they've established that they both come in peace, the hackles lie back down.

It is difficult to see raised hackles in long-haired dogs such as the Chow Chow. However, two breeds of dogs have naturally raised hackles: the Rhodesian Ridgeback and the Thai Ridgeback. They are occasionally seen in ridgeback mixes as well. Raised hackles in these breeds does not mean the dog is aggressive.

The portion of teeth exposed, the depth of facial wrinkles along a dog's muzzle, and the position of the ears can communicate a range of emotions from excitement to fear. Coupled with a dog's body position and vocalizations, facial expressions are good indicators of a dog's intentions.

Dogs generally bare their teeth out of fear, from aggression, for predation, or when play fighting. The extent of teeth and gum exposure indicates the level of a dog's aggression and intention to attack. A dog who is exposing a small portion of his teeth is probably just giving a warning. As more of the teeth are exposed, the threat becomes more serious.

Once a dog is exposing the whole of his front teeth and gums, the threat is imminent.

There are dogs who also expose teeth in a "smile." Although it is unusual, some dogs appear to actually smile in a friendly way as a greeting or in a state of excitement. Unlike the grimace or snarl, when the teeth are exposed in a menacing manner, this smile is quite friendly and benign in nature. Experts postulate that it stems from a submissive posture that wolves sometimes take, or it may be a function of the flehmen behavior, which is a secondary, more primitive, method of communication involving the olfactory system. The flehmen behavior sends olfactory messages to the brain through a lobe above the canine incisors rather than through the nose.

This humanlike smile may also simply be a function of our close relationship with dogs— dogs often imitate humans and quickly pick up on behaviors that cause humans to laugh or otherwise provide positive feedback. Tail chasing, for example, is a behavioral oddity that's often perpetuated by a human response to a chance occurrence.

Dogs have a second type of smile that is, for lack of another descriptor, a canine smile. Some dogs when relaxed and content display an open-mouth smile that slightly exposes the teeth and causes facial wrinkling at the corners of the mouth. It is often accompanied by half-closed eyes and a relaxed posture.

Facial wrinkles correspond closely with baring teeth. As a dog becomes increasingly agitated, frightened, or aggressive, his lips draw back farther and farther in a snarl, causing facial

Some dogs exhibit what is often called a canine smile or grin.

wrinkles. An aggressive dog who is ready to attack has facial wrinkles that extend from the top of his curled-up lips to above his nose.

One distinction that can help you differentiate between an aggressive dog who is snarling and showing teeth and one who is smiling and showing teeth is the lack of severe facial wrinkles in the latter. Dogs exhibiting a canine smile have only relaxed wrinkles that form at the corners of the mouth.

According to a study published in a 2007 issue of the *Journal of the American Veterinary Medical Association* and performed at Colorado State University's College of Veterinary Medicine and Biomedical Sciences, the lunar cycle affects dog health. Veterinarians at CSU's Veterinary Medical Center found that the risk of emergencies such as cardiac arrest, epileptic seizures, and trauma was greater on days the moon was waxing gibbous, full, or waning gibbous.

Body Language at a Glance

To help you interpret this all-body communication, here's a brief glossary of basic dog gestures and postures.

Head

Head high: self-confident and interested in what he sees, hears, or smells

Head high, neck arched: confident; displaying superior rank over another dog

Head high, tilted to side: interested and curious

Head and neck horizontal, body stiff, slight crouch, leaning forward: ready to rush forward but waiting for the right moment; may be inquisitive or aggressive

Head and neck horizontal or lowered below horizontal, body stiff, slight crouch, leaning backward: ready to escape; may snap or bite if cornered

Head horizontal or lower than horizontal, turned to one side, cheek turned upward: showing the desire to appease

Head horizontal or lower than horizontal, body curved so head and tail face same direction: cornered, fearful, and feeling self-protective; the dog is likely to snap or bite if approached

Head drooped, nose down or tucked toward chest, eyes averted, slight crouch: lacking confidence, showing submissive deference to a higher-ranking individual

Ears

Lifted, openings facing forward: strong interest

Lifted only partway, openings forward: interested but not yet eager to approach

Lifted halfway, openings sideways: interested but worried

Lowered, openings down or turned backward: worried, desiring to escape

Lowered, plastered to sides of head: alarm or fear; the dog desires to escape but may be afraid to move and may snap or bite if approached when cornered

Eyes

Hard, intent stare that does not break away: dominant, may be predatory or aggressive

Eyes averted: submissive, may be fearful

Eyes that move toward and away from a person or animal: fearful or anxious

Body Posture

Skulking posture, dog stays close to the ground: submissive, fearful, may be fear-aggressive

Standing tall, stiff, rising up on paws, leaning forward: confident, curious, and excited but may be aggressive or predatory

Bows with front legs extended, head down, and rump in the air: playful and friendly, initiating interaction

On back, belly exposed: submissive, may be fearful

Tail

Above Horizontal

Tail high, stiff, and still: assessing the situation for danger; ready for conflict

High and wagging stiffly like a metronome: displaying dominance and willingness for combat

High and wagging stiffly in a short arc: willing to interact in a friendly manner with a dog of similar rank if the other dog doesn't start combat; indicating possible sexual interest

Waving gently in a wide arc: friendly, interested, and enthusiastic

Horizontal

Tail stiff and still, straight out behind dog: interested, assessing the situation, and will likely follow or chase if the object of interest retreats or flees

Tail still: interested but not yet ready to move forward

Tail horizontal with tip drooping: undecided whether to approach or retreat

Below Horizontal

Wagging gently: friendly but lacking confidence

Tucked and wagging: lacking confidence and rank but is not combative; he will allow a slow approach but may panic and flee if rushed

Tucked and still: fearful, will retreat if approached and may bite if cornered

Tail tucked tightly, dog lying on side or back, possibly also urinating: showing full submission to a higher-ranking individual

CHAPTER 30

Socializing Your Dog

The simple fact is that dogs without socialization and training are more likely to end up with behavioral problems—and ultimately be surrendered to animal shelters—than are dogs who receive consistent training throughout their lives. This means that socializing and training your dog may be the kindest thing you ever do for him. If you have a dog who behaves well inside and outside the home, you'll want to spend more time with him. You will find that being in his company is wonderful, not a chore, and even your friends will enjoy having him around. Like all of the other necessities we provide our dogs—food, shelter, and attention—socializing and training are requirements, not bonuses.

Socialization

Puppies, just like children, need exposure to the world so they can come to understand

Young puppies should begin to be socialized before they leave their whelping homes.

what it's all about. If you keep your puppy secluded in your house and yard, he will grow up afraid of the world around him. It's your job to expose him to many things and help him understand that the world is full of exciting new experiences. If you do this, your puppy will grow up to be a healthy, well-adjusted dog.

The socialization process begins during the first several weeks after the puppies are born. They learn to share with their littermates and to accept human touch. They learn to play nicely and to display proper submissiveness with their mother. As the weeks progress, they begin to interact outside of their canine family—meeting the rest of the members of the household and other visitors. They may be exposed to inside and outside noises, such as vacuum cleaners and planes flying overhead, and to different surfaces such as linoleum, carpet, and grass. After your new puppy arrives in your home, socialization will continue to be one of the most important aspects of his training.

Puppies who are not socialized often have a variety of behavior problems when they grow up. When an unsocialized dog leaves the safety of his house or yard, he may become aggressive, anxious, have difficulty focusing, become fearful of other dogs and strangers, or become shy. The last thing you want is a dog who suffers from some or all of these problems simply because he never received proper socialization as a puppy. Socializing your puppy is easy and fun, and it is definitely worthwhile.

Your puppy may act afraid in some situations, and that is normal. The best way to help him get over his fears is to act unafraid yourself

Puppies exposed to livestock at a young age will have fewer fears of these large animals as adults.

and even be enthusiastic about whatever is going on. Avoid the temptation to coddle your puppy and appease his fears. Unlike children, puppies perceive coddling as encouragement of fearful behavior and will become even more fearful in response. Talk to your puppy in a happy voice and act as if whatever is scaring him is the most fun thing in the world. This will do wonders to relieve his fears. Our dogs take cues from us, and if we act as if it's no big deal, they often decide to react the same way.

To live happily with people, dogs have to learn to be handled from a young age. Throughout your dog's life, you will need to bathe him, groom him, and clip his nails. Your veterinarian will need to be able to exam your dog, and if you plan to compete with your dog in obedience or conformation, others have to be able to handle him as well. All this will be made a lot easier if you teach your puppy to tolerate or even enjoy these activities when he's young.

It's vital that your puppy learn to like or at least tolerate handling by children, too. Even if you don't have kids of your own, your puppy will come into contact with these small humans throughout his life, and you need him to be reliable and safe when in the presence of little ones.

Your own kids can do wonders to help socialize your puppy. It is best if your children have enough self-control that they can learn

Bring your pup with you during your daily activities, including gardening, running errands, and visiting friends. The more you expose him to as a puppy, the less fearful he will be as an adult.

Socialize your puppy to calm children as soon as possible.

them that yelling and running around is scary to a young dog, so they need to be relaxed. Most kids will understand the idea that the puppy will be scared and will cooperate. If you can, have kids come over at least once a week to visit with your puppy. As he gets older and learns that children are fun, they can start playing with him. By the time your puppy is six months old, he should be comfortable around children and even seek out their company. However, no matter how good a friendship your dog and children develop, they should never be left unsupervised together.

Eventually, you will be taking your puppy on walks outside of your yard, so he needs to get used to wearing a collar and leash. Fit him with a lightweight buckle collar, and have him wear it for a while. He'll probably scratch at it at first and act as if it's driving him crazy. Limit his collar-wearing sessions to half an hour at first and then over about a week work up to all day.

Once your puppy is used to his collar, attach a lightweight leash to it, and let him walk around while you hold the other end. Don't try to control his movements yet. Just let him wander wherever he wants. Do this for a couple of minutes a day until he's used to the collar and leash.

Puppies need to be socialized to other animals as well because they have a tendency to be obnoxious with other animals in the household, especially cats. They follow the cats around, bark at them, and sometimes give chase. Most of the time this behavior is just meant as play, but cats view it as harassment.

Do not allow your puppy to chase your cat, bark at her, or control her movements by forbidding her to walk in certain areas of the house or room. Remember, your cat was there first and she has the right to live a

to treat the puppy gently and with respect. Teach your kids not to carry the puppy around, not to bother him when he's eating, and never to hit him or be mean to him. If your kids are calm and quiet around your puppy and treat him with love and respect, he will grow up to love your children. This affection for kids most likely will extend to other children outside the family, as long as they treat your dog with respect.

If you don't have your own children, you will need to find friends' or relatives' kids who can help you socialize your puppy. All you need is one or two kids at least five or six years old to come over to play with your puppy. Since most kids love puppies, this shouldn't be too hard to pull off.

Ask the kids to be quiet and calm with the puppy so he's not frightened. Explain to

Adding a Second Dog to Your Home

Introducing a new dog to your family may be disconcerting to your current dog. If he is used to having you all to himself, he may be jealous of the attention you pay to the new dog. There are some things you can do to ease the social transition for both of them:

- When you do something fun with one dog, make sure the other gets something good, too.
- Teach your dogs to take turns by saying each dog's name before you hand him a treat or a toy. This will teach them to wait to hear their names before taking an item from you.
- If either dog gets too pushy or rowdy with the other or tries to guard you as private property, give him a time-out alone for five to ten minutes.
- When you're not home to supervise, keep the dogs separated until their relationship is stable.

peaceful life without constant harassment from the puppy.

Don't allow your puppy to have access to your cat unless you are present to supervise the interaction. If your puppy starts bothering the cat, put a leash on him, and give him the command *leave it*. This is a good opportunity to begin teaching him this important com-

mand. Enforce the command by picking up the leash and bringing your puppy toward you. Do this consistently each time your puppy begins to harass the cat.

Other animals such as birds, rodents, and reptiles may also fall victim to your puppy's harassment if you don't intercede. Use the same method to teach your puppy to

Dogs can get along with cats as long as they are introduced early in life.

leave these pets alone. If you are consistent, your puppy will eventually learn that your other pets don't appreciate his attempts to play. In time, he should leave them alone. If you find that your dog doesn't back off and becomes obsessed or aggressive with any of your other pets, consult a professional trainer for advice.

The process of socializing your puppy to an older dog in the home will take some time. Keep your puppy on a leash when with existing household dogs until everyone is comfortable. Let the older dog go to the puppy to investigate. He'll probably sniff him all over and may exhibit some dominant postures. Most puppies respond to this with appropriately submissive behaviors such as licking the older dog's muzzle, flipping on his back and exposing his tummy, or even urinating. If the puppy becomes too boisterous or does not exhibit suitably submissive postures, your older dog may scold him with a gruff bark or growl. He may even pin him down and hold him until the puppy is calmer. All of these responses are normal and will help your puppy mature into a respectful adult. However, if your older dog is consistently aggressive or injures your puppy, consult a professional trainer. You should also seek the advice of a professional trainer if your existing

A new puppy will be naturally submissive to your older dog. Do not interfere when your dog disciplines the puppy, who needs to be taught proper behavior.

dog refuses to acknowledge the new puppy. Sometimes extra help is needed to integrate a household, and in some cases a family dog simply will not accept an interloper. When adopting your puppy from a breeder or shelter, be sure you have the option of returning the puppy if your existing dog will not accept him. Your older dog should come first.

You can help keep the proper balance by making sure to provide your older dog with as much or more attention as the new puppy, always feeding and giving the older dog treats and toys first, and generally respecting his role as the elder statesman. Eventually your dogs will work out their hierarchy but for now, your old friend should be top dog. Never leave a puppy alone with an older dog, even if they seem to get along well when supervised. An older, larger dog can seriously injure a young puppy. Keep your puppy warm and secure in his crate when you aren't able to supervise.

Because you don't want your puppy to spend his entire life within the four walls of your home, it's important for you to socialize him to all the fun and scary things the world has to offer. Take him to outdoor malls and markets, busy parks, and downtown streets. Introduce him to strangers and encourage all types of people to pet him. Always bring an ample supply of treats to lubricate friendships.

It's also a good idea to periodically leave your puppy in the care of someone else for an afternoon, a day, or even a week during the first year of his life. This could be a friend, a relative, or a boarding kennel. It's good for your puppy to experience life without you for short periods of time so he's knows he can be OK, even when Mom or Dad isn't around.

In addition to taking your older puppy to different places, give him new experiences close to home. Look for opportunities to go up and down stairs with him. Have him walk over plastic garbage bags laid flat on the ground. Sit in the kitchen with him while the dishwasher is running, and keep him outside with you while you are mowing the lawn. Let him be in the next room when you turn on the vacuum for the first time, and gradually let him approach it if he desires. Run appliances, drop pans on the floor, and generally make a ruckus, keeping it jolly and fun for your puppy all the while. If he acts fearful, introduce him to the source of the fear slowly but with a lot of treats and upbeat happy talk.

Puppy Timeline

Before you begin teaching your puppy about the world around him, it helps to understand how puppies develop. Much like children, puppies go through different stages of development. During a child's development, she learns such skills as how to interact with other human beings, how to coordinate her body, and how to use her mind. During a puppy's developmental stages, he learns such skills as being independent of his mother and siblings, accepting humans as his pack members, and following

A Bull Terrier puppy at five weeks of age begins to investigate the world around him and discover exciting new things.

commands. Socializing and training should be done in accordance with your puppy's natural development—pushing young puppies into potentially frightening situations or expecting too much out of an immature pup can backfire.

Newborn to Two Months

A puppy's most important development takes place during the time he is with his mother

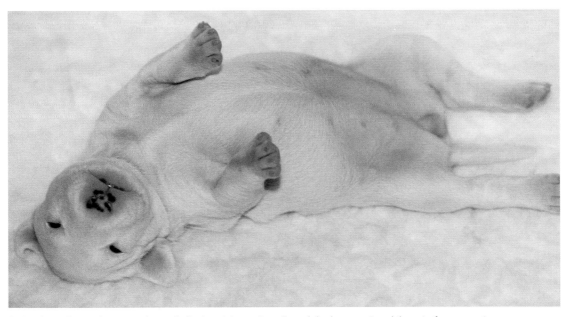

At 25 days of age, the puppy has a limited social repertoire, though he has mastered the art of puppy cuteness.

and siblings. During the first 20 days of life, a puppy learns to coordinate his muscles and recognize his family members. From the ages of 21 to 35 days, he learns the proper way to behave around his canine family and learns to accept people. At the age of 5 weeks, the puppy begins to venture away from his mother and siblings and become a bit more independent. While with his mother and siblings, the puppy learns how to play and interact with other dogs. He also learns to control his bite and share with his littermates. If he is not exposed to people during this time, he can develop fears that will inhibit his ability to function well in human society. If he is isolated from other dogs or taken away from his mother and littermates too early, he may develop a fear of other dogs that can lead to dog aggression.

Puppies who leave their litters before eight weeks should receive extra socialization with friendly dogs to ensure that they learn how to positively interact with other animals. Failure to provide this socialization for your puppy can lead to a lifetime of anxiety and severe dog aggression.

Two to Three Months

Around the age of 8 or 9 weeks, most puppies go off to their new homes. They adapt best to their new surroundings at 9 weeks of age.

During the ages of 9 to 12 weeks, it's especially important for a puppy to be exposed to a number of different objects and situations so he can learn to accept them as part of his environment. Puppies at this age have not developed complete immunity to the many diseases that can plague them, so it's impor-

This eight-week-old Cairn Terrier puppy has been socialized, groomed for the first time, and is wearing his first real collar—all ready for his new home.

Breeders carefully monitor the weight and development of each puppy in the litter.

Puppies can now be crate-trained and can begin to be house-trained. Most puppies take to crate-training easily and find comfort in the warm, dark space of a crate. Some puppies catch on to house-training right away, while others need a few months to become reliably clean in the home. You can also begin teaching him some basic commands, such as sitting for food and watching you when asked to. There are even some puppy kindergarten classes that will enroll these young pups, although most are limited to puppies three months or older.

Young puppies are naturally curious and eager to explore their surroundings. They want to test their teeth on new materials and sniff and taste new substances. Unfortunately, the human world yields a number of dangers for curious puppies, and misbehaviors such as chewing shoes and eating tissue can become habits. So puppies should be kept in a safe place, like a crate, at all times. Some people keep track of their puppies by attaching one end of a leash to their belt and the other end to the puppy.

Three to Six Months

At the age of 12 weeks, puppies should attend puppy kindergarten. Attending obedience classes gives puppies the opportunity to socialize with other dogs and new people and to experience a new environment. Most puppy training schools require proof of vaccination to help keep the puppies safe from disease.

When puppies reach the age of 17 weeks, they're old enough to venture out on longer walks around the neighborhood. They should continue to be exposed to as many different environments and situations as possible. Parks, beaches, and local shopping districts are good places to go. For health reasons, sniffing around busy canine potty areas is still not recommended and shouldn't be allowed until puppies are at least 6 months old.

tant to keep them away from strange dogs and other puppies during this time. However, that doesn't mean he shouldn't be exposed to a lot of fun and upbeat experiences. Take him for walks to the park, to your local coffee shop, and to friends' homes. Do not let him sniff feces, which can carry dangerous bacteria. If you know calm and friendly adult dogs who are up-to-date on their shots, allow your puppy to visit with them to reinforce the appropriate puppy etiquette he began learning from his mom and littermates. At home, puppies can be exposed to a variety of things without their health being at risk. These can include other pets in the home, children (include kids other than the ones who live with you), bicycles, vacuum cleaners (turned off so as not to frighten them), and other such items.

As long as you take normal safety precautions, young pups can go to parks and even beaches. Don't let your pet sniff around dog potty areas until he is at least six months old.

upbeat and safe because at this time a puppy can easily develop fears that he will carry throughout his life. This is especially important when it comes to exposure to children and other dogs. If you don't have your own children, make a concerted effort to find a willing parent to help socialize your puppy. To ensure that your puppy has a good impression of children, introduce him to well-behaved children over five who are experienced with dogs. Be sure they understand how to be gentle with a puppy before introductions. Keep introducing him to friendly adult dogs and puppies.

At three to six months of age, puppies can begin to learn important commands like *sit, stay, down, come, leave it,* and *drop it* in earnest. Although they should already have been introduced to some basic commands, they are now old enough to understand and retain the lessons. They still have plenty of puppy energy and curiosity, though, so this is no time to let your guard down.

Some trainers call the three- to six-month age the fear imprint stage. During this stage, puppies make important decisions about what is and isn't safe in their environment. It's vital to keep exposure to new things and situations

Six to Twelve Months

By the age of six months, a puppy can go anywhere. Take him camping and on hikes. Take him to outdoor parties and to a child's soccer

---

Go Wild and Freeze

Go Wild and Freeze is a game that gives you an off switch for your dog's excitement and helps prevent jumping. First, teach your dog to sit for a treat. Next, wave your arms and hop around, your dog will likely begin bouncing and playing along with you. After a moment, stop, stand tall, ask your dog to sit, and reward him with a treat when he obeys.

After your dog learns to play this game with you, add family members and friends to the mix. Show them how to cue and reward your dog for sitting, then give each player a treat and call, "Go wild!" Everyone should bounce around and make happy noise until you say "Freeze," then all players must stop and stand tall. The person nearest the dog asks him to sit and rewards him. Then you call "Go wild!" and begin another round.

This game is great for teaching children and dogs to play safely together. Kids learn how to get the dog to sit, which keeps him from jumping on them, and how to calm him when he gets too rowdy in play. Dogs learn that when kids stop moving they should too and that it's more rewarding to sit than to jump. Adults should always supervise play between children and dogs so they don't accidentally frighten or hurt each other.

game. Take him to a riding stable that allows dogs so he can get a look at the horses (keep him on leash and under full control). Take him to street fairs and practice heeling. Allow people to pet him so he has the chance to meet plenty of strangers.

Puppies at this age are still highly energetic, and they are nearly full grown, with adult teeth and strength. Cute puppy misbehavior becomes annoying and even threatening by this age. Jumping up and nipping can potentially cause major injury when done by an 80-pound "teenager." Not surprisingly, this is the time many active, untrained dogs land in animal shelters.

It's vital to keep up the training during this time. Sometimes puppies can become stubborn or conveniently forget training at this age. Maintaining daily training helps counter these tendencies. You can enroll your teenaged puppy in a more advanced training class, where the skills that were learned in puppy kindergarten can be reinforced and new commands like *heel* and *long stays* can be learned.

Your pup may need an increase in exercise and outside stimulus at this age, but remember he's still not done growing. Jumping, running on slippery surfaces, and other jarring activities should be discouraged until he is fully grown. However, because he has received his shots and is out of the prime danger zone for infectious diseases, he can regularly visit dog parks and other dog-friendly places where he is sure to get plenty of playtime and interaction with other dogs.

Socializing and training a puppy appropriately throughout his first year of development produces an adult dog who is unafraid of new situations, is in less danger because he is under voice control, and is well received by friends and strangers alike. This puppy is well on his way to a healthy, happy adulthood.

Older puppies will delight in every new experience, from playing in the snow to lounging in the sand.

CHAPTER 31

Training Your Dog

Training starts in puppyhood and continues throughout a dog's life, whether you're teaching basic obedience commands or training for competitive events. The time you invest in training your dog will pay off down the road with a happy, well-adjusted canine who is a much-loved member of your family. The end result—a dog who is a joy to live with—is more than just reward for the work you put into training.

One of the reasons dogs respond so well to training is that every dog needs someone to look up to. The social order of dogs is such that every dog must have a leader or be a leader. If you don't step up to the plate as leader, your dog will either appoint himself to the job (bad), or if he doesn't have the temperament of a leader, he may become an insecure mess (also

Teach your dog that you are the most important thing in his life.

bad). Dogs who are trained know that their human companions are in charge, need to be respected, and have things under control. This creates peace of mind for the dog and a pleasant living experience for the person.

For the past several thousand years, human beings have asked dogs to work for them. Look at all the different dog breeds out there and the myriad jobs they were bred to do: herding, guarding, hauling, hunting. Each of these tasks requires a dog who is enthusiastic about his job. But in our modern society, dogs often find themselves without a job. For some dogs, depending on age, breed, and individual temperament, it's a bigger problem than for others. A young, active Border Collie without a job will bounce off the walls, while an elderly Pomeranian without regular tasks will be only mildly bored. For dogs who like having something to do, training is a great way to fit the bill. A dog who is trained and can perform even simple tasks like sit and stay is a dog who sees himself with a job to do.

You may even decide to get him involved in a canine sport, which can simulate the work his breed was developed for. Herding dogs, gun dogs, and northern dogs often find satisfaction in herding trials, field trials, and recreational sledding. This makes for a happier dog who is less likely to look for other, less appropriate ways—like chewing up your couch or herding the kids around the yard—to spend his time and energy.

You Are the Boss
The first thing your puppy needs to learn is that you are the boss. This training should begin as soon as your new pup enters your

home. All dogs need a leader, and it's important that you establish yourself as the boss early in your dog's life. If your dog recognizes your authority, he will be more obedient, more secure, and easier to control. You can communicate to your dog that you are the leader in a number of different ways.

Being the leader means being first. Teach your puppy to wait for you to go through doorways before he is allowed to enter or exit a room. You can do this by keeping him on a leash and going through a door first, with him following behind you. If he tries to rush ahead of you, use the leash to bring him back. Put him in a sit-stay, walk through the door yourself, and then invite him to follow. Reward him when he obeys.

In puppy kindergarten or any other canine activity, paying attention to you is one of the first lessons a puppy learns. To learn commands and tricks, your puppy must first learn to focus on you when he's asked to. Teach him that making eye contact is good by asking him to look at you and then giving him a treat when he looks at your face or makes eye contact. Repeat this exercise until he automatically looks at your eyes, instead of the people walking by or the treat behind your back, when you are interacting.

Your puppy will see you as the leader if you are the one who determines when he plays and eats. Schedule playtime for your puppy and be the one to initiate it. Feed your puppy his daily meals yourself, and use treats in training to help him see you as the source of his food. Don't chase your puppy or play tug of war to take his toys away. Instead, teach him to give you his ball or other toys on command, saying "drop it," or using another verbal cue. When playing tug or fetch games, occasionally ask your puppy to give you the toy and then offer it back to him; he'll quickly learn that acquiescing continues the fun.

Using a treat, teach your dog to look at you when you ask him to. This will help with training throughout his life.

Always end games with the toy in your hands, not your dog's mouth.

As the leader, you need to establish food control right from the start. In the wild, it's natural for a dog to protect his food from other dogs and animals, but it's unacceptable for a dog to do this in the home. Food possessiveness can be the most dangerous and problematic canine behavior. It can lead to serious bites and a general sense of the dog controlling the home, rather than the other way around.

You can do a number of things to establish that you are in control of the food. Always ask your puppy to sit and leave it before allowing him to eat from his bowl. You should begin teaching him the basic *sit* and *leave it* commands as soon as you bring him home, if only to use them at mealtime. Later, you can incorporate these commands into the rest of his training regimen. The *leave it* command is different than the *stay* command in that it is used to prevent your dog from moving toward or taking an object. Asking him to leave a food or toy item reinforces that you make the decisions about what he eats or plays with and helps keep him safe. Puppies should never be allowed to eat scraps on the ground or floor without your permission.

Make your puppy earn his food by feeding him his meals one piece of kibble at a time, asking him to perform a command or trick for each piece of kibble. If your puppy is possessive, you can do this at each meal, but it's also good to do this a couple of times a week as reinforcement for any puppy. You can also interrupt your puppy's eating to offer him an extraspecial treat or to just hand feed him a few pieces of kibble; he'll learn that human hands in the food bowl mean good things. Do this at least once at every meal for his first couple of months in

Some owners use remote control collars to teach dogs certain skills and to discourage barking and other misbehaviors. However, many trainers discourage use of these devices.

your home. Keep up this training throughout his life by hand feeding or placing a treat in his bowl several times a week.

Training Equipment

To properly train your dog, it's important to have the right equipment. The pet supply industry offers an array of collars, leashes, and other training devices that can prove helpful when teaching your dog the ropes.

Collars

The kind of collar you choose for your dog depends on the type and level of training you're pursuing and on your dog's individual personality. When training young puppies, the

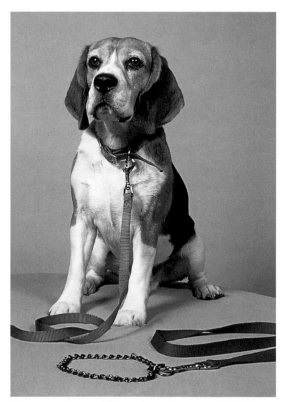

Be sure you have all the equipment you need to train your pup right.

best type of collar to use is a flat buckle collar made either of nylon or leather. This is the most basic collar and will help your puppy get used to wearing something around his neck.

For training older puppies and adult dogs—particularly those who are difficult to control—a chain collar (sometimes called a choke collar) is popular. People use chain collars to apply pressure around the dog's neck to check unwanted behavior. It's important to put this collar on correctly (the chain must be looped through the ring properly so it releases when pressure is removed), and to never leave it on a dog when he is unsupervised. Not all trainers like these collars because they can cause tracheal injuries when used incorrectly, and they rely on negative reinforcement in the form of pain to teach a behavior. They are still a mainstay in some training classes, though, and are often used when training high-energy or stubborn dogs.

A milder version of the chain collar is the half-check collar. Half-check collars are usually leather or nylon with a small section of chain that attaches to the leash. These collars provide less pressure than a chain collar does during training but more than a flat buckle collar does. The half-check collar has become increasingly popular as an alternative to the sometimes controversial chain collar. Sometimes the term *Martingale* collar is also used for the half-check collar. However, a traditional Martingale collar is a soft choke collar made of leather, nylon, or cotton. It consists of a double loop, with a larger neck loop and a smaller control loop that tightens when the dog pulls. The benefit of the Martingale collar is that it provides control but tightens only to a certain point so the dog is not choked. The Martingale collar was orig-

An enthusiastic dog tries on a head halter and a half-check collar.

inally developed for sighthounds and other dogs whose necks are larger than their heads. Martingale and half-check collars have become increasingly popular with trainers because they provide excellent control. They are sometimes called limited or partial slip collars.

The prong collar is also considered controversial because of its potential for misuse in the wrong hands and its dependence on negative reinforcement. This is a metal chain collar with tips that point inward toward the dog's neck. When the dog pulls, the points put considerable pressure on the dog's neck, thus discouraging pulling. Many trainers believe that prong collars are a valuable training tool if used by a knowledgeable trainer, but they don't recommend these collars for inexperienced dog owners.

Another collar that should be used only with the assistance of a professional trainer is the electric collar, also known as the shock collar. This collar features a battery operated mechanism that a person can use to administer a moderate shock to the dog's neck when he does something he shouldn't. It is often used for excessive barking (the dog is automatically shocked when he barks) and for training at long distances; for example, when teaching a dog to hunt in the field. Some trainers believe electric collars are useful for dogs who do not respond to other types of training. But many people, including a number of trainers and animal welfare activists, feel these collars are inhumane and ineffective. A gentler way to keep dogs from barking excessively is the citronella collar. This device automatically shoots off a spray of harmless citronella when the dog barks, providing an odor that is unpleasant to the dog and thus acts as a correction.

A gentle alternative to using collars for training is the head halter, which is much like the halter used on a horse. A head halter for

If using a chain collar, you should ask a trainer to show you the proper method. Incorrect usage can lead to trachea injuries.

dogs takes advantage of the dog's natural behavior by exerting slight pressure on the back of the dog's neck and muzzle, which causes him to pull backward rather than forward, and reestablishes the handler's position of top dog. Halters are designed to help train dogs who have a tendency to pull on leash.

Slip collars are a combination of collar and leash, which are used primarily by dog show exhibitors. They consist of a thin rope of nylon with a slip knot loop at the end that slips easily on and off a dog's head. Slip collars are designed for dogs who are well trained.

There are two different types of harnesses: those used for training and those used as an alternative to collars for small dogs with fragile necks, medical conditions such as a collapsed trachea, and a history of escaping from collars. The leash attaches to a tab at the back of the harness rather than at the neck. Standard harnesses are designed to attach to a leash without any additional control. Training harnesses have straps designed to restrain the front part of the dog's torso and chest, gently discouraging a dog's tendency to pull.

Leashes

An assortment of leashes can be found on the market today, each with its own practical and aesthetic appeal. When purchasing a leash, consider your dog's size and age, keeping in mind that small dogs should have lightweight leashes and large dogs should have stronger, heavier leashes. Length is also a factor. Most leashes come in 4-foot, 6-foot, or 8-foot lengths. For basic training, 6-foot leashes are usually recommended. The longer leashes are used when training requires you to be farther away from your dog.

Leashes come in a variety of materials. The most cost-effective leash on the market today is the nylon leash. Available in a variety of colors and designs, nylon leashes are adequate for most dogs and are consistently popular. They are both for training and for everyday use. But for those who are willing to spend a little extra for something nice, the leash of choice is made of leather. These leashes are luxurious and attractive, strong and easy to grip. A cotton leash is easier on the hands than nylon or leather is, especially if the dog tends to pull. It is lightweight and durable. Cotton leashes can be found in lengths up to 30 feet, making them valuable for training sessions in unenclosed outdoor areas.

Retractable leashes can also be quite long. They extend and retract with the dog as he moves around. A retractable leash is not recommended for dogs who aren't yet trained to walk calmly on a fixed-length leash. Some trainers believe these leashes encourage dogs to pull. A retractable leash also provides less control than a standard leash does.

If you plan to leave a leash on your dog in the house so you can train him more easily, a drag leash is your best option. This lightweight leash does not have a handle loop at the end so it can be safely dragged by your dog without the possibility of snagging on furniture or getting caught in his legs.

Your pup may have little use for the leash and collar at first, but he will quickly get used to them.

For situations when you need to keep your dog close to you, a traffic leash can be useful. Usually made of leather, traffic leashes are between 15 to 18 inches long and feature a large handle loop. A large dog can easily be held close to your body if equipped with a traffic leash.

For training on agility equipment or in any other activity that involves obstacles, many people prefer to use a training tab, a short leash about 8 inches long. The benefit of the training tab is that it does not get caught in equipment or tangled in a dog's legs, but it still allows you some control over the dog, either when leading him through an obstacle, or catching him as he tries to run off. It's especially useful for young, exuberant dogs who become overexcited during training sessions.

Training Methods

There are many different methods of training, and it's important to know about them before you begin training your dog. Some are widely popular, and others have become controversial or are only slowly gaining acceptance.

Group training can be an excellent way for both you and your dog to learn new skills.

Three training methods especially well known are positive reinforcement training, correction-based training, and clicker training.

The most widely accepted type of training today is based on positive reinforcement. This method emphasizes praise and reward, and de-emphasizes punishment, or corrections. The reward can range from food treats to positive verbal encouragement to petting and to play. Most modern trainers use a combination of positive reinforcement and minor corrections, such as a quick leash jerk or vocal correction, while some use strictly positive methods.

The principles of positive reinforcement are relatively simple. By asking the dog to do

Positive reinforcement greatly enhances a dog's interest in learning, so always end your dog's training sessions on a positive note, with a lot of praise, a fun game, or a tasty treat.

what you want and then rewarding him when he complies, you are teaching him to obey you. Treats and praise are great rewards from the dog's point of view. And in time, a dog who is trained with positive reinforcement and mild correction learns exactly what he needs to do, and then corrections are rarely, if ever, needed. The result is a happy dog who enjoys learning and catches on quickly.

Most modern trainers recommend that people look for a professional who primarily uses positive reinforcement when shopping for a trainer or training class. This is especially true when looking for a puppy kindergarten class because the way your dog is trained as a puppy will affect his attitude about training for the rest of his life.

The traditional correction-based training was the norm 20 years ago. However, it's rare these days to find a trainer who works only in this old method of training, where dogs were simply punished for doing something wrong and never rewarded for doing something right. In this type of training, the absence of punishment is considered the reward. Corrections include leash corrections, scruff shakes, hitting, shocking, and negative verbal corrections.

Most trainers now believe that correction-based training is less effective than other, more positive methods because dogs learn better when they are rewarded for proper behavior than they do when they are only punished for improper behavior. When a dog is only being corrected for improper behavior, he is forced to try a number of other behaviors to find the one that pleases the trainer, so training takes more time. In addition, many trainers believe that dogs who receive positive training enjoy their work and show an enthusiasm not seen in dogs trained exclusively through negative reinforcement. Correction-based training is no longer recommended by most dog behavior experts.

Clicker training is a positive training method that is recommended by many experts. A clicker is used to give dogs precise instructions. The clicker is a small handheld device that makes a clicking sound when you press it. It is used to tell the dog when he has done something right at the exact moment he is doing it, thus instantly rewarding him. Clicker training was first developed in the 1950s by well-known animal trainer Karen Pryor to teach tricks to dolphins. It is now often used to teach canine activities such as agility and obedience.

The idea behind the clicker is that normal rewards are always delayed—saying "good dog" or giving a treat usually means the dog is rewarded a few seconds after he's completed the command. He may even be leaving the sit position by the time you're done rewarding him. Because of the delay, it is difficult for the dog to understand exactly what you are rewarding him for: the sitting action, the sit

Clicker training is becoming increasingly popular as a positive method of behavior training.

Teach your pup to associate the clicker with something positive by repeatedly clicking and rewarding with small treats.

itself, or standing up from a sit. A click is an instantaneous marker with no ambiguity.

The clicker is also used to shape dog behavior, giving the dog positive feedback for learning a new behavior one step at a time. For example, a dog is taught to shake hands through shaping by clicking when the dog happens to lift his paw. Once the dog offers his paw to you reliably, the cue or vocal command is introduced. The dog is then clicked for lifting his paw when you say "shake."

Before introducing your dog to the clicker, practice using the clicker device without your dog so that you are comfortable with it. By pushing and releasing the springy metal of the clicker, you can produce a two-toned click. Put your dog in another room while you practice so your dog can get used to the clicking noise from a distance.

To teach your dog using the clicker method, you must first teach him to associate the click with something good. Start with some very small delicious treats in one hand and the clicker in the other. Put the clicker behind your back, click it, and give your dog a treat. Do this about 40 times in a row to teach your dog to associate the click with the treat. You're successful when your dog starts to look for a treat when you click. Your dog may begin to relate the click to the treat right away, or it may take 20 or 25 repetitions. Even if he begins to look for the treat right away, follow through with 40 repetitions to ensure that he understands.

You are now ready to teach your dog using the clicker. Train him to do basic obedience commands by shaping his behaviors. Click when you catch him in a sit or a down and give him a treat. After he begins to associate the sit with the click and offers the behavior, you can add the verbal cue "sit" and then click. Another method to teaching sit with a clicker is to train sit in the traditional method, by luring the dog into the sit position, and then clicking.

You can get creative with the clicker and teach your dog all kinds of tricks, if you are so inclined. You'll find it's much easier to teach tricks when you're able to communicate exactly what behaviors you are asking for. Some owners find that it is difficult to juggle the clicker, the treats, and the dog. Taking advantage of a few pieces of equipment will help. Use a small clicker, rather than a large one, which is harder to hold. Most clickers have a small hole through which you can thread a lanyard or a wrist coil so you can hang the clicker from your neck or wrist. This keeps your hands free when you're not clicking. Another important piece of clicker equipment, which works for all positive training methods, is a treat bag. A treat bag is a small, sturdy bag that clips to your belt or waistband and can be drawn tight with a drawstring. There are also treat bags made with extra pockets for all your clicker equipment.

To find a good trainer, ask for referrals from your veterinarian and dog-loving friends.

Formal Training

While some people prefer to train their dogs at home themselves or with a private trainer, the best avenue of learning for most dogs is in obedience class. By beginning your dog's training in a class setting, you can get the help of an instructor. You also have the benefit of working with your dog in a setting where distractions are present, and your dog has the chance to socialize with other dogs.

In a class, your dog will learn commands as part of a group. He will probably receive some individual instruction if he (or you) is having difficulty with a particular command, but this will be limited to the number of instructors and the class size. For this reason, it's best to choose a class with no more than 10 students per instructor. Most instructors make time available to speak with individual owners for a few minutes before and after each class.

Even though you take your dog to class, you still need to do some training on your own. While classes tend to run for about an

Zoomies

Whether you call it zoomies or going on a tear, if you have a puppy you know what it is. Puppies from about three to six months of age tend to have sudden bursts of high energy. Without warning, they zoom around the house or yard as if they've gone loony. In this wild mood, they may nip at people as they dash by or grab something they shouldn't and run off with it, inviting a chase. Zoomies usually last five or ten minutes and occur most often during the evening when puppies need to release excess energy before settling down to sleep. These energy bursts are a normal part of puppyhood, so you needn't try to stop them.

- Two puppies the same age may zoom around together and often an adult dog can be persuaded to join in, but if your puppy is your only dog, you might try joining in the fun yourself. You can turn zoomies into a game that you can steer in a positive direction.

- To keep your puppy from grabbing objects or people while he zooms around, encourage him to carry one of his own toys. Wave or wiggle the toy to get your puppy's attention, then either hand it off to him as he dashes by or toss it into his path so he can snatch it from the floor. Say "take it" or "get it" when you offer or throw the toy so your puppy will know he has your permission to grab it.

- If you hand your puppy a toy, make sure you offer something large enough so his teeth won't collide with your fingers. A thick knotted rope or a big floppy toy works well. If you'd rather your dog not grab things from your hand, even in play, throw the toy instead. This is also a good strategy when playing with a dog who uses his teeth too roughly.

- Zoomies are fun and good exercise for puppies, who will grow out of this bursting-with-energy stage within a few months on their own. Young adult dogs have these energy bursts, too, but less frequently than pups do.

- Just guide your puppy during zoomies and enjoy the hilarity while it lasts. The world can be a far too serious place—let your puppy help you cultivate the playful side of your own behavior.

hour once a week, you'll be expected to do 15 to 30 minutes of homework each day to reinforce the skills and commands you've learned in that week's class. The time should be broken up throughout the day with several 5- to 10-minute sessions. A puppy will probably do best with three 5-minute sessions. A good instructor provides students with a training handbook as a guide.

If you are planning to take only one formal training class with your dog, make it puppy kindergarten. Here, dogs learn the basics they need to become good citizens. They interact with other puppies and people, learn the basic commands such as *sit* and *down*, and learn how to focus on you even with the distraction of a roomful of potential playmates. More important, you learn how to

According to a study conducted by the National Council on Pet Population Study and Policy, the following are the top 10 reasons dogs are relinquished to shelters: moving, refusal by landlord to permit a pet, too many animals in the household, cost of pet maintenance, owner having personal problems, inadequate facilities, no homes for dog's littermates, no time for the dog, pet illness, and biting.

teach your dog. A good puppy kindergarten instructor will give you the skills you need to help integrate your puppy into your home. You also will get the chance to ask questions about behavior issues your puppy may be having and to decide whether your puppy needs additional training beyond puppy kindergarten basics. It's also an excellent bonding experience for you and your puppy and likely a memory you will cherish.

Instructors in group classes rarely have time to spend a significant amount of time on individual problems. If you are having a particular problem with your dog, private trainers are the most helpful. Aggression is a common problem that prompts people to seek the help of a private trainer. People with unruly dogs who they simply can't control often find help through private trainers.

If private training appeals to you, you can hire a trainer to come to your home and teach you how to handle your dog. Bear in mind, this is a lot more expensive than going to a class, but it is probably the best option when dealing with a specific behavior problem that requires one-on-one training. It's important to choose a trainer who is going to teach you how to train your dog, not just do the work for you.

In the past, it was popular among dog owners to send their dogs away to school. In recent years, however, this has become increasingly uncommon, and for good reason. While your dog may learn myriad commands in record speed when working with a

Enjoy the zoomies while they last because soon enough your pup will be a sedate older dog with too much decorum to run slapdash through mud puddles.

professional trainer, this training won't last at home. Your dog may exit a boarding training facility with amazing abilities, but those abilities won't do either of you any good if you have not been taught to train your dog. Training is a lifelong endeavor, something you and your dog must work on together. Just because your dog has mastered basic commands now, doesn't mean you can rest on your laurels. He will need continual and consistent reinforcement of the lessons he's learned. Old dogs can learn new tricks but they can also forget them. Learning the basic commands is not the end of your dog training; rather, it's the beginning of a lifetime education.

How intelligent are dogs? A Border Collie named Rico, studied by psychologist Julia Fischer at the Max-Planck Institute for Evolutionary Anthropology in Leipzig, Germany, has a vocabulary of more than 200 words. His abilities are comparable to those of a three-year-old child. Rico, a family dog, demonstrated his smarts by, among other things, selecting a new toy from among familiar ones, even though it was referred to by a name he'd never heard before.

Use treats to teach simple commands such as sit, down, and leave it.

Choosing a Trainer

Whether you are looking for a private trainer to come to your home and work with your dog or you are looking for a good class to attend, give a lot of thought to the person who will be guiding your dog through his training lessons.

The best way to choose either a private trainer or an obedience school instructor is through word of mouth. Ask other dog owners you know for a referral. Find out which trainers or instructors they like and why they like them. Seek out someone who uses positive reinforcement as his or her main philosophy of training. If you can't get a referral from another dog owner, ask your veterinarian. Vet's offices often refer dog owners to trainers and obedience instructors.

Once you have the name of a trainer or instructor, your next task is to evaluate that person and decide whether you want to work with her. If you are looking at a private trainer, ask for a consultation. The trainer will usually come to your home and meet with you and your dog. Ask the trainer what kinds of methods she uses and how she plans to help your dog with his problem. Look for a trainer who is knowledgeable in dog behavior. Ask for credentials such as a degree from a dog training school, considerable experience as a trainer, training titles acquired in competition, and participation in a dog training organization such as the Association of Pet Dog Trainers (APDT).

Obedience instructors teach basic training to dogs and people, so they don't need to be as qualified as private trainers who train dogs with serious behavioral problems. When you have a referral to an obedience school, go to a class and watch the instructor in action, making sure she uses positive reinforcement with the dogs and provides careful instruction to the owners.

A good instructor should be willing to answer specific questions about your dog's behavior and should be available for further questions for at least five minutes before and after class. If she seems disinterested in helping you, find another trainer. You want your obedience instructor to be good with people as well as with dogs because your dog isn't the only one learning; you are learning the methods and skills needed to train your dog.

Just as people may develop memory problems as they age, so do dogs. You can help keep your dog's mind alert by offering him puzzles like Kong toys or Buster Cubes filled with food and by playing games such as hide-and-seek with treats. Memory-improving medication may also be of benefit, so talk to your veterinarian.

Puppy Training

Much of the training you do with your puppy will take place at home. This is true even if you decide to continue on to adult obedience classes or any other activity training. All good teachers give homework, and dog trainers are no exception.

Some people think puppies are too young to be trained, but nothing could be further from the truth. Puppyhood is prime training time for dogs. Nature designed their little brains to learn as much as possible to help prepare them for the world of adulthood. Puppy training can begin as early as eight weeks of age. You can begin teaching your young puppy certain rules of the house and a few basic obedience commands.

Training Principles

Important points to keep in mind when training your puppy are reinforcement, both positive and negative; consistency; practice; and prevention.

Always use positive reinforcement, and use it frequently. That means whenever your dog does something right, reward him, either with food, praise, or both. He will catch on quickly that doing what you ask gets him something nice in return.

Don't be afraid to use verbal corrections when needed. The word *no* is as vital to the good behavior of a dog as it is to a child. If your dog is doing something he shouldn't, don't be afraid to say "no chew" or "no bite." Adding the word *no* to the behavior your dog is committing makes your point. Be stern to make an impression, but be sure to control your emotions. Anger should never be a factor when you are training your dog. Always give the verbal correction while the action is taking place. Correcting your dog any time after he has committed his crime will not teach him anything.

Consistency is important when training. People often forget this and then can't understand why their dog doesn't learn. Know the rules in your own mind, and then enforce them every single time. If you let your dog get away with responding to your commands only some of the time, you soon won't be able to get him to pay attention to you at all. And don't repeat commands. Teach your dog that he must come, sit, or stay the first time you give the order.

Always practice and keep practicing. Don't assume that once your dog has learned basic obedience that he never has to brush up on it again. Practice and reinforce what he knows on a regular basis throughout his life. That way, when you need him to perform one of his commands on the spot, he will have it fresh in his mind.

Preventing your dog from establishing a bad habit is the best way to keep him from performing that behavior. If a dog is allowed to potty in the house, he learns that it is OK to potty in the house. And, if he's allowed as a puppy to nip or to chew, it will be difficult to break him of these behaviors when he grows up.

Crate-training your dog will be a boon to house-training as well as provide your pup a warm, safe place of his own.

Crate-Training

Crate-training is one of the best things you can ever do for your dog. Some people are adverse to the idea of crate-training because they think it is tantamount to keeping a dog in a cage. If used properly, however, a crate is a humane way to handle a dog. Crate-training works because dogs have a strong denning instinct and like to sleep in small, confined places. The crate serves as a safe place for a dog to escape to when he's tired or anxious. It provides a dog with security and a permanent bed that you can take with you wherever you go. And dogs who travel in crates are safer than those who don't. To top things off, crate-training is an invaluable tool for house-training.

The best time to crate-train a dog is when he's a young puppy. At this age, puppies are most open to learning and appreciate the security that a crate can bring. When intro-ducing your puppy to a crate, it's important to convince him that the crate is a wonderful place to be. You'll do this with the help of food and toys.

First, you need to purchase a crate for your puppy. Crates come in two general styles: plastic airline crates and wire mesh crates. The type of crate you choose is a matter of per-sonal preference, although plastic airline crates seem to provide the greatest sense of security for dogs because they have solid pan-els. Another advantage is that the plastic crates can be used to ship your dog by airplane, whereas the wire mesh crates can't. Whichever style you choose, you want a crate that is large enough for your puppy to be able to stand up and turn around comfortably, but not so large that he can get far away from any mess he might make. (This is especially important if you plan to use the crate for house-training.)

Most breeders and trainers agree that crate-training is the preferred method of house-training young puppies of most breeds.

House-training accidents should be expected for the first few months. Be consistent and proactive until the puppy is a year old.

In general, puppies avoid eliminating when they know they cannot move away from their waste. Your new puppy is rapidly growing, which means one of two things: you buy a puppy-size crate now and another when he reaches (or comes close to) his adult size, or you buy an adult-size crate with divider panels that can be adjusted as your puppy grows.

Decide where you want to keep your dog's crate. It's best if your dog can sleep with you in your bedroom, since this counts as time spent with you and gives your dog a greater sense of belonging. If you decide not to keep the crate in your bedroom, place it in an area of the house that is neither too hot nor too drafty and not so heavily trafficked that your dog won't be able to get his needed rest. At the same time, the crate should not be relegated to a basement or other out-of-the-way location; dogs want to be able to hear and smell their people around them.

To introduce your puppy to the crate, feed him his meals in the crate, leaving the door open. Start by putting the bowl inside the crate near the entrance, and then gradually move it farther into the crate over several days as your dog seems comfortable.

You can also toss a toy or a treat into the crate whenever you have the opportunity. This will encourage your puppy to go into the crate and will help him associate it with something pleasant.

Whenever your puppy enters the crate, give him a command word or phrase that you want to use to tell him to go into the crate. He'll come to associate that word with entering the crate and will learn to go to his crate whenever you give the command. This is an excellent tool to use when your puppy is underfoot or impertinent or it's time for bed. Your command can be anything from the traditional *kennel* to *go to bed*.

Once your puppy is comfortable entering the crate and spending time in it with the door open, you can close the door. Try this for the first time when your puppy is eating his meal. He probably won't notice that the door is shut until he has finished eating. If he paws at the door and whines to get out, say "quiet" and wait until he is silent before you let him out. Letting him out of the crate while he's whining and pawing will teach him that carrying on works when he wants his way and will inhibit him from becoming comfortable in his crate. By opening the door when he whines, you provide tacit agreement that the crate is scary.

Keep doing this with every meal until your puppy has learned to finish his meal and quietly wait to be let out of the crate. Once he has become comfortable, you can start lengthening the amount of time he stays in the crate. Eventually, ask him to enter the crate at times other than dinnertime. Place a dog biscuit or another treat in the crate and give him the crate command. If he's comfortable with the crate, he shouldn't hesitate to enter it and enjoy his treat with the door closed. Always keep a fun toy or two in the crate to keep him occupied. Provide both a hard chew toy like a Nylabone or Kong and a soft fuzzy toy so he'll have a toy to fit his mood. Any toy you leave in your puppy's crate should be sturdy and safe. Fuzzy toys should not have holes, tears, or squeakers, should be labeled safe for children over three, and should be machine washable. Some stuffings are not safe for ingestion; for crate use, an unstuffed lamb's wool toy works well. Rope toys are also good options. Never leave rawhides, hooves, or pigs' ears in your puppy's crate.

Although the crate is a valuable tool, it's important to remember that it should not be overused. Do not leave your puppy in the crate for more than four hours, except at night when you are sleeping. If you need to confine your dog for more than four hours at a time, keep him in the kitchen or another area of the house where he'll have more room to stretch his legs.

If you do not have a separate, dog-friendly room, use doggy gates to secure the dog in the room. Keep the crate in this closed off area so that your pup has a cozy place to which to retreat. On the other side of the room, you may choose to use paper as a soiling site. If you work, try to come home at lunch to provide playtime for your new pup. Consider hiring a dog walker or asking a neighbor to stop by once or twice a day.

House-Training

The importance of house-training can't be overemphasized. Your puppy must learn to relieve himself outdoors as soon as he comes to live with you. Otherwise, he will have bad habits that you will have a hard time coping with in the future.

Some owners choose to paper train their dogs; however, this can extend the period needed for house-training.

Litter Box and Paper Training

House-training a dog to use a litter box or paper can be a boon for high rise apartment dwellers. Just because a dog is litter-box or paper trained, though, doesn't mean he won't need to go outside. Dogs still need to get outside daily to walk and play.

To train your dog to use a litter box, use clay litter, newspapers, or another absorbent material in the box. Dogs are less picky than cats are about the material, but be sure to use the same material consistently. Litter boxes and litter made for dogs are available in different sizes at pet supply stores, or you can use a standard cat pan if you have a smaller dog.

At first, it may be a good idea to leave the litter slightly dirty to attract the dog back to the litter box. Place your dog in the box when you see him showing signs that he has to go, like sniffing and circling. Say "go potty" or provide another cue that you want him to associate with using the box. Praise him when he eliminates in the litter box. If he eliminates outside of it, say "no" and immediately lift him or lead him into the box and encourage him to go there. Praise him if he does.

To paper train, cover an area of an uncarpeted room with a thick layer of newspapers. Be sure it is away from where your dog eats. Then use the same method as discussed above for litter box training. When he shows signs of needing to go, place him on the thick layer of newspaper where you want him to go. Praise him when he eliminates on the papers; if he misses say "no" and put him on the paper. Use a commercial product that simulates the scent of urine, available at pet supply stores, to attract him to the paper, or treat the paper with some of his own urine. When you leave the house, confine him in the papered area. If he has used the papers while you were gone, praise him. Slowly decrease the amount of paper over time, until only a small area is covered with paper and he is trained to go to that spot.

Whatever method of house-training you use, notice the times when your dog or puppy usually has to go, such as after waking or eating, and keep him on a schedule. Be patient and give him a lot of praise when he eliminates where he is supposed to. Never punish your dog when he has an accident; instead, use positive reinforcement when he does the right thing. Remember, some dogs learn quickly, while others may take months to house-train.

There are two important tricks to ease house-training: crate-training and eliminating on command. By using a crate, you're able to take advantage of your dog's denning instinct, which is strong even in young puppies; it keeps them from soiling the place where they sleep. Use a command such as *go potty* every time you take your puppy outside to eliminate. He will soon associate the command with the act. Learning to eliminate on command reinforces that your puppy's business is done outdoors at your discretion, not indoors when the urge hits. It is also handy when the weather is bad or if you are in a hurry.

House-training, like other training, is about preventing bad habits. The quickest way to house-train a puppy is to avoid establishing the habit of eliminating indoors. When your puppy is inside, keep him in his crate or close by you so you can keep an eye on him. You may even want to keep him on a leash attached to your belt. Take him outside to relieve himself as frequently as possible. If your puppy is young (8 to 12 weeks), he'll need to go outside every two hours. He should be able to make it through the night, without going potty by this age, so don't feel that you have to set your alarm to get up every two hours. However, if he whines during the night, take him out and encourage him to relieve himself. Once your puppy is older, you won't have to take him out as frequently, although the more you do, the faster he will learn to eliminate outdoors.

When you bring your puppy outside, make sure he eliminates before you begin playing with him. In the beginning, keep him on a leash and lead him to the same area of the yard each and every time. When he begins to eliminate, give the word or phrase you have chosen for his bathroom command. After you give the command and he is doing his business, praise him gently. Be careful not to distract him as you praise him since you don't want him to stop what he's doing. It's important during this training time to be patient. It takes some puppies quite a while to catch on, while others get the idea fairly quickly.

If your puppy has an accident indoors, don't overreact. The old methods of hitting a dog with a rolled-up newspaper or rubbing his nose in his mistake are not only inhumane but also ineffective. Instead, do not react to the mistake if it happened more than four seconds before you noticed it. If you catch your puppy in the act, loudly say "ah-ah!" or "whoops!" to interrupt the action, grab his leash, and lead him outside to his bathroom spot. Don't stop to find a leash if it's not immediately accessible, simply scoop him up or lead him by his collar. Quick, decisive action is paramount. He will probably continue eliminating once he gets outside, so praise him effusively.

If you repeatedly find messes in the house or in an area where your dog is confined (including his crate), you need to figure out what is going wrong in your training process. You may need to give your puppy more frequent breaks outdoors to do his business. You may also need to confine him to a smaller crate or area. If the crate is too big, your puppy will be able to get away from his mess and won't be inclined to hold it.

It can take anywhere from a few weeks to a few months to house-train a puppy. The amount of time it takes depends a lot on the individual dog. If you work outside the home and your puppy must resort to eliminating

---

When a dog shakes an object held in his mouth, he is displaying behavior from his days of hunting and killing small animals for food. Dog breeds, such as terriers, that were originally developed to quickly kill a large number of rodents display this behavior most often.

---

on paper in a confined area, house-training will take longer. Consider hiring a pet sitter to drop by at least once a day to reinforce training. By the time your dog is five months old, he should be reliable in the house. Keep in mind that although he may be reliable in *your* house, he may not be as well behaved in someone else's home. If you go to someone's house to visit, make sure your puppy does his business before you go indoors, and then keep a close eye on him.

If your puppy does have an accident in your home, it's vital that you clean all traces of feces or urine thoroughly. Otherwise, the puppy will assume that this is a proper place for elimination and will continue to eliminate in the same spot over and over again. To thoroughly clean the spot, remove and soak up all waste matter, then thoroughly douse the affected area with a commercial pet cleaning product. These products utilize enzymes to neutralize urine and fecal stains and are available at pet supply stores. Be sure to follow the package directions. Once cleaned, keep your puppy away from the area—if it is a communal area, then cover with an overturned laundry basket or punched aluminum. If the smell lingers despite your cleaning efforts, it's likely you didn't get everything. Pet supply stores sell black lights which will allow you to find errant stains.

Basic Commands

Puppies not only need to learn the rules of the house and how to fit into the world, but they also should learn some basic commands. This is important because a little puppy will someday grow up to be a bigger dog (or even a giant dog), and you need to be able to control your dog. Dogs who are obedience trained are generally better behaved and easier to live with.

You can start introducing your puppy to obedience training as young as nine weeks. This is when he should learn to wear a leash and collar and when he can begin learning some basic commands, including *sit* and *down*, and some behavioral commands, including *leave it*, and *drop it*.

When training your puppy, remember that positive reinforcement works best. Every time your puppy does something right, give him a food treat and plenty of praise in the form of happy talk. You'll be amazed at how eagerly your puppy will want to please you. If your puppy makes a mistake, do not punish him. Instead, ignore the mistake and set him up for success by repeating the command and ensuring that he will comply. Remember, puppies have a short attention span. Training should be brief and upbeat; don't give your puppy a chance to become bored. Provide breaks during training by giving the release command and playing a game or just by running around together.

The release command creates a beginning and an end to every command you give. Although *OK* is the most common release command, you can use whatever word works for you and your puppy, just be sure to use that command consistently. Many trainers recommend against using *OK* simply because it is such a common word. If your dog is in a down-stay during a lively party, chances are there are going to be a few occasions when a guest says "OK." If this is a concern to you, come up with an alternative release command; *go play* or *all done* are two popular alternatives.

If luring your dog to sit doesn't work, don't push down on his hips; this can strain his joints. Instead, run your hand along his back and down his tail and then gently push behind his knees, where his back legs naturally bend.

One of the most useful commands you can teach your puppy is *leave it*. This command is used whenever you want your puppy to stop doing what he's doing. It not only can save your dinner, but it also can save your puppy's life. If he is about to eat the steak you just dropped on the floor, you can say "leave it" and he'll stop in his tracks. If he's chasing a cat into the street, you can say "leave it" to get him to stop. If he is about to put something hazardous in his mouth, *leave it* will motive him to cease and desist.

To teach the *leave it* command, you must have your dog under leash control. Put a piece of food on the ground and walk by it with your puppy. When he approaches to investigate the item, say "leave it" and pull him away. Then say "good leave it" and give him a scratch or a treat. Practice this repeatedly with food items, toys, or anything else that stirs your puppy's curiosity.

Other ways to reinforce the *leave it* command are to keep an empty soda can filled with coins or a spray bottle filled with water handy. When your puppy approaches something he shouldn't, say "leave it." If he ignores you, give him a squirt with the bottle or toss the can of coins near him. However, some trainers discourage this. As long as you are consistent, your puppy should learn the command quickly.

When your puppy has something in his mouth that you want him to relinquish, the *drop it* command comes in handy. *Drop it* tells the puppy to let go of whatever he is holding. The best way to teach *drop it* is by trading with your puppy. If he's holding one of his toys in his mouth, get one of his favorite treats and then ask him to drop the toy as you offer him the treat. When he drops the toy, give him the treat. Do this often and you will find that your puppy will instantly drop on command. If your puppy refuses the command, gently press your fingers into the gap behind his canines, this should cause him to release the object. Praise him and offer something in exchange. You can reinforce the *drop it* command by using a toy to play tug with your puppy and periodically asking him to drop it. Ask him to sit, then return the toy and continue to play. Remember to always end a tug game with control over the toy.

One of the easiest commands you can teach your puppy is to *sit*. You can train your puppy to sit by using a treat lure. Stand in front of your puppy while holding a treat in one hand. Starting directly above his nose, slowly raise the treat upward in a vertical line and slightly out. As his head lifts to follow the treat, your puppy's rump should drop to the ground. Make sure he keeps his front paws on the ground. Once the pup is sitting, give him the treat and praise him. When he's consistently sitting with the treat

You can lure your pup into a sit by raising a treat in front of his nose. As his nose goes up, his butt will go down.

lure, introduce the *sit* command. He will quickly associate the action with the command and his performance with receiving a reward.

Teaching your puppy to come when called can save his life in a dangerous situation, and it allows him off-leash freedom in a safe environment. To teach the *come* command, you want to get your puppy to think coming to you is a really good thing. With a treat in hand, say your dog's name and "come" and run in the opposite direction from your dog. He will probably chase after you. As soon as he does, stop, wait for him to run up to you, then praise him verbally and give him the treat. Do this several times a day for a few weeks until you don't have to run for him to come right when you call him.

Another way to practice *come* is to get a few friends each with a handful of treats to sit in a large circle. Have each person call the puppy one at a time. When your puppy responds appropriately, he gets a treat. Your puppy soon learns to respond to the *come* command.

You can also use a long leash when teaching the *come* command. If your puppy doesn't respond to your first command of *come,* simply draw in the leash gently but firmly. Praise him and give him a treat once he's in front of you.

Stay is an important command to maintain control over your dog. It may even save his life someday.

To reinforce the *come* command throughout your dog's life, occasionally call him simply to give him a treat. Don't reserve the *come* command for ending play; this will quickly teach your puppy not to respond. Never ask your dog to come and then scold him.

Stay is an important command because it enables you to control your puppy off leash. You can use *stay* when you need your puppy to

Practicing commands with an adult dog reinforces the dog's education. Alternate hand signals, voice commands, and whistles in the dog's training.

stand or sit in one place. This can be in any situation from outside in the park to inside your house during dinner time. Before you can teach your puppy to stay, you must teach him to sit. You will then incorporate *stay* into your *sit* command.

Start by telling your puppy to sit. Although you won't be holding the leash, attach a leash to his collar so you can bring him quickly under control if decides to make a dash for it. With particularly exuberant puppies, you might want to recruit a helper to stand behind the puppy and hold the leash. While standing about 6 inches in front of him, present your open hand to his face; it should be flat with the palm side facing him. Say "stay" at the same time. Give your puppy a treat, saying "good stay." Continue to give him treats at 2- to 3-second intervals. If

he moves out of the stay position, do not give him a treat. Repeat this until he is staying reliably for 10 seconds. Then step back about a half foot and ask him to stay. If making this move is challenging for your puppy, you may need a partner to stand next to him and give him treats as he stays. If your puppy moves toward you during that time, put him back where he was and ask him to sit again, and then to stay. Although he may grasp the concept in one training session, it's unlikely he'll retain it, so start each training session in the initial position and then gradually increase distance.

Once your puppy sits quietly for 10 seconds, release him and give him a treat. Be sure to offer plenty of verbal praise. Practice this daily until your puppy consistently stays for 10 seconds. You can then ask him to hold the stay for 20 seconds. As your pup becomes comfortable at each amount of time, gradually increase the distance as well. Be consistent about making your puppy hold the stay until you release him. That means every time he breaks the stay, you walk him back into place and start over.

Once your puppy is reliable at staying while on a leash, you can graduate to teaching the *stay* command off leash in an enclosed area. Again, increase the time and distance

Once your dog is confident doing a sit, you can begin to teach him down.

you ask him to hold the stay as he gets better and better at it.

Down is a great command to teach your puppy if you like the idea of having voice control over him. Combine it with the *stay* command and you can keep your puppy in one spot under control for an extended period of time.

If your puppy already knows the *sit* command, the *down* command will be easy to teach. Put your puppy in a sit position and hold a treat in front of his nose. Lower the treat straight down to the floor by his feet, saying his name followed by the *down* command. Your puppy will lower his head to try to get the treat. As he does this, pull the treat away from him, still at floor level. You may need to put one hand on his rump to ensure that he does not stand up and simply walk toward the treat. You can also pull his front legs out and gently set him in the down position. He'll probably need to be shown only once or twice before he figures out what you are asking for. Once his entire body is down on the ground, give him the treat. Once your pup is comfortable in the down position, you can increase duration over several days of training sessions by offering him a treat but not allowing him to take it immediately. Say "good down" and then release him.

Another way to teach the down command is to say "Down, good down" every time you see your puppy lying down. He'll soon learn to associate the word down with being in that position. Then try giving the command when he's not lying down. When he responds correctly, say "good down" and give him a treat.

When your puppy reliably responds to the *down* and *sit-stay* commands, you can add the *down-stay* command. Teach the down-stay using the same technique as you used when teaching the sit-stay. Ask him to hold the down-stay for a longer and longer period of time. Eventually, when your puppy becomes an adult, you should be able to walk away from him and leave him in the down-stay.

The down-stay command is a natural extension of the sit-stay exercise. Practice in an area that is free from distractions.

Although pet dogs don't need to learn a perfect heel, they should be able to walk nicely on a leash.

Unless you plan to compete in obedience or conformation with your dog, it isn't necessary for him to perfect a flawless heel. What is vital, however, is that he learn to walk nicely on a leash. Teaching your puppy to walk quietly beside you on leash is important because you don't want him to drag you down the sidewalk or zigzag along in front of or behind you. Dogs who know how to walk quietly on leash are much more pleasant to take for walks and definitely make better companions.

It's important to teach your puppy how to walk properly on leash early because once a puppy develops the habit of pulling, it is difficult to correct. While your puppy is young, he is learning to accept the leash, and he's taking short walks where he follows you or walks alongside you. Once he is no longer a tiny puppy, you should start teaching him the proper way to walk on a leash.

To teach your puppy to walk beside you, work with him in an outdoor area with mini-

mal distractions. This could be a quiet park or the sidewalk in front of your house. Be sure to bring treats with you. Wait until your puppy is relaxed and focused on you, and stand in front of him holding the leash. Hold a treat to his face and then back up. As you do, call his name to follow you. When he does this, praise him verbally and give him the treat. If he doesn't come toward you, keep encouraging him until he steps forward. If he likes treats, it won't be long before he figures out what you want.

If you lose his attention during the session and he starts pulling away from you, lure him back to you using a treat. While he's looking at you, enthusiastically tell him he's a good boy. Encourage him to follow you, and if he does, reward him with additional treats.

When you have convinced your puppy to pay close attention to you using this method, move on to the next step. This may take several days or it may take several weeks. Then using the same method, walk forward away from your puppy with your back to him. When he comes toward you, he will probably move up beside you. Steer him to the left side of your body, and once he's taken a few steps this way, praise him and give him a treat. If he starts getting ahead of you and pulling, stop

You can begin training your dog for many sports when he is just a pup.

Competitive obedience training can be a bonding experience for dog and owner.

this is to keep training sessions short and sweet. Use a lot of fun and tasty rewards and always use a jolly voice. Training sessions are not the time to reprimand your dog. If he isn't learning a command, shrug it off and try again tomorrow. Puppies have bad days just as people do. Never keep a session going so long that your puppy becomes bored or restless, and don't allow yourself to become frustrated—your puppy will pick up on this very quickly. Don't work on any one command for more than five minutes, and always end your session before either of you begin to tire. At the end of your training session, reward your puppy for his hard work with a play session and a lot of praise.

Beyond Puppy Training

Even after your dog has graduated from puppy kindergarten class and has learned the basic commands and what's expected of him at home, your job as dog trainer isn't done. You need to reinforce what your puppy has learned to ensure that he knows his place in the household and retains the training he learned as a youngster.

You can do this at home on your own or by taking more obedience classes. Obedience training for adult dogs is similar to puppy class except more precision is required. If you are fortunate enough to have a good training facility near you, you can take classes that emphasize manners at home as well as those that train for competitive events.

If you want to take your dog further along in the training process, you can opt to participate in any of a variety of dog activities that will provide you with different training opportunities. Some of the activities are competitive and will enable you to attend events that will allow you to earn titles for your dog. Other activities are noncompetitive and are just for your dog's education and enjoyment.

until the leash is taut and he can't continue. If he continues to strain forward, take a few steps backward. This will get his attention back on you, at which time you should start walking forward again. Do this each time he begins to pull. When he looks at you, praise him or give him a treat. You'll probably need to do this a number of times before he catches on, especially if he's already in the habit of pulling.

Be consistent when training your puppy to walk properly on a leash. Find the patience to teach him how to do this before you start walking him regularly. If he gets into the habit of pulling when you walk, you'll have a hard time breaking him of this habit and people will be reluctant to take the poor puppy out for walks.

Whatever you are teaching your puppy, it is imperative that you end every training session on an upbeat note. The best way to do

Before training for sports or other activities, dogs must know basic obedience.

The Canine Good Citizen

This program is a great way to test your dog's obedience skills and comfort level in public situations. The CGC certification program stresses basic good manners for dogs as well as responsible caretaking on the part of people. Any dog, purebred or mixed breed, can earn a CGC.

Dogs who pass the 10-step test receive a certificate from the American Kennel Club commemorating the achievement. A CGC certificate can be crucial in getting your dog approved for an apartment rental or purchase of a co-op unit with strict pet requirements. A dog who can pass the CGC is also ready to begin training for activities such as agility, obedience, tracking, and other canine performance events. Most important, dogs with this level of training are a pleasure to live with. At home or in the community, their people can

count on them to respond to commands and to display good behavior in the presence of other people and dogs.

The CGC test is available through dog trainers and dog clubs. It has 10 parts: accepting a friendly stranger; sitting politely for petting; appearance and grooming; walking on a loose lead; walking through a crowd; sit, down, stay, and come on command; reaction to another dog; reaction to distraction; and supervised separation.

A dog who is trained to walk on a leash receives more walks and less discipline.

The CGC test is performed with the dog on leash, wearing a buckle or slip collar made of leather, fabric, or chain. No other type of collar is permitted. Be sure to bring your dog's brush or comb for the appearance and grooming evaluation.

If you'd like to earn a CGC certificate for your dog, it's a good idea to train him to behave properly from puppyhood. Teach him not to jump up on people, socialize him with other dogs, and take him to obedience class so he can learn the recall, to walk on leash, and the *sit, stay,* and *down* commands. Have other people handle him throughout his young life so he doesn't become overly anxious when left with someone he doesn't know. If you do all this, your dog should easily be able to earn a CGC certificate by the time he is one year old.

If your dog is an adult and has not received any training as a youngster, you will have to work harder to educate him so he's able to earn a CGC certificate. A dog's behavior toward other dogs is well established by the time he's an adult. If your dog tends to be aggressive with other canines, he may not be able to earn a CGC certificate. If he simply gets out of control around other dogs and wants to play, you can teach him to control his impulses through obedience training. If your dog is aggressive toward strangers, you need to work with a trainer to solve this problem before you even attempt the CGC test. Otherwise, you'll quickly be dismissed from the test.

Teaching your dog what he needs to know to pass the CGC test is not only fun but also incredibly rewarding. Any dog who receives a CGC award is a dog who is a joy to live with.

Training for Activities

You can prepare your puppy for any number of activities early in life. The first step is ensuring that your puppy is well socialized and knows the basic commands. He should be comfortable in new situations with other dogs and many types of people. He should also be used to training in a variety of settings, from dog parks to your backyard. You need to teach him to work past distractions.

To excel in a canine activity, you and your puppy have to work together, so teaching him to focus on you when training is important, and he should always be under your voice control. To allow him the freedom to learn a new activity, a steadfast recall is imperative.

There are many activities in which you can participate with your dog, including Flyball, canine freestyle, tracking, search and rescue, Frisbee, going to ground, and many more. Therapy work, competitive obedience, and agility are among the most popular—following are guidelines to getting started in each of the three. For other activities such as search and rescue and Flyball, there are a number of things you can do to prepare a puppy for future success. Teach him to use his nose by hiding treats and toys and by encouraging him to search for them; find out what type of play or reward most motivates him; and build his coordination by playing catch and introducing him to safe ground-level obstacles.

One of the most rewarding noncompetitive activities for dog owners is therapy dog work. Therapy dogs have the training and temperament to accompany their owners to nursing homes, orphanages, hospitals, and other facilities to help people in need. The

A 2002 Harvard University study suggests that some dogs outperform chimpanzees on some tests of cognitive ability. One test gauged the animals' ability to read signals from people who were indicating the location of hidden food. Dogs far outperformed captive-raised chimpanzees when it came to understanding the cues humans gave in this test.

emotional benefits of therapy dog visits to people confined to institutions are well documented. Researchers have shown that animal-assisted therapy effectively reduces the loneliness of residents in long-term care facilities, and rehabilitation patients take more interest in their treatments when working with a dog. Therapy dogs are of special benefit in child-related programs, where they have successfully worked with children suffering from emotional trauma and abuse and dealing with long-term hospitalization. The rewards for dog owners who participate in therapy dog work are also significant.

To train your dog for therapy dog work, you should start with basic obedience training when your dog is young. If your dog is already an adult, it's not too late to teach him the basics. You should be in control of your dog at all times, and he should be friendly without being overly boisterous. If your dog is not easy to handle when he's excited—especially when meeting new people—you need to work on this in an obedience class setting.

Have your dog participate in the American Kennel Club's Canine Good Citizen (CGC) Program. If your dog can pass this test, he may be a good candidate for therapy dog work. You can also request that your dog be given the Therapy Dogs International, Inc. (TDI) requirements on the CGC test, which will give you a greater idea if he is therapy dog material. These requirements test your dog's reaction to medical equipment and persons with infirmities, as well as his obedience to the *leave it* command and his willingness to gently interact with strangers. If he passes, you will be able to register your dog with TDI.

Once your dog is in control and has mastered basic obedience, you may want to enroll him in a workshop designed specifically for therapy dog work. These workshops provide opportunities for your dog to encounter the types of situations he would experience in a real therapy work setting and enable you to learn how to deal with each event. The Delta Society and TDI are two therapy dog organizations that provide these types of workshops.

People who enjoy training their dogs in obedience often want to take it to the next level and participate in competitive obedience. Precision is the name of the game in this type of competition, and dogs are judged on how quickly, enthusiastically, and accurately they perform the commands they are given during a trial.

The best way to train your dog for competitive obedience is to enlist the help of a trainer. Many dog training facilities offer competitive obedience classes for handlers who wish to earn AKC obedience titles on their AKC-registered purebred dogs and for those who have mixed-breed dogs who want to compete in trials sponsored by other organizations. Look for a teacher who has put a number of AKC obedience titles on his or her dogs and who is good at helping you learn how to get the best performance from your dog.

Before you can enter a competitive obedience training class, your dog needs to know basic obedience. You should then familiarize yourself with the AKC obedience competition rules to get an idea of what your dog will be

---

Researchers in Sweden and Denmark have identified five basic traits common to all dogs: playfulness, curiosity/fearlessness, tendency to chase, sociability, and aggressiveness. The researchers analyzed standardized behavioral tests given by the Swedish Working Dogs Association to 15,329 dogs representing 164 breeds.

Source: Mark Derr, "What Makes Dogs Tick? The Search for Answers." The New York Times, *section F, August 19, 2003.*

---

expected to do. In essence, your competitive obedience training will build on your dog's basic obedience skills and require him to perform those skills with greater precision. At the novice level, your dog is expected to heel on leash at your side, sit when you stop the heel, follow you through a figure eight, come when called, stay in a long sit and a long down, and stand for examination.

It's important to practice these exercises every day if you expect to earn an obedience title on your dog. Start practicing in a quiet, secluded area so you and your dog can pay full attention to your work. After a couple of months of training, start practicing in an area where distractions abound, such as a park. Your dog must be able to focus on you in a show setting surrounded by a lot of activity, so you will have to teach him to pay attention to you regardless of what is going on around him.

Use positive rewards when teaching your dog. Figure out what motivates your dog, and use that to make him happy after a job well done. Some dogs prefer treats, while others will do just about anything for you if they know a game of ball is to follow.

One of the fastest growing and most popular of all canine activities is agility. This sport requires teamwork between handler and dog, and it is a lot of fun for both. In agility competition, a dog races through an obstacle course that includes elements such as an A-frame, a dog walk (the canine version of a catwalk), a tunnel, assorted jumps, a pause table, a teeter, and weave poles. The arrangement of the obstacles changes from event to event, so a course is never familiar to the dogs participating in a competition. A dog races through the obstacle course with his handler running alongside him to direct him to the correct obstacle. The goal, other than having fun, is for the dog to get through the course as quickly as possible with the fewest faults.

You can start training an agility dog with equipment in your backyard, moving up to regulation equipment as his comfort level increases.

If you have a puppy and know that you want to compete in agility in the future, start training him now, since it's always easier for a dog to negotiate obstacles as an adult if he's been exposed to them as a puppy. Begin with basic obedience, since all agility dogs must be reliable in the down, sit, and stay. Basic obedience also teaches your dog to focus on you, which is a crucial element in agility competition. Then some of the other ways to prepare your puppy for agility is to get him used to climbing and walking on different surfaces. You can put down a plastic tarp and encourage him to walk on it, or you can build a low, sturdy table with a sheet of plywood and four bricks for legs that he can jump on. Get your puppy used to running through tunnels, too. You can purchase nylon tunnels made for children. They are available at most toy stores.

Once your puppy is six months old, he may be eligible to join a puppy agility class, where he

Young puppies enjoy being exposed to agility obstacles. These exercises do well to prepare the pup for actual agility trials later in life.

will learn to negotiate each of the individual obstacles in a way that is safe for his developing body. Call a local dog training or agility club to get a reference to a puppy agility class in your area. After your puppy graduates from puppy agility class, you are ready for regular agility classes, which will prepare you and your dog for competition.

It's very important to use positive reinforcement in the form of treats, toys, and praise when teaching agility to your dog. You want your dog to be happy and to enjoy himself, and he must be enthusiastic if you are going to successfully compete in this sport. You never want to push your dog too fast. A bad experience on the teeter or A-frame can create a severe fear of these obstacles. Wait until your dog is completely confident on equipment before asking him to put on the gas.

Practice is also vital in agility training. Most agility classes meet once a week, but you are expected to practice your training in between. Certain obstacles like the weave poles are more difficult for dogs to master, and so they require considerable practice at home. If you are serious about your agility training, you'll want to purchase some obstacles to keep in your backyard so you can practice with your dog. These items are available through agility supply Internet sites. Or, if you are handy, you can build your own or improvise. For example, a row of cheap plungers can make for excellent weave practice.

While your dog is learning how to negotiate the obstacles and follow your direction, you will be learning how to run the course. The way you move your body and your arms, the sound of your voice, and your entire attitude will affect the way your dog performs in agility. You'll find that you need to learn how to navigate this exciting sport as much as your dog does.

Training for Tricks

Teaching your dog to do tricks is a fun way to practice training skills—for both of you. Trick training builds on your dog's basic obedience skills as well as on his natural behaviors, such as spinning, bowing, or lifting a paw. And tricks are not only fun to do at home. If you're interested in animal-assisted therapy, for instance, you can develop tricks into a routine that your dog performs at nursing homes or children's hospitals. If your dog's tricks are really good, he might even win a prize for them at a just-for-fun dog show. If nothing else, your friends and neighbors will be impressed by his talents and your training skills.

To begin teaching tricks to your dog, first observe his normal behaviors. Does he like to stand on his hind legs or chase his tail? When he wakes up from a nap, does he give a big stretch, paws forward and rear end up in the air? Does he have a habit of lifting a paw when he sits or tapping you on the leg if he wants something? All of these natural body movements can be developed into tricks such as Dance, Beg, Shake, and more.

Remember that sometimes the tricks your dog does best will be the ones that come naturally to him. For instance, retrievers and spaniels are really good at learning *fetch*, but hounds are likely to look at you and yawn if you throw a ball and expect them to go get it.

More Tricks for Treats

Here's a list of other fun tricks you can try to teach your dog, from easy to amazing:

Walk backward

Wave

Crawl

Ring bell with nose or paw

Roll over

Cover eyes

Fetch TV remote

Sneeze

Take money from someone else and bring it to you

Balance treat on nose

Put toys away

Stop, drop, and roll to demonstrate fire safety technique

Dogs who enjoy getting tummy rubs are more willing to learn *roll over* than are dogs who are reluctant to show you their bellies. Dogs who love to bark will learn *speak* more quickly than dogs who never utter a sound will. That's the other good thing about teaching tricks. You can turn an annoying behavior such as licking or barking into a trick that can be turned on or off with a command.

Key Tips

- Start with behaviors that your dog already does naturally.
- Practice only a few minutes at a time, but practice several times daily.
- Use lots of praise, play, and treats when your dog does something right.
- Be patient. It can take a while to teach some tricks, especially if they don't come naturally to your dog.
- Always end the training session when your dog has been successful.

Fetch

For many dogs, this is a natural. First, choose a ball or other item that's appropriate for your dog's size. A tennis ball is just right for some big puppies or adult dogs, but you may need a smaller ball or toy for a little puppy or small dog. Try several items until you find the one your dog likes best. He may prefer a fuzzy stuffed toy to a ball or dumbbell.

With your dog on a long lead such as piece of clothesline, show him the ball and let him get excited about it. Then toss it in your yard or down the hall (make sure it won't hit anything breakable). At first, throw it only a short distance so it's easy for him to bring it back to you.

If he runs after it and brings it back, you've got a winner! Say "Good fetch!" in a happy, high-pitched tone of voice. If you're really lucky, he'll bring it back and then sit in

The fetch game comes naturally to most energetic dogs. Returning the fetched item may require more effort than the actual fetching does.

front of you with it in his mouth. Congratulations! You've got a natural retriever on your hands.

If he runs after it but doesn't bring it back, use the line to encourage him to come back toward you. When he reaches you, say "Good fetch!" Show him a treat and say "Give it!" He should willingly drop the toy or ball and take the treat. (This is a great deal because it allows you to practice two commands in one.)

Once he's in the habit of bringing the toy back to you, start tossing it farther, and then start tossing it when he's not wearing the lead. When he has this trick down pat, take it up a notch by teaching him to retrieve different items such as your keys, the newspaper, your slippers, and so on. Dogs are capable of learning different words for different items, so this can become a useful trick indeed.

Kiss

Lots of puppies love to lick faces. Turn this natural behavior into a trick by saying "Give me a kiss" every time your puppy licks you. The idea is to teach him to associate the spo-

ken phrase "Give me a kiss" with licking you. Soon, you should be able to say "Give me a kiss" and have him respond with the licking behavior.

Eskimo Kiss: Some dogs don't lick but they do touch with their noses. Using the same technique described above, say "Eskimo kiss" whenever he touches you on the face or nose with his nose.

When he's learned *kiss* or *eskimo kiss*, teach the opposite: *no kiss.* This comes in handy when your dog is around people who don't appreciate canine kisses or when you've just applied your makeup for a big evening out. If your puppy tries to lick you without being given the *kiss* command, firmly say "no kiss" and turn your face away. Walk away if you have to so that your dog learns that trying to lick you without being given permission means he loses your attention. You must repeat this every time your dog tries to lick you unless you have first said "Give me a kiss."

Spin

This is an easy trick for even older dogs to learn. Hold a treat in front of your dog's nose, say "Spin!" then move it in a circle behind him. He will eagerly follow the path of the treat until he's made a complete revolution. At that point, say "Good spin!" and give him the treat. Practice frequently and watch your dog closely during other times. He'll eventually start offering you a spin all on his own. Be sure to keep treats around the house so you can reward him when he does. But if they aren't handy, he'll be just as pleased with a "Good spin!"

Have your dog learn to spin in both directions. Say "Spin right" or "Spin left" or use two different words for each direction: *spin* for left and *twirl* for right, for example. Just be sure you remember which is which.

Shake

Teach this by first showing your dog what you want. Take his paw in your hand and say "Shake." Do this over and over for a couple of minutes several times a day. When you've done this for a while, start saying "Shake" without taking your dog's paw. See if he offers it to you on his own. If he does, say "Good shake!" and give him a treat. If he doesn't, back up and spend a little more time showing him what you want. Eventually, he'll learn to associate the word *shake* with giving you his paw. Once he's learned this, graduate to "Other paw" or "High five."

Play Dead

Every time you see your dog lying on his back or side, point your finger at him and say "Bang!" or "Play dead!" Then give him a treat. Your dog should quickly learn to associate the

The high five evolves out of the dog's mastery of the shake. Owners enjoy this display as much as the dogs do themselves.

word *bang* with lying on his back or side. If he starts to come to you and offer the behavior, give him lots of happy praise. Then start saying "Bang!" before he does the behavior. If he responds by lying on his back or side, say "Good Bang!" and give him a treat. Start extending the length of time he must lie there "dead" before he gets a treat. Once he gets good at it, try combining "Spin" with "Bang" for a dramatic "death scene."

Bow

This is another trick that involves giving a name to a natural behavior and rewarding your dog every time you see it. When your dog gets up in the morning or after a nap, it's likely that his first action is to give a big stretch—paws forward and rear end up in the air. Whenever you see him do this, say "Bow." Then proceed as described above for "Play dead." Once your dog knows a variety of tricks, Bow is a great way to end his floor show.

Training Adult Dogs

Many of us choose to adopt adult dogs from animal shelters or dog rescue organizations. There are a number of wonderful adult dogs available, but many need some extra training when they come into their new homes. The primary difference between training a fully grown dog and a puppy is that an adult dog already has established behaviors and attitudes. Whereas puppies are virtual blank slates and are easily molded, adult dogs have habits that may need to be changed or broken. A dog may have come from a wonderful home where the owner has passed away or from a neglectful home where he never saw the inside of a house or walked on a leash. Many private rescue organizations are able to work with dogs for several months, getting them ready for their new homes. Large animal shelters have less time for this.

Practice your training whenever you get a chance. Going over basic commands for 10 or 15 minutes each day will help establish them in your dog's mind.

Newly adopted dogs may be well versed in *sit*, *down*, and *stay*, or they may need the most basic of training from walking on linoleum to knowing their names. Many have learned bad habits like soiling in the house, chewing furniture, or being food possessive. For these reasons, training an adult dog can be a much greater challenge than training a puppy. The adult dog has to unlearn his previous behavior and replace it with the new behavior. It can be done, but it takes more work than training a puppy.

Although many adult dogs adopted from animal shelters or rescue organizations lack training, they often catch on quickly once they've bonded with their new owners. Patience is the order of the day for dogs who

have not received prior training. With the right amount of work and kindness, most of these dogs eventually learn the basics.

Many of these rescue dogs also need careful, nonthreatening socialization. Expose your new dog to happy, friendly sights and sounds slowly and with plenty of happy talk and tasty treats. Bring him with you when you go to the store, the park, or to a friend's home, and ask helpers to offer him treats and butt scratches. If he shows signs of nervousness, you're moving too fast. Instead of bringing him to a park where there is a lot of busy activity, walk him close to the park, offering treats and jolly encouragement. As he relaxes, you can take him closer to the park. If he ever shows any signs of aggression, contact an animal trainer or behaviorist to help you through this transition safely.

Many rescue dogs are not crate-trained. Teaching an adult dog to use a crate can be a challenge. You will need plenty of patience. Begin by purchasing a crate that is big enough to allow your adult dog to stand up and turn around, but not so large that he can get far away from any soiling accidents that may occur inside the crate. Put the crate in an area of the house that is frequented often by the family, and leave the door open. Start by feeding all of your dog's meals in the crate. At first, place the bowl near the edge of the doorway, and then slowly move it farther and farther into the crate. Depending on the confidence of your new dog, this may take a day or several weeks. Eventually, your dog should have to go all the way into the crate to get his food. Don't close the door behind him at first; let him come and go as he pleases.

Young adult dogs tend to have high energy levels and short attention spans. A trainer can help you contain their exuberance.

A rescue dog often requires some remedial training. He may need to learn to stay off furniture and how to navigate certain surfaces and structures, such as linoleum and stairs.

In addition to feeding your dog in the crate, periodically put a favorite toy or treat inside it to encourage your dog to go in. If your dog goes into the crate and stays there to play with his toy or eat the treat, be sure to leave the door open so he can leave whenever he wants.

Once your dog goes in and out of the crate freely, try closing the crate door for brief periods of time while he is inside. Start with just a minute and gradually increase the time over several days until your dog is in the crate with the door closed for 10 or 15 minutes at a time. If you are lucky, your dog won't be alarmed when he discovers the door is closed. However, your dog may suddenly panic and start barking or clawing at the door. If this is the case, correct him by saying "no." Do not let him out of the crate until he is quiet. Then, begin the process again starting from the beginning. Your dog may be reluctant to go back into the crate at first, but when he discovers the door will stay open, he will grow more confident. Meanwhile, be sure to gradually work up to closing the crate door once again. This time, increase the time the door is closed more gradually so your dog can get used to being confined at a slower pace. With time and patience, most adult dogs can learn to like the crate. If

you find yourself with a dog who is too claustrophobic to tolerate crate-training, consider consulting a certified animal behaviorist for help. Another option may be a wire crate, which your dog may find less claustrophobic, or an x-pen—essentially a wire pen enclosure with no floor or ceiling. The benefit of the x-pen is that it can be set up anywhere; however, it won't work with jumpers who can escape by leaping over the sides.

A common behavior problem for adult rescue dogs is poor house-training. Dogs who have been kept outside all their lives do not know proper etiquette while indoors. Some dogs were allowed inside but were never house-trained. In other situations, rescue dogs have lived most if not all of their lives in kennels. In all of these cases, the dogs need a lesson in house-training.

As with puppies, successful crate-training will be a huge boon to house-training your new dog. Once your dog is crate-trained, it is imperative that you keep him in the crate or secured with doggy gates when you can't watch him. Most dogs are loathe to eliminate where they must sleep and will hold it until you let them out to potty. It is far more effective to house-

This rescued German Shepherd mix proves that anything is possible with a determined dog and a loving owner. "Destiny Rose" moves like lightning on three legs.

train a dog by avoiding, rather than punishing, accidents. Take him outside on a leash as often as you can. At some point he will urinate or defecate outside. When he does, make a very big deal about this. Praise him profusely with petting and a happy voice, and give him a treat. Repeat this for a few weeks, and his habit of eliminating indoors should be replaced with going outside. To get your dog to associate a word command with eliminating, say the command whenever you catch him urinating or defecating in an appropriate place.

As your dog seems to catch on, you can give him more time loose in the house, but always with a leash dragging behind him. If you catch him starting to eliminate indoors, yell "No!" and lead him outside to an appropriate spot. He may not continue to do his business outside right away, so you may have to be outside with him for a while. But when he does, praise him heartily and give him a treat.

The key to success with this method is essentially the same as it is with puppies: never give the dog the opportunity to eliminate indoors. You are trying to break him of the habit of going in the house and replace it with the habit of going outside. Therefore, you have to have control over your dog at all times to ensure that he doesn't go indoors.

Just as with house-training, many rescue dogs do not know they are supposed to come when called because no one ever bothered to teach them. They may not even know their own names. If you are trying to train an adult dog who ignores you when you call him, first find out what he likes best in the way of food and play to help motive him.

Start out by putting the dog on a long leash, and have his favorite treat or toy in your pocket. Hold the leash so your dog has about 6 feet of line. Wait until he is distracted, and then say his name followed by the *come* com-

Providing a safe haven in the home for a rescued puppy or adult, as well as proper chew toys, is the basis of a successful new beginning.

mand. As soon as you finish saying the command, reel him toward you, showing him the treat or toy. When he gets to you, give him his reward (feed him the treat or play with the toy) and tell him he's a good dog.

Repeat this process several times a day for many days, gradually extending the length of the leash so your dog is farther and farther away from you. Meanwhile, remember that you are trying to break your dog of the habit of ignoring people who call him, so don't give him the chance to fall back into his old behavior. Call him to you only when you can reinforce your command; that is, when your dog is on a leash.

If you have done a good job motivating your dog with a toy or treat, you will soon see that when you call your dog, he comes toward you. Once he is doing this consistently, you can practice this training in an enclosed area. Remove the leash, and then give the *come* command. If your dog ignores you, do not repeat the command. Instead, go back to working with him on the leash and try a different toy or treat. Your dog won't be ready to repeat this second step until he is completely focused on you when you call him.

CHAPTER 32

Problem Behaviors

Every dog has a few problem behaviors that will need to be addressed throughout his life. The best tactic is to be aware of the factors that cause problem behaviors to prevent them from forming in the first place. The information in this chapter addresses the causes of most common behavior problems so you can deal with them proactively—before they start. If unwanted behavior is already occurring, this chapter suggests proven ways to rectify the problem.

Barking

Dogs bark for many reasons, so it's easy for barking to become an excessive habit. In fact, barking is one of the most widespread behavior problems. An underexercised dog may bark excessively because barking provides physical activity that's otherwise lacking in his daily routine. A healthy young dog needs at least one hour of vigorous running and playing every day. Without sufficient exercise, a dog may become antsy and start barking at everything that moves, just for something to do. If barking is becoming a problem and your dog gets less than an hour of vigorous exercise daily, try increasing his activity level. Take him for long walks or hikes, preferably up and down hills. Teach him to fetch, take him swimming, or train him in agility or another energetic sport.

If you don't have time to exercise your dog for at least an hour each day, find someone who can. You can take your dog to doggy day care, which offers energetic playtime for dog-friendly dogs, or you can hire a pet sitter or dog walker to exercise your dog. If hiring a professional isn't feasible, find a neighbor or friend who is willing to exercise your dog.

Barking is one of the most common problem behaviors in dogs. It often stems from easily resolved issues.

Even a well-exercised dog might bark excessively when home alone because barking provides entertainment. One way to decrease boredom barking is to provide something more interesting for the dog to do with his mouth. Food-dispensing toys work great for this. These toys come in different shapes, textures, and sizes but all have a hollow space inside for hiding food. The food comes out bit by bit as the dog chews and manipulates the toy, keeping him focused and quiet for quite some time. If your barker spends more than a few hours alone, consider leaving two or more food-dispensing toys stuffed with different flavors. All that chewing will satisfy your dog's need for activity, and he

Signs of Problem Behavior

It is important to recognize potential problem behaviors before they become serious. Here are some behaviors that may indicate a need for training, socialization, or veterinary treatment. Be aware, though, that many of these behaviors are exhibited at certain times by most dogs. They become worrisome when they are exhibited often, at inappropriate times, or in combination with other inappropriate or aggressive behaviors.

- aggressive barking
- begging
- biting
- digging
- chasing people or other dogs
- chewing or destroying things
- escaping
- grabbing things
- growling
- guarding food or toys
- herding people or other animals
- inching closer when commanded to stay
- jumping up
- lip curling
- lunging at other dogs
- lying on top of people
- mouthing
- nipping

- playing keep away
- playing tug-of-war with leash
- pulling on leash
- pushing between people or other animals for attention
- repeatedly fetching after playtime has ended
- repeatedly pushing rear end against person for scratching
- running away when called
- snapping
- snarling
- showing teeth
- staring
- taking food from the table or counter
- tugging or nipping clothing
- urinating on bed
- urinating or defecating in house
- whining

will spend most of his time occupied with the toys. After he empties the food puzzles, your dog will probably take a nice nap to recover from all that work.

If your dog is indoors and barking at what he sees outdoors, obscure his view of the excitement. If he stands on a chair or couch to bark at outdoor happenings, rearrange the furniture so this isn't possible. If when outdoors your dog barks at neighbors or passersby, try confining him to a more secluded area of the yard. A section of opaque fencing or strategically planted foliage can be useful for limiting a dog's view without creating an unsightly barrier. If appearances are unimportant, a plastic tarp

stretched between two fence posts or trees may serve well.

Adopting a second dog as a companion for your barker with the hope he will stop barking seldom works. Usually it just increases the noise. Two dogs together often bark more than twice as much as one.

A number of products on the market promise a quick fix for excessive barking. The most popular of these are electronic sensor collars that deliver an aversive consequence when the dog barks. There are also bark-activated noisemakers you can place near where the dog habitually barks to discourage him. The sudden sound startles the dog, interrupting his focus on what he's barking at. When the dog stops barking after hearing the sound from the collar, give him praise for being quiet.

Although these collars and other devices may temporarily reduce barking, they often become less effective as the dog gets accustomed to the punishment.

Antibark collars that release a burst of harmless but strong-smelling citronella when triggered by barking are useful for some dogs. The sudden release of scent startles and distracts the dog, similar to the way the sound-type antibark collars work. Some dogs, however, figure out that if they bark nonstop for a while they can empty the citronella reservoir on the collar. Then they can bark all they want the rest of the day without triggering any more bursts of citronella.

It's possible to debark a dog surgically, but this is a drastic measure that should not be considered unless other possibilities have been exhausted. On each side of a dog's larynx is a fold of tissue that tightens and vibrates when the dog barks. Debarking surgery removes this tissue so the bark doesn't resonate normally.

Dogs who have been debarked do not actually stop barking; their voice is just muted to a raspy whisper. In many cases, the dog's voice gradually returns, necessitating successive surgeries to retain the effect. A debarked dog is at greater risk for choking on food.

Guarding Food and People

It's normal for animals in the wild to protect prized resources such as food from other animals, but it's inappropriate and dangerous for a companion dog to guard possessions such as food and toys from people. Some dogs growl or snap if they fear someone might take away their food, lashing out at anyone who approaches while they're eating. A dog who guards his food cannot safely be free-fed because if a bowl of kib-

ble is always available, the dog will constantly be on guard. Instead of free-feeding your protective dog, give him measured meals at regular intervals (three to four meals per day for puppies, one to two for dogs over one year). Put the food bowl down, give your dog a half hour to eat, and then pick up the bowl and any remaining food. Put it away until the next mealtime. If your dog has ever bitten someone in defense of his bowl, have an experienced professional trainer or behaviorist assess your dog's behavior and determine the safest way to proceed with his training.

Training to prevent food guarding is best begun while a dog is young, before he forms the habit, but adult dogs can also be trained. Start by teaching your dog to sit, lie down, and do simple tricks for treat rewards, and feed him the treats by hand. When your dog understands how to earn food rewards, have

Food possessiveness can be problematic and requires commitment to a desensitization regimen.

family members and dog-loving friends cue him to do his tricks and hand-feed the rewards. Children should do this only under adult supervision, only if they're comfortable around dogs, and only if the dog is friendly and gentle with kids.

Then teach your dog that wonderful things will happen when people are nearby while he's eating. Here are some exercises to teach every dog that people are food providers, not food stealers. Follow the exercises step by step, and be sure your dog is comfortable with each step before moving onto the next:

1. Feed your dog half of his meal. When he finishes, pick up the empty bowl, add the second helping, and give it back.
2. While your dog is eating, talk quietly, and gently pat or stroke him while intermittently dropping special treats into his bowl.
3. Take away your dog's bowl before he's finished, add some superdelicious goodies, and give it back.

Guarding food can be one of the most dangerous problem behaviors in dogs. Small children are especially at risk around a food-possessive dog. To curtail resource guarding in multidog households, do not free-feed. Instead, offer each dog his meal at a set time. Give each an allotted amount of time to eat, then remove the food. Similarly, always supervise play and chewing of highly prized toys. Some dogs, for instance, will fight over smelly chew toys such as rawhides, pig hooves, and bones. Give these to dogs separately, and put them away when the dogs are done chewing. If your training efforts do not work, seek professional guidance.

Some dogs consider their favorite person a resource worth guarding and will behave possessively when anyone else tries to share that person's attention. The possessive dog crowds other pets away from the person, wedging himself between them and threatening or actually biting what he perceives as competition. When a dog does this, owners may think he's protecting them from imagined harm, but the dog is simply staking his turf, claiming the person as real estate.

This behavior can become a serious problem if the dog starts warding off family members or friends who show affection or sit too close to the guarded person. This behavior is fairly common with small dogs who are habitually carried or held in their owners' laps. The little dog assumes a higher-ranking position when lifted and held near human eye level, and he feels secure in his owner's arms. The dog feels bigger and may believe his owner will back him up should he need help in a conflict.

The best way to end the lap dog's reign of terror is to lower his perceived rank. The moment your little dog starts acting aggressively toward a friendly person or pet, gently set him on the floor. If he continues his display, emphasize your message by carrying him straight to his time-out area, his crate or his bed, and leaving him there by himself for five to ten minutes. After that, allow him to walk back into the room with you, but don't pick him up or hold him in your lap. If he behaves politely, give him pleasant attention. If he tries to guard you again, calmly put him back on a time-out.

Large dogs also sometimes try to guard people they view as their property. If your dog is pushy and persistent about guarding you but doesn't act aggressive, ask him to lie down when he begins guarding you. That will keep him from wedging himself between you and the perceived threat and will also put him into a lower-ranking posture than if he were standing up. If he lies down on command, praise him and let him know you approve. Divide yourself between the dog and the friend, giving the dog intermittent attention, petting, and praise as he lies there politely. If he gets up or tries to guard you again, put him on a time-out for five to ten minutes, then let him rejoin you and give him another chance to behave politely. Your dog will learn that sharing your attention with others is the only way he can have some of that attention himself.

Noise Sensitivity

A dog's sense of hearing is far more sensitive than ours, and many dogs become overwhelmed by sudden loud sounds. Fireworks or thunder will make some dogs so anxious that they whine, tremble, and may try to escape. If you can predict which sounds scare your dog, you may be able to reduce his startle reaction by playing music or television fairly loudly in the background. Some dogs do best when made comfortable in the basement during fireworks or thunderstorms. If you are with your dog during those scary times, stay upbeat and act as if you actually like the noise. Don't hover and croon, "It's OK, it's OK," because to a dog that sounds as if you're worried, too, and he won't believe things are fine at all.

Some dogs can gradually be desensitized to scary sounds by playing recordings of thunder or fireworks in the background while the dog plays or eats or receives a relaxing massage. Start the soundtrack very quietly at first, gradually turning up the volume as the dog tolerates the sounds without showing any anxiety. If this type of desensitization program is rushed, however, it can worsen fears by overwhelming the dog. In extreme cases of sound sensitivity, veterinarians will sometimes prescribe calming medication to be administered during stressful times or in conjunction with a gradual desensitization program.

Chasing

Chasing moving objects is related both to prey drive and protection. Most pet dogs don't need to supplement their diets by hunting, but many still feel the urge to chase moving objects like cars, bikes, birds, cats, or joggers. In chase mode, a dog doesn't think about safety or social rules, so if your dog is a chaser, keep him adequately confined. Chasing is usually visually stimulated, so blocking your dog's view of exciting movement helps minimize the behavior.

Some dogs become extremely agitated when they are prevented by walls, windows, or fences from chasing a strange dog running by. Sometimes this buildup of frustration is vented by attacking another pet in the household or even by biting the owner if suddenly restrained at those moments. This is known as redirected or displaced aggression. Most dogs can be trained out of this behavior by gradually increasing their excitement threshold. Start by rewarding your dog for remaining calm while close to low-level distractions or at a distance

Some dogs will chase anything, from cars to water hoses.

Keeping your dog well exercised can help alleviate problem behaviors related to boredom and excess energy.

from higher-level distractions. Gradually include stronger distractions or move closer to exciting stimuli, continuing to reward your dog for calm behavior. Don't push too fast; give your dog plenty of positive exposure at a low level of excitement before moving on to a higher level. Until this training is firmly in place, dogs who redirect their frustrated aggression must not be left alone with other pets.

As an outlet for his natural drive, give a dog who likes to chase things plenty of exercise, including opportunities to play directed chase games. Your dog may enjoy playing chase with you, which is OK if you make the object of the game to catch up with you and sit for treats or toy rewards. Avoid chasing your dog because this tends to reinforce a dog's annoying habit of dancing just out of reach when you call him.

Playing fetch is a positive chase-related game that provides miles of running for the dog but is easy on the handler. Another game involves a fishing pole or buggy whip with a long cord at the tip attached to a tennis ball or small toy. The handler stands or sits in the center and swings the pole in a big circle while the dog chases the toy around and around trying to catch it.

Another undesirable chase-related behavior that combines the chase drive with territorial aggression and barrier frustration is fence fighting. It is usually caused by sharing a boundary with what a dog perceives as a rival dog. Blocking the view through the fence so the dogs can't see each other usually stops this behavior, but some dogs will continue as long as just a fence separates them. In this situation, it may be necessary to either move the dogs to nonadjacent areas of their yards or put up a second fence several feet from the original to create a buffer zone between them.

Another chase-related misbehavior includes aggression toward mail carriers and other delivery persons. To a dog, these people are trespassers who enter his property without being welcomed by his owners, then quickly leave. Delivery persons leave in a hurry because they're on a tight schedule, but dogs think their chasing and barking is what drives these people away, so this behavior is automatically reinforced every time it occurs. If the delivery person makes threatening gestures toward the dog, this only increases the dog's certainty he should chase him away.

This situation can often be prevented by introducing puppies to as many friendly delivery persons as possible. Let your puppy meet your postal carrier and regular delivery persons; give your puppy treats in their presence and hand them goodies to give to your puppy, if they're willing. Order a lot of doggy toys and treats from pet supply catalogs, so delivered parcels frequently have something wonderful in them for your puppy.

If your dog chases delivery persons, you must securely confine him from the route those people take to your door. Many state laws require that the public be permitted access to your front door, and many delivery persons are required by company rules to carry pepper spray as protection against dogs who approach aggressively.

Eating Behavior Problems

Eating is a favorite hobby for many dogs and it's also a necessity for survival. In addition to food guarding, there are a number of eating-related behaviors that can get out of control. Some are related to health, while others are guided by social factors. Pay attention to physical and emotional changes in your dog's eating habits and deal with them before they become extreme.

Getting into the garbage isn't just irritating, it's also potentially dangerous. Chicken bones, glass shards, and rotten food are all common trash bin hazards for dogs.

Wild canines gorge when food is plentiful and fast when supplies are lean. Our pet dogs seem to retain their instinct to gorge, but food is so readily available that there are no fasting periods between feasts. Overeating regularly leads to overweight dogs with deteriorating health, so if your dog tends to put on weight, take charge and limit his food intake.

Many dogs swallow their food without much chewing, and some bolt it down so quickly they tend to choke. Eating too quickly can lead to bloat, or gastric torsion. Here are some ways to slow down an overeager eater:

Soak dry food: Before feeding your dog, soak his dry food in an equal amount of water or broth until the kibble absorbs all the liquid it can hold. Dogs are less likely to choke on softened food, even if they gulp it down.

Use a rock: Put a big, smooth, rounded rock in the food bowl so instead of having room for wide-mouthed gulping, the dog has to eat around it.

Divide meals: Divide the dog's daily ration of food into more frequent meals so he is never famished at mealtimes.

Use puzzle toys: Stuff up to half of the dog's meal into several food-dispensing puzzle toys so he must work the food out a few pieces at a time.

Freeze food: Fill rubber food-dispensing toys with soaked and softened kibble, then freeze them before offering them to the dog.

Most healthy dogs are enthusiastic eaters, so when a dog refuses food, you should suspect he doesn't feel well. Instead of trying to tempt a poor appetite by adding gravy to the bowl, remove the uneaten food and let your dog skip that meal. It's likely his appetite will return by the next meal. If he refuses successive meals and shows any other signs of discomfort, see your veterinarian.

If your dog is healthy but regularly turns up his nose at dinner unless you provide sauces and side dishes, you have probably taught him to do that. Finicky eaters are made, not born. If you enjoy catering to your dog and don't mind his fussiness, just make sure any additions to his menu are healthy and balanced. Many people cook for their dogs or feed them wholesome raw foods, and the dogs enjoy vibrant good health.

If you'd rather your dog accept simple fare as offered, then choose a high-quality dog food. Allow your dog twenty minutes to eat his meal, then remove any remaining food until the next mealtime. When he gets hungry and realizes there's only one dish on the menu, he will give up his fussiness and enjoy what's in front of him.

If your dog seems healthy, energetic, and happy but frequently skips meals, he may have found an alternate food source. Dogs with opportunity will snack from garbage cans, compost bins, and other animals' food bowls. Sometimes people feed their neighbors' dogs, even those who are penned or otherwise confined, without asking permission.

Garbage and trash are tempting and hazardous for dogs. Spoiled food or gobs of grease can cause serious illness. Broken glass and discarded razor blades can cut noses, tongues, or paws. Wads of hair from a person's comb or brush can cause fatal blockages if ingested. Strands of used dental floss can cut through a dog's intestines. To reduce odors and make trash less tempting, rinse out food containers before discarding them. And protect your dog from his natural appetite and curiosity by dog-proofing your trash.

Most kitchen trash is kept either tightly lidded or in a closet or cabinet, but bathroom trash is often left out in the open. To make bathroom trash less attractive, keep a container of cayenne pepper handy, and shake a good-sized dash or two of it into the trash basket on top of each item you discard. The first time your puppy follows his nose to the bathroom trash, he will discover an unpleasant surprise. One experience may be sufficient, but in case your puppy decides to try it again, continue treating the trash with cayenne for at least three months.

Dogs are both hunters and scavengers. A bored dog will start looking for something to do—preferably something that involves food. Dogs can smell food left on counters and tables, and many will grab it if they can. This habit usually debuts when a puppy gets tall enough to stand on his hind legs and reach countertops with his front paws. Some dogs even figure out how to use a chair or a bench to gain additional altitude. Dogs are natural scavengers, so food left unguarded is considered fair game in dog society.

After one or two successful experiences counter surfing, a dog usually makes it a habit. If you've noticed food mysteriously disappearing lately, you may have a counter surfer on your hands. This habit isn't just annoying, it can be dangerous or fatal because many common people foods, including chocolate, onions, and raisins, can cause serious health problems for dogs.

Counter surfing is hugely self-rewarding and much easier to prevent than change, so don't let it get started. With good management, your dog will not get a chance to develop this habit. If he's already discovered there are easy pickings on counters and tables, you'll need to change some of your own habits for a while. Keep counters and tables clear of unguarded food, and keep your dog out of the kitchen when you're not there to supervise.

Dogs are good at solving puzzles and challenges to obtain food. You can use food as training rewards and give your dog several brief training sessions throughout the day. He will learn to get goodies directly from you for doing tricks and tasks. This is a good way to provide a dog with mental exercise and an approved way to snag his snacks.

It may also help to feed your counter surfer more frequent meals, so hunger doesn't trigger a search for food. If the dog is underweight, give him an extra meal each day. If he's a healthy weight, give him the same total amount of food but divide it into more meals. Part of the dog's daily ration could be stuffed into a food-dispensing toy, so it takes some effort to get it out and satisfies the dog's inclination to figure out ways to get food. Although some trainers advocate booby trapping counters to discourage counter surfers, this technique isn't always effective. If the booby trap isn't scary enough, it can simply add to the excitement of the challenge, but higher intensity booby traps can possibly injure the dog.

It's normal for dogs to show interest in eating nonfood items. They seek out certain grasses, take a few bites, and sometimes they vomit up the grass, sometimes they don't. Eating a small quantity of grass is not a problem. But your dog may feel ill if he eats a lot of grass. Dogs sometimes also swallow dirt, rocks, hair, paper, or wood for various reasons, including hunger, curiosity, boredom, nutrient deficiency, or digestive disturbances. Swallowing some materials like rocks or wads of hair can cause life-threatening internal blockages. If your dog consumes nonfood items, have him examined by a veterinarian to rule out health problems.

The most common nonfood item that dogs eat is feces. Called coprophagia, feces-eating is one of the dog behaviors people complain about most. Dogs may eat their own feces, feces from other dogs, or cat feces. If you live on a farm, there's likely a cornucopia of feces for your dog to ingest. Fortunately, eating feces isn't harmful to dogs.

Unfortunately, the habit is highly undesirable for humans who, in addition to disliking the idea of their dog eating feces, really dislike the idea of being licked by a dog who

Puppies often chew inappropriate items. Discourage this by keeping your possessions off the floor and giving him good chewing alternatives.

has just eaten feces. And dogs who snack from cat litter boxes may also be ingesting a great deal of chemically treated clay, which could cause intestinal obstructions.

It's unknown why dogs eat feces, but the habit probably stems from a number of normal behaviors found in wild animals. Eating the feces of other animals may provide additional nutrients such as iron. Eating their own feces may stem from an instinct to hide their tracks from predators. Many dogs seem to like the taste of feces; if they didn't, they probably wouldn't keep doing it.

Preventing coprophagia is more a matter of management than training. To keep your dog from eating his own feces, follow him outside when he goes potty, and clean up

feces immediately. Keep your yard clean of feces. When on walks, keep your dog from sniffing—and quickly gulping down—feces. If you have cats, keep their litter boxes in an area inaccessible by your dog. One method is to use a door chain on the room where the litter box is kept. With the chain on, the door is open wide enough for an average cat but not for an average dog.

Begging is one of the more common complaints among dog owners. Teaching your dog not to beg is easy: simply avoid establishing the habit in the first place. One of the reasons begging becomes so entrenched is because owners teach their dogs to do it by rewarding the behavior with a treat. Of course the dog thinks begging is proper behavior. Every time a dog receives food for begging, the habit becomes that much more difficult to break. A begging dog begs at every opportunity; he doesn't understand the difference between begging when it's just the two of you and begging when there are out-of-town guests.

To avoid begging behavior in your dog, never give him food you are eating or food off your plate. Even if you are going to give him a few choice table scraps, wait a few minutes after dinner and scrape them into his bowl out of his sight. This way he won't relate the food he receives to the food on your plate. Be

Begging can be irritating, but fortunately it's easily preventable. Just don't feed your dog from your plate—ever.

consistent. Never give your dog food when he begs, and establish a clear end to treat giving. After giving him a biscuit or two say "all gone" or another cue, and do not under any circumstances give him another treat.

It is difficult to control the actions of other people, which can make teaching your dog not to beg more challenging. Many visitors like to slip food to a dog without asking the owner's permission. Politely ask your guests not to feed your dog. If you are planning a party, you might even put a sign around your dog's neck informing guests of your house rule. Don't be embarrassed to enforce your rules with guests. Many people won't take you seriously, so be emphatic.

Impolite and Unsafe Behaviors

Many dog behaviors such as jumping up on people, herding people, crotch sniffing, and pulling on leashes seem rude, and others such as nipping, not coming when called, and dashing through doors compromise safety for the dog or the people around him. These behaviors can be changed by teaching the dog activities that will help him practice better, safer manners.

When dogs meet their canine buddies, they often jump all over each other in a happy, boisterous greeting. Your dog may want to greet you that same way, but you probably prefer a less intense greeting. The old-fashioned cure for jumping involved punishing the dog, but to be effective, punishment had to be delivered by everyone the dog greeted, which is impossible for children and difficult for many adults. Even when punishment was faithfully applied, many dogs acted as if being shoved or kneed in the chest made jumping more fun, like bouncing off another dog.

It's more effective (also easier) to teach a dog to sit when he wants attention than to punish him for jumping. If your dog is persistent and fast with his jumping, you might start his sit-for-greeting lessons from the opposite side of a fence or gate. This also teaches your dog not to jump against gates when people are entering. From one side of a barrier—a baby gate across a doorway works well—cue your dog to sit, reward him with a treat, and pet him. If he jumps up, step back and stand calmly until he sits again either on his own or in response to a cue. When he remembers not to jump up a few times in a row, leave the area for a few minutes and return. That will increase the excitement level and allow fur-

What was adorable six months ago when this German Shepherd was a puppy is now annoying and potentially dangerous.

ther training progress. When your dog learns to greet you politely from the other side of the gate, repeat the sit-for-greeting exercise without the barrier. Your dog will start to get the idea right away, probably with the first lesson, but it will take several weeks of practice for the new polite greeting behavior to completely replace the old, much-practiced jumping.

For good manners with visitors, teach your dog to sit on a mat. A mat or small rug is a visual and tactile area, easy for the dog to go to and know he's in the right place. The mat can be placed wherever you want the dog to be while visitors are arriving. For toy breeds, a stool or chair works well instead of a mat because it gets the dog up off the ground so he isn't likely to be stepped on in the excitement of arrivals.

Herding is another behavior that is considered rude. Dogs with herding ancestry often try to control the movement of humans the same as they would sheep or cattle. This may include nipping at feet or legs from the side or from behind, as well as body blocking from the front to make people turn or stop. These maneuvers can be annoying for adults and frightening for children, and they may result in bruised ankles, torn clothing, and nasty falls.

To stop your dog from herding people, teach him that it won't work on you. If he blocks you from the front, gently shuffle into him as if you didn't notice him there. Be careful not to trip over him, and keep your feet close to the ground to avoid stepping on his paws.

If your dog tries to herd you by grabbing your shoe or the leg of your pants, stop moving and stand calmly. Stare straight ahead, ignoring your dog until he stops. Then ask him to sit, praise him for that, and then start walking again. If your dog repeats the behavior, have him sit again. If he does it a third time, give him a five minute time-out.

Young puppies from herding breeds, like this baby Old English Sheepdog, should learn the difference between children and livestock at an early age.

Herding isn't the only time a dog will nip. Dogs nip each other when they romp, and some even try to play this game with their human friends. Prevent the nipping habit by never playing mouth-hand games with a puppy. Keep puppy toys handy at all times so you can substitute a toy for your flesh if your puppy starts getting excited and nippy. A puppy who nips when excited shouldn't be left unsupervised around children until he learns gentler play.

When your puppy nips, cry out as if in serious pain. Puppies under eight weeks will respond to a high-pitched yelp, but past that age most react to it by nipping harder, as if disrespecting a whiney playmate. For those puppies, use a lower pitched *ouch* and sound as if you're injured and insulted. If your puppy ignores your cry and keeps nipping, calmly give him a five minute time-out. Confine him in his crate or pen, or leave the play area yourself for about five minutes.

Don't let your dog dictate when he comes in from out doors. Ignore scratching, barking, and whining; allow him into the house only when he's calm.

When you return, speak softly and stroke your puppy. If he's gentle, end the time-out. If he's still nippy, give him ten or fifteen more minutes, then check on him again. He will probably be asleep by then; puppies are often nippiest when they need a nap.

Crotch sniffing is one of the more embarrassing behaviors we endure from our dogs. It's natural for dogs to sniff each other's personal places, so it's not surprising they'd try to sniff ours as well. Most of us don't appreciate this and prefer dogs not be so nosey. One way to end crotch sniffing is to teach your dog to sit when greeting you. That way he won't have as much range of motion as when standing and you'll be able to position yourself and your guests so your dog's nose can't reach your crotch.

If your dog is intent on sniffing, sweep your hand across your crotch, palm toward your body, lightly bumping the side of the dog's nose with the edge of your hand. Don't do this forcefully; simply sweep your hand back and forth a few times as if brushing away dust. This will work best if you act as if you don't notice the dog while you're doing it. As soon as he moves his nose away, stop sweeping your hand back and forth and greet your dog.

It can be embarrassing if your dog doesn't come when he's called, but an unreliable recall can also be dangerous for your dog. If he chases a cat across the street and ignores your call, he could end up being hit by a car. To prevent such a tragedy, it's important to teach your dog to come when called. Start by making coming to you the most wonderful thing your dog can imagine. This means you always reward him for coming and you never call your dog to punish him or do anything he dislikes. If your dog habitually ignores your call, keep him on a leash or a long line when in unfenced areas until he's coming reliably when called.

To teach your dog to come when called, start by calling him when he's already coming toward you. Say "come" or "here," and if your dog is slow to come, playfully back away a few steps, teasing him to catch you. Praise him as soon as he begins to approach and reward him with a treat, a toy, or a game when he gets to you. Vary the rewards you use, but make sure they're always something your dog likes a lot. Do this at least a dozen times a day in dif-

Dogs urinate to empty their bladders and to mark their territories. Male dogs lift a leg to urinate, thus depositing their scents at nose level. Some female dogs may raise a hind leg when urinating, and some even raise both hind legs off the ground to urinate against a vertical object.

Bellybands

Some male dogs, especially the little ones, mark indoors so quickly that even if you're vigilant you may not be able to stop them. A useful management aid for these boys Is a bellyband: a soft, wide cloth belt with a pouch that holds absorbent pads. The band fastens around the dog so if he marks, the pad catches the urine and protects the target. Bellybands can be purchased through pet supply stores and catalogs or can be made fairly easily at home.

Measure an 18- to 24-inch-wide strip of cloth to fit around your dog's middle, leaving a couple of inches extra at each end for finishing. Fold the cloth along its full length into thirds, then sew hook and loop fastener strips at each end (hooks at one, loops at the other). Tuck a standard sanitary pad into the fold, wrap the belt comfortably snug where it needs to be around your dog, and fasten the ends together. Check pads frequently and change when soiled.

ferent situations so that your dog forms a solid habit of coming when called no matter what's happening nearby.

Another potentially dangerous behavior is dashing through doors. To a dog, an open door looks like a personal invitation to go through to the ever-exciting outdoors, so carefully close all outside doors. Doors left ajar are common in homes with children and visitors coming and going. Dogs quickly learn to take advantage of carelessness, so consider installing springs on your gates and outer doors so they automatically close.

For safety's sake, teach your dog to wait for permission before going through doors or gates. While the dog is learning this important safety rule, make sure everyone in the family knows he or she must tell your dog to wait before opening a door that leads outside.

Start by taking your dog to the door on leash. As you reach for the doorknob, tell your dog to wait. Touch the doorknob but don't open the door, then praise and treat your dog. Open the door slightly (be ready to stop your dog if he moves forward), then close the door and reward your dog. Repeat this process, opening the door wider each time. If your dog moves before you give permission, close the door and pause ten seconds before starting again. When your dog waits with the door

wide open, praise, treat, and permit him through. Make the wait gradually longer before releasing your dog to go through the door. When he can wait ten seconds before being released, gradually start adding distractions outside like people playing catch, dogs being walked, kids on bikes. When your dog resists temptations like these without bolting outside, he's ready to progress to off-leash work. It will likely take several weeks of practice for this to become a habit.

When you start off-leash training to wait at doors, attach a 10- to 20-foot-long lead or sturdy cord to your dog's collar before removing the leash. Stand on the long line or tie it to something immovable if you suspect your dog may bolt when the leash comes off. When you unsnap the leash, your dog will think he's free, but the long line will prevent escape in case he does decide to bolt.

Going for a walk with your dog can be one of the best activities the two of you do together. But a dog pulling on his leash while on a walk makes for an unpleasant outing. A dog pulls on his leash because he wants to go faster and explore more ground, and as long as pulling works he'll keep doing it. To prevent or fix a leash-pulling habit, teach your dog that pulling actually slows him down.

Clip the leash onto your dog's collar or harness, tell your dog "let's go," and start to walk. As soon as your dog begins to pull, slow down as if his pulling were operating your brakes. If he continues to pull, come to a complete stop. Stand still until he quits pulling, and then walk again. If your dog pulls for more than three seconds after you've stopped, begin to back up very slowly. The dog, noticing he's losing ground, will turn and look at you to find out why. When he does, the leash will loosen slightly. Immediately praise your dog and start walking again.

If your dog is very strong or pulls so hard he gasps or coughs, try using a head collar for easier walking. This dog-size version of a horse halter works by leverage, not pain or force, gently turning the dog's head to the side when he pulls. If the dog wants to look straight ahead, he has to stop pulling and allow the lead to go loose. With a head collar, a small or frail person can easily walk a large, strong dog.

Behavior Problems Related to Elimination

Some dogs are easier to house-train than others are. Physical development and general health play a role in this, but mismanagement and miscommunication cause most problems with elimination behavior.

Sometimes puppies realize they should eliminate outside but don't know how to ask to be let out. You can easily solve this dilemma by hanging a bell from the doorknob of the door leading to the potty area. Every time you take your puppy out to do his business, ring the bell before you open the door. Puppies notice the connection between the bell ringing and the door opening so readily on their own that they don't really need to be taught. Within a few days to a week, you'll hear that bell ring and when you go to the door

Whole (unaltered) male dogs will mark their territory through urination. The owner must correct these behaviors before bad habits are cemented.

(hurry!) there will be your good little pup waiting to be let out.

Many puppies and even some adult dogs crouch and urinate when they greet people they perceive as high ranking. This is a normal canine gesture of submission, intended to placate higher-ups. A high-ranking dog appreciates this behavior as a sign of respect, but most people find it annoying and would prefer drier greetings.

Puppies generally outgrow submissive urination by maturity, although some continue into adulthood. To change this behavior, it's critical you not scold the dog or act displeased. Scolding or punishing submissive urination will cause the dog to offer even more extreme submission to appease you. He will crouch lower and grovel around while peeing, or perhaps flip onto his back and wet his own belly.

It's best to greet a dog with this habit outdoors, where you won't need to mop up urine afterwards. Keep walking when saying hello to the puppy so he has no opportunity to squat and piddle. Reaching down over a puppy to pet him will often elicit submissive urination because leaning over a dog's head and shoulder is a dominant position. Don't pet the dog until his excitement wanes.

Supply your pup with a selection of playthings, including balls, plush toys, and chew toys.

When you do greet him, lean to the side of the dog or crouch down so that you are not looming over him.

Marking is another form of elimination that can turn into a problem. Marking is urinating for the purpose of leaving a message. Dogs mark to communicate fear or friendliness, to flirt, to express rank, to claim resources, to blaze trails, and to leave their calling card for dogs who follow. Marking is a big part of canine social life. It isn't about bladder relief, it's about communication.

Dogs who mark a lot, especially those who target high, usually have a dominant attitude and a high rank. Intact males usually mark more than neutered males do. Neutering a male who marks inappropriately won't stop the behavior, but it usually reduces the behavior substantially. Neutered or not, male dogs can urinate higher than females and tend to mark more objects, which means male marking causes more problems—especially when it occurs indoors.

Popular indoor marking targets are table legs, door frames, and the side or front corners of sofas and chairs. Usually a dog refreshes his marks daily, sometimes more often. To discourage indoor marking, thoroughly clean all the spots your dog marks using a preparation designed to eliminate urine stains and odors. A dog can smell a urine signature no matter how well a spot is cleaned, though, so don't allow your dog unsupervised access to that area.

Punishing a dog after he marks seldom causes him to stop marking. Catching him in the act, stopping him, and rushing him immediately outdoors helps somewhat, but it's better to prevent opportunities for inappropriate marking before the behavior becomes a habit.

If the habit is longstanding, it may take three or more months of management and training for a dog to give up marking indoors. During this time, the dog must never go alone into areas of your home he has previously marked. He does need to spend supervised time in those areas, though, so he can learn to be there without marking.

To help prevent indoor marking, take your dog outside to urinate at least once every two hours. This will give him ample opportunity to mark appropriately, and it will also keep his bladder as empty as possible. When you aren't able to monitor your dog closely, keep him crated. But remember, for good health, a crated dog needs opportunities to urinate and exercise every few hours during the day.

Outdoors, dogs mark trees, posts, hydrants, and other upright landmarks with urine. If your dog marks items outdoors such as lawn furniture or the kids' playhouse, you can train him to mark more appropriate targets. Blot up some of your dog's urine with a paper towel, and smear it on approved spots in the yard. Take your dog on leashed walks around the yard, stopping at places you've selected for him to mark. When your dog catches a whiff of his signature there, he will naturally want to mark that spot. Encourage him with praise. Take your dog to the approved marking areas daily to renew his mark and deepen his habit of going there. Soon he will head for those spots on his own.

Many dogs will chew on things that smell like their owners, from shoes, socks, and gloves to remote controls and steering wheels.

Destructive Behaviors

Some normal dog behaviors involve chewing, tearing things apart, and digging holes. Although normal, these behaviors can ruin personal belongings and make a mess of the house or yard. Most destructive behaviors are manageable and can be controlled if you anticipate them and provide other outlets for your dog's energy.

Chewing is natural and healthy for dogs: it keeps teeth clean, jaws strong, and it's an enjoyable way to pass time. The wild canine diet requires a lot of hard chewing just to survive. Commercial dog foods may be nutritious, but they don't provide sufficient chewing exercise to satisfy, so most dogs seek other items to gnaw. Dogs have no concept of the monetary value of items they chew. To them, value is measured in satisfaction.

Anticipate chewing mistakes your dog might make by getting down to his level and checking around. Curiosity will attract dogs to anything that sticks out or hangs down—handles and knobs, furniture corners, long drapes, houseplant leaves, and fringe. Dogs like the comforting scent of their favorite people, so they chew items worn close to the skin or held in the hand, for example pens, books, eyeglasses, computer mouses, hats, gloves, and underwear. Dogs are drawn to food smells and will chew nonfood items scented with food, including TV remotes (pizza, buttered popcorn), car steering wheels (fast-food burgers), and rugs or other floor coverings (food spills).

To help keep your dog from chewing your belongings, teach him to exercise his jaws on chew bones and toys. Sometimes a dog prefers a soft toy, but other times only a hard chew will satisfy, so provide toys of different textures. Personally present new chew toys to your dog

Treats can help you train your pup and solve unwanted behaviors. Keep them small to avoid a pudgy pup.

Dogs, especially puppies, often chew (and sometimes swallow) objects like paper and wire. They do this for varied reasons, including hunger, digestive upset, or boredom and curiosity. To prevent this habit from forming, limit access to areas with forbidden temptations, and guide your dog's chewing preferences by encouraging play with interesting textured and flavored toys.

Trade treats and toy rewards for what your dog has in his mouth so he learns to willingly release whatever he has. Ask him to release a toy and give him treats. Then return the original toy to him so he learns the trade-up game is very rewarding. Soon you'll be able to reclaim both toys and stolen objects without a dramatic (and likely unproductive) chase. Anything a dog chews on can possibly be dangerous so there's no such thing as a completely safe chew toy. Check all dog toys for loose parts that could be removed and swallowed or choked on. If toys become small enough to swallow, discard them.

If electric wires dangle within your dog's reach, he might experimentally chew through their plastic insulation and be seriously burned or shocked. Aversive tasting antichew products can be applied to wires that can't be moved or hidden, but some dogs don't mind the flavor and will chew anyway. It's better to keep your dog out of that room until he's not chewing household items at all.

Some puppies become curious about plants in the house and yard and may munch on leaves that dangle within reach. This can be dangerous because many flowers and ornamental plants contain toxic substances. If you have houseplants or garden plants, find out which varieties are toxic to dogs and keep teething puppies away.

Some puppies ignore potted plants but eat the soil they're rooted in. To prevent this, cover the soil with a collar of metal hardware

instead of just leaving them for him to discover on his own. This will help your dog differentiate between his own toys and the many other items he finds around the house.

Teach your dog to chew his own toys by keeping at least two available at all times. When your dog chews something he shouldn't, interrupt him by diverting attention to an approved toy. Praise him for chewing on his toy. The replacement toy will work best if it is of similar texture to the forbidden item; provide a cloth toy if your dog was chewing fabric or a more solid toy if he was gnawing hard plastic or wood.

Some breeds of dogs may be predisposed to a fear of storms. Herding breeds such as Collies and German Shepherds, and hounds such as Beagles and Basset Hounds, seem to be more disposed to storm phobias than other dogs are. Storm phobia is also common in sporting and working breeds. Behaviorists are not sure what frightens dogs the most—the booming thunder, lightning flashes, howling wind, or noise of rain on the roof. Dogs may even be reacting to a change in air pressure or electrical charge in the air, as some become upset even before the storm actually hits.

cloth or window screening. Cut a circle the diameter of the inside of the pot, then slice from the edge to the center and make a smaller doughnut hole there for the plant's stem. Place the collar around the plant to protect the soil from the puppy.

Digging is another natural behavior that can go awry. Certain breeds have a heritage that makes them especially dedicated diggers. Dachshunds were bred to pursue badgers down dark narrow tunnels into subterranean dens. Terriers were bred to hunt rats and other vermin that burrow underground or under rock piles. Spitzes (from Pomeranians to Malamutes) evolved in northern climates where they'd dig mice to eat, bury chunks of large carcasses for later, and tunnel through permafrost to make underground birthing dens in the warmer soil below. For these breeds, digging is a lifestyle that's seldom outgrown.

These days, dogs dig for exercise, to alleviate boredom, to bury treasures, to make comfortable resting spots, to hunt rodents, and to explore underground scents and sounds. Adolescent puppies bursting with energy and strength especially enjoy digging; and the bigger the pup, the bigger the holes. Many outgrow their digging habit by adulthood, but some become lifelong excavators.

To discourage outdoor digging, fill in any unapproved holes your dog has dug in the yard, and give him an approved spot to dig. Start a good hole in a place where it won't be in the way, or fill a toy sandbox with digging material. Teach your dog to dig in the approved spot by partially burying a few treats or toys and encouraging your dog to discover them. If he doesn't immediately catch on, playfully dig up a couple of the treasures while he watches. Let him see and sniff the goodies, then partially rebury them for him to uncover.

Each day for a week or so, go with your dog to the approved digging spot and encourage him to dig there, praising and applauding his efforts. If he tries digging in an unapproved area, interrupt him, take him to the approved hole, and praise him for digging there.

Freshly turned earth is tempting to dogs, so if your dog digs at his old spots after you've filled them, fill them again, but this time add a scoop of your dog's poop near the top, then finish filling with a couple of inches of clean soil. Most dogs prefer to avoid their own feces and will hesitate to dig a poop-tainted hole. This trick won't work with puppies and dogs who eat or play with their own feces. If your dog does this, you'll need to keep him away from the old holes until he learns to dig only in the approved hole.

Some dogs take their digging inside, where they bury toys and bones beside or under the cushions of a couch or chair or tuck them under someone's bedcovers. Dogs instinctively bury bones to hide them from others. If the hiding spot is discovered and the treasure is gone when the dog returns, he will seek a more secure hiding place in the future. When you see your dog hiding a treasure in your furniture, wait until he finishes, then go retrieve the item and put it somewhere out of the dog's reach for an hour or so before giving

Escape behavior is genetic in some dogs. If you are unable to stop his desire to escape, adjust his environment so he can't get out.

Some dogs are born to dig. If you can't end his desire to dig up your garden beds, you may at least be able to direct his digging to a more desirable site.

it back. Watch him to be sure he doesn't try to hide the item in the same spot or in another piece of furniture. If he does, go steal it again.

Periodically check favorite hiding spots to be sure your dog hasn't buried something when you weren't watching. If you find one of his treasures, take it and put it in a different spot, somewhere the dog will accidentally find it. Your dog will be puzzled to find the item there. When he notices that treasures keep disappearing from under the cushions, he will find more secure, hopefully more appropriate, places to cache his stash.

If your dog digs under the fence to escape, try filling his escape hole with bricks and rocks or a mixture of rocks and the dog's feces. If that doesn't stop the escape excava-

tions, dig a trench a foot or more deep along the bottom of the fence line. Attach poultry fencing or other wire mesh to the bottom of the existing fence, push it down into the trench, and bury it. Another solution is to use electric livestock wire. (Check local ordinances to make sure electric fences aren't prohibited.) Install one strand of the wire 6 to 12 inches from the ground. Attach it to your fence with 6-inch plastic insulators made for that purpose. When your dog puts his head near the bottom of the fence to dig under it, he will get a small shock that is unpleasant enough to make him stop.

The most common reasons dogs try to escape are boredom, lack of exercise, and a desire to mate. Attempts to escape can be ended

What is DAP? The acronym DAP stands for "dog-appeasing pheromone." Pheromones are biological or chemical substances that influence sexual and other behaviors in animals. DAP is a synthetic pheromone that mimics the pheromones produced when a female dog lactates. Used in conjunction with behavior modification techniques, it can sometimes help ease a dog's anxieties. DAP is available in spray form or as a diffuser that can be plugged into a wall outlet.

by providing your dog with an hour or more of vigorous physical exercise, ongoing training for mental exercise, and plenty of social contact with the family every day. Neutering dogs eliminates their drive to find mates and ends hormonally motivated escape attempts.

Anxious Behaviors

A dog is an emotional creature, and his behavior reflects his emotional state. Dogs can form long-lasting memories—either positive or negative—from emotionally charged events. Happy experiences cause dogs to repeat those events, sometimes leading to behaviors resembling addictions. Unpleasant or frightening experiences can cause fear and anxiety that result in repetitive avoidance-related behavior. Behaviors attached to strong emotions can take time to change, but helping your dog through the process will reduce his anxiety and positively affect your relationship with him.

Dogs can develop obsessive behaviors, repeating the same action or sequence over and over beyond the point of physical exhaustion. Some of the most common obsessions are spinning in circles and chasing flies or glimmers of light. A favorite game can also become an obsession. This happens fairly often with fetch: the dog retrieves a certain object endlessly and finds ways to manipulate people into continuing to throw.

The best way to prevent obsessions is to teach your dog a lot of rewarding games and tricks so he doesn't get stuck on just one. Get him involved in varied activities that use different skills. Don't let your dog con you into playing a repetitive game; take charge and change the game before you both get into a rut. To interrupt spinning, for example, call the dog and reward him for coming, then initiate some other activity to break the pattern. Obsessions usually start innocently enough, with a patterned behavior the dog enjoys. The more fre-

Many dogs whine, pace, bark, and become destructive when left alone.

quently the dog engages in the behavior, the stronger the pattern becomes. Soon the pattern takes on a life of its own, and the dog seems to do it repeatedly, without thinking.

Some dogs exhibit anxious behavior in cars. Car sickness can have both physical and psychological causes. The motion of the vehicle, the sensation of scenery whizzing past, or the odor of exhaust fumes or tobacco smoke can trigger it. Some dogs don't get carsick their first several rides but become so if going on trips becomes associated with unpleasant or frightening experiences. Being in any kind of traffic accident, even a minor one, can initiate car sickness. It's also common for dogs to develop car sickness if the only place they have been taken to by car

It is estimated that 10 to 15 percent of dogs experience some type of separation anxiety.

Source: The American Animal Hospital Association 2004

are unpleasant places, such as the veterinary clinic, a boarding facility, or an animal shelter where they were abandoned.

The signs of car sickness build from rapid panting and light drooling to thick ropes of saliva and then often to vomiting. Many carsick dogs develop such a strong aversion to riding in vehicles that they try to avoid getting in, then start drooling as soon as the door closes behind them, even before the engine is started. By this point, the problem is both physical and psychological.

Some dogs are less carsick when riding in a crate or on the floor where they can't see

Let your adult dog get accustomed to the vehicle before attempting to take him for a ride. Some dogs are natural passengers and others hate the experience.

out. Sometimes the position of the dog makes a difference. Facing forward is often worst; some dogs do well positioned sideways to the motion or facing toward the back of the vehicle.

To conquer car sickness, take your dog for very short, frequent rides to extremely rewarding destinations. That may mean driving only half a block, then getting out and playing and relaxing for half an hour before turning around and driving the half block back home. Gradually lengthen the ride, making sure to keep all destinations pleasant.

While your dog learns that car rides are safe and fun, it may help to give him medication that alleviates nausea but won't reduce his enjoyment of the destination. Some anti-nausea drugs cause drowsiness, so ask your veterinarian to advise you about medication and other treatment options.

In contrast to dogs who become anxious in cars, some dogs experience separation anxiety when they are left at home. They may pant and shake, pace or run back and forth, hide under furniture, rip curtains from windows, dig holes through walls and chew through doors trying to escape. Gradual desensitization helps many dogs recover from separation anxiety. To desensitize your dog to your absence, start by leaving him for just a minute and then returning. Increase the separation for a few more minutes and then return. Gradually increase the periods that you and your dog are separated.

But if that doesn't work, there are medications that can help many dogs recover from severe separation anxiety. Your veterinarian can advise you on this.

It's much easier to prevent separation anxiety than to cure it, and proper crate-training is the way to go. When your dog is a puppy, give him an hour of pleasant quiet time alone each day. Start by taking him outside to relieve himself, then settle him comfortably in his crate with a soft pad and a chew bone or food-dispensing toy. You might turn on the radio for company and to partially cover environmental sounds that might worry him. Then leave. Be matter-of-fact about leaving: no long, emotional good-byes. See that your puppy is safe and comfortable, then go. Your return should not be a big deal either. Say hello to your puppy, let him out of his crate, and take him to the potty area. The less of a production you make of your comings and goings, the calmer your puppy will be.

If your dog shows mild signs of separation anxiety, you may be able to desensitize his fears by following the prevention protocol above. If your dog is severely anxious, consult your veterinarian.

Pushy Behaviors

Some of the behaviors your dog exhibits such as leaning on you and licking you may simply be related to how much he enjoys being with you. Although he is just showing affection, some of his attention-seeking behaviors can be irritating.

If your dog leans against you while you're petting him, don't try to push him away because he'll just push back against the extra support. Instead, take a 6-inch step away so your dog loses his balance. If your dog repositions himself and leans against you again, repeat that small step away. Continue repeating until your dog sits or stands beside you without using you as a leaning post.

If you're sitting in a chair petting your dog and he leans against you, slide your chair a few inches away, which again will cause him to lose his balance. If you can't slide your chair away, simply take your hands off your dog and stop petting when he leans. Wait until he supports himself before you start petting again. Your dog will soon realize that you won't pet him while he's leaning on you, and he will stop leaning.

Pushy dogs can be annoying. Discourage pushy behaviors by controlling the interaction with your dog.

Sometimes affectionate licking or kissing can become excessive and difficult to stop. Discourage prolonged licking so it doesn't become a habit. If you don't mind a few doggy kisses, let your dog lick once or twice, then say enough and move slightly away so he stops. It also helps to teach your dog to lick only on command ("give a kiss"), making this form of affection from your dog unacceptable unless you ask for it.

Teach your dog to give a kiss:

1. Place one hand on your dog's chest and the other on the side of his neck. This will allow you to gently push him away if he gets overexcited.
2. Put your face near your dog's. Say "kisses" and make a series of quiet kissing sounds. Most puppies and many adults will immediately start licking.
3. If yours doesn't lick when he hears the cue, smear a dot of cream cheese on your cheek and try again.
4. As soon as your dog licks, praise and offer a treat. This both rewards the dog and stops the licking before he gets carried away.

Teach your dog to receive a kiss:

1. Place one hand on your dog's neck and gently hold his muzzle with the other. This protects from nips while your dog learns to kiss gently.
2. Kiss your dog's cheek or the top of his head, then give a treat.
3. When he accepts kisses calmly, try the procedure without restraining him. Keep your hands ready to block in case he moves too fast.

Health-Related Behavior Problems

A surprising number of health problems can often first make their appearance as inappropriate behavior. Any uncharacteristic behavior or sudden change in habit should be viewed as a possible sign that your dog does not feel well. If, for example, your dog is fully housetrained, then suddenly starts soiling, or if he's normally friendly then suddenly turns irritable, a check-up is needed. Schedule an appointment with your veterinarian to rule out illness as the underlying cause of these problems. These are a few of the behaviors a dog may exhibit when ill:

- Urinating on a bed, couch, or soft chair
- Urinating indoors within minutes of returning from outside
- Defecating indoors
- Unexpected aggression when touched or approached
- Pacing or whining excessively
- Persistent thirst and frequent urination
- Overeating or refusal to eat or drink
- Eating his own or another dog's feces
- Eating hair, rocks, sand, or other nonfood items
- Frequently eating a large amount of grass
- Constantly licking or chewing himself in one particular spot
- Refusal or reluctance to sit

Training alone won't solve a behavior problem if it is a result of pain or illness. First, rule out any medical issues that might be causing your dog's misbehavior. Then, if necessary, teach him better manners later on when your dog feels well.

Additional health-related behavior problems include panting and sudden rage syndrome. A dog doesn't sweat over his whole body the way we do; he sweats mainly through his footpads. The primary way dogs cool themselves is by panting, breathing rapidly with mouth open and tongue out. As a dog gets hotter, he exposes more of his tongue and opens his mouth wider to increase the moist surface area for evaporative cooling. Dogs also pant when they're nervous, much as we might perspire when worried.

A dog who pants excessively may be either overheated or very anxious. Excessive panting is a symptom, not just an irritant. If your dog is playing and begins to pant excessively, stop the game, move him to a shady area, and give him water. If he pants excessively in the car or during a thunderstorm, respond as you would if he exhibited other signs of fear or nervousness by acting calm and not adding to his unease.

Sudden rage syndrome is an unpredictable and unusual type of aggression in which a calm dog without apparent provocation suddenly flies into a rage and attacks anyone who touches him or comes near. After the outburst of aggression passes, the dog often behaves as if nothing unusual has happened. Some take a nap.

Sudden rage syndrome seems to be triggered by a neurological abnormality. It is seen most often in spaniels but also appears in other breed types. This form of aggression is rare. Because sudden rage syndrome is likely hereditary, there is no way to prevent it other than not breeding dogs with this condition. Fortunately, it is rare.

Moving Beyond Problem Behaviors

Despite what may sometimes seem to be conflicting evidence, your dog doesn't want to annoy you. He wants nothing more than to please you, but it's up to you to teach him the way to do so. Dogs aren't born knowing how to live in harmony with humans; what outrages us is perfectly acceptable in the canine world. By working closely with your dog to prevent unwanted behavior and by correcting it before it becomes a habit, you will make the job of training your dog that much easier. For entrenched problem behaviors, your work may be more difficult, but it's certainly not impossible. Devote yourself to helping your dog live in harmony with you and your family and you will both receive lifelong benefits.

A well-trained dog is a happy dog.

Dogs and Work

Since the beginning, dogs and people have worked together. Had we not, it's unlikely we would have ever come to share our lives so completely. Dogs have been beasts of burden, pulling heavy carts and turning spits; herding dogs; livestock guardians; police and military dogs; and assistance dogs for those with disabilities. In the course of their work for us, they have been celebrated and denigrated, prized and neglected.

In addition to the work we do together and the work dogs do for us, there are times when we work to support and care for dogs. Many dog lovers find that working with a dog or working to ensure the care of dogs can bring a high level of personal satisfaction.

CHAPTER 33

Dogs Who Work

Dogs work for people in many ways: as guides and hearing dogs, as herders and livestock guardians, and as searchers and rescuers. Their roles as workers have adapted constantly since humans first domesticated them. Although their first use was probably as accidental guards in villages, they eventually accompanied humans when they hunted, helping people track, subdue, and retrieve prey. Then, when humans began to keep livestock, dogs served as herders and livestock guardians. They helped move herds from one grazing pasture to another and watched over flocks when they were grazing far from the village.

Eventually, dogs were bred for everything from companionship to meat. They were used in almost every part of the planet. After the Industrial Revolution, dogs were used less in their traditional agricultural and hunting capacities, but their skills were eventually adapted for use in the modern world. Dogs now serve in low- and high-tech capacities. Some sniff out drugs, explosives, and currency; others continue in age-old traditions of herding sheep and watching over goats on rural farms.

In urban and suburban settings, dogs are best known for their assistance, protection, and detection work. For almost a century, dogs have been actively used in the United States to assist blind, deaf, and physically challenged handlers. And police dogs have become an increasingly common presence in large American cities—serving to pursue and subdue suspects, detect contraband substances such as narcotics and weapons, and search for missing victims. Search and rescue dogs have proved to be a boon to rescue efforts, searching for and rescuing both lost hikers and victims caught in the path of natural and human-made disasters. Search and rescue dogs are invaluable in finding living and deceased victims in collapsed buildings and infrastructure after cataclysmic events such as terrorist attacks or natural disasters.

Our close relationship with dogs is based on their ability to work for us. Were it not for their abilities to help us hunt, guard, and herd, it is unlikely they would have been domesticated to such a great extent. Nor would we have developed the hundreds of breeds that exist, most originally bred to serve humans in a particular job.

As long as they are well cared for, many dogs will thrive on having a job to do.

The National Bird Dog Museum in Tennessee houses art, photography, and memorabilia related to pointing dog and retriever breeds, hunting and field trial activities, and shooting sports. The most famous bird dogs in history are represented among the portraits and exhibits, and the museum displays the works of many notable sport dog artists and sculptors.

The museum provides information on the origins of hunting breeds, their development through the centuries, and performance in the field. A diorama containing the stuffed remains of Count Noble, a setter that arrived in the United States in 1880 and went on to prove his excellence as a field performer and sire of champions, is on permanent display in the museum.

Our dependence on dogs to serve us in such a variety of capacities has not always ensured them humane treatment at the hands of humans. We praise military dogs for saving thousands of lives during the Vietnam War, but we abandoned all but a few hundred military dogs when our troops pulled out. And until 2000, all U.S. military dogs were summarily euthanized when they could no longer work. Animals in the entertainment industry were once routinely physically manipulated, injured, and even killed in the pursuit of a film shot or audience reaction. But advances have been made concerning the humane treatment of working dogs. In 2000, a Congressional bill forced the military to pursue adoption for military dogs who can no longer work, and federal and state animal welfare laws prohibit injuring a dog in the course of his work. As our understanding of dogs' skills and capacities increase, our ability to use them for both our benefit and theirs increases as well.

Hunting was one of the first jobs dogs did for us. Their role as hunters is the basis of much of the work they continue to do, including herding, detection work, and search and rescue. Today, however, the use of hunting dogs in the United States has been largely adapted as a sport or a hobby rather than a full-time job. There are many ways to test the skills and aptitude of hunting dogs, including hunt tests and field trials.

Born to Work

Although not all dogs are born to work, some thrive only when provided a job. There are breeds of dogs that have been developed for hundreds even thousands of years for a certain task. When denied that or a similar job, these dogs may react with anxiety, aggression, or depression. Some dogs may create their own

The Animal Welfare Act sets minimum standards of care and treatment regarding housing, handling, sanitation, nutrition, water, veterinary care, and protection from extreme weather and temperatures. Regulated businesses are encouraged to exceed the minimum standards.

Draft work was once common for dogs. They pulled coaches and milk and laundry trucks.

job—invariably one you don't want them to do such as gardening (digging up the flower garden), remodeling (chewing through dry wall), and guarding (keeping the house safe against any and all intruders, including passersby and postal workers).

Some of the dogs who are most likely to have problems when faced with a jobless life are those bred to work tirelessly for long periods. Herding dogs, for example, have been used for thousands of years to separate and move livestock. They may work in close confines, such as in a stable or paddock, or they may move livestock across tens or hundreds of miles. They were bred to be tenacious, fearless, untiring, and bold. When you take a Border Collie, Australian Shepherd, or Australian Cattle Dog and provide them with a warm bed and a yard but no exercise, the consequences can be traumatic for all involved. These dogs may roam, bark incessantly, herd children or other ani-

mals, dig obsessively, become aggressive, or simply bounce off the walls in an effort to diffuse their natural energy. Many of these dogs are turned over to animal shelters because their needs are misunderstood. Gun dogs and terriers are other breeds with high energy demands. Without a real or simulated job, they can become destructive or anxiety ridden.

There are also dogs who have no interest in working. For example, most companion dogs were bred to be devoted companions to doting humans. Their job is to relax in a lap and be adored. Companion dogs aren't the only ones to shun the idea of work. Energy inclinations are highly individual among dogs, just as they are among people. There are couch potato pointers and energy-to-spare Pomeranians. And working drive isn't all about high energy. Guardian dogs, for example, are often very mellow aside from their protective instincts. Aside from its great size, the Mastiff is likely the best apartment dog there is.

Most types of canine work require the dog to be a willing participant, and dogs simply won't work, or won't work well, if they don't want to. To keep a dog interested and willing, canine work is almost exclusively done on a play/reward system. Dogs in training are rewarded with a toy, a treat, or a play session. The work itself is part of the reward because it is perceived by the dog as play. Herding dogs, for instance, can't wait to get into a paddock and move sheep; they often require no additional reward for their work. When a dog is searching for a missing person, he is really searching for the toy that he knows will be provided him when and if he finds the victim. A popular misperception is that a search and rescue dog becomes depressed when he hasn't made a find after an extended period of time. In fact, he becomes dispirited and bored because the game isn't having its usual pay off. This is why search and rescue dog

Dogs work best when they receive positive encouragement.

handlers simulate finds every few hours while doing search work: to keep the dog interested in the game. You can see how this works at home with your own dog by hiding a toy and encouraging him to find it. At first, each time he finds it and brings it to you, play a vigorous game of tug or fetch. Then stop playing with the toy when your dog brings it to you. After several repetitions, he will lose interest. The game is no longer fun.

Don't worry too much if your dog was bred to move cattle over hundreds of miles but instead lives in a three-bedroom suburban ranch house. There are plenty of ways a conscientious owner can re-create the conditions of canine work. Recreational herding, agility, flyball, Frisbee, earth trials, and field trials are all good alternatives. Daily workouts, including walking, swimming, hiking, running, or accompanying you while you bicycle or inline skate are also good activities for high-energy working breeds. Sledding is a traditional canine job that is now a popular sport.

Assistance Dogs

Assistance dogs are those dogs who assist people with some type of physical challenge, be it hearing, sight, or mobility related. All assistance dogs are covered by the Americans with Disabilities Act (ADA), which was passed in 1990 and protects public access for people with disabilities. This means that disabled people and the tools they use, including dogs, must be allowed access to public places. As a result of the ADA, assistance dogs are legally entitled to go anywhere their handlers go, be it a restaurant, a theater, or a hotel. Although adherence to the ADA was not immediate, public awareness has grown quickly. As a result of advocacy of those in the disabled and assistance dog communities, it continues to grow. Acceptance of guide dogs has grown more quickly than for other assistance dogs.

Special-needs dogs, such as this one provided by the North Star Foundation (www.northstardog.com), assist autistic children and their families.

There is a common misunderstanding that only guide dogs are covered by the ADA. This, too, is beginning to change.

ADA rules take precedence over local or state laws governing the presence of animals in public spaces. According to the ADA, service animals that must be granted access to public places include signal dogs who indicate sounds to people who are hearing-impaired, dogs who pull wheelchairs or carry or pick up items for people whose mobility is impaired, dogs who alert people to impending seizures, and dogs who help people maintain their balance. Business owners may not require documentation that the dog is a service animal and may not segregate the dog and handler from other patrons. Service dogs are not pets, and posting a "no pets allowed" sign does not relieve business owners of the obligation to permit service dogs. The only

From quality time spent with his young master, North Star Dog "Charlie" offers companionship, encouragement, and lots of smiles.

time service animals may be excluded from the premises is if they pose a direct threat to the health or safety of others.

Assistance Dog Training

In most cases, assistance dogs are trained by individuals in nonprofit organizations. The dogs may be adopted from shelters or they may be bred by the organization. If raised from puppies, assistance dogs generally live with foster families for their first 12 to 18 months of life. Then they are returned to the nonprofit organization for training. Dogs adopted at an older age begin their education right away with basic good citizen training as well as training specific to their future jobs. They may remain at the organization for up to six months, depending on the job the dog is intended to do.

Once the dog's initial training is complete, handler training begins. In most cases, new handlers come to the organization for a week to a month for intensive training. They learn to trust the assistance dogs, give them commands, and teach them new commands. At the end of training, each handler is matched with the dog who suits him or her best. The assistance dog and handler now work together as a team. Most assistance dog training organizations provide follow-up training and support throughout the career of the dog-and-handler team.

Not all dogs make it through the rigorous training, however. In fact, less than 25 percent of potential assistance dogs are ultimately placed with a handler. This applies to dogs who are bred for assistance work and those who are adopted from shelters. Dogs may be released from the program for medical reasons, for behavioral issues, or simply because they don't enjoy working. Some dogs are believed to be better suited for other jobs. A dog who is not structurally sound enough for

Although it is still uncommon, assistance dogs are beginning to work with children with disabilities.

the rigorous physical work of a guide or service dog can still make an excellent hearing dog and may be offered to another agency for their program. Some dogs who are released from assistance dog training programs become search and rescue dogs, prison guard dogs, or acting dogs. Others are deemed to be excellent pets and are adopted out to loving families or individuals.

Once a nonprofit group makes a commitment to an animal, it is responsible for that animal throughout his life. If the dog is released early in his training, the organization finds him another job or a suitable home. Dogs who retire are cared for equally well. Most assistance dog handlers are unable to keep their working dogs once they are retired. Caring for two dogs may be too difficult physically, and jealousy and competition can be problematic for both the new dog and the retired dog. Retired dogs are placed for adoption through the nonprofit organization that originally trained them. Many dogs end up with the same foster families that cared for them 8 or 10 years before.

A service dog can help expand the world of a person with mobility limitations.

Service Dogs

Service dogs help people with physical mobility limitations reach high or low places, open doors, and turn on lights. They may help around the house by moving the wet laundry to the dryer, or they may help in public by pulling a wheelchair up a steep incline. Some service dogs may also detect and warn their handlers of seizures before they happen and respond to medical emergencies by pushing a button preset for an emergency contact. Service dogs range in their job descriptions. Many handlers rely on their dogs to pick up dropped items or reach high countertops. Service dogs must be large and strong enough to do physical chores for their handlers. Many are Labrador Retrievers, Golden Retrievers, or mixes of these breeds, although there are also German Shepherd Dogs, Rottweilers, and other herding, gun, or guardian breeds and mixed breeds

The German government established the first school for training guide dogs following World War I. The school benefited veterans blinded in the war. In the United States, two of the oldest guide dog schools are The Seeing Eye, founded in 1929, and Leader Dogs for the Blind, founded in 1939. The breeds of dog most often used for this work are German Shepherd Dogs, Golden Retrievers, Labrador Retrievers, and Golden/Labrador mixes, although some schools also use breeds such as Poodles and Boxers.

working as service dogs. Although some service dog organizations breed dogs especially to serve in this role, others adopt young adult dogs from shelters. They are matched with a person after working with a group for a week to a month.

Because every person's physical limitations are different, it's important the dogs be capable of learning new commands and tasks once they are placed with a handler. While one handler may need to be pulled up inclines, another handler may be partially ambulatory and only need to lean on the dog when navigating the home or office. Most service dogs are used in a variety of activities both inside and outside the home.

Service dog handlers often rely on their dogs for emotional support as well as physical help. This is especially true for handlers who have suffered traumatic injuries that have substantially changed their lives. For many with disabilities, leaving their homes and interacting with the public is difficult. Having a dog alongside them can bring comfort and security as well as an incentive to get up and be active each day.

For quadriplegics and other people who cannot use their arms, service dogs serve an extremely important task by being able to dial preprogrammed phone numbers on the telephone. Knowing they have access to 911 or other emergency aid brings enormous comfort to these people. Having a service dog may even allow them to live independently.

Guide Dogs

Guide dogs were first used in Europe and were introduced to the United States by an article in the *Saturday Evening Post* in 1927. The first U.S. guide dog organization, The Seeing Eye, was opened in 1929, followed by Leader Dogs for the Blind, Inc., in 1939. The popularity of guide dogs increased greatly in the 1940s, when soldiers who were blinded during World War II began investigating their use. These young, healthy men were unwilling to give up their independence, and the guide dogs helped them maintain their independent lives. The use of guide dogs was the impetus behind developing other types of assistance dogs.

Most guide dog organizations breed dogs specifically to serve as guide dogs. Although the original guide dogs were German Shepherd Dogs or shepherd mixes, modern-day guide dogs may be purebred Labrador Retrievers, Golden Retrievers, German Shepherd Dogs, or Labrador/Golden Retriever mixes. As with service dog work, guide dog work is physically demanding, so dogs must be large, strong, and physically sound.

In most cases, guide dogs are bred and raised by a nonprofit organization. The organizations closely evaluate the physical, mental, and emotional strengths of dams and sires in order to breed the best puppy candidates possible. Potential guide dogs spend the first eight weeks of their lives with their dams (mothers) in a whelping home. Then they are returned to the guide dog center, where they are evaluated for health problems. Each healthy puppy is placed with a foster family for the next year of life. In the foster homes, the dogs are socialized and taught the basics of good dog citizenship. At about 15 months of age, they are returned to the guide dog center, where they learn how to be guide dogs. After about 6 months of training, they are matched with a group of incoming guide dog handler candidates. Throughout the month-long class they work with a number of potential guide dog handlers; at the end, each dog is matched with a handler with whom he lives for the rest of his working life.

Not all dogs are right for guide dog work. Dogs may be cut from the program at eight weeks for medical problems or after their fos-

A guide dog can allow a blind person the opportunity to move around independently, even to take hikes.

such as a curb or stairs. When crossing a street, the handler listens for traffic flow and tells the dog when to cross. However, guide dogs are trained to be intelligently disobedient. If the handler tells a dog to proceed and a car is speeding around the corner, the dog will stop the handler from continuing, even stepping into the handler's path to stop her.

In addition, guide dogs learn a number of commands specific to their handlers' needs. For example, a handler who works in an office building may train her dog to find the elevator. Other handlers may teach their dogs to find items by commanding, *ATM, door,* or *chair.* Because handlers have different levels of sight and a range of lifestyles, guide dogs must be able to learn new commands appropriate for their particular jobs.

Guide dogs do most of their work outside of the home, so they have distinct on and off hours. When they go home at night and the harness comes off, they're pets free to lounge in the grass and play with other family pets. When the harness comes out in the morning, they're all business. Whenever a guide dog is in public wearing his harness, he is working and is prohibited even from licking or scratching himself. Even lying on the floor under a restaurant table is considered work; the dog is not allowed to eat crumbs or beg. Because it is difficult to determine whether a dog is actively working or not, it's important that you always ask before petting or approaching a guide dog. Guide dogs must be able to focus intensely. Distracting a guide dog can be dangerous for him and his handler. When asked, many guide dog handlers will refuse to allow you to pet their guide dog. Don't be offended; they are doing what is best for their working team.

ter placement because they simply don't have the drive or interest to work. Some dogs are cut from the program after being placed with a handler. These dogs are either placed for adoption or are made candidates for other assistance dog uses or other jobs. For example, some failed guide dogs make good service dogs or even search and rescue dogs.

Contrary to popular perception, guide dogs do not lead their handlers. Rather, the handler tells the dog where to go and the dog looks out for overhead obstacles, such as a tree branch or a sign, and incline changes,

Hearing Dogs

Hearing dogs are quickly gaining use among the deaf and hard of hearing. They are

Hearing dogs alert their handlers to doorbells, telephone rings, and oven timers.

calling the handler's name. Sometimes they do active alerts, where they run back and forth between their handler and the source of the sound, while other times they do passive alerts, staying with the handler or at the source of the sound.

Their uses can be as dramatic as notifying a deaf or hearing-impaired person to a fire alarm or as routine as letting a handler know that the coffee is done. Besides alerting to fire alarms, doorbells, door knocks, and their handler's name, most hearing dogs are trained to alert to the sound of a timer. The timer is then used in a variety of ways: as an alarm clock, as a cooking timer when making coffee or boiling water, or even when running a bath. This way the dog doesn't need to learn a new command each time a new alarm clock or tea kettle is bought.

Although many deaf people use their hearing dog only inside the home, others find it useful for the dog to accompany them on errands or to work. Although not trained to respond to dangers in the same way that a guide dog is, a hearing dog has a natural reaction to loud or ominous noises—something that helps a deaf person be aware of her surroundings. At work, a hearing dog can notify the handler when the phone rings or when an office mate requires the handler's attention.

Hearing dogs, like service and guide dogs, are provided full access under the ADA. However, many hearing dog organizations may train dogs differently for use inside and outside of the home. If a handler has a hearing dog who is trained only for home use, the organization may require that the hearing dog not wear his working vest and abide by all rules for pet dogs when outside the home.

Most hearing dog organizations obtain their dogs from shelters or breed rescue organizations. They receive rigorous training through a hearing organization and are then matched with a group of potential

trained to recognize certain sounds and to notify their handlers when they hear those sounds. A hearing dog generally alerts his handler to a noise by sitting in front of her or pawing the handler. Some hearing dogs are trained to have different alerts for different sounds or to touch colored rugs to indicate a certain sound: for example, one rug indicates a doorbell and another rug indicates someone

A Global Positioning System collar or backpack, sized for dogs weighing 30 pounds or more, can pinpoint your lost dog's location in 10 to 60 seconds. The GPS is activated by a phone call, and when the system locates the dog, it sends back an SMS position update. If the system can't find the dog, it transmits the dog's last known location. A new version is coming out that will be sized for small dogs.

Police dogs are commonly used by law enforcement departments in U.S. cities.

hearing dog handlers for further training for one week to one month. At the end of handler training, each handler is matched with a hearing dog.

As with all potential assistance dogs, not all hearing dogs make it through the long and challenging training process. These dogs are placed up for adoption. Dogs who are not able to stay in their working home after retirement are also placed for adoption by the hearing dog organization.

Because hearing dogs do not do any physical labor, they can be any size and do not need to be as physically sound as guide or service dogs are. There are also fewer restrictions on the age of beginning hearing dogs. Terriers often make good hearing dogs because their hearing is acute and they tend to react to sound. Terriers' small size also makes them popular among hearing dog handlers, who may want a dog who can be easily kept in an apartment or easily lifted and controlled. For people who lose their hearing with age, small dogs can fit more easily into their lifestyle, especially if they live in a retirement home or apartment.

Hearing dogs can range from 4 to 80 pounds and can be of almost any breed or breed mix, as long as their hearing is superb and their drive is high.

There are also assistance dogs who provide emotional support for people with severe mental and emotional problems; however, this a fairly new area of assistance dog work.

Police Dogs

A majority of major U.S. cities now have at least one canine cop, and some have many. Dogs were first officially used by police units in Germany and Belgium starting in the late 1800s. By the early 1900s, their use had expanded to England, France, Hungary, Australia, and Italy. Police dogs were first used in the United States by the New York City Police Department starting in 1907. They are now used by thousands of police departments across the country.

Police dogs are often German Shepherd Dogs, Belgian Malinois, and Rottweilers. Dogs are used by law enforcement for many jobs. There are tracking dogs, usually Bloodhounds, who are used to track suspects and victims. There are also patrol dogs, who are used to detect illicit substances, such as weapons and narcotics, and to pursue and subdue suspects. Patrol dogs are trained in bite work, which is a nonlethal method to apprehend suspects. It consists of the dog latching onto a limb and not letting go until the handler gives him a command to release the suspect, which is usually once the police officer has physical control over the person.

Police dogs work day in and day out with their human partners. They ride with their partners throughout the work day and generally go home with them at night. In the past, some police dogs were kenneled during their off time, but experts now believe that police dogs are better socialized and

German Shepherd Dogs have long been called "Police Dogs," due to their prominence in this field. The breed's strength, agility, and high trainability have all contributed to their success as police dogs.

less prone to aggressiveness when they live in a family setting.

Although police dogs are generally bred and raised in Europe, there are some preliminary attempts at establishing U.S. breed programs. Police dogs who do not succeed in their work are either placed in other, more suitable jobs; adopted out to families; or kept as pets by their former partners. Most retired police dogs are kept by their human partners.

The use of police dogs is popular for many reasons. Tracking dogs have proved to be highly effective in finding both suspects and victims. They are also objective, with none of the personal biases that can affect a human police officer's decision making. Their finds hold up well under examination and in trials. Patrol dogs are able to subdue suspects in a nonlethal way, and their presence often helps prevent a violent response when a suspect is approached by police officers. Because of this, police dogs save the lives of both suspect and police, minimizing the situations in which an officer must resort to using her weapon.

Although canine police are often perceived as being vicious, they are simply doing what they are trained to do, just as any working dog does. For example, police dogs may subdue a suspect by biting a limb and shaking it vigorously. The dogs are trained to do this through the use of a bite sleeve, a heavily padded sleeve worn by a simulated suspect. A handler gives the command for a dog to bite. Once the dog is latched onto the sleeve, the dog and simulated suspect play a game of tug. The game ends when the handler orders the dog to release the sleeve. In other words, bite work is almost exactly the same as a tug game you play with your dog, the difference being your dog bites a rope or plush toy. Police dogs bite harder when a suspect resists and lighter when the suspect surrenders. They release the suspect immediately upon their handler's command. The bite has enough force to subdue a suspect but not enough to cause serious injury.

That said, police dog work has not always been used effectively or ethically. For example, the brutal use of police dogs for crowd control during the civil rights movement tainted the program for many decades.

The work dogs do reflects the morality of those who train and handle them. While dogs have done enormous good through the years, they have also been trained to serve in jobs that victimized innocent people. In addition to the police dogs used against peaceful marchers during the civil rights movement, guard dogs were used to intimidate and terrorize prisoners in concentration camps during World War II. Despite this, police dogs do serve as effective public relations tools. Officers who work with canine partners are generally viewed as easier to approach and as less threatening. Police dog teams are active in school visits, particularly with antidrug programs, and do regular exhibitions for the public.

Military Dogs

Dogs have been used in war throughout recorded history. The Romans bred large mastiffs and affixed them with spiked collars before going into battle. During the First World War, the French, Germans, and English all used dogs in battle; by the Second World War, the Americans also had inducted canine combatants.

Although the United States did not officially use dogs in wartime until World War II, dogs were unofficially present in every battle in American history. During the American Revolution, soldiers routinely brought their hunting dogs with them into battle—as companions and as watchdogs. During the Civil War, soldiers on both sides were known to have dogs in their company. Some American soldiers adopted dogs while serving during World War I—stray dogs were common in the bombed-out European cities and on the battlefields. Some of these dogs ended up serving as messengers; others became mascots for military units; and most served unofficial duties as guards and therapy dogs.

By World War II, American dogs were being actively solicited for military duty.

Military dogs serve as sentries, detection dogs, scouts, and patrol dogs.

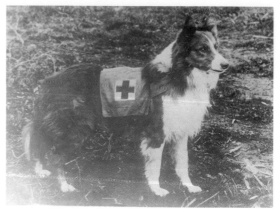

European dogs were used as Red Cross dogs during the First and Second World Wars.

Most of the dogs used during the war were loaned by patriotic American families who wanted to contribute to the war effort. In all, 19,000 dogs were recruited from civilian life; of these about 55 percent passed their training and made it into the military, serving as patrol dogs, scout dogs, and sentry dogs. After the war, most of the surviving dogs were returned to their families, where they resumed their lives as pets. Dogs are attributed to saving thousands of lives during World War II. The Marines used dogs, particularly Dobermans, in the Pacific Theater. On the island of Guam, 25 Marine Dobermans died in the line of duty. A life-size sculpture of a Doberman Pinscher on Guam memorializes their service.

Since World War II, dogs have continued to be a part of the U.S. military. They were used in the Korean War, the Vietnam War, the Persian Gulf War, and in the wars in Afghanistan and Iraq. Today, military dogs serve in a variety of ways: they are explosive, weapon, and mine detection dogs and scout and patrol dogs.

Although the World War II dogs were deployed under the direction of the Quartermaster Corps, after World War II military dogs were moved under the authority of the Air Force. The military policies toward dogs were altered dramatically following World War

II. The Air Force initiated a military dog breeding program and reclassified military dogs as equipment. As such, they were neither ranked nor decorated for their military service. Dogs who did not make it through training or who were retired because of advanced age or behavioral or medical problems were euthanized. Military dogs lived their entire lives within military kennels.

As a result of pressure by military dog handler associations and other dog lovers, Congress unanimously passed a bill in 2000, ordering the Air Force to attempt to adopt out dogs who were being retired due to injury, age, or unsuitability. Public Law No: 106-446 requires that retired military dogs who are healthy and safe be made available for adoption. The retired military dogs go through a rigorous screening process to ensure that they do not behave aggressively once they are in a private home.

Vietnam

Vietnam is among the most notorious events in canine war history. More than 4,000 dogs were deployed during the war, but only about 250 returned to the United States. Although the dogs who served in Vietnam are credited with saving more than ten thousand human lives, they were left in Vietnam when the United

States pulled out. There has never been an official explanation, although some Air Force officials claim the dogs had a tropical disease that could be spread to American animals. This claim is heavily disputed by military dog advocates and Vietnam dog handlers. Officially, Vietnam dogs were left as part of the military equipment that was given to the South Vietnamese as the United States pulled out. It is presumed that after the fall of Saigon, most of the military dogs were killed for food or let loose to starve to death or become feral.

Vietnam dog handlers have been active in questioning the government's explanation for the dogs' abandonment and have been successful in establishing several official memorials to the military dogs who served in Vietnam. A documentary about the Vietnam War dogs, *War-Dogs*, also helped publicize the fate of the Vietnam dogs.

Modern Military Dogs

Today, several hundred military working dogs—primarily German Shepherds, Dutch Shepherds, and Belgian Malinois—serve in the sand and heat of Afghanistan and Iraq, where they are used for guard duty, crowd control, tracking, and bomb detection.

Some military dogs serve a new purpose. Labrador Retrievers Boe and Budge were deployed to Iraq as therapy dogs to help troops control the stress in their lives and communicate more easily about problems they may be having. And specially trained service dogs help wounded veterans carry objects, pick up dropped items, provide balance, and simply to readjust to civilian life.

Herding Dogs

Humans have used herding dogs for thousands of years. Herding is one of the first jobs for which dogs were actively utilized. While some modern herders are involved only in herding as a hobby and for competition, there are still many herding dogs working hard on farms throughout the world. Herding dogs are precious commodities for ranchers, who point out that a herding dog can do the work of several people when it comes to separating and moving livestock.

Herding dogs are especially valued in Australia, where they are still used to move sheep and cattle over wide ranges. It is said that Australia was built on the back of the Australian Kelpie, a dog used mostly for

An Australian Shepherd herds sheep in an enclosed paddock.

Military working dogs in Afghanistan and Iraq have some special needs because of the dry climate and blowing sand they're exposed to. Many of them were suffering corneal ulcerations and recurrent conjunctivitis. A donation of Doggles, protective eyewear for dogs, made a difference. Army veterinarians and dog handlers saw a huge decrease in the number of eye injuries that were occurring in those environments.

Livestock guardians work independently of humans, protecting their charges in enclosed spaces or on grazing land.

sheep herding. Herding dogs are also commonly used in Europe, Canada, North Africa, and the western United States. The most commonly used herders are Australian Shepherds, Border Collies, Australian Cattle Dogs, and Australian Kelpies.

Herding dogs may be used on anything from large cattle ranches to small dairy farms. They herd any livestock, including cattle, sheep, and goats. Handlers work with their dogs from the ground or from horseback. Cattle ranchers generally work on horseback.

Herding work varies: the dogs may be used for a cattle run, moving thousands of head of cattle over many miles, or they may be used to move one sheep from one barn stall to another. Herding breeds work in different ways. Some are hard dogs who nip and bite at the heels of the livestock. This style of herding is common when working with cattle. It is commonly associated with dogs such as the Australian Cattle Dog and the low-slung Corgi. Sheep herding dogs tend to use more eye, meaning that they direct the movement

of the livestock with a fixed gaze. This use of eye is easy to see in Australian Shepherds, Border Collies, and Australian Kelpies.

Herders must be able to stop and start on a dime and respond immediately to commands from their handlers. However, a good herding dog will override a command from his handler if the command puts the dog, the livestock, or the handler in jeopardy. Like guide dogs, herders are encouraged to be intelligently disobedient.

Most herding dogs have a strong on-off switch. When working, they are tireless, moving cattle across many miles and for many hours at a time. When not working, they tend to be calm but alert. Herding dogs are known for their strong attachment to one person.

Livestock Guardians

Livestock guardians are among the few working dogs who do not work closely with people. In fact, their ability to work depends on the fact that they don't bond with people. The guardians are large, protective dogs who watch over livestock in paddocks or in open grazing areas. Originally, they were developed to guard livestock that were grazing away from shepherds for several months at a time. Now, however, the encroachment of civilization on wildlife has made livestock far more vulnerable to predators than their ancestors were. Wild predators often do not have ample hunting grounds and turn to farms and ranches for easy prey. Ranchers may use livestock guardians within paddocks when other predator controls have failed.

These dogs are fierce protectors and will protect their livestock from any threat, including humans and other dogs, as well as large predators such as mountain lions, cougars, panthers, and bears. They have been known to fight bears and mountain lions to the death. Livestock guardians are used in Europe and parts of the Middle East and Asia, as well as in Canada and the United States. Among the live-

Therapy dogs have been shown to alleviate stress and boredom for patients confined to long-term hospitalization and nursing care.

Cassidy the Rottweiler, who lives with owner Becky Buffum in Austin, Texas, hasn't let a missing leg stop her from doing anything. She excelled at agility and lure coursing at dog camp, clocked 19 miles per hour at a "fastest dog" contest, and makes frequent visits to retirement homes and schools as a therapy dog.

stock guardian breeds are Great Pyrenees, Akbash Dogs, and Anatolian Shepherd Dogs.

Livestock guardians are taught their work less by training than by environmental stimulus. Once the puppies are weaned from their mothers, they are placed with the animals they will someday protect, be they goats, sheep, llamas, or cattle. By growing up with the livestock, they bond so tightly with them that they will protect them as they would their own babies. Human and canine contact is kept to a minimum—only enough so that they are not aggressive toward their human owners. The United States Department of Agriculture (USDA) advocates the use of livestock guardians as a dependable method of predator deterrence.

Therapy Dogs

Although therapy dogs are usually pet dogs who perform work in the area of human therapy, what they do is rarely just a hobby. Most therapy dog teams make a high level of commitment: visiting a specific hospital or facility as many as four times a week and receiving extensive training. In addition to a high level of training, most facilities require that therapy dogs be certified by a national therapy dog organization. The two foremost national certification organizations are Therapy Dogs International, Inc. (TDI), and the Delta Society. Local organizations often require additional training and certification beyond that provided by the national groups.

Although they can be big or small, all therapy dogs must be well behaved and very friendly with people.

Therapy dogs may participate in animal-assisted activities (AAA), animal-assisted therapy (AAT), literacy therapy, or grief therapy. Each type of dog therapy requires a distinct set of skills and behavioral types.

Animal-assisted activities are the most basic type of animal therapy. These dogs simply spend time with patients, or they may participate in agility or obedience exhibitions for hospital patients. They visit patients at hospital or nursing facilities or visit at-risk, developmentally disabled or physically disabled children in schools or residential facilities. These dogs serve the function of a pet dog by providing companionship and entertainment. They are the most common therapy dogs currently used. They must be well trained and nonaggressive toward people and animals. Most facilities require the dogs be certified by TDI or the Delta Society. Some facilities also require additional training or certification through a regional therapy group.

Animal-assisted therapy is a more formal form of dog therapy. Dogs in AAT usually work in rehabilitation departments and play an important role in motivating and assisting patients in physical therapy. Patients may brush the dogs, throw balls to them, or walk them as an alternative to doing therapy with inanimate objects. One common activity is for patients to buckle and unbuckle a collar and clip on and clip off a leash instead of using the traditional dress-board that aids rehab patients in manual dexterity. These dogs may assist patients by providing mobility support, and there are some who introduce disabled patients to the benefits of a service dog. Many rehabilitation therapists believe that using a dog instead of traditional equipment is a strong motivator for rehab patients to participate in physical therapy.

AAT dogs must be certified by TDI or the Delta Society. Facilities usually require that AAT dogs have additional training or certification through a local organization or the facility itself. Some facilities have initiated their own programs, training and certifying their own therapy dogs.

Literacy Therapy

Literacy therapy is a fairly new form of canine therapy that is quickly gaining acceptance. Literacy therapy dogs provide a safe place for children with learning difficulties to read aloud. Although these dogs usually require national certification, they are much more passive participants than dogs in other forms of therapy. Literacy therapy is considered ideal for calm, older dogs who are content to lie with a head in the lap of a child for an hour or so while he or she reads to them.

Therapy Dogs International has a Disaster Stress Relief unit that is deployed upon official invitation from federal or state agencies or from other agencies in need of its services.

The use of literacy therapy dogs stems from the theory that children with reading problems often suffer a social stigma as much as a learning disability. Taunts from peers can compound learning disabilities, leading to a dislike, even fear, of reading. By reading to a dog, the children encounter a nonjudgmental, passive listener. The handler also plays a role, encouraging the child to look up words to help the dog understand the story or encouraging the child by saying the dog enjoys the story or thinks the story is scary.

Grief Therapy

Grief therapy dogs are used by therapists to help counsel and console people after a trauma of some kind. They have been used to help calm children in the aftermath of school shootings or other violent events, to provide firefighters a mental break during grueling forest fires, and to console and distract victims of earthquakes, tornadoes, or fires. During the past several years, the use of grief therapy dogs has become more actively embraced by disaster relief organizations. This has much to do with the use of grief therapy dogs in the aftermath of the attacks on the World Trade Center and the Pentagon.

After September 11, 2001, New York City reserved a pier to assist families affected by the World Trade Center attack. There, therapy dogs associated with the ASPCA and the Delta Society were made available to those looking for canine comfort. Grief therapy dogs were also used in Washington, D.C.

The Red Cross and other relief organizations were surprised by the popularity of the therapy dogs: they were well received not only by victims' families but also by laid-off workers seeking economic relief and job assistance at the pier and by aid workers themselves. The dogs were cathartic and comforting for many, especially children. The dogs even accompanied relatives when they visited Ground Zero to lay flowers on the site. Although grief therapy dogs existed before 2001, the events provided a catalyst for relief agencies to include dogs as part of future disaster relief work.

Since then, the comforting presence of therapy dogs has helped people mend after California's wildfires in 2003 and Hurricane Katrina in 2005, to name just two notable disasters after which visits from therapy dogs have made a difference. For people who may have lost everything, therapy dogs are calming and reassuring.

But there's more to this type of therapy work than just being there for people. Dogs and handlers trained in crisis response receive intensive training that includes such airport simulations as riding an escalator, being frisked by security, and boarding a plane. They encounter firefighters in full uniform; bright lights; shrieking sirens; and other sights, sounds, and smells that might accompany a disaster scene. Only then are they ready to start meeting with victims and responders, both of whom benefit from their presence.

Detection Dogs

Although there are detection dogs who work for the armed forces or for the police department, detection dogs serve in other capacities as well. These dogs use their noses to sniff out contraband drugs, weapons, explosives, currency, and banned agricultural products. There are even dogs who have been trained to

---

Can dogs predict earthquakes? A public health doctor in Japan is researching the possibility. In findings presented at a seismology conference in 2003, Kiyoshi Shimamura reported that complaints about erratic dog behavior jumped 18 percent in the two months before and after a major earthquake struck Kobe in 1995.

Bloodhounds are often used by police departments to track missing victims and suspects.

Dogs can be trained to find anything detectable by scent—their olfactory skills are so heightened that they can smell drugs or explosives even when hidden in food or other powerful-smelling substances. In fact, their olfactory senses are so well developed, dogs smell not only the ketchup on a hamburger but also every distinct ingredient in the ketchup as well. This means that a dog can sniff out and zero in (alert) on the scent of vinegar through the competing smells of the tomato paste and onion powder that makes up the ketchup as well as the bun, meat, lettuce, and pickles that make up the rest of the meal.

Detection dogs must have more than just a great sense of smell; they also have to have a highly developed work drive. They must be easily motivated by a toy, praise, or food reward. Depending on their job specifications, whether they work around the public, need to work on top of cargo containers, or must cover large areas of terrain, detection dogs may be large or small.

The Department of Homeland Security trains dogs to detect explosives on airlines or in baggage. These explosive-detecting dogs were formerly overseen by the Federal Aviation Administration (FAA) and then the Transportation Safety Agency (TSA) to screen baggage and airplanes before they take off so disasters such as the explosion of Pan Am Flight 103 over Lockerbie, Scotland, in 1988 are prevented. According to experts, explosive-detecting dogs are not only highly accurate but also more mobile and less expensive than human-made equipment.

detect termites in homes and melanoma cells on human skin.

Dogs have olfactory senses that are far more efficient than humans' are. In the wild, dogs use these skills to hunt and to scavenge. We, however, have trained dogs to use these skills to serve us in a variety of ways. They save lives, protect agriculture and wildlife, and even deter terrorists—all through their amazing sense of smell.

Dogs have been used effectively as drug detectors by police units around the United States. This Belgian Malinois is proving the power of his able sniffer.

Dogs also serve to keep substances out of the United States, such as undeclared currency, illegal drugs, contraband fruits and vegetables, and protected or potentially harmful wildlife. In Guam, Jack Russell Terriers are trained to detect brown snakes in cargo to prevent them from leaving the island. Brown snakes have had a devastating effect on the indigenous wildlife of Guam, and officials hope to prevent the same experience on other Pacific islands such as Hawaii.

The Beagle Brigade, which also operates under the Department of Homeland Security as part of the U.S. Customs and Border Protection (CBP) Canine Enforcement Program, is a group composed of trained Beagles and their handlers who work to keep certain fruits, vegetables, and meats out of the United States. Because many foods carry microscopic pests that could decimate American agriculture, these dogs perform an important function. The dogs sniff passenger baggage at airports and cars at border cross-

ings, looking for anything from pork to guavas to fresh ginger. Beagles were chosen for this important job because they have highly attuned noses and are considered to be less threatening to the public than are larger Labrador Retrievers or German Shepherd Dogs.

Most Americans are familiar with the U.S. Customs and Border Protection dogs seen at border crossings, airports, and ship ports. Under the U.S. Customs and Border Protection Canine Enforcement Program, dogs sniff passengers, luggage, cars, airplanes, ships, and cargo, looking for drugs, currency, ammunition, and concealed people. Recently, they've added explosives to their repertoire.

Many detection dogs are adopted from animal shelters. The CBP has trainers who actively seek appropriate dogs from U.S. shelters. These dogs receive intense training both with and without their new handlers. Other detection dogs are career-change dogs, who did not have the drive or ability to be guide

Urban, or disaster, search and rescue dogs have received increased attention in the United States since the attacks of 9/11 and Hurricane Katrina.

dogs or herding dogs but whose playfulness and excellent sense of smell make them ideal for detection work. Although most detection dogs who work for the U.S. government are kenneled when not working, they are almost always retired to the handler who has worked with them the longest. They generally retire between 8 and 10 years of age, or when they lose interest in their work.

Search and Rescue Dogs

Search and rescue dogs may be media sweet-hearts, but they're also highly trained, highly efficient workers. Search and rescue dogs search for living or dead human beings who are missing. They may search in wilderness or in suburban areas, in snow or in water. Search and rescue dogs must have a strong play and toy

Not all search and rescue dogs are Labs or German Shepherds. The smallest rescue dog to serve at the World Trade Center was Ricky, a Rat Terrier from Seattle, Washington.

drive. Although they have been used for centuries in Europe, they've been embraced only during the last 20 to 30 years in the United States. Most search and rescue dogs are handled by private citizens, although there is an increasing number of search and rescue dogs

Water recovery is a unique type of search and rescue work. Dogs search for drowning victims rather than missing people.

Tony Zintsmaster and Kaiser of Indiana Task Force 1 were among the first responders to Ground Zero on the evening of September 11, 2001.

owned and trained by ski patrol units, firefighters, and rural police departments.

The training for search and rescue dogs is done in increments. The dog is taught first to alert by barking, sitting, or scratching for a toy or other object. He then progresses to alerting on a toy in a handler's hand. It is gradually made more complex when the handler hides the object in increasingly difficult locations. Trainers sometimes use what is called a bark box: the handler hides inside a wooden box, and the door opens when the dog exhibits an alert. The dog then learns to exhibit the same alert on any human smell. Some dogs are also taught to search for human remains through the use of cadaver scent.

In some disciplines, the alert is specifically taught, while other handlers allow the dogs to choose their own alert, believing it encourages

The most up-to-date hunting dogs in Finland carry cell phones to work. Benefon, a Finnish cellular phone manufacturer, offers a wireless phone that uses a Global Positioning System chipset to track the locations of dogs in the field. Hunters can also issue verbal commands by dialing their dogs.

a stronger, more consistent alert. The reward also varies: it can be a chew toy, a ball, a piece of fire hose, or even, rarely, a food reward. Dogs who are play motivated will receive a brisk game of tug-of-war or catch in addition to the toy as a reward for finding the missing/hiding person.

Urban search and rescue dogs are found at such disaster scenes as the bombing of the Murrah Building in Oklahoma City; the destruction of the World Trade Center in 2001; and the aftermaths of Hurricane Katrina, the 2004 tsunami in Asia, and the 2008 earthquake in China. In such situations, dogs can become depressed when they find only dead bodies, so at intervals their handlers set up "live" finds to

Dogs were both rescuers and rescued in the aftermath of Hurricane Katrina along the Gulf Coast in 2004.

Avalanche specialist Patti Burnett, author of Avalanche Hasty Search, *unloads from the helicopter at an avalanche deployment.*

help restore the dogs' morale. Search and rescue dogs and their handlers may work up to 18 hours a day and travel around the world at their own expense when disaster calls for their skills.

There are two types of wilderness search and rescue dogs: air scent and trailing dogs. Air scent dogs pick up the scent of any person in an area, while trailing dogs look for the particular scent of one person. Air scent dogs are usually used for very large areas; for example, when a hiker is missing and searchers can narrow the search only to a 20- or 50-mile circumference. Trailing dogs are used to find a person who left from a known location and is believed to be on foot and within a relatively short distance; for example, an Alzheimer's patient who has wandered from a home within a suburban neighborhood. The dog is supplied the missing person's scent from a scent article, which may be an article of clothing or other object the missing person has held. Sometimes the two types of dogs are used together. The air

scent dog searches for a general human scent; when it gets "on scent," or finds a scent trail to follow, the trailing dog is brought in to determine whether it is the scent of the missing person and to follow the scent more accurately to the person.

Avalanche dogs are used to find people buried in the snow. The victims may be skiers or snowboarders, hikers, or even motorists. Avalanches can even bury people in their homes. These dogs are trained specifically to search for people under a blanket of snow and to scratch and bark at the snow when they get on scent. To reinforce the drive to get to the victim, avalanche dogs are usually taught to self-reward—to actually take the toy, be it a glove or a tennis ball, from the victim, pulling a glove off a hand or a ball from inside a jacket.

Water searches are considerably different from other types of search and rescue, requiring dogs who not only have highly developed olfactory senses and a work drive but also a higher level of tenacity. These dogs do not do

Water rescue, saving a person who has fallen out of a boat, as this Newfoundland is demonstrating, differs from water searches to recover the bodies of drowned victims.

rescues but rather recoveries, finding drowned victims. Because there is no live victim and because the payout, or reward, is delayed, it is difficult to keep these dogs interested and motivated. In training, handlers use everything from divers to scentillators, to simulate victims of drowning.

Wilderness search and rescue dogs are certified by regional organizations rather than a national organization. They are generally deployed through local sheriff departments.

Search and rescue dogs come from a variety of sources; they may be purebred dogs or adopted from animal shelters. Some handlers choose dogs based on particular criteria such as a strong drive and an excellent nose, while others fall into search and rescue when looking for a hobby. For the most part, search and rescue dogs live with their handlers throughout their lives and retire in their own homes. They are rarely kenneled.

Disaster, sometimes called urban, search and rescue dogs have received a great deal of attention in the United States since the Oklahoma City bombing and September 11 attacks. They have been actively trained and certified in the United States for the only last

20 to 30 years but have been used in Europe much longer. Disaster dogs are certified through the Federal Emergency Management Agency (FEMA) and deployed through Urban Search and Rescue (USAR) task forces. Although some disaster teams are affiliated with local fire departments or rescue agencies, most handlers are private citizens who fund their own training.

Avalanche and mountain rescue dogs are used to find people buried in snow, often under extreme, dangerous conditions.

Disaster dogs are trained in much the same way as other search and rescue dogs are trained, but in addition to finding a victim, they must learn to navigate unusual and dangerous terrain. They are used to search for both living and dead human beings trapped in buildings or infrastructures that have collapsed by natural or intentional causes, including tornadoes, fires, earthquakes, and explosions. Disaster dogs must have an extremely strong play drive and they must be extremely agile. In their work, they navigate upended trees and rocks, splintered wood and metal beams, shards of glass, and a number of other unexpected elements. Disaster sites are unpredictable—with several-stories-deep chasms, tenuous structures, diminished light, and dangerous toxins. These dogs must be able to climb ladders and be comfortable being strapped to a rappelling handler's back or tied into a transport basket.

Disaster search and rescue teams train for long hours—usually three to four times a week for the first year of training and one to two times a week thereafter. To maintain their skills, most disaster teams are members of disaster search and rescue organizations that organize and facilitate training.

Dogs in Entertainment

Dogs have served as entertainers in many ways throughout history. They entertained the masses in Rome in public combat, pitted against large predators or one another, and later they played similar roles in the United Kingdom and the United States by bull baiting and pit fighting. They were also part of traveling circuses and sideshows, entertaining audiences with their ability to balance balls, do back flips, and ride horses. Dogs are still sometimes seen in circuses or as intermission entertainment at rodeos. They also provide entertainment through Greyhound races, dog shows (such as the Westminster Kennel Club Dog Show), and herding exhibitions.

Many forms of entertainment work have been curtailed because they are dangerous or inhumane for the dogs or for other participants. Bull baiting and pit fighting is illegal everywhere in the United States, and Greyhound racing has been banned in many

---

Balto, the Wonder Dog

A sled dog named Balto gained fame in 1925 for his part in stopping a diphtheria epidemic. In Nome, Alaska, a dangerous outbreak of the disease was threatening the town's children. The only antitoxin serum was almost 1,000 miles away in Anchorage. Because of treacherous weather and mechanical problems, the only planes available had been grounded. Instead, the serum was taken by train 298 miles to Nenana, still 674 miles from Nome, and dispatched the rest of the way to Nome by teams of sled dogs. Twenty mushers and more than 100 dogs ran in legs over the next six days. Balto was the lead dog in the final team.

Balto became famous throughout the United States, but eventually he and the other dogs in the team became a traveling sideshow attraction. A Cleveland businessman discovered that the dogs were being mistreated and brought them to Cleveland, where they lived out the rest of their lives comfortably. Balto's remains are on display at the Cleveland Museum of Natural History. A statue in his honor was erected in New York City's Central Park, where it still stands today. Incidentally, the heroism of Balto and his musher, Gunnar Kaasen, is widely disputed. Most historians believe the true heroes of the run were lead dog Togo and his musher, Leonhard Seppala, who carried the serum through the most treacherous part of the route.

The American Humane Association (AHA) oversees the treatment of dogs and other animals in television and film through the AHA Film and Television Unit, which opened in Los Angeles in 1940. The organization has sole authority, through a contract with the Screen Actors Guild, to monitor the treatment of animal actors in movies and television shows. AHA's authority includes American produced movies and shows filmed in this country and abroad.

AHA works closely with producers and animal trainers to review the animal action prior to the beginning of filming. Areas reviewed include safety measures, stunts, camera angles, special effects, lighting, make-up, and costumes. During filming, AHA inspects facilities where animals are housed and cared for during production and examines sets prior to filming each workday to ensure the animals' well-being.

Following filming, AHA writes a review of the production describing how the animal action was accomplished. Each production is rated based exclusively on how the animals were treated during filming. Those productions rated Acceptable qualify for the official end-credit disclaimer from AHA. To see ratings of current movies, go to www.AHAfilm.org.

states. Many cities no longer allow circuses featuring animals within their city limits.

The entertainment media we most relate dogs with are TV and film. Dogs have a long history in film—they are still the most popular animals in the movie and TV business. As with other forms of animal entertainment, there are a number of ethical concerns regarding the use of animals in TV and film. In the past, animals have been subjected to neglect, torture, even death, in the pursuit of a good shot. Now, film studios and TV networks come under the oversight of the American Humane Association (AHA) and the Humane Society of the United States (HSUS). These organizations oversee the use of animals on film sets and provide an approval rating for films based on the treatment of the animals used in filming. Most film companies now welcome the scrutiny of these organizations in order to obtain their approval rating.

Dogs were once commonly used as circus and sideshow entertainment.

Researchers at Montana State University are studying whether dogs can be trained to find the spotted knapweed, a noxious weed that is a problem throughout Western range land. The weed impacts agricultural production and wildlife habitat and is estimated to cost Montana's economy $42 million per year. The first dog being trained to find the weed is named Knapweed Nightmare.

One of Hollywood's most famous canines, here's "Benji" escaping in an exciting scene from one of the Benji movies.

Dogs first appeared in movies during the silent film era. Rin Tin Tin, one of history's most famous dog stars, was seen in 1922 in the film *The Man from Hell's River*. Other early films that featured dogs are *The Adventures of the Masked Phantom* (1938) and *Almost a Gentleman* (1939). Recently, dogs have starred in movies such as *Babe, Air Bud, Snow Dogs*, and *Underdog*.

Since its inception, dogs have been a staple on television—from cameos on shows like *The Brady Bunch*, which had a dog who lasted only one season, to regular cast members on shows such as *Lassie* and, more recently, *Mad About You, Frasier, Lost,* and *Desperate Housewives*. On the latter show, the character Carlos has a guide dog, Roxy, and insists she be allowed to sleep on the bed.

Termite-tracking dogs are hired by pest-control companies. Beagles are a popular breed to use for the task. Dogs can find termites under floors, in soil, and in walls. A group of dogs tested by researchers at the University of Florida was found to be 92 to 98 percent accurate in locating termites.

Although dogs on television and film appear to have supercanine knowledge and skills, in fact, their behavior is the product of rigorous training. Although Lassie seemed to know Timmy was in danger, an off-screen trainer was directing his moves. That's not to say that animal actors aren't intelligent, just not in the way they are represented on screen. Animal trainers have to shape normal canine behavior and learn how to cue emotions, or what appear to be emotions. For example, the hot, tired dog in a movie is actually a well-hydrated actor who probably just popped out of an air-conditioned trailer.

The vast majority of dogs used in television and film are rescued from animal shelters or rescue organizations. Many dogs who become animal actors are high-energy animals who fit poorly into a family environment. Sometimes a trainer rescues a dog and the dog begins a lifelong career as an animal actor. *Frasier's* Eddie, for example, is a rescue dog who has worked nonstop. Other times, a large number of dogs are needed for a movie but the trainer does not plan to keep working with all of them. In this situation, the dogs must be rehomed with an adoptive family. Ethical trainers never return dogs to animal shelters and always work to place off-the-job dogs in the best homes possible. Occasionally, pet dogs are recruited for a film or TV show. These dogs are returned to their homes when the movie or TV shoot is complete.

New Jobs for Dogs

Not all of the work dogs do continues to be pertinent today. Some jobs have ended because we have a better appreciation of dogs' basic needs, others because they have become anachronistic. Two hundred years ago, dogs were used for everything from turning grain wheels and cooking spits to pulling milk wagons and killing rats. But even as these jobs have disappeared, new jobs have taken their place. For every canine job displaced by industrialization and technology, a canine job has been created. Most new work for dogs is based on the skills bred and developed for centuries for other jobs.

Hunting dogs and herding dogs are especially prized in many of the new jobs that have arisen in recent years. Their agility, strength, intelligence, keen sense of smell, and eagerness to please are easily redirected toward new endeavors.

Dogs Saving Wildlife

One of the ongoing problems caused by the rapid suburbanization of America is the loss of wildlife habitat. As humans encroach on the spaces wildlife once called home, animals are increasingly becoming commonplace in human territories. And as we have destroyed sources of food and eased their natural suspicion of humans, more animals are venturing into these new human neighborhoods to scavenge for food, sometimes causing damage or even injuring humans in the process. Our

Gone fishing. Even working dogs have opportunities for rest and relaxation.

As old jobs become obsolete, many dogs have found new lines of work.

recreational and travel pursuits also put us at odds with wildlife.

Many western regions in the United States have found that the loss of wilderness areas and the increasing interaction among people and animals have led to a sharp increase in bear and human encounters. Unfortunately, these encounters often fare worst for the bears, who, if they cannot be safely relocated, may be euthanized. To avoid this scenario, traditional bear-hunting dogs are now being used to dissuade bears from entering human-occupied areas, including suburban neighborhoods and campsites. Karelian Bear Dogs are Russian dogs traditionally used to hunt bears who are now used to

harass and intimidate bears and generally convince them that humans and their canine companions are to be avoided. The less comfortable bears are in human environments, the less likely they'll end up paying with their lives for indiscriminate dumpster diving.

Gun and herding dogs are taught to chase birds from airport tarmacs to keep so-called bird strikes at a minimum. Bird strikes occur when a flock of birds collides with an aircraft. Birds can be sucked into the engines, causing mechanical failure, or actually damage the wings or the hull. According to the Federal Aviation Administration (FAA), bird strikes are a serious safety issue in aviation. There are approximately 2,000 bird strikes involving commercial airlines each year.

Dogs are also used to harass birds such as geese and gulls, whose excrement and sometimes aggressive behavior can be a nuisance. In New Jersey, Connecticut, New York, Massachusetts, and other states, businesses have sprung up that use Border Collies to scare away wild geese from parks, ball fields, golf courses, hotels, and even luxury auto dealers.

Dogs do more than harass wildlife, however. Sometimes they take an active role in saving animals at risk. At the Center for Conservation Biology at the University of Washington in Seattle, dogs are used to sniff out the scat of endangered species. The program was started in 1997 by Center director Samuel Wasser. He enlisted dog trainer Barbara Davenport, owner of Pack Leader Dog Training in Washington, for help. Davenport recruits potential scat smelling dogs, which include Golden Retrievers, Labrador Retrievers, German Shepherds, and other high-energy dogs from animal shelters. Training uses a reward-based system and takes about six weeks.

A 9-year-old German Shepherd Dog named Camas has been trained to sniff out invasive plants in Montana, such as dyer's woad, which crowd out beneficial native plants. Such weeds affect agricultural production and wildlife habitat as well as the economy, costing hundreds of millions of dollars per year in Western states.

The specially trained canine sleuths find the scat of kit foxes, grizzly bears, bobcats, fishers, and other animals. They can detect up to 18 species and differentiate between the scat of different animals whose scat looks similar. They work on land and even from boats in the sea. In one pilot study, the dogs detected the floating feces of 50-ton North Atlantic right whales. They have helped researchers in the United States and Canada.

Scat-sniffing dogs in Russia assist researchers a bit differently than their North American counterparts do. For studies of endangered Amur tigers in Russian forests, researchers bring the relatively easy-to-find scat to the dogs. The dogs then sniff it to identify individual tigers against a collection of scat of known tigers. Dogs cannot be released into the forests to do this work, however, as the tigers are aggressive to dogs.

Researchers use scat to gain valuable information on animals' range, population size, gender, stress, fertility status, and diet. The use of scat-sniffing dogs is noninvasive compared with the traditional method of tracking by fitting study animals with radio collars. Using dogs also allows researchers to go into remote areas without affecting the animals' natural behaviors. And because dogs can find scat much more quickly than humans can, there is minimal disturbance to wildlife.

Until the scat dogs came on the scene, researchers searched for droppings by sight. Since the program began, the dogs have found four times the amount of samples that were found using visual methods.

A German Wirehaired Pointer in Olathe, Kansas, works for the Salvation Army. The dog, named Providence, rings the bell, takes donations from peoples' hands, and even puts the money in the kettle.

The fearless Karelian Bear Dog, a Russian bear-hunting breed, is used to protect humans by intimidating bears from public campgrounds and parks.

New Forms of Detection

There are also a number of new ways in which dogs' amazing noses are being used. On the medical forefront, early studies indicate that dogs may be able to detect malignant melanoma. The phenomenon was first noted in an April 1989 issue of the British medical journal, *The Lancet*. Two doctors cited a case where a woman's dog repeatedly nosed at a mole on her leg, even attempting to bite it off.

Herding dogs trained to become "Geese Police" are employed to chase geese from any location where they are unwanted, from airport runways to cemeteries.

The woman had the mole removed, and it was discovered to be malignant melanoma. This case incited several small studies, which seemed to confirm the woman's experience. British scientists have taken the concept one step further by attempting to determine whether dogs can detect prostate cancer in human urine.

Animal researchers have also found that canine noses serve well in studying populations of wild animals. The use of dogs to find the scat of endangered species has allowed researchers to collect more data in shorter periods of time. Dogs have been used to find the feces of animals ranging from grizzly bears and wolves to 50-ton right whales.

The use of detection dogs is even finding a niche in the realty world. Dogs are being used by home owners, house inspectors, and realtors to find such banes as toxic mold and termites. These dogs are trained to alert on a particular scent by using repetition and satisfying rewards in much the same way other types of detection dogs are trained. Using dogs in this way works particularly well because finding mold or termites often involves drilling into wood. Sometimes infestations cannot be found until significant damage has been done. Dogs can find the problem right from the start, and walls and tile are no barrier to their sense of smell.

Working for Dogs and Humans

The work dogs do can be multifaceted, benefiting both the dogs and the people they work with. But there is one way in which the work dogs do that radically benefits not only the dogs but also the handlers, the recipients, and the community.

In the early 1980s, a Washington State nun, in partnership with the Delta Society and the Washington State Department of Corrections, established the first prison-based dog training program in the United States. Called the Prison Pet Partnership, the program recruits female inmates to train dogs rescued from animal shelters to become service dogs. The motivation behind the program is to provide trained service dogs to disabled citizens, to rescue dogs who would likely be euthanized, and to help rehabilitate

Prison assistance dog training programs are life changing for everyone involved: the inmates, the dog recipients, and the dogs themselves.

inmates while providing them with vocational training.

As with all service dog training programs, the dogs receive rigorous training until they are deemed ready to be matched with a handler. They then receive an additional week of training with a group of potential recipients and are ultimately matched with the person they will work with for the next 8 to 10 years. Dogs who do not complete the program receive the benefit of basic good citizen training and are adopted out to appropriate homes.

The success of the program was so immediate and compelling that the program was quickly replicated throughout the country. There are now hundreds of these programs in correctional facilities throughout the United States. The fundamental idea has also been extended to other rehabilitative programs for at-risk youth and juvenile offenders and for those with mental illness. In some programs, the dogs continue to be trained for service work; in others, dogs are simply provided basic training to prepare them for adoption.

As with all successful dog work, the dogs receive as much as they give.

The Work of Dogs

In one way or another, all dogs work. Some serve as companions and watch dogs and provide emotional support. Other dogs are carefully bred and trained to do specific tasks, including assisting those with disabilities, law enforcement, and search and rescue. The job a dog does, however, should depend as much on his desire as his breeding or training. Some dogs want nothing more than to work long hours at the side of their favorite person, while others are more than happy to serve as lifelong companions. Whatever job your dog does, he should feel safe, satisfied, and well cared for while doing it.

CHAPTER 34

Careers

Many dog lovers wish they could spend their workdays—not just their leisure time—in the company of canines. Perhaps they merely enjoy being around dogs, or maybe they feel they've developed skills and knowledge that could be parlayed into a fulfilling career. But is a career with dogs just a pipe dream or is it a possibility?

People do earn a pleasurable and profitable living working with dogs. Their careers involve caring for dogs, educating the public about dog issues, training dogs, and working as part of a human-dog team.

Caring for Dogs

Careers that involve taking care of dogs range widely, from offering medical treatment (veterinarians and veterinary technicians) to providing food and comfort (animal caretakers) to tending to dogs' special aesthetic needs (groomers).

Veterinarian

Being a veterinarian can be an ideal job for a dog lover. More than half of the veterinarians in the United States work in private practice clinics in which they see primarily small companion animals such as cats and dogs. Veterinarians need to be comfortable with and interested in other animals, too, because these small private clinics may also care for other animals such as birds, reptiles, hamsters, guinea pigs, and rabbits.

The primary duties of a veterinarian in a clinical practice include diagnosing diseases and other health problems, vaccinating for diseases like rabies and distemper, prescribing medication for ill or injured animals, tending to fractures and other injuries, performing surgery, and giving advice to pet owners about animal behavior and proper nutrition. Veterinarians who work for animal shelters have similar duties, although spaying and neutering, and even euthanizing animals may make up a greater part of their jobs.

Veterinary practice is a promising occupation. Employment of veterinarians is expected to increase 35 percent through 2016, much faster than the average for all occupations. At least half of these jobs will be replacing veterinarians who retire or leave the labor force. About 75 percent of veterinarians in the United States are employed in solo or group practices, according to the American Veterinary Medical Association (AVMA).

Working conditions for veterinarians vary with the choice of specialty. Most vets who

There are expanding opportunities in the field of veterinary medicine.

work for private practices can count on usually working regular hours and receiving a steady income with good benefits. On the other hand, the hours can be long: over one-third of full-time veterinarians work 50 hours or more per week. Vets who work for a group practice may be expected to take turns being on call for weekend or night emergencies. Solo practitioners are even more likely to work extended hours.

Becoming a veterinarian demands a high level of commitment and strong academic skills. You need first to obtain a four-year undergraduate education. You should specialize in premed courses such as mathematics, organic and inorganic chemistry, physics, biology, biochemistry, and genetics. You also need to take courses that apply more specifically to your veterinary goals, such as zoology, animal nutrition, and animal biology. In addition, most veterinary colleges require a strong grounding in core subjects such as English, the social sciences, and the humanities. Some universities have specific preveterinary classes, but at other universities aspiring veterinarians take their prerequisites through premed and biology classes. After completing four years of undergraduate studies, you need another four years at an accredited college of veterinary medicine. From there, you graduate with a doctorate in veterinary medicine (called either a DVM or VMD, depending on the school). At most schools, you have the option of earning a PhD at the same time.

There are 28 accredited veterinary schools in the United States. Admission to such schools is very competitive. Since 1983, the number of American veterinary schools has not risen, whereas the number of candidates has risen significantly. In 1998, only about one out of every three applicants was accepted to veterinary school. Your chances of getting in are higher if you are a resident of a state that has a public,

state-funded veterinary college—such schools reserve most of their slots for in-state applicants.

Veterinary schools require GPAs that range from 2.5 to 3.2, but the GPAs of students actually admitted average 3.0 or higher. Depending on which college you are applying to, you must also submit test scores from the Graduate Record Examination (GRE), Veterinary College Admission Test (VCAT), or the Medical College Admission Test (MCAT). In addition to looking for high grades and test scores, schools favor applicants who have gained relevant experience by working or volunteering in veterinary clinics or animal shelters. The more formal your experience, the more advantageous it is. Schools expect you to demonstrate a strong motivation for a veterinary career and a desire to work with animals.

Veterinarians, like human doctors, can specialize in different kinds of medicine. Some schools gear their courses specifically toward specialized career paths; others offer a more generalized curriculum. Most students focus on basic veterinary science for the first two years, then come the laboratory work and clinical procedure studies such as surgery, diagnosis, and treatment of animal diseases. Veterinarians must also complete a one-year internship to specialize in a particular clinical area or work with particular types of animals. If you seek board certification in a specialty, you must complete a two- to three-year residency in which you undergo intensive training.

Finally, a veterinarian needs to be licensed. Every state requires a license, but the requirements vary. They invariably include both the completion of a DVM program (or its equivalent) and the passage of a national board examination. Most states also require passage of an examination covering state laws and regulations, and some states also test clinical competency.

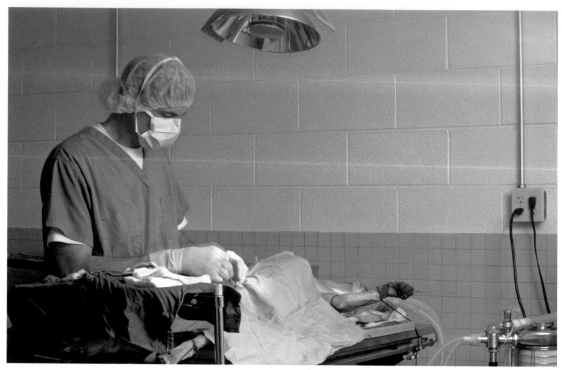

As part of their jobs, veterinarians provide preventive care, treat illnesses, and perform surgery.

Your education is not over when you become a veterinarian. It is important to keep up with new scientific discoveries and technological advances. Continuing education for veterinarians is required in 45 states.

For those who finish veterinary school, there generally is great career potential. The prospects for veterinarians with training in cardiology, dentistry, acupuncture, and hip-replacement surgery are particularly good.

The number of pet dogs is expected to increase more slowly from 2005 to 2015 than it did from 1995 to 2005. This could affect veterinarians who practice in animal hospitals or clinics. This trend is counter-balanced, however, by the cat population, which is increasing faster. This means that dog-loving veterinarians should be prepared to treat more cats. Another positive trend is that pet owners are becoming aware of and more likely to seek out nontraditional vet-

erinary services such as preventive dental care, acupuncture, and chiropractic, along with more traditional services.

Contemporary dog owners are also more willing to pay for intensive care than they were in the past. And recent medical advancements add to the treatments that veterinarians are able to offer.

In 2006, the median annual income of veterinarians was $71,990. Most veterinarians earned between $56,450 and $94,880. According to a survey by the American Veterinary Medical Association (AVMA), average starting salaries of veterinary medical college graduates in 2006 ranged from about $40,000 to $61,000, depending on the type of practice and the geographic region.

Veterinary Technician

The work of a veterinary technician is very much like the work of a nurse. Duties vary from practice to practice, but in general, vet techs administer and monitor anesthesia, perform medical tests, prepare vaccines for administering to patients, take blood samples, prepare tissue samples, and perform laboratory tests. They also maintain equipment and keep instruments sterilized. Vet techs work under the direct supervision of a veterinarian. The job of a vet tech requires patience and empathy to treat sick and injured animals and deal with distraught owners.

To become a veterinary technician, you must graduate from a vet tech program, which is usually a two-year course of study leading to an Associate in Applied Science. You may also have to pass a certification exam. Veterinary technician programs require a high school diploma and many look for a strong foundation in science. In the United States, there are more than 70 college programs in veterinary technology accredited by the AVMA. These programs cover general subjects like mathematics, chemistry, and biology. They also offer more specialized courses such as biochemistry, physiology, anatomy, parasitology, and nutrition. Many students gain experience by working summer jobs at clinics or shelters in the process of obtaining their degrees.

Some states require that veterinary technicians become licensed or certified after receiving the vet tech degree. The requirements vary—check with the AVMA for specific information. Many veterinary technicians stay on the cutting edge of their profession by joining professional associations such as the North American Veterinary Technician Association. This allows them to network with others and stay up to date in their field at professional meetings.

There are many job opportunities for vet techs in a variety of settings. In 2006 there were approximately 71,000 vet techs employed in the United States, and employment is expected to grow much faster than average from 2006 to 2015. Vet techs can find employment anywhere that veterinarians work.

Veterinary Assistant

Animal caretakers who work in veterinary offices are often called veterinary assistants. They differ from vet techs in terms of their qualifications and their duties. Veterinary assistants are responsible for performing daily tasks that ensure the well-being of the animals at the hospital. This may include providing food and water, examining the animals for signs of illness or injury, and cleaning cages. Veterinary assistants may also help with the preparation and sterilization of laboratory or surgical equipment. They may help vets by holding the animals during examination and treatment. Under the supervision of veterinarians or veterinary technicians, they may administer medication and provide some postoperative care. Such caretakers may also, depending on the size of the clinic, be respon-

Veterinary technicians have the opportunity to do a lot of hands-on care of dogs and other animals.

Working at a boarding facility is demanding, but it also includes lots of doggy playtime.

sible for communication with the animals' owners and at the front desk (which may include answering phones, greeting owners and patients, making appointments, and keeping records). The need for veterinary assistants is expected to grow much faster than other occupations from 2005 to 2015. The primary source of training is on-the-job.

Boarding and Day Care

There are a number of boarding, day care, pet sitting, and pet walking businesses currently in operation, especially in urban areas. Some of these are small, one- or two-person businesses, while others are large-scale pet care compa-

Take Your Dog To Work Day allows dog owners to bring their canine companions into participating workplaces each June. Pet Sitters International began the campaign in 1999 to encourage employers to offer pet-friendly benefits that help pet owners care for their animals.

nies. Commercial boarding facilities are the most likely to hire outside workers. Many of these facilities also offer day care services for companion animals.

Boarding and day care facilities need animal caretakers, just as veterinary hospitals do. These workers tend to the everyday care of animals. In addition to feeding, watering, grooming, and bathing the animals, animal caretakers clean and disinfect their cages and exercise and play with them. At a day care, animal caretakers may be responsible for supervising dog play groups and keeping notes on the dogs' interactions. They may also be responsible for communicating with owners about their dogs, working the front desk, and greeting clients.

Animal caretakers usually learn their trade on the job. Often, caretakers start as volunteers and work their way into staff positions as they become available. The advantage of going this route is that it allows you the opportunity to determine whether you like the work and possess the requisite abilities to be an animal caretaker. In larger kennels, there may be opportunities for animal caretakers to be promoted to positions such as kennel supervisor, manager, and assistant manager.

The job of an animal caretaker is necessary and rewarding but not always glamorous. The daily duties involve dirty, difficult, and sometimes tedious work. This work generally involves a lot of kneeling, bending, stooping, and lifting. You may be exposed to infected animals and can be bitten or scratched. You may have to lift or restrain large dogs. And you will almost certainly be in contact with animal waste.

The jobs are plentiful, but this probably has to do with the high rate of turnover resulting from low pay. In 2006, the median pay for nonfarm animal caretakers was $8.72 per hour. Despite the low rate of pay, the work is steady, and many workers receive benefits including paid health and life insurance, a pension plan, and sick days.

Other types of day care include dog walking and pet sitting. These jobs involve taking care of dogs who are left alone when their owners are at work or out of town. Dog walkers take dogs out to relieve themselves and for exercise several times a day. A dog walker might take individual dogs out for a short period—not longer than one hour—or she might take a large group of dogs out at the same time, perhaps to a rural area or off-leash park, where they can run and play for hours. Dog walkers may also be responsible for providing food or water to dogs during the day.

Pet sitters care for dogs when their owners have gone away on business trips or vacations. Pet sitters take care of dogs in their own homes. Many owners prefer this arrangement because it is more convenient for them and because the dog does not have to experience the anxiety of being in a strange place in addition to being separated from his owner. It also precludes the possibility that the dog will pick up a disease from other animals kept in a kennel.

Pet sitters are expected to care for all of the pets a family has, which may include cats, birds, fish, rabbits, and even snakes. Pet sitters may also perform the general duties of a house sitter, such as watering the plants, turning the lights on and off, and bringing in the mail and newspaper. Each dog has his own needs and each owner has her own expectations, so the amount of time a pet sitter spends at a house varies. Dogs may need to be walked or they may simply require some time in the yard.

Pet sitting and dog walking are growing occupations because so many people are out of their houses all day for work. Today's two-income families are more likely to have pets than families of the past were, but they have less time to spend with them. Many dogs require more exercise and interaction than can be provided in the mornings and evenings. Some pet sitters and dog walkers are also hired by elderly or infirm people who are not able to fully care for their pets but do not want to give them up.

Groomers

Groomers specialize in maintaining an animal's appearance. They may work in special grooming shops, kennels, clinics, or pet sup-

In the 1890s, the U.S. Postal Service had its own unofficial mascot. Owney, a homeless mixed-breed dog, was taken in by postal workers in Albany, New York. During his lifetime, Owney followed postal workers on their daily rounds, traveling more than 140,000 miles. He died in 1897, and his stuffed body was put on display at the National Postal Museum in Washington, D.C., where it remains.

ply stores. A typical grooming shop has two or three full-time employees. Besides tending to the aesthetic care of animals, the job of a groomer may include selling pet care products, answering telephones and scheduling appointments, and communicating with clients about their dogs' needs and dispositions. A basic knowledge of medical conditions affecting companion animals is helpful because groomers often are the first to see undiagnosed problems such as skin or ear infections. The services provided by groomers include nail clipping, ear and teeth cleaning, bathing, and flea dipping, as well as brushing, combing, and clipping the coat.

There are several ways to become a dog groomer. Most learn on the job through an informal apprenticeship, usually lasting about 6 to 10 weeks, with a more experienced groomer. If you choose to take this path, it is important to check the credentials and reputation of the groomer you apprentice with. Beginning groomers usually start with a single duty, such as bathing and drying, and eventually take responsibility for greater portions of the grooming process. After receiving your training, you may continue to work for other groomers, or consider starting your own shop. If you work for an established shop, you will probably be paid by commission. A typical rate is 50 percent of the amount paid by the customer.

There is no standard license for groomers, nor are there educational standards that all groomers must meet. There are, however, state licensed grooming schools that prepare students for voluntary certification. Completing such a program may take from 4

Some lucky people get to bring their dogs to work with them. In a survey by www.dog friendly.com, 14 percent of respondents said that they take their dogs to work every day.

Groomers must begin as apprentices. If you are interested in a career as a groomer, talk to a local shop about working or volunteering there on a part-time basis.

to 18 weeks. You can then become certified by the National Dog Groomers Association of American (NDGAA) by passing an examination that includes both a written section as well as a demonstration of practical skills.

Once they become professionals, many groomers continue their education by participating in training programs, reading trade journals, and attending seminars and conventions, often as members of a professional association.

Many dogs need to be groomed to stay in good health and maintain their appearance. Thus, groomers will always be needed in both small towns and big cities. Like other animal caretakers, most dog groomers are not well paid, earning a median hourly wage of $8.39 in 2004. However, a well-run grooming business in a good location may earn its owner a comfortable living.

Protection and Advocacy

There are several ways to earn a living while protecting the welfare of dogs and other animals. Rewarding careers are available in public animal control agencies or private shelters or humane societies. These jobs can involve working directly with animals, but such organizations also employ individuals to educate the public about animal welfare.

Animal Control and Government Shelters

Animal control agencies routinely employ administrators, clerical workers, veterinarians, technicians, animal care attendants, and animal control officers. They are run by the city, county, state, or federal government. Their function is to protect the health and safety of both humans and animals. They are legally obligated to patrol for and impound stray animals, investigate complaints about nuisance or injuries caused by dogs or strays, and investigate incidents of animal cruelty and neglect. Some animal control jobs involve working closely with animals, others are administrative.

Animal control officers work to protect the community from dangerous animals and protect animals from abuse and mistreatment. Animal control officers investigate kennels, pet shops, and other places where animals are kept, including private homes, to ensure compliance with animal welfare regulations. They also sometimes rescue trapped or injured animals, conduct pet care and obedience classes, and enforce licensing laws, including picking up strays. They may work in conjunction with the police or other government departments, or with private humane societies.

In their duties as investigators of cruelty and mistreatment, animal control officers (also referred to as humane law enforcement [HLE] officers) have the power to enforce laws and licensing regulations, which may include making arrests. Thus, this job includes many of the risks incurred by other law enforcement officers. Animal control and humane law enforcement officers must know the local animal

Animal control officers must be advocates for the dogs in their care. However, officers may also be responsible for picking up stray dogs and euthanizing animals.

ordinances and be able to enforce them in a calm and professional manner. The ability to make sound judgments in stressful circumstances is an important part of the job.

The basic requirements for becoming an animal control or HLE officer are a high school diploma and possibly some undergraduate courses in criminology and veterinary technology or animal science. The most significant source of training is on the job, acquired under the guidance of an experienced officer. Some states, however, require certification, which may be offered by the National Animal Control Association (NACA) or a state-level animal control association.

Employment prospects for animal control officers are good because municipalities continue to fund public shelters.

Shelter attendants in public shelters have essentially the same duties as veterinary and kennel assistants do. Besides basic feeding, cleaning, and grooming, shelter attendants may also keep records, answer telephone inquiries, screen potential adopters, and even serve as adoption counselors, giving advice to prospective dog adopters. They

Humane society workers provide daily care for the animals kept in their shelters.

able through the Humane Society of the United States (HSUS) and the National Animal Control Association (NACA). Through these workshops, you may learn how to conduct cruelty investigations, how to humanely euthanize shelter animals, and how to capture and restrain large animals. Animal caretakers in shelters may, with experience and additional training, have opportunities for promotion to positions such as animal control officer, adoption coordinator, assistant shelter manager, and shelter director. Many shelter attendants get their start as volunteers. Animal caretaker jobs in public and private shelters are largely the same.

In general, shelter attendants make better salaries than other animal caretakers. Local government workers, such as shelter employees, earned a median hourly rate of $11.80 in 2000. The job market for these positions is strong.

Shelters also have veterinary clinics that provide care for abandoned dogs who are sick and injured, and spaying and neutering services for the community. They may even operate a mobile spay/neuter clinic. These shelters may be headed by a chief veterinarian and employ other veterinarians and technicians that report to her. Shelter medicine, though not a board-certified specialty recognized by the AVMA, is an area of veterinary medicine that requires special knowledge and skills. It is necessary to have a working knowledge of almost all areas of veterinary medicine and to bring them together in a practical and innovative manner.

Animal control agencies are headed by directors. This chief administrator oversees the agency's programs and personnel. Education or experience in business or public administration is required. These administrators must have strong communication skills and be adept at working with people. They must be well organized to ensure that the

know the dogs in their care well, so they are often better able than anyone else to match them appropriately with new owners. Some shelter attendants may also serve as animal control officers and be responsible for dealing with reports of animal abuse and cruelty.

Compared with other animal caretaking positions, those working for shelters may have greater contact with the public. This involves keeping a calm and professional demeanor, especially when dealing with situations involving abuse and neglect. Shelter attendants may also have some veterinary duties such as vaccinating newly admitted animals and euthanizing animals.

Being a shelter attendant does not require formalized training, but there are educational programs and workshops avail-

Do dogs understand calculus? Mathematician Tim Pennings of Michigan thinks so. After watching his dog retrieve a ball from the ocean, Pennings measured the dog's route, plotted the points on a graph, and discovered the dog innately used the fastest route possible. Pennings wrote about his findings in the mathematics journal of Hope College where he works.

shelter runs smoothly, and must be familiar with and committed to upholding the animal control laws of their communities.

A shelter usually has a manager who is responsible for its day-to-day operations. Depending on the size of the agency and where it is located, the director and manager may each have a staff of assistants. Shelters, both private and public, also hire bookkeepers, receptionists, computer technicians, store clerks, custodians, event promotion coordinators, public relations officers, handypersons, and data entry clerks. Education requirements and salaries vary according to the position and the location.

Humane Societies/Private, Nonprofit Shelters

Private shelters differ from public animal control agencies primarily in terms of their underlying philosophies. The sole purpose of a humane shelter is to alleviate the suffering of animals. Animal control agencies, on the other hand, are also charged with ensuring that animals do not create problems for the human residents of a community. This difference in goals affects the operating procedures of the shelter. Many humane shelters, for example, do not use euthanasia except when an animal is terminally ill and in pain. Government agencies may not be bound by these ethical positions, although it is increasingly common for government shelters to avoid euthanizing healthy, adoptable animals. In recent years, the difference between public and private shelters has narrowed and, in fact, many private shelters now function as city or county shelters under government contracts.

In general, whether you decide to work for a private or public shelter, it is a good idea to carefully investigate the policies of any shelter you are considering for employment. There is a great deal of variation in policies,

As a humane society employee, you may be expected to perform a range of activities, from grooming dogs to exercising and training them to cleaning pet waste.

even within the category of private humane societies. They differ in terms of the type of kennels used, whether they euthanize or not, and whether they ever turn animals away. Some shelters take any animal brought to its door; others take only healthy cats and dogs.

In private shelters, there are jobs that involve a lot of contact with dogs and others that do not. Many are nonprofit agencies and are organized accordingly. They employ administrative and managerial workers, as well as clerical workers such as receptionists, records clerks, and bookkeepers. As nonprofits, they utilize the service of volunteers and often require a volunteer coordinator to manage them. In addition, they hire humane investigators and/or law enforcement officers, veterinarians, veterinary technicians, and animal attendants.

The jobs of veterinarians, veterinary technicians, and animal caretakers in private clinics are almost identical to those of their counterparts in public shelters.

Animal Welfare and Adoption Groups

Here are three examples of the many organizations that exist to better the lives of unwanted and abused animals:

Best Friends Animal Sanctuary in Angel Canyon, Utah, is the nation's largest sanctuary for abandoned and abused dogs, cats, horses, and other animals. Animals come to the 3,000-acre sanctuary from all over the country, and each day there are at least 1,800 animals at the facility. Best Friends seeks to place adoptable animals in loving homes. Those who are sick, very old, or who have suffered extreme trauma are kept at the sanctuary for the rest of their lives.

Best Friends was begun in Arizona in the 1970s by a group of animal lovers who rescued animals from shelters, rehabilitated them, and attempted to find homes for them. The number of unadoptable animals grew, and eventually a permanent home was needed for the organization. The sanctuary was established in Angel Canyon in the early 1980s.

Hearts United for Animals in Auburn, Nebraska, is a no-kill shelter and animal welfare organization located on two farms with a total of 105 acres. There are approximately 250 dogs at the farms at any one time. They also rescue cats, but their numbers are small. Dogs who cannot be adopted stay at the shelter for the rest of their lives. The largest of the two shelter facilities is located on a 65-acre tree farm and features specialty housing that includes soft beds, covered patios, and dog play houses for dogs up for adoption. On the grounds of the shelter is a spay/neuter clinic, grooming salon, memorial park, and an agility field.

North Shore Animal League America in Port Washington, New York, began its legacy of helping unwanted animals working out of a garage in 1944. Since then, the organization has become one of the largest pet adoption agencies in the world. Animals are rescued from shelters and overcrowded animal organizations throughout the country and brought to North Shore's no-kill adoption center, which houses approximately 350 dogs, puppies, cats, and kittens. Trained counselors work with adopters to ensure that animals are placed in good homes. In addition to rescue and adoption efforts, North Shore also has humane education and public outreach programs.

As with public animal control agencies, private shelters may employ humane investigators (also sometimes called cruelty investigators). They have the responsibility of picking up strays, rescuing injured animals, and investigating reported cases of abandonment, abuse, and neglect. Humane investigators are empowered to issue citations and may even help prosecute offenders.

Although they work for private nonprofit organizations, humane investigators have the same law enforcement power as any other peace officer. They investigate cases of animal abuse and neglect, and they rescue animals that are trapped or in danger. To become a humane investigator, you must have a high school education, and taking some relevant undergraduate courses is

The ASPCA is the oldest humane organization in the United States. Its mission is to provide effective means for the prevention of cruelty to animals throughout the United States. Toward this goal, the ASPCA provides national leadership in humane education, public awareness, government affairs and public policy, shelter support, animal medical services, and animal placement. Its New York City headquarters houses a full-service animal hospital, behavior therapy center, adoption facility, and humane law enforcement department. The ASPCA is a privately funded, not-for-profit organization, employing 300 people in seven offices nationwide.

a plus. Certification may be required in some states.

In small communities, it may not be possible to find full-time work as a humane investigator. Salaries are also higher in urban areas. It is possible to be promoted from humane investigator to a supervisory position or a position in shelter management. Because there are so few positions, competition for the jobs may be fierce. It is a good idea to distinguish yourself as a volunteer with an organization you wish to work for.

Because private shelters are nonprofit corporations, they operate with volunteers who take on many of the duties performed by paid employees in similar governmental organizations. Because there are so many volunteers and because they are charged with such serious responsibilities, workers in private shelters often require extensive training and direction. The staff person responsible for this is the volunteer coordinator.

A volunteer coordinator must have excellent communication and supervisory skills. She must also be knowledgeable about the structure and operations of the shelter and have strong organizational abilities.

Private shelters are headed by an executive director who has overall responsibility for running all departments and programs in the shelter. A shelter might also have an administrative director who works more directly with membership recruitment and fund-raising efforts. Such a person may also be responsible for personnel decisions. These jobs require the ability to solve problems, a head for business, and human resource skills. They are similar to the job of the director of an animal control office, except there is a much stronger emphasis on fundraising and development. To become a shelter administrator, you generally need an undergraduate degree in business administration and prior experience in managing an animal shelter. This is usually obtained by working your way up within the shelter's administrative hierarchy.

Larger shelters also have a shelter manager who is responsible for the daily operation of the kennels. You can become a shelter manager by being promoted from an animal attendant position. A liberal arts degree helps you qualify, particularly if it includes relevant courses in animal science and business administration. Most nonprofit shelters also have marketing and development positions and a number of administrative and clerical jobs.

Education and Advocacy

There are a number of professionals who devote their efforts to educating the public about animal welfare. They may be employed by nonprofit or governmental shelters, by national animal welfare organizations, or by activist animal rights organizations.

Many shelters employ humane educators to teach others, particularly children, about animals' needs and abilities. The particular message varies with the organization represented, but all humane educators try to

---

With seven million members and constituents, the Humane Society of the United States (HSUS) is the world's largest animal protection organization. Founded in 1954, HSUS promotes the protection of all animals, including companion dogs and cats, wild animals, and research and food animals. HSUS aims to combat animal abuse and exploitation.

The organization comprises 10 regional offices; 4 affiliates; an international arm; and 250 staff members, including veterinarians, wildlife biologists, lawyers, and animal behaviorists. While HSUS does not oversee local animal shelters or societies, it does work closely with them, helping create standards and guidelines. HSUS is a nonprofit organization.

impart reverence for life, and values such as tolerance and compassion toward both people and animals.

These educators visit grade schools and teach students about pet care, animal needs, overpopulation problems, and the responsibilities of pet owners. They may also talk about what humane societies are and what they do. Sometimes students tour the shelters. Often, educators provide students with informational packets and sometimes even videos and tapes produced by the shelter.

In some larger organizations, the humane educator is part of a department of humane education. These shelters may employ a director as well as a staff of several humane educators. Such large shelters may provide humane education not only to schools but also to libraries, museums, and even other shelters.

Being a humane educator requires the ability to work well with children and animals, excellent communication and public speaking skills, and a high degree of creativity. It is useful, but not necessary, to have a teaching degree. It is also preferable to have a minor in a relevant area, such as animal science, and coursework in journalism, public relations, or environmental education. If you want to become a director of a humane education department, you will probably need a master's degree in education and courses in writing and public speaking. The HSUS offers workshops through the National Association for the Advancement of Humane Education. Pay as a humane educator depends on the size of

the organization and the community being served. In general, humane educators receive a higher salary in urban areas.

Animal welfare is often advocated by lobbyists. A lobbyist for canine and other animal issues works to pass bills in support of animal welfare (such as strengthening animal cruelty laws) by educating and trying to influence the legislators who vote on them. Major humane organizations hire lobbyists. For example, the American Society for the Prevention of Cruelty to Animals (ASPCA) employs lobbyists in its Department of Government Affairs. Lobbyists are usually lawyers. Becoming a lawyer involves earning a bachelor's degree, completing an additional three years of law school, and passing the bar examination of the state in which you plan to practice. Large humane organizations also need lawyers for the same reasons other organizations do: to review and negotiate contracts and ensure legality of organization policies and practices, among other things. Lobbyists are not usually involved in working with dogs but support their interests instead.

Training and Handling

Some dog lovers work with dogs who have special skills. Others help dogs develop such skills. These are handlers and trainers.

There are many different kinds of dog trainers. Most are obedience trainers, but there are also those who train service and working dogs and those with advanced degrees and specialized skills, such as applied animal behaviorists. Some trainers work mainly with individual animals, others teach large classes. Trainers work in many settings, including shelters, private businesses, homes, even the sets of movies and television shows.

Handlers, on the other hand, work with dogs after they have been trained (although they will likely continue to train the dog on an

---

The verb *muse* probably originated from the Middle French *muser*, which is related to the English *muzzle*. *Muser* meant "to stand with muzzle in the air." Over time, it came to be applied to people who think meditatively about something. The noun *muse*, "a source of inspiration," has a different origin.

Working dog handlers work with animals who have specialized skills.

ongoing basis). These jobs range from exhibiting dogs at shows to working as part of a dog-human team in a police K9 unit.

Obedience Trainer

Obedience trainers teach dogs to behave and follow their owner's commands. For example, training can be used to teach dogs not to chew up furniture and clothing, jump up on the furniture, or bark excessively. Effective training may also involve teaching people the skills and techniques they need to train their own dogs.

There are no licensing requirements or educational standards for dog trainers in most states. Most trainers learn their trade through an apprenticeship, through on-the-job training, or by volunteering. Many, however, take college courses in animal behavior, veterinary technology, and psychology, which makes them more attractive for employment.

If you feel that training is the career for you, you might begin as a volunteer at a training facility until a position is available. Some organizations require an apprentice to work for as long as five years with an experienced trainer. Choose the facility or trainer you apprentice with carefully. Since there are no set standards, there is tremendous variation in both the quality of training and the methods used. It is important to select an instructor or facility whose philosophy is consistent with your own.

You can also attend a dog training academy. These schools, however, are expensive and usually not accredited. In addition, they do not all offer a high-quality education in dog training. Another consideration is that dog training facilities may wish to train you in their own methods. If you're interested in attending a dog training school, get some names of graduates, and contact them to ask about their experience and whether they are presently working as trainers.

The National Association of Dog Obedience Instructors (NADOI) is trying to put into place professional standards for certification of trainers and accreditation of trainer academies. The NADOI offers something like an accreditation program, with members of NADOI being required to undergo a rigorous examination and peer evaluation process. The Association of Pet Dog Trainers (APDT) is another professional organization for dog trainers. While membership in the APDT is open to all, the organization has implemented a certification program and predicts that its program will become the standard in the industry.

If you want to be a trainer, prepare yourself by finding out as much about dogs and dog training as you can. Volunteering or working in kennels, reading books and other publications about dogs, attending dog shows and obedience classes, and interviewing people in the field will give you a better understanding of the career you are preparing to enter.

There is strong demand for qualified obedience trainers. The need is expected to grow as higher numbers of owners seek behavior modification services for their animals. In 2006, the median pay of all animal trainers was $12.65 per hour. There is great variation in pay rates—the lowest 10 percent made less than $7.66 and the top 10 percent made more than $22.42.

Animal Behaviorist

When a dog develops severe behavior problems, one option available to owners is to send the animal to therapy. Therapists for dogs are called applied animal behaviorists. They deal with highly inappropriate behavior such as aggression, compulsive behaviors, separation anxiety, and other fears and phobias. Initially working with the dog's veterinarian to rule out physical disorders, the behaviorist creates an individualized plan to help the dog develop more acceptable behavior patterns. This plan may involve drug therapy as well as behavior modification techniques such as desensitization and counter conditioning, in which a dog is gradually exposed to the object of his phobia while associating it with pleasurable activities such as eating and playing.

There are far fewer applied animal behaviorists than trainers. As of May 2003, there were only 36 certified applied animal behaviorists listed by the Animal Behavior Society. Generally, animal behaviorists hold advanced degrees—usually a PhD—in animal behavior

The word *adulation* originates from the Latin word *adulari*, which means "to fawn on" and, in its earliest origin, "to wag the tail." By the eighteenth century, the meaning of *adulation* had come to be what we know today, "excessive praise or admiration."

Being a dog trainer requires ongoing education. Good trainers attend seminars and conferences, read journals and new training books, and keep up with any changes in the industry.

theory and its application. A typical educational path would be to earn a BA or BS in biology or psychology and then an MS or PhD in animal behavior, zoology, or animal psychology. One difficulty with this profession is the financial obligations that are incurred in attaining an advanced degree. The extent of these obligations depends on the choice of graduate school and opportunity for financial assistance.

Generally, applied animal behaviorists do not specialize in companion animals in school because few graduate programs offer such courses. Certification is provided through the Animal Behavior Society and is based on both education and experience.

This is a very new profession, and it is difficult to predict what its future will hold.

Applied animal behaviorists have had success solving behavior problems and perhaps even preventing the abandonment of troubled pets. Applied animal behaviorists have started successful businesses, but it takes hard work to get these businesses going. As with any small business, a financial investment is required. Some applied animal behaviorists are bivocational, holding research posts at major universities.

Similar to applied animal behaviorists are veterinary behaviorists. These are veterinarians who focus on animal behavior. Board certification by the AVMA became available for this area in 1995. Veterinary behaviorists rule out physical causes of a problem, and then recommend behavior modification techniques and/or nutritional or drug therapies to solve it. This combination of skills is what distinguishes veterinary behaviorists from applied animal behaviorists.

Board-certified veterinary behaviorists are those who have passed a test given by the American College of Veterinary Behaviorists. They may have also completed a residency program in animal behavior after their graduation from veterinary school.

Show Dog Handlers

Some professionals are hired by the owners of show dogs to exhibit their animals at conformation shows. These handlers must be experts at bringing out the best in a dog. Many handlers also care for the dogs full time, serving as trainers, groomers, and companions for these catwalk canines.

This is a great job for those who enjoy being in the spotlight, but it also involves a lot of work. To become a show dog handler, you must have several years of experience with purebreds, then complete an apprenticeship with a qualified handler. Expert handlers are often members of the Professional Handler's Association, which sets standards of ethics and performance. Handlers with a good reputation and results are able to earn great financial rewards for their hard work.

Training and Handling Working Dogs

There are a variety of jobs that involve training and working with dogs who have special skills. These are dogs who can sniff out bombs, guide their blind owners across a busy street, or perform on a movie set like a seasoned pro. Training and assisting such talented canines can be an exciting and rewarding career.

Before a working dog is placed with his handler, he generally receives some initial training. Military, police, detection, and assistance dogs are all trained in their areas of expertise before being placed with their handlers, from whom they receive additional training. Because assistance dogs work for as well as with their handlers, they generally require more intense initial training than other working dogs do.

Show dog handlers often care for their charges on a full-time basis, providing grooming, exercise, and affection.

Some trainers specialize in teaching dogs to help people with special kinds of problems. There are guide dogs for the blind, hearing dogs for the hearing impaired, and service dogs for people with mobility challenges.

Training a service dog may take several years. Only well-qualified dogs make it through the training, so part of the job of a trainer is determining and continuously evaluating whether a dog has the correct attributes to become a service dog. The culmination of formal training involves working intensively with the dog and his future owner for a period of up to four weeks.

Many people are attracted to the idea of a career working with dogs and at the same time providing help to disabled populations. Therefore, there is a great deal of competition for the few positions of training service dogs. Many training programs are nonprofits and rely on volunteers for much of the work, and staff trainers are usually not paid very well. Qualifications needed for the job include physical strength and prior experience with animals, such as working in a kennel or clinic. An educational background in animal science or veterinary technology is preferred. If you are committed to obtaining an assistance dog training position, the best way to start is as a volunteer at an established organization. Such apprenticeships can last as long as three years.

There are also administrative, public relations, and volunteer coordinator jobs available at most assistance dog training facilities.

Some careers involve not just training dogs but also accompanying them and per-

Training a detection dog requires many hours of hard work for both the handler and the dog.

forming duties as part of a canine-human team. Dogs are used to detect explosives, narcotics, and prohibited agricultural products; as tracking dogs for the police and military; as therapy dogs for residents of hospitals or nursing homes; and to herd sheep and cattle on ranches. In many of these occupations, dogs work closely with a human handler.

Police dogs work with officers to search buildings for substances or criminals, subdue suspects, for crowd control, and to track missing people. If you want to work with police dogs, you will have to become a law enforcement officer. Doing so involves meeting stringent fitness requirements and passing written and physical examinations. You may also need an educational background in criminal justice—either a two-year or a four-year degree.

Police dog (K9) handlers are chosen because they have an excellent record as

---

I am called a dog because I fawn on those who give me anything, I yelp at those who refuse, and I set my teeth in rascals.

—*Diogenes the Cynic, Fourth Century B.C.E.*

police officers and an interest in working with dogs. Most large police departments have at least one human-canine team, and some have many.

Handlers and their dogs receive extended training that continues throughout their working life. The length and intensity of training varies among police departments and is based on the money allocated to the program and the strength of the program. Most police dog programs are funded by outside, nonprofit organizations rather than through the police department itself. Other than a police officer's salary, the cost of special canine equipment, training, and even the dog himself is paid for by donations and fund-raising.

Police dogs have often received some training before being matched with a police officer, but most of the essential training is conducted as a team. The officer is expected to continue her dog's training throughout his working life. Police dogs are taught to act aggressively on command but are socialized to be obedient and docile in other circumstances. Police dogs almost always live with their handlers and their families. When they retire, they either continue to live with their handlers or, on rare occasions, are adopted by private citizens.

The U.S. Customs Service hires canine enforcement officers (CEOs) to work with drug, currency, and explosive detection dogs. Together, these dogs and their handlers are fast, mobile, and accurate. In 2002, the Customs Service began a pilot program to use dogs for bomb detection as part of homeland security efforts. These dogs are able to detect the smell of explosives on cargo or people.

Most U.S. Customs dogs are adopted from animal shelters. Training is ongoing throughout the dog's working career. Dogs live in kennels but spend their days with their handlers. Most dogs have one handler throughout their

careers. In most cases, the handler adopts the dog upon his retirement.

It takes four years of college (or a combination of college and work experience) to qualify for an entry-level position as a CEO. The position requires self-motivation, patience, strong communication skills, and the ability to stay calm in volatile situations, along with a high degree of physical stamina. Previous law enforcement or military service experience is preferred. The Customs Service hires only U.S. citizens who pass a background check and medical and drug screenings. If you are selected, you will complete 15 weeks of enforcement, dog handling, and firearms training.

Canine enforcement officers receive good pay and an attractive federal benefits package, which includes health and life insurance, a retirement plan, and paid vacation and holi-

Police dog handlers and their animals are partners for life. Most of the dogs live with their handlers and retire to their handlers' homes.

days. The government offers tuition assistance for job-related education, and there are opportunities for advancement. It may also be possible to earn a significant amount of overtime pay in some positions.

The U.S. Department of Agriculture (USDA) also hires dog handlers, called plant protection and quarantine (PPQ) canine officers, to maintain security at ports of entry into the country. The dogs specialize in sniffing out prohibited agricultural products. There are also Jack Russell Terriers positioned in Guam who are trained to detect brown snakes to prevent the snakes from being transported out of the country in cargo shipments.

Beagles are used as agricultural detection dogs because of their acute sense of smell and excellent people skills. As a group, the dogs and their handlers are referred to as the Beagle Brigade. As of 2002, there were 131 Beagles working for the U.S. government in this capacity, all of whom require handlers. These dogs usually come from shelters and are often adopted by their handlers at retirement. During their active careers, these dogs live in kennels, but handlers are encouraged to get to know their dogs well so that they can recognize small changes in their behavior.

The job involves walking around the inspection area and mingling with passengers arriving on international flights or at other ports of entrance such as Canadian and Mexican border crossings. Working dogs can distinguish among 50 different scents. When a dog detects something forbidden, he alerts his handler by sitting near the person or baggage. Handlers reward the dogs with food treats.

The words *dogged* and *dogging* stem from hunting dogs. A dogged person is one who is determined and persistent. The dictionary definition of *dogging* is "hunting, tracking, or following like a hound."

The basic educational requirement for a PPQ canine officer is a four-year degree with a major in agriculture or a biological science and at least 20 semester credits in relevant coursework. To be considered for this position, you also should be able to demonstrate superior academic achievement or some post-baccalaureate coursework or experience. Strong communication skills and previous experience in training, handling, and caring for dogs will also make you a more desirable candidate. After they are hired, handlers complete 9 weeks of USDA technical training and 10 weeks of canine training. In 2001, PPQ canine officers made between $25,000 and $40,000 per year.

Dogs are used to search for survivors of natural and human-made disasters. For the most part, handlers of search and rescue dogs are volunteers, not paid professionals. It may be possible to work with a search and rescue dog as part of your job if you already work for a ski patrol unit or a fire department. This would mean obtaining additional training with an organization such as the National Disaster Search Dog Foundation (NDSDF).

Dogs (and their handlers) can also have careers in the field of entertainment. Dogs are used in movies, television shows, commercials, and special performances. Many trainers who work with entertainment dogs are independent contractors with a company that supplies animals to movie and TV productions. Payment varies based on the type of entertainment job a dog does, whether he is performing tricks at birthday parties or is the star of a big-budget movie.

Trainers work as apprentices with established trainers before taking on their own projects. This type of dog training can be financially lucrative and rewarding for those with the skills and experience.

Working with dogs can be very rewarding but also requires considerable personal sacrifice, including lower wages and sometimes dangerous job duties.

Other Careers for Dog Lovers

There are many options for dog enthusiasts who are willing and able to create their own opportunities. Dog lovers might be able to find work within the publishing field. Each of the numerous books and magazines about dogs requires writers, editors, photographers, and/or illustrators, as well as other editorial staff. These careers are attractive to many people, so it may be hard to find a position. Obtaining training and thoroughly developing your natural talents through education and work experience are important.

Writers and editors generally have undergraduate degrees in the liberal arts, especially in areas such as communications, journalism, or English. It is valuable to have publication experience in high school or college, which can be obtained by working for the school newspaper. Anyone with strong writing skills and a great deal of knowledge about the topic could potentially be a pet writer. Trainers, for example, sometimes write books or articles to promote successful techniques.

While editors are generally on the staff of a magazine or book publisher, writers and photographers usually work in a freelance capacity. This essentially means going into business for yourself. If you chose the freelancing career path, you will experience the benefits of greater freedom as well as the risks attendant upon starting your own business.

Salaries in dog-related publishing are equivalent to those in other niche areas of publishing. Depending on region and organization, pay ranges from about $20,000 a year for beginning editors to over $60,000 a year for senior editors. There are also administrative, sales, and production positions.

If talking and thinking about dogs throughout your workday is appealing to you, you may also look into pet product companies and pet supply stores. Companies that design and manufacture dog toys, dog food, and dog-related novelties all need designers; public relations people; marketing and salespeople; administrative staff; managers; and human resources personnel. Pet supply stores, especially large chain stores such as PetSmart and PETCO, have positions in the stores themselves as well as in their corporate headquarters. Store positions include cashiers, groomers, and managers and corporate level jobs include administrative, sales, and management positions.

The salaries at pet-related companies are equivalent to those in other industries. Strengthen your eligibility for one of these positions through courses and work experience.

Starting Your Own Business

There are many possibilities for dog-related businesses that you can start yourself. A groomer may work for a kennel or pet supply store, but it is also possible for her to start up her own business. For many, the idea of having a neighborhood business and building up a clientele of loyal patrons has great appeal. In addition to the basic duties of any groomer, the groomer owning her own business is responsible for making business decisions and putting in place practical working procedures. She must select a good location, balancing convenience for customers with the need for low overhead costs. She is responsible for hiring and managing employees, such as other groomers, an accountant or bookkeeper, and perhaps a receptionist. The groomer may also need a veterinarian on call, an insurance agent, and a lawyer. A private grooming shop owner sets her own fees, which depend on both the local neighborhood and the type of services she offers.

Pet sitting and dog walking services tend to be small one- or two-person businesses. To get a job in this field, you may have to start your own service. Pet sitting and dog walking can be a flexible full- or part-time job. Demand usually peaks during summers, so you might limit your operation to that time (a great summer job for teachers), but it is possible to sustain a year-round business. You can work alone or hire other sitters and build up a larger practice. It is a good idea to make up a service contract with each client, specifying everything that the owner wants done. Obtain emergency phone numbers and information about the dog from the owner in advance. Meetings should be set up with owners in their homes before the job starts so you can get to know the dog and determine whether he has any behavior problems that would make him unsuitable for your services.

Compared with some businesses, starting a home-based pet-sitting operation requires only a minimal initial investment. You'll need liability insurance, a telephone and answering machine, a computer, and some business cards and flyers. You and all employees should be bonded and insured. Any employees you hire must be responsible and thoroughly trained. Consider advertising your services; pet supply stores and veterinary clinics will probably be willing to post your flyers or business cards. You also might advertise at dog shows and with groomers or breeders.

Because you own your own business, you can set your own rates. How much you can reasonably ask, however, will vary according to your location. Pet sitters generally charge by the day and require a down payment. The

Entrepreneurial types may have creative ways to combine their love of dogs with other skills and passions. Love to cook? How about starting a dog bakery, a dog-friendly café, or a natural dog food company?

National Association of Professional Pet Sitters recommends rates.

A career similar to pet sitting is running a day care for dogs. This is a facility where owners can drop off their dogs before work and pick them up at the end of the day. Dogs are fed, cared for, and played with during the day.

Opening a doggy day care requires a larger initial investment because you must lease or buy space and retrofit the space to make it appropriate to care for animals, but it provides better opportunities to grow your business. This business also should be insured and bonded.

Another possible home-based business is transporting dogs to and from the airport, veterinarian, or groomer. To be a dog transporter requires only the willingness to work with animals and a van or a truck. You might also run a dog transport operation out of a kennel or pet supply shop. It is useful to be able to offer boarding as well, since a dog who arrives home from a trip before his owner does might need to be kept in a kennel for a short stay. Operating a pet taxi and boarding service means being on call 24 hours a day, seven days a week, all year round, but the need for this service may not be great enough for you to make it your full-time job. This business, too, should be licensed, bonded, and insured.

There are no educational or training requirements for pet transporters (apart from a driver's license), but there is a professional organization, the Independent Pet and Animal Transportation Association, which you can join.

While many dog-related businesses involve animal care, there are also careers in retail. The primary example is running a pet supply store. It is true that discount chain stores have eaten into the pet retail business. However, most communities can support multiple pet stores, and many customers opt for the convenience and comfort of shopping at a neighborhood store run by someone they know and trust. There is also an increasing market for specialty and boutique pet supply stores.

To own a pet supply store, you need to love pets—not just dogs but cats, fish, birds, and other species—and you must be comfortable communicating with pet owners. You should be knowledgeable about pet nutrition and care. You will probably sell a wide variety of pet-related merchandise, including food, cages, collars, training supplies, toys, shampoos, and books.

To get started, enlist the services of an accountant, an attorney, and an insurance agent. You will also need a reliable pet product supplier. You may want to hire an assistant or two. You will be most successful if you are responsive to the needs of your customers and their pets.

As a pet supply store owner, selling live animals is a bad idea. Purebred dogs and cats available to pet retailers often come from unethical large-scale breeding operations, often called puppy mills, or from backyard breeders who do not screen their animals for genetic or temperament disorders. There is also an increasing disdain of stores that sell pets by the pet-owning public. Instead of selling animals, make your facilities available to pet rescue organizations. Carefully research and compile a list of excellent breeders, shelters, and rescues so you can reliably suggest reputable dog sources to customers. By letting customers know that you are working to alleviate pet overpopulation as well as helping them find a perfect pet, you will only increase customer loyalty.

There are many other possible businesses for dog enthusiasts. The only limit is your imagination (and, perhaps, available start-up money). You could run a summer camp for dogs. You could own and operate a pet cemetery or provide caskets or headstones. Health insurance for pets is becoming more common; you might start a dog insurance agency. You could even work for a Greyhound adoption center that matches retired racing animals with private owners.

Is It Right for You?

If you are considering a career with dogs, go through a personal inventory of your skills and interests. Not everyone is cut out for a career with dogs. The rewards of being a dog owner or hobbyist are also great, and you may find these roles more appealing when you consider the downsides of many dog-related careers. Ask yourself whether you are willing to work long hours, live on a modest income, move to an area where jobs are more plentiful, and perhaps complete years of specialized training in order to achieve your goals. Consider your skills: Can you

He is your friend, your partner, your defender, your dog. You are his life, his love, his leader. He will be yours, faithful and true, to the last beat of his heart. You owe it to him to be worthy of such devotion.
—*Unknown*

make sound decisions in stressful situations? Are you good at relating to people (as well as dogs), even people who are upset or grieving? How strong are your writing and speaking skills? Do you excel in math or science?

Finally, keep in mind that a deep concern for the welfare of dogs is necessary but is not in itself sufficient to be successful in any of these jobs.

If you decide to pursue a dog-related career, there are things you can do right away to get started. If you are in school (whether high school or college), look into courses that will give you the knowledge and skills you'll need. Talk to people who are working in the career you are considering; people who are dedicated to their profession are generally delighted to share their knowledge with newcomers to the field. Read books and look at Web sites in the area of your interest. A great start for many careers is to volunteer at your local shelter or clinic. You not only will be improving your chances of getting a job (or getting accepted into a training program), you also will be getting an early start in a life of contributing toward the health and welfare of our canine companions. Good luck!

If you love dogs and have the appropriate skills, a canine career may be for you.

Glossaries

Breed Pronunciation Guide

Affenpinscher (AFF-en-pin-shur)

Ainu (I-new)

Akbash Dog (AK-bash Dog)

Akita (A-KEE-ta)

Alaskan Klee Kai (Alaskan Klee Ki)

Alpine Dachsbracke (Alpine DOX-brack)

Appenzeller (APP-un-zell-er)

Ariegeois (Ar-ERZH-wa)

Azawakh (OZ-a-wahk)

Barbet (Bar-BAY)

Basenji (Ba-SEN-gee)

Basset Artésien Normand
   (Bas-SAY Ar-TESS-ee-en Nor-MAN)

Basset Bleu de Gascogne (Bas-SAY Bluh day Gas-CONE)

Basset Fauve de Bretagne
   (Bas-SAY Fove day Bret-TAN-ye)

Beauceron (BO-sir-on)

Belgian Malinois (Belgian MAL-in-wa)

Belgian Tervuren (Belgian Tur-VUR-en)

Belgian Laekenois (Belgian LAKE-in-wa)

Berger Picard (Bear-jay Pee-CAR)

Berger de Pyrenees (Bear-jay day PEER-en-ees)

Bichon Frisé (BEE-shon Free-ZAY)

Bleu de Gascogne (Bluh day Gas-CONE)

Bolognese (Bo-luh-NAZE)

Borzoi (BORE-zoy)

Bouvier des Flandres (BOO-vee-ay day FLAND)

Bracco Italiano (BRAH-co Ee-tal-ee-AH-no)

Braque du Bourbonnais (Brack doo Bore-bon-nay)

Braque Français (Brack Fron-SAY)

Braque Saint-Germain (Brack San-JAR-man)

Briard (BREE-ard)

Briquet Griffon Vendéen (Bree-kay Grief-ON Von-DAYNE)

Cane Corso (CAH-nay CORE-so)

Caucasian Ovcharka (Caw-kay-zhon Of-char-ka)

Cesky Fousek (CHESS-key Fow-sek)

Cesky Terrier (CHESS-key Terrier)

Chart Polski (SHAR Pole-ski)

Chinese Shar-Pei (Chinese Shar-PAY)

Chinook (SHIN-ook)

Coton de Tuléar (Ko-TAUN day Too-LEAR)

Danish Broholmer (Danish Bro-hol-mer)

Deutscher Wachtelhund (Doyt-cher VACH-tel-hoond)

Dogo Argentino (DOUGH-go Argentino)

Dogue de Bordeaux (Dog day Bore-DOUGH)

Drentse Patrijshond (Drents Pa-trij-hond)

Entlebucher (ENT-el-boo-ker)

Épagneul Bleu de Picardie
   (AY-pah-nul Bluh day Pee-CAR-dee)

Épagneul Picard (AY-pah-nul Pee-CAR)

Épagneul Pont-Audemer (AY-pah-nul PON Au-de-may)

Fila Brasileiro (FEEL-ah Bra-see-yair-o)

Finnish Lapphund / Swedish Lapphund (Finnish or Swedish LAP-hoond)

Glen of Imaal Terrier (Glen of EE-mahl Terrier)

Grand Anglo-Français (Gron Ang-LO-Fron-SAY)

Grand Basset Griffon Vendéen
   (Gron Bass-SAY GRIEF-on Von-DAYNE)

Grand Gascon-Saintongeois/Petit Gascon-Saintongeois
(Gron Gas-CON- San-TONG-wa/Pet-EE Gas-CONE
San-TONG-wa)

Great Pyrenees (Great PEER-en-eez)

Griffon Fauve de Bretagne
(Grief-ON Fove-ve day Bre-TAN-ya)

Griffon Nivernais (Grief-ON Nee-ver-NEH)

Hamiltonstövare (Ham-il-ton-STO-var)

Havanese (HAH-vah-neez)

Hovawart (Hov-a-VORT)

Ibizan Hound (Ee-BEE-thun Hound)

Jagdterrier (Yack-terrier)

Kai (Kye-ee)

Kangal Dog (Kang-al Dog)

Keeshond (KAYS-hoond)

Komondor (KOM-mon-door)

Kooikerhondje (Koy-ker-hund-yuh)

Kraški Ovčar (Kras-ski Of-car)

Kuvasz (KOO-vas)

Large Münsterländer (Large MOON-ster-lon-der)

Lhasa Apso (LAH-sa AHP-so)

Löwchen (LEUV-shen)

Lundehund (Loon-da-hoond)

Mudi (MOO-dy)

Norwegian Buhund (Norwegian BOO-hoond)

Owczarek Podhalanski (Of-char-ek Po-dal-LON-ski)

Papillon (PAP-ee-yon)

Pekingese (PEEK-in-eez)

Perdiguero Português (PAIR-de-GAIR-o
Port-u-GAZE)

Perdiguero de Burgos (PAIR-de-GAIR-o day Bur-gos)

Perdiguero Navarro (PAiR-de-GAIR-o Na-VAR-o)

Petit Basset Griffon Vendéen
(Puh-TEE Bas-SAY Grief-ON Von-DAYNE)

Porcelaine (POUR-sell-len)

Presa Canario (PRES-sa Can-AIR-ee-o)

Pudelpointer (POO-del-pointer)

Puli (POO-lee)

Pumi (POO-mee)

Saluki (Sa-LOO-kee)

Samoyed (SAM-mee-yud)

Sarplaninac (Shar-pla-NEE-natz)

Schapendoes (Ska-PEN-doz)

Schipperke (SKIP-er-kee)

Shiba Inu (SHEE-ba EE-new)

Shih Tzu (SHEET-zoo)

Sloughi (SLEW-ghee)

Slovac Cuvac (Slovac chew-votch)

Small Münsterländer (Small MOON-ster-lon-der)

South Russian Ovcharka (South Russian Of-char-ka)

Spinone Italiano (spee-NO-nee Ee-tal-ee-AH-no)

Stabyhoun (Sta-BAY-hoon)

Swedish Vallhund (Swedish VAL-hoond)

Tosa Ken (TOE-za Ken)

Vizsla (VEESH-la)

Weimaraner (WHY-mer-ron-er)

Wirehaired Pointing Griffon
(Wirehaired Pointing Grief-ON)

Xoloitzcuintli (Show-low-EATS-queent-lee)

Dog Show Speak

Dog shows have a language of their own. The following is a sample of dog show terms, courtesy of Bo Bengtson's Best in Show *(Kennel Club Books):*

agent: term used by AKC to indicate a dog's handler

all-breed show: conformation show for all breeds

all-rounder judge: judge approved for all (or, used loosely, most) breeds

American Kennel Club: the largest and most influential organization governing purebred dog activities in the United States

Award of Merit: unofficial award available at selected, usually large, AKC shows. Abbreviated as AOM.

bait: object or food (usually dried liver or dog cookie) used by a handler to attract the dog's attention during judging

Best in Show: the dog judged as best in a show; the only dog undefeated in Breed, Group, and Best in Show competition at that event

Best in Specialty Show: the dog judged as best in a show limited to only one breed

Best of Breed: the dog judged as best of its breed in a show

Best of Opposite Sex: the dog judged as best of its sex in a show but defeated by the Best of Breed winner

Best of Winners: the dog judged as best of Winners Dog and Winners Bitch in a show

breed standard: written description of characteristics possessed by each breed

brindle: coat pattern including stripes of black hair against a lighter (usually brown, grey or fawn) background

champion: title conferred by most national kennel clubs to dogs that have fulfilled certain specified requirements at conformation shows, sometimes including performance achievements

conformation: form and structure; arrangement of body parts

double handling: the act of attracting a dog's attention during judging by a person outside the ring to make the dog look alert or show better

Dual Champion: a dog who has won titles both in conformation and performance

Fédération Cynologique Internationale: international organization that governs competition at dog shows in most of the world, with the major exceptions of the United States, Canada, United Kingdom, and Australia. Abbreviated as FCI.

gait: a dog's movement, action

group: designated division of breeds, primarily in order to facilitate judging: the number of groups at shows in North America and the United Kingdom is seven; at FCI shows, ten.

Junior Showmanship: classes for young handlers between the ages of 9 and 18 in which the abilities of the handlers, not the quality of the dogs, are taken into account

major: a United States Winners Dog or Winners Bitch award that consists of 3, 4, or 5 points; at least two majors must be part of the 15 points required for the AKC champion title

match: informal dog show at which championship points are not awarded

Miscellaneous class: US class for breeds not yet fully recognized by AKC

parent club: national organization representing a specific breed

parti-color: dog with two or more distinct broken body colors, one of which is white

pedigree: written record of a dog's ancestry, usually incorporating at least three generations (parents, grandparents, and great-grandparents)

points: (1) credits toward a champion title at shows in, for example, the United States, Canada, and Australia; the number of points awarded on each occasion is usually dependent on the number of competitors defeated: (2)

credits in the annual ratings, where usually one point is awarded per defeated competitor in Breed, Group, and Best in Show competitions

professional handler: person who makes a livelihood from showing dogs for a fee

purebred: dog whose sire and dam belong to the same recognized breed

registration certificate: document issued by the national kennel club to the owner of a dog that includes the dog's individual registration number, date of birth, parentage, breeder, owner, and so on

Reserve Winners: award to a dog that has been defeated only by the Winners Dog or by the Winners Bitch

ring steward: person in charge of the running of a ring during judging, distributing armbands, getting the right dogs into the ring for each class, preparing ribbons, etc.

special: US champion, especially a top-quality champion worth campaigning

Specials class: US champion class for both dogs and bitches

Specialty: a dog show in which only a single breed competes. (AR's insert

type: the combined characteristics that distinguish one breed from another or dogs of one family within a breed from another family

Winners (Dog or Bitch): US award given to the best nonchampion dog and bitch in each breed

Activities

agility: A competition in which dogs coached by their handlers run a course that includes jumps, tunnels, weave poles, and other obstacles. The goal is to finish the course in the shortest time with the fewest faults.

canine disc: A competition or performance in which a handler throws a Frisbee or other disc for a dog to chase and catch

Canine Good Citizen (CGC): A title and certificate that is awarded to dogs passing minimum standards for good behavior; a program that tests behavior

carting: A sport in which a dog is hitched by harness to a cart and pulls a handler riding in the cart.

conformation: A dog show that judges dogs on how closely they fit the breed standard. The coat, body structure, temperament, and gait, are judged.

drafting: A sport in which a dog is hitched by harness to a loaded cart or wagon and pulls the heavy load as far as he can. Carting, weight pulling, and sledding are all drafting sports.

earthdog trial: A simulated hunt that tests the skills of small terriers and dachshunds who follow and corner prey underground

flyball: A relay race in which teams of four dogs each race over four hurdles to a flyball box, catch a ball, then return over the four hurdles

freestyle: A choreographed dance routine set to music performed by both dog and handler

herding trial: A competition that tests a dog's herding skills, which include his ability to respond to his handler and think on his own

hunting field trial: An organized competition that tests the skills of hunting dogs against one another; includes flushing, retrieving, and trailing

hunting test: A test in which individual dogs' hunting skills are evaluated against a standard

lure coursing: A race run by sighthounds chasing an artificial lure around a large field

obedience trial: An event in which a dog's training and handler's control of the dog is judged. Dogs must be able to follow commands and be skilled at scent discrimination and directed jumping.

Schutzhund: A test of a dog's skills in three areas: obedience, tracking, and protection

skijoring: Cross-country skiing with a dog. One to three dogs pull a handler on skis.

sledding: A race in which a handler operates a sled that is being pulled by from 2 to 24 dogs. Races are run in heats and may span several days.

therapy: A treatment in which dogs act as catalysts for people suffering with illness or injury or struggling with learning or emotional problems

tracking: A competition that tests a dog's ability to follow an aged scent trail for a specified distance over varying terrain

weight pull: A competition that tests a dog's strength by having him pull a cart with a heavy load as far as he can. The dog who pulls the heaviest load the farthest wins the competition.

Medical Terms

abscess: an infected, pus-filled pocket beneath the skin

acquired: caused by environmental factors, not inherited

acute: occurring intensely and suddenly

alopecia: loss of hair

alter: spay or castrate

anaphylactic shock: life threatening allergic response

anemia: reduced number of red blood cells

anorexia: loss of appetite

bacteria: single-celled organisms that cause disease by secreting toxins that affect cells or by invading cells and reproducing inside them

cherry eye: swelling of the gland behind a dog's third eyelid that causes both the gland and eyelid to protrude. The gland is pink and appears round

chronic: lasting over a long period of time

congenital: present at birth

conjunctivitis: inflammation of the membrane covering the inner surface of the eyelids; commonly called pinkeye

coprophagia: eating feces

crop: amputation of part of the ears so they stand erect

cryptorchid: a condition of testicles that have not descended into the scrotum

cyst: sac or pocket of fluid or soft matter

dewclaw: a vestigial digit that does not reach the ground and is found on the foot

dock: amputation or partial amputation of the tail

ectropian: rolling outward of the eyelids

Elizabethan collar: cone-shaped collar used to prevent dogs from reaching wounds to chew or lick

entropian: rolling inward of the eyelids

estrus: period when female accepts mating

euthanasia: painless termination of a life

genetic: having to do with characteristics inherited through the genes

heat: term for estrus period

hip dysplasia: inherited condition in which tissue develops abnormally and the hip joint does not fit together tightly

hot spot: an inflamed, bald area on skin caused by rubbing, scratching, licking, or biting; also called pyotraumatic dermatitis

incontinence: uncontrolled leaking of urine; most common in older female dogs

kennel cough: contagious bronchial disease caused by viruses and bacteria. It is characterized by a dry, raspy cough

keratoconjunctivitis sicca: eye condition caused by a lack of tears; dry eyes.

lick granuloma: damaged tissue sores resulting from excessive licking

melena: black, tarry stool caused by bleeding

monorchid: an individual who has only one testicle descended into the scrotum

neuter: to alter

obese: a dog who is extremely overweight

parasite: an organism that feeds off of a host; includes fleas, ticks, mites, and worms

pica: a craving to eat nonfood substances

spay: removal of ovaries and uterus to prevent reproduction

titer: blood test that measures the concentration of an antibody to a disease

tumor: abnormal new tissue growth with no function; it can be malignant or benign

ulcer: a small, painful sore in the stomach or intestinal lining

vaccine: a preparation that triggers protective immune responses against disease when introduced into the body

virus: a small, infectious microorganism that reproduces within living cells

whelp: to give birth to puppies

zoonosis: a condition that can be passed from one species to another. Rabies is one example of a zoonotic disease.

Coat Color Terms

ASCOB: any solid color other than black

badger: a mix of brown, black, gray, and white hairs

blaze: a strip of white down the center of the face

belton: term used to describe spots of hair that are lighter or darker than the base color (ticking or roaning) in English Setters only

blue: a grayish blue

blue merle: black markings on a grayish blue background

brindle: dark and light streaking that looks like tiger stripes

café au lait: creamy brown

chestnut: reddish brown

chocolate: brown

cream: off white

dead grass: tan

fawn: a reddish-brown yellow

grizzle: mixture of white hairs with black or red hairs

harlequin: patchy black or gray on white (this term is usually reserved for Great Danes)

hound color (or marked): white with tan and black patches

landseer: black-and-white Newfoundland

lemon: yellow

lion color: reddish tan

liver: deep reddish brown

mahogany: dull reddish brown

mask: dark color on the face

merle: dark splotches against a lighter background of the same color

mottled: dark, round splotches on a lighter background

mustard: muted yellow

parti-colored: Patches of two colors or more

piebald (or pied): large splotches of two or more colors

roan: mix of colored hairs with white hairs

ruby: mahogany red

rust: reddish brown

sable: black-tipped silver, gold, gray, brown, or fawn hairs

sandy: sand colored, tan

seal: black with a reddish tint

sedge: reddish yellow

stag red (stag): deep red with black hairs

wheaten: wheat colored, tan

tawny: brownish orange

ticking: little spots of color lighter or darker than the base color

Dog Ear Types

bat ear: forward-facing erect ear that is broad at the base and rounded on top (example: French Bulldog)

bell ear: a wide ear (example: Cocker Spaniel)

button ear: an ear that folds forward and covers the inside of the ear (example: Parson Russell Terrier)

cropped ear: Drop ear cut to stand erect (example: some Boxers)

drop ear: an ear that folds over and hangs down instead of being erect; also called a pendant ear (example: Labrador Retriever)

hound ear: a rounded drop ear (example: Basset Hound)

natural ear: an ear that isn't cropped (example: Labrador Retriever)

pendant ear: also called a drop ear

prick ear: a pointy ear that stands up; erect ear (example: German Shepherd Dog)

rose ear: a small ear that folds over and back (example: American Pit Bull Terrier)

semiprick ear: an erect ear with just the tips folding forward (example: Collie)

tulip ear: a wide erect ear with the edges curving in (example: Bull Terrier)

Dog Tail Types

bee-sting tail: a short, straight tapered tail (example: Pointer)

brush tail: a bushy tail (example: Australian Cattle Dog)

bobtail: naturally tailless or naturally docked tail (example: Australian Shepherd; Old English Sheepdog)

carrot tail: a tail shaped like an upside-down carrot and carried straight up (example: West Highland White Terrier)

corkscrew tail: a spiral tail (example: Pug)

crank tail: a tail carried low and shaped like a crank (example: Scottish Deerhound)

curled tail: a tail that curls over the back (example: Alaskan Malamute)

docked tail: a tail that is shortened by being cut (example: some Doberman Pinschers)

double curl tail: a tail that curls twice over the back (example: Akita)

flag tail: a long tail that is carried high with long silky hair on it (example: Irish Setter)

gay tail: a tail carried higher than the back (example: Brussels Griffon)

hook tail: a tail that hangs down and curves up at the bottom (example: Greyhound) another term for a bee-sting tail

horizontal tail: another term for bee-sting tail

otter tail: a long tail that is thick and rounded and has hair parted on its underside (example: Labrador Retriever)

plume tail: a tail with feathering (example: Gordon Setter)

pump handle: a long tail that is carried up (example: Black and Tan Coonhound)

rat tail: a long tail with curls of fur covering most of it but the tip, which is almost hairless (example: Irish Water Spaniel)

ring tail: a tail carried up and curled almost in a circle (example: Afghan Hound)

saber tail: a tail carried like a sword in a semicircle (example: Siberian Husky

screw tail: another term for a corkscrew tail

sickle tail: another term for a saber tail

whip tail: a pointed tail carried straight out and stiffly (example: Bull Terrier)

Terms in Breed Standards

almond eye: a narrow eye shaped like an almond

apple head: a round skull

bad mouth: a mouth with crooked teeth; incorrect bite

bandy leg: an outward-bending leg; bowleg

barrel hock: a hock (ankle) that turns out, causing the foot to toe in; divergent hock; spread hock

beefy: overdeveloped hindquarters

bird of prey eyes: usually harsh-looking light yellowish eyes

blocky: a cube-shaped head

bodied-up: well developed and mature

bossy: over-developed shoulder muscles

brick-shaped: rectangular

broken coat: wirehaired

broken-down ear: a deformed ear that lacks correct carriage

brush coat: a coat that is short, straight, and stiff

brush: a thick and bushy tail

bull neck: a thick and powerful neck

burr: inside of ear

butterfly: a dark nose that has areas without pigment

cat foot: a foot that is neat and round and has close-set arched toes

cheeky: prominent round cheeks

Chippendale front: forelegs that turn out at the elbows, are close at the pasterns (area of foot above toes) and have feet that turn out; fiddle front

china eye: a clear blue or light blue eye

chiseled: having a smooth, clean-cut head

close-coupled: having a short loin

coarse: unrefined

cobby: stocky

compact: short-bodied

corky: lively and alert

cow hocks: hocks (ankles) that are turned inward

dish-faced: having a slightly concave foreface

divergent hock: a hock (ankle) that turns out, causing the feet to toe in; barrel hock; spread hock

domed: a skull that is evenly curved on top

down-faced: having a muzzle that slopes downward

dry: a skull or neck with tight, smooth skin

dudley nose: a flesh-colored nose

ewe neck: a neck with a concave topline

filbert ear: an ear shaped like a filbert, or hazelnut

filled-up face: a smooth face that isn't excessively muscular

flat-sided: having ribs that are too flat

fluffy: a long coat with exaggerated feathering

foxy: a sharp face with a pointy nose

frog face: a face with a receding, often overshot jaw

goose neck: a long neck; swan neck

hare foot: a long, narrow foot

haw eyes: eyes with the third eyelid, or nictitating membrane, visible

lippy: having loosely hanging lips

loaded shoulders: shoulders with overdeveloped muscles

loose slung: having muscles that are attached at the shoulders too loosely

making a wheel: a tail that is circling over the back

oblique shoulders: sloping shoulders

oblique eyes: eyes that slant upward from inner corner to outer corner

oval chest: a chest that is deeper than it is wide

overhang: a prominent brow

paper foot: a flat foot with a thin pad

pig eyes: small eyes set close together

pigeon breast: a narrow chest with a projecting breastbone

pigeon-toed: having turned-in toes

plume: fringy long hair on a tail

racy: tall and lean

rangy: tall, long, slim, and lanky

skully: a skull that is thick and coarse

slab-sided: having flat ribs

snipy: a weak, pointed, muzzle

snow nose: a black nose that gets a pink streak in winter; winter nose

snowshoe feet: feet that are slightly webbed

spike tail: a short, straight, tapering tail

squirrel tail: a tail carried up and curving forward over the back

throatiness: a throat with excess skin

tuck-up: narrow at the loin

turn-up: a foreface that turns up

varminty: having an intense, bright, expression

walleye: a whitish or light blue eye

Grooming Tools

clippers: Electric clippers for cutting and shaping

combination brush: A slicker brush on one side for removing dead hair, and a bristle brush on the other side for everyday brushing

cream rinse or conditioner: Adds body and reduces static electricity following shampoo

dog shampoo: Shampoos that are specially formulated for dogs and come in a variety of types, including medicated, tearless, flea control, bluing, texturizing, and moisturizing

double-sided comb: Stainless steel comb with wide teeth on one end and finer teeth on the other used for general grooming, removing undercoat, and flea control

ear-cleaning solution: Mineral oil or a commercial ear cleaner used to clean and reduce odor and excess moisture in ears. Commercial ear cleaners come in liquid, cream, and powder form. The powder cleaner is also used to help grip and remove hair from ears.

eye drops: Specially made drops or mineral oil that protect eyes during bathing

flea comb: Fine-toothed comb for catching fleas and removing undercoat

grooming glove or mitt: A glove with rubber nubs for shining and controlling shedding, especially useful in single-coated dogs

grooming rake: A comblike device used to pull out undercoat and remove mats and tangles. A rake has one to three rows of wide teeth and a long handle for easy gripping. It is especially useful for dogs with double coats.

grooming table: A waist-high table that dogs on most grooming tables.

hair dryer: For drying and/or fluffing after bathing. Groomers can use a hand-held standard dryer or a dryer designed for dogs. Dog dryers come in handheld varieties and canister styles with short legs. Hose attachments direct air flow.

mat splitter: A tool with razor-sharp teeth used to cut through mats

nail clippers: Clippers used to cut dog toenails. They come in guillotine, scissors, pliers, and power types.

natural or rubber bristle brush: A brush with long bristles used for shining and smoothing the coat

nonskid rubber mat: A rubber mat placed in the bottom of a sink or a tub to keep a dog from slipping when being bathed

pin brush: A brush with round tips on the bristles to avoid skin abrasions. It is popularly used for long-haired dogs.

pumice stone: A porous stone that is brushed across the coat. It collects dead undercoat and smooths and shines the outer coat.

rubber curry brush: An oval brush with small, flexible rubber teeth that massages skin, speeds up shedding, and adds shine

shears or scissors: Scissors used for trimming and thinning the coat and for cutting out mats

shedding blade: A saw-toothed device used to thin heavy shedding coats

slicker brush: A brush with closely clustered wire or rubber bristles. It removes dead hair to reduce shedding and is useful for removing mats.

stripping tool or knife: A knife-shaped tool with a handle and a toothed blade used to pluck dead hair from wire-haired dogs

styptic pencil/powder: Contracts the blood vessels to stop a clipped nail from bleeding

toothbrush or finger brush: A standard-sized toothbrush or a brush made to fit over a finger, which is used to clean canine teeth

toothpaste (canine): Toothpaste that is safe for dogs to swallow and made in flavors they enjoy

tweezers or ear forceps: Used to remove hair from ears. Ear forceps are stainless steel devices resembling scissors in appearance that grip hair for pulling.

Resources

Books

Note: Starred (*) items are deemed suitable for children.

Activities
Agility
Agility Fun the Hobday Way, Vol. 1: Agility Training for Puppies
by Ruth Hobday
Clean Run Productions, 1998

Agility Fun the Hobday Way, Vol. 2: Steps for Obstacle Training
by Ruth Hobday
Clean Run Productions, 1998

Agility Fun the Hobday Way, Vol. 3: Further Lessons for Beginners
by Ruth Hobday
Clean Run Productions, 1999

All About Agility
by Jacqueline O'Neil
Howell Book House, 1999

Enjoying Dog Agility, 2nd Edition
by Julie Daniels
Kennel Club Books, 2009

Excelling at Dog Agility: Book 1: Obstacle Training
by Jane Simmons-Moake
Flashpaws Productions, 1999

Excelling at Dog Agility: Book 2: Sequence Training
by Jane Simmons-Moake
Flashpaws Productions, 2000

Excelling at Dog Agility: Book 3: Advanced Skills Training
by Jane Simmons-Moake
Flashpaws Productions, 2003

Introduction to Dog Agility
by Margaret H. Bonham
Barron's Educational Series, 2000

Switching Sides: Making the Transition from Obedience to Agility
by Kay Guetzloff
Gulf Publishing, 1999

Canine Freestyle
Dancing with Dogs: A Step-by-Step Guide to Freestyle
by Richard Curtis
Ringpress Books Ltd., 2003

Dancing with Your Dog: The Book
by Sandra Davis
Sandra Davis Musical Freestyle, 1999

Conformation
Best in Show: The World of Show Dogs and Dog Shows
by Bo Bengtson
Kennel Club Books, 2008

Born to Win, Breed to Succeed, 2nd Edition
by Patricia Craige Trotter
Kennel Club Books, 2009

Canine Terminology
by Harold R. Spira
Dogwise, 2001

The Forsyth Guide to Successful Dog Showing
by Robert and Jane Forsyth
Howell, 1975

Frank Sabella's The Art of Handling Show Dogs
by Frank Sabella and Shirlee Kalstone
B & E Publications, 1980

Going for the Blue: Inside the World of Show Dogs and Dog Shows
by Roger A. Caras
Diane Publishing Company, 2001

The Joy of Breeding Your Own Show Dog
by Ann Seranne
Howell/Wiley, 2004

New Secrets of Successful Show Dog Handling
by Peter Green and Mario Migliorini
Alpine, 2002

The Nicholas Guide to Dog Judging
by Anna Katherine Nicholas
Howell, 1989

The Science and Techniques of Judging Dogs
by Robert J. Berndt
Alpine, 2001

Showing Your Dog: An International Guide for Fanciers
by Juliette Cunliffe with Ann Hearn and Dr. Robert Pollet
Kennel Club Books, 2004

The Simple Guide to Showing Your Dog
by Richard G. Beauchamp
TFH, 2003

Solving the Mysteries of Breed Type
by Richard G. Beauchamp
Kennel Club Books, 2008

The Winning Edge: Show Ring Secrets
by George C. Alston with Connie Vanacore
Howell, 1992

Winning with Purebred Dogs: Success By Design
by Dr. Alvin Grossman and Beverly Grossman
Doral, 1992

Disc Dogs
Flying Dogs: How to Teach Your Dog to Catch a Flying Disc
by Jake Jensen
Infinity Plus One, 1998

Skyhoundz Images
by Peter Bloeme
Skyhoundz, 1998

Earthdog
Dig In!: Earthdog Training Made Easy
by Mario Migliorini
Wiley Publishing Inc., 1997

Earthdog Ins and Outs: Guiding Natural Instincts for Success in Earthdog Tests and Den Trials
by Jo Ann Frier-Murza
OTR Publications, 1998

Flyball
Flying High: The Complete Book of Flyball
by Joan Payne
KDB Publishing, 1996

Flyball Racing: The Dog Sport for Everyone
by Lonnie Olson
Howell Book House, 1997

Flyball Training: Start to Finish
by Jacqueline Parkin
Alpine Publications, 1996

General
Beyond Fetch: Fun, Interactive Activities for You and Your Dog
by D. Caroline Coile, PhD
Howell Book House, 2003

Doggy Days: Dozens and Dozens of Outdoor Activities for You and Your Best Friend
by Joe and Melanie Borgenicht
Ten Speed Press, 2001

Fun and Games with Your Dog: Expert Advice on a Variety of Activities for You and Your Pet
by Gerd Ludwig, et al.
Barron's Educational Series, 1996

Healthy Dog: The Ultimate Fitness Guide for You and Your Dog
by Arden Moore
BowTie Press, 2004

Hiking with Dogs: Becoming a Wilderness-Wise Dog Owner
by Linda Mullally
Falcon, 1999

Ruffing It: The Complete Guide to Camping with Dogs
by Mardi Richmond and Melanee L. Barash
Alpine Publications, 1998

The Simple Guide to Getting Active with Your Dog
by Margaret H. Bonham
TFH Publications, 2002

Herding
A Way of Life: Sheepdog Training, Handling and Trialling
by H. Glyn Jones and Barbara C. Collins
Diamond Farm Book Publications, 2002

Herding Dogs: Selecting and Training the Working Farm Dog
by Christine H. Renna
Kennel Club Books, 2008

Training the Sheep Dog
by Thomas Longton and Barbara Sykes
Crowood Press, 2003

Hunting and Field Trials
Canine Tracking Guide: Training the All-Purpose Tracker
by Don Abney
Kennel Club Books, 2008

Dog Training: Retrievers and Pointers, at Home and in the Field (The Complete Hunter)
by Jason A. Smith
Creative Publishing International, 2003

How to Help Gun Dogs Train Themselves: Taking Advantage of Early Conditioned Learning
by Joan Bailey
Swan Valley Press, 2004

Hunting with Spaniels: Training Your Flushing Dog
by Paul Morrison
Kennel Club Books, 2008

The Labrador Shooting Dog
by Mike Gould
Clinetop Press, 1999

Retriever Madness: Training the World's Favorite Gundog
by Nona Kilgore Bauer
Kennel Club Books, 2008

Scenting on the Wind: Scent Work for Hunting Dogs
by Susan Bulanda
Doral Publishing, 2003

Training Pointing Dogs: All the Answers to All Your Questions
by Paul Long
The Lyons Press, 1985

Training Retrievers and Spaniels to Hunt 'Em Up!
by Joe Arnette and George Hickox
Down East Books, 2000

Training the Hunting Retriever
by Jerome B. Robinson
The Lyons Press, 1999

Lure Coursing
Lure Coursing: Field Trialing for Sighthounds and How to Take Part
by Arthur S. Beaman
Wiley Publishing Inc., 1993

Obedience
A Beginner's Guide to Competitive Obedience
by Wendy Beasley
TFH Publications, 1999

Competitive Obedience: A Step-by-Step Guide
by Paddy Coughlan
Ringpress Books Ltd, 2003

Competitive Obedience for Winners
by Brian McGovern
Trafalgar Square, 2000

Expert Obedience Training for Dogs
by Winifred Gibson Strickland
Howell Book House, 2003

Remembering to Breathe: Inside Dog Obedience Competition
by Willard Bailey
Infinity Publishing, 2003

Schutzhund
Advanced Schutzhund
by Ivan Balabanov and Karen Duet
Howell Book House, 1999

K9 Schutzhund Training: A Manual for Tracking, Obedience and Protection
by Resi Gerritson and Ruud Haak
Detselig Enterprises Ltd., 2000

Schutzhund: Theory and Training Methods
by Susan Barwig and Stewart Hilliard,
Howell Book House, 1991

Sledding and Skijoring
Mush: A Beginner's Manual of Sled Dog Training
by Bella Levorsen and Sierra Nevada Dog Drivers Inc.
Barkleigh Productions, 1999

Skijor with Your Dog
by Mari Hoe-Raitto and Carol Kaynor
OK Publishing, 1992

The Speed Mushing Manual: How to Train Racing Sled Dogs
by Jim Welch
Sirius Publishing, 1989

Boarding/Pet Sitting
Boarding Your Dog: How to Make Your Dog's Stay Happy, Comfortable, and Safe (Storey Country Wisdom Bulletin)
by Pat Storer
Storey Books, 2001

The Dog Sitter's Handbook: A Personalized Guide for Your Pet's Caregiver
by Karen Anderson
Willow Creek Press, 2001

Careers
A Day in the Life of a Veterinarian
by Mary Bowman-Kruhm
Rosen Publishing Group Inc., 1999*

Careers for Animal Lovers
by Russell Shorto, et al.
Choices: The Millbrook Press, 1992*

Careers for Animal Lovers and Other Zoological Types
by Louise Miller
McGraw-Hill, 2000

Career Success with Pets
by Kim Barber
Howell Book House, 1996

Careers with Animals
by Audrey Pavia
Barron's Educational Series, 2001

Careers with Animals
by The Humane Society of the United States and Willow Ann Sirch
Fulcrum Publishing, 2000*

How to Make Big Money Grooming Small Dogs: The Absolute Amateur's Guide to Profitable, Professional Canine Styling
by Robert S. Whitman
Protective Specialties Development Group, 1995

I Want to Be a Veterinarian
by Stephanie Maze
Harcourt Trade, 1999*

Operating Your Own Pet Sitting Business Kit: Lessons Learned from Successful Pet Sitters ... What Works & Why!
by Vicky Whelan
Pet Sitting and Pet Related Services, 1999

Opportunities in Animal and Pet Care Careers
by Mary Price Lee and Richard S. Lee
McGraw-Hill/Contemporary Publishing Group, 2001

Opportunities in Veterinary Medicine Careers
by Robert E. Swope
McGraw-Hill/Contemporary Books, 2001

Pet Sitting for Profit: A Complete Manual for Success
by Patti J. Moran
Howell Book House, 1997

Starting a Pet Sitting Business
by William S. Foster
Hancock House Publishers, 1990

The World of Work: Choosing a Career in Animal Care
by Jane Hurwitz
Rosen Publishing Group Inc., 1997

General
ASPCA Complete Guide to Dogs: Everything You Need to Know About Choosing and Caring for Your Pet
by Sheldon L. Gerstenfeld, VMD, et al.
Chronicle Books LLC, 1999

The Complete Dog Owner's Manual: How to Raise a Happy, Healthy Dog
by Amy Marder, VMD
Chain Sales, 1998

Complete Guide to Dog Care
by Peter Larkin, DVM
Lorenz Books, 1999

The Complete Idiot's Guide to Getting and Owning a Dog
by Sheila Webster Boneham, PhD
Alpha Books, 2002

Dog Law: A Plain English Legal Guide for Dog Owners and Their Neighbors
by Mary Randolph
Nolo Press, 2001

Dogs for Dummies
by Gina Spadafori
Wiley Publishing Inc., 2000

Dogs for Kids: Everything You Need to Know About Dogs
by Kristin Mehus-Roe
BowTie Press, 2007

The Dog Owner's Manual: Operating Instructions, Troubleshooting Tips, and Advice on Lifetime Maintenance
by David Brunner, et al.
Quirk Books, 2004

The Humane Society of the United States Complete Guide to Dog Care: Everything You Need to Know to Keep Your Dog Healthy and Happy
by Marion S. Lane
Little, Brown and Company, 2001

Puppies for Dummies
by Sarah Hodgson
Wiley Publishing Inc., 2000

The Puppy Owner's Manual: Solutions to All Your Puppy Problems in an Easy-to-Follow Question and Answer Format
by Diana Delmar
Storey Books, 2001

Puppy Owner's Survival Manual: Everything You Need to Know to Raise a Happy, Healthy Well-Behaved Pet
by Julia Barnes and Matthew Brash
Sterling, 2002

Solutions: An All-in-One Reference for Raising a Happy and Healthy Dog
by Mordecai Siegal and Matthew Margolis
Simon and Schuster, 2002

You and Your Puppy: Training and Health Care for Puppy's First Year
by James DeBitetto, DVM, and Sarah Hodgson
Howell Book House, 2000

Grooming
A Dog Owner's Guide to Grooming Your Dog: A Practical Step-by-Step Program for Maintaining and Improving Your Dog's Appearance
by Suzanne Ruiz
Tetra Press, 1996

The All Breed Dog Grooming Guide
by Sam Kohl
Aaronco Pet Products, 2002

Grooming Your Dog: A Natural and Herbal Approach
by Paula Kephart
Storey Books, 2000

Guide to Home Pet Grooming
by Chris C. Pinney
Barron's Educational Series, 1990

Poodle Clipping and Grooming: The International Reference
by Shirlee Kalstone
Howell Book House, 2000

The Simple Guide to Grooming Your Dog
by Eve Adamson and Sandy Roth
TFH Publications, 2004

The Stone Guide to Dog Grooming for All Breeds
by Ben and Pearl Stone
Howell Book House, 1981

Ultimate Dog Grooming: The Complete Guide to 170 Breeds
by Eileen Geeson, et al.
Firefly Books, 2002

Health
The 5-Minute Veterinary Consult: Canine & Feline
by Larry Tilley and Francis W.K. Smith
Lippincott, Williams and Wilkins, 2000

8 Weeks to a Healthy Dog: An Easy to Follow Program for the Life of Your Dog
by Shawn Messonnier, DVM
Rodale Press, 2003

A–Z of Dog Diseases & Health Problems: Signs, Diagnoses, Causes, Treatment
by Dick Lane and Neil Ewart
Ringpress Books Ltd., 1997

A Lifetime Guide to Practical Pet Care: Better Health and Happier Homes for Dogs and Cats
by Jeff Nichol, DVM
Prentice Hall Trade, 2001

The Angell Memorial Animal Hospital Book of Wellness and Preventive Care for Dogs
by Darlene Arden
McGraw-Hill, 2002

Anti-Aging for Dogs: A Longevity Program for Man's Best Friend
by John Simon, DVM, and Steve Duno
St. Martin's Press, 1999

Ask the Vet About Dogs: Easy Answers to Commonly Asked Questions
by Leslie Sinclair
BowTie Press, 2003

Canine Epilepsy: An Owner's Guide to Living With and Without Seizures
by Caroline Levin
Lantern Publications, 2002

Canine Massage: A Complete Reference Manual
by Jean-Pierre Hourdebaigt
Dogwise Publishing, 2003

Caring for Your Dog: The Complete Canine Home Reference
by Bruce Fogle, DVM
DK Publishing, 2002

Complete Care for Your Aging Dog
by Amy D. Shojai
New American Library, 2003

Complete Dog Care: The Essential Guide to Looking After Your Pet
by Peter Larkin, DVM
Southwater Publishing, 2003

Complete Holistic Dog Book: Home Health Care for Our Canine Companions
by Jan Allegretti and
Katy Sommers
Celestial Arts, 2003

The Complete Idiot's Guide to Dog Health and Nutrition
by Margaret Bonham and James M. Wingert, DVM
Alpha Books, 2003

Comprehensive Health Care for Dogs: A Practical Guide to Identifying and Treating Your Dog's Ailments
by James E. McKay
Creative Publishing International, 2001

The Contented Canine: A Guide to Successful Pet Parenting for Dog Owners
by Lowell Ackerman, DVM
iUniverse, 2001

Control of Canine Genetic Diseases
by George A. Padgett
Howell Book House, 1998

The Doctors Book of Home Remedies for Dogs and Cats
by the Editors of Prevention Magazine Health Books
Bantam Books, 1998

Dog Health & Nutrition for Dummies
by M. Christine Zink, DVM, PhD
Wiley Publishing Inc., 2001

Dog Owner's Home Veterinary Handbook
by James Giffen, MD, and Liisa Carlson, DVM
Howell Book House, 1999

Dog Owner's Manual
by Bruce Fogle, DVM
DK Publishing, 2003

The Dog's Drugstore: A Dog Owner's Guide to Nonprescription Drugs and Their Safe Use in Veterinary Home-Care
by Richard Redding, DVM, MSC, PhD, and Myrna Papurt, DVM, BSc
St. Martin's Press, 2000

The Dog's Health from A to Z: The Ultimate Handy Guide for Every Owner
by John Bleby and Gerald Bishop
David and Charles Publishers, 2003

Dr. Pitcairn's Complete Guide to Natural Health for Dogs & Cats
by Richard H. Pitcairn, DVM, PhD, and Susan Hubble Pitcairn Rodale Press, 1995

Dr. Khalsa's Natural Dog: A Holistic Guide for Healthier Dogs
by Deva Khalsa, DVM
Kennel Club Books, 2009

The Essential Puppy Guide
by Miriam Fields-Babineau
TFH Publications, 2001

Eternal Puppy: Groundbreaking Veterinary Advances to Enrich Your Senior Dog's Life
by Janice Willard, DVM
Kennel Club Books, 2008

The Genetic Connection: A Guide to Health Problems in Purebred Dogs
by Lowell Ackerman, DVM
American Animal Hospital Association, 1999

Getting in Touch with Your Dog: An Easy, Gentle Way to Better Health and Behavior
by Linda Tellington-Jones
Trafalgar Square, 2001

Guide to Skin and Haircoat Problems in Dogs
by Lowell Ackerman, DVM
Alpine Publishing, 1994

Hands-On Dog Care: The Complete Book of Canine First Aid
by Sue Copeland and John Hamil, DVM
Doral Publishing, 2000

Healing Pets with Nature's Miracle Cures
by Henry Pasternak, DVM
Highlands Veterinary Hospital, 2001

Herbs for Pets: The Natural Approach for Enhancing Your Companion's Life
by Gregory L. Tilford and Mary L. Wulff
BowTie Press, 2009

The Holistic Dog Book: Canine Care for the 21st Century
by Denise Flaim and Michael W. Fox
Howell Book House, 2003

Holistic Guide for a Healthy Dog
by Wendy Volhard and Kerry Brown, DVM
Howell Book House, 2000

Is My Dog OK? How to Know ... When Your Dog Won't Say
by Jeff Nichol, DVM
Prentice Hall Press, 2001

It's a Dog's Life and Medical Journal
by Franceen Hill
Taffy Lynn Company, 2001

Love Me or Leash Me: 50 Simple Ways to Keep Me a Happy, Healthy and Well-Behaved Companion
by Anne Bobby
Black Dog and Leventhal Publishing, 2001

Natural Healing for Dogs and Cats
by the Editors of Prevention Magazine Health Books
St. Martin's Press, 2001

Natural Health Bible for Dogs & Cats: Your A-Z Guide to Over 200 Conditions, Herbs, Vitamins, and Supplements
by Shawn Messonnier, DVM
Prima Lifestyles, 2001

Naturally Healthy Dogs
by Carol Osborne
Todtri Productions Ltd., 2003

Natural Remedies for Dogs and Cats
by C. J. Puotinen
NTC/Contemporary Publishing, 1999

The Natural Way for Dogs and Cats: Natural Treatments, Remedies and Diet for Your Pet
by Midi Fairgrieve
C W Daniel Publishing, 2001

The Nature of Animal Healing: The Definitive Holistic Medicine Guide to Caring for Your Dog and Cat
by Martin Goldstein, DVM
Ballantine Books, 2000

New Choices in Natural Healing for Dogs & Cats
by Amy D. Shojai
Rodale Press, 2001

Owner's Guide to Dog Health
by Lowell Ackerman, DVM
TFH Publications, 1996

Pet Care in the New Century: Cutting-Edge Medicine for Dogs and Cats
by Amy D. Shojai
New American Library, 2001

Pet First Aid: Cats and Dogs
by Bobbie Mammato, DVM
StayWell, 1997

Pets Living With Cancer: A Pet Owner's Resource
by Robin Downing, DVM
American Animal Hospital Association Press, 2000

Pills for Pets: The A to Z Guide to Drugs and Medications for Your Animal Companion
by Debra Eldredge
Citadel Press, 2003

The First Aid Companion for Dogs & Cats (Prevention Pets)
by Amy D. Shojai
Rodale Press, 2001

The Simple Guide to a Healthy Dog
by Eve Adamson
TFH Publications, 2002

Ultimate Dog Care: A Complete Veterinary Guide
by Sue Guthrie, et al.
Howell Book House, 2002

Vaccine Guide for Dogs and Cats: What Every Pet Lover Should Know
by Catherine Diodati
New Atlantean Press, 2003

The Veterinarians' Guide to Natural Remedies for Dogs: Safe and Effective Alternative Treatments and Healing Techniques from the Nation's Top Holistic Veterinarians
by Martin Zucker
Three Rivers Press, 2002

The Veterinarians' Guide to Your Dog's Symptoms
by Michael Garvey, DVM, et al.
Villard Books, 1999

The Well Adjusted Dog: Canine Chiropractic Methods You Can DO Yourself
by Daniel Kamen, DC
Brookline Books, 1997

The Well-Connected Dog: A Guide to Canine Acupressure
by Amy Snow, et al.
Tallgrass Publishing, 1999

The Well Dog Book: The Classic Comprehensive Handbook of Dog Care
by Terri McGinnis, DVM
Random House, 1996

What's up with My Dog: The Only Visual Guide to Symptoms and First Aid
by Bruce Fogle, DVM
DK Publishing, 2002

Why is Cancer Killing Our Pets?: How You Can Protect and Treat Your Animal Companion
by Deborah Straw
Healing Arts Press, 2000

You and Your Puppy: Training and Health Care for Puppy's First Year
by James DeBitetto, DVM, and Sarah Hodgson
Howell Book House, 1995

Your Older Dog: A Complete Guide to Helping Your Dog Live a Longer and Healthier Life
by Jean Callahan
Fireside, 2001

Nutrition

Barker's Grub: Easy Wholesome Home Cooking for Your Dog
by Rudy Edalati
Three Rivers Press, 2001

Better Food for Dogs: A Complete Cookbook and Nutrition Guide
by David Bastin, et al.
Robert Rose Inc., 2003

Canine and Feline Nutrition: A Resource for Companion Animal Professionals, Second Edition
edited by Linda P. Case
Mosby, 2000

Canine Nutrition: Choosing the Best Food for Your Breed
by William Cusick
Doral Publishing, 1997

Canine Nutrition: What Every Owner, Breeder, and Trainer Should Know
by Lowell Ackerman, DVM
Alpine Publications, 1999

Coffman's Comparative Reference Guide to Dog Food
by Howard D. Coffman
PigDog Press, 1998

The Complete Idiot's Guide to Dog Health and Nutrition
by Margaret Bonham and James M. Wingert, DVM
Alpha Books, 2003

The Consumer's Guide to Dog Food: What's in Dog Food, Why It's There, and How to Choose the Best Food for Your Dog
by Liz Palika
Howell Book House, 1996

Doggy Desserts: Homemade Treats for Happy, Healthy Dogs
by Cheryl Gianfrancesco
BowTie Press, 2007

Dr. Jane's Natural Care for a Healthy, Happy Dog: The Complete Guide to Nutrition and Health
by Jane R. Bicks
Penguin USA, 1999

Dog Health and Nutrition for Dummies
by M. Christine Zink, DVM, PhD
Wiley Publishing Inc., 2001

The Dog: Its Behavior, Nutrition, and Health
by Linda P. Case and Kerry Helms
Blackwell Publishing, 1999

Earl Mindell's Nutrition & Health for Dogs: Keep Your Dog Healthy and Happy with Natural Preventative Care and Remedies
by Earl Mindell and Elizabeth Renaghan
Prima Lifestyles, 1998

Feeding Your Dog for Life: The Real Facts About Proper Nutrition
by Diane Morgan
Doral Publishing, 2002

Fitness Planner for Your Dog
by Linda Waniorek
Barron's Educational Series, 2001

Foods Pets Die For: Shocking Facts About Pet Food
by Ann N. Martin
NewSage Press, 2003

Home-Prepared Dog & Cat Diets: The Healthful Alternative
by Donald R. Strombeck
Blackwell Publishing, 1999

Manual of Veterinary Dietetics
by C. A. Tony Buffington, et al.
W. B. Saunders, 2004

The Maxi Lifespan Diet for Dogs: A Scientific Feeding Plan that Will Extend the Maximum Lifespan of Your Dog
by Robert Haas
Bonus Books, 2004

Nutrition for Dogs
by Maryann Mott
TFH Publications, 2001

Natural Nutrition for Dogs and Cats: The Ultimate Pet Diet
by Kymythy
R. Schultze Hay House, 1999

Obligate Carnivore: Cats, Dogs, and What it Really Means to be Vegan
by Jed Gillen
Steinhoist Books, 2003

Raw Dog Food: Make it Easy for You and Your Dog
by Carina Beth MacDonald
Dogwise Publishing, 2003

Raw Meaty Bones Promote Health
by Tom Lonsdale
Rivetco P/L, 2001

Real Food for Dogs: 50 Vet-Approved Recipes to Please the Canine Gastronome
by Arden Moore
Storey Books, 2001

Recent Advances in Canine and Feline Nutrition: Volume III
edited by Gregory A. Reinhart, PhD, and Daniel P. Carey, DVM
Orange Frazer Press, 2000

Super Nutrition for Dogs n' Cats: Preventive Medicine for Your Pets!
by Nina Anderson and Dr. Howard Peiper
Safe Goods, 2000

The Waltham Book of Clinical Nutrition of the Dog and Cat, 2nd Edition
edited by Josephine M. Wills and Kenneth W. Simpson
Butterworth-Heinemann Medical, 1994

Waltham Book of Companion Animal Nutrition
edited by I. H. Burger
Butterworth-Heinemann Medical, 1993

Pet Loss

Angel Pawprints: Reflections on Loving and Losing a Canine Companion
by Laurel E. Hunt
Hyperion Press, 2000

Because of Flowers and Dancers
by Sandra S. Brackenridge
Veterinary Practice Publishing, 1994*

Blessing the Bridge: What Animals Teach Us About Death, Dying, and Beyond
by Rita M. Reynolds
NewSage Press, 2001

Children and Pet Loss: A Guide for Helping
by Marty Tousley
Our Pals, 1996*

Cold Noses at the Pearly Gates
by Gary Kurz
Cold Noses, 1997

Coping with Sorrow on the Loss of Your Pet
by Moira Anderson
Alpine Publications Inc., 1996

Dog Heaven
by Cynthia Rylant
Scholastic Trade, 1995*

Goodbye, Friend: Healing Wisdom for Anyone Who
Has Ever Lost a Pet
by Gary Kowalski
Stillpoint Publishing, 1997

Good-bye My Friend: Tributes, Poems, Prose, and Other
Ways to Remember Your Pet
by Michele Lanci-Altomare
BowTie Press, 2000

Grieving the Death of a Pet
by Betty J. Carmack
Augsburg Fortress Publishers, 2003

It's Okay to Cry
by Maria Luz Quintana, et al.
K and K Communications, 1998

The Loss of a Pet
by Wallace Sife
Howell Book House, 1998

Pet Loss: A Thoughtful Guide for Adults and Children
by Herbert A. Nieburg
Harper Perennial, 1996

Preparing for the Loss of Your Pet
by M. Milani
Prima Publishing, 1998

Sometimes It Breaks Your Heart
by Dr. Richard Orzeck
Purrfect Love Publishing, 2000

When Only the Love Remains: The Pain of Pet Loss
by Emily Margaret Stuparyk
Hushion House Publishing Ltd., 2000

Purebred

Barron's Encyclopedia of Dog Breeds
by D. Caroline Coile, PhD
Barron's Educational Series, 1998

Choosing a Puppy: Finding Your Ideal Canine Mate
by Amy Fernandez
BowTie Press, 2009

The Complete Dog Book, 19th Edition Revised
by the American Kennel Club
Howell Book House, 1998

The Complete Encyclopedia of Dogs: Includes Caring for
Your Dog and Descriptions of Breeds from Around the
World
by Esther J. J. Verhoef-Verhallen
Book Sales, 2004

Dogs: The Ultimate Dictionary of Over 1,000 Breeds
by Desmond Morris
Trafalgar Square Publishing, 2002

The Encyclopedia of Dog Breeds
by Juliette Cunliffe
Parragon Publishing, 2001

The Illustrated Encyclopedia of Dog Breeds
by Joan Palmer
Book Sales, 1997

Legacy of the Dog: The Ultimate Illustrated Guide to
over 200 Dog Breeds
by Tetsu Yamazaki and Toyoharu Kojima
Chronicle Books, 1995

The New Encyclopedia of the Dog
by Bruce Fogle, DVM
DK Publishing, 2000

The Ultimate Encyclopedia of Dogs: Dog Breeds & Dog
Care
by Peter Larkin, DVM, and Mike Stockman
Lorenz Books, 2003

Your Purebred Puppy: A Buyer's Guide
by Michele Welton
Owl Books, 2000

Rescue and Welfare

A Century of Caring: A History of the Guelph Humane Society
by Bob Rutter
Evanston Publishing Inc., 1993

Canine Caper: Real Life Tales of a Female Pet Vigilante
by Rose Block and Delilah Ahrendt
New Horizon Press, 2001

The Humane Societies: A Voice for the Animals
by Shelley Sateren Silver
Burdett Press, 1996*

Man and Beast
by J. R. Helton
Abiqua Press Inc., 2001

One at a Time: A Week in an American Animal Shelter
by Diane Leigh and Marilee Geyer
No Voice Unheard, 2003

Out of Harm's Way: The Extraordinary True Story of One Woman's Lifelong Devotion to Animal Rescue
by Terri Crisp with Samantha Glen
Pocket Books, 1996

Purebred Rescue Dog Adoption: Rewards and Realities
by Liz Palika
Howell Book House, 2004

Rescue Me! Your Guide to Selecting, Adopting, and Caring for a Shelter or Rescue Dog
by Bardi McLennan
Kennel Club Books, 2007

Second Chances: More Tales of Found Dogs
by Elise Lufkin
The Lyons Press, 2003

Second Start: Creative Rehoming for Dogs
by Jacqueline O'Neil
Wiley Publishing Inc., 1997

Speaking out for Animals: True Stories About Real People Who Rescue Animals
edited by Kim W. Stallwood
Lantern Books, 2001

Successful Dog Adoption
by Sue Sternberg
Howell Book House, 2003

To the Rescue: Helping Homeless Purebred Dogs
by Barbara Curtiss
Writers Club Press, 2001

Purebred Rescue Dog Adoption: Rewards and Realities
by Liz Palika
Howell Book House, 2004

Training and Behavior

The ABCs of Positive Training: A Rewarding Approach for All Owners
by Miriam Fields-Babineau
Kennel Club Books, 2005

After You Get Your Puppy: The Clock is Ticking!
by Ian Dunbar, DVM
James and Kenneth Publishing, 2001

Aggression in Dogs: Practical Management, Prevention and Behaviour Modification
by Brenda Aloff
Dogwise Publishing, 2002

Ain't Misbehavin': The Groundbreaking Program for Happy, Well-Behaved Pets and Their People
by John C. Wright, PhD with Judi Wright Lashnits
Rodale Press, 2001

All Dogs Need Some Training
by Liz Palika
Howell Book House, 1997

American Kennel Club Dog Care and Training
by the American Kennel Club
Howell Book House, 2002

The Art of Raising a Puppy
by the Monks of New Skete
Little, Brown and Company, 1991

ASPCA Dog Training
by Bruce Fogle, DVM
DK Publishing Inc., 1999

Before You Get Your Puppy
by Ian Dunbar, DVM
James and Kenneth Publishing, 2001

Beginning Family Dog Training
by Patricia McConnell, PhD
Dog's Best Friend Ltd., 1996

Better Dog Behavior: Correcting and Curing Bad Habits
by Charlotte Schwartz
Kennel Club Books, 2004

Beyond Basic Dog Training
by Diane L. Bauman
Howell Book House, 2003

Bones Would Rain from the Sky: Deepening Our Relationships with Dogs
by Suzanne Clothier
Warner Books, 2002

The Canine Good Citizen: Every Dog Can Be One
by Jack Volhard and Wendy Volhard
Howell Book House, 1997

The Cautious Canine: How to Help Dogs Conquer Their Fears
by Patricia B. McConnell, PhD
Dog's Best Friend Ltd., 1998

Childproofing Your Dog: A Complete Guide to Preparing Your Dog for the Children in Your Life
by Brian Kilcommons and Sarah Wilson
Warner Books, 1994

Click for Joy! Questions and Answers from Clicker Trainers and Their Dogs
by Melissa C. Alexander
Sunshine Books, 2003

Clicker Fun: Dog Tricks and Games Using Positive Reinforcement
by Deborah Jones
Howln Moon Press, 1998

Clicker Training for Obedience: Shaping Top Performance—Positively
by Morgan Spector
Sunshine Books, 1999

The Clicker Workbook: A Beginner's Guide
by Deborah Jones, PhD
Howln Moon Press, 1999

Clicking With Your Dog: Step-by-Step in Pictures
by Peggy Tillman
Sunshine Books, 2001

The Complete Idiot's Guide to Positive Dog Training
by Pamela Dennison
Alpha Books, 2003

Crate Training Your Dog (A Storey Country Wisdom Bulletin)
by Pat Storer
Storey Books, 2000

Culture Clash: A Revolutionary New Way of Understanding the Relationship Between Humans and Domestic Dogs
by Jean Donaldson
James and Kenneth Publishing, 1997

Doctor Dunbar's Good Little Dog Book
by Ian Dunbar, DVM
James and Kenneth Publishing, 2003

Dog Behavior: An Owner's Guide to a Happy, Healthy Pet
by Ian Dunbar, DVM
Howell Book House, 1996

Dog-Friendly Dog Training
by Andrea Arden
Howell Book House, 1999

The Dog Listener: Learn How to Communicate with Your Dog for Willing Cooperation
by Jan Fennell
HarperResource, 2004

Dog Talk: Training Your Dog through a Canine Point of View
by John Ross and Barbara McKinney
St. Martin's Press, 1995

Dog Training: A Lifelong Guide: Top Trainers Share Their Secrets
by Arden Moore
BowTie Press, 2002

Dog Training for Dummies
by Jack Volhard and Wendy Volhard
Wiley Publishing Inc., 2001

Dog Training with a Head Halter
by Miriam Fields-Babineau
Barron's Educational Series, 2000

Dogperfect: The User Friendly Guide to a Well-Behaved Dog
by Sarah Hodgson
Wiley Publishing Inc., 1995

Dogs Are From Neptune
by Jean Donaldson
Lasar Multimedia Productions, 1998

Dogs on the Couch: Behavior Therapy for Training and Caring for Your Dog
by Larry Lachman and Frank Mickadeit
Overlook Press, 2002

Don't Shoot the Dog: The New Art of Teaching and Training
by Karen Pryor
Bantam Books, 1999

Feeling Outnumbered? How to Manage and Enjoy Your Multi-Dog Household
by Karen B. London, PhD, and Patricia B. McConnell, PhD
Dog's Best Friend Ltd., 2001

Feisty Fido: Help for the Leash Aggressive Dog
by Patricia B. McConnell, PhD, and Karen B. London, PhD
Dog's Best Friend Ltd., 2003

Finding a Balance: Issues of Power in the Human/Dog Relationship
by Suzanne Clothier
Flying Dog Press, 1996

Getting Started: Clicker Training for Dogs
by Karen Pryor
Sunshine Books, 2002

Good Dog! Simple Training for Successful Behavior
by Donna Chandler
Emmis Books, 2004

Good Owners, Great Dogs: A Training Manual for Humans and Their Canine Companions
by Brian Kilcommons and Sarah Wilson
Warner Books Inc., 1999

Help for Your Shy Dog: Turning Your Terrified Dog into a Terrific Pet
by Deborah Wood
Howell Book House, 1999

House-training Your Dog: A Practical Plan for Dogs of All Ages
by Charlotte Schwartz
Kennel Club Books, 2005

How Dogs Learn
by Mary R. Burch, PhD, and Jon S. Bailey, PhD
Howell Book House, 1999

How Dogs Think: Understanding the Canine Mind
by Stanley Coren
Free Press, 2004

How to Be the Leader of the Pack…And Have Your Dog Love You For It!
by Patricia B. McConnell, PhD
Dog's Best Friend Ltd., 1996

How to Be Your Dog's Best Friend
by the Monks of New Skete
Little, Brown and Company, 2002

How to Behave So Your Dog Behaves
by Sophia A. Yin
TFH Publications, 2004

How to Raise a Puppy You Can Live With
by Clarice Rutherford and David H. Neil
Alpine Publishing, 1999

How to Speak Dog: Mastering the Art of Dog-Human Communication
by Stanley Coren
Free Press, 2001

How to Teach a New Dog Old Tricks: Sirius Puppy Training
by Ian Dunbar, DVM
James and Kenneth Publishing, 1998

I'll Be Home Soon: How to Prevent and Treat Separation Anxiety
by Patricia B. McConnell, PhD
Dog's Best Friend Ltd., 2000

The Latchkey Dog: How the Way You Live Shapes the Behavior of the Dog You Love
by Jodi Andersen
HarperResource, 2002

Mine! A Guide to Resource Guarding in Dogs
by Jean Donaldson
Kinship Communications/San Francisco-SPCA, 2002

Mother Knows Best: The Natural Way to Train Your Dog
by Carol Lea Benjamin
Howell Book House, 2002

New Knowledge of Dog Behavior
by Clarence Pfaffenberger
Dogwise Publishing, 2001

101 Essential Tips: Training Your Dog
by Bruce Fogle, DVM
DK Publishing, 1997

The Only Dog Training Book You'll Ever Need: From Avoiding Accidents to Banishing Barking, the Basics for Raising a Well-Behaved Dog
by Gerilyn J. Bielakiewicz
Adams Media Corp., 2004

The Other End of the Leash: Why We Do What We Do Around Dogs
by Patricia B. McConnell, PhD
Ballantine Books, 2002

Positive Perspectives: Love Your Dog, Train Your Dog
by Pat B. Miller
Dogwise Publishing, 2003

Positive Puppy Training Works
by Joel Walton
David and James Publishers, 2002

The Power of Positive Dog Training
by Pat Miller
Howell Book House, 2001

The Puppy Pack: Making the Most of Puppy's First Year
by Sara John
BowTie Press, 2008

Puppy Preschool: Raising Your Puppy Right—Right from the Start!
by John Ross and Barbara McKinney
St. Martin's Press, 1996

Puppy Primer
by Brenda Scidmore and Patricia B. McConnell, PhD
Dog's Best Friend Ltd., 1996

Puppy School: Everything You Need to Know to Raise the Perfect Pup
by Maggie Holt and Stella Sweeting
Rodale Press, 2004

Puppy Training: Owner's Week-by-Week Training Guide
by Charlotte Schwartz
Kennel Club Books, 2003

Puppy Training: Raising a Well-Mannered Family Dog
by Miriam Fields-Babineau and Bardi McLennan
BowTie Press, 2009

Rover, Don't Roll Over: Compassionate Training Guide for Dogs and Their People
by Jody Rosengarten
Ten Speed Press, 2004

The Secret Lives of Dogs: The Real Reasons Behind 52 Mysterious Canine Behaviors
by Jana Murphy
Rodale Press, 2000

Shelby Marlo's New Art of Dog Training: Balancing Love and Discipline
by Shelby Marlo
McGraw-Hill/Contemporary Books, 2000

Smarter Than You Think: A Revolutionary Approach to Teaching and Understanding Your Dog in Just a Few Hours
by Paul Loeb and Suzanne Hlavacek
Pocket Books, 1998

So Your Dog's Not Lassie: Tips for Training Difficult Dogs and Independent Breeds
by Betty Fisher and Suzanne Delzio
HarperResource, 1998

Teaching Basic Obedience: Train the Owner, Train the Dog
by Alexandra Powe Allred
TFH Publications Inc., 2001

Training Your Mixed Breed
by Miriam Fields-Babineau
Kennel Club Books, 2005

Training Your Puppy in 5 Minutes: A Quick, Easy and Humane Approach
by Miriam Fields-Babineau
Kennel Club Books, 2005

Train Your Dog, Change Your Life: An Interactive Training Program for Individuals, Families, and Their Dogs
by Maureen Ross and Gary Ross
Wiley Publishing Inc., 2001

Training in No Time
by Amy Ammen
Howell Book House, 1995

25 Stupid Mistakes Dogs Owners Make
by Janine Adams
Gramercy Books, 2003

Understanding "Dog Mind": Guide to Bringing out the Best in Your Dog
by Bonnie Bergin
Little, Brown and Company, 2000

What Color Is Your Dog? Train Your Dog Based on His Personality "Color"
by Joel Silverman
Kennel Club Books, 2009

What is My Dog Thinking?: The Essential Guide to Understanding Pet Behavior
by Gwen Bailey
Thunder Bay Press, 2003

Why Dogs Do That: A Collection of Curious Canine Behaviors
by Tom Davis
Willow Creek Press, 1998

Travel

A Dog's World: True Stories of Man's Best Friend on the Road
edited by Christine Hunsicker
Travelers' Tales Guides, 1998

Cruising with Your Four-Footed Friends: The Basics of Boat Travel with Your Cat or Dog
by Diana Jessie
Seaworthy Publications, 2003

DogFriendly.com's United States and Canada Dog Travel Guide
by the Editors of DogFriendly.com
DogFriendly.com Inc., 2004

DogFriendly.com's California and Nevada Dog Travel Guide
by Tara Kain
DogFriendly.com Inc., 2004

Dog-Friendly New England: A Traveler's Companion
by Trisha Blanchet
Countryman Press, 2003

The Dog Lover's Companion Series
Avalon Travel Publishing:
- *The Dog Lover's Companion to Boston: The Inside Scoop on Where to Take Your Dog*
  by JoAnna Downey and Christian Lau, 2002
- *The Dog Lover's Companion to the Bay Area: The Inside Scoop on Where to Take Your Dog*
  by Maria Goodavage, 2002
- *The Dog Lover's Companion to Chicago: The Inside Scoop on Where to Take Your Dog*
  by Margaret Littman, 2003
- *The Dog Lover's Companion to California: The Inside Scoop on Where to Take Your Dog*
  by Maria Goodavage, 2002
- *The Dog Lover's Companion to Florida: The Inside Scoop on Where to Take Your Dog*
  by Sally Deneen and Robert McClure, 2001
- *The Dog Lover's Companion to New England: The Inside Scoop on Where to Take Your Dog*
  by JoAnna Downey and Christian Lau, 2004
- *The Dog Lover's Companion to New York City: The Inside Scoop on Where to Take Your Dog*
  by JoAnna Downey and Christian Lau, 2002
- *The Dog Lover's Companion to Seattle: The Inside Scoop on Where to Take Your Dog*
  by Steve Giordano, 2001
- *The Dog Lover's Companion to Washington D.C. and Baltimore: The Inside Scoop on Where to Take Your Dog*
  by Ann and Don Oldenburg, 2003

Doin' Arizona with Your Pooch!: Where to Stay, What to Do, and How to Do It
by Eileen Barish
Pet-Friendly Publications Inc., 1996

Doin' California with Your Pooch!: Thousands of Dog-Friendly Hikes and Hotels, Plus Travel and Training Tips
by Eileen Barish
Pet-Friendly Publications Inc., 2002

Doin' the Northwest with Your Pooch!: Thousands of Dog-Friendly Hikes and Hotels, Plus Travel and Training Tips
by Eileen Barish
Pet-Friendly Publications Inc., 2002

Doin' New York with Your Pooch!: Eileen's Directory of Dog-Friendly Lodging and Outdoor Recreation in New York State
by Eileen Barish
Pet-Friendly Publications, Inc. 1997

Fido's Finest: Traveling With Your Pet... In Style! Colorado Edition
by Bridgette K. Maxwell
1st Books Library, 2003

Fodor's Road Guide USA: Where to Stay with Your Pet
by Andrea Arden
Fodor's, 2001

Globetrotting Pets: An International Travel Guide
by David Forsythe
Island Publishing, 2003

Great Vacations for You and Your Dog Abroad
by Martin Management Books staff,
Martin Management Books, 1996

Great Vacations for You and Your Dog, USA, 2003-04
by Martin Management Books staff,
Martin Management Books, 2003

Mobil Travel Guide: On the Road with Your Pet
by the Editors of the Mobil Travel Guide
Mobil Travel Guide, 2004

The Pet Travel and Fun Authority of Best-of-State Places to Play, Stay & Have Fun along the Way
by M. E. Nelson
Annenberg Communications, 2001

Pets on the Go: The Definitive Pet Accommodation and Vacation Guide
by Dawn Habgood and Robert Habgood
Dawbert Press, 2002

Pets on the Go: Eastern United States
by Dawn Habgood and Robert Habgood
Dawbert Press, 2004

The Portable PetsWelcome.com: The Complete Guide to Traveling with Your Pet
by Fred N. Grayson and Chris Kingsley
Howell Book House, 2001

Traveling with Dogs (Basic Training, Caring & Understanding Library)
by Nona Kilgore Bauer
Chelsea House Publishers, 1998*

Traveling with Your Pet—The AAA Petbook
by Automobile Association of America
Automobile Association of America, 2003

Vacationing with Your Pet: Eileen's Directory of Pet-Friendly Lodging in the United States & Canada
by Eileen Barish
Pet-Friendly Publications, Inc., 2001

Working Dogs

Avalanche! Hasty Search: The Care and Training of the Avalanche Search and Rescue Dogs
by Patti Burnett
Doral Publishing, 2003

Bomb Detection Dogs (Dogs at Work Series)
by Charles George and Linda George
Capstone Press, 1998*

Companion Animals in Human Health
by Cindy Wilson and Dennis Turner
SAGE Publications, 1997

Creature Comfort: Animals That Heal
by Bernie Graham
Prometheus Books, 2000

Dog Heroes of September 11th: A Tribute to America's Search and Rescue Dogs
by Nona Kilgore Bauer
Kennel Club Books, 2006

Dog Heroes: Saving Lives and Protecting America
by Jen Bidner
The Lyons Press, 2002

DOGNY: America's Tribute to Search and Rescue Dogs
by the American Kennel Club
TFH Publications, 2002

Dogs with Jobs: Working Dogs Around the World
by Merrily Weisbord and Kim Kachanoff, DVM
Atria Books, 2000

Enthusiastic Tracking, The Step-by-Step Training Manual
by William R. Sanders
Rime Publications, 1998

Guide Dogs: From Puppies to Partners
by Diana Lawrenson
Allen and Unwin, 2002*

Guide to Search and Rescue Dogs
by Angela Eaton Snovak
Barron's Educational Series, 2004

Handbook on Animal-Assisted Therapy: Theoretical Foundations and Guidelines for Practice
by Aubrey Fine
Academic Press, 2000

The Healing Power of Pets: Harnessing the Ability of Pets to Make and Keep People Happy and Healthy
by Marty Becker
Hyperion Press, 2002

Helping Hounds: The Story of Assistance Dogs
by Allison Hornsby
Ringpress Books Ltd., 2000

Hero Dogs: Courageous Canines in Action
by Donna M. Jackson
Megan Tingley, 2003*

K9 Explosive Detection
by Ron Mistafa
Detselig Enterprises Ltd., 1998

K9 Scent Detection
by Jan Kaldenbach
Detselig Enterprises Ltd., 1998

K9 Schutzhund Training: A Manual For Tracking, Obedience and Protection
by Resi Gerritson and Ruud Haak
Detselig Enterprises Ltd., 2000

Love Heels: Tales from Canine Companions for Independence
by Patricia Dibsie
Yorkville Press, 2003

Police Dog Tactics
by Sandy Bryson
Detselig Enterprises Ltd., 2000

Ready! The Training of the Search and Rescue Dog
by Susan Bulanda
Doral Publishing, 1995

Scent and the Scenting Dog
by William G. Sjrotuck
Barkleigh Productions, Inc., 2000

Search and Rescue Dogs: Training the K-9 Hero
by American Rescue Dog Association
Howell Book House, 2002

Smoke Alarm Training for Your Dog
by Anders Hallgren
Hallwig Publishing, 2002

Teamwork: A Dog Training Manual for People With Disabilities
by Stewart Nordensson and Lydia Kelley
Top Dog Publications, 1997

Teamwork II: A Dog Training Manual for People With Disabilities (Service Exercises)
by Stewart Nordensson and Lydia Kelley
Top Dog Publications, 1998

Therapy Dogs: Training Your Dog to Help Others
by Kathy Diamond Davis
Dogwise Publishing, 2002

Therapy Pets: The Animal-Human Healing Partnership
by Jacqueline J. Crawford, Karen A. Pomerinke, and Donald W. Smith
Prometheus Books, 2003

Tracking Dog: Theory and Methods
by Glen R. Johnson
Barkleigh Productions, Inc., 1999

Wanted: Animal Volunteers
by Mary R. Burch
Howell Book House, 2002

Working as a Therapy Dog: Observations and Tips from an Experienced Therapy Dog
by Lorna Stanart
Hispen Books, 2003

Working Dogs
by Carrie Owens
Prima Lifestyles, 1999

Working Dogs: Tales from Animal Planet's K-9 to 5 World
by Colleen Needles, Kit Carlson, and Kim Levin
Discovery Books, 2000

Working Dogs: Training for Sheep and Cattle
by Colin Seis
Butterworth-Heinemann, 1995

Working Dogs: True Stories of Dogs and Their Handlers
by Kristin Mehus-Roe
BowTie Press, 2003

Organizations

Activities

Agility

Canine Performance Events, Inc.
P.O. Box 805
South Lyon, MI 48178
www.k9cpe.com

North American Dog Agility Council (NADAC)
11522 South Highway 3
Cataldo, ID 83810
www.nadac.com

United States Dog Agility Association, Inc. (USDAA)
P.O. Box 850955
Richardson, TX 75085-0955
(972) 487-2200, www.usdaa.com

Canine Freestyle

Canine Freestyle Federation
4207 Minton Drive
Fairfax, VA 22032
www.canine-freestyle.org

Musical Dog Sport Association
www.musicaldogsport.org

World Canine Freestyle Organization (WCFO)
P.O. Box 350122
Brooklyn, NY 11235-2525
(718) 332-8336
www.worldcaninefreestyle.org

Disc Dogs

Ashley Whippet Enterprises
PO Box 9435
Anaheim, CA 92812
(714) 488-1042 , www.ashleywhippet.com

International Disc Dog Handlers Association (IDDHA)
1690 Julius Bridge Road
Ballground, GA 30107
(770) 735-6200
www.iddha.com

Skyhoundz
1015C Collier Road
Atlanta, GA 30318
(404) 350-9343
www.skyhoundz.com

Earthdog

American Working Terrier Association (AWTA)
Ann Wendland, Secretary
15720 State Highway 16
Capay, CA 95607
(530) 796-2278
www.dirt-dog.com/awta

Jack Russell Terrier Club of America (JRTCA)
P.O. Box 4527
Lutherville, MD 21094-4527
(410) 561-3655
www.terrier.com

Flyball

North American Flyball Association
1400 West Devon Avenue, 512
Chicago, IL 60660
(800) 318-6312
www.flyball.org

General

Dog Scouts of America (DSA)
5068 Nestel Road E
St. Helen, MI 48656
(989) 389-2000
www.dogscouts.com; www.dogscouts.org

Herding

American Herding Breed Association (AHBA)
www.ahba-herding.org

American Tending Breeds Association (ATBA)
2318 Little Road
Perkiomenville, PA 18074
www.atba-herding.org

Australian Shepherd Club of America (ASCA)
P.O. Box 3790
Bryan, TX 77805-3790
(979) 778-1082
www.asca.org

United States Border Collie Handlers Association (USBCHA)
2915 Anderson Lane
Crawford, TX 76638
(254) 486-2500
www.usbcha.com

Hunting and Field Trials

Ames Plantation
P.O. Box 389
Grand Junction, TN 38039
(901) 878-1067
www.amesplantation.org

Bird Dog Foundation
P.O. Box 774
505 Highway 57 W
Grand Junction, TN 38039
(731) 764-2058
www.birddogfoundation.com

National Bird Hunters Association (NBHA)
P.O. Box 68
Winfield, AL 35594
(205) 487-3001; (800) 239-5464
www.nbhafuturity.com

National Shoot to Retrieve Association (NSTRA)
226 North Mill Street, 2
Plainfield, IN 46168
(317) 839-4059
www.nstra.org

North American Hunting Retriever Association (NAHRA)
P.O. Box 5159
Fredericksburg, VA 22403
(540) 899-7620
www.nahra.org

North American Versatile Hunting Dog Association
(NAVHDA)
PO Box 520
Arlington Heights, IL 60006
(847) 253-6488
www.navhda.org

United States Complete Shooting Dog Association
(USCSDA)
3329 Redlawn Road
Boydton, VA 23917
(434) 738-9757
www.uscomplete.org

Lure Coursing

American Sighthound Field Association (ASFA)
www.asfa.org

Obedience

Rally O
Association of Pet Dog Trainers (APDT)
(800) 738-3647
www.apdt.com/rallyo/index.htm

Sledding and Skijoring

International Federation of Sleddog Sports (IFSS)
3381 Troy Brett Trail
Duluth, MN 55803
(218) 525-4012
www.sleddogsport.com; www.sleddogsportdata.org

International Sled Dog Racing Association
(ISDRA)
22702 Rebel Road
Merrifield, MN 56465
(218) 765-4297
www.isdra.org

Schutzhund

Landesverband DVG America/DVG America
Sandi Purdy, Secretary
2101 South Westmoreland Road
Red Oak, TX 75154
(972) 617-2988
www.dvgamerica.com

United Schutzhund Clubs of America (USA)
3810 Paule Avenue
St. Louis, MO 63125-1718
(314) 638-9686
www.germanshepherddog.com

Boarding and Pet Sitting

American Boarding Kennel Association
(ABKA)
702 East Pikes Peak Avenue
Colorado Springs, CO 80909
(719) 667-1600
www.abka.com

National Association of Professional Pet Sitters (NAPPS)
17000 Commerce Parkway, Suite C
Mt. Laurel, NJ 08054
(856) 439-0324; (800) 296-7387
www.petsitters.org

Pet Sitters Associates, LLC
3520 McElroy Street
Eau Claire, WI 54701
(800) 872-2941 (access code 25); (715) 831-6004
www.petsitllc.com

Pet Sitters International
201 East King Street
King, NC 27021- 9161
(336) 983-9222
www.petsit.com

Careers

American Society of Animal Science (ASAS)
1111 North Dunlap Avenue
Savoy, IL 61874
(217) 356-9050
www.asas.org

Association of American Veterinary Medical Colleges (AAVMC)
1101 Vermont Avenue NW, Suite 301
Washington, DC 20005
(202) 371-9195
www.aavmc.org

Dog Writers Association of America c/o Pat Santi, Secretary
173 Union Road
Coatesville, PA 19320
(610) 384- 2436
www.dwaa.org

Humane Society University
Humane Society of the United States
2100 L Street, NW
Washington, D.C., 20037
(202) 452-1100
www.humanesocietyu.org

International Association of Canine Professionals
P.O. Box 560156
Montverde, FL 34756-0156
(407) 469-2008
www.dogpro.org

National Animal Control Association (NACA)
P.O. Box 480851
Kansas City, MO 64148
(913) 768-1319
www.nacanet.org

National Association for Humane and Environmental
Education (NAHEE)
67 Norwich Essex Turnpike
East Haddam, CT 06423-0362
(860) 434-8666
www.nahee.org

National Association of Veterinary Technicians in
America, Inc. (NAVTA)
P.O. Box 224
Battle Ground, IN 47920
(765) 742-2216
www.navta.net

World Wide Pet Industry Association (WWPIA)
135 West Lemon Avenue
Monrovia, CA 91016
(626) 447-2222; (800) 999-7295
www.wwpia.com

General

American Dog Owners Association, Inc. (ADOA)
1654 Columbia Turnpike
Castleton, NY 12033
(518) 477-8469
www.adoa.org

American Pet Association (APA)
P.O. Box 7172
Boulder, CO 80306
(800) 272-7387
www.apapets.com

Grooming

International Internet Groomers Alliance
www.groomers.net/iiga/

International Professional Groomers, Inc.
120 Turner Avenue
Elk Grove Village, IL 60007
(847) 758-1938
www.ipgcmg.org

International Society of Canine Cosmetologists
(ISCC)
2702 Covington Drive
Garland, TX 75040
(972) 414-9715
www.petstylist.com/ISCC/ISCCMain.htm

National Dog Groomers Association of America, Inc.
(NDGAA)
P.O. Box 101
Clark, PA 16113
(724) 962-2711
www.nationaldoggroomers.com

Health

Academy of Veterinary Homeopathy
P.O. Box 9280
Wilmington, DE 19809
(866) 652-1590
www.theavh.org

American Academy of Veterinary Acupuncture (AAVA)
66 Morris Avenue, Suite 2A
Springfield, NJ 07081
(973) 379-1100

American Animal Hospital Association (AAHA)
12575 West Bayaud Avenue
Lakewood, CO 80228
(303) 986-2800
www.aahanet.org

American Holistic Veterinary Medical Association (AHVMA)
2218 Old Emmorton Road
Bel Air, MD 21015
(410) 569-0795
www.ahvma.org

American Kennel Club Canine Health Foundation (CHF)
P.O. Box 37941
Raleigh, NC 27627-7941
(888) 682-9696
www.akcchf.org

American Veterinary Chiropractic Association
442154 East 140 Road
Bluejacket, OK 74333
(918) 784-2231
www.animalchiropractic.org

American Veterinary Dental College (AVDC)
University of Pennsylvania, VHUP 3113
3900 Delancey Street
Philadelphia, PA 19104-6043
(215) 573-8135
www.avdc.org

American Veterinary Medical Association (AVMA)
1931 North Meacham Road, Suite 100
Schaumburg, IL 60173-4360
(847) 925-8070
www.avma.org

American Veterinary Medical Foundation (AVMF)
1931 North Meacham Road, Suite 100
Schaumburg, IL 60173-4360
(800) 248-2862, ext. 4355
www.avmf.org

Canine Health Information Center (CHIC)
2300 East Nifong Boulevard
Columbia, MO 65201-3856
(573) 442-0418
www.caninehealthinfo.org

International Veterinary Acupuncture Society (IVAS)
P.O. Box 271395
Ft. Collins, CO 80527-1395
(970) 266-0666
www.ivas.org

Morris Animal Foundation
45 Inverness Drive E
Englewood, CO 80112
(800) 243-2345
www.morrisanimalfoundation.org

Orthopedic Foundation for Animals (OFFA)
2300 East Nifong Boulevard
Columbia, MO 65201-3856
(573) 442-0418
www.offa.org

SPAY USA
2261 Broadbridge Avenue
Stratford, CT 06614
(203) 377-1116
www.spayusa.org

Veterinary Medical Database
(including Canine Eye Registration Foundation (CERF))
Purdue University, CERF/Lynn Hall
625 Harrison Street
West Lafayette, IN 47907-2026
(765) 494-8179
www.vmdb.org

VetGen Veterinary Genetics Services
3728 Plaza Drive, Suite 1
Ann Arbor, MI 48108
(734) 669-8440
www.vetgen.com

Nutrition

Association of American Feed Control Officials, Inc.
P.O. Box 478
Oxford, IN 47971
(765) 385-1029
www.aafco.org

American College of Veterinary Nutrition
Dr. Wilbur Amand, Executive Director
6 North Pennell Road
Media, PA 19063
www.acvn.org

Pet Food Institute (PFI)
2025 M Street NW, Suite 800
Washington, D.C. 20036
(202) 367-1120
www.petfoodinstitute.org

U.S. Food and Drug Administration (FDA)
5600 Fishers Lane
Rockville, MD 20857
(888) 463-6332
www.fda.gov

Pet Loss

American Society for the Prevention of Cruelty to
Animals (ASPCA) Pet Loss Support Program
424 East 92nd Street
New York, NY 10128-6804
(212) 876-7700, ext. 4355, Pet Loss Hotline: (800) 946-4646
www.aspca.org

The Association for Pet Loss and Bereavement (APLB)
P.O. Box 106
Brooklyn, NY 11230
(718) 382-0690
www.aplb.org

Pet Loss Support Web Sites and Hotlines

ASPCA Pet Loss Hotline
(800) 946-4646
www.aspca.org

Chicago Veterinary Medical Association Hotline
(630) 325-1600

Colorado State University Pet Loss Support Hotline and Web Site
(970) 297-1242
www.argusinstitute.colostate.edu/grief.htm

Cornell University Pet Loss Support Hotline and Web Site:
(607) 253-3932
http://web.vet.cornell.edu/public/petloss/

Iowa State University Pet Loss Support Hotline and Web Site:
(888) 478-7574
www.vetmed.iastate.edu/animals/petloss

Michigan State University Pet Loss Support Hotline and
Web Site:
(517) 432-2696
cvm.msu.edu/petloss/index.htm

Ohio State University Pet Loss Support Hotline:
(614) 292-1823

Tufts University Pet Loss Support Hotline and Web Site:
(508) 839-7966
www.tufts.edu/vet/petloss

University of California, Davis Pet Loss Hotline and
Web Site
(530) 752-3602; (800) 565-1526
www.vetmed.ucdavis.edu/petloss.index.htm

University of Illinois Pet Loss Hotline and Web Site:
(217) 244-2273; (877) 394-2273
www.cvm.uiuc.edu/CARE

University of Minnesota Pet Loss Web Site:
www.petcare.umn.edu/Grief/Support_Services.htm

Virginia-Maryland Regional College of Veterinary
Medicine Pet Loss Hotline and Web Site:
(540) 231-8038
http://www.vetmed.vt.edu/Organization/Clinical/petloss/petloss.html

Washington State University Pet Loss Hotline and Web Site:
(509) 335-5704
www.vetmed.wsu.edu/plhl/home/index.asp

Registries

American Kennel Club (AKC)
260 Madison Avenue
New York, NY 10016
(212) 696-8200
www.akc.org

American Mixed Breed Obedience Registration (AMBOR)
179 Niblick Road, 113
Paso Robles, CA 93446
(805) 226-9275
www.amborusa.org

American Rare Breed Association (ARBA)
9921 Frank Tippett Road
Cheltenham, MD 20623
(301) 868-5718
www.arba.org

Fédération Cynologique Internationale (FCI)
13 Place Albert 1er
B-6530 Thuin, Belgium
(011) 327 1591238
www.fci.be

Mixed Breed Dog Clubs of America (MBDCA)
13884 State Route 104
Lucasville, OH 45648-8586
(740) 259-3941
www.mbdca.org

United Kennel Club (UKC)
100 East Kilgore Road
Kalamazoo, MI 49002-5584
(269) 343-9020
www.ukcdogs.com

Rescue and Welfare

American Humane Association
63 Inverness Drive E
Englewood, CO 80112
(800) 227-4645; (303) 792-9900
www.americanhumane.org

American Society for the Prevention of Cruelty to
Animals (ASPCA)
424 East 92nd Street
New York, NY 10128
(212) 876-7700
www.aspca.org

Animal Legal Defense Fund (ALDF)
127 Fourth Street
Petaluma, CA 94952
(707) 769-7771
www.aldf.org

Animal Protection Institute of America (API)
PO Box 22505
Sacramento, CA 95822
(916) 447-3085
www.api4animals.org

Animal Rights Coalition
P.O. Box 8750
Minneapolis, MN 55419
(612) 822-6161
www.animalrightscoalition.com

Animal Welfare Institute (AWI)
P.O. Box 3650
Washington, DC 20027
(703) 836-4300
www.awionline.org

Association of Veterinarians for Animal Rights
(AVAR)
P.O. Box 208
Davis, CA 95617-0208
(530) 759-8106
www.avar.org

Humane Society of the United States (HSUS)
2100 L Street, NW
Washington, DC 20037
(202) 452-1100
www.hsus.org

In Defense of Animals (IDA)
131 Camino Alto
Mill Valley, CA 94941
(415) 388-9641
www.idausa.org

People for the Ethical Treatment of Animals (PETA)
501 Front Street
Norfolk, VA 23510
(757) 622-PETA (7382)
www.peta.com

Psychologists for the Ethical Treatment of Animals
(PSYETA)
P.O. Box 1297
Washington Grove, MD 20880
(301) 963-4751
www.psyeta.org

Training and Behavior

American College of Veterinary Behaviorists
Department of Small Animal Medicine and Surgery
Texas A&M University
College Station, TX 77843-4474
(979) 845-2351
www.veterinarybehaviorists.org

American Temperament Test Society, Inc.
P.O. Box 4093
St. Louis, MO 63136
(314) 869-6103
www.atts.org

American Veterinary Society of Animal Behavior
c/o Steven Feldman, D.V.M.
1535 Rugby Circle
Thousand Oaks, CA 91360
www.avma.org/avsab

Animal Behavior Society
Indiana University
2611 East Tenth Street, Office 170
Bloomington, IN 47408
(812) 856-5541
www.animalbehavior.org

The Association of Pet Dog Trainers
(800) 738-3647
www.apdt.com

Canadian Association of Professional Pet Dog Trainers
P.O. Box 59011
Whitby, ON L1N 0A4 Canada
(877) SIT-STAY
www.cappdt.ca

Cornell University College of Veterinary Medicine
Animal Behavior Clinic
Ithaca, NY 14853-6401
(607) 253-3450
www.vet.cornell.edu/abc

Dumb Friends League
Animal Behavior Services
2080 South Quebec Street
Denver, CO 80231
(303) 696-4941; (877) 738-0217
www.ddfl.org

National Association of Dog Obedience Instructors
PMB 369
729 Grapevine Highway
Hurst, TX 76054-2085
www.nadoi.org

Purdue University School of Veterinary Medicine,
Veterinary Teaching Hospital
Animal Behavior Clinic
625 Harrison Street
West Lafayette, IN 47907-2026
(765) 494-1107
www.vet.purdue.edu/animalbehavior/index.htm

University of California—Davis, School of Veterinary
Medicine
Behavior Service
One Shields Avenue
Davis, CA 95616
(530) 752-1393
www.vmth.ucdavis.edu

Washington State University College of Veterinary
Medicine
Veterinary Behavior Service
P.O. Box 6470
Pullman, WA 99164-7060
(509) 335-0711
www.vetmed.wsu.edu/depts-behavior/index.asp

Travel
Animal Transportation Association (ATA)
111 East Loop N
Houston, TX 77029
(713) 532-2177
www.aata-animaltransport.org

Companion Air Corporation
1640 Grand Oak Way
Wellington, FL 33414
(561) 615-1120
www.companionair.com

Fido Friendly Travel Club (includes magazine subscription)
P.O. Box 91836
Long Beach, CA 90809
(888) 881-5861
www.fidofriendlytravelclub.com

Independent Pet and Animal Transportation Association
International, Inc. (IPATA)
745 Winding Trail
Holly Lake Ranch, TX 75755
(903) 769-2267
www.ipata.com

International Air Transport Association (IATA)
800 Place Victoria
PO Box 113
Montreal Quebec H4Z1M1
(800) 716-6326
www.iata.org

Working Dogs

Assistance Dogs International
P.O. Box 5174
Santa Rosa, CA 95402
www.adionline.org

Canine Companions for Independence
2965 Dutton Avenue
Santa Rosa, 95407
(800) 572-2275
www.caninecompanions.org; www.cci.org

Canine Search and Recovery, Inc. (CSAR)
2120 County Road 323
Palmyra, MO 63461
(573) 769-2782
www.csar.org

Delta Society
875 124th Avenue NE, Suite 101
Bellevue, WA 98005-2531
(425) 226-7357
www.deltasociety.org

Dogs for the Deaf
10175 Wheeler Road
Central Point, OR 97502
(541) 826-9220 V/TDD; (800) 990-3647
www.dogsforthedeaf.org

Guide Dogs of America
13445 Glenoaks Boulevard
Sylmar, CA 91342
(818) 362-5834; (800) 459-4843
www.guidedogsofamerica.org

International Association of Assistance Dog Partners (IAADP)
38691 Filly Drive
Sterling Heights, MI 48310
(586) 826-3938
www.iaadp.org

International Guide Dog Federation
Hillfields, Burghfield Common
Reading, United Kingdom RG7 3YG
44-118-983-1990
www.ifgdsb.org.uk

National Association for Search and Rescue (NASAR)
4500 Southgate Place, Suite 100
Chantilly, VA 20151
(703) 222-6277
www.nasar.org

National Education of Assistance Dogs Service (NEADS)
P.O. Box 213
West Boylston, MA 01583
(978) 422-9064
www.neads.org

National Narcotic Detector Dog Association (NNDDA)
379 Country Road 105
Carthage, TX 75633
(888) 289-0070 (no late calls as this is a number to a private home)
www.nndda.org;
www.nndda.com

North American Police Work Dog Association (NAPWDA)
4222 Manchester Avenue
Perry, OH 44081
(888)-4CANINE
www.napwda.com

Paws with a Cause
National Headquarters
4646 South Division
Wayland, MI 49348
(616) 877-PAWS; (800) 253-PAWS
www.pawswithacause.org

The Seeing Eye, Inc.
P.O. Box 375
Morristown, NJ 07693-0375
(973) 539-4425
www.seeingeye.org

Therapy Dogs International, Inc. (TDI)
88 Bartley Road
Flanders, NJ 07836
(973) 252-9800
www.tdi-dog.org

United States Police Canine Association (USPCA)
P.O. Box 80
Springboro, OH 45066
(800) 531-1614
www.uspcak9.com

U. S. War Dogs Association, Inc.
1313 Mt. Holly Road
Burlington, NJ 08016
(609) 747-9340
www.uswardogs.org

Vietnam Dog Handler Association
www.vdhaonline.org

Periodicals

Activities
Agility
Agility Action On-line Magazine
219 Deanna Place
Windsor, CA 95492
(707) 838-3265
www.agilityaction.com

Clean Run Magazine
35 North Chicopee Street
Chicopee, MA 01020
(800) 311-6503
www.cleanrun.com

Training for Agility
Popular Dogs Series
P.O. Box 6050
Mission Viejo, CA 92690-6050
(888) 644-8387
www.animalnetwork.com

General
Athletic and Working Dog Newsletter
1550 Opelika Road,
Suite 6115
Auburn, AL 36830
http://sportsvet.com

Dog & Handler
234 Butternut Hill Road
Guilford, VT 05301
(802) 254-1209
www.dogandhandler.com

Front and Finish magazine
P.O. Box 333
Galesburg, IL 61402-0333
(309) 344-1333
www.frontandfinish.com

Tricks and Games
Popular Dogs Series
P.O. Box 6050
Mission Viejo, CA 92690-6050
(888) 644-8387
www.animalnetwork.com

Herding
American Border Collie Magazine
218 Stagecoach Lane
Crawford, TX 76638
(434) 263-5550
www.americanbordercolliemagazine.com

The National Stock Dog Magazine
P.O. Box 402
Butler, IN 46721
(260) 868-2670
www.nationalstockdog.com

Stockdogs
P.O. Box 995
Mancos, CO 81328
(970) 533-1375
www.stockdogsmagazine.com

The Working Border Collie
14933 Kirkwood Road
Sidney, OH 45365
(937) 492-2215
www.working-border-collie.com

Hunting
American Field, the Sportsman's Journal
542 South Dearborn Street,
Suite 1350
Chicago, IL 60605
(312) 663-9797
www.americanfield.com

Bird Dog and Retriever News
563 17th Avenue NW
New Brighton, MN 55112
(651) 636-8045; (612) 868-9169
www.bird-dog-news.com

Coonhound Bloodlines
100 East Kilgore Road
Kalamazoo, MI 49002-5584
(269) 343-9020
www.ukcdogs.com

Field Trial Magazine
P.O. Box 298
Milan, NH 03588
(800) 615-8392
www.fielddog.com/ftm

Gun Dog
6420 Wilshire Blvd
Los Angeles, CA 90040
(800) 800-7724
www.primediainc.com

Hunting Retriever
100 East Kilgore Road
Kalamazoo, MI 49002-5584
(269) 343-9020
www.ukcdogs.com

North American Versatile Hunting Dog
116 West Eastman,
Suite 204
Arlington Heights, IL 60004-5914
(847) 253-6488
www.navhda.com

Pointing Dog Journal
P.O. Box 509
Traverse City, MI 49685
(800) 447-7367
www.pointingdogjournal.com

Retriever Journal
P.O. Box 509
Traverse City, MI 49685
(800) 447-7367
www.retrieverjournal.com

Retrievers Online magazine
1457 Heights Road, Rural Route 3
Lindsay, Ontario, K9V 4R3
Canada
(705) 793-3556
www.retrieversonline.com

Lure Coursing
Sighthound Review
10177 Blue River Hills Road
Manhattan, KS 66503
(785) 485-2992
www.sighthoundreview.com

Obedience
Training for Obedience
Popular Dogs Series
P.O. Box 6050
Mission Viejo, CA 92690-6050
(888) 644-8387
www.animalnetwork.com

Sledding
Mushing
P.O. Box 149-NET
Ester, AK 99725-0149
(907) 479-0454
www.mushing.com

Careers
APDT Chronicle of the Dog newsletter
Association of Pet Dog Trainers
5096 Sand Road SE
Iowa City, IA 52240-8217
1-800-738-3647
www.apdt.com

Groomers Voice
National Dog Groomers Association of America, Inc.
P.O. Box 101
Clark, PA 16113
(724) 962-2711
www.nationaldoggroomers.com

International Association of Canine Professionals Newsletter
P.O. Box 560156
Montverde, FL 34756-0156
(407) 469-2008
www.dogpro.org

JAVMA: Journal of the American Veterinary Medical Association
1931 North Meacham Road, Suite 100
Schaumburg, IL 60173-4360
(847) 925-8070
www.avma.org

The NAVTA Journal
National Association of Veterinary Technicians in
America, Inc.
P.O. Box 224
Battle Ground, IN 47920
(765) 742-2216
www.navta.net

Veterinary Economics
8033 Flint Street
Lenexa, KS 66214
(800) 346-0085
www.vetmedpub.com

Veterinary Medicine
8033 Flint Street
Lenexa, KS 66214
(800) 346-0085
www.vetmedpub.com

General

Animal Fair
545 8th Avenue, Suite 401
New York, NY 10018
(212) 629-0392
www.animalfair.com

Bark
2810 Eighth Street
Berkeley, CA 94710
(877) 227-5639
www.thebark.com

Dog Fancy
P.O. Box 6050
Mission Viejo, CA 92690-6050
(888) 644-8387
www.animalnetwork.com

Dog & Kennel
7 Dundas Circle,
Suite L
Greensboro, NC 27407
(336) 292-4047
www.dogandkennel.com

Dog World
P.O. Box 6050
Mission Viejo, CA 92690-6050
(888) 644-8387
www.animalnetwork.com

Dogs for Kids*
P.O. Box 6050
Mission Viejo, CA 92690-6050
(888) 644-8387
www.animalnetwork.com

Dogs' Life: The Magazine for Today's Dog
311 Jethro Lane
Yorktown, VA 23692
(757) 833-7411
www.riverbankpress.com

Good Dog! On-line Consumer Magazine for Dog Owners
William Becker
P.O. Box 7076
Huntington Woods, MI 48070
(480) 503-3001
www.gooddogmagazine.com

Modern Dog
1941 Whyte Avenue
Vancouver, BC, Canada V6J1B4
Canada
(604) 734-3131
www.moderndog.ca

Puppies USA
P.O. Box 6050
Mission Viejo, CA 92690-6050
(888) 644-8387
www.animalnetwork.com

Health

Dog Watch
P.O. Box 420235
Palm Coast, FL 32142-0235
(800) 829-5574
www.vet.cornell.edu/publicresources/dog.htm

Pet Health Newspage electronic newsletter
Kansas State University, Media Relations and Marketing
9 Anderson Hall
Manhattan, KS 66506-0117
(785) 532-6415
www.mediarelations.ksu.edu/WEB/News/NewsReleases/
pethealth.html

Whole Dog Journal
P.O. Box 420234
Palm Coast, FL 32142-0234
(800) 829-9165
www.whole-dog-journal.com

Your Dog
PO Box 420235
Palm Coast, FL 32142-0235
(800) 829-5116
www.tufts.edu/vet/publications/yourdog

Pet Loss

Association for Pet Loss and Bereavement Quarterly Newsletter
P.O. Box 106
Brooklyn, NY 11230
(718) 382-0690
www.aplb.org

Pet Sitting

World of Professional Pet Sitting: Annual Pet Owner's Issue
Pet Sitters International
201 East King Street
King, NC 27021-9161
(336) 983-9222
www.petsit.com

Purebred

AKC Family Dog
260 Madison Avenue
New York, NY 10016
(212) 696-8200
www.akc.org

AKC Gazette
260 Madison Avenue
New York, NY 10016
(212) 696-8200
www.akc.org

Bloodlines
100 East Kilgore Road
Kalamazoo, MI 49002-5584
(269) 343-9020
www.ukcdogs.com

The Canine Chronicle Online
4727 NW 80th Avenue
Ocala, FL 34482
(352) 369-1104
www.caninechronicle.com

Dogs In Review
P.O. Box 6050
Mission Viejo, CA 92690-6050
(888) 644-8387
www.animalnetwork.com

Dog News
1115 Broadway
New York, NY 10010
(212) 462-9588
www.dognews.com

Dogs USA
P.O. Box 6050
Mission Viejo, CA 92690-6050
(888) 644-8387
www.animalnetwork.com

Hoflin Dog Breed Magazines
4401 Zephyr Street
Wheat Ridge, CO 80033
(303) 420-2222
www.hoflin.com

Just Labs
P.O. Box 968
Traverse City, MI 49685
(800) 447-7367
www.justlabsmagazine.com www.villagepress/justlabs.com

Popular Dog Series
P.O. Box 6050
Mission Viejo, CA 92690-6050
(888) 644-8387
www.animalnetwork.com

Rescue and Welfare

All Animals, The Humane Society of the United States
2100 L Street, NW
Washington, DC 20037
(301) 548-7722
www.animalsheltering.com

Animal Sheltering Magazine
The Humane Society of the United States
2100 L Street, NW
Washington, DC 20037
(301) 548-7722
www.animalsheltering.com

ASPCA Animal Watch
American Society for the Prevention of Cruelty to Animals
424 East 92nd Street
New York, NY 10128-6804
(212) 876-7700
www.aspca.org

ASPCA News Alert on-line newsletter
American Society for the Prevention of Cruelty to Animals
424 East 92nd Street
New York, NY 10128-6804
(212) 876-7700
www.aspca.org

Protecting Animals
American Humane Association
63 Inverness Drive E
Englewood, CO 80112
(303) 792-9900
www.americanhumane.org

Training and Behavior

Clicker Journal
39233 Fox Hill Road
Leesburg, VA 20175
www.clickertrain.com

Clicker Training
Popular Dogs Series
P.O. Box 6050
Mission Viejo, CA 92690-6050
(888) 644-8387
www.animalnetwork.com

Off-Lead & Natural Pet Magazine
6 State Road 113
Mechanicsburg, PA 17050
(717) 691-3388
www.off-lead.com

Pet Behavior Newsletter
P.O. Box 1658
Grants Pass, OR 97526
(541) 476-5775
www.webtrail.com/petbehavior/pbnews.html

Training and Behavior
Popular Dogs Series
P.O. Box 6050
Mission Viejo, CA 92690-6050
(888) 644-8387
www.animalnetwork.com

Training Your Puppy
Popular Dogs Series
P.O. Box 6050
Mission Viejo, CA 92690-6050
(888) 644-8387
www.animalnetwork.com

Travel

DogGone Newsletter (online)
P.O. Box 1846
Boulder, CO 80517
(303) 449-2527; (888) DOGTRAVEL
www.doggonefun.com

Fido Friendly magazine
P.O. Box 91836
Long Beach, CA 90809
(888) 881-5861
www.fidofriendly.com

Working Dogs

Athletic and Working Dog Newsletter
1550 Opelika Road, Suite 6115
Auburn, AL 36830
www.sportsvet.com

Video and Audio

Note: Starred (*) items are deemed suitable for children.

Activities

Agility

Competitive Agility Training with Jane Simmons-Moake: Vol.1 —Obstacles
Canine Training Systems, 1998, VHS

Competitive Agility Training with Jane Simmons-Moake: Vol.2 —Sequence Training
Canine Training Systems, 1998, VHS

Competitive Agility Training with Jane Simmons-Moake: Vol.3 —Advanced Skills
Canine Training Systems, 1998, VHS

Jump into Agility: AKC Agility Program Video
American Kennel Club, 2000, VHS

Training Your Agility Dog, with Peter Lewis
Leerburg Video & Kennel, VHS/DVD

Canine Freestyle

Dancing With Your Dog 1: Getting Started
Dancing Dogs Video, 1997, VHS

Dancing With Your Dog 2: Getting the Rhythm
Dancing Dogs Video, 1997, VHS

Dancing With Your Dog 3: Getting Applause
Dancing Dogs Video, 1997, VHS

Disc Dog

Dog, Disc, and Wind
Glen Speckert, 1997, CD-Rom

Frisbee Dogs: Throwing Video
PRB and Associates, Skyhoundz, 1996, VHS

Frisbee Dogs: Training Video
PRB and Associates, Skyhoundz, 1995, VHS

Earthdog

Gone to Ground: Jack Russell Terrier Video
Canine Training Systems, 1997, VHS/DVD

Flyball

Spring Loaded's Expert Flyball Training Series, Vol. 1: Foundations of Puppy Training with Lee and Angie Heighton
Blended Planet Productions, 2003, VHS and DVD

Spring Loaded's Expert Flyball Training Series, Vol. 2: Introduction to the Jumps and Box with Team Spring Loaded
Blended Planet Productions, 2003, VHS and DVD

Herding

Herding I: Overview
Canine Training Systems, 1989, VHS

Herding II: Young Dogs
Canine Training Systems, 1989, VHS

Herding III: Penning and Shedding
Canine Training Systems, 1989, VHS

Hunting

Game Dog
Mid-Carolina Media, 2002, VHS/DVD

Gun Dog
Mid-Carolina Media, 2002, VHS/DVD

Water Dog
Mid-Carolina Media, 2002, VHS/DVD

Obedience

Obedience Without Conflict, Tape 1: Clear Communication
Canine Training Systems, 2002, VHS & DVD

Obedience Without Conflict, Tape 2: The Game
Canine Training Systems, 2003, VHS & DVD

The Foundations of Competitive Obedience, Tape 1: Basic Skills
Canine Training Systems, 1997, VHS

The Foundations of Competitive Obedience, Tape 2: Teaching Precision
Canine Training Systems, 1997, VHS

Schutzhund

Handler Training for a Schutzhund I Trial
Leerburg Video and Kennel, VHS/DVD

Schutzhund Overview
Canine Training Systems, VHS

Schutzhund the Dog Sport
Leerburg Video and Kennel, 2003, VHS

Tracking

*The Foundations of Competitive Tracking,
Audio Tapes 1 and 2*
Canine Training Systems, 1999, VHS

General

All by Myself: Taking Care of My Pet *
BigKids Productions, 2003, VHS

*Dog Care Guide: Professional Advice for a Happier,
Healthier, Loving Dog*
Warner Home Video, 1997, VHS

Dog's Best Friend: They Really Like Us
WGBH Boston Video, 1995, VHS

Eyewitness Dog
Dorling Kindersley, 1995, VHS

It's A Dog's Life: Puppy's First Year
Bonneville Video, 1998, VHS

Wagging Tails: Dog and Puppy Music
New Market Sales, 1996, VHS

Grooming

Dog Grooming: The How-To Video Guide
Media Consultants, 1994, VHS

*Doggie Cuts: A Complete Step-by-Step Guide to
Cutting and Grooming Your Own Dog's Hair at Home*
The Kevin Martin Corporation, 1996, VHS/DVD

Grooming Your Dog: Basic Haircuts
MJM/A.R.T. Productions, 2002, VHS

In-Home Grooming: Long Coat Dogs
Increase Video, 1997, VHS

Show Off Your Dog: Grooming Basics
A.R.T. Productions, 1997, VHS

Health

*Ask Dr. Jim About Dogs: A Video Guide to the Most
Common Questions About Dog*
Tapeworm, 1998, VHS

*Bodywork for Dogs—Connecting Through Massage,
Acupressure and Intuitive Touch*
Animals Healing, Inc., 2002, VHS

Caring for a Handicapped Pet: A Holistic Approach
Sheba the Quad Dog Productions, 2002, VHS/DVD

Pet Emergency First Aid: Dogs
Apogee Entertainment, 1998, VHS

Massage Your Dog the Lang Way: Volumes 1 and 2
The Lang Institute for Canine Health, VHS

The Tellington TTouch for Happier, Healthier Dogs
Walt Disney Home Video, 1992, VHS

Pet Loss

Journey Through Pet Loss
by Deborah Antinori
YokoSpirit Publishing, 2000, audio book

*Legacies of Love: A Gentle Guide to Healing from the
Loss of Your Animal Loved One*
by Teresa Wagner
Matters of the Heart Publishing, 1998, audio book

Purebred

*American Kennel Club Breed Identification Boxed Set
(seven videos divided by AKC breed groups)*
American Kennel Club, VHS

American Kennel Club Video Series: Breed Standards Videos
American Kennel Club, VHS

The Right Companion: The DVD Guide to Dog Breeds
Jason Video Inc., 2004, DVD

Rescue and Welfare

Breaking the Cycles of Violence
The Latham Foundation, 2004, VHS

Shelter Dogs
Red Hen Productions, Inc., 2003, VHS/DVD

Training and Behavior

Beginners Guide to Dog Care and Training
American Kennel Club, 2003, VHS

Brian Donovan's The Nipping, Chewing, Digging, Garbage Raiding, Won't Come when Called Dog Training System, Part I
Dog Star Productions, 1998, VHS

Bringing Up Puppy with Uncle Matty
WGBH Boston, 2000, VHS

Calming Signals: What Your Dog Tells You Video
Hanalei Pets, 2000, VHS

Canine Behavior Program: Body Postures and Evaluating Behavioral Health
Animal Care Training, 2000, VHS

Canine Courtesy, Step-by-Step Solutions for Training Your Dog
American Production, 1997, VHS

Click & Fix
Canine Training Systems, 1999, VHS

Click & Go
Canine Training Systems, 1999, VHS

Clicker Magic
Sunshine Books, 1997, VHS

Dog Aggression: Biting
James and Kenneth Publishing, 1998, VHS

Dog Aggression: Fighting
James and Kenneth Publishing, 1998, VHS

Dog Obedience: Expert Advice for Easy Training and Care
Northstar Entertainment, 1999, VHS

Dog Training for Children*
James and Kenneth Publishing, 1996, VHS

Family Dog
Mid-Carolina Media, 2002, VHS

Gentle Leader Step by Step Training
Premier Pet Products, 1998, VHS

The How of Bow Wow: Building, Proofing and Polishing Behaviors
Take a Bow... Wow!, 2003, VHS,

Paw-sitive Dog Training
Goldenbrook Kennels, 1998, VHS

Puppy Love: Raise Your Dog the Clicker Way
Sunshine Books, 1999, VHS

Puppy Smarts: Lessons for a Lifetime
PuppySmarts, 2003, VHS/DVD/CD

Raising Your Dogs with the Monks of New Skete Three-Volume Video Set
One Leg Up Productions, 1996, VHS

Smart Training: Basic Obedience for the Companion Dog
Triple Crown Dog Academy, 2000, VHS

The TTouch for Dogs and Puppies
Goldhil Home Media, 1999, VHS

The Third Way 4-Video Set
Third Way Publications, 1999, VHS

Tips on Training
American Kennel Club, VHS

Train Your Dog
Picture Palace, Inc., 2003, DVD

Training Dogs with Dunbar
James and Kenneth Publishing, 1996, VHS

Training Dogs with John Fisher
Hyperactive Films, Ltd., 1995, VHS

Training that Works for Your Dog, with April Frost
Increase Video, 1995, VHS

Training the Dog in the Human Pack
Hyperactive Films Ltd., 1995, VHS

Uncle Matty's Guide to Doggy Problems
WGBH Boston, 1999, VHS

Unleash Your Dog's Potential
Trafalgar Square, 2001, VHS

Woof! A Guide to Dog Training
WGBH Boston, 1998, VHS

Woof! It's A Dog's Life Series*
WGBH Boston, 1999, VHS

Working Dogs
Partners in Independence
International Association of Assistance Dogs Partners, 2001, VHS

Pets Helping People, Video and Manual
Delta Society, 1999, VHS

Teamwork for People with Disabilities
Top Dog, 2003, VHS

Training Narcotics Detection Dogs
Leerburg Video and Kennel, VHS/DVD

Training Police Service Dogs
Leerburg Video and Kennel, 2002, VHS/DVD

Training Police Tracking Dogs (Tracking Through Drive)
Leerburg Video and Kennel, VHS/DVD

Web Sites

Activities

Agility
www.agilityability.com: Agility Ability: Dog Agility Central; Comprehensive agility information site

www.agilitynet.com: AgilityNet; UK agility site

Disc Dog
www.discdogezine.com: Disc DogEzine; Quarterly e-zine for disc dog enthusiasts

Earthdog
www.dirt-dog.com: Dirt-Dog.com; Links to articles and information on earthdogs, lure coursing clubs; especially focused on Jack Russell Terriers

Flyball
www.flyball.com: Flyball; Web ring for flyball enthusiasts
www.flyballdogs.com: Flyball Home Page; Flyball information and products. Online portal for the North American Flyball Association (NAFA)

www.i-flyball.com: i-Flyball; Information about flyball

General
www.dog-play.com: Dog-Play: Activities for Dogs; Web site with information on various dog sports and activities

www.dogpatch.org: The Dogpatch; Information on activities including disc dogs, herding, and obedience; links to other canine sites

Herding
www.geocities.com/Heartland/Ranch/5093: German Shepherd Dogs in Herding; Training and historical information on German Shepherd Dogs in herding

www.glassportal.com/herding: Herding on the Web; Portal to herding information, resources, and training tips

www.stockdog.com: The Stockdog Server; Information on working stock dogs and competition

Hunting and Field Trials
www.americanfield.com: American Field: The Sportsman's Journal; Lists bird dog field trials throughout the country

www.coonhounds.com: Coonhound Central; Types of coonhounds and their hunting uses

www.dogtrial.com: Dogtrial.com; Field trial results and calendar; information on pointing dog field trials

www.fielddog.com: Fielddog.com; Field trial and bird dog hunting resources

www.fieldtrialnews.com: Field Trial News; Information on field trials, hunt tests, and shows, sponsored by pointing dog clubs

www.pointingdog.com: Pointingdog.com; Site about pointing dogs

www.treehound.com: Tree Hound; Site with hound breed definitions, info on other hunting breeds, hound terms, and the sound of hounds when they have treed their quarry

www.uplandbirddog.com: UplandBirdDog.com: Information for Bird Dog and Hunting Enthusiasts; Bird dog training site

www.versatiledogs.com: Versatile Dogs: Dedicated to Pointing Dogs, Retrievers, and Spaniels; Training information and message board for sporting dog enthusiasts

Lure Coursing
www.sighthounds.com: Sighthounds.com; Lure coursing information, events, clubs, and links

Schutzhund

home1.gte.net/exec/SCHH.htm: Schutzhund Web ring; a collection of sites with information, pictures, and event information related to schutzhund

www.finographics.com/schutzhund: Schutzhund: Schutzhund Training; Collection of articles about schutzhund

www.schutzhund.com: Schutzhund.com: The Voice of the Dog Sports Fan; Membership site for schutzhund enthusiasts

www.uniteddobermanclub.com/schutz.htm: United Doberman Club: The Sport of Schutzhund; Background, competition, and training information on schutzhund

Sledding and Skijoring

www.dogsled.com: Dogsled.com; Sled dog racing site includes articles on the sport and prominent mushers, upcoming events, and recent results

www.iditarod.com: Iditarod Trail Sled Dog Race; Official site of the Iditarod sled dog race with general information and race updates

www.skijornow.com: Skijor Now; The Skijorer's Source; Training tips and products for skijoring

www.sleddogcentral.com: Sled Dog Central; Online sled dog advertising and information source

General

www.thedogpark.com: The Dog Park; Web site with dog park information and directories to other pet care services

www.petplace.com: Petplace.com; Information on caring for dogs and other pets

www.dogwise.com/forums: Dogwise; Behavior, training, obedience, health, nutrition, and general dog information

www.dogforum.info: Dog Forum: The Dog Info Site; Information related to canine health, training, and breeds

www.canismajor.com/dog: Dog Owner's Guide; Online magazine with links to hundreds of Web sites and articles on a wide variety of dog-related topics

www.cyberpet.com/cyberdog: Cyber Pet: Dog Mission Central; Articles, dog photos, and links

www.digitaldog.com: DigitalDog; Dog tales, breed info, and training tips

www.dog.com: Dog.com: A Dog's Best Friend; Search engine for thousands of canine-related sites

www.dogchannel.com: Dog Fancy Magazine online; General dog information

www.doginfomat.com: The Dog Infomat; Provides links to dog health, behavior, and general information

www.doglogic.com: DogLogic; Articles and links to canine Web sites for all breeds

www.dogomania.com: Dogomania; Dog-related search engine and database for FCI, UKC, AKC, and KC standards for all breeds; dog registries for nearly 600 dog breeds

www.happyandhealthypets.com: Happy and Healthy Pets; E-zine providing information and articles for pet owners

www.kidsanddogs.bravepages.com: How to Love Your Dog; Child-oriented guide to dog care

www.newpet.com: Newpet; Offers tips for new or prospective dog owners

www.srdogs.com: The Senior Dogs Project; Offers tips on healthcare and general information on living with older dogs

Grooming

www.bathing-a-dog.com: Bathing a Dog; Provides tips for bathing your dog

www.breedneeds.com: Breed Needs; Advice on grooming and grooming tools for different breeds

www.dogparlor.com: DogParlor; Professional dog grooming site offering grooming information and other articles of interest about dogs

www.findagroomer.com: Find a Groomer Directory for Pet Owners; Directory of pet groomers throughout the U.S.

www.groomers.com: The Groomers Lounge; Professional dog groomers' site with "Ask the Groomer" section

www.groomteamusa.com: Groom Team U.S.A., Inc.; A nonprofit organization that encourages pet stylists to improve their skills and offers the opportunity for professional stylists to represent the U.S. at World Team Competitions

www.petgroomer.com: PetGroomer.com: Where Pet Grooming is Everything; Resource site for professional pet groomers and those interested in the profession

n.webring.com/hub?ring=petgroom: Pet Groomers; Web ring offering links to pages of professional dog groomers and grooming information

Health

www.altvetmed.com: Alt Vet Med; Information on complementary and alternative treatments in veterinary medicine

www.ani-med.com: AniMed Pet Care Information; Pet health information tips sponsored by the ASPCA

www.animalhealthchannel.com: Animal Health Channel; Pet health and behavior information and online health videos

www.belfield.com/home.html: Your Animal's Health; Online natural pet health magazine

www.caninesincrisis.org: Canines in Crisis: People for Pets Exchange; Discussion and information site for owners of dogs with cancer and various other diseases

www.fda.gov/cvm/default.html: Center for Veterinary Medicine; Information and news from the U.S. Food and Drug Administration

www.goodnewsforpets.com: GoodNewsforPets.com: The Source for Pet News; Online newsletter with information on veterinary research and animal health

www.healthypet.com: HealthyPet.com; American Animal Hospital Association-sponsored site with veterinary health information, as well as many other topics related to general dog care and training

www.merckvetmanual.com: The Merck Veterinary Manual; An online manual of veterinary care information used by veterinarians and animal health professionals

www.petdental.com: Pet Dental: Pets Need Dental Care, Too; Dental information site sponsored by Hill's Pet Nutrition, the American Veterinary Medical Association, and veterinary dental organizations

www.peteducation.com: PetEducation.com; more than 2,500 articles on pet care from Doctors Foster and Smith

www.thepetcenter.com: ThePetCenter.com: The Internet Animal Hospital; offers information on pet health

www.vetgate.ac.uk: VetGate; UK site offering free access to a catalog of Internet sites covering animal health

www.vetinfo.com: Vetinfo: A Veterinary Information Service; Site maintained by veterinarians, with an extensive selection of animal health information

www.vetmed.wsu.edu/ClientEd: Pet Health Topics: Washington State University College of Veterinary Medicine; General information on pet health care and treatment

www.vetmedicine.about.com: About Veterinary Medicine; Guide to dog diseases and general health information

www.veterinarypartner.com: VeterinaryPartner.com: Veterinary Information Network (VIN); Animal health information

www.aahabv.org: The American Association of Human-Animal Bond Veterinarians; Site exploring the veterinary aspects of the human-animal bond

Nutrition

www.barfworld.com: BARFWorld.com: Biologically Appropriate Raw Food (BARF); Information about feeding your pet a biologically appropriate diet

www.hillspet.com: Hill's Pet Nutrition: Hill's Pet Food Manufacturer; Includes a general section on nutrition and health

www.iams.com: Iams: Dog and Cat Nutrition; Includes Dog Nutrition Factbook section

www.petdiets.com: PetDIETS.com; Nutrition advice and homemade diets from veterinary nutritionists

www.purina.com/dogs/nutrition.asp: Purina: Nutrition; Purina pet food home page; information on diets, nutrients, and pet food labeling

Pet Loss

www.aplb.org: The Association for Pet Loss and Bereavement, Inc.; Support source for pet loss

www.petloss.com: Pet Loss Grief Support Web site; Pet loss support information

www.pet-loss.net: PetLoss.com: Pet Loss Grief Support Web site; Articles on surviving pet loss as well as state-by-state guide to support groups and counselors

www.rainbowsbridge.com: Rainbows Bridge; Site offering memorials to lost pets and information on dealing with loss

Pet Sitting

www.petsitusa.com: Petsit U.S.A.; Online database for locating pet sitters, dog walkers, and pet daycare. Provides checklist for interviewing pet care providers and pet sitting preparation tips

Purebred

canismax.angelcities.com/breeds.htm: Canis Max: The Web site for Large Dog Enthusiasts; Discusses 43 large dog breeds

www.dogbreedinfo.com: Dog Breed Info Center; Descriptions of dog breeds and breeder listings

www.dogpatch.org/dogs/breed.cfm: Great Dog Breed Pages; Articles and multiple links to information about purebred dogs

www.dogwatch.net: Dog Watch; Provides information and updates on breed-specific legislation

www.dogweb.nl/hondenrassen/dogbreeds.html: The Dog Breeds Alphabet; A Netherlands-based breed encyclopedia

Rescue and Welfare

www.petfinder.com: Petfinder.com: Adopt a Homeless Pet; Web site that allows rescue groups to post available dogs from throughout the country

www.deafdogs.org: Deaf Dog Education Action Fund; Advocacy site for deaf dogs

www.dogfind.com: Dog Find!; Web site dedicated to reuniting lost or stolen animals with their families

www.theanimalrescuesite.com: The Animal Rescue Site; Dedicated to feeding animals in shelters

Training and Behavior

www.animalbehavior.org/Applied/CAAB_directory.html: Directory of Certified Applied Animal Behaviorists; International listing from the Animal Behavior Society

www.animal.discovery.com/fansites/evets/yelpline/yelpline.html: Animal Planet: Yelpline; Part of the Humane Society of the United States Pets for Life campaign, providing information to solve behavioral problems

www.clickersolutions.com: ClickerSolutions; Provides clicker training information

www.clickertrain.com: Corally Burmaster's Clicker Training Center; Clicker training information and site of publisher of Clicker Training Journal

www.clickertraining.com: Karen Pryor Clickertraining; Web site maintained by a founder of clicker training

www.dogtrainingbasics.com: Dog Training Basics; Training tips from a professional dog behavior consultant and trainer

www.flyingdogpress.com: Flying Dog Press; Features a collection of training and behavior articles from the author of Bones Would Rain from the Sky

www.101-dog-training-tips.com: 101 Dog Training Tips; Training site that gives tips for training dogs and dog behavior programs

www.perfectpaws.com: Perfect Paws: Articles on dog training and behavior from author, trainer, and behavior consultant Gwen Bohnenkamp

www.uwsp.edu/psych/dog/dog.htm: Dr. P's Dog Training; University of Wisconsin–Stevens Point; Virtual library of information about dog training and behavior

www.webtrail.com/petbehavior: Pet Behavior Resources; Information from author and behavior expert William E. Campbell

Travel

www.airlines.org: Air Transport Association of America, Inc.; Offers an online publication, Air Travel for Your Dog and Cat

www.dogfriendly.com: DogFriendly.com; Online newsletter and thousands of dog-friendly accommodations, restaurants, and attractions, as well as tips on traveling with dogs

www.hikewithyourdog.com: Hike With Your Dog!; Dog-friendly parks and national park dog regulations

www.hotdogholidays.com: Hot Dog Holidays; Accommodations in Europe for people traveling with dogs

www.petsonthego.com: Pets on the Go!: Pet Travel Unleashed; General information on traveling with pets and listings of pet-friendly places

www.petswelcome.com: Petswelcome.com; thousands of pet-friendly lodgings and attractions and tips on traveling with pets

www.pettravel.com: PetTravel.com: Worldwide Travel Guide for Pet Owners; Lists accommodations and services that welcome pets

www.petvacations.com: Pet Vacations; Pet-friendly accommodations, travel tips, and more

www.takeyourpet.com: TakeYourPet.com; Membership Web site that offers online information and free newsletter about traveling with pets

www.traveldog.com: TravelDog.com; Membership Web site offering pet-friendly listings in the U.S. and Canada

www.travelingpets.com: Traveling U.S.A.: The Online Guide for Road Travel and Recreation; Tips on traveling with pets and finding accommodations

Working Dogs

www.cofc.edu/~huntc/service.html: Service and Therapy Dogs; Web site about service and therapy dogs from Dr. Caroline Hunt, a professor at the College of Charleston

www.fbi.gov/kids/dogs/doghome.htm: FBI Working Dogs; Educational Web site (geared toward grades K–12) about the working dogs of the Federal Bureau of Investigation*

www.inch.com/~dogs/service.html: American Dog Trainers Network; Provides a listing of service dog resources by state, also includes international and assistance dog resource listings

www.sardog.org: Search and Rescue News Resource; Search and rescue dog resource site with training information, equipment links, news articles, and pictures

www.workingdogweb.com: WorkingDogWeb; Articles and links to working dog and dog sports information

www.workingdogs.com: Working Dogs Cyberzine; Includes information on working and sporting dogs and an online bookstore featuring working and sporting dog books and videos

Bibliography

Chapter Material

Section One
Books
Budiansky, Stephen. 2000. *The Truth about Dogs: An inquiry into the ancestry, social conventions, mental habits, and moral fiber of Canis familiaris.* New York: Viking Press.

Caras, Roger, and H. Knight. 1998. *A Dog Is Listening: The way some of our closest friends view us.* New York: Galahad Books.

Coppinger, Raymond, and L. Coppinger. 2001. Dogs: *A startling new understanding of canine origin, behavior, and evolution.* New York: Scribner.

Coren, Stanley. 1995. *The Intelligence of Dogs: A guide to the thoughts, emotions, and inner lives of our canine companions.* New York: Bantam Books.

Coren, Stanley. 2002. *The Pawprints of History: Dogs and the course of human events.* New York: Free Press.

Dale-Green, Patricia. 1967. *Lore of the Dog.* Boston: Houghton Mifflin.

Leach, Maria. 1961. *God Had a Dog: Folklore of the dog.* New Brunswick, NJ: Rutgers University Press.

Mery, Fernand. 1968. *The Life, History and Magic of the Dog.* New York: Grosset and Dunlap.

Organizations and Web Sites
American Society for the Prevention of Cruelty to Animals
Animal Planet.com: The Wolf Within
Delta Society
Dog Genome Project
Humane Society of the United States
Molecular Evolution of the Dog Family:
www.kc.net/~wolf2dog/wayne2.htm
Veterinary Genetics Lab

Section Two
Books
American Kennel Club Staff. 1998. *The Complete Dog Book,* 19th edition. Hoboken, NJ: Howell Book House.

DeVito, Carlo, and Amy Ammen. 1999. *The Everything Dog Book.* Avon, MA: Adams Media Corporation.

Gerstenfeld, Sheldon L., VMD, and J. L. Schultz. 1999. ASPCA *Complete Guide to Dogs.* San Francisco: Chronicle Books.

Hoffman, Matthew, ed. 1998. *Dogs: The ultimate care guide.* Emmaus, PA: Rodale Press.

Lane, Marion S. 2001. *The Humane Society of the United States Complete Guide to Dog Care: Everything you need to keep your dog healthy and happy.* Boston: Little, Brown, and Company.

Periodicals
Dog Fancy
Dog World
Popular Dogs Series

Organizations and Web Sites
American Kennel Club
American Society for the Prevention of Cruelty to Animals
Delta Society
Fédération Cynologique Internationale
Humane Society of the United States
Petfinder.org

Section Three
Books
DeVito, Carlo, and Amy Ammen. 1999. *The Everything Dog Book.* Avon, MA: Adams Media Corporation.

Fogle, Bruce. 1993. ASPCA *Complete Dog Care Manual.* New York: DK Publishing.

Gerstenfeld, Sheldon L., VMD, and J. L. Schultz. 1999. ASPCA *Complete Guide to Dogs.* San Francisco: Chronicle Books.

Hoffman, Matthew, ed. 1998. Dogs: *The ultimate care guide. Emmaus,* PA: Rodale Press.

Lane, Marion S. 2001. *The Humane Society of the United States Complete Guide to Dog Care: Everything you need to keep your dog healthy and happy.* Boston: Little, Brown, and Company.

Presutti, R. John, DO. 2001. *Prevention and Treatment of Dog Bites*. American Family Physician: 63:1567-72, 1573-4.

Shojai, Amy. 2003. *Complete Care for Your Aging Dog*. New York: New American Library.

Organizations and Web Sites

Air Transport Association
All Dog Sports Club
American Kennel Club
American Mixed Breed Obedience Registration
American Sighthound Field Association
American Society for the Prevention of Cruelty to Animals
Australian Shepherd Club of America, Inc.
Companion Air
The Dachshund Network
Delta Society
Dogfriendly.com
Dog Infomat
Dogpark.com
Federal Emergency Management Agency
Humane Society of the United States
International Federation of Sleddog Sports
International Sled Dog Racing Association
LV/DVG America
Mixed Breed Dog Clubs of America
Moraine Tracking Club
Nordkyn Outfitters
North American Dog Agility Council, Inc.
North American Flyball Association
North American Hunting Retriever Association
Petfinder.com
PetPlace.com
Save Our Strays
Tri-State Alaskan Malamute Club
United Schutzhund Clubs of America
United States Dog Agility Association
United States Border Collie Handler's Association
World Canine Freestyle Organization
YourDog.net

Periodicals

Clean Run magazine
Dog Fancy
Dog World
Training for Agility: Popular Dogs Series
Training for Obedience: Popular Dogs Series
Tricks and Games: Teach Your Dog: Popular Dogs Series

Section Four

Books

American Kennel Club Staff. 1998. *The Complete Dog Book,* 19th edition. Hoboken, NJ: Howell Book House.

Coile, D. Caroline, and Michele Earle-Bridges. 2005. *Barron's Encyclopedia of Dog Breeds*, 2nd edition. Hauppauge, NY: Barron's Educational Series.

DeVito, Carlo, and Amy Ammen. 1999. *The Everything Dog Book. Avon,* MA: Adams Media Corporation.

Fogle, Bruce. 2000. *The New Encyclopedia of the Dog.* New York: DK Publishing.

Gerstenfeld, Sheldon L., VMD, and J. L. Schultz. 1999. ASPCA *Complete Guide to Dogs.* San Francisco: Chronicle Books.

Hoffman, Matthew, ed. 1998. *Dogs: The ultimate care guide.* Emmaus, PA: Rodale Press.

Lane, Marion S. 2001. *The Humane Society of the United States Complete Guide to Dog Care: Everything you need to keep your dog healthy and happy.* Boston: Little, Brown, and Company.

Wilcox, Bonnie, and Chris Walkowicz. 1995. *The Atlas of Dog Breeds of the World.* Neptune City, NJ: TFH Publications.

Organizations and Web Sites

Affenpinscher Club of America
Afghan Hound Club of America, Inc.
Airedale Terrier Club of America
Akbash Dogs International
Akita Club of America
Alaskan Malamute Club of America, Inc. (Leneia R. Rogowski)
American Azawakh Association (Deb Kidwell)
American Catahoula Association
American Belgian Malinois Club
American Belgian Tervuren Club
American Black and Tan Coonhound Club
The American Bloodhound Club
The American Bouvier des Flandres Club
American Boxer Club, Inc.
The American Brittany Club (Mary Jo Trimble)
American Brussels Griffon Association

American Bulldog Association
American Bulldog Rescue
American Canine Association
American Cavalier King Charles Spaniel Club, Inc.
American Chesapeake Club
American Chinese Crested Club (Dianne Mullikin)
American Eskimo Dog Home Page
American Foxhound Club, Inc. (Kay Phillips)
The American Fox Terrier Club
American Kennel Club
American Lhasa Apso Club
American Maltese Association
American Manchester Terrier Club
The American Miniature Schnauzer Club
American Norfolk Terrier Association
American Pit Bull Terrier Association
American Pointer Club, Inc. (Karin Kashe)
The American Polish Lowland Sheepdog Club, Inc.
   (Carol Hales)
American Pomeranian Club, Inc. (Cindy Boulware)
American Rare Breed Association
American Rottweiler Club
American Sealyham Terrier Club
American Shetland Sheepdog Association
American Shih Tzu Club, Inc.
American Sloughi Association (Ermine Moreau-Sipiere)
American Spaniel Club, Inc.
American Tibetan Mastiff Association
The American Water Spaniel Club, Inc.
American Water Spaniel Field Association
The American Whippet Club
American Wirehaired Pointing Griffon Association
The Anatolian Shepherd Dog Club of America (Genia Kyres)
Aniwa.com
Appenzell Mountain Dog Club of America, UKC (Audrey Lyke)
Association Burkinabe Idi du Sahel
Australian Cattle Dog Club of America
Australian Cattle Dog Social Club of North Queensland
Australian Shepherd Club of America, Inc.
The Australian Terrier Club of America, Inc.
Barbet Club of America
Basenji Club of America
Basenji Rescue & Transport
Basset Hound Club of America, Inc. (Robert Booth)
Bearded Collie Club of America
Beauceron Club of America
Beauceron Club of Canada
Bedlington Terrier Club of America
The Belgian Sheepdog Club of America (Jill Miller)

The Bergamasco Sheepdog Club of America
Bernese Mountain Dog Club of America, Inc. (Chris
   Walkowicz)
Bichon Frise Club of America, Inc.
Black Russian Terrier Club–Golden Gate
Bleu De Gascogne Club of America
Bluetick Breeders and Coonhunters Association
Bolognese Club of America (Jacquelyn Engle)
Border Collie Society of America
Border Terrier Club of America
Borzoi Club of America, Inc.
Boston Terrier Club of America, Inc.
The Boykin Spaniel Society
Briard Club of America (Dr. M. Lana Sheer)
Broholmerselskabet (Ulla Sellerup)
The Bulldog Club of America
Bull Terrier Club of America, Inc.
Cairn Terrier Club of America
The Canaan Dog Club of America
Canadian Eskimo Dog Association of Canada
Canadian Kennel Club
Cane Corso Preservation Society
Cardigan Welsh Corgi Club of America (Susan Buxton)
The Carolina Dog Association (Jane Gunnell)
Catahoula EZine
Catahoula Owners, Breeders, and Research Association
Caucasian Ovcharka (Mountain Dog) Club of America
   (Stacey Kubyn, Angie Wheat)
Cavalier King Charles Spaniel Club–USA, Inc.
Central Asian Shepherd Society of America (Jeannine De
   Palma)
Chart Polski Association of America (Lisa Pinto)
Chinese Shar-Pei Club of America, Inc. (Gayle Gold)
Chinook Owners Association, Inc. (Jessica Maurer)
The Chow Chow Club, Inc.
Club du Braque Français
Club du Griffon Nivernais (Roger Goby)
Club du Griffon Vendeen
Club National de l'Épagneul Français (Canada)
Clumber Spaniel Club of America
Clumber Spaniel Club of Canada
Collie Club of America (Sara Futh)
The Colonial Schipperke Club
Continental Kennel Club
The Coton de Tulear Club of America (Laurie Spalding,
   Dr. Robert Jay Russell)
Curly-Coated Retriever Club of America (Yvonne Cooper)
Dachshund Club of America, Inc. (Andra O'Connell)
Dalmatian Club of America

Dandie Dinmont Terrier Club of America
Dansk Stabyhoun Klubb
De Nederlandse Schapendoes
Deutscher Wachtelhund of America (Dave Pepe)
Doberman Pinscher Club of America (Bob Vandiver)
Dog Breed Info Center
Dogo Argentino Club of America
Dogo Canario Club of America
Dogs Downunder
Dogue de Bordeaux Society (Andrea Switzer)
English Setter Association of America
English Shepherd Club
English Springer Spaniel Field Trial Association
Foundation (Frances A. Nelson)
English Toy Spaniel Club of America (Tom O'Neal)
Entlebucher Mountain Dog Club of America
The Estrela Mountain Dog Association of America
    (Camille Pentland)
Fédération Cynologique Internationale
Fényes Dezs Mudi Klub
Field Spaniel Society of America, Inc.
Fila Brasileiro Club of America
The Finnish Lapphund Club of Great Britain
The Finnish Spitz Club of America (Leslie Carlson-Elliott)
Flat-Coated Retriever Society of America
Fox Terrier Network
The French Bulldog Club of America (Jan Grebe)
German Eurasier-Klub
German Jagdterrier Club of America
German Jagdterrier Registry
The German Longhaired Pointer Club (UK)
German Pinscher Club of America (Renee Phillips)
German Shepherd Dog Club of America
German Shorthaired Pointer Club of America (Susan Clemons)
The German Wirehaired Pointer Club of America
The Giant Schnauzer Club of America, Inc.
Glen of Imaal Terrier Club
Golden Retriever Club of America
Gordon Setter Club of America, Inc.
The Great Dane Club of America, Inc. (Lynda Moriarty)
Great Pyrenees Club of America (Ruth A. Marcy)
The Greater Swiss Mountain Dog Club of America
    (Kathy Spencer)
Greyhound Club of America (Sue LeMieux)
GSD Rescue
Hamiltonstövare Club of Great Britain
Harrier Club of America (Ellen Parr)
Havanese Club of America
Havanese Heart

Hokkaido-Inu Museum (Kazuhiro Takada)
The Hovawart Club of Great Britain
Ibizan Hound Club of the United States (Nancy Turchi)
Icelandic Sheepdog Association
International Cane Corso Federation
International Leonberger Union
International Sarplaninac Club (Dagmar Cestrova)
Irish Red and White Setter Club
Irish Setter Club of America (Connie Vanacore)
Irish Terrier Club of America
The Irish Water Spaniel Club of America (Florence Blecher)
The Irish Wolfhound Club of America, Inc.
Israel Canaan Dog Club of America, Inc.
Italian Greyhound Club of America (Lilian Barber)
Jack Russell Terrier Club of America
Japanese Chin Club of America
The Jindo Club of America
Keeshond Club of America (Carolyn Schaldecker)
Kennel Club
Kerry Blue Terrier Foundation
Komondor Club of America
Kooikerhondje Club of Canada (Diane Lumsden)
Kuvasz Club of America
The Labrador Retriever Club, Inc.
The Large Munsterlander Club of North America
Leonberger Club of America
Les Amis du Berger Picard
The Lowchen Club of Canada
Mastiff Club of America (C. Cuthbert)
The Miniature Bull Terrier Club of America
    (Christine Burton)
Miniature Pinscher Club of America, Inc.
National Beagle Club of America
The National Brussels Griffon Club
National Cesky Terrier Club
National Rat Terrier Association
The National Shiba Club of America, Inc. (Jacey Holden)
Newfoundland Club of America (Ann Thibault)
New Guinea Singing Dog Conservation Society (Janice
    Koler-Matznick)
North American Bracco Italiano Club
North American Kai Association
Northwest Alaskan Klee Kai Association (Carroll Parkison)
The Norwegian Buhund Club of America
Norwegian Elkhound Association of America
Norwegian Kennel Club (Anne Indergaard)
The Norwegian Lundehund Club of America, Inc. (Debby
    G. Morris)
Norwegian Polar Dog Association

The Norwich and Norfolk Terrier Club
Nova Scotia Duck Tolling Retriever Club (USA)
  (Gretchen Botner)
Old English Sheepdog Club of America (Chris Lawrenz)
The Otterhound Club of America
Papillon Club of America
The Patterdale Club of America
The Pekingese Club of America
Pembroke Welsh Corgi Club of America, Inc. (Deborah
  S. Harper)
Peruvian Inca Orchid Club of America (Debby G. Morris)
Petit Basset Griffon Vendeen Club of America
Pharaoh Hound Club of America
Polish Tatra Sheepdog Club of America
The Poodle Club of America
The Portuguese Water Dog Club of America, Inc.
Pudelpointer Club of North America
Pug Dog Club of America (Warren Hudson)
Puli Club of America
Pyrenean Journal
Pyrenean Shepherd Club of America
Rat Terrier Club of America
Rhodesian Ridgeback Club of the United States
Saint Bernard Club of America
Saluki Club of America
Scottish Deerhound Club of America
Scottish Terrier Club of America (Cindy Cooke)
Samoyed Club of America, Inc.
Second Chance Filas
Siberian Husky Club of America, Inc.
Silky Terrier Club of America
Skye Terrier Club of America (Chris Crowell and Marcia
  Scherer)
Slovac Cuvac Club of America (Herb and Sheryl Rose)
Sloughi Fanciers Association of America
Small Munsterlander Club of North America, Inc.
Soft Coated Wheaten Terrier Club of America, Inc. (Ann Leigh)
SOS Galgos
Southern California Chihuahua Club
Spanish Water Dog Association of America (Craig Pope)
Spinone Club of America
The Staffordshire Bull Terrier Club of America
Staffordshire Terrier Club of America
The Standard Schnauzer Club of America
Sussex Spaniel Association
Swedish Kennel Club
Swedish Lapphund Club (Ambjörn Lindqvist)
Swedish Vallhund Club of America (Gail Smyka)
Teddy Roosevelt Terrier Association

ThaiDog.org
Tibetan Spaniel Club of America
Tibetan Terrier Club of America
Troika, Ovcharka International (Diane Sari)
United Kennel Club
United States Kerry Blue Terrier Club
United States Lakeland Terrier Club, Inc.
United States Neapolitan Mastiff Club
U.S. Coton de Tulear Club
The Vizsla Club of America, Inc.
Weimaraner Club of America
The Welsh Springer Spaniel Club of America, Inc. (Sue Healy)
Welsh Terrier Club of America, Inc.
West Highland Terrier Club of America (Daphne Gentry)
The Working Kelpie (North American Australian Kelpie
  Registry, Inc.)
Xoloitzcuintle Club USA
Yorkshire Terrier Club of America, Inc.

Periodicals

Dog Fancy
Dog World
Popular Dog Series

Section Five
Books

Eldredge, Debra M., DVM, James. M. Giffin, MD, and
Liisa D. Carlson, DVM. 2007. *Dog Owner's Home
Veterinary Handbook, 4th edition.* Hoboken, NJ: Howell
Book House.

Siegal, Mordecai, ed. 1995. UC Davis *Book of Dogs: The
complete medical reference guide for dogs and puppies.*
New York: HarperCollins.

Experts

Gregory M. Acland, BVSc
Gustavo Aguirre, VMD, PhD
Jerold Bell, DVM
Jan Bellows, DVM
Robin Downing, DVM
Deb Eldredge, DVM
John Hamil, DVM
Alicia Karas, DVM
Doug Mansfield, DVM
Amy Marder, VMD
Shawn Messonier, DVM
Brook Niemiec, DVM
Al Raymond, DVM

James Ross, DVM
Frank J. M. Verstraete, DVM
Jerry Woodfield, DVM
Michele Yasson, DVM

Section Six
Books

Adamson, Eve. 2002. *The Simple Guide to a Healthy Dog*. Neptune City, NJ: TFH Publications.

Association of American Feed Control Officials Incorporated. Official Publication 2001.

Edalati, Rudy. 2001. *Barker's Grub: Easy wholesome home cooking for your dog*. New York: Three Rivers Press.

Giffin, James. M., MD, and Liisa D. Carlson, DVM. 1999. *Dog Owner's Home Veterinary Handbook, 3rd edition*. Hoboken, NJ: Howell Book House.

Glover, Harry. 1978. *A Standard Guide to Pure-bred Dogs*. New York: McGraw-Hill.

Hamlyn, Paul. 1962. *Dogs Dogs Dogs Dogs Dogs Dogs*. London: Westbrook House.

Kalstone, Shirlee. 2001. *Poodle Clipping and Grooming: The international reference, third edition*. Hoboken, NJ: Howell Book House.

Moore, Arden. 2001. *Real Food for Dogs: 50 vet-approved recipes to please the canine gastronome*. North Adams, MA: Storey Books.

Pitcairn, Richard H., DVM, PhD, and Susan Hubble Pitcairn. 1995. *Dr. Pitcairn's Complete Guide to Natural Health for Dogs and Cats, new updated edition*. Emmaus, PA: Rodale Press.

Stone, Ben, and Pearl Stone. 1981. *The Stone Guide to Dog Grooming for All Breeds*. Hoboken, NJ: Howell Book House.

Volhard, Wendy, and Kerry Brown, DVM. 2000. *Holistic Guide for a Healthy Dog, 2nd edition*. Hoboken, NJ: Howell Book House.

Walin, Dorothy. 1986. *The Art and Business of Professional Grooming*. Loveland, CO: Alpine Publications, Inc.

Wilcox, Bonnie, and Chris Walkowicz. 1995. *The Atlas of Dog Breeds of the World*. Neptune City, NJ: TFH Publications.

Zink, M. Christine, DVM, PhD. 2001. *Dog Health and Nutrition for Dummies*. New York: John Wiley & Sons.

Experts
Denise Trapani, DVM

Organizations and Web Sites
American Kennel Club
Canine Connections
Canines.com/library
Dog Owner's Guide: canismajor.com/dog/
TheDogPark.com
EDogLovers.com
GroomTeamUSA.com
Intergroom.com
NationalDogGroomers.com
PetCo.com
PetGroomer.com
PetPlace.com
PetSmart.com
WagnTails.com

Section Seven
Books

Coren, Stanley. 2001. *How to Speak Dog: Mastering the art of dog-human communication*. New York: Free Press.

Donaldson, Jean. 1998. *Dogs Are from Neptune: Candid answers to urgent questions about aggression and other aspects of dog behavior*. Montreal: Lasar Multimedia Productions Inc.

McConnell, Patricia, PhD. 2002. *The Other End of the Leash: Why we do what we do around dogs*. New York: Ballantine Books.

The Monks of New Skete. 1991. *The Art of Raising a Puppy*. Boston: Little, Brown and Company.

The Monks of New Skete. 2002. *How to Be Your Dog's Best Friend*. Boston: Little, Brown and Company.

Pryor, Karen. 1999. *Don't Shoot the Dog! The new art of teaching and training*. New York: Bantam Books.

Pryor, Karen. 2002. *Getting Started: Clicker Training for Dogs.* Auckland, NZ: Sunshine Books.

Experts
September Morn
Liz Palika

Periodicals and Newspapers
Bark Magazine
Clicker Training: Popular Dogs Series
Dog Fancy
Dog World
Training and Behavior: Popular Dogs Series
Training Your Puppy: Popular Dogs Series

Section Eight
Books
Barber, Kim. 1996. *Career Success with Pets.* Hoboken, NJ: Howell Book House. Bowman-

Kruhm, Mary. 1999. *A Day in the Life of a Veterinarian.* New York: Rosen Publishing Group, Inc.

Caras, Roger. 1984. *A Celebration of Dogs.* New York: Crown Publishing Group, Inc.

Clark, A. J., ed. 1998. *Animal Breeding: Technology for the 21st century.* New York: Gordon & Breach Publishing Group.

Coren, Stanley. 2002. *The Pawprints of History: Dogs and the course of human events.* New York: Free Press.

Foster, William S. 1990. *Starting a Pet Sitting Business.* Blaine, WA: Hancock House Publishers.

Hurwitz, Jane. 1997. *Choosing a Career in Animal Care (World of Work).* New York: Rosen Publishing Group, Inc.

Lee, Mary Price, and Richard S. Lee. 2001. *Opportunities in Animal and Pet Care Careers.* Lincoln, IL: VGM Career Books.

Mehus-Roe, Kristin. 2003. *Working Dogs: True stories of dogs and their handlers.* Irvine, CA: BowTie Press.

Miller, Louise. 1991. *Careers for Animal Lovers & Other Zoological Types.* Lincoln, IL: VGM Career Books.

Moran, Patti J. 1992. *Pet Sitting for Profit: A complete manual for success.* Hoboken, NJ: Howell Book House.

Rutter, Bob. 1993. *A Century of Caring: A history of the Guelph Humane Society.* Louisville, KY: Evanston Publishing Inc.

Sateren, Shelley S. 1996. *The Humane Societies: A voice for the animals.* Englewood Cliffs, NJ: Silver Burdett Press.

Shorto, Russell. 1992. *Careers for Animal Lovers.* Brookfield, CT: Millbrook Press.

Sirch, Willow Ann. 2000. *Careers with Animals: The Humane Society of the United States.* Golden, CO: Fulcrum Publishing.

Whelan, Vicky. 1999. *Operating Your Own Pet Sitting Business Kit: Lessons learned from successful pet sitters … what works & why!* Middletown, NJ: Pet Sitting and Pet Related Services.

Whitman, Robert S. 1995. *How to Make Big Money Grooming Small Dogs: The absolute amateur's guide to profitable, professional canine styling.* Philadelphia: Protective Specialties Development Group.

Organizations and Web Sites
American Boarding Kennels Association
American College of Veterinary Behaviorists
American Grooming Shop Association
American Humane Association
American Kennel Club
American Pet Boarding Association
American Red Cross
American Society for the Prevention of Cruelty to Animals
American Veterinary Medical Association
American Veterinary Society of Animal Behavior
Animal and Plant Health Inspection Service
Animal Behavior Society
The Animal Control Academy (sponsored by the Humane Society of the United States)
Animal Legal Defense Fund
Animal Transportation Association
Assistance Dogs International, Inc.
Association of American Veterinary Medical Colleges
Association of Pet Dog Trainers

Beagle Brigade
Canine Companions for Independence
Canine Enforcement Training Center
Coalition to Protect Animals in Entertainment
Colorado Search and Rescue
Delta Society
Department of Defense Military Working Dog Center
Dogs for the Blind
Dogs for the Deaf, Inc.
Dog Writers Association of America
Federal Emergency Management Administration
Guide Dog Foundation for the Blind
Guide Dogs for the Blind
Humane Society of the United States
Independent Pet and Animal Transportation Association
International Association of Assistance Dog Partners
International Professional Groomers, Inc.
King County Search Dogs
National Animal Control Association
National Association for Humane and Environmental Education
National Association of Dog Obedience Instructors
National Association of Professional Pet Sitters
National Disaster Search Dog Foundation

National Dog Groomers Association of America, Inc.
National Education for Assistance Dog Services
National Urban Search and Rescue Response System
North American Veterinary Technician Association
People for the Ethical Treatment of Animals
Pet Sitters International
Quartermaster Museum—War Dogs
Therapy Dogs International
Transportation Security Administration Canine Explosives Unit, U.S. Department of Transportation
United Kennel Club
United States Customs and Border Protection
United States Department of Agriculture
United States Department of Labor Occupational Outlook Handbook
U.S. Council of Dog Guide Schools
U.S. Customs Canine Enforcement Program
U.S. Fish and Wildlife Service
Vietnam Dog Handlers Association
Washington State Correctional Center for Women Prison Pet Partnership Program
World Wide Pet Supply Association

Sidebar Material

Books

Barnette, Martha. 2003. *Dog Days and Dandelions.* New York: St. Martin's Press.

Bartlett, John. 1992. *Bartlett's Familiar Quotations.* Boston: Little, Brown and Company.

Case, Linda P. 1999. *The Dog: Its behavior, nutrition and health.* Ames, IA: Iowa State University Press.

DeVito, Carlo, and Amy Ammen. 1999. *The Everything Dog Book.* Avon, MA: Adams Media Corporation.

Fogle, Bruce. 1995. *The Encyclopedia of the Dog.* New York: DK Publishing.

Fogle, Bruce. 2000. *The New Encyclopedia of the Dog.* New York: DK Publishing.

Periodicals/Newspapers/Articles

American Animal Hospital Association. 2001. *Pet Owners Survey.*

American Pet Products Manufacturers Association. *2003/2004 Survey.*

Associated Press. 2004. "A Traveler's Tail." CNN.com (accessed January 3, 2004).

Associated Press. 2003. "Norman the Wonder Beagle." www.cbsnews.com/stories/2003/05/19/national/main554454.shtml?.

Deneen, Sally. 2002. "Under the Sea." *Dog Fancy*, August.

ABC News Web site. 2003. "Foes to Friends." abcnews.go.com/sections/GMA/GoodMorningAmerica/GMA020225AnimalHouse.html.

Guidry, Virginia Parker. 2001. "Take It Slow and Easy with Your Senior Dog." *Dog Fancy*, August.

Reuters. 2001. "'Dog Boy' Rescued." abcnews.go.com/sections/world/DailyNews/dogboy 010619.html.

Sheils, Colleen. 2002. "Picture This: How to take better portraits of your dog." *Dog Fancy*, November.

Wong, Lawson. 2003. Sony Aibo ERS-7. abcnews.go.com /sections/scitech/WeekendWarrior/techtv_AiboERS7Review 031024.html.

Organizations and Web Sites
Amazon.com
American Animal Hospital Association
American Kennel Club
Animal Instincts
AnimalPlanet.com
Auburn University's College of Veterinary Medicine
Black Dog Accessories
Bow Wow Meow
Cleveland Museum of Natural History
Dilbert.com
DogFriendly.com
DogQuotes.com
DogsInTheNews.com
DogSaver.com
DomainsForYourPet.com
Earthsky.com
The Gallup Organization
GroomTeam USA
Guinness World Records
Kansas State University, Pet Health News
National Aeronautics and Space Administration (NASA)
PetEducation.com
Purina.com
RoadsideAmerica.com
Roadside Attractions LLC
SitStay.com
Society for the Prevention of Cruelty to Animals Los
   Angeles
TheDogpatch.com
Veterinary Information Network
WorldWideWords.org

Section One
Books
Coren, Stanley. 2002. *The Pawprints of History: Dogs and the course of human events*. New York: Free Press.

Fogle, Bruce. 1995. *The Encyclopedia of the Dog*. New York: DK Publishing.

Muir, John. 1990. *Stickeen*. Berkeley, CA: Heyday Books.

Steinbeck, John. 1962. *Travels with Charley: In search of America*. New York: Penguin Books.

Thurston, Mary Elizabeth. 1996. *The Lost History of the Canine Race: Our 15,000-year love affair with dogs*. Kansas City: Andrews McMeel Publishing.

Periodicals and Newspapers
ABC News official Web site. 2001. "The Next 'Benji.'" abcnews.go.com/sections/primetime/2020/PRIME TIME_011213_benji2_feature.html.
Associated Press. 2003.

"New Benji Is Doggone Good." *Edmonton Sun,* September 7. Brouillette, Renee. 2002.

"Dogs Smile on Steinbeck Centennial." *Dog Fancy,* February. Fisher, Sally. 2002.

"Hot Dog Hall of Fame." *Melbourne Sunday Herald Sun*, June 9.

"Frank Inn, Famed Animal Trainer Dies." www.freere public.com/focus/f-chat/723481/posts. Jablon, Robert. 2002.

Frazier, Joseph B. 2003. "Canine Companion Went With Explorers Into the Unknown." *Associated Press*, July 31. Green, Susie. 2001.

"Pablo's Dog Days." *The Guardian,* September 8. Microsoft Encarta Online Encyclopedia. 2003.

"Lewis and Clark Expedition." encarta.msn.com/encyclopedia_761569929/Lewis_and Clark_Expedition.html. Recer, Paul. 2003.

"Scientists Map Dog's Genetic Structure." *Associated Press,* September 25.
Roback, Diane, Jason Britton, and Debbie Hochman Turvey. 2001.

"All-Time Bestselling Children's Books." *Publisher's Weekly,* December 17.
Rubenstein, Steve. 2001.

"Why New Yorker Is Going to the Dogs." *San Francisco Chronicle,* December 8.
Tipton, Abby. 2002.

"Did You Know?"
magma.nationalgeographic.com/ngm/0204/feature5/.
University of Virginia Web site.

"The Journals of Lewis and Clark."
xroads.virginia.edu/~HYPER/JOURNALS/toc.html.

Organizations and Web Sites
The Adventures of Rin Tin Tin: www.skypoint.com/mem bers/joycek19/rinty.htm
Amazon.com
American Humane Association
American Humane Association, Film and TV Unit
American Kennel Club
American Society for the Prevention of Cruelty to Animals
AncientGames.com
Antiquibles.com
ARFkids.com
AskTheMeatman.com
BBC.co.uk
Best Friends Animal Society
Chicago Public Library Online Reference
DogFancy.com
DogSaver.com
Encarta Online Encyclopedia
GameCabinet.com
Hearts United for Animals
Hollywood Chamber of Commerce
Humane Society of the United States
LaurelAndHardyCentral.com
Iams.com
Museum of Texas Tech University Web site
Nefertiti.iwebland.com
North Shore Animal League America
PBS.org
Rintintin.com
RoadsideAmerica.com
Sierra Club
Silent-Movies.com
Who2.com
Wild Dog Foundation
The Wolf Education and Research Center
University of Wisconsin Department of Astronomy
WorkingDogWeb

Section Two
Books
Brickell, Christopher, and Judith D. Zuk (eds.).
The American Horticultural Society A-Z Encylopedia of Garden Plants. New York: DK Publishing.

Cooper, Paulette, and Paul Noble. 1999. *277 Secrets Your Dog Wants You to Know: A doggie bag of unusual and useful information.* Berkeley, CA: Ten Speed Press.

Lane, Marion S. 2001. *The Humane Society of the United States Complete Guide to Dog Care: Everything you need to keep your dog healthy and happy.* Boston: Little, Brown, and Company.

The Monks of New Skete. 2002. *How to Be Your Dog's Best Friend.* Boston: Little, Brown and Company.

Prevention Magazine Health Books, eds. 1996. *The Doctors Book of Home Remedies.* Emmaus, PA: Rodale Press.

Periodicals/Newspapers/Articles
Adamson, Eve. 2002. "Dog Proofing Checklist." *Dog Fancy,* April.

Dolder, Linda K., DVM. 2003. "Metaldehyde Toxicosis." *Veterinary Medicine,* March.

Volmer, Petra A., DVM. 2002. "How Dangerous Are Winter and Spring Holiday Plants to Pets?" *Veterinary Medicine,* December.

Organizations and Web Sites
Allerpet
American Animal Hospital Association
American College of Allergy, Asthma and Immunology
American Humane Association
American Kennel Club
American Society for Prevention of Cruelty to Animals
ASPCA Animal Poison Control Center

DogFriendly.com
DrLarryPetVet.com
Dumb Friends League
Humane Society of Denver
Humane Society of the United States
Iams.com
National Institute of Environmental Health Sciences
PestProducts.net/flycontrol
PetPlace.com
United Kennel Club
Veterinary Information for Dog Owners
Veterinary Information Network, Pet Care Forum's Opinion Poll
Veterinary Support Personnel Network

Section Three
Books
American Kennel Club Staff. 1998. *The Complete Dog Book, 19th edition.* Hoboken, NJ: Howell Book House.

Arden, Darlene. 2002. *The Angell Memorial Animal Hospital Book of Wellness and Preventive Care for Dogs.* New York: McGraw-Hill.

Cooper, Paulette, and Paul Noble. 1999. *277 Secrets Your Dog Wants You to Know: A doggie bag of unusual and useful information.* Berkeley, CA: Ten Speed Press.

DeVito, Carlo, and Amy Ammen. 1999. *The Everything Dog Book.* Avon, MA: Adams Media Corporation.

Miller, Cynthia D. 1999. *Canine Adventures.* Yuba City, CA: Animalia Publishing Company.

Moore, Arden. 2000. *50 Simple Ways to Pamper Your Dog.* North Adams, MA: Storey Books.

Prevention Magazine Health Books, eds. 1996. *The Doctors Book of Home Remedies.* Emmaus, PA: Rodale Press.

Richmond, Mardi, and Melanie L. Barash. 1999. *Ruffing It: The complete guide to camping with dogs.* Loveland, CO: Alpine Publications.

Thornton, Kim. 1997. *Why Do Dogs Do That?* Irvine, CA: BowTie Press.

Thurston, Mary Elizabeth. 1996. *The Lost History of the Canine Race: Our 15,000-year love affair with dogs.* Kansas City: Andrews McMeel Publishing.

Veterinary Market Statistics. 2002. *U.S. Pet Ownership and Demographic Sourcebook.*

Periodicals and Newspapers
American Boarding Kennel Association press release. 2003. "ABKA Notes Industry Trends Reflected in 2002 Boarding Kennel Statistics," August.

American Veterinary Medical Foundation. 2003. *Newsletter*, September–December.

AVMA Task Force on Canine Aggression and Human Canine Interactions. 2001. "A Community Approach to Dog Bite Prevention." *Journal of the American Veterinary Medical Association* (JAVMA), June 1.

Dingeman, Robbie. 2002. "Hoku Dog Name to Da Max." *Honolulu Advertiser,* August 14.

Dog and Kennel. 2003. "Using GPS to Track Pets." November.

Dog Fancy, Newshound section. 2002. "Toward Parental Rights," August.

Emerson, Dan. 2003. "How to Lobby for a Dog Park." *Dog Fancy,* September.

Finke, Beth. 2003. "When the Coping Gets Tough." *Dog Fancy,* May.

Fogle, Jean M. 2002. "Let the Games Begin." *Dog Fancy,* August.

Horowitz, Donna. 2003. "Outfitting Firefighters to Save Pets' Lives." *Los Angeles Times*, October 20.

Kirkwood, Kyra. 2002. "Dog Owner's Guide to Home Insurance." *Dog Fancy,* November.

Mifflin, Krista. 2003. "Dog Safety for Kids." dogs.about .com/cs/childrenanddogs/a/child_safety.htm.

Moore, Arden. 2002. "Child's Play." *Dog Fancy*, April.

Purina. *State of the American Pet Survey.*

Singer, Glenn. 2002. "Seven Facts to Fight Fleas and Ticks." *Dog Fancy*, May.

Turner, Debbye, DVM. 2002. "When the Dog Bites." www.cbsnews.com/stories/2002/07/10/earlyshow/contributors/debbyeturner/main514774.shtml.

Organizations and Web Sites
Airtight Investigations Security Company
Air Transport Association
American Animal Hospital Association
American Herding Breed Association
American Humane Association
American Kennel Club (Daisy Okas)
American Mixed Breed Obedience Registration
American Pet Products Association
American Sighthound Field Association
American Society for the Prevention of Cruelty to Animals
American Veterinary Medical Association (Dr. Gail Golab)
American Working Terrier Association
Australian Shepherd Club of America, Inc.
Bureau of Consular Affairs, U.S. Department of State
Canine Freestyle Federation, Inc.
Centers for Disease Control and Prevention
Consulate General of France
Delta Society
DogFriendly.com
Dog Owner's Guide: canismajor.com/dog/
Dog-Play.com
Embassy of Italy in the United States
Embassy of the Federal Republic of Germany
Family Dog Training Center: FamilyDogOnline.com
Flyball.com
Fodors.com
Guinness World Records
Hawaii Department of Agriculture
Humane Society of the United States
International Federation of Sleddog Sports
International Sled Dog Racing Association
Kennel Club
LV/DVG America
Ministry of Agriculture, Forestry and Fisheries of Japan
Mixed Breed Dog Clubs of America
National Capital Air Canines
National Council on Pet Population Study and Policy
National Pet Owners Association
North American Dog Agility Council, Inc.
North American Flyball Association
North American Hunting Retriever Association
Oakland Dog Owner's Group
Pet Doors USA, Inc.
PetSmart.com
Purina Pet Institute
ShowDogSuperSite.com
Skyhoundz (Peter Bloeme)
Stock Dog Server
Travel Industry Association of America
United Kennel Club (Michelle Morgan)
United Schutzhund Clubs of America
United States Border Collie Handler's Association
United States Department of Agriculture
United States Dog Agility Association, Inc. (Heather Smith)
Unity Marketing
University of Minnesota College of Veterinary Medicine Web site
U.K. Department for Environment, Food and Rural Affairs
Westminster Kennel Club (David Frei)
World Canine Freestyle Organization
Yale University Library Online

Section Four
Books
American Kennel Club Staff. 1998. *The Complete Dog Book, 19th edition.* Hoboken, NJ. Howell Book House.

Barnette, Martha. 2003. *Dog Days and Dandelions.* New York: St. Martin's Press.

Coile, D. Caroline, and Michele Earle-Bridges. 1998. *Barron's Encyclopedia of Dog Breeds.* Hauppauge, NY: Barron's Educational Series.

Coren, Stanley. 1995. *The Intelligence of Dogs: A guide to the thoughts, emotions, and inner lives of our canine companions.* New York: Bantam Books.

Coren, Stanley. 1998. *Why We Love the Dogs We Do.* New York: Free Press.

Fogle, Bruce. 2002. *Caring for Your Dog.* New York: DK Publishing.

Fogle, Bruce. 1995. *The Encyclopedia of the Dog.* New York: DK Publishing.

Fredricks, Anita, and Grant Fredricks. 2003. *History of the Schipperke.* Olympia: WA: Blumoon.

Guinness World Records, eds. 2003. *Guinness Book of World Records, 2004.* London: Guinness World Records Limited.

Guinness World Records, eds. 2002. *Guinness Book of World Records, 2003.* London: Guinness World Records Ltd.

Hausman, Gerald, and Loretta Hausman. 1997. *The Mythology of Dogs.* New York: St. Martin's Press.

Periodicals and Newspapers

Adamson, Eve. 2001. "More Than a Pretty Face." *Dog Fancy,* December.

Carney, Steve. 2001. "They're Little Love Sponges." *Dog Fancy,* September.

Dearth, Kim D. R. 2002. "American Bulldog." *Dog World,* December.

Dearth, Kim D. R. 2001. "The Old Country Charm of the Old English Sheepdog." *Dog World,* March.

Dearth, Kim D. R. 2001. "Swiss Bliss: The Greater Swiss Mountain Dog." *Dog World,* May.

Dingeman, Robbie. 2002. "Hoku Dog Name to Da Max." *Honolulu Advertiser,* August 14.

Müller, Alfred. 2003. "Origins and History of Eurasiers." Translated by Ellen Conzelmann. www.eurasier-online.de /inhalt_e.htm.

Saluny, Susan. 2003. "New York's Top Dog? It Depends on the Zip Code." *New York Times,* October 24.

Organizations and Web Sites

Affenpinscher Club of America
Airedale Terrier Club of America
Akita Club of America
American Bullmastiff Association
American Foxhound Club, Inc.
American Kennel Club
American Lhasa Apso Club
American Rare Breed Association
American Shetland Sheepdog Association
American Sighthound Field Association (Jack Helder)

Ames Plantation and the National Field Trial Champion Association
Aniwa.com
Asian and Hong Kong Dachshund Society
Australian National Kennel Council
Australian Terrier Club of America
BarkBytes.com
Bleu De Gascogne Club of America
Border Collie Society of America
Boston Terrier Club of America, Inc.
BriardWorld.net/herding
Canadian Kennel Club (Justin Foucalt)
The Canine Chronicle
Chinese Shar-Pei Club of America
Continental Kennel Club
Curly-Coated Retriever Club of America
Dalmatian Club of America
Dog Breed Info Center
DogOMania.com
Dog Yarn Shop and Custom Spinning
English Setter Association of America
English Shepherd Club
Fédération Cynologique Internationale
Finnish Kennel Club
The French Bull Dog Club of America
Guinness World Records
Iams.com
Kennel Club (Cathy Hayward)
Komondor Club of America
North American Kai Association
Norwegian Lundehund Club of America, Inc.
Office of the Governor of Louisiana Web site
Old English Sheepdog Club of America
The Otterhound Club of America
Papillon Club of America
Pharaoh Hound Club of America
Portugal Web site: portugal-live.net/UK/mountains.html
Portuguese Water Dog Club of America
Presa-Canario-Canary-Dogs.com
PuppyShop.com
Saint Bernard Club of America
Samoyed Club of America, Inc.
SchnauzerWare.org
Scottish Deerhound Club of America
Skye Terrier Club of America
Southern California Chihuahua Club
Thai Ridgeback Dog Online
Tibetan Mastiff Club of America, Inc.
TrailsEndEstrela.com

United Doberman Club
United Kennel Club (Sara Jonas, Todd Morgan, Steve Vanduine)
University of Minnesota College of Veterinary Medicine
VIPFibers.com
West Highland White Terrier Club of America
Westminster Kennel Club (David Frei)

Section Five
Books
Case, Linda P. 1999. *The Dog: Its behavior, nutrition and health.* Ames, IA: Iowa State University Press.

Dodman, Nicholas, DVM. 1999. *Dogs Behaving Badly: An A–to–Z guide to understanding and curing behavioral problems in dogs.* New York: Bantam Books.

Fogle, Bruce. 2002. *Caring for Your Dog.* New York: DK Publishing.

Fogle, Bruce. 1995. *The Encyclopedia of the Dog.* New York: DK Publishing.

Lane, Marion S. 2001. *The Humane Society of the United States Complete Guide to Dog Care: Everything you need to keep your dog healthy and happy.* Boston: Little, Brown, and Company.

Experts
Dr. Fred Oehme, professor of toxicology and pathbiology and director of Kansas State University's comparative toxicology laboratories

Periodicals/Newspapers/Articles
Bertram, Susan H., DVM. "Contact Lenses for Your Dog?" www.dogfancy.com.

CBS News Web site. 2003. "Blood Donor Dogs." www.cbsnews.com/stories/2003/05/30/earlyshow/saturday/main556301.shtml.

Dog Fancy, Checkup section. 2002. "Be Your Dog's Dental Detective." August.

Dunn, T. J., Jr., DVM. "Tongue Talk." www.thepetcenter.com/gen/tongue.html.

Feldman, Lori H., DVM, and Henry J. Feldman, MD. 1996. "Save A Life: Learn Animal CPR." EMS Provider and Pet Owner brochure.

Howl, Joanne Healey, DVM. "The Bionic Dog." www.dogfancy.com.

Kirkwood, Kyra. 2003. "Vaccinations: Not If, But When." *Dog Fancy,* June.

Moore, Arden. 2001. "Forever Young." *Dog Fancy*, September.

Serafin, Barry. 2003. "Old Dog, New Life." poochdogpark.com/OldDogNewLife.htm.

Singer, Glenn. 2002. "Allergy Control—It's Simple." *Dog Fancy,* June.

Organizations and Web Sites
Alliance for Contraception in Cats & Dogs Web site
All Pets Dental Clinic
All Pets Veterinary Clinic
American Animal Hospital Association
American Association of Housecall Veterinarians
American Heartworm Society
American Kennel Club
American Red Cross
American Veterinary Medical Association
Animal Health Institute
ASPCA Ani-Med Web site
Bayer Animal Health
Canine Online: All about Dogs Origins, Design, Functions and Genetics
DFW Pug Rescue Club, Inc.
Dog Beach Dentistry
DogFancy.com
HealthyPet.com
PetDental.com
PetPlace.com
RescueCritters.com
Sergeant's Pet Products
VetDentistry.com
Veterinary Information Network, Pet Care Forum's Opinion Poll
VeterinaryPartner.com
Veternet.com
Washington State University College of Veterinary Medicine

Section Six
Books
American Kennel Club Staff. 1998. *The Complete Dog Book, 19th edition.* Hoboken, NJ: Howell Book House.

Arden, Darlene. 2002. *The Angell Memorial Animal Hospital Book of Wellness and Preventive Care for Dogs.* New York: McGraw-Hill.

Fogle, Bruce. 2002. *Caring for Your Dog.* New York: DK Publishing.

Fogle, Bruce. 1995. *The Encyclopedia of the Dog.* New York: DK Publishing.

Experts
William Pollak, DVM

Periodicals and Newspapers
Wong, Lawson. 2003. "Alpha Omega Soft iSeePet." abcnews.com, Science and Technology section (accessed September 19).

Organizations and Web Sites
The CEO Refresher (Pam Danzinger):
   http://www.refresher.com/!umi2004.htm
Chomp, Inc.
CycleDog.com
DogFancy.com
FancyPetsGrooming.com
Guinness World Records
Pet Food Institute
PetSmart.com
Recipe Goldmine, LLC
RecipeSource.com
Sergeant's Pet Products
Three Dog Bakery
University of Minnesota College of Veterinary Medicine
Veterinary Information Network, Pet Care Forum's Opinion Poll
Waltham

Section Seven
Books
Fogle, Bruce. 2002. *Caring for Your Dog.* New York: DK Publishing.

Fogle, Bruce. 1995. *The Encyclopedia of the Dog.* New York: DK Publishing.

Lane, Marion S. 2001. *The Humane Society of the United States Complete Guide to Dog Care: Everything you need to keep your dog healthy and happy.* Boston: Little, Brown, and Company.

Nichol, Jeff, DVM. 2001. *Is My Dog Okay? How to know when your dog won't say.* Upper Saddle River, NJ: Prentice Hall Press.

Pinney, Chris C., DVM. 2003. *Complete Home Veterinary Guide, third edition.* New York: McGraw-Hill.

Prevention Magazine Health Books, eds. 1996. *The Doctors Book of Home Remedies.* Emmaus, PA: Rodale Press.

Shojai, Amy. 1999. *The Purina Encyclopedia of Dog Care.* New York: Ballantine Books.

Periodicals and Newspapers
Derr, Mark. 2003. "What Makes Dogs Tick? The search for answers." *New York Times,* August 19.

Moran, Peggy. 2001. "Pest Control: Reducing Bothersome Behaviors." *Dog World,* February.

Reed, Christopher. 2003. "Best Friend Bests Chimp." *Harvard Magazine,* March/April.

Organizations and Web Sites
American Animal Hospital Association
American Dog Trainers Network
American Kennel Club
American Pet Association Web site
American Society for the Prevention of Cruelty to Animals
Courteous Canines, Inc.
Guinness World Records
Humane Society of Silicon Valley
Humane Society of the United States
Leeds Castle
PetCo.com
PetSmart.com
Purina.com
Waltham

Section Eight
Books
Freedman, Lew. 1999. *Father of the Iditarod: The Joe Redington Story.* Kenmore, WA: Epicenter Press, Inc.

Periodicals and Newspapers
Associated Press. 2003. "Can dogs be trained to sniff out problem weeds?" www.cnn.com/2003/TECH/science/12/31/offbeat.weed.sniffer.ap/.

Curtis, Dr. Paul D., and Dr. Jeff Jackson. 1999. "Controlling Critters in Golf-Course Landscapes." grounds-mag.com/mag/grounds_maintenance_controlling_critters_golfcourse/index.html.

Denney, Alicia. 2003. "Bell Ringing Dog is Salvation Army's Best Friend." *Kansas City Star,* November 22.

Dye, Lee. 2003. "Good Dog: Mathematician explains how his dog understands calculus." more.abcnews.go.com/sections/scitech/dyehard/dyehard030529.html.

Hesseldahl, Arik. 2002. "Dogs with Phone Numbers." forbes.com/2002/08/28/0828tentech.html.

Meadows, Robin. 2002. "Scat Sniffing Dogs." *Zoogoer Magazine,* September/October.

Moll, Maryann. 2003. "Scat Dogs Sniff Out Endangered Species Feces." news.nationalgeographic.com/news/2003/10/1001 031001_scatdogs.html.

Reuters. 2003. "Brides ask for bomb sniffing dogs." www.cnn.com/2003/WORLD/americas/05/25/bogota.dogs/.

Simmons, Morgan. 2002. "Dog Finds Termites Right under His Nose." *Scripps Howard News Service,* July 20.

Organizations and Web Sites

Alliance for Contraception in Cats & Dogs (ACCD) Web site
Alaska Native Heritage Center
Alaska State Museums
American War Dog Association
Animal Planet
Association of Companion Animal Behavior Counselors Web site
Border Collie Rescue
Colorado Division of Wildlife
DogFriendly.com
EMagazine.com
FactMonster.com
Guide Dogs for the Blind
Guide Dogs of the Desert International
Iditarod Trail Sled Dog Race Web site
National Geographic Web site
Montana Weed Control Association
Museums Alaska Web site
National Bird Dog Museum
PetPlace.com
Pet Sitters International
The Seeing Eye

Contributors

Eve Adamson is an award-winning writer and author of over 25 books, including most recently *The Simple Guide to Grooming Your Dog, Your Outta Control Adopted Dog,* and *The Simple Guide to a Healthy Dog.* She is a contributing editor to *Dog Fancy* magazine and frequent contributor to many other pet publications. She lives in Iowa City, Iowa, with her two sons and two small terriers of undetermined origin.

Vicki Hogue-Davies is a freelance book, magazine, and business writer from California. She has written pet columns for *Ladies' Home Journal*, contributed to several animal magazines, and is the author of two horse-related books.

Siri Mehus is a dog lover and graduate student in communication studies. She lives in Austin, Texas, with her husband, daughter, and 15-year-old dog, Patsy.

September B. Morn is a dog trainer and freelance writer. She holds a degree in psychology and has authored several training books, including *Training Your Labrador Retriever.* September is a frequent contributor to many dog publications and is the "Ask Dog Fancy" columnist for *Dog Fancy* magazine. She lives in Bellingham, Washington, with her four dogs and enjoys showing in agility, obedience, and conformation.

Audrey Pavia is a freelance writer specializing in animal subjects. She is a former managing editor of *Dog Fancy* magazine and former senior editor of the *American Kennel Club Gazette*. She has authored six books on dogs as well as books on a number of other animals.

Allan Reznik has been involved in the world of purebred dogs—as a breeder, exhibitor, journalist and author—for more than three decades. His work has won awards from the Dog Writers Association of America and the Alliance of Purebred Dog Writers, and he discusses dogs regularly on national TV and radio. He was a celebrity judge on the CBS reality series "Greatest American Dog." Allan is Editor-in-Chief of *Dogs in Review* magazine, and Editor-at-Large of *Dog World* and *Dog Fancy.* A Southern California resident, he shows Tibetan Mastiffs and Cavalier King Charles Spaniels.

Kathy Salzberg is a Nationally Certified Master Groomer and a freelance writer who frequently writes about pets. She is a former columnist for *Groom & Board* and the author of *How to Start a Home-Based Pet Care Business.* With her daughter and business partner, Missi, Kathy owns and operates The Village Groomer in Walpole, Massachusetts. Kathy shares her home with three cats and a French Bulldog.

Kim Campbell Thornton is an award-winning freelance writer. She is a frequent contributor to various dog magazines and has written a number of books on dog breeds, care, and training. She lives in Lake Forest, California, with her husband and three Cavalier King Charles Spaniels.

Photo Credits

The Publisher would like to thank the following individuals for contributing photographs:

Principle Photographers:

Norvia Behling
Paulette Braun
Tara Darling
Daniel Dempster
Dwight Dyke
Cheryl A. Ertelt
Isabelle Francais
Billy Hustace
Carol Ann Johnson
David Johnson

Cris Kelly
Bonnie Nance
Cindy Rogers
Heidi Schoenemann
Dale Spartas
Renee Stockdale
Judith Strom
Alice Su
Alice van Kempen

Additional Contributors:

Christopher Appoldt
Art Resource, NY:
  Erich Lessing
  Scala
  Snark
Berndt Brinkmann
Patti Burnett
Chelle Calbert
The Canine Chronicle
Christina Chan
Click the Photo Connection
David Dalton
Tony Demin/Mulberry Square Productions, Inc.
Shirley Fernandez
Franklin D. Roosevelt Library
Donnie Gilpin
Andrea Jemolo
Samantha Johnson
Bette Kaplan
Library of Congress, Prints and Photographs Division:
  FSA/OWI Collection
World's Transportation Commission Photograph
    Collection

Joan Marcus
Kristin Mehus-Roe
Minnesota French Spaniels
Steven Robertson
Connie Summers
Smithsonian Institution
Steve Sourifmann
Karen Taylor
Todd Tripp
Robert White
The William Secord Gallery, New York
Bob Winsett
Kerrin Winter-Churchill
WPA Poster Collection
Carolyn Zalewski/North Star Foundation, Inc.
Robert Zena/Geese Police®, Inc.
Tony Zintsmaster/Dog Heroes of September 11th
Zoombak

Illustrations by Laurie O'Keefe

Index

Note: Page numbers in **bold** indicate a breed profile.

bonding, 528–30, 577, 611
genetic link, 25
grieving dogs, 202
living together, 23
overview, 19
tetanus shot for dog bites, 65
See also dog ownership
Hungarian Vizsla, **398–99**, 507
hunting breeds
field trials and hunt tests, 186, 188, 736–37
in Islamic religion, 31
in medieval Europe, 24
overview, 667
resources, 737–38, 754, 761–62, 766, 769
Hunting Dogs constellation, 32
Hunt tests, 186, 188, 736-37
Hurricane Katrina, 40, 145, 147, 149, 683, 686–87
hydrotherapy, 429
hyperglycemia, 506
hypertension (high blood pressure), 475–76, 477
hypoallergenic dogs, 70, 71
hypoglycemia, 506–7
hypothyroidism, 462, 467, 508

I
Ibizan Hound, **313**
ibuprofen poisoning, 119, 123
Iceland Dog, **313–14**
Icelandic Sheepdog, **313–14**
Iceland Spitz, **313–14**
ICH (infectious canine hepatitis), 434
identification, 152–54
idii 'n illeli, **225**
Ifugao people of the Philippine islands, 34–35
IGRs (insect growth regulators), 441
illnesses
anemia, 444, 446–47, 476, 551

autoimmune hemolytic anemia, 496, 497
bloat, 174, 484–85
drug-resistant staph, 450
exhaustion, 193
heat exhaustion, 192
heatstroke, 173, 174, 192
overview, 142–43
signs of, 433
See also heart; immune system; infections; infectious diseases
Illyrian Shepherd Dog, **372–73**
imaging technology, 520–21
imidacloprid, 441
immune system
autoimmune diseases, 496–97
autoimmune hemolytic anemia, 497
and ear infections, 465, 467
herbal enhancement, 425
immune-mediated arthritis, 496, 497
maternal immunity, 432
nutritional support for, 567
overview, 495–97
See also allergies of dogs
immune-mediated arthritis, 496, 497
immune-mediated canine diabetes, 506
immunizations, 54, 430–33, 436, 444, 499, 509
impolite and unsafe behaviors, 649–53
Inca Hairless Dog, 354–55
Incas, 58
incontinence, 486
India, 24, 32, 34, 36
Indians' Dog (Carolina Dog), 82, 261, 414
indoor marking problems, 654
Industrial Revolution, 25
infections
abscesses and cysts, 462, 473, 519

of anal glands, 485, 542–43
bladder infections, 486
from brucellosis, 499
ear infection prevention, 467–68
ear infections, 81, 463, 465–67
of eccrine glands, 473
eye infections, 469–70
methicillin-resistant *Staphylococcus intermedius,* 450
microscopic exam of organisms, 520
nasal cavity role in prevention, 481
periodontal disease, 438–39, 483
from puncture wounds, 457
See also antibiotic therapy; bacterial infections; parasites, internal
infectious canine hepatitis (ICH), 434
infectious diseases
canine influenza, 434
distemper, 433–34
infectious canine hepatitis, 434
overview, 430, 436
parvovirus, 435, 436, 437, 520
rabies, 63, 65, 436, 437, 525
inherited conditions. *See* genetics and heredity
injuries
moving your injured dog, 143
muzzling your dog, 63, 143, 144
insect bites and stings, 452, 453
insect growth regulators (IGRs), 441
Institute for Genomic Research and the